BEST-EVER
Slow Cooker
One-pot & Casserole
COOKBOOK

BEST-EVER
Slow Cooker
One-pot & Casserole
COOKBOOK

Tasty and tender meals with all the nutrients locked in – over 400 easy-to-prepare step-by-step recipes shown in 1700 superb photographs

Catherine Atkinson and Jenni Fleetwood

HERMES
HOUSE

This edition is published by Hermes House

Hermes House is an imprint of Anness Publishing Ltd
Hermes House, 88–89 Blackfriars Road, London SE1 8HA
tel. 020 7401 2077; fax 020 7633 9499
www.hermeshouse.com; www.annesspublishing.com

If you like the images in this book and would like to investigate
using them for publishing, promotions or advertising, please visit
our website www.practicalpictures.com for more information.

A CIP catalogue record for this book is available from the British
Library.

Publisher: Joanna Lorenz
Editorial Director: Helen Sudell
Editorial Readers: Richard McGinlay, Joy Wotton and
  Jay Thundercliffe
Designer: Nigel Partridge
Photography: Karl Adamson, Edward Allwright, Steve Baxter, Nicki
Dowey, James Duncan, Ian Garlick, Michelle Garrett, Amanda
Heywood, Janine Hosegood, David Jordan, David King, Don Last,
William Adams-Lingwood, Patrick McLeavey, Thomas Odulate,
Craig Robertson, Bridget Sargeson, Sam Stowell
Recipes: Catherine Atkinson, Jane Bamforth, Alex Barker, Valerie
Barrett, Michelle Berriedale-Johnson, Judy Bastyra, Kit Chan,
Jacqueline Clarke, Carole Clements, Matthew Drennan, Sarah
Edmonds, Joanna Farrow, Brian Glover, Nicola Graimes, Juliet
Harbutt, Christine Ingram, Becky Johnson, Lucy Knox, Lesley
Mackley, Sally Mansfield, Sallie Morris, Jennie Shapter, Anne
Sheasby, Marlena Spieler, Steven Wheeler, Kate Whiteman,
Rosemary Wilkinson, Elizabeth Wolf-Cohen, Jeni Wright
Production Controller: Pedro Nelson

10 9 8 7 6 5 4 3 2

Previously published in two separate volumes: *One-pot, Slow-pot
and Clay-pot Cooking* and *The Slow Cooker Recipe Book.*

NOTES

Bracketed terms are for American readers.
For all recipes, quantities are given in both metric and imperial
measures and, where appropriate, measures are also
given in standard cups and spoons. Follow one set, but not a
mixture because they are not interchangeable.

Standard spoon and cup measures are level. 1 tsp = 5ml, 1 tbsp =
15ml, 1 cup = 250ml/8fl oz
Australian standard tablespoons are 20ml. Australian readers
should use 3 tsp in place of 1 tbsp for measuring small quantities
of gelatine, cornflour, salt etc.
Medium (US large) eggs are used unless otherwise stated.

Nutritional Analysis of recipes: The nutritional analyses on
recipe pages are calculated per portion (i.e. serving or item),
unless otherwise stated. If the recipe gives a range, such as Serves
4–6, then the nutritional analysis will be for the smaller portion
size, i.e. 6 diners.
Measurements for sodium do not include salt added to taste.

CONTENTS

Introduction   **6**
Slow cooker basics   10
Slow cooker equipment   12
One-pot equipment   14
Clay-pot equipment   16
Beef   20
Lamb/pork   22
Poultry and game   24
Fish and shellfish   28
Vegetables   30
Grains, pasta and beans   32
Fruits   34
Herbs, spices and flavourings   36

Basic techniques
Making stock   40
Making soups   42
Making marinades   44
Making stews and casseroles   46
Braising   50
Toppings   52
Pot-roasting   54
Poaching   56
Using the slow cooker as a bain-marie   58
Making steamed puddings and desserts   60
Making cakes   62
Making savoury sauces   64
Making sweet sauces   66
Making fondues   68
Making preserves   70
Slow cooker safety   72
One-pot cooking techniques   74
Clay-pot cooking techniques   76

The recipes
Slow cooker soups   **80**
One-pot, clay-pot soups   **98**
Slow cooker first courses and light meals   118
One-pot, clay-pot first courses and
    light meals   134
Slow cooker fish and shellfish   162
One-pot, clay-pot fish and shellfish   186
Slow cooker poultry and game   212
One-pot, clay-pot poultry and game   240
Slow cooker meat   278
One-pot, clay-pot meat   312
Slow cooker vegetarian and side dishes   350
One-pot, clay-pot vegetarian and
    side dishes   370
Slow cooker desserts and cakes   436
One-pot clay-pot desserts   466
Slow cooker preserves and drinks   490

Useful addresses   506
Index   507

INTRODUCTION

Long, slow cooking techniques have been used for centuries. From the earliest times, cooks discovered that meat roasted in the dying embers of the fire, or in a pot of gently bubbling stock suspended well above the flames, produced the tenderest results with rich, well-balanced flavours.

Cooking methods have developed and improved over the years, but no drastic changes were seen until the reduction of staff employed in richer households meant that very few people still had a cook who would spend the entire day preparing food.

Along with the gradual introduction of controllable range cookers and, eventually, the introduction of modern gas and electric ovens came an increased demand for dishes requiring less cooking time. In the latter half of the 20th century, more women went out to work, and time-saving became all-important.

Food manufacturers thrived on the sale of prepared ingredients that could reduce the number of hours spent in

Below: The gentle heat of the slow cooker means that delicate fish cooks beautifully.

the kitchen. Canned and dried soups, dehydrated prepared vegetables, main meals and "instant" desserts became very popular at the end of the 1960s and continued to be so throughout the 1970s.

The story of slow cooking

In the mid-1970s, the slow cooker was invented. It was originally designed for making baked beans and was marketed to the public as an appliance that would cook a wholesome meal unattended, ready to be served after a hard day's work. As such it caught the attention of those with busy working lives. It lived up to its promise, and busy working mothers, families and students soon discovered its delights. The slow cooker's popularity continued for a decade.

However, with the booming economy years in the late 1980s and 1990s, the demand for economical cuts of meat fell. They were replaced by lean prime cuts, such as chicken breast portions and beef steak, which were more suited to fast cooking methods, such as grilling, broiling and stir-frying. Time-saving appliances appeared on the scene,

Above: Impressive terrines can be made using the slow cooker as a bain-marie.

including the microwave – and with their arrival, many slow cookers were left to gather dust.

Changing attitudes

Towards the end of the 20th century and in the new millennium, there has been a change in attitudes towards food and a reverse in eating trends. Many people now demand natural food, with fewer artificial chemicals and more nutrients and flavour, rather than instant, quick-fix food. Genetically modified produce has not been welcomed and sales of organic food have rocketed, along with requests for less tender, tastier cuts of meat. Slow-simmered casseroles, home-made soups and traditional desserts are back in fashion, and so are slow cookers.

From tasty, wholesome family food to sophisticated entertaining, a slow cooker is a superb way to create wonderfully tender and flavour-packed meals. Its reputation for making delicious soups and succulent stews is well known, and the slow cooker is far more versatile than many people realize.

Because the slow cooker cooks gently, without the vigorous bubbling or fierce heat of some other cooking methods, delicate food, such as fish, fruit and vegetables, won't break up even after long cooking. Used as a bain-marie the slow cooker can produce divine creamy "baked" custards, the lightest sponge desserts, and tasty terrines and pâtés. The constant temperature makes it perfect for keeping party punches steaming hot and simmering preserves so that the flavours mingle, making ready-to-eat preserves that don't need to be left to mature.

There are many advantages to using a slow cooker. Not only does it produce delicious dishes with well-developed flavours, but once the food is in the slow cooker you can usually turn it on and forget about it. Because the slow cooker uses less electricity than a light bulb, it can be left unattended, which means you can be away from the kitchen all day and return when ready to serve.

Some slow cookers have timers that automatically switch to the warm setting when the food is cooked, and this is ideal for households who eat at different times. The remaining portions will still be deliciously moist for latecomers, and won't be overcooked or dry. As an added bonus, little steam or smell escapes from slow cookers.

You will be pleasantly surprised at the range of uses of the slow cooker. Although traditionally associated with cold weather foods, such as warming

Below: Pastry toppings for traditional pies are oven-cooked to retain their crispness.

casseroles, soups and stews, you can also make delicious hot weather dishes, such as chilled pâtés and terrines, light fish dishes and summery Mediterranean-style pasta meals. The slow cooker really is invaluable when it is warm outside and you don't want to be confined to a steamy kitchen, with the oven pumping out heat. Simply switch on the slow cooker and leave it to it while you get on with more important things.

Below: Individual servings can be cooked in single-portion ramekins in the slow cooker.

Above: The slow cooker makes excellent steamed chocolate and fruit puddings.

One-pot and clay-pot cooking

You can still take advantage of the benefits that a slow cooker brings by making meals cooked in just one pot, whether it be a large casserole dish, a clay baking dish or a wok. Nourishing soups, delectable stews, spicy stir fries, robust roasts, creamy risottos and citrus custards all can be cooked in one-pot dishes. They are easy to prepare, a pleasure to serve and the perfect choice for family and friends.

As with the slow cooker, cooking in a single pot is wonderfully liberating. All that is needed is a bit of leisurely preparation, and then the cook can relax, secure in the knowledge that there will be no last-minute sauces to make, and no tricky toppings to produce. Serving a selection of side dishes would defeat the object of one-pot cooking (and is largely unnecessary when vegetables are included anyway), so you have the perfect excuse for offering only the simplest accompaniments, sparing yourself the anxiety that comes with trying to get everything ready at precisely the same time.

One-pot dishes will seldom spoil if not eaten the moment they are ready. Some, like curries and casseroles, actually improve if made the day before, so that all the flavours can bed down together and blend. Stir-fries, pasta and rice dishes need last-minute cooking, but if the preparation is done in advance, the effort is minimal.

This style of cooking is perfect for everyone from single students to those cooking for a large family. The meal can be cooked in the oven, on top of the stove or even in a free-standing appliance like a microwave oven or electric frying pan. There's very little washing up, and if there are any leftovers, you may well be able to transform them into tasty pie fillings, simply by sandwiching them inside ready-rolled puff pastry or filo.

The benefits of one-pot and clay-pot cooking

One-pot cooking can also be extremely healthy, especially if you use a clay pot, which ensures that vitamins and minerals are retained. This ancient form of cooking seals in all the food's natural juices by enclosing it in a porous clay container that has been soaked in water. As the container heats up, the water turns to steam, keeping the contents beautifully moist and tender. The only other liquid is that which comes from the food itself, so the full flavour of the food can be appreciated.

There's nothing new about cooking in clay. Thousands of years ago, hunters discovered that coating small birds and animals in clay before baking them in an open fire kept the meat juicy and

Above: Paella, a classic one-pot seafood and rice dish from Spain, is traditionally cooked in a shallow, two-handled pan.

Left: A whole chicken cooked with forty cloves of garlic makes the perfect pot-roast, and it, like other one-pot dishes, needs little attention once it is in the oven.

Below: Clay pots come in a whole host of sizes and shapes. These tiny shallow cazuelas can be used to bake individual portions of both savoury and sweet tarts, roasted vegetables and custards.

Left: The tall, conical tagine from north Africa is one of the many ancient clay pot designs that are still widely used today.

results every time. For each type of dish there is a chapter devoted to slow cooker recipes followed by a chapter for one-pot and clay-pot recipes so that you can easily find recipes to suit your chosen method of cooking.

Most recipes are based on a family of four people, but if you have a small or large slow cooker or pan the quantities can easily be halved to serve two, or doubled for eight. All recipes have been thoroughly tested, but it is important to get to know your slow cooker, as times can vary from one model to another. After trying a few recipes, you will know whether your slow cooker is faster or slower, and you will be able to adjust the recipe cooking times accordingly.

Below: A glazed clay pot ensures that the flavours don't soak into the pot, which means that it can be used for both sweet and savoury dishes.

prevented it from burning. Chipping off the clay and throwing it away was wasteful and time-consuming, however. Clay pots were a huge improvement, and this material was used by many of the ancient civilizations. Today, clay pots based on ancient designs are still widely used all over the world. In North Africa, it is the conical tagine; in China, the sand pot; in Spain, the cazuela; and in France, the daubière and tian.

Chicken bricks, bean pots and clay pots come in all shapes and sizes. They need to be treated kindly, but are surprisingly durable. If you've never used one – or have forgotten just how good they make food taste – there is plenty of inspiration, along with ideas for other delicious one-pot dishes of every kind, contained within these pages.

Using this book

Ideal for the first-time slow-cooker user, as well as the more experienced slow-cooker fan, this book also offers practical advice and plenty more recipes that can be cooked just on the hob in any large pan or slowly in the oven in a clay pot. It contains a wonderfully detailed reference section with everything you need to know about ingredients, equipment and techniques, so that you can feel completely confident.

Once you have mastered the basics, turn to the recipe chapters for a selection of all-time classics as well as unusual recipes that are sure to become household favourites. Step-by-step photographs show the key preparation stages of each recipe to give successful

SLOW COOKER BASICS

The basic principle behind the slow cooker is that it cooks food very slowly at a low temperature. The heat gradually builds up and is then maintained at an even temperature throughout cooking, to give perfect, tender results. Slow cookers are very simple and economical to use. They have a low wattage that consumes about the same amount of electricity as a light bulb, which makes them environmentally friendly as well.

Choosing a slow cooker

There is a very wide selection of slow cookers available. They come in a range of sizes, shapes, colours and prices, and it is these factors that you will need to think about before you decide which type of slow cooker is right for you.

When slow cookers were first manufactured, the earthenware or ceramic pots were permanently fixed into the heat-resistant plastic or aluminium outer casing. While it is still possible to buy models made this way, most modern versions have a removable cooking pot that fits snugly into an inner metal casing. The heating elements are safely situated between the inner and outer casings. This newer style not only simplifies washing up, but allows the cooking pot to be lifted out and taken to the table as a serving dish. In addition, food can be browned in the oven or under the grill (broiler) without causing damage to the outer casing.

The heat-resistant lid may be made of toughened glass or ceramic. The former has the advantage of allowing you to monitor the food's cooking progress without lifting off the lid and losing heat and moisture, although this may be hindered to some extent by steam and condensation gathering on the inside of the lid.

The range of designs and colours of slow cookers has increased in recent years. The original round-shaped rustic cream and brown design with ceramic lid is still available, but alongside it you will now find much more contemporary-looking white, stainless steel and brightly coloured models that will fit well in a bright, modern kitchen.

Slow cookers may be round or oval in shape. Round ones are superb for cooking casseroles, steaming desserts and cooking cakes in round tins (pans), while the oval version is better for pot-roasted meats and for use with loaf tins (pans) and terrines.

The size of different slow cookers can vary enormously – from a small 600ml/ 1 pint/2½ cup cooking pot to a huge 6.5 litre/11¼ pint/26¼ cup one. Of all the sizes, the most popular size is probably 3.5 litres/6 pints/14¼ cups, which will enable you to cook a wide range of dishes and easily cater for four people. However, the smaller versions, intended for cooking just one or two portions at a time, are a great asset for single people and couples and take up less space in the kitchen. They are also perfect for making hot dips and fondues.

Below: Oval-shaped slow cookers are perfect for cooking certain types of food, such as pot-roasted joints of meat, long, loaf-shaped terrines, and small whole fish.

Temperature settings

The cooking temperatures and settings on slow cookers vary slightly from model to model. The most basic (but perfectly adequate) models have three settings: off, low and high. When the slow cooker is switched to low, the food will barely simmer, and at the highest setting it will cook at a simmer or even boil.

Other models have an additional medium setting and some also have an auto setting. The auto setting is thermostatically controlled, so that the cooking temperature builds up to high, maintains it for a short time, then automatically switches to low to maintain the heat. It normally takes about an hour for the slow cooker to reach the "high" temperature, but this depends on the quantity of food being cooked and its initial temperature.

Most slow cooker models also have a power indicator light that remains on constantly during cooking – although in a few models it may switch off to indicate that the optimum temperature has been reached, so check the instructions.

Using a new slow cooker

Every model of slow cooker varies slightly, so it is important to read the manufacturer's instructions carefully before using. Even when using the same settings, some cookers will cook slower or faster than others.

To cover all models of slow cooker, the recipes in this book offer a range of cooking times. Depending on whether your own model cooks more slowly or quickly, you will either need to use the longer or shorter timing, or somewhere in between. Once you have used your new cooker a few times, it will be easy to know at a glance which cooking time you need to use.

Preheating

Some slow cookers need to be preheated on high for 15–20 minutes before cooking. However, always check the instructions first because some models heat up quickly, making this step unnecessary, and the manufacturer may advise against heating the slow cooker when empty.

To preheat the slow cooker, place the empty cooking pot and lid in the slow cooker base and switch the temperature on to the high setting. While the slow cooker heats up, prepare the ingredients for the recipe.

Slow cooker care

Always remove any labels and tags from a new slow cooker, then wash the ceramic cooking pot well in hot soapy water, rinse and dry thoroughly.

After use, the slow cooker should be switched off before removing the ceramic cooking pot. If you don't want to wash the pot immediately after serving the food, it can be filled with warm water and left to soak for as long as necessary. However, do not immerse the entire pot in water for long periods of time because the base is usually porous and soaking may damage the pot. Very few cooking pots are dishwasher-proof, but it is worth checking the manufacturer's instructions; these should also inform you whether the cooking pot can be used on the stovetop or in the oven, microwave or freezer.

Never plunge the hot cooking pot into cold water immediately after use, or pour boiling water into an empty cold cooking pot. Subjecting it to a sudden change in temperature could cause it to crack. As with all electrical appliances, never immerse the outer casing in water or fill it with water. Nor should you use the metal inner casing without the ceramic cooking pot.

Scouring pads and abrasive cleaners will damage the outside of the cooker, so use a damp soapy cloth to clean it.

Above: Smaller slow cookers intended for cooking just one or two portions at a time are an asset for single people and couples.

During cooking, the cooking pot and lid will become very hot, so always use oven gloves when handling. The outer casing may also become hot after long cooking, so care should be taken when touching this, too.

The first few times you use a slow cooker, you may notice a slight odour. This is caused by the burning off of manufacturing residues, which is normal, and will lessen and disappear after time. After several months, the glaze on the cooking pot may become crackled; this is common with glazed stoneware and will not affect the slow cooker's efficiency.

Adapting your own recipes

Conventional recipes can be adapted for cooking in a slow cooker. The easiest way to adapt a recipe is to find a similar one in this book and use it as a guide to adapt the original recipe. As a general rule, the liquid content of a dish cooked conventionally can be reduced by as much as half in a slow cooker. Check towards the end of cooking time and add more hot liquid if necessary.

Tips for success

During cooking, steam will condense on the lid of the slow cooker, then slowly trickle back into the pot. This helps to form a seal around the lid, retaining heat, flavour and cooking smells. If possible, avoid lifting the lid during cooking because this will cause heat loss and lengthen the cooking time. Unless a recipe states otherwise, the slow cooker should be left undisturbed. There is no need to stir food frequently because the even cooking and low temperature help to prevent food from sticking or bubbling over. Should you need to lift the lid though, add an extra 15–20 minutes to the cooking time to make up for the heat lost.

If at the end of the cooking time the food is not quite ready, replace the lid and switch the slow cooker to high to speed up the cooking process. Once ready, many dishes can be kept hot for an hour or so without risk of spoiling, by switching the slow cooker to low.

Guide to cooking times

You can often introduce some flexibility to the total cooking time by adjusting the temperature setting. Certain foods, however, are only successful if cooked at the specified setting. Cakes, for example, should always be cooked on high for the entire cooking time, and pot-roasted meats and egg-based recipes should usually be started on high (or auto) for the first hour of cooking, then reduced. For dishes such as soups and casseroles, the cooking time may be shortened or extended to suit your needs by cooking on a higher or lower setting. As a rough guide, the cooking time on high is just over half that on low.

Low	Medium	High
6–8 hours	4–6 hours	3–4 hours
8–10 hours	6–8 hours	5–6 hours
10–12 hours	8–10 hours	7–8 hours

SLOW COOKER EQUIPMENT

To make most slow cooker recipes, you will only need a slow cooker. Stocks, soups, stews, casseroles, compotes and pot roasts can all simply be cooked in the ceramic cooking pot. However, to make other dishes, such as cakes and pâtés that are cooked in a bain-marie, you will need suitable cookware that is watertight and which will fit inside the ceramic cooking pot.

Cake tins/pans

When cooking cakes in the slow cooker, always use cake tins that have a fixed, non-removable base, rather than loose-based or springform tins. Before use, check that the tin is completely watertight by filling it with water and leaving it to stand for an hour; if it leaks it is not suitable. You should also check that the tin will fit inside the ceramic cooking pot before you prepare and fill it with mixture.

While it is important that the tin has a strong rigid shape, heat will penetrate more quickly if lighter, thinner tins are used. When using heavy-gauge metal tins, you will need to allow an extra 15–20 minutes cooking time.

Generally, round slow cookers can accommodate larger round and square cake tins than oval cookers. A 20cm/8in round tin or a 17.5cm/6½in square tin should fit comfortably in a 5 litre/8¾pint/20 cup round cooker, providing the sides of the tins are straight and

there is no protruding lip or side handle. Oval cookers can also be used for round and square tins, if necessary, but the size will obviously be more limited.

The recipes in this book state which size and shape of tin to use. Try to stick to these as closely as possible – if the tin is too large you will end up with a shallow cake; if it is too small the mixture may overflow. Bear in mind, too, that the length of cooking time and the texture of the cake may be affected if the wrong tin is used.

Loaf tins/pans

Perfect for making terrines, pâtés and loaf-shaped cakes, these sturdy long, narrow metal tins are better suited to cooking in an oval-shaped slow cooker, which will accommodate their shape conveniently. A 3.5 litre/6 pint/14 cup oval slow cooker will hold a straight-sided 900g/2lb loaf tin or Balmoral – a barrel-shaped ridged tin.

Ring tins/pans

Kugelhopf tins and deep, ring-shaped tins that are not too wide, are excellent for using in a slow cooker. The hollow tube in the centre conducts heat into the middle of the cake, helping it to cook quickly and evenly. Ideally choose

Below: Classic rectangular loaf tins are very useful for making terrines and chunky, country-style cooked pâtés.

Above: Rectangular, round and heart-shaped tins can be used in the slow cooker as long as they fit comfortably inside the pot.

a tin with a central tube that is just a little higher than the outer rim of the tin. However, you should also check that the tin fits inside the slow cooker, and that the cooker lid can still fit tightly on top of the ceramic cooking pot when the tin is inside.

Other shaped tins/pans

There are many other shapes of tin that may also be used in the slow cooker. These include small heart-, petal-, oval-, and hexagon-shaped tins. Before buying a tin to use in a slow cooker, it may be worth taking the internal measurement of the ceramic cooking pot first, to be sure the tin will fit inside.

Dariole moulds

These little sandcastle-shaped tins are usually made of matt aluminium and come in various sizes, although moulds with a 65mm/2½in diameter are the most popular. Dariole moulds are useful for making single-portion sized cakes, desserts and timbales, and are particularly good for making individual baked custards.

Soufflé and ramekin dishes

These pretty round dishes can be used as an alternative to metal cake tins, as well as for cooking pâtés and mousses. They are always straight-sided and may be made of glass, heatproof porcelain or stoneware. Glass or porcelain are preferable because they conduct heat more quickly to the food inside. When using these dishes for cake making, it is better to choose one with a perfectly flat base; occasionally they are slightly domed. Individual soufflé and ramekin dishes are miniature versions and can be used to make small, individual cakes, pâtés and desserts such as baked custards.

Terrines

Usually rectangular in shape, these dishes may be made of porcelain, cast iron or earthenware. When used to make pâté, they may double up as a serving dish. Some earthenware terrines aren't glazed, so are unsuitable for use in a bain-marie in a slow cooker. A loaf tin makes a good substitute.

Left: Meat thermometers are used to check that meat is cooked through.

Pudding bowls

Traditionally made of white earthenware, but also made of toughened glass, aluminium or polypropylene, pudding bowls have sloping sides, which make the top much wider than the base. They are ideal for making sweet and savoury steamed puddings and can also be used to melt chocolate, butter and similar ingredients in a bain-marie in the slow cooker. Bowls made from aluminium may have a clip-on lid with a handle attached. They are very good for making steamed meat and plain sponge puddings, because heat is conducted quickly. They are unsuitable for making acidic fruit desserts or similarly acidic recipes because the acid will react with the metal.

Below: Soufflé dishes and ramekins can be used inside the slow cooker to make steamed desserts, custards and pâtés.

Above: Metal pudding bowls with a clip-on lid and handle for easy lifting are great for making steamed meat puddings.

Meat thermometers

These useful instruments are the most reliable way of checking that meat is thoroughly cooked – this is particularly important for poultry, which can pass on the salmonella bacteria when raw or partially cooked. Most thermometers have a stainless steel body and a glass dial. By piercing the meat near the centre towards the end of the cooking time, you can check the temperature inside the meat. The meat is ready to eat when the pointer on the dial reaches the appropriate wording; there are indications for types of meat including chicken, beef, lamb and pork, as well as readings within some of those categories for rare, medium and well-cooked meat. Choose a thermometer with a thin probe, so that it doesn't make large holes in the meat, causing juices to be lost. Do not leave the thermometer inside the meat during cooking because exposure to steam in the slow cooker could damage the dial. Immediately after use, rinse the probe in hot soapy water and wipe it clean; don't immerse the thermometer in water.

ONE-POT EQUIPMENT

If you are going to do a lot of cooking in just one pot, make it a good one. There's no point in planning a pot-roast for the whole family, only to find you haven't got a big enough pan, or that the one you have has a wobbly base. It is equally irritating to discover that your only decent casserole has a crack in it, or can only be used in the oven and not on top of the stove. Choose your cookware with care; it is worth investing in good quality equipment that will last.

Right:
Stainless-steel pans with a heavy base are a good choice for one-pot cooking.

Above: Frying pans with metal handles can be used under the grill (broiler) and in the oven.

For one-pot cooking, you need a large pan with a heavy base, which will conduct the heat evenly and help to prevent the food from scorching should you inadvertently allow the amount of liquid to get too low. A good quality stainless-steel pan would be an excellent choice, but it is important to choose one with an aluminium or copper base, since stainless steel does not conduct heat well. For long, slow cooking, cast-iron pans coated in vitreous enamel, are ideal, as they can also be used in the oven. When buying a frying pan, choose one with a heavy base. When cooking a frittata or a dessert such as tarte Tatin, it is essential to use a frying pan with a handle that can withstand the heat of the grill (broiler) or oven; a point worth considering when you are buying a new frying pan.

Woks

One of the most useful items in the kitchen, the wok need not be reserved solely for stir-frying. It is the ideal pan for quick-cooked creamy dishes such as beef Stroganoff. The wok can also be used for making a risotto. Woks that

Pots and Pans

When you are buying cooking equipment, it is very tempting to opt for a set of shiny pans, rather than individual items that might suit your purposes – and your personal circumstances – better.

Below left: A large pot with metal handles can be used on top of the stove and in the oven.

Left: Woks have either one or two handles.

Right: When buying casseroles, it is a good idea to choose different shapes and sizes.

Casseroles

For one-pot cooking, choose a casserole that is big enough to serve six, even if you usually cook for four. This will give you plenty of room for stirring the contents without risking splashes and scalds. The ideal pot will be one that can be used on top of the stove as well as inside it, so that if you do need to do any pre-cooking, or if cooking juices need to be reduced by boiling, you will not need a second container. If you buy several casseroles, vary the shapes as well as the sizes. For cooking a whole chicken, for instance, an oval is more useful than a round dish. Look at the handles, too. It is important that they are easy to grasp, and that they do not become so hot that they are liable to burn you, even when you are using an oven glove. Appearance will obviously be a consideration, since you will be serving straight from the casserole, but consider practical aspects too.

Baking Dishes

There are plenty of one-pot recipes that benefit from being cooked in large, shallow dishes, from oven-roasted vegetables to layered potato bakes. Buy several different shapes, bearing in mind the size of your oven. Having two rectangular dishes that will fit side by side can be a real boon if you want to cook one meal for serving immediately and another for the freezer.

Ramekins

You will also find it useful to have six or eight ovenproof ramekin dishes, for baking single portions, such as individual soufflés and oven-baked desserts.

Below: Choose two ovenproof baking dishes that will fit next to each other in your oven.

have a flat base can be used on all types of cooker. They can have either one or two handles. Those with two handles are good for deep-frying and general cooking, while the wok with one handle is designed especially for stir-frying. The single handle makes the wok easy to pick up so that the ingredients can be stirred and tossed in the wok at the same time.

FLAMEPROOF CASSEROLES

The most versatile casseroles are also flameproof and so can be used on top of the stove and under the grill (broiler) as well as in the oven.

CLAY-POT EQUIPMENT

Visit any market in any town the world over, and you will find clay cooking pots for sale. Some will be rough, rustic items, only suitable for display, but others – like the Spanish cazuela or the North African tagine – will be intended not for the tourist trade, but for everyday cooking. Before buying, always seek local advice as to the durability and safety of the items, especially as regards any glazes that might be used. Buying a boxed item from a reputable store may not be as romantic, but it is probably more sensible. Clay cooking pots need special treatment, and it makes sense to follow the instructions that come with your particular utensil.

Romertopfs
Perhaps the most familiar unglazed clay pots are those produced by Romertopf. Their extensive range includes items suitable for cooking meat, fish, vegetables, fruit, even bread and cakes. The classic Romertopf is a rectangular pot with a deep, wide base and a domed lid. These come in several sizes. Other shapes include a long oval, suitable for accommodating a whole fish. This has a glazed base, to prevent liquid from penetrating the porous clay and leaving behind a lingering fishy smell.

Lids are designed to fit snugly, so that they cannot accidentally slip off, but there is a narrow gap between the lid and the base that allows any excess steam to escape from the clay pot.

Left: The classic, high, domed Romertopf dish (top) and a large oval clay pot that is especially designed for cooking whole fish.

Right: This deep, pan-shaped clay pot is designed for cooking bean dishes, but would also be good for baking potatoes, and for cooking soups and stews that have lots of liquid.

Above: The shape of these deep-based clay pots makes them ideal for baking potatoes and cooking beans and pulses.

Bean Pot/Potato Brick
There are several shapes of these deep, round pots. Some have a handle for easy lifting. Made entirely from clay, the pots have a domed lid. Although these pots are especially suitable for slowly cooking beans and pulses, they can also be used for soups and stews, and the shape is ideal for cooking both large and small potatoes. The potatoes are bathed in a layer of steam, which keeps them moist during cooking.

Whatever you are cooking, the pot and lid should first be soaked in water, then placed in a cold oven after the ingredients have been added.

Above: *This large chicken brick is designed to hold a whole bird.*

Garlic Baker

This small terracotta dish with a domed lid is used for baking garlic. Like all clay pots, it must be placed in a cold oven and heated gradually. There is no need to soak the pot in water first. The inside of the dish is glazed, so the garlic juices will not permeate it. The baker will accommodate four to six garlic bulbs. A small cross must be cut in the top of each garlic bulb, or the tops can be sliced off, to prevent them from bursting during cooking. The steam they release will be trapped under the domed lid of the garlic baker, and will keep the garlic cloves beautifully moist and tender. The garlic baker can also be used in a microwave oven.

Onion Baker

This clay pot looks like a larger version of the garlic baker. It consists of a shallow terracotta dish with a high, domed lid; it will accommodate four medium-sized onions, and can also be used for cooking onion wedges, shallots or baby onions. The lid can be soaked in water first, so that it releases steam during cooking. The steam helps to tenderize the onions. Towards the end of cooking, the lid should be removed so that the onions turn brown and become caramelized.

Above:
The onion baker (left) and the garlic baker both have high, domed lids that are designed to trap steam during cooking.

Chicken Brick

This is a large, unglazed fire clay cooking dish with a high lid. The largest ones are designed to hold a whole chicken, guinea fowl or duck, but can also be used to cook any large piece of meat or poultry. Smaller chicken bricks are ideal for small birds and portions. There is no need to add fat or liquid to the pot unless the recipe specifically requires this.

Chinese Sand Pot

This covered earthenware pot, which is sometimes called a Chinese casserole, is usually glazed on the inside only and reinforced on the outside with wire. It comes from China, where it was originally used to cook stews over a slow charcoal fire. Several shapes and sizes are available. They are not expensive and can be bought in Asian and Chinese food and cooking equipment stores. The sand pot is ideal for slow-cooked dishes such as soups and stews that are baked in the oven. Do not use sand pots on top of the stove unless the manufacturer recommends this. Sand pots are fairly fragile, and are prone to crack easily. They do not need to be soaked before baking but like other clay pots are best placed in a cold oven.

Tagine

This North African cooking pot consists of a large, shallow base and a tall, conical lid. The dish that is cooked in it is also known as a tagine.

Left: The Chinese sand pot was designed for cooking over a slow charcoal fire, but it is equally at home in a modern oven.

The food is placed in the base. As it cooks, steam rises and is trapped in the lid, keeping the food moist. Tagines are traditionally made from glazed brown earthenware, sometimes with a slightly rounded base. They come in a range of sizes, from small individual tagines to family-size ones that measure at least 20cm/8in across. There is also a modern version, with a heavy, cast-iron base and a glazed earthenware lid. Unlike the traditional tagine, which can only be used in the oven, or on a barbecue whose coals have been dowsed with sand, this design can also be used on top of the stove. This is very convenient, since it means that onions, vegetables and other ingredients such as meat and poultry can be browned in the base before the lid is fitted and the tagine is placed in the oven. Some glazed earthenware tagines can be used on top of the stove on a low heat, but it is best to use a heat diffuser; always check the manufacturer's instructions.

Above: The traditional tagine (above left) has a shallow base and a tall, conical lid, while the contemporary version (right) has a deeper, larger base.

WHAT'S IN A NAME?

Clay, earthenware, terracotta, stoneware – we use the terms interchangeably, but are they all the same thing? Clay is essentially the raw material; it is a fine-grained mix of mineral origin that occurs in sedimentary rocks and soils. It is malleable when moist, but hardens when it is heated. When pots that are made from clay are baked, they become earthenware.

Terracotta is an Italian word that means "baked earth". It has come to refer to a type of hard, brownish-red earthenware that is traditionally left unglazed.

Stoneware is stronger than earthenware, having been fired at a higher temperature. It is usually perfectly safe to put stoneware in a hot oven, but always check the manufacturer's instructions.

Cazuelas

These shallow, lidless earthenware dishes originated in Spain. They are made in a variety of sizes. The smallest, suitable for Catalan-style sweet custards, measure 10–12.5cm/4–5in across, while the largest – used for cooking savoury dishes in the oven – measure 38cm/15in or even more. They vary in depth from about 2.5cm/1in to 7.5cm/3in. Cazuelas are either partially glazed on the outside, and fully glazed inside, or glazed inside and out. Neither type are soaked in water before use. After a while, the glaze on the cazuela may develop a slightly "crazed" appearance, but this is completely natural and will not affect the performance of the dish.

Individual cazuelas can be used for cooking single portions of all sorts of one-pot dishes, but they are ideal for making individual upside-down tarts. The lightly fried vegetables are spread out on the cazuelas, topped with rounds of puff pastry, then baked in the oven. The tarts are then inverted on serving plates.

Left: *Spanish cazuelas come in a range of sizes and depths. The smallest are perfect for individual oven-baked custards, while the largest are good for slow-cooked stews and vegetable bakes, but will also accommodate whole fish and poultry as well as large joints of meat.*

Tian

This traditional French baking dish originated in Provence. It is a shallow, usually oval, earthenware dish, and is used for baking vegetables, sometimes with rice and eggs. The dish that is cooked in it is also called a tian.

Right: *Oval-shaped tians originated in Provence and are traditionally used for baking vegetables, but the shape is ideal for other oven-baked, one-pot dishes.*

Glazed Earthenware Bakeware

A wide selection of glazed ovenproof earthenware is available. These dishes can often be put straight into a hot oven, or used under a hot grill (broiler) for browning. They are also suitable for use in the freezer. Unlike clay pots and porous earthenware, they do not need to be soaked in water before use and will not absorb food flavours and become tainted.

Right: *A wide range of glazed earthenware bakeware is available – these dishes can often be used in the oven and under the grill.*

INGREDIENTS: BEEF

Enjoyed all over the world, there are dozens of classic beef dishes, from the British Sunday roast, to French boeuf bourguignonne, German sauerbraten and Russian stroganoff. Beef's popularity is partly due to its versatility. There are many different cuts of beef, and many of these are suitable for a range of cooking methods. Tender fillet, for example, is perfect for cutting into steaks for grilling (broiling), strips for stir-frying, or baked whole, wrapped in pastry. Other cuts, such as the less expensive shin of beef, are unsuitable for roasting or grilling but are wonderful in stews and braised dishes – and are perfect for slow cooker cooking.

Buying and storing

As with all meat, the flavour and texture of beef is determined by the breed of the animal, its feed, the environment in which it is reared and, ultimately, by the process of slaughtering and the treatment of meat before it is cooked. While pork and lamb tend to come from very young animals, beef usually comes from those aged between 18 months and 2 years.

Beef should be hung to allow the flavour to develop and the texture to improve, preferably for at least two weeks. Well-matured beef has a deep, rich burgundy colour, not a bright red hue, and the fat is a creamy colour, or yellow, if the animal was grass-fed. Maturing is an expensive process because some water content will be lost through evaporation, so expect to pay a little more for well-hung meat. The leanest looking joint isn't always the best: for pot-roasting, casseroling

Above: Topside, also known as top round or top rump, is a fairly lean cut of beef that is best slowly braised or pot-roasted.

and braising, a marbling of fat running through the meat will provide flavour and basting to keep the meat moist.

Beef should be kept on a low shelf in the refrigerator, below any cooked foods and ingredients that will be eaten raw. When buying pre-packed meat, check and observe the eat-by date. Whether pre-packed or loose, minced (ground) and cubed beef should be used within 1–2 days of buying; chops and small joints should be used within 3 days, and larger joints within 4–5 days.

Cuts of beef

Butchering techniques differ according to regional and cultural traditions, and also from country to country. Good butchers and larger supermarkets offer a range of cuts and it is worth asking for their advice when buying.

Generally, cuts from the top of the animal, along the middle of the back, are tender because the muscles in this area do relatively little work. These are prime cuts that are good for quick cooking techniques, such as grilling (broiling) and pan-frying, and tend to be the most expensive. Cuts from the neck, shoulders and lower legs are full of flavour, but the texture is coarser and tougher because these are the parts of the animal that work the hardest. They require longer cooking by moist methods to ensure tender results – it is these cuts that are perfectly suited to cooking in the slow cooker. Slow, gentle stewing results in meltingly tender meat and a further developed flavour.

Left (from top): Thick flank makes good braising steak; thin flank produces rich-flavoured steaks and is best suited to slow, moist methods of cooking. Skirt and onglet, which is taken from the skirt area, are lean cuts with a coarse texture that become moist and tender when slowly braised.

Below: Neck is one of the less tender beef cuts but is delicious braised or stewed.

Blade or chuck These cuts come from the top forequarter and are relatively lean, marbled with just a little fat that keeps the meat moist. They are usually boned and sold together as braising steak. The long, gentle cooking of a slow cooker helps to tenderize the meat and intensifies its flavour. These cuts suit pot-roasting, casseroling and braising.

Brisket This may be bought on the bone or boned and rolled and comes from the lower part of the shoulder. It can be a fatty and somewhat tough cut of meat, but is excellent pot-roasted, braised or stewed in the slow cooker. It may also be salted or spiced before cooking, and served cold in thin slices.

Clod and neck Sometimes referred to as "sticking", these cuts come from the neck area and are fairly lean. They are often sold cut up as "stewing" steak. Slightly leaner than blade or chuck, they may also be sold minced (ground).

Fillet/tenderloin, rump/round, sirloin steak These lean, tender cuts from the back are usually cut into steaks for grilling (broiling) or frying, or into strips for stir-frying, and occasionally they are used for roasting. They may be included in braised slow cooker recipes, particularly those cooked on a high setting, but there is little point in using such cuts in casseroles and similar long-cooked dishes, where less expensive cuts produce more flavourful results.

Flank Lean thick flank, or top rump, comes from the hindquarter. In a whole piece, it is ideal for pot-roasting in the slow cooker. It is also sold thickly sliced as braising steak. Thin flank can be fatty and gristly. It can be stewed but is often sold minced (ground).

Leg and shin/foreshank The leg cut comes from the hind legs of the animal and the shin from the forelegs. The shin is a tough cut that responds well to slow cooking. It is usually sold in slices with the bone in the centre and sinews and connective tissue running though; these and the marrow from the bones give the cooked meat a rich, gelatinous quality.

Minced/ground beef This is made from meat from any part of the animal, which has been passed through a mincer. It can be used to make meat sauces and meatballs in the slow cooker. As a general rule, the paler the meat the higher the fat content, so look for dark meat with less fat.

Rib Fore rib and wing, or prime rib, are expensive joints, best served roasted. For the slow cooker, choose middle rib. It is a fairly lean joint, and best boned before braising or pot-roasting.

Silverside/round pot roast This is lean, but tough, and is excellent for pot-roasts and braised dishes. It is often salted and gently cooked, then pressed and served cold.

Skirt/flank steak This thin braising cut can also be pot-roasted. It has a lean but somewhat coarse texture, and can be fast-fried or cooked very slowly, making it an ideal cut for the slow cooker.

VEAL

This meat comes from young calves so is very tender and lean. Most cuts are not well suited to cooking in the slow cooker. Exceptions are shoulder of veal, also known as the oyster, which is sometimes cut into chunks for casseroles; and the knuckle, the bonier end of the hind leg, which can be cut into slices and used to make the Italian stew osso bucco.

BRING OUT THE TASTE

Beef is a well-flavoured meat that is delicious cooked with robust ingredients and served with spicy accompaniments. Peppery mustards and spicy horseradish are classic accompaniments, while wasabi, a sharp-tasting Japanese horseradish gives a more unusual twist.

Other Asian flavourings, such as soy sauce and ginger, also work well. Perfect vegetable partners include potatoes, leeks, onions, parsnips, celery and celeriac.

Above: Chuck steak (top) and brisket (bottom) are tough cuts, but both have an excellent flavour. They are perfectly suited to long, slow stewing, which gives deliciously moist results.

Below: Knuckle (top) and shoulder (bottom) are two of the few cuts of veal suitable for slow cooker cooking.

LAMB

Though lamb cuts do not usually need tenderizing, the fragrant flavour of the meat is intensified by slow cooking. It is enjoyed around the world in a wealth of pot-roasts, casseroles, stews, tagines, curries and braised dishes.

Buying and storing

Lamb comes from animals that are less than a year old; spring lamb comes from animals that are between five and seven months old. Meat from older sheep is known as mutton and has a darker colour and stronger flavour; it is rarely available. Look for firm, slightly pink lamb with a fine-grained texture. The younger the animal, the paler the meat. The fat should be creamy white, firm and waxy. Avoid any meat that looks dark, dry or grainy.

Lamb should be kept covered on a low shelf in the refrigerator. Pre-packed meat can be left in its packaging and used by the date given on the packet. When buying loose meat, steaks and chops will keep for 2–3 days, while larger joints will keep for up to 5 days.

Above: Tender chump chops are good pan-fried, grilled or braised.

Below: A small leg of lamb can be pot-roasted in the slow cooker; steaks cut from the leg are good for braises and casseroles.

Cuts of lamb

The lean, tender prime cuts are taken from the top of the lamb along the middle of the back and are often grilled (broiled), fried or roasted. However, they may also be cooked using slow, moist methods. Tougher cuts from the neck and lower legs respond we to slow cooker methods.

Breast This inexpensive cut is fairly fatty and is often served boned and rolled, sometimes wit stuffing. It can be braised in the s cooker, but trim off the visible fa

Chops and cutlets Chump or loi and leg chops are thick tender chops. Best-end chops or cutlets and middle neck cutlets are thinner and should be trimmed of fat before slow cooking.

Leg This is the prime roasting joint and is often divided into two pieces: the knuckle or shank end, and the leg fillet. The shank is a flavourful cut and is good pot-roasted or gently braised. A small leg of lamb may be pot-roasted on the bone in a large or oval slow cooker, or it can be boned and stuffed. It may also be cut into leg steaks or cubed.

Middle neck and scrag end Relatively cheap and made tender by long, slow cooking, these are used in dishes such as Lancashire hot-pot and Irish stew.

Saddle of lamb Also called a double loin of lamb, this tender roasting joint is too big to cook in a slow cooker.

Shoulder This roasting joint from the forequarter is fattier than the leg, so should be trimmed before pot-roasting on or off the bone. Boneless shoulder can be cubed for casseroles.

Above: Tender noisettes cut from the rolled, boned loin (top) are better suited to quick cooking techniques, while lamb cutlets (bottom) are great for braised dishes.

PERFECT PARTNERS

Fragrant herbs and fruity flavours go well with lamb. Dried fruit is a common addition to lamb dishes all over the world; rosemary, thyme and mint are popular herbs; and garlic and salty additions, such as anchovies and olives, are widely used in Mediterranean dishes. Vegetables that go well with lamb include new potatoes, peas, carrots and beans such as haricot (navy) and flageolet.

Below: Dried prunes make a tasty addition to a Moroccan lamb tagine.

PORK

This light meat is rich-tasting and very versatile. It is also particularly good for slow cooking: whole joints can be pot-roasted, bacon and gammon can be poached, chops can be braised, and cubes of meat stewed. Pork products, such as sausages and minced (ground) pork, are also fabulous cooked in the slow cooker, in dishes such as hearty stews and chunky pâtés and terrines.

Buying and storing

Traditionally, fresh pork was a food for late autumn. Pigs were fattened through the summertime to provide fresh and cured meats during the colder months. However, with modern storage techniques, pork is no longer a seasonal meat and is available all the year round.

Pork should be a pale brownish-pink in colour with a smooth, moist, fine-grained texture. The fat should look white and firm. In older animals, the meat darkens to a deeper colour and the flesh is coarser and less tender.

Hygiene is very important when handling pork, and great care should be taken not to contaminate other foods with the meat juices. Store pork on a low shelf in the refrigerator, below any food that will be eaten raw. Keep pre-packed meat in its packaging and observe the use-by dates. Minced (ground) pork can be kept for up to 2 days, while pork chops and joints can be kept for 3 days.

Above: Loin chops (top) and chump chops (bottom) are very good for braising.

Cuts of pork

Belly/side This cut can be rolled and tied to make a neat joint and pot-roasted, or used for mincing and making sausages or terrines. Once a very fatty cut, today's belly pork tends to be leaner.

Chops Large and bony chump chops come from the hind loin, and leaner loin chops from the foreloin. Both are good for braising. (A loin joint is better suited to oven-roasting than slow cooking.)

Leg/ham Often weighing more than 4.5kg/10lb, this cut is too big to be cooked in the slow cooker. However, it can be cut into two joints: the knuckle (shank) and the fillet. The knuckle can be pot-roasted, but is better oven-roasted. Leg fillet is cut across the top of the leg and is very tender. Leg steaks, cut from the top of the leg, are good for braising.

Neck end Cuts from this area include the spare rib, which is often cut into spare rib chops (different from Chinese-style spare ribs, which are cut from the belly). They are good for braising.

Shoulder/blade Taken from the fore end and sold on or off the bone, this can be pot-roasted, but is usually trimmed, cubed and casseroled.

Tenderloin/fillet This lean, boneless, fine-textured piece of meat can be sliced into medallions or split lengthways, stuffed and tied. It may be cooked on a high setting in the slow cooker.

CLASSIC FLAVOURINGS

Pork is widely eaten in Europe, Asia and South and Central America. Because of its rich taste and texture, it goes well with fruity and acidic accompaniments. In England, Germany and France, apples are a popular choice, while in New England, cranberries are favoured. In other cuisines, peaches, apricots and pineapple are all used. Pungent herbs and spices, such as sage, rosemary, thyme and juniper, are often added to pork dishes, and throughout Europe cabbage is a popular vegetable accompaniment.

OFFAL

Known as variety meats in the United States, offal refers to all the offcuts from the carcass, including the organs, tail, feet and head. Most offal is rich and highly flavoured; it may be eaten on its own in a dish, but is often used together with other meats — for example, in steak and kidney pie and in terrines and pâtés. Many types of offal are good cooked in a slow cooker, particularly heart, tongue and pig's trotters, which become deliciously tender with slow, moist, gentle cooking. Unlike meat, which is often hung and matured for several weeks before using, offal does not keep well and should be bought very fresh and used quickly.

Bacon, ham and gammon

These are cured cuts of pork. Bacon is usually cured meat taken from the back and sides of the pig. Ham is the hind leg of a pig cut from the whole side, then cured separately. Gammon is the name of the whole hind leg cut from a side of bacon after curing. Cooked gammon is now often referred to as ham. These joints respond well to poaching in the slow cooker, as long cooking makes them very tender. Bacon chops and gammon steaks are also good braised. Strips of bacon are often fried in a pan before adding to slow cooker stews.

Above: Rolled belly of pork is perfect for pot-roasting in the slow cooker.

POULTRY and GAME

The term poultry covers domesticated birds, including chicken, turkey, duck, goose and guinea fowl, while game refers to wild birds and animals hunted for food, including pheasant, quail, wild rabbit and venison. However, many game birds and animals are now farmed.

SMALL POULTRY

Chicken is probably the most popular of all small poultry, but there are many other types that are just as good.

Buying and storing

When buying fresh or chilled poultry, choose birds with soft blemish-free skin. Because poultry is highly susceptible to bacterial growth, keep poultry well chilled. Place loose poultry in a deep dish and cover loosely, check pre-packed poultry to make sure that the packs are sealed and place on a plate, then store in the coldest part of the refrigerator. Check inside whole birds and remove any giblets. Always wash hands, utensils and surfaces after handling poultry.

When using frozen poultry, the safest way to thaw it is in the refrigerator. Place in a suitable container and leave to defrost: for a 900g–1.3kg/2–3lb bird, allow about 30 hours in the refrigerator, or 8 hours at room temperature; for a 2.25kg/5lb chicken, allow about 48 hours in the refrigerator, or 10 hours at room temperature. Once thawed or partially thawed, it should not be refrozen.

Below (from left to right): Corn-fed, free-range and organic chickens are widely available.

Types of small poultry

Poussin This is the French name for a young chicken that is only four to six weeks old and weighs 350–675g/ 12oz–1½lb. These are very tender, with little fat, and will serve one or two people. They are ideal for pot-roasting, which gives moist, tender results.

Spring chicken These are sometimes called double poussins and will easily serve two. They are slightly larger birds, between six and ten weeks old, and weigh about 900g/2lb.

Roasting chicken Sometimes known as a roaster, these prime birds are about 12 weeks old. They usually weigh about 1.3kg/3lb but they may be as big as 3kg/ 6–7lb. The larger the bird, the better its value, because the proportion of meat to bone will be higher. They can be pot-roasted whole or in portions, poached, braised or stewed.

Stewing or boiling chicken Rarely available from supermarkets, these birds are over one year old and tend to be large. Too tough for roasting, they are full of flavour and perfect for the slow cooker as they need slow simmering. Either poach or use for soups and stews.

Guinea fowl These domestic fowl originated from the coast of Guinea in West Africa, hence their name. These birds are about the same size as a spring chicken. The flesh is delicate with a slightly gamey flavour. They can be cooked in the same way as chicken, but because they are quite dry, they respond best to moist cooking such as pot-roasting, braising and stewing.

FARMING CONDITIONS

While intensively reared chickens are the least expensive, many cooks agree that free-range, organic and corn-fed birds are tastier. Free-range chickens are not raised in factory conditions and have access to open-air runs. Unlike intensively reared birds, their growth isn't accelerated by their feed and restricted movement. Because free-range birds grow and develop more slowly, they are older by the time they reach the desired weight, and therefore better flavoured. Corn-fed chickens have a lurid, bright yellow skin. This is partly due to their diet of corn (maize), but is often intensified by additional colouring in the feed. They are rarely free-range and may be reared intensively. Organic chickens are fed on a natural diet and are raised in humane conditions.

Cuts of chicken

A wide range of chicken portions are available fresh and frozen and are sold either individually, or in large, more economical packs. They may be sold on or off the bone.

Chicken quarters may be either leg joints or wing joints that have a portion of breast meat attached. The leg joint may be divided into thighs, small well-flavoured dark meat joints, and drumsticks. Both need relatively long cooking in the slow cooker because the meat is compact.

Tender breast portions are entirely white meat; they are sold on or off the bone and may be skinned or unskinned. Portions on the bone have the most flavour when stewed or braised. Boneless chicken breast portions are sometimes referred to as fillets. The very small strips of chicken that can be found under the chicken breast are often sold separately. Supremes are chicken breast portions that include the wingbone, while part-boned breasts still have the short piece of bone leading into the wing and the fine strip of breastbone.

Jointing small poultry

This method of jointing can also be used for game birds, such as pheasant.

1 With the breast uppermost, use a sharp knife to remove the leg between the thigh and carcass. Cut, angling the knife inwards, through the ball and socket joint. Repeat with the other leg.

2 Using poultry shears, cut along the breastbone, between the breast sections. Turn the bird over and cut out the backbone. Using poultry shears, cut off the wing tips at the first joint.

3 Cut each breast section in half, leaving a portion of the breast attached to the wing. Next, cut each leg through the knee joint to separate the thigh and drumstick, making eight portions in all.

TURKEY

These substantial birds have dense meat that is lean and succulent. Fully grown, a turkey can weigh over 9kg/20lb and feed over twenty people. Whole birds won't fit in a slow cooker, but prepared joints and cuts are perfect for slow cooking.

Skinless, boneless breast fillets can be used in many different dishes. Turkey drumsticks can be large enough to provide a meal for three to four people. They can be pot-roasted, but are better braised or stewed until tender. Diced turkey is usually darker meat from the thigh or leg, and is ideal for casseroles and pâtés. Minced (ground) turkey can be used as an alternative to minced beef.

DUCK

Flavourful, juicy and rich, duck is much fattier than chicken or turkey, with a higher proportion of bone to meat. Birds under 2 months old are called ducklings and are slightly leaner and more tender, but with less flavour. Wild duck has a stronger, more gamey taste than farmed duck, but can be cooked in the same way. The slow cooker is unsuitable for cooking whole birds because of their awkward shape and fat content. However, duck breast portions can be used, providing the thick layer of fat is removed. Breast portions weigh about 225g/8oz, making a generous serving for one. Skinned duck portions are ideal for braising, especially in citrus or fruit sauces, which tenderize and flavour.

Jointing a duck

Because ducks have a high proportion of bone to meat, it is better to cut the bird into four portions, dividing an equal amount of meat between them.

1 Place the duck, breast side up, on a board. Using poultry shears, trim off the wing tips at the first joint. Pull back the skin at the neck end and cut out the wishbone. Cut the breast in half from the tail end to the neck.

Above: Turkey is a versatile as well as economical meat.

2 Separate the bird into two halves by cutting along each side of the backbone. Remove the backbone and discard.

3 Cut each portion in half, sharing the meat as evenly as possible between the four portions.

GOOSE

These large, fatty birds are difficult to rear intensively, so fresh birds are usually only available from the late autumn until Christmas. Goose is much better suited to oven-roasting than cooking gently in the slow cooker.

GAME

Once hard to come by, game is now readily available from the supermarket. Fresh wild game remains seasonal and is only available during the months when hunting is allowed. Many types of game are now farmed and available year-round, while wild game is available frozen. Game can be divided into two types: game birds and furred game, which includes rabbit, hare, wild boar and venison.

Buying and storing

Larger supermarkets and specialist butchers offer a good choice of game when in season and should be able to offer you advice on preparation and cooking. Game birds will not look as perfect as poultry, but check that they are not too damaged. Pheasant should be even in shape with a pleasant gamey aroma. Partridge will have a slightly stronger game smell and soft pale flesh. When buying grouse and quail, look for a moist fresh skin and choose birds with a high proportion of meat to bone.

Right: A brace of pheasant.

Below: Tiny quail are often farmed.

Below: Mallard is the most commonly available wild duck.

Below: Pigeon.

Birds that are sold in sealed packaging should be left in their packing and used by the date indicated. If you buy a bird "loose" from the butcher, remove the packaging when you get home, rinse the bird under cold running water and pat dry with kitchen paper. Put the bird in a deep dish to catch any drips and cover it tightly with clear film (plastic wrap). Store game birds in the coldest part of the refrigerator and use within two days of purchase or freeze straight away. Before cooking wild game birds, rub your fingertips over the surface to try to locate any tiny balls of lead shot that may be left in them, then carefully cut them out with kitchen scissors or a filleting knife and discard.

Types of game bird

Very young and tender birds are often roasted or spatchcocked and grilled (broiled), but most older game birds benefit from moist cooking techniques, as pot-roasting, stewing or raising. When pot-roasting y game birds, such as cock heasant, wrap rashers (slices) of streaky (fatty) bacon around the bird, then tie in place with string. This will help to baste and flavour the meat.

Pheasant One of the most plentiful of game birds, these are usually raised on managed estates in a similar manner to free-range farming. Traditionally they were sold in pairs, known as a brace (one male and one female). The tender hen pheasant would be roasted and the cock pheasant hung and stewed. In practice, supermarket pheasants are always young and tender. For the best results, pot-roast or stew pheasants. One bird should serve three or four people.

Grouse Native to Scotland, these birds feed on highland heather, which gives them a rich gamey flavour. They are quite small and

will serve one or two people. Ptarmigan and capercaillie are members of the grouse family, but are considered to have an inferior flavour compared to grouse. Young birds may be pot-roasted, but need to be kept moist with a layer of fat or streaky bacon over the breast. They are good stewed.

Partridge There are two main types: French or red-legged partridge, and the smaller English or grey-legged partridge, which has a better flavour. At their prime (around three months old), they weigh about 450g/1lb and it is usual to serve one per person. Older birds should always be casseroled or braised.

Wild duck These are less fatty than farmed ducks, so smaller ones may be cooked whole in a large slow cooker. Choose inland ducks because those from saltwater areas may have a fishy flavour.

Pigeon Wild and wood pigeon has a strong flavour and can be stewed slowly to tenderize the meat. Another traditional way of cooking an older bird is in a steamed pudding, often with beef steak inside a suet crust. Young pigeon is known as squab. They are reared commercially, although they are usually only available in the spring.

Quail This is now a protected species, so quail on sale will have been farmed. They are tiny, so you will need two per person for a main course. They may be pot-roasted whole.

FURRED GAME

Most game needs to be hung before cooking to tenderize the flesh and develop the flavour. However, this is usually done by the butcher, so the meat is ready for cooking when you buy it.

Game is cooked in the same way as other meats and recipes for similar types of meat are usually interchangeable. For example, wild boar can often be used instead of pork, farmed rabbit instead of chicken, and venison in place of beef in many recipes. Mature game should always be cooked using gentle, moist heat, such as braising and stewing, making it ideal for the slow cooker.

Deer

The word venison was once used to describe the meat of any animal killed for food by hunting. Today, in Britain and Australia, the term venison only refers to the meat from deer, although in North America it also includes meat from the reindeer, moose, caribou, elk and antelope. Venison from deer is a lean, dark, close-textured meat. Much of it is now farmed and is more tender, with a slightly milder flavour, than venison from wild deer. Prime cuts, such as loin and fillet, are best roasted and served rare. Other cuts, such as shin, neck and shoulder, benefit from marinating (red wine and juniper is traditional); they then need long and gentle cooking to tenderize and bring out the flavour of the meat.

Wild boar

Although hunted to extinction in Britain in the 17th century, wild boar is still found in Europe, central Asia and North Africa. The meat is dark-coloured with a strong flavour and little fat, so it benefits from marinades with a little added oil. It can be cooked in exactly the same way as pork, but care must be taken because the meat is dry and can easily become tough. Moist cooking methods work best.

Rabbit and hare

Although these animals belong to the same family, the meat is very different. Rabbit, especially if it has been farmed, is a paler, milder meat, similar to chicken. Hare, or jack rabbit as it is known in the United States, has a very strong, dark gamey flesh. The saddle of both can be roasted, but other cuts are best slowly stewed. Boneless rabbit and hare meat can be used in steamed puddings, terrines and pâtés. Older hares are traditionally jugged (cooked in a casserole set over a pan of simmering water to temper the heat) to give deliciously tender results. Cooking gently in the slow cooker gives similar results.

Above and right: Rabbit saddle is best roasted. Other rabbit cuts should be stewed.

Above and left: Cultivated hare has lean, dark meat and is available whole or in pieces.

Jointing a rabbit

A whole rabbit can be jointed into five pieces or more, depending on its size.

1 To joint a skinned and cleaned rabbit, use a large filleting knife to cut between the ball and socket joint at the top of each thigh to remove the hind legs.

2 Cut the body into three pieces. This will give you five pieces – two forelegs, two hind legs and the saddle.

Above and left: Venison cuts that benefit from long, slow cooking include shin, shoulder and neck (above left to right) and haunch (left).

FISH and SHELLFISH

The slow cooker is great for cooking fish, allowing the subtle flavour to develop slowly and also helping to retain the fish's shape as it cooks. Fish dishes that can be made in the slow cooker include terrines, soups, risottos and pasta dishes, as well as simple steamed and poached fish. The slow cooker is also good for cooking many dishes containing raw and cooked shellfish. However, it is not suitable for cooking live shellfish, such as mussels and lobsters, because these require brief, fast boiling.

Most shellfish benefit from short cooking and should be added towards the end of cooking time, particularly when using pre-cooked shellfish. One exception is squid, which requires either very brief or very long, slow cooking; anything in between gives tough results.

Buying and cooking

Always buy the freshest fish and shellfish available, from a supplier with a high turnover, and prepare and cook it within 24 hours. Fish and shellfish should smell fresh; if it has an unpleasant fishy or ammoniac odour, it is past its best. Most fish and shellfish from the supermarket has already been frozen, so shouldn't be refrozen; check this when you buy.

PREPARING FISH

Fish can be divided into two types: white and oily. These, in turn, can be divided into round and flat fish, which require slightly different preparation and cooking.

Round fish

This group includes white-fleshed fish such as cod, coley and haddock, and oily fish such as salmon and mackerel. They have rounded bodies and eyes on either side of the head. The flesh is usually firm with largish flakes when cooked. Many are too big to be cooked whole in the slow cooker, so need to be sliced into steaks or filleted. A good fishmonger will often do this for you.

1 To remove the scales, place the fish on a large sheet of newspaper. Scrape a fish scaler or knife against the skin, working from the tail to the head.

2 Using a filleting knife or thin, sharp knife, slit the fish open along the belly from the gills to the tail vent. Carefully scrape out the innards with a spoon, then rinse well under running water, inside and out. Cut off the head using a sharp knife.

3 To fillet the fish, lay it on its side, tail away from you. Make an incision along the backbone from head to tail, cutting through behind the gills. Starting at the head end, slide the knife between the fillet and bones to release the fillet.

4 To skin the fillet, lay it skin side down. Make a cut at the tail end, cutting through the flesh, but not the skin, so that the fillet can be lifted away slightly. Hold the tail firmly and "saw" the knife between the skin and flesh.

Flat fish

This group includes sole and plaice. Both eyes lie on their upper side and, because they lead an inactive life on the seabed, the flesh tends to be very delicate.

1 Place the fish, light side down, on a board. Make a cut down the centre using a sharp filleting knife, following the backbone, then make a second cut round the head.

2 Slide the knife under one fish fillet, inserting the blade between the flesh and bones. Holding the loosened corner, cut the flesh from the bones. Remove the second fillet in the same way, then turn the fish over and repeat.

3 The skins may be removed in the same manner as for round fish.

PREPARING SHELLFISH

You can often ask the fishmonger to prepare shellfish for you, but it is also easy to prepare at home.

Prawns/shrimp

Raw prawns may be cooked in their shells or peeled first. The dark intestinal vein is usually removed.

1 To peel, grip the head between your forefinger and thumb. Holding the body with your other hand, gently pull until the head comes off. Remove the legs and peel the shell from the body. The tail may be pulled away or left on.

2 To remove the dark intestinal vein, make a shallow cut down the centre of the back and pull out the vein using a knife blade or a cocktail stick (toothpick).

Preparing squid

Unlike other shellfish, which have their protective shell on the outside, the shell of the squid is found inside its body.

1 Hold the body of the squid in one hand and the tentacles in the other and gently pull apart. Cut the tentacles away from the head just below the eyes and discard the head.

2 Remove the "quill" and soft innards from the body and discard. Peel off the thin membrane, then rinse the body and tentacles under cold running water.

3 Using a sharp knife, slice the body into rings, or cut it into large pieces and lightly score in a criss-cross pattern.

COOKING FISH

Fish is well suited to simple cooking methods that retain its natural juices. Unlike meat, fish should be removed from the slow cooker as soon as it is done, otherwise it will become dry. It is ready when the flesh is still slightly translucent when eased away from the bone, and flakes easily.

Poaching

This is a good method for cooking large, fairly firm pieces of fish, such as steaks or chunky fillets. It can also be used for small whole fish. Fish stock, wine, water and milk can all be used for poaching.

1 Lightly grease the base of the ceramic cooking pot. Place four 175–225g/6–8oz salmon fillets or similar in the base, leaving space between each one.

2 Pour over 150ml/¼ pint/⅔ cup dry white wine and 300ml/½ pint/1¼ cups of boiling fish stock or water. Add a pinch of salt, 2 black peppercorns, a few slices of onion, 1 bay leaf and a sprig of fresh parsley.

3 Cover the pot with the lid and switch the slow cooker to high. Cook for 45 minutes–1½ hours, or until cooked. Serve with melted butter or a sauce, or leave to cool and serve with salad.

Braising

This method cooks the fish in a small amount of liquid, so that it is partly poached and partly steamed. It is a good technique for delicate flat fish fillets. Rolling the fish fillets helps to protect them during cooking and allows you to add a filling for extra flavour.

1 Pour slightly less than 5mm/¼in white wine, cider or fish stock into the ceramic cooking pot and switch the slow cooker to high. Cover with the lid.

2 Blend 25g/1oz butter with lemon or orange rind, salt and pepper. Place four large, skinned lemon sole fillets on a board and spread each with the butter.

3 Roll up the fillet to enclose the filling and carefully place in the base of the ceramic cooking pot, with the loose end tucked underneath.

4 Sprinkle the fish with 15ml/1 tbsp lemon juice. Cover with the lid and cook for 45 minutes–1½ hours, or until the fish is opaque and cooked. Transfer to serving plates. Stir a little sour cream and chopped fresh parsley, dill or coriander (cilantro) into the cooking juices and spoon over the fish.

VEGETABLES

Cooking vegetables in the slow cooker is a good way to ensure they are tender without being overcooked, which can spoil their texture and subtle flavours.

Onions

An essential ingredient in many slow cooker recipes, they take a long time to cook so are often fried in oil before adding to the slow cooker.

Different types of onion have varying degrees of pungency. Large, yellow onions (often called Spanish or Bermuda onions) are mild. Smaller, white onions, the most common type, have a stronger flavour; red onions are mild and sweet. Leeks are part of the onion family and have a milder flavour than onions; they cook more quickly. Garlic adds

Above: The onion family includes spring onions, red and white onions, and brown and banana shallots.

flavour; the taste it imparts is milder when whole or sliced, and stronger when crushed or chopped. Slow cooking tames the pungency, so you may need to increase the amount in dishes cooked for more than 4 hours. Spring onions (scallions) are usually used raw, but have a delicate flavour when cooked.

Roots and tubers

These vegetables, which include carrots, swedes (rutabagas), turnips, parsnips and potatoes, have a dense, sometimes starchy flesh. They take the longest time to cook in the slow cooker.

Cut roots and tubers into small pieces, no larger than 2.5cm/1in thick, and place in the base of the ceramic cooking pot, which is the hottest part during cooking. The vegetables should be immersed in the cooking liquid to ensure they soften, and to protect those roots and tubers, such as potatoes, that will discolour if exposed to air.

In braised dishes that use only a little liquid, it may be necessary to layer the ingredients. It does not matter if some of the meat on the surface is not covered with cooking liquid, as it will cook in the steam. If the dish contains ingredients that do not require long cooking, such as fish, sauté the root vegetables first.

Mushrooms

These add a deep colour and rich taste to many dishes. They give off a lot of liquid, so if you add extra mushrooms to a recipe, adjust the liquid content.

Button (white), chestnut and flat mushrooms are the most common cultivated types. Button mushrooms have a mild taste; small whole ones are good in casseroles. Flat mushrooms have a stronger flavour and are usually sliced or left whole and stuffed. Chestnut mushrooms have a darker brown skin, firmer texture and a stronger, nuttier taste than buttons. Large ones are known as field (portabello) mushrooms and have a meaty taste.

Field mushrooms, field blewitts, ceps, morels and shiitake mushrooms are wild varieties with intense flavours. Delicate mushrooms, such as oyster and enoki, should be added to the slow cooker near the end of cooking. Dried mushrooms are used to thicken dishes by absorbing liquid. They should be pre-soaked in boiling water for a few minutes before adding, to remove any grit or dirt.

CLEANING LEEKS

Leeks usually need careful cleaning to remove grit and dirt in the leaves.

1 Trim the root and coarse green tops and discard. Remove any damaged or tough outer leaves.

2 Slit the top green part lengthways about a third of the way down. Rinse well under cold running water, separating the layers as you do so.

Above: Mushrooms have a distinctive taste and meaty texture.

Pumpkins and squashes

These come in many shapes, sizes and colours. Cooking in the slow cooker helps to develop their flavour and retain their firm texture. They tend to produce a lot of liquid during cooking, so don't add too much extra liquid to braised dishes containing pumpkins or squashes.

Squashes can be divided into two varieties: summer and winter. Winter squashes have a dense, fibrous flesh and include pumpkins and butternut and acorn squashes. They all have sweet-tasting, deep-orange flesh. Summer squashes include patty pans and courgettes (zucchini). They are picked young and have a high water content and delicate flesh that cooks quickly, so be careful not to overcook.

Shoot vegetables

This category covers a large number of vegetables, which vary widely in appearance and characteristics. Some, such as fennel, chicory and celery, respond well to slow cooking, while others, such as asparagus and globe artichokes, are better cooked using conventional methods.

VEGETABLE FRUITS

Although tomatoes, (bell) peppers and aubergines (eggplant) are all used as vegetables, botanically they are fruits.

Tomatoes

Great for slow cooking, these add a rich colour and flavour to many dishes. They are juicy, so can be used as part of the cooking liquid. Long cooking can make the skins tough and seeds bitter, so these are best removed before cooking.

Sweet peppers

Known as bell peppers in the United States, these come in many colours, including red, orange, yellow, green and purple. Green peppers are the unripe stage of peppers of other colours, such as red. Green peppers tend to lose their colour and become bitter in slow cooked dishes, unless they are cut into very small pieces and added towards the end of cooking.

Below (from left): Butternut, acorn and patty pan squashes make a great addition to slow cooked dishes.

Aubergines/eggplant

There are many types of aubergine, from large, glossy, dark-purple ones to the small, creamy-white egg-shaped ones that gave rise to the American name "eggplant". Very large aubergines may be slightly bitter, so should be salted after slicing or cubing and left for half an hour, then rinsed well. This process is also useful for drawing out liquid that would dilute the sauce of the dish.

Brassicas and green leafy vegetables

Brassicas, such as broccoli and cauliflower, should be broken or cut into small sprigs to ensure they cook evenly in the slow cooker. When using leafy vegetables, such as cabbage and spinach, shred them very finely and always add to hot liquid so they cook in the shortest possible time to retain their taste and texture.

CANNED AND FROZEN VEGETABLES

These make a useful last-minute addition to many dishes. They are particularly good time-savers because they require no further preparation. Cooked, canned vegetables should be well drained, then simply added 15 minutes before the end of cooking time.

Frozen vegetables, such as peas and corn, should be defrosted first and need a little more cooking. (For speedy defrosting, they can be placed in a strainer under cool running water.) Once added to the slow cooker, they should be cooked for 15–20 minutes.

GRAINS, PASTA and BEANS

Cereal grains, pasta and beans are all very versatile and can be used as a main ingredient or an accompaniment. Classic slow cooker dishes that use grains, pasta and beans as the main ingredient include risottos, pilaffs, lasagne, pasta bakes and bean stews and curries.

RICE

Ordinary long grain rice doesn't cook well in the slow cooker, but easy-cook (converted) rice gives excellent results. Also known as par-boiled rice, it is soaked in water and then steamed under pressure, making it difficult to overcook. The grains remain separate during cooking, so it is particularly good for slow cooking, where the water bubbles very gently, if at all. The dry grains may appear more yellow than normal rice, but this coloration disappears during cooking, and when fully cooked the rice becomes bright white.

TYPES OF EASY-COOK RICE

As well as white, long grain easy-cook (converted) rice, there are several other varieties, all with their own unique cooking properties.

Easy-cook brown rice Also known as easy-cook wholegrain rice, this is the whole rice grain complete with bran. It has a chewier texture and nuttier flavour than white long grain rice, and stands up best of all to long, slow cooking, still holding its shape after several hours on high.

Easy-cook basmati rice Basmati rice is grown in northern India, the Punjab, parts of Pakistan and in the foothills of the Himalayas. It has a unique taste and texture, and the word *basmati* means "fragrant one" in Hindi. Basmati is particularly good in pilafs and for serving with spicy Indian-style dishes.

Easy-cook Italian rice Sometimes labelled easy-cook risotto rice, this rice has short plump grains and a high proportion of starch, which gives a rich, creamy texture to dishes such as risotto.

Making slow cooker rice

A simple savoury rice dish can be made easily in the slow cooker, and makes a good accompaniment for four people.

1 Grease the bottom of the ceramic cooking pot with 15g/½oz/1 tbsp butter, or 15ml/1 tbsp sunflower oil. Sprinkle 4–6 very finely chopped spring onions (scallions) over the butter or oil. Switch the slow cooker to high and leave to cook for 20 minutes.

2 Add 1.5ml/¼ tsp ground turmeric or a pinch of saffron strands and 750ml/1¼ pints/3 cups boiling vegetable stock to the pot. If the stock is unseasoned, add a pinch of salt as well.

3 Sprinkle 300g/10oz/generous 1½ cups easy-cook rice over the stock and stir well. Cover and cook for about 1 hour, or until the rice is tender and the stock has been absorbed. Serve hot, or put into a shallow dish, stir in 30ml/2 tbsp vinaigrette, and serve warm or cold.

Making risotto

A good risotto should be creamy and moist. Cooked conventionally, this is achieved by adding the cooking liquid gradually and stirring constantly. The gentle heat of the slow cooker and the use of easy-cook Italian rice means that the liquid can be added in one go to produce a creamy risotto. This recipe for Risotto alla Milanese serves 3–4 people.

1 Gently fry 1 finely chopped onion in 15g/½oz/1 tbsp butter and 15ml/1 tbsp olive oil in a frying pan until soft. Pour in 120ml/4fl oz/½ cup dry white wine and heat until steaming but not boiling.

2 Transfer the mixture to the ceramic cooking pot and switch the slow cooker to high. Cover with the lid and cook for about 30 minutes, until boiling.

3 Sprinkle 225g/8oz/1¼ cups easy-cook Italian rice and a pinch of saffron strands into the pot. Pour in 750ml/1¼ pints/3 cups boiling stock. Stir well, re-cover and cook for about 45 minutes, stirring once halfway through cooking. The rice should be almost tender and most of the stock absorbed.

4 Turn off the slow cooker. Sprinkle 50g/2oz/¾ cup freshly grated Parmesan cheese into the risotto and stir, then season with freshly ground black pepper.

5 Cover the pot and leave to stand for about 5 minutes to allow the risotto to finish cooking. Taste and adjust the seasoning if necessary, then serve with fine shavings of Parmesan.

COOK'S TIP

This recipe is for the classic Risotto alla Milanese, but the ingredients can be varied to create other risotto dishes. Try stirring pan-fried mushrooms or chopped cooked chicken into the risotto 15 minutes before the end of cooking.

OTHER GRAINS

As well as rice, there are many other grains that can be cooked successfully in a slow cooker. Whole grains, such as barley, quinoa and whole wheat, can be served as an accompaniment instead of rice or potatoes, or as part of a main course. Whole rye grains need to be soaked in cold water overnight before cooking. This is not necessary for most grains, although pre-soaking will shorten the cooking time.

Cooking grains

The cooking times vary from grain to grain; quinoa and millet take the least time, while grains such as barley and rye take much longer. To speed up cooking and enhance the flavour, fry grains in a little oil for 2–3 minutes, before transferring to the slow cooker.

1 Allow about 75g/3oz per person for part of a main course. If the quantity of cooking liquid is not indicated on the packet, place the grains in a measuring jug (cup) to check their volume, then measure three parts boiling water or stock to one part grain (millet is the exception, and needs four parts water).

2 Rinse the grains in a sieve under cold running water, then place in the ceramic cooking pot and pour over the water or stock. Cover and cook on high for 40 minutes–2 hours, or until tender.

PASTA

Both ordinary and easy-cook pastas can be used in the slow cooker. The latter gives the best results, but is not suitable for "all-day cooking"; the final result will be soft and soggy. As a general rule, pasta made from 100 per cent durum wheat holds its shape better than the varieties made with eggs (all'uova). Fresh pasta is not suitable for slow cookers because it requires fast boiling in a large quantity of water. There is a huge range of pasta shapes, and the shape and size will affect cooking times.

"Pre-cooked" lasagne sheets layered with meat or vegetables and white or cheese sauces, and stuffed cannelloni tubes, covered with white or cheese sauce, will take about 2 hours on high, or 1 hour on high followed by 2 hours on low. The time taken will also be affected by the initial temperature of the sauces; the hotter they are to start with, the quicker the pasta will cook.

Large and medium shapes added to almost-cooked casseroles or near-boiling sauces will take 30–45 minutes on high. They will take less time if there is plenty of free cooking liquid, and if the sauce is thin. Wholemeal (whole-wheat) pasta will take 10 minutes longer than white.

Small shapes, such as soup pasta, will take about 20 minutes on high. These can also be used to thicken casseroles or soups towards the end of cooking; the pasta absorbs some of the liquid.

BEANS

The slow cooker was invented for the commercial cooking of baked beans, cooking haricot beans until perfectly tender, while still keeping their shape. The slow cooker is therefore great for cooking all dried beans, peas and lentils.

Cooking beans

Most beans, peas and lentils need to be soaked before cooking, but soaking times depend on the variety and also the age of the beans. Red lentils and split peas need no soaking; most beans should be soaked for at least 6 hours and some, such as chickpeas, for 8–12 hours. Beans should not be left to soak for more than 24 hours. When they are fully soaked, the skin should look plump and smooth.

1 Put the beans in a large bowl, cover with at least twice their volume of cold water and leave to soak.

2 Drain the beans, then rinse under cold running water. Place the pulses in a large pan and cover with cold water. Pour over enough cold water to come about 4cm/1½in above the beans. Bring to the boil and boil rapidly, uncovered, for 10–15 minutes. (All beans, except for lentils and gunga peas, should be boiled fast before being transferred to the slow cooker to destroy toxins.)

3 Remove the pan from the heat and skim off any froth on the surface. Leave to cool for 5 minutes, then transfer the beans and cooking liquid to the ceramic cooking pot. The liquid should cover the pulses by at least 2cm/¾in; if necessary, top up with a little boiling water.

4 Add flavouring ingredients, such as bay leaves or sprigs of thyme, but do not add salt or acidic ingredients, such as tomato juice – these will toughen the beans and prevent them cooking properly. Cover with the lid and cook on high for 1¼–5 hours. (Cooking times vary according to the type of bean: kidney beans take about 1½ hours and soya beans take 4½–5 hours. Canned beans or peas only need to be added to a dish about 30 minutes before the end of cooking time to warm through.)

FRUITS

The gentle simmering of the slow cooker makes it ideal for cooking all kinds of fruit to perfection. It is particularly good for poaching delicate fruits that have a tendency to break up during cooking, including soft fruits, such as currants and rhubarb. It can also be used to make desserts, such as cobblers and crumbles.

PREPARING FRUIT

Many fruits need only simple preparation, such as washing, while others need to be peeled, cored, seeded or stoned (pitted) before they are cooked.

Peeling

Fruits such as apples, pears and peaches should be peeled before cooking.

To peel fruits such as apples and pears, use a vegetable peeler or a small paring knife to pare off the skin in thin strips. Apples can also be peeled in one single, spiral strip.

To peel fruits such as peaches and apricots, loosen the skins first. Make a tiny nick in the skin, then place in a bowl. Pour over boiling water to cover and leave for 20–30 seconds. Lift out using a slotted spoon, rinse under cold water, and the skin should peel off easily.

Coring

Tough cores, pips and stems should be removed from fruit before cooking so that they do not spoil the dish.

When cooking chunks of fruit, first cut the fruit lengthways into quarters. Remove the central core and pips using a small knife, then peel and chop into smaller pieces as required.

When cooking whole fruits (for example, baked apples) you will need a special corer. Place the sharp "blade" of the corer over the stem end of the fruit, press down firmly and twist. The core will come out with the corer.

Removing stones/pits

Hard stones should always be removed from fruit before cooking, since they will become loose as the fruit cooks.

To stone larger fruits such as plums and apricots, cut around the crease in the fruit. Twist the halves apart, then carefully lever out the stone using the point of a small knife.

To stone cherries, it is easiest to use a special cherry stoner. Put the fruit in the stoner, with the end where the stalk was facing upwards. Push the bar into the fruit to eject the stone.

COOKING FRUIT

Fruit can be cooked in all kinds of ways in a slow cooker, which is good for stewing and poaching, and can be used for "baking" as well.

Poaching and stewing

These techniques are slightly different. Poaching cooks fruit in a hot syrup, and is good for pears, stone fruits, and figs. Stewing is used for fruit such as apples, berries and rhubarb.

1 To stew rhubarb, cut 900g/2lb rhubarb into 2.5cm/1in pieces. Put into the ceramic cooking pot with 150–200g/5–7oz/¾–1 cup caster (superfine) sugar, sprinkling it between the layers. Pour over the juice of 1 large orange and 120ml/4fl oz/½ cup water.

2 Switch the slow cooker to high and cook for 1½ hours, or until the rhubarb is tender but still holds its shape. Stir gently halfway through cooking.

Baking

Fruits such as whole apples, halved peaches and figs can be "baked" in the slow cooker, with just a tiny amount of liquid to start the cooking process.

1 To make baked apples, you can use either cooking or eating apples. Keeping the fruits whole, remove the cores, then score the skin around the circumference.

2 Blend together 115g/4oz/½ cup soft light brown sugar and 50g/2oz/¼ cup finely chopped dried fruit and use to fill the apples. Top each with a piece of butter and place in the ceramic pot on a square of foil shaped to form a saucer.

3 Pour 150ml/¼ pint/⅔ cup very hot water around the foil squares. Cover and cook on high for 2–3 hours. If using cooking apples, check frequently and remove as soon as they are tender; if overcooked, they may collapse.

To bake nectarines, figs and oranges, place the halved or sliced fruits in the buttered ceramic cooking pot. Sprinkle a little lemon juice and sugar over each one and dot with butter. Pour 75ml/5 tbsp water around the fruit, cover and cook on high for 1½–2 hours, or until tender.

Making compotes

Compotes can be made with a single fruit, or several different types, cooked in a flavoured syrup. They may be served hot or cold, as a dessert or for breakfast. The fruits should be ripe but still firm.

When using a slow cooker, all the fruits can be added at the same time, rather than in order of their cooking time. When using dried fruit, less extra sugar is needed because the fruit is already very sweet.

1 Put 200g/7oz/1 cup sugar in the ceramic cooking pot with 300ml/½ pint/1¼ cups cold water. Add flavouring ingredients such as lemon rind.

2 Switch the slow cooker to high and heat for about 30 minutes, then stir until the sugar dissolves completely. Cover the cooking pot with the lid and heat for a further 30–45 minutes.

3 Add the fruit to the syrup. This could be 450g/1lb each prepared peaches, apricots and cherries, or 450g/1lb each halved pears, plums and apple slices. Cover and cook for 1–3 hours, or until the fruit is tender. Serve hot or allow to cool and transfer to a bowl before chilling. The compote will keep for several days in the refrigerator.

Making cobblers

Stewed and canned fruit are perfect for making these traditional baked desserts. Adding a little of the juice or syrup with the fruit produces steam and helps the cobbler to rise.

1 Lightly grease the ceramic cooking pot with unsalted (sweet) butter. Add the fruit, cover the cooking pot with the lid and switch the slow cooker to high. Canned fruit, such as peaches and berries, should be cooked for about 1 hour until hot and steaming; uncooked fruit, such as apple slices, should be cooked for 2–3 hours until tender.

2 When the fruit is nearly ready, make the cobbler topping. Sift 50g/2oz/½ cup plain (all-purpose) flour, 5ml/1 tsp baking powder and a pinch of salt into a bowl. Rub in 40g/1½oz/3 tbsp butter, then add the finely grated rind of ½ lemon. Stir in 75ml/2½fl oz/⅓ cup milk to make a thick batter and spoon over the fruit. Cover and cook on high for 45 minutes–1 hour, or until a skewer inserted into the topping comes out clean.

Making crumbles

Crumbles made in a slow cooker do not brown in the same way as conventional crumbles, but using brown flour, oats, butter and crunchy sugar and a fairly dry fruit mixture gives similar results.

1 Combine prepared fruit such as apple and peach slices with a little sugar and 5ml/1 tsp cornflour (cornstarch). Add 30ml/2 tbsp fruit juice or water and switch the slow cooker to high.

2 Place 75g/3oz/¾ cup wholemeal (whole-wheat) flour and 50g/2oz/½ cup jumbo oats in a mixing bowl. Rub in 75g/3oz/6 tbsp butter. Stir in 50g/2oz/¼ cup demerara (raw) sugar, then sprinkle over the fruit. Cover and cook for 3–4 hours, or until the fruit and topping are cooked.

HERBS, SPICES and FLAVOURINGS

The judicious use of flavourings is the key to successful cooking. Some dishes require just a subtle hint, while others need more robust flavourings.

HERBS

While fresh herbs are usually considered superior, for slow cooker dishes dried herbs are often better. Delicate fresh leaves lose their pungency and colour with long cooking, whereas dried herbs release their flavour slowly. As a general rule, fresh herbs should be added about 30 minutes before the end of cooking, or just before serving.

Some herbs dry more successfully than others. Thyme, marjoram, oregano and sage dry very well, while parsley and chives lose their potency and colour; it is better to use these herbs fresh at the end of cooking. Dried herb mixtures are often well flavoured and worth using.

Buy dried herbs from a reliable source with a quick turnover and look for small packets. "Freeze dried" herbs have a good fresh flavour. Store dried herbs in a cool, dark place for 6–9 months. Try to buy fresh herbs on the day you need them. They will keep for several days stored in the refrigerator.

Below: *Robustly flavoured rosemary and sage should be used sparingly.*

Tender herbs

These herbs have soft, fragile leaves and need careful handling. They should be added in the last few minutes of cooking time, or to the finished dish. Popular tender herbs include pungent basil, which goes well with tomatoes and Mediterranean-style dishes; anise-scented chervil, dill and tarragon, which go well with fish, eggs and cream sauces; strong, refreshing mint; aromatic coriander (cilantro); lovage with its mild taste of celery; and the great all-rounder, parsley.

Robust herbs

These usually have tough, woody stems and pungent leaves and can withstand long cooking. They should be added at the start of slow cooking to extract and mellow their flavour, then removed just before serving. Popular robust herbs include richly flavoured bay leaves, which are used in stocks, casseroles, marinades and some sweet dishes; fragrant, aromatic oregano, marjoram and thyme, which are very good in Mediterranean-style dishes; robust rosemary, which goes well with lamb; pungent sage, which complements pork; and aromatic kaffir lime leaves, which are used in Thai and Malaysian dishes.

SPICES

Warm, fragrant spices are usually added at the beginning of cooking time. However, some may become bitter if cooked for many hours, and should be added partway through cooking. Most spices are better used whole, rather than ground, in slow cooker dishes. Store spices in a cool, dark place and check the sell-by date before using; they lose their taste and aroma with age. Whole spices will keep for up to 1 year; ground spices start to lose their pungency after about 6 months.

Left: *Delicate dill has a mild aniseed flavour that goes well with fish.*

Hot spices

Many spices add heat to dishes – some give just a hint of warmth, others a fierce heat. The main hot spices are chilli, ginger, pepper and mustard.

There are more than 200 types of chilli, with varying shape, size, colour and potency. They can be bought fresh, dried, flaked or ground. Chilli powder may be hot or mild – from red hot cayenne pepper to mild, sweet paprika. There are also chilli sauces, such as Tabasco or Thai chilli sauce. All chillies and chilli products can become bitter with long cooking and should be added partway through cooking.

Sweet, peppery ginger is used in both sweet and savoury dishes and is available fresh, dried, ground and preserved in syrup. Its close relative, galangal, is used in many South-east Asian dishes. Warm, spicy fresh turmeric looks similar to fresh root ginger and is used in curries.

Black, white and green peppercorns add a peppery bite to dishes. Black are the most aromatic. Black, brown and white mustard seeds have a much more pungent aroma and kick, with the black seeds being the hottest. The heat diminishes with cooking, so add towards the end of cooking time.

Fragrant spices

Some plants are grown for their fragrant, aromatic seeds. These are sold whole and ground. Long, slow cooking softens the whole seeds and releases their taste. Popular seed spices include warm, aromatic cumin and coriander, which are used in Indian, North African and Middle Eastern dishes; pungent caraway seeds, which feature in many European dishes, especially pork- and cabbage-based ones, as well as baked recipes such as rye bread and sweet seed cake; and poppy seeds, which are often used in desserts in eastern Europe, and are also a popular topping for crusty bread. Other fragrant spices include warming allspice, cinnamon, cassia and nutmeg; aromatic cardamom pods; pungent cloves; scented star anise; vanilla, which is mainly used in sweet dishes; gin-scented juniper berries, which go well with pork, game and cabbage; delicate, bitter-sweet saffron, which is often used in rice and fish dishes; and sour tamarind, which is widely used in Indian and South-east Asian cooking.

Above: There are many different varieties of chilli.

Spice mixtures

As well as individual spices, there are a number of ground spice mixes that are widely used in both sweet and savoury dishes. Popular mixes include mixed spice (apple pie spice), which is used in cakes and desserts; Chinese five-spice powder, which is used in many savoury Chinese and Asian dishes; garam masala, a popular Indian spice mix that is added towards the end of cooking; and a wide variety of curry powders that vary in strength from mild to very hot. Jars of curry paste are also available.

OTHER FLAVOURINGS

As well as herbs and spices, there are many other flavourings that can be used to enliven dishes – ranging from pungent sauces to delicate flower waters.

Savoury sauces

There are many savoury sauces that can be used to boost the flavour of dishes. They are strongly flavoured and often salty, so usually only a splash or two is required. Mushroom ketchup and Worcestershire sauce can add a rich, rounded flavour to stews and casseroles. Dark and light soy sauce and other soy-based sauces, such as hoisin, are good in Asian-style braised dishes and soups. Fermented fish sauces are common in many cuisines and include anchovy sauce, oyster sauce and nam pla (Thai fish sauce). They should be added at the beginning of cooking.

Sweet extracts

These have a rich, fragrant aroma and are usually used to flavour sweet dishes. You only need a little, sometimes just a few drops, to flavour a whole dish. Look for the real thing, and avoid artificial flavourings. Almond and vanilla extract are used to flavour cakes and desserts. Orange flower water and rose water have a delicate fragrance and should be added towards the end of cooking for the best flavour.

Alcohol

Because of the gentle heat, alcohol evaporates more slowly in a slow cooker, resulting in a stronger flavour. When adapting conventional recipes, the amount of alcohol should be reduced slightly. Beer, cider and wine can be used in marinades and casseroles. Fortified wines, such as sherry, port, Marsala and Madeira, can be used to enrich both sweet and savoury dishes; a few spoonfuls should be added towards the end of cooking. Colourless fruit spirits, such as kirsch, and sweet liqueurs, such as amaretto, can be used to flavour desserts and sweet dishes.

GRINDING SPICES

Where ground spices are called for in a recipe, it is better to use whole spices and grind them yourself.

1 Dry-fry whole spices in a heavy frying pan, shaking the pan over a medium-high heat for 1–2 minutes until the aroma is released.

2 Place the spices in a mortar and grind to a powder. To grind a larger quantity of spices, it is easier to use an electric spice grinder or a coffee grinder used solely for the purpose.

MAKING STOCK

A good stock forms the foundation of many dishes, from simple soups and classic sauces to warming casseroles and pot-roasts. Although ready-made stocks are available from supermarkets, making your own is easy and inexpensive. Most butchers and fishmongers will supply meat and fish bones and trimmings.

Making stock in a large pan on the stovetop is a simple process, but using a slow cooker is even easier because it can be left to bubble unattended for hours. A good stock must be simmered gently (rapid boiling will make it go cloudy) so the slow cooker comes into its own, keeping the stock at a bare simmer.

There are two types of stock: brown stock, where the bones and vegetables are roasted in the oven first, and white stock, where ingredients are only boiled. Clean vegetable peelings, celery leaves and the stalks from fresh herbs are useful additions, providing extra flavour.

Always start making a stock with cold water; ideally this and any vegetables should be at room temperature. Use whole peppercorns because long cooking makes ground pepper taste bitter. If you make stock without salt, it can be used in dishes that include salty ingredients, such as smoked meats and fish, and as a base for reduced sauces.

Below: The ingredients used for stock can be varied according to what is available.

A good stock should be beautifully clear. Fat and other impurities will make it cloudy, so it is important to skim these off as the stock comes to simmering point, and at least once during cooking. Strain the stock through a sieve placed over a bowl and leave to drip slowly, rather than squeezing the vegetables, which will spoil the clarity.

For the following recipes, you will need a slow cooker with a capacity of at least 3.5 litres/6 pints/10¼ cups. If your slow cooker is too small, the recipes can be halved, but the cooking times remain the same.

Basic meat stock

Used for meat dishes, such as casseroles, and as a base for light soups, basic meat stock is traditionally made from veal bones. Beef bones will also make a good stock but with a stronger flavour. Lamb bones may also be used, but this stock can only be used for lamb dishes. Some recipes include lean stewing meat, such as shin of beef, which gives a much meatier flavour. For this option, you will need 450g/1lb each bones and meat.

MAKES ABOUT 1.2 LITRES/2 PINTS/5 CUPS

675g/1½lb beef or veal bones
1 onion, unpeeled and quartered
1 carrot, sliced
1 stick celery, sliced
6 black peppercorns
1 fresh bouquet garni
about 1.2 litres/2 pints/5 cups cold water

1 Using a meat cleaver, chop any large bones, so that they will fit into the slow cooker. (Cutting the bones into pieces will increase the flavour of the stock.)

2 Place the vegetables in the ceramic cooking pot. Add the peppercorns and bouquet garni, then place the bones on top, packing them tightly so that they fit in a single layer. Pour over the water, adding a little more, if necessary, to cover the bones, but leaving a space of at least 4cm/1½in between the water and the top of the pot. Cover and cook on high or auto for 2 hours.

3 Using a slotted spoon, skim off any scum and turn the temperature to low or leave on auto and cook for 5 hours.

4 Strain the stock through a fine strainer and leave to cool. This should be done quickly, ideally over a bowl of iced water.

5 Chill the stock for at least 4 hours, then remove the fat from the surface.

Brown meat stock

This stock is used as the base for classic beef consommé and other clear soups such as French onion soup. It also adds depth to the colour and flavour of casseroles and braised meat dishes. The secret to the stock's rich colour and flavour lies in the way the onion and bones are caramelized before simmering. However, take care not to let them burn, or the final stock will taste bitter.

MAKES ABOUT 1.2 LITRES/2 PINTS/5 CUPS

675g/1½lb beef or veal bones
1 onion, unpeeled and quartered
1 carrot, sliced
1 stick celery, sliced
6 black peppercorns
1 fresh bouquet garni
about 1.2 litres/2 pints/5 cups cold water

1 Preheat the oven to 220°C/425°F/ Gas 7. Using a meat cleaver, chop up the large bones, then place in a large, heavy roasting pan. Roast for 15 minutes, turning several times during cooking.

2 Add the vegetables to the pan and cook for 15 minutes more, until the bones are well browned and the vegetables lightly tinged with colour.

3 Transfer the bones and vegetables to the slow cooker, adding the peppercorns and bouquet garni. Pour in enough water to just cover, allowing a space of at least 4cm/1½in between the water and the top of the cooking pot. Cover with the lid and cook on high or auto for 2 hours.

4 Using a slotted spoon, skim off any scum, then reduce the temperature to low or leave on auto. Cook for 4 hours.

5 Strain the stock through a fine strainer into a bowl and cool quickly. Cover and chill or freeze. Remove the fat from the surface of the stock before using.

STORING STOCK

Fresh stock should be covered and stored in the refrigerator as soon as it is cool, then used within 3 days. If it will not be needed in this time, freeze it in small quantities – 300ml/ ½ pint/1¼ cups is ideal. Line square-sided containers with freezer bags, leaving plenty overhanging the sides. Pour the measured stock into the bags, then freeze until solid. Remove the bags of stock, seal, label and stack the blocks in the freezer.

White poultry stock

Raw poultry bones, chicken wings or a cooked poultry carcass can be used to make this stock. It makes an excellent base for soups, white sauces and for braising or stewing white meats. Including the onion skins does not add a great deal of extra flavour, but gives the stock a lovely, rich golden colour.

MAKES ABOUT 1 LITRE/1¾ PINTS/4 CUPS

1 fresh or cooked poultry carcass
1 onion, unpeeled and roughly chopped
1 leek, roughly chopped
1 celery stick, sliced
1 carrot, sliced
6 white peppercorns
2 sprigs fresh thyme
2 bay leaves
about 1 litre/1¾ pints/4 cups cold water

1 Using poultry shears, cut the carcass into pieces, so that they will fit into the slow cooker. (This will also help to extract the flavour from the bones.)

2 Place the chopped onion, leek, celery and carrot in the base of the ceramic cooking pot. Sprinkle over the peppercorns, then add the herbs and top with the chopped poultry carcass.

3 Pour over the water, adding a little more to cover the chicken carcass, if necessary, but leaving a space of at least 4cm/1½in between the water and the top of the ceramic cooking pot. Cover the pot with the lid, then cook on high or auto for 2 hours.

4 Using a slotted spoon, skim off any scum that has risen to the surface of the stock. Reduce the temperature to low or leave on auto, re-cover and cook for a further 3–4 hours.

5 Strain the stock through a fine strainer into a bowl and cool quickly, ideally over a bowl of iced water.

6 Cover the stock and store in the refrigerator, or freeze. Before using, remove the fat that has risen to the surface of the stock.

TURKEY GIBLET STOCK

This stock can be made in exactly the same way as white poultry stock. Use the giblets (including the liver) and neck of the turkey in place of the poultry carcass and pour over 900ml/1½ pints/3¾ cups water.

Fish Stock

This light broth can be used as the base for delicate fish soups and hearty stews, as well as for poaching. It is the quickest and most easily made of all stocks.

Unlike other stocks, fish stock should not be simmered for very long, otherwise it will become bitter. Once the stock has come to simmering point (which will take about 1 hour), it should be kept at a bare simmer for no more than 1 hour.

Use only the bones of white fish such as sole and plaice. (The bones of oily fish such as mackerel are unsuitable.) Heads may be added, but the eyes and gills should be removed because these will spoil the final flavour. You can also use prawn (shrimp) shells. The vegetables should be sliced finely to extract as much flavour as possible during cooking. To make a stock with a richer flavour, you can replace about 150ml/¼ pint/⅔ cup of the water with dry white wine.

MAKES ABOUT 900ML/1½ PINTS/3¾ CUPS

900g/2lb fish bones and trimmings
2 carrots, finely sliced
1 onion, peeled and sliced
6 white peppercorns
1 bouquet garni
900ml/1½ pints/3¾ cups water

1 Rinse the fish bones and trimmings well under cold water and cut any larger bones or pieces into several chunks so that they will easily fit inside the ceramic cooking pot.

2 Arrange the vegetables in the base of the cooking pot. Sprinkle over the peppercorns, add the bouquet garni and place the fish bones on top.

3 Pour the cold water into the pot, adding a little more to cover the bones, if necessary, but leaving a space of at least 4cm/1½in between the water and the top of the cooking pot. Cover with the lid, then cook on high or auto for 1 hour until simmering.

4 Using a slotted spoon, skim off any scum that has risen to the surface. Reduce the temperature to low or leave on auto, re-cover and cook for 1 hour. (Do not cook for longer than this.)

5 Using a fine sieve – or a course sieve lined with muslin (cheesecloth) that has been briefly held under running water – pour the stock into a bowl, then cool quickly, ideally in a bowl of iced water. Cover with clear film (plastic wrap) and store in the refrigerator, or freeze.

Vegetable stock

You can vary the vegetables used in this recipe, but be sure to wash them well and chop fairly small. Strong-tasting vegetables, such as turnips and parsnips, should be used in small quantities; their flavour will dominate otherwise. Starchy vegetables, such as potatoes, should be avoided; they will make the stock cloudy.

MAKES ABOUT 1.5 LITRES/2½ PINTS/
6¼ CUPS

1 large onion, left unpeeled
  and chopped
1 leek, roughly chopped
2 carrots, thinly sliced
1 celery stick, thinly sliced
2 bay leaves
1 sprig fresh thyme
a few fresh parsley stalks
6 white peppercorns
about 1.5 litres/2½ pints/6¼ cups water

1 Put the vegetables, herbs and peppercorns in the ceramic cooking pot and pour over the water. Cover and cook on high or auto for 2 hours.

2 Using a slotted spoon, skim off any scum. Reduce the temperature to low, or leave on auto, and cook for 2 hours.

3 Strain the stock through a fine sieve into a bowl and leave to cool. Cover and store in the refrigerator, or freeze.

Removing fat

Before using stock, the fat should be removed. The easiest way to do this is by cooling, then chilling the stock.

Pour the stock into a bowl, cover and leave undisturbed in the refrigerator for at least 4 hours, or overnight. The fat will rise to the surface, setting in visible globules or a single layer if there is a lot of fat in the stock. Simply lift the fat from the top, or scoop off with a spoon.

1 If you don't have time to let the stock cool, let it settle for a few minutes, then skim off as much fat as possible, using a slotted spoon.

2 Next, draw a sheet of absorbent kitchen paper across the top to soak up any remaining surface fat. You may need to use two or three pieces of paper to remove the fat completely.

Another way to remove the fat is to leave the stock to cool, then lower several ice cubes into it. Gently move the ice cubes around for a few seconds, then remove. The fat will solidify and cling to the ice cubes, making it easy to remove. (This method will only work if the stock is cool.)

Reducing stocks

After straining and removing the fat from stock, it can be concentrated by returning it to the slow cooker and cooking uncovered on high for several hours to allow some of the water to evaporate. However, if you need a very concentrated stock, for a reduced sauce for example, the slow cooker is not suitable. To make very concentrated stocks, pour the stock into a pan and boil rapidly on the stovetop.

READY-MADE STOCKS
If you do not have time to make your own stock, cartons of fresh stock can be found in the chiller cabinets of many supermarkets. These make a good substitute. Good-quality bouillon powders and liquid stocks may also be used, but take care with stock cubes because they are often strongly flavoured and high in salt. Make them only in the recommended strength and use in robustly flavoured dishes.

MAKING SOUPS

Although many slow cooker soup recipes have lengthy cooking times, the actual preparation time for most is minimal, and they can then be left simmering on a low setting all day or overnight. Most soups benefit from long, gentle cooking, so there is no need to worry if they are left for a little longer than intended.

A good home-made stock forms the base of many soups so it is well worth making large batches of stock and freezing it in convenient quantities. Alternatively, use good-quality ready-made stock from the supermarket.

There are two basic techniques for making slow cooker soups. The easiest is to place the prepared ingredients in the ceramic cooking pot with either cold or near-boiling stock. This produces a fresh-flavoured soup with a low fat content and is a good method for vegetable soups. However, it is less suitable for recipes containing onions, which take a long time to soften. The second, more usual, method is to sauté or fry onions, other vegetables and/or meat in a frying pan before placing in the cooking pot. In some recipes, vegetables are simply softened, but in others they may be lightly browned, giving a richer flavour and deeper colour.

Mixed vegetable soup

Almost any vegetable can be made into soup, but for the best results, use the freshest, seasonal ingredients.

SERVES 4–6

675g/1½lb mixed vegetables, such as
  carrots, celery, parsnips, potatoes
25g/1oz/2 tbsp butter
1 onion, finely chopped
5ml/1 tsp dried mixed herbs
900ml/1½ pints/3¾ cups near-boiling
  vegetable stock
150ml/¼ pint/⅔ cup milk or single
  (light) cream (optional)
salt and ground black pepper

1 Prepare the mixed vegetables, then cut them into 5mm/¼in slices, sticks or dice to ensure that they cook evenly and within the recommended time.

2 Melt the butter in a frying pan, add the onion and fry gently, stirring frequently, for 10 minutes, until softened, but not coloured.

3 Add the chopped vegetables to the pan and fry for 2–3 minutes. Transfer the vegetables to the ceramic cooking pot and switch the slow cooker to low.

4 Sprinkle over the dried mixed herbs, then pour in the stock. If you are using vegetables with a high water content, such as courgettes (zucchini) or squash, reduce the quantity of liquid. Others, such as potatoes and dried vegetables, soak up cooking juices, so add a little more liquid to compensate. (Bear in mind that it is easier to dilute the soup at the end of cooking, than to try to thicken a watery soup.)

5 Make sure that there is a gap of at least 2cm/¾in between the liquid and the top of the slow cooker, then cover with the lid and cook for 7–12 hours, or until the vegetables are tender.

6 If using milk or cream, stir this in and cook for a further 30 minutes to bring the soup back to boiling point. (Do not heat for longer than this because long heating may cause the soup to separate.) Season to taste, then serve.

ADAPTING SOUP RECIPES

Use this simple mixed vegetable soup recipe as a guide for making other soups. If you want to add meat or poultry to the soup, add it to the ceramic cooking pot at the start of cooking and cook on high for at least 1 hour before reducing the heat to low. If you want to use fresh rather than dried herbs, stir in twice the quantity at the end of cooking time. Rather than using plain stock, use a mixture of stock and tomato juice, or a moderate amount of white wine or cider. Instead of stirring in cream, try adding crème fraîche instead.

Above: Using a hand blender is one of the easiest ways to make smooth soups, but be sure to keep the blade submerged in the soup to avoid spattering.

Puréeing soups

A few ladlefuls of soup can be puréed, then stirred back into the remaining soup to thicken it, or the entire soup can be puréed to make a wonderfully smooth, velvety soup. When making chilled puréed soup, it is best to adjust the consistency after chilling because the soup will thicken considerably as it cools.

The simplest way to make puréed soup is using a hand-held blender. It can be puréed while still in the slow cooker, and will not need reheating. You can also use a food processor or blender, but do not over-fill it because it may flood over the top. Most soups will need to be processed in two or more batches and, unless being served cold, will need to be reheated in the slow cooker or in a pan on the stovetop.

Soft vegetable soups can be puréed by hand. Press the mixture through a fine stainless steel or plastic sieve, using a wooden "mushroom" or a large spoon. Alternatively, press the vegetables through a mouli-légumes, then stir in the cooking liquid. The soup will need to be reheated if serving hot.

Thickening soups

There are several ways to thicken soups. Cornflour (cornstarch) or arrowroot are probably the simplest. They can be blended with a little cold water to make a smooth paste, then stirred or whisked into the hot soup. Cornflour will thicken boiling liquid instantly, but takes about 10 minutes to lose its raw flavour. Arrowroot thickens as soon as it reaches boiling point, but will become slightly thinner with prolonged cooking, so add in the last few minutes of cooking.

Plain (all-purpose) flour can be sprinkled over fried onions before stirring in the stock, or blended with an equal quantity of softened butter or double (heavy) cream and whisked into the finished soup a little a time, cooking for a few minutes to thicken. Allow the soup to cook for at least 5 minutes to avoid a raw flour flavour.

Beaten eggs, egg yolks or a mixture of eggs and cream can be used to thicken and enrich smooth soups. Always turn off the heat and allow the soup to cool slightly before whisking in the egg mixture, otherwise it may curdle.

Breadcrumbs are sometimes used to thicken rustic and chilled soups. The breadcrumbs are stirred into the finished soup to soak up and thicken the liquid.

Garnishing soups

Adding a pretty garnish gives the final flourish as you serve soup, and can be as simple or complex as you like. A swirl of cream, crème fraîche or yogurt, followed by a sprinkling of paprika or ground black pepper, can look great with smooth soups. Fresh chopped herbs make another simple but stylish garnish, adding colour, flavour and texture. Use strong herbs, such as sage and rosemary, in moderation.

For a richly flavoured garnish, try adding a spoonful or swirl of pesto. It works especially well with Italian and Mediterranean soups. Grated, shaved or crumbled cheeses also work well and are particularly good with vegetable and bean soups. Strongly flavoured cheeses, such as Parmesan, Cheddar or a crumbly cheese, such as Stilton, are ideal.

To add more substance, flavour and texture to soups, try sprinkling over croûtons or fried breadcrumbs. These are a classic soup garnish and they add a crunchy texture that works with both smooth and chunky soups. To make croûtons, cut thick slices of day-old bread (any type will do) into cubes. Shallow-fry in hot olive oil, turning them continuously, so that the cubes brown evenly, then drain on kitchen paper. Fried breadcrumbs can be made in the same way, but need less cooking time. To oven-bake croûtons, toss them in a little oil, then bake in a shallow roasting pan at 200°C/400°F/Gas 6 for 12–15 minutes.

Grilled cheesy croûtes are the classic topping for French onion soup and can make a dramatic impact floating on top of a bowl of steaming hot soup. Simply rub thin slices of day-old baguette with peeled garlic cloves, then lightly toast both sides under a hot grill (broiler). Sprinkle one side with grated Cheddar or Parmesan cheese, or sliced goat's cheese, and put under a hot grill until melted. Float one or two croûtes on top of the soup just before serving.

Below: Crispy croûtes coated in melted, bubbling cheese make an impressive garnish for a simple blended soup.

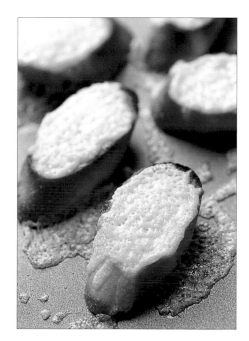

MAKING MARINADES

Marinating tenderizes and flavours meat, poultry, game, fish and even vegetables and cheese. Although tenderizing may not be necessary when using a slow cooker, it is worth doing for the flavour. There are three basic types of marinade: moist, dry and paste. Always use a non-metallic dish for marinating.

Basic moist marinade

Moist marinades are usually made with oil and vinegar, or other acidic ingredients, such as wine, fruit juice or yogurt. They add moisture as well as flavour.

Red meat, poultry and game can be marinated for up to 2 hours at room temperature, or up to 24 hours in the refrigerator; small pieces of meat, such as steaks, chops and cutlets, should be marinated for no more than 2 hours at room temperature, or 12 hours in the refrigerator; whole fish, fish fillets and steaks should be marinated for up to 30 minutes at room temperature, or 2 hours in the refrigerator; vegetables need 30 minutes at room temperature, or 2 hours in the refrigerator; cheeses and tofu can be marinated for 1 hour at room temperature, or about 8 hours in the refrigerator.

SUFFICIENT FOR 900G/2LB MEAT OR FISH OR 675G/1½LB VEGETABLES

90ml/6 tbsp olive oil
15–30ml/1–2 tbsp cider vinegar
1 garlic clove, crushed
5ml/1 tsp dried thyme
2.5ml/½ tsp crushed peppercorns

1 Combine all the ingredients, using 15ml/1 tbsp vinegar for fish and 30ml/2 tbsp vinegar for meat or vegetables.

2 If you are marinating meat or fish with skin, make several shallow slashes in each piece, then place in a shallow dish.

3 Drizzle or brush the marinade over the food, making sure the pieces are completely covered, then leave to marinate, turning the pieces regularly.

Other moist marinades

You can make several other marinades, using the same techniques and timings as for the basic moist marinade.

Spicy yogurt marinade: Combine 175ml/6fl oz/1 cup plain yogurt, 2 crushed garlic cloves, 2.5ml/½ tsp each ground cumin and cinnamon and crushed black peppercorns, a pinch each of ground ginger, ground cloves, cayenne pepper and salt. Use for chicken, lamb and fish.

Hoisin marinade: Combine 175ml/6fl oz/1 cup hoisin sauce, 30ml/2 tbsp each sesame oil, dry sherry and rice vinegar, 4 finely chopped garlic cloves, 2.5ml/½ tsp soft light brown sugar, 1.5ml/¼ tsp five-spice powder. Use this Chinese marinade for chops and chicken pieces.

Coconut and pineapple: Blend ¼ peeled, chopped pineapple, juice of ½ lime and 150ml/¼ pint/⅔ cup coconut milk in a food processor. Use for chicken and pork.

Thai: Soak 30ml/2 tbsp tamarind pulp in 45ml/3 tbsp boiling water until softened, then press through a fine sieve into a pan. Finely chop 1 lemon grass stalk, 2.5cm/1in piece fresh galangal or ginger, 2 shallots, 2 garlic cloves, 2 seeded green chillies and 2 kaffir lime leaves and place in a blender with 30ml/2 tbsp each groundnut (peanut) oil and dark soy sauce. Blend to a paste and add to the pan. Bring to the boil, then leave to cool. Use for beef, pork or chicken.

Wine: Combine 75ml/5 tbsp wine, 30ml/2 tbsp olive oil, 2 finely chopped shallots, a pinch of dried herbs or 10ml/2 tsp chopped fresh herbs, such as rosemary. Use red wine for red meat and duck, and white wine for chicken and fish.

Basic dry marinade

Also known as dry rubs, these herb and spice mixtures are rubbed into food shortly before cooking. They are used purely for flavouring and so are best used on fattier pieces of meat, oily fish, or for braised dishes. You can vary the flavour by using different spices, such as cardamom, dry-roasted cumin seeds or a little chilli powder, or try a dried herb mixture with some grated citrus rind.

SUFFICIENT FOR 900G/2LB MEAT OR FISH

15ml/1 tbsp dried thyme
15ml/1 tbsp dried oregano
15ml/1 tbsp garlic granules
15ml/1 tbsp ground cumin
15ml/1 tbsp ground paprika
2.5ml/½ tsp cayenne pepper
2.5ml/½ tsp ground black pepper

1 Combine the ingredients in a bowl, then transfer the mixture to a shallow dish and spread out in an even layer.

2 Press each piece of meat or fish into the mixture to coat evenly, then gently shake off any excess. Arrange on a dish, cover with clear film (plastic wrap) and leave to marinate at room temperature for 30 minutes, or use immediately.

Paste marinades

Because these coat the food, it should be cooked above the level of the liquid – such as on a bed of vegetables.

Herb paste: Heat 50g/2oz/¼ cup butter in a frying pan and gently fry 115g/4oz finely chopped shallots and 1.5ml/¼ tsp fennel seeds until the shallots are soft. Remove from the heat and stir in 2.5cm/1in piece grated fresh ginger, 30ml/2 tbsp each chopped fresh dill and parsley and 15ml/1 tbsp finely chopped capers. Stir in 15–30ml/1–2 tbsp sunflower oil to make a paste. Spread over chicken pieces or tuck under the skin, or use to fill the cavity of whole fish. Marinate for up to 1 hour at room temperature, or cook straight away. Use for food with a short cooking time.

Mexican chilli paste: Combine the finely grated rind of 1 lime, 4 crushed garlic cloves, 30ml/2 tbsp mild chilli powder, 15ml/1 tbsp ground paprika, 5ml/1 tsp ground cumin, 2.5ml/½ tsp dried oregano and a pinch each of ground cinnamon and salt. Stir in 15ml/1 tbsp olive oil and enough lime juice to make into a paste. Use for chicken and pork. Marinate for up to 1 hour at room temperature, or cook straight away.

Tandoori paste: Mix together 30ml/ 2 tbsp each ground coriander, cumin and garlic powder, 15ml/1 tbsp each paprika and ground ginger and 10ml/2 tsp each ground turmeric and chilli powder with enough groundnut (peanut) oil to make a paste. Use for lamb, beef, chicken and oily fish. Marinate for up to 2 hours at room temperature, or cover and leave overnight in the refrigerator. Scrape off the excess paste before cooking.

Fruit marinades

Certain fruits contain enzymes that soften the fibres of meat and tougher seafood, such as squid. Papaya, pineapple and kiwi fruit all contain papain, which breaks down protein and is used in commercial tenderizers. Add a little of the juice to a marinade, or slice the fruit and place on top of the meat or fish and leave for no longer than 15 minutes.

MARINATING TIPS

• The thicker a piece of food is, the longer it will need to marinate.
• When marinating meats such as game and white fish that can become dry during cooking, choose marinades containing less vinegar, wine or fruit juice. These are suitable for fattier meats, such as lamb, and oily fish.
• During humid weather or in a warm kitchen, it is safer to marinate meat and fish in the refrigerator. In cooler weather, or for short marinating times, it is safe to leave the food at room temperature.
• As a general rule, dry herbs are better than fresh for marinades. When using fresh woody herbs, such as rosemary and thyme, crush the leaves to release their aroma.
• If you are frying or grilling (broiling) marinated food before adding it to the slow cooker, pat it dry on kitchen paper first.
• Avoid adding salt to marinades; this will draw moisture from the food. If you want to season with salt, do so after marinating.

MAKING STEWS and CASSEROLES

The slow cooker's gentle, constant heat makes it perfect for making stews and casseroles. The lengthy cooking allows all cuts of meat to become tender and succulent, and even the toughest pieces can be turned into a flavoursome meal.

Stews, casseroles, carbonnades, hot-pots and navarins are all names for what is, essentially, the same type of dish – meat and/or vegetables cooked in liquid in a cooking pot. Originally, the word stew described such dishes cooked on the stovetop, while casserole described dishes cooked in the oven, but now the names are largely interchangeable.

Choosing the right cut

Ideal meats for slow cooking are the cheaper cuts, such as brisket, chuck steak, blade-bone, shank and knuckle. These cuts come from the part of the animal (usually the front) that has worked hardest, so have a looser texture and a good marbling of fat. During cooking, the connective tissues and fat dissolve to create a rich gravy and the fibres open up and allow moisture to penetrate, making them juicy. These cuts also have far greater flavour than very lean ones.

More expensive cuts of meat, such as fine-grained and densely-textured sirloin steak and pork fillet, are delicious when cooked to rare or medium by quick-frying or grilling (broiling). However, they are less suitable for slow cooking because the tightness of the fibres prevents them absorbing the liquid around them. This means that although they become tender when cooked in a slow cooker, the final stew will lack succulence and flavour.

Cutting meat into cubes

Tougher cuts of meat, such as stewing steak, cook more evenly and quickly if they are cut into small, even-size cubes; 2.5cm/1in is ideal. They should be slightly larger than the vegetables being cooked in the stew because these will take a little longer to cook than the meat. Although excess fat should be removed, some marbling is useful for keeping the meat moist. Any excess fat can be skimmed off after cooking.

1 Trim the meat, cutting off the excess fat and any gristle, sinew or membranes while it is in one piece.

2 Using a large sharp knife, cut the meat across the grain into 2.5cm/1in thick slices. These slices can be used for stews and casseroles. Cutting across the grain makes the fibres shorter so that the meat is more tender.

3 To cut the meat into cubes, first cut the slices lengthways into thick strips. Remove any fat or gristle as you go.

4 Cut each strip crossways into 2.5cm/1in cubes. (When preparing meats such as shoulder of lamb, it may not be possible to cut into perfect cubes. Simply cut into evenly-sized pieces, removing any fat or gristle as you go.)

Preparing chops

These are usually sold ready-prepared and fairly lean, but it is usually worth trimming a little before cooking. This will help them cook, look and taste better.

1 Using sharp kitchen scissors or a sharp knife, remove the excess fat, cutting around the contours of the chop and leaving a little less than 5mm/1/4in fat on the edge of each chop.

2 If you are going to pre-fry chops, such as bacon or gammon, before adding to the slow cooker, make shallow cuts with the knife all around the edge. The edge of the meat will then fan out during frying, preventing the meat curling up, so that it stays in constant contact with the frying pan.

Preparing poultry

A variety of chicken and game portions can be used in stews and casseroles – from whole or diced breast portions, to drumsticks and thighs. Leaving the bones in the meat during cooking will enhance the flavour, or you may remove them (saving to use for stock) if you prefer. Generally, it is better to remove poultry skin before casseroling because it won't crispen during the moist cooking.

To skin breast fillets, carefully pull the skin and thin membrane away from the meat. If you like, use a small, sharp knife to cut the meat off the rib bone and any remaining breastbone. Turn the breast portion over and remove the thin, white central tendons from the meat.

To prepare escalopes (US scallops), cut the breast in half horizontally, holding your hand on top of the chicken breast as you cut. A chicken breast portion will yield two escalopes, a duck breast portion three, and turkey four or more.

To skin and bone chicken thighs, use a sharp knife to loosen the skin, then pull it away from the meat. Carefully cut the flesh lengthways along the main thigh bone, then cut the bone out, trimming the meat close to it.

Preparing vegetables

One of the unusual characteristics of slow cooking is that many types of vegetables take longer to cook than meat. To ensure that they cook within the recommended time, they should be cut into even-size pieces slightly smaller than the meat.

When preparing onions, slice them thinly or chop finely. If you want to have chunkier pieces, fry them until they are soft before adding to the slow cooker, because onion takes a long time to cook in a slow cooker.

Hard root vegetables such as carrots, potatoes and turnips take the longest time to cook in the slow cooker. Cut them into 5mm/¼in dice, slices or sticks. (Potatoes discolour when exposed to air, so make sure they are covered with liquid during cooking.)

COOK'S TIP

Some vegetables, such as (bell) peppers, become bitter if cooked too long and some types, especially green peppers, may discolour. They cook fairly quickly, so add these to the slow cooker 45 minutes–1 hour before the end of cooking time.

LIQUIDS FOR CASSEROLES AND STEWS

The finished sauce is provided by a mixture of the juices from the meat and vegetables and the liquid that is added at the start of cooking. The long cooking time ensures plenty of flavour if you use water, although other liquids will give the dish a richer finish. You may need to adjust the quantity of liquid used, according to the main ingredients in the dish; vegetables such as mushrooms, for example, will give out a lot of moisture that will thin the sauce.

Stock Home-made stock is preferable, but you can use ready-made fresh stock, or good-quality stock cubes or bouillon powder. Make these to the correct strength (you may only need a small portion of stock cube) because too much can produce an over-salty, artificial flavour. Try to use the flavour of stock that matches the dish. If you haven't got the appropriate meat stock, use vegetable stock instead.

Wine Red or white wine will add extra flavour and its acidity will help to tenderize the meat. Choose a wine that you enjoy drinking because a really cheap, acidic wine will spoil the finished dish. Generally, it is preferable to use a mixture of wine and stock, rather than wine alone.

Cider This flavours and tenderizes meat in the same way as wine, and is excellent in chicken and pork dishes, especially ones containing fruit. Unless you require a very sweet finish, use dry or medium (hard) cider.

Beer Pale or brown ale or stout makes a rich dark sauce and cooks without a hint of its original bitterness. Too much can be overpowering, though, so use a mixture of beer and stock.

Tomatoes These add flavour to the dish. You can use chopped fresh or canned tomatoes, passata (bottled strained tomatoes), concentrated purée (paste), or tomato juice.

BASIC TECHNIQUES

There are two basic ways of making slow cooker stews and casseroles: a simple one-step method, where cold raw ingredients are placed in the ceramic cooking pot, and a second method in which the meat and some or all of the vegetables are fried beforehand.

Making a one-step stew

Irish stew is a classic one-step stew, and the recipe given here is a perfect guide to cooking any stew using this technique. All the ingredients are placed in the ceramic cooking pot without pre-frying. This reduces preparation time and is also suitable for those on a reduced-fat diet.

The stock or cooking liquid is usually cold, but may be hot to speed up the cooking process. For the tenderest results, casseroles should be cooked on a low setting. However, when the ingredients are cold to begin with, and especially if cooking larger pieces of meat, it is better to start the cooking on the high or auto setting for 1–2 hours.

SERVES 4

900g/2lb boned shoulder of lamb
    or 8 neck of lamb chops
450g/1lb onions
900g/2lb potatoes
1 carrot, sliced (optional)
sprig of thyme or bay leaf (optional)
about 600ml/1 pint/2½ cups lamb
    or vegetable stock
salt and ground black pepper

1 Using a sharp knife, trim all excess fat from the lamb, then cut the meat into 3cm/1¼in pieces. (If using lamb chops, these may be left whole.)

2 Using a sharp knife, slice the onions and potatoes as thinly as possible.

3 Place the onions at the bottom of the ceramic cooking pot, then arrange the potatoes, carrot and herbs, if using, on top and finally the meat. Lightly season each layer with salt and pepper.

4 Pour the stock over the meat. If necessary, add a little more stock to cover the meat. Cover the slow cooker with the lid and cook on auto or high for 2 hours.

5 Using a large spoon, skim off any scum that has risen to the surface. Re-cover the pot and leave on auto or switch to low and cook for a further 4–6 hours, or until the meat and vegetables are very tender and juicy.

Making a pre-fried stew

This method is used for the majority of stews and casseroles, because it adds colour and an intense rich flavour. The natural sugars in the ingredients are broken down by pre-frying and the sweet, complex flavours are released. While pre-cooking meat improves the taste and appearance of the cooked casserole, it is also useful to give vegetables the same treatment, especially onions because they take much longer to tenderize than meat in a slow cooker.

SERVES 4–6

900g/2lb lean stewing steak
45ml/3 tbsp plain (all-purpose) flour
50g/2oz/¼ cup butter
30ml/2 tbsp oil
12 baby (pearl) onions, peeled
115g/4oz button (white) mushrooms
1 garlic clove, crushed
300ml/½ pint/1¼ cups red wine
150ml/¼ pint/⅔ cup near-boiling
    beef stock
1 bay leaf
30ml/2 tbsp chopped fresh parsley
salt and ground black pepper

1 Trim the meat and cut into 2.5cm/1in cubes. Season the flour with salt and black pepper and either spread out on a plate or place in a plastic bag. Roll the meat in the flour, or add a few cubes at a time to the bag, shaking until coated, then remove and coat the next batch. Shake off any excess and reserve.

2 Melt half the butter with half of the oil in a large frying pan. (If you prefer, you can reduce the fat slightly by using a non-stick frying pan.)

3 When the butter sizzles, fry the meat in two or three batches. (Do not try to cook too much meat at once because it will start to stew, rather than brown.) Turn the meat frequently, so that it browns on all sides. Lift the meat out of the pan with a slotted spoon and transfer to the ceramic cooking pot.

4 Heat the remaining butter and oil in the frying pan, then add the onions and cook until glazed and golden brown. Transfer to the ceramic cooking pot using a slotted spoon. Add the mushrooms and garlic to the pan and cook for 2–3 minutes until browned, then transfer to the cooking pot.

5 Sprinkle any remaining flour into the pan juices and stir to mix. Gradually mix in the red wine, followed by the stock.

6 Stir the sauce to loosen any sediment from the base of the pan and heat to simmering point. Pour over the meat and vegetables, and add the bay leaf, pressing it down into the liquid.

7 Cover the slow cooker with the lid and switch to high or auto. Cook for 1 hour, then leave on auto or switch to low and cook for a further 6–8 hours, or until the meat and vegetables are tender. Alternatively, cook on high throughout for 4–5 hours. Sprinkle over the parsley just before serving.

Thickening stews

There are many different ways to thicken the sauces of stews and casseroles.
Flour Meat is often fried before being put in the ceramic cooking pot, and can be first dusted in flour, which will act as a thickener for the juices as the meat cooks. Do not over-brown the flour as this gives it a bitter flavour; only fry until light brown.

Alternatively, you can add flour towards the end of cooking time by whisking in a paste made from equal quantities of flour and butter. Allow extra cooking time to allow the flour to cook and lose its "raw" flavour.

Cornflour/cornstarch or arrowroot

These very fine flours can both be used as thickeners. They should be blended with a little water or other cold liquid before being stirred into the stew.

Pasta and rice If it becomes obvious part-way through cooking that the stew or casserole will be too thin, you can stir in a little pasta or easy-cook (converted) rice, which will absorb some of the liquid. These should be added about 45 minutes before the end of cooking time. (Lentils and grains, such as pearl barley, will also act as thickeners, but these must be added early in the cooking time to cook thoroughly.)
Reduction If the sauce is too thin when cooking is complete, lift out the meat and vegetables with a slotted spoon and set aside. Pour the liquid into a wide pan or frying pan and boil fast to reduce the liquid. Add the meat and vegetables to the reduced sauce and gently reheat. This is a useful technique with delicate fish and chicken, which may break up if overcooked.

Skimming off fat

If the dish has produced a lot of fat during cooking, you may wish to remove it before serving. Most will rise to the surface so that you can simply skim it off the top, using a large kitchen spoon. Further fat can be removed using absorbent kitchen paper. Simply rest the kitchen paper on the surface of the stew and remove as soon as it has soaked up the fat. If you have made the dish in advance, chill it in the refrigerator so that the fat solidifies on the top of the stew or casserole. It can then be lifted or scooped off.

BRAISING

This technique involves slow cooking in very little liquid in a dish with a tight-fitting lid; the trapped steam keeps the food moist during cooking. Instead of cutting meat into small chunks, it is sliced into larger, even-size pieces, or in some cases, such as chops or lamb shanks, left whole. Braising also works well for large pieces of firm, meaty fish which can be placed on a bed of vegetables, with just enough liquid to cover these. The slow cooker is perfect for braising because the heat is so gentle, and the lid forms a tight seal, so that any steam condenses on the inside of the lid and trickles back into the pot.

Preparing meat for braising

Always trim excess fat from meat before braising, then skim any fat from the surface before serving. To ensure even cooking, all the pieces of meat should be of a similar thickness.

1 Cut the meat into slices about 2cm/¾in thick. At the narrower end cut slightly thicker slices.

2 Place the thicker slices on a chopping board, cover with a sheet of greaseproof (waxed) paper and gently beat with a rolling pin or meat mallet to flatten.

If you want to pound all the meat, to help tenderize it, you can start by cutting it all into thick slices, about 3cm/1in thick, then pounding it to flatten.

Braising lamb shanks

On the whole lamb joints are tender and quite fatty and do not benefit from being braised. Lamb shanks, however, are lean and tough so benefit from long, slow, moist cooking. Thickly sliced meat, such as braising steak, and small joints, such as topside, can be cooked in the same way.

SERVES 4

4 lamb shanks
1 red onion, very finely chopped
1 garlic clove, crushed
sprig of fresh thyme
5ml/1 tsp chopped fresh rosemary
5ml/1 tsp ground paprika
15ml/1 tbsp balsamic vinegar
60ml/4 tbsp olive oil
175ml/6fl oz/¾ cup red wine
150ml/¼ pint/⅔ cup lamb
   or vegetable stock
chopped fresh parsley
salt and ground black pepper

1 Using the point of a sharp knife, gently prick the shanks at intervals all over.

2 Combine the onion, garlic, thyme, rosemary, paprika, vinegar and 30ml/2 tbsp of the oil. Brush over the shanks, place in a shallow, non-metallic dish, cover and leave to marinate for 2 hours at room temperature, or up to 24 hours in the refrigerator. (Marinating starts the tenderizing process, but is not essential.)

3 Brush the marinade off the lamb and set aside. Heat the remaining 30ml/2 tbsp oil in a frying pan and lightly brown the shanks all over. Transfer to the ceramic cooking pot and season with salt and pepper.

4 Add the reserved marinade to the frying pan and pour in the wine and stock. Bring almost to the boil, stirring, then pour over the shanks.

5 Cover with the lid and switch to high or auto. Cook for 1 hour, then leave on auto or reduce to low and cook for a further 6–8 hours, or until very tender, turning the meat halfway through.

6 Using a slotted spoon, transfer the lamb shanks to a warmed serving plate. Skim off any fat from the cooking juices, then check the seasoning. Stir in the parsley and spoon over the shanks.

Braising red cabbage

Many types of vegetable respond well to braising, becoming meltingly tender with an intense flavour. Red cabbage is used here, but fennel and celery are also very good braised. Fennel should be cut into thin, even slices from the top through the root end; sticks of celery can be left whole or cut into shorter pieces.

SERVES 4–6

1 red cabbage, about 900g/2lb
450g/1lb cooking apples, peeled, cored
   and chopped
30ml/2 tbsp soft light or dark brown sugar
30ml/2 tbsp red wine vinegar
175g/6fl oz/¾ cup near-boiling water
salt and ground black pepper

1 Discard the tough outer leaves of the cabbage, cut it into quarters and remove the hard stalk. Shred the cabbage finely.

2 Put the cabbage, apples, sugar, vinegar, salt and pepper into the ceramic cooking pot and toss together. Pack down firmly, then pour over the water.

3 Cover with the lid and switch to high for 3–4 hours, or to low for 6–8 hours, stirring halfway through.

Reheating braised dishes, casseroles and stews

Braised dishes, casseroles and stews are often served the day after they are made because their flavour improves with keeping and reheating. The improvement in taste is less obvious in dishes made in the slow cooker because the long gentle cooking has already allowed the flavours to develop and mingle. However, if you do plan to reheat a dish, it is important to cool it as quickly as possible – but you should never plunge the hot ceramic cooking pot into cold water because this may cause it to crack.

1 When cooking is complete, remove the ceramic cooking pot from the slow cooker, and place on a pot stand for at least 10 minutes, taking off the lid to allow steam to escape. (Do not remove the lid for braised vegetables; you want to retain the moisture with these.)

2 Place the ceramic cooking pot in a washing-up bowl of cool but not very cold water. Leave for about 15 minutes, or until the surrounding water starts to feel warm. (Don't overfill the bowl or the water may overflow into the prepared dish; the water should come just over halfway up the cooking pot.)

3 Remove the ceramic cooking pot and pour away the warmed water. Refill the bowl with very cold water, replace the ceramic cooking pot and add a few ice cubes or frozen ice packs to speed up the cooling process. Leave until the food is completely cool.

4 Cover the ceramic cooking pot with the lid and place in the refrigerator until needed, or transfer the contents to another container, if you prefer.

5 The slow cooker is not suitable for reheating the dish. It will take too long for the contents to reheat to ensure food safety. Check whether the ceramic cooking pot is suitable for use on the stovetop or in the oven. Remove the dish from the refrigerator at least 30 minutes before reheating.

6 If necessary, transfer the food to a suitable pan or casserole dish, then reheat gently over a low heat on the stovetop, or in the oven at 170°C/325°F/Gas 3, until simmering. For safety, meat dishes must come to a gentle simmer and be maintained at that temperature for at least 30 minutes. Any fresh herbs should be added at this stage, a few minutes before serving.

TOPPINGS

Adding a topping to casseroles and braised dishes can transform them into a special meal. It is also an easy way to create a one-pot meal with no need for extra accompaniments. Many toppings are arranged on top of the casserole or braise and cooked as an integral part of the dish. Others are cooked separately, then served with the dish.

Dumplings

These are ideal for casseroles and stews, but are unsuitable for braised dishes because they need plenty of simmering liquid to cook in. If the casserole is cooking on a low setting, increase the temperature to high about 30 minutes before adding the dumplings. This recipe makes enough to serve four.

1 Sift 115g/4oz/1 cup self-raising (self-rising) flour and a little salt and pepper into a mixing bowl. Stir in 50g/2oz shredded beef or vegetable suet. Mix in about 75ml/5 tbsp chilled water to make a soft but not sticky dough.

2 Using floured hands, shape the mixture into 8 medium or 12 small round dumplings. Alternatively, roll out into a "rope" with a diameter of about 2.5cm/1in and cut off 2.5cm/1in pieces.

3 Remove the lid from the slow cooker. Working quickly so that heat isn't lost, lower the dumplings into the casserole, spacing them slightly apart. Cover and cook on high for 45 minutes–1 hour, or until well risen and firm. Do not lift the lid during cooking, or the dumplings won't rise properly. (Alternatively, the dumplings can be cooked separately in a covered shallow pan of simmering stock for 30 minutes. Lift out using a slotted spoon and serve with the casserole.)

FLAVOURING DUMPLINGS

Dumplings can be flavoured in many ways. Good choices include herbs or flavoured liquids, such as stock, white wine or cider, instead of water.
Herb and mustard dumplings go well with rich beef casseroles. Sift 5ml/1 tsp mustard powder with the flour and stir in 30–45ml/2–3 tbsp chopped fresh parsley.
Lemon and tarragon dumplings are good with chicken, turkey and fish casseroles. Stir in the finely grated rind of ½ lemon and 45ml/3 tbsp chopped fresh tarragon.
Caraway and sour cream dumplings work well with beef and veal goulash. Stir in 5ml/1 tsp caraway seeds and mix the dry ingredients together with a mixture of half sour cream and half chilled water.
Mushroom dumplings go well with beef and pork casseroles. Stir 50g/2oz very finely chopped mushrooms into the dumpling mixture.
Rosemary dumplings are good with lamb casseroles. Stir in 2.5–5ml/½–1 tsp chopped fresh rosemary.

Potato toppings

Sliced, grated and mashed potatoes make a good topping for casseroles and some braised dishes. If you like, they can be browned in the oven or under a grill (broiler) before serving. Sliced and grated potatoes are usually added at the beginning of cooking; mashed potatoes are added towards the end. All these recipes make enough to serve four.

Sliced potato topping: Thinly slice 675g/1½lb potatoes and arrange over the top of the casserole at the beginning of cooking. Make sure there is just enough liquid to cover the potatoes. Cover with the lid and cook on low for 8–10 hours, or on high for 4–5 hours, until tender. To brown the top before serving, brush the potatoes with a little melted butter and place under a hot grill (broiler) for 3–4 minutes.

Grated potato topping: Grate 675g/1½lb potatoes, then blanch in boiling salted water for 5 minutes. Drain well and squeeze out any excess liquid. Stir in 15ml/1 tbsp melted butter or olive oil, then sprinkle evenly over the surface of the casserole. Cook on low for 4–6 hours, or on high for 2–3 hours. If you like, brown under the grill.

Creamy mashed potato topping: Boil 900g/2lb peeled floury potatoes (such as King Edward or Maris Piper) until tender. Drain well, return to the pan and add 50g/2oz/¼ cup butter, or 30ml/2 tbsp olive oil. Mash with a potato masher until smooth, then beat in 75ml/5 tbsp hot milk or cream, salt, pepper and grated nutmeg. Spoon on top of the casserole or braised dish, spreading out evenly. Cover and cook in the slow cooker for 1 hour. Alternatively, bake in an oven preheated to 190°C/375°F/ Gas 5 for 30 minutes, or brown the top under a medium grill (broiler).

Polenta toppings

This golden-yellow cornmeal topping goes well with Mediterranean-style stews. Mixed with flour, milk and egg, polenta makes a cornbread topping.

Basic polenta topping: Bring 2 litres/ 3½ pints/8 cups water with 5ml/1 tsp salt to the boil in a large, heavy pan. Remove the pan from the heat and pour in 375g/13oz/3 cups fine polenta, whisking continuously. Return the pan to the heat and stir for 15 minutes, until thick. Season well with salt and pepper. This soft polenta can be used in the same way as mashed potato topping.

Polenta triangles: Spoon the basic polenta mixture on to a wet board and spread out to 1cm/½in thick. Leave to set for 1 hour, then cut into triangles. One hour before the end of cooking time, arrange the polenta on top of the casserole. To serve, brush with olive oil, sprinkle with grated Parmesan cheese and grill.

Cornbread topping: Mix 175g/6oz/ 1½ cups fine cornmeal with 15ml/1 tbsp wholemeal (whole-wheat) flour and 5ml/1 tsp baking powder. Make a well in the centre and add 1 beaten egg and 175ml/6fl oz/¾ cup milk. Mix, then quickly spoon over the top of the casserole. Cover and cook for 1 hour until firm. If you like, brown under a grill.

Crumble toppings

These can be cooked in the slow cooker, but are much better baked in the oven. They work well with braised dishes and chunky casseroles with only a little sauce or gravy. This recipe serves four.

1 Sift 175g/6oz/1½ cups plain (all-purpose) white or wholemeal (whole-wheat) flour and a pinch of salt into a bowl. Rub in 90g/3½oz/7 tbsp butter or margarine until the mixture resembles very fine breadcrumbs.

2 Stir in 50g/2oz/½ cup chopped nuts, or 30–45ml/2–3 tbsp porridge oats, 25g/1oz grated mature (sharp) Cheddar cheese, or 25g/1oz sunflower seeds.

3 Preheat the oven to 190°C/375°F/ Gas 5. Sprinkle the topping over the casserole in an even layer, then bake uncovered for 30 minutes until golden.

Bread toppings

Sliced, cubed or crumbled, many types of bread may be used, from sliced white to textured wholegrain.

Breadcrumb topping: Preheat the oven to 150°C/300°F/Gas 2. Combine 75g/3oz/1½ cups breadcrumbs with 30ml/2 tbsp chopped fresh parsley and 2 finely chopped garlic cloves. Sprinkle over the casserole and bake for about 30–40 minutes until golden.

Cheesy French bread topping: Lightly toast 6–12 thick slices of day-old baguette on both sides. Rub one side of each slice with a halved garlic clove, then spread with a little French mustard. Sprinkle over 115g/4oz/1 cup coarsely grated Gruyère cheese and grill until the cheese bubbles. Arrange on top of the casserole and serve immediately.

POT-ROASTING

This method of cooking small or large joints of meat and whole poultry in a small amount of liquid, usually with herbs and vegetables, is ideal for less tender cuts of meat, poultry and game that are low in natural fat. It makes them wonderfully succulent and tender and minimizes shrinkage. The meat is nearly always browned before being placed in the slow cooker with a little liquid and other ingredients. Sometimes the meat is marinated before cooking, especially beef and game, which can be dry.

When choosing joints of meat for pot-roasting, small pieces weighing no more than 1.2kg/2½lb are ideal. If the meat is irregularly shaped it will cook less uniformly and may be awkward to carve, so boned joints such as sirloin, silverside and topside should be tied; shoulder of lamb should be both boned and tied before pot-roasting.

Tying a boneless joint

You will need fine string for tying joints of meat. Store it in a plastic bag or box, rather than leaving loose in a drawer, so that it does not get dirty.

1 Roll or arrange the meat joint into a neat shape. Tie it lengthways with a piece of string. This should be pulled tightly and double-knotted because the meat will shrink a little during cooking. (You may need to ask someone to help you do this.)

2 Tie the joint widthways at regular intervals about 2.5cm/1in apart, knotting and trimming the ends of string as you go. Apply even pressure when tying each length of string to keep the shape of the joint as neat as possible.

Boning a shoulder of lamb

Lamb shoulder is made up of three bones: the flat blade bone, the thin arm bone and the knuckle.

1 Place the shoulder on a board and trim off any excess fat. Insert a sharp knife into the larger end of the lamb joint, then slice it along the flat blade bone, working towards the centre. Turn the meat over and repeat on the other side. Twist out the blade bone.

2 Put the lamb, skin side down, on the board. Cut along the line of the arm and knuckle bones, scraping the meat off the bones, then remove them.

3 Cut through the flesh where the blade bone was and open out the meat. It can now be stuffed, then rolled and tied.

Tying a shoulder *en ballon*

As an alternative to rolling and tying a shoulder of lamb, it can be tied *en ballon*; this is a round cushion shape that is served sliced into wedges.

1 Lay the meat out flat, skin side down. If you like, spoon stuffing into the middle. Pull one corner of the joint into the centre and secure it with a skewer.

2 Do the same with the other four corners, tucking in the remains of the shank and securing them by tying a loop of string around the "ballon".

3 Turn the joint over and continue tying loops of string at even spaces around the ballon, to make six or eight sections. Tie a knot at the crossover point on each side as you go.

Pot-roasting brisket of beef

Other cuts of beef, such as silverside and topside of beef, can be cooked in this way. Stuffed breast or shoulder of lamb also work very well.

SERVES 4–6

1.2kg/2½lb rolled brisket
25g/1oz/2 tbsp beef dripping
   or white vegetable fat
2 onions, cut into 8 wedges
2 carrots, quartered
2 sticks celery, cut into 5cm/2in lengths
2 bay leaves
2 sprigs of fresh thyme
300ml/½ pint/1¼ cups near-boiling
   beef stock
salt and ground black pepper

1 Season the meat well with salt and pepper. Heat the dripping or vegetable fat in a large, heavy pan until hot. Add the meat and turn frequently using two spoons until browned. If the fat gets too hot before the meat is browned, add a little cold butter to cool it. Lift out the meat and transfer to a plate.

2 Pour away some of the fat, leaving about 15ml/1 tbsp in the pan. Add the onions, carrots and celery and cook for a few minutes or until lightly browned and beginning to soften. Browning the vegetables will add flavour and colour to the pot-roast, but take care not to darken them too much or the stock will become bitter. Arrange a single layer of vegetables in the base of the cooking pot, then place the meat on top, adding any juices from the plate. Put the remaining vegetables around the sides of the meat and tuck in the fresh herbs.

3 Pour the stock into the pan and bring to the boil, stirring in any sediment.

4 Pour the stock over the meat and vegetables; it should barely cover them, leaving most of the meat exposed.

5 Cover the slow cooker with the lid and switch to high. Cook for 4 hours, then reduce the temperature to low and cook for a further 2–3 hours, or until the meat is cooked through and very tender. Once or twice during cooking, turn the meat and baste. Avoid using any sharp utensils when doing so because they may puncture the outer layer and allow juices to escape.

6 Lift out the meat and place on a warmed serving dish. Cover with a piece of foil and leave it to rest; 15 minutes will be sufficient to allow the fibres to relax and let the juices settle, making the meat easier to carve.

7 Meanwhile, skim any fat from the juices and stock in the cooking pot. Serve as a gravy with the meat. (If you like, thicken the juices with cornflour or arrowroot first.) Normally the vegetables are discarded, but these may be served with the meat as well.

Pot-roasting chicken

A whole chicken can be pot-roasted in exactly the same way as a joint of beef or lamb, but this technique is unsuitable for large chickens weighing more than 1.6kg/3½lb. Avoid stuffing the cavity, although you may add a quartered onion or lemon for flavouring.

SERVES 4

150ml/¼ pint/⅔ cup dry white wine
   or dry (hard) cider
2 bay leaves
1.2–1.3kg/2½–3lb chicken
1 lemon, quartered
15ml/1 tbsp sunflower oil
25g/1oz/2 tbsp unsalted (sweet) butter
150ml/¼ pint/⅔ cup boiling chicken stock
15ml/1 tbsp cornflour (cornstarch) blended
   with 30ml/2 tbsp water or wine
salt and ground black pepper

1 Pour the wine into the ceramic cooking pot. Add the bay leaves and switch the slow cooker to high. Meanwhile, rinse or wipe the chicken and pat dry using kitchen paper. Season the cavity, then add the lemon quarters.

2 Heat the oil and butter in a heavy frying pan. Brown the chicken on all sides, then transfer it to the ceramic cooking pot. If the chicken has been trussed, untie it before placing in the cooking pot. This will allow the heat to penetrate more easily.

3 Pour the stock over the chicken, then cover with the lid and cook on high for 3½–4½ hours, or until the juices run clear when pierced with a thin knife or skewer, or a meat thermometer inserted into the thickest part of the thigh reads 77°C/170°F. (Chicken and other poultry must be cooked on high throughout.)

4 Lift the chicken out of the cooking pot, place on a warmed serving dish, cover with foil and leave to rest for 10–15 minutes before serving. Meanwhile, skim the juices, stir in the cornflour mixture and cook on high for 10 minutes, then serve as a sauce.

POACHING

This gentle method of cooking keeps food wonderfully moist. It differs from boiling because the heat is so low that only the occasional bubble breaks the surface of the liquid. It is ideal for delicate meats, such as poultry and fish, which can overcook and disintegrate if fiercely boiled. Poaching also allows you to skim off the scum and fat that faster boiling would bubble back into the liquid, making it cloudy and spoiling the flavour. The slow cooker is perfect for poaching because it keeps the heat constant and steady and needs little attention.

Poaching chicken

Unlike pot-roasting, the slow cooker can be used for poaching large chickens and other poultry, although it is important to check that it will fit comfortably in the ceramic cooking pot. There should be enough space for it to be completely immersed in liquid and room for liquid to circulate around the sides. Because the cavity of the bird will be filled with poaching liquid, the bird will be cooked from the inside and the outside.

SERVES 4

1.3kg/3lb oven-ready chicken
1 onion
2 carrots
2 leeks
2 celery sticks
a few fresh parsley stalks
2 bay leaves
6 black peppercorns
2.5ml/½ tsp salt

1 Remove any trussing string from the chicken. Remove any loose pieces of fat from inside the chicken, then rinse the cavity under cold water and place the chicken in the ceramic cooking pot.

2 Trim the onion at the stem and root end, but do not peel (the skin will add a rich golden colour to the stock). Cut the onion into six or eight wedges. Wash and trim the carrots, leeks and celery, then roughly chop or slice them and add to the cooking pot, packing them in around the chicken.

3 Tie the herbs together and add to the pot with the peppercorns and salt.

4 Pour in enough near-boiling water to just cover the chicken, pouring it over the vegetables and the chicken. Cover with the lid, switch the slow cooker to high and cook for 1 hour.

5 Skim off any scum and fat using a slotted spoon. Re-cover the pot and cook for 2–2½ hours, or until the chicken is cooked and tender. To check the chicken is cooked, insert a meat thermometer into the thickest part, where the thigh joins the body; it should read 77°C/170°F. (Alternatively, insert a skewer into the thickest part; the juices should show no traces of pink. If they are clear, lift the chicken out of the pot and double-check on the other side.)

6 Remove the chicken from the pot, using a large fork inserted into the cavity to lift it up. Leave the chicken to rest for 10 minutes before carving. Alternatively, if you plan to eat the chicken cold, leave it to cool completely on a wire rack placed over a large plate to catch any drips. (The wire rack will allow air to circulate around the chicken, helping it to cool more quickly.)

7 Leave the cooking liquid to cool for a few minutes, then ladle into a colander set over a large bowl. Leave to drip; do not press the vegetables or the stock will become cloudy. Cool the stock quickly by placing the bowl in cold water.

8 If you plan to eat the chicken cold, as soon as it is cool, cover with clear film (plastic wrap) and store in the refrigerator. (Leave the skin on because this will help to keep the meat moist.) Use within 2 days of cooking.

9 When the stock is cool, cover with clear film (plastic wrap) and place in the refrigerator. Any fat in the stock will rise to the surface and can be removed easily and discarded. The stock can be kept for up to 3 days, or it can be frozen in airtight containers for up to 6 months.

Poaching gammon

Gammon is the cured hind leg of the bacon pig. Once cooked, it is known as ham. When serving the meat in slices, poaching is the best cooking method, producing tender, juicy results. However, if you wish to serve it whole, it can be glazed after poaching and briefly baked.

SERVES 6–8

1.8kg/4lb boned middle gammon joint
1 onion
6 whole cloves
2 carrots, halved
1 bouquet garni
10 black peppercorns
dry (hard) cider (optional)

1 Place the meat in the ceramic cooking pot, cover with cold water and leave to soak for 2–24 hours to remove the salt. (Mild cured gammon shouldn't need long soaking, but it is preferable to soak smoked gammon for the longer time.)

2 Drain the gammon, then return it to the cooking pot. Peel the onion, stud with the cloves and add to the pot with the carrots, herbs and peppercorns. If you find it difficult to squeeze the onion down the side of the gammon, halve it.

3 Pour in enough cold water, or cider or a mixture of the two, to just cover the gammon. Switch the slow cooker to high, cover with the lid and cook for 1 hour. Skim off any scum using a slotted spoon, then re-cover and cook for a further 4–5 hours. Check and skim the surface once or twice during cooking.

4 Lift the ham out of the pot and place on a board. Slice and serve hot, or allow to cool, then wrap in foil and store in the refrigerator for up to 5 days.

5 Strain the cooking liquid into a bowl and leave to cool. (Taste the stock when hot; if it is very salty, use sparingly in dishes and do not add additional salt.) Chill the stock and remove any fat from the surface. Store in the refrigerator and use within 2 days. Alternatively, freeze for up to 6 months.

GLAZING HAMS

After poaching, lift the ham into a foil-lined baking dish and leave to cool for 15 minutes. Snip the string off the ham, then slice off the rind, leaving a thin, even layer of fat. Score the fat in diagonal lines, then score in the opposite direction to make a diamond pattern. Brush the warm joint with about 45ml/3 tbsp lime marmalade and sprinkle with 45ml/ 3 tbsp demerara (raw) sugar. Push whole cloves into the corners of the diamond shapes after glazing, if you like. Bake at 220°C/425°F/Gas 7 for about 20 minutes, until the fat is brown and crisp. Serve hot or cold.

Poaching fish

The delicate texture of fish benefits from simple cooking. Poaching brings out its flavour and keeps it moist. Both whole fish and fillets can be poached in the slow cooker, but first check that there is enough room for the fish, as well as space to manoeuvre a fish slice (spatula).

Fish can be poached in cold liquid, but it will retain its shape and texture if added to hot liquid. Larger pieces of fish, such as steaks or cutlets, will take no more than 45 minutes on high, or 1½–2 hours on low, but take care not to overcook and check frequently. Fish is ready when the flesh is only slightly translucent when eased away from the bone, or flakes easily when tested with the point of a sharp knife or skewer.

Poaching fruit

Apples, pears, stone fruits, such as plums, and soft fruit, such as figs, can be poached whole, halved or sliced. Even fragile fruit, such as rhubarb, will retain its shape when cooked in a slow cooker. Cooking times will depend on the size and ripeness of the fruit, but as a rough guide, tender fruit, such as figs and rhubarb, will take about 1½ hours on high; ripe or near-ripe fruit, such as plums or apples, will take about 2 hours on high; and harder, less ripe fruit, such as pears, will take 3–5 hours on high, or 6–8 hours on low.

The classic poaching liquid is syrup and usually consists of 1 part sugar to 2 parts water. Flavouring ingredients such as a pared strip of lemon rind or spices can be added to the liquid, as can red or white wine, cider or fruit juice sweetened with sugar.

1 Put the sugar, poaching liquid and any flavourings into the ceramic cooking pot and switch the slow cooker to high. Cook for 1 hour, stirring occasionally to dissolve the sugar.

2 Add the fruit, cover and cook until the fruit is barely tender. Leave the fruit to cool in the syrup, or remove and place in a serving dish. Strain the syrup over the fruit, or simmer gently to thicken.

USING the SLOW COOKER as a BAIN-MARIE

While many dishes are cooked directly in the ceramic cooking pot, others may be cooked in a bain-marie – in a tin (pan) or dish placed inside the cooking pot and surrounded by barely simmering water. This technique is good for making pâtés, terrines, cakes, steamed puddings and custard-based desserts. To allow the water to move freely around the cooking container, an upturned saucer or metal pastry ring is often placed on the base of the cooking pot. This is important if the cooking pot has a slightly concave base.

MAKING PÂTÉS AND TERRINES

When raw meat and eggs are used, make sure that the depth of the mixture is no greater than 6cm/2¼in, otherwise the pâté may not cook thoroughly. This is especially important with pork and chicken. A 450g/1lb terrine or loaf tin measuring about 20 x 10 x 5.5cm/ 8 x 4 x 2¼in and holding a volume of 900ml/1½ pints/3¾ cups is an ideal size.

Making classic pork pâté

You can use this recipe as a guide for making other pâtés. You can vary the proportions of the main ingredients, and can use lean minced (ground) beef or pork in place of the veal.

SERVES 6

225g/8oz rindless smoked streaky (fatty) bacon rashers (strips)
225g/8oz boneless belly of pork
175g/6oz veal
115g/4oz chicken livers
45ml/3 tbsp dry white wine
15ml/1 tbsp brandy
2.5ml/½ tsp dried thyme
2.5ml/½ tsp dried rosemary
1 garlic clove, crushed
2.5ml/½ tsp salt
1.5ml/¼ tsp ground mace
ground black pepper

1 Place an upturned saucer or metal pastry cutter in the base of the ceramic cooking pot. Pour in about 2.5cm/1in of very hot water, then turn the slow cooker to high.

2 Taking 150g/5oz of the bacon, stretch one rasher at a time on a board using the back of a large knife. Use to line a 450g/1lb loaf tin, or a 900ml/1½ pint/ 3¾ cup round dish, leaving the bacon overhanging the sides.

3 Finely chop the remaining bacon and place in a large bowl. Trim the belly of pork, veal and chicken livers, then mince (grind) using the medium blade of a mincer, or place in a food processor and chop roughly. Add to the bowl.

4 Spoon the white wine and brandy over the meat. Add the herbs, garlic and seasonings, then mix well. Transfer the mixture to the tin or dish, pressing down lightly. Fold the overhanging bacon over the top of the filling, then cover with a piece of foil.

5 Place the pâté in the slow cooker, then pour enough very hot water around it to come nearly to the top. Cook on high for 4–6 hours. To test whether the pâté is cooked, push a thin skewer into the centre and press lightly around the edges of the hole; the liquid should be clear, not cloudy or pink.

6 Carefully remove the pâté from the slow cooker and leave to cool on a wire rack. Cover and chill for several hours, then unmould and keep covered until ready to serve. (If you like, the pâté can be pressed before chilling.)

PRESSING PÂTÉS

After cooling the cooked pâté, you may "press" it to give it a slightly firmer texture and to make it easier to slice. Cover the pâté with greaseproof (waxed) paper or clear film (plastic wrap). Top with a board that fits exactly inside the tin (pan) and place several weights or cans on the board. (Alternatively, use bags of rice or lentils, which can be moulded to fit into the top of the tin.) Leave until completely cool, then chill overnight (still weighted if you want a really firm texture).

Making mousseline pâté

A mousseline pâté has a light, smooth, creamy texture. Allow plenty of time to prepare it because you will need to chill the mixture between each stage. Mousseline pâtés are extremely rich, so serve thinly sliced with bread or salad.

SERVES 8

15g/½oz/1 tbsp butter
1 shallot, finely chopped
15ml/1 tbsp brandy or sherry
225g/8oz skinless chicken breast portion
50g/2oz chicken livers, trimmed
15ml/1 tbsp fresh white breadcrumbs
1 egg, separated
300ml/½ pint/1¼ cups double (heavy) cream
salt and ground white pepper

1 Lightly oil and line a 450g/1lb loaf or terrine tin (pan), or a 900ml/1½ pint/3¾ cup baking dish, with baking parchment. Melt the butter in a small pan, add the shallot and cook for about 5 minutes until soft. Turn off the heat, then stir in the brandy or sherry. Place the mixture in a bowl and leave to cool.

2 Meanwhile, roughly chop the chicken breast portion and livers, then place in a food processor and purée for about 30 seconds. Add the shallot mixture and breadcrumbs to the chicken and process until very smooth. Return the mixture to the bowl and chill for 30 minutes.

3 Meanwhile, place an upturned saucer or metal pastry cutter in the bottom of the ceramic cooking pot. Pour in about 2.5cm/1in of very hot water, then turn the slow cooker to high.

4 Set the bowl of chicken purée over a larger bowl filled with crushed ice and water. Lightly whisk the egg white with a fork until frothy and beat into the purée, a little at a time. Beat in the egg yolk.

5 Gradually add the cream, mixing well between each addition. Season with salt and white pepper, then spoon the mixture into the prepared tin and level the top. Cover with clear film (plastic wrap) or foil.

6 Place the tin or terrine in the slow cooker, then pour enough hot water around to come nearly to the top. Cook on high for 3–4 hours, or until firm.

7 Carefully remove the pâté from the slow cooker and leave to cool on a wire rack. Chill well before slicing and serving.

Making a studded terrine

Attractive terrines can be made using the mousseline mixture and studding it with vegetables or layering it with other meats, such as strips of chicken or ham.

SERVES 8

75g/3oz fine asparagus stalks
75g/3oz green beans, topped and tailed
115g/4oz carrots, peeled and cut into matchstick strips
½ quantity mousseline pâté mixture

1 Lightly oil and line a 450g/1lb loaf tin or terrine, or a 900ml/1½ pint/3¾ cup baking dish, with baking parchment. Cook the vegetables, one type at a time, in boiling water for 1 minute. Drain, plunge into cold water, then drain again.

2 Spread a layer of the mixture in the bottom of the tin. Arrange the asparagus lengthways, with gaps between each, then cover with a thin layer of the pâté.

3 Repeat the layers using the beans and carrots and finishing with the remaining pâté mixture. Smooth the top. Cover with clear film (plastic wrap) or foil and cook in the same way as the chicken mousseline for 2½–3½ hours.

MAKING STEAMED PUDDINGS and DESSERTS

The slow cooker is perfect for cooking sticky steamed sponges and custards. It keeps the water at a very gentle simmer, reducing the risk of the water bubbling up and spoiling the dish.

Making a steamed sponge

Sponge puddings cooked in steam have a surprisingly light, moist texture. They were traditionally made using shredded beef or vegetarian suet, but this modern version uses a creamed cake mixture. Make sure that all the ingredients are at room temperature before you start.

SERVES 4–6

115g/4oz/½ cup butter, at room
   temperature
115g/4oz/generous ½ cup caster
   (superfine) sugar
2.5ml/½ tsp vanilla essence
   (extract)
2 eggs, lightly beaten
175g/6oz/1½ cups self-raising
   (self-rising) flour
about 45ml/3 tbsp milk

1 Place an upturned saucer or metal pastry cutter in the bottom of the ceramic cooking pot. Pour in 2.5cm/1in very hot water, then preheat the slow cooker on high. Grease a 900ml/ 1½ pint/3¾ cup pudding bowl and line the base with a piece of greaseproof (waxed) paper or baking parchment.

2 Cream the butter, sugar and vanilla essence together in a large mixing bowl until pale and fluffy. Add the eggs, a little at a time, beating thoroughly. If the mixture begins to curdle, beat in a spoonful of the flour.

3 Sift half the flour over the creamed mixture and fold in using a large metal spoon. Sift over the rest and fold in with 30ml/2 tbsp of the milk. If necessary, add the remaining milk to make a soft dropping consistency, then spoon into the pudding bowl.

4 Cover the pudding with greaseproof paper and foil and tie with string. Lower into the slow cooker, then pour enough water around the bowl to come halfway up the sides. Cover with the lid and cook on high for 4–5 hours, or until well risen and springy to the touch. Lift out of the slow cooker and remove the foil. Turn out on to a serving plate, peel off the paper and serve.

HOW TO COVER A STEAMED PUDDING

1 Brush a sheet of greaseproof (waxed) paper with softened butter, then place the unbuttered side on a sheet of foil. Make a pleat about 2cm/¾in wide in the middle to allow the pudding to rise. (If fresh fruit is included in the pudding, you must use greaseproof paper; otherwise, a double piece of foil may be used.)

2 Cover the bowl with the pleated greaseproof paper and foil, allowing it to overlap the rim by 2.5cm/1in. Tie the foil securely with fine string.

3 Make a loop with the string at the top of the bowl to make a secure handle. This will enable the bowl to be lifted in and out of the ceramic cooking pot easily.

Making baked egg custard

A lightly set, creamy-textured custard is ideal for serving hot or cold. It can be enjoyed on its own or with all manner of desserts, such as fruit pies, steamed sponges and crumbles.

SERVES 4–6

butter or flavourless oil, for greasing
475ml/16fl oz/2 cups milk
3 eggs
45ml/3 tbsp caster (superfine) sugar
pinch of freshly grated nutmeg

1 Place an upturned saucer or metal pastry cutter in the bottom of the ceramic cooking pot. Pour in about 2.5cm/1in of very hot water, then turn the slow cooker to high.

2 Lightly grease the base and sides of a 900ml/1½ pint/3¾ cup heatproof dish. Heat the milk in a pan until it is steaming hot, without letting it boil.

3 Whisk the eggs and sugar lightly in a bowl, then slowly pour over the hot milk, whisking all the time. Strain the mixture through a fine sieve (strainer) into the prepared dish and sprinkle the top with a little grated nutmeg.

4 Cover the dish with clear film (plastic wrap) and place in the slow cooker. Pour in enough near-boiling water to come just over halfway up the sides of the dish. Put the lid on the slow cooker, then switch to the low setting and cook for 4 hours, or until the custard is lightly set. Serve hot or cold.

Making crème brûlée

You can use the basic baked egg custard mixture to make other custard-based desserts, such as crème brûlée, which is a rich, creamy baked custard topped with a crisp layer of caramelized sugar.

1 Make the custard, whisking 5ml/1 tsp vanilla essence (extract) into the egg and sugar mixture, then use 150ml/¼ pint/ ⅔ cup double (heavy) cream and 300ml/ ½ pint/1¼ cups single (light) cream in place of the milk.

2 Strain the custard into a jug (pitcher), then pour into four or six individual ramekins (custard cups), first making sure that the ramekins will fit inside the cooking pot in a single layer.

3 Cover each dish with clear film (plastic wrap), then place in the ceramic cooking pot. Pour enough near-boiling water around the dishes to come three-quarters of the way up the sides. Cover with the lid and cook on low for about 3 hours, or until set.

4 Remove the custards from the slow cooker and leave to cool. Sprinkle the tops with 115g/4oz/½ cup caster (superfine) sugar. Place under a hot grill (broiler) and cook until the sugar melts and caramelizes. Cool, then chill.

Making bread and butter pudding

This favourite dessert can be made using the classic baked custard mixture.

1 Make the custard using 300ml/½ pint/ 1¼ cups milk and 75ml/2½fl oz/⅓ cup double (heavy) cream.

2 Butter 8 medium slices of bread, then cut each in half diagonally. Arrange the slices in a 1 litre/1¾ pint/4 cup, buttered baking dish, first making sure that it will fit in the cooking pot.

3 Pour the custard over the bread and sprinkle 30ml/2 tbsp demerara (raw) sugar and a little grated nutmeg over the top. Cover with clear film (plastic wrap) and put the dish in the cooking pot. Pour enough near-boiling water around the dish to come two-thirds up the sides. Cover with a lid and cook on high for 3–4 hours, or until the custard has set. Serve the pudding warm.

Making cheese and vegetable strata

This savoury bread and butter pudding can be made using the baked custard mixture. Simply leave out the sugar and season well with salt and black pepper.

1 Cook 1 thinly sliced leek and 1 large finely chopped onion in 25g/1oz/2 tbsp butter until soft. Stir in 30ml/2 tbsp chopped fresh chives or parsley.

2 Remove the crusts from 8 slices of bread, then cut into fingers. Arrange one-third of the bread fingers in a buttered 1.75 litre/3 pint/7½ cup soufflé dish. Top with half the vegetable mixture. Repeat the layers, ending with bread.

3 Pour the custard mixture over the strata, then sprinkle 75g/3oz/¾ cup finely grated Cheddar cheese over the top. Cover with buttered foil, then put in the ceramic cooking pot and pour enough near-boiling water around the dish to come halfway up the sides. Cover and cook on high for 3–4 hours until lightly set. Cut into wedges and serve warm.

Making rice pudding

Cooked in the slow cooker, rice pudding is wonderfully rich and creamy. Unlike baked versions it doesn't form a thick skin on the top. Add flavourings such as grated nutmeg at the beginning, or part-way through cooking.

SERVES 4–6

25g/1oz/2 tbsp softened butter
75g/3oz/generous ⅓ cup pudding rice, rinsed and drained
50g/2oz/4 tbsp caster (superfine) sugar
750ml/1¼ pints/3 cups milk
175ml/6fl oz/¾ cup evaporated (unsweetened condensed) milk

1 Thickly butter the ceramic cooking pot, taking it about half-way up the sides. Add the rice, sugar, milk, evaporated milk and any flavourings and stir to mix.

2 Cover with the lid and cook on high for 3–4 hours, or on low for 5–6 hours, until the rice is cooked and most of the milk has been absorbed.

3 Stir the pudding at least twice during the last 2 hours of cooking. If the mixture gets too thick towards the end, stir in a little more milk.

MAKING CAKES

Many cakes can be made successfully in a slow cooker – in particular, moist cake mixtures, such as carrot cake and gingerbread, that normally require long cooking at low temperatures. These types of cake usually benefit from being left to mature before eating, but this is not necessary when they are cooked in the slow cooker. The slow cooker is also good for making lightly textured, rich-flavoured sponge cakes. However, it is not suitable for whisked sponges and cakes because these need fast cooking at a high temperature.

Cakes can be cooked either in a tin (pan) with a fixed base or in a straight-sided soufflé dish. Before you line a tin and fill it with cake mixture, make sure it will fit in the ceramic cooking pot. It is a good idea to test that the tin is watertight: fill it with water and leave for a few minutes to check for leakages.

The baking tin should be lined with greaseproof (waxed) paper that has been greased with a little flavourless oil, or baking parchment. This makes it easier to remove the cake from the tin.

Base-lining
Some recipes only require the base of the tin (pan) to be lined. This technique can be used to line any shape of tin, whether round, square or rectangular.

Place the tin on a sheet of greaseproof (waxed) paper or baking parchment and, using a pencil, draw round the tin. Cut just inside the line so that the paper will fit neatly inside the tin. Using a sheet of kitchen paper drizzled with a flavourless oil, grease the inside of the tin and place the lining paper in the base, pressing it right into the corners.

Lining round cookware
The sides, as well as the base, of a tin or soufflé dish will often need to be lined.

1 Place the tin (pan) or soufflé dish on a sheet of greaseproof (waxed) paper and draw round it. Cut inside the line. Cut strips of paper, about 1cm/½in wider than the depth of the tin or dish. Fold up the bottom edge by 1cm/½in, then make cuts about 1cm/½in apart from the edge of the paper to the fold.

2 Brush the inside of the tin or dish with oil, then position the paper strips around the side of the tin so that the snipped edge sits on the base. Place the paper circle in the base.

Lining a square tin
You can line a square tin (pan) with a single piece of greaseproof paper.

Put the tin on a square of greaseproof paper, which allows the depth of the tin on all four sides. Draw around the base of the tin. Cut in from the edge to each corner of the square. Fold in each side along its pencil line, making a firm crease. Lightly brush the inside of the tin with oil, then fit the paper inside, making sure it fits well into the corners.

Lining a loaf tin
Unlike a square tin (pan), it is easier to line a loaf tin with two strips of paper.

1 Cut a strip of greaseproof paper the length of the tin base and wide enough to cover the base and long sides. Cut another strip of paper, the same width as the tin base and long enough to cover the base and ends of the tin.

2 Lightly brush the inside of the tin with oil, then press the two pieces of paper into position, creasing it where it meets the edges of the base of the tin.

Making dark chocolate cake
Steaming in the slow cooker gives this rich cake a deliciously moist crumb.

SERVES 8–10

175g/6oz/¾ cup butter, at room
    temperature
115g/4oz/½ cup soft light brown sugar
50g/2oz/¼ cup clear honey
3 eggs, lightly beaten
150g/5oz/1¼ cups self-raising
    (self-rising) flour
25g/1oz/¼ cup unsweetened
    cocoa powder
10ml/2 tsp milk
5ml/1 tsp vanilla essence (extract)
whipped cream, for the filling (optional)

1 Place an upturned saucer or metal pastry cutter in the ceramic cooking pot. Pour in 2.5cm/1in of very hot water, then switch the slow cooker to high.

2 Grease and line a 16cm/7in fixed-base round cake tin (pan) or soufflé dish, at least 7.5cm/3in deep.

3 Put the butter, sugar and honey in a bowl and cream together until pale and fluffy. Beat the eggs into the creamed mixture a little a time, beating well after each addition. If the mixture curdles, mix in a little of the measured flour.

4 Sift the flour and cocoa over the cake mixture. Using a large metal spoon, gently fold in with the milk and vanilla essence. Spoon the mixture into the prepared tin and level the surface.

5 Loosely cover the cake tin with lightly oiled foil. Put the tin in the ceramic cooking pot and then pour enough near-boiling water around the tin to come just over halfway up the sides.

6 Cover with the lid and cook on high for 3 hours. To test if the cake is cooked, insert a skewer into the centre of the cake. Leave for a few seconds, then remove; it should come away clean. If any mixture sticks to the skewer, re-cover and cook for 30 minutes more.

7 Remove the cake from the ceramic cooking pot and place on a wire rack for 10 minutes before turning out of the tin. Leave to cool, then cut in half and fill with whipped cream, if you like.

DECORATING CAKES

Cakes cooked in a slow cooker darken in colour but they do not brown in the same way as an oven-baked cake. As a result, many will benefit from decorating.

Decorating uncooked cakes

Many cakes can be decorated before they are cooked in the slow cooker. Note that light sponges and wet cake mixtures cannot hold heavy decorations.

Glistening sugar is an easy and effective way of decorating cakes. Different types of sugar can be sprinkled over the top of an uncooked cake. Good choices include caster (superfine) sugar, larger crystals of granulated or demerara (raw) sugar, and brown sugar crystals.

Chopped and flaked (sliced) nuts can be sprinkled over cakes in the same way as sugar. Toast them first.

Halved nuts and glacé (candied) fruits can be arranged in decorative patterns on fruit cakes and stiff cake batters. After cooking, brush over a little warmed honey or sugar syrup to glaze.

Decorating cooked cakes

After cooking, cakes can be decorated in a number of different ways.

Icing or frosting can transform a simple cake into something special. To make fudge frosting, break 50g/2oz plain (semisweet) chocolate into the cooking pot and add 225g/8oz/2 cups sifted icing (confectioners') sugar, 50g/2oz/¼ cup butter, 45ml/3 tbsp milk and 5ml/1 tsp vanilla essence (extract). Switch the slow cooker to high for 15–25 minutes, or until the chocolate has melted. Remove the cooking pot, stir to mix, then beat until thick and spread over the cake.

American frosting can be made by placing a bowl in the ceramic cooking pot, then pouring enough near-boiling water around the bowl to come just over halfway up the sides. Switch the slow cooker to high. Place 350g/12oz caster (superfine) sugar in the bowl with 2.5ml/½ tsp cream of tartar and 2 egg whites. Whisk continuously until the mixture holds its shape. Spread over the cake in peaks.

MAKING SAVOURY SAUCES

Sauces add flavour, colour, texture and moisture to food. Many can be made in the slow cooker, from classic simmered sauces to emulsions that are made by using the slow cooker as a bain-marie. Here are just a selection of classic sauces that can be used for cooking or for serving with other dishes.

Making fresh tomato sauce

This sauce can be used as the base for pasta dishes, or can be combined with meat or poultry to make a rich cooking sauce. You can use 2 × 400g/14oz cans chopped plum tomatoes instead of fresh, if you prefer. This recipe will make about 475ml/16fl oz/2 cups.

1 Pour 15ml/1 tbsp olive oil into the ceramic cooking pot. Add 2 crushed garlic cloves and the finely grated zest of ½ lemon. Stir, then cover with the lid and switch the slow cooker to high. Cook for 15 minutes.

2 Peel and roughly chop 900g/2lb ripe tomatoes and add to the cooking pot with 60ml/4 tbsp vegetable stock or red wine, 5ml/1 tsp dried oregano and a pinch of caster (superfine) sugar. Stir to combine, then cover with the lid and cook on low for 3 hours.

3 Stir in 30–45ml/2–3 tbsp chopped fresh basil and season to taste with salt and ground black pepper.

Making white sauce

To make white sauce in a slow cooker, heat the milk, then whisk in a mixture of butter and flour. This recipe will make about 475ml/16fl oz/2 cups.

1 Pour 400ml/14fl oz/1⅔ cups milk into the ceramic cooking pot. Add flavouring ingredients (such as a bay leaf, a blade of mace, a few parsley stalks, half a peeled onion and 4 black peppercorns). Switch the slow cooker to high and heat for 1 hour, or until simmering.

2 Blend 20g/¾oz/1½ tbsp softened butter with 20g/¾oz/scant ¼ cup plain (all-purpose) flour to make a paste.

3 Remove the flavouring ingredients from the milk using a slotted spoon. Add the paste in small spoonfuls and whisk into the hot milk until thickened.

4 Cover with the lid and cook for about 30 minutes, stirring occasionally. Season with salt and extra pepper if needed.

HOT EMULSION SAUCES

These rich, creamy sauces can be made very successfully using the slow cooker as a bain-marie.

Making hollandaise sauce

The rich flavour of hollandaise sauce goes well with fish, shellfish and many vegetables. Take your time making it because it may curdle if the butter is added too quickly. This recipe will make about 300ml/½ pint/1¼ cups.

1 About 30 minutes before making the sauce, remove 150g/5oz/¾ cup unsalted (sweet) butter from the refrigerator. Cut into tiny cubes and leave to come to room temperature.

2 Pour about 5cm/2in near-boiling water into the ceramic cooking pot. Cover the slow cooker with the lid to retain the heat and switch to high.

3 Put 60ml/4 tbsp white wine vinegar in a pan with 4 black peppercorns, 1 bay leaf and 1 blade of mace (optional). Bring to the boil and simmer until reduced to 15ml/1 tbsp. Remove from the heat and dip the base of the pan into cold water to prevent further evaporation.

4 Beat 3 egg yolks with 15g/½oz/1 tbsp of the butter and a pinch of salt in a heatproof bowl that will fit in the slow cooker. Strain in the reduced vinegar. Place the bowl in the ceramic cooking pot and pour enough boiling water around the bowl to come just over halfway up the sides. Whisk for about 3 minutes until beginning to thicken.

5 Beat in the remaining butter a little at a time, making sure that each addition of butter is completely incorporated before adding the next. The mixture will slowly thicken and emulsify. Season with salt and ground black pepper. Switch the slow cooker to low and keep the hollandaise warm for up to 1 hour. (If the sauce starts to curdle, add an ice cube and whisk vigorously; the sauce should combine. If this doesn't work, whisk 1 egg yolk with 15ml/1 tbsp lukewarm water and slowly whisk into the separated sauce.)

Making beurre blanc

This simple butter sauce is served with poached or grilled (broiled) fish and poultry. It can be varied by adding chopped fresh herbs, such as chives or chervil, to the finished sauce. It is extremely rich, and only a small amount is needed per serving. This recipe will make about 250ml/8fl oz/1 cup.

1 Pour about 5cm/2in of near-boiling water into the ceramic cooking pot. Cover with the lid and switch the slow cooker to high.

2 Pour 45ml/3 tbsp each of white wine and white wine vinegar into a pan. Add 2 finely chopped shallots and bring to the boil. Simmer until reduced to about 15ml/1 tbsp liquid.

3 Strain the mixture into a heatproof bowl that will fit in the slow cooker, then pour enough boiling water around the bowl to come halfway up the sides.

4 Whisk in 225g/8oz/1 cup chilled diced butter, adding it piece by piece and making sure that each addition is completely incorporated before adding the next. Season with salt and ground black pepper before serving.

Making a sabayon sauce

Light and airy sabayon sauce is thickened with egg. It goes well with vegetable and pastry dishes. This recipe will make about 300ml/½ pint/1¼ cups.

1 Half-fill the ceramic cooking pot with near-boiling water, cover with the lid and switch to high.

2 Place a heatproof bowl over the water in the slow cooker; the base should just touch the water but the rest of the bowl should be above the water. Place 4 egg yolks with 15ml/1 tbsp white wine vinegar in the bowl and whisk until pale. Add 90ml/6 tbsp red or white wine or stock and whisk again.

3 When the sauce is thick and frothy, season to taste and serve immediately.

MAKING SWEET SAUCES

A sweet sauce adds the finishing touch to a dessert, and the slow cooker is excellent for making fruit purées, creamy custards and rich chocolate sauces.

Making fresh fruit coulis

Cooking soft fruits, such as raspberries, blackberries, blueberries, blackcurrants, plums, cherries and apricots, brings out their natural flavour. This recipe will make about 350ml/12fl oz/1½ cups.

1 Put 350g/12oz/3 cups prepared fruit in the ceramic cooking pot with 45ml/ 3 tbsp water. Stir in a little sugar and add a dash of lemon juice. Cover with the lid and cook on high for 1–1½ hours or until very soft.

2 Remove the cooking pot from the slow cooker and leave to cool slightly. Pour the fruit into a food processor or blender and process until smooth. Press the purée through a sieve (strainer) to remove any seeds or skins.

3 Taste the sauce and stir in a little more sugar or lemon juice, if needed. Cover and chill until required. If you like, stir in 45ml/3 tbsp liqueur, such as Kirsch, before serving. The coulis can be stored in the refrigerator for up to 5 days.

Making dried fruit sauce

Dried fruits, such as apricots, can also be made into sauces. This recipe will make about 600ml/1 pint/scant 2½ cups.

1 Place 175g/6oz dried apricots in the ceramic cooking pot, pour over 475ml/ 16fl oz/2 cups orange juice, cover and leave to soak overnight.

2 Place the ceramic pot in the slow cooker and cook on high for 1 hour, or until the apricots are tender. Purée in a food processor or blender and serve warm or cold. If necessary, dilute the sauce with a little extra fruit juice.

Making custard

Custard is the classic dessert sauce and can also be used as the basis for many desserts. The slow cooker maintains a gentle, constant heat, so the custard can be made directly in the ceramic cooking pot, rather than in a bain-marie. It can be served hot or cold, and can also be flavoured: try stirring 75g/3oz chopped plain (semisweet) chocolate or 45ml/ 3 tbsp rum or brandy into hot custard. For extra richness, replace some of the milk with single (light) or double (heavy) cream. This recipe will make about 600ml/1 pint/2½ cups.

1 Pour 475ml/16fl oz/2 cups of milk into the ceramic cooking pot. Split a vanilla pod (bean) lengthways and add it to the milk. Heat on high for 1 hour, or until the milk reaches boiling point.

2 Meanwhile, whisk together 5 egg yolks and 90g/3½ oz/scant ½ cup caster (superfine) sugar in a bowl until the mixture is pale and thick.

3 Whisk 5ml/1 tsp cornflour (cornstarch) into the egg mixture. (This will help the custard to thicken and prevent curdling.)

4 Remove the vanilla pod and pour the hot milk over the egg mixture, whisking all the time. Pour the mixture back into the ceramic cooking pot and stir until slightly thickened. Bring the custard to simmering point; do not let it boil or it may curdle. Cook until it is thick enough to coat the back of a wooden spoon.

Making sabayon sauce

This frothy sauce goes well with elegant desserts and dainty pastries. This recipe makes about 450ml/¾ pint/scant 2 cups.

1 Pour about 5cm/2in near-boiling water into the ceramic cooking pot. Cover with the lid and switch to high.

2 Put 4 eggs and 50g/2oz/¼ cup caster (superfine) sugar in a heatproof bowl, first checking that it will fit comfortably in the slow cooker. Beat well until the mixture becomes a paler colour, then whisk in 100ml/3½fl oz/generous ½ cup sweet white wine.

3 Place the bowl in the ceramic cooking pot and pour enough boiling water around it to come just over halfway up the sides. Continue whisking the sauce for 10 minutes until it is very thick and frothy. Serve hot or cold.

Making creamy chocolate sauce

This dark, velvety smooth sauce should be served with desserts that can stand up to its deep, rich flavour.

1 Pour 200ml/7fl oz/scant 1 cup double (heavy) cream, 60ml/4 tbsp milk and 2.5ml/½ tsp vanilla essence (extract) into the ceramic cooking pot. Switch the slow cooker to high and heat for about 45 minutes.

2 Turn off the slow cooker. Add 150g/ 5oz chopped dark (bittersweet) chocolate and stir continuously until it has melted. Serve warm.

Making glossy chocolate sauce

This sweet pouring sauce is ideal for serving with profiteroles and ice cream.

Put 225g/8oz chopped plain (semisweet) chocolate, 60ml/4 tbsp golden (light corn) syrup, 60ml/4 tbsp water and 25g/1oz/ 2 tbsp unsalted (sweet) butter into the ceramic cooking pot. Switch the slow cooker to high and heat, stirring, for 30 minutes until melted. Serve warm.

Making white chocolate sauce

This sweet creamy sauce is good served warm with fresh summer fruits.

1 Pour about 5cm/2in very hot water into the cooking pot. Cover with the lid and switch the slow cooker to high.

2 Put 200g/7oz white chocolate and 30ml/2 tbsp double (heavy) cream into a heatproof bowl. Place in the cooking pot and pour enough near-boiling water around the bowl to touch the base.

3 Stir until melted, then stir in 60ml/ 4 tbsp double (heavy) cream and 60ml/4 tbsp milk. Heat for 5 minutes, then remove from the heat and whisk.

Making caramel sauce

This rich, creamy sauce is delicious poured over sweet pastries and pastry desserts.

1 Put 25g/1oz/2 tbsp unsalted (sweet) butter and 75g/3oz/6 tbsp soft dark brown sugar in the ceramic cooking pot. Switch the slow cooker to high and heat for about 20 minutes, stirring occasionally, until the butter has melted and the sugar has dissolved.

2 Stir 150ml/¼ pint/⅔ cup double (heavy) cream into the sauce and cook for 20 minutes, stirring occasionally, until smooth. Serve warm or cold.

Making butterscotch sauce

This buttery sauce is very sweet and rich and should be served in small quantities.

1 Put 50g/2oz/¼ cup unsalted (sweet) butter, 75g/3oz/6 tbsp soft light brown sugar, 50g/2oz/¼ cup caster (superfine) sugar and 150g/5oz/scant ½ cup golden (light corn) syrup into the ceramic cooking pot. Heat on high for 20 minutes, stirring, until the sugar has dissolved.

2 Gradually stir in 150ml/¼ pint/⅔ cup double (heavy) cream and 5ml/1 tsp vanilla essence (extract). Serve warm.

MAKING FONDUES

Fondues are tremendous fun for informal entertaining, and if you already own a slow cooker you won't need a special fondue set to keep the dip warm at the table. The smaller models of slow cooker are ideal for fondue-making because they are deeper and the mixture needs to be at least 5cm/2in deep for dipping. Cheese, chocolate and butterscotch fondues can all be made in the slow cooker. Meat fondues cooked in hot oil are unsuitable because the slow cooker does not reach a high enough temperature.

Making cheese fondue

There are many versions and variations of this hot cheese dip. The classic Swiss cheese fondue, traditionally enjoyed after an exhausting day of Alpine skiing, usually uses hard cheeses, such as Emmenthal and Gruyère, and slightly softer ones, such as Appenzeller.

This basic recipe serves four to six people and can be used as a guide for creating your own variations. Try using beer, cider, ale or milk in place of the white wine, or add brandy in place of Kirsch. Alternatively, you can vary the cheese, using mature (sharp) Cheddar or Monterey Jack. You can buy packets of cheese mixtures for fondues but check the label carefully; *fromage fondu* is a term for a blended cheese product and not a cheese for fondue-making.

1 Rub the inside of the ceramic cooking pot with the cut half of a clove of garlic. This will impart a subtle flavour to the fondue. Pour in 150ml/¼ pint/⅔ cup dry white wine. Cover with the lid, then switch the slow cooker to high and heat for 45 minutes.

2 In a small bowl, blend 10ml/2 tsp cornflour (cornstarch) with 15ml/1 tbsp Kirsch to make a smooth paste, then stir in a pinch of freshly grated nutmeg and season well with ground black pepper.

3 Stir the cornflour mixture into the hot wine until thickened and smooth. (The cornflour will help to prevent the fondue separating once the cheese is added.)

4 Sprinkle 225g/8oz grated Gruyère or Emmenthal cheese over the wine and stir until completely melted. Switch the slow cooker to low and continue stirring until the fondue is thoroughly blended and smooth. Add a little more wine if the mixture seems too thick. The fondue is now ready to serve, or can be kept warm on low for up to an hour.

SPECIALITY FONDUES
While the Swiss fondue is classic, other countries have their own versions. *Fonduta* is a creamy fondue made with Fontina cheese from the Piedmontese region of Italy. The Dutch *kaasdoop* is a similar hot cheese dip. The French make fondue using Comte and Beaufort cheese.

SAVOURY DIPPERS
Savoury fondues are usually served with cubes of crusty bread, which are speared on to long-handled forks for dipping: Swiss tradition has it that anyone who loses their piece of bread in the fondue has to pay a forfeit. There are lots of other foods that can be dipped into the fondue as an alternative to bread:

• Crispy bacon rolls: rinded streaky (fatty) bacon rashers (strips) cut in half widthways, rolled and skewered, then grilled (broiled) or oven-baked.
• Cooked cocktail sausages.

• Small whole mushrooms, grilled (broiled) or lightly fried.

• Vegetable crudités such as florets of raw cauliflower.

Making chocolate fondue

This smooth, not-too-sweet fondue makes a deliciously indulgent dessert. It is made using equal quantities of chocolate and cream, so you can easily increase the quantities to feed more people, if necessary. This recipe makes enough to serve four people.

If you prefer, you can use other types of chocolate, such as milk or white; be sure to choose a good quality chocolate that is intended for melting because many brands of eating chocolate are difficult to melt.

This recipe can also be used as a guide for a fudge fondue. Simply omit the liqueur and add 65g/2½oz chopped caramel chocolate bars in place of the dark (bittersweet) chocolate.

1 Pour 150ml/¼ pint/⅔ cup double (heavy) cream into the ceramic cooking pot and switch the slow cooker to high. Stir in 15ml/1 tbsp orange or coffee liqueur, then cover with the lid and heat for about 30 minutes.

2 Finely chop 150g/5oz dark (bittersweet) chocolate and sprinkle over the hot cream mixture. Stir with a wooden spoon until melted and well blended, then switch the slow cooker to low.

3 Keep the chocolate fondue warm for up to 30 minutes, or serve immediately. For a thicker fondue, turn off the slow cooker and leave to cool for 10 minutes.

Butterscotch fondue

This rich, creamy fondue is especially good served with sweet fruits, such as pineapples, pears and bananas. This recipe will serve four to six people.

1 Cut 115g/4oz/½ cup unsalted (sweet) butter into small cubes and place in the ceramic cooking pot. Add 115g/4oz/ 1 cup dark muscovado (molasses) sugar and heat on high for about 15 minutes, until the butter starts to melt.

2 Pour in 200ml/7fl oz/scant 1 cup double (heavy) cream and stir until the sugar dissolves.

3 Stir in 2.5ml/½ tsp vanilla essence (extract), then cover with the lid and cook on high for 30 minutes, stirring occasionally, until the sauce is smooth and creamy. Switch the slow cooker to low and keep warm for up to 1 hour.

4 Before serving, turn off the slow cooker and leave for 10 minutes to allow the sauce to cool and thicken slightly.

SWEET DIPPERS

As with savoury fondues, there are all manner of sweet and fruity treats that you can dip into hot chocolate or butterscotch fondues.

• Pink and white marshmallows, bitesize strawberries and marzipan cut into small shapes.

• Fresh fruits such as seedless grapes, tangerine segments, pineapple cubes, sliced figs and kiwis. (Toss any fruits that are likely to discolour, such as apples, in a little orange juice.)

• Plain cake, such as Madeira or fruit cake, cut into small cubes. Cut up the cake a few hours before serving to allow it to dry out and firm up.

MAKING PRESERVES

The slow cooker is excellent for making chutneys, curds and syrups. Although it is unsuitable for making jams and jellies because the temperatures reached are too low to achieve setting point, it can be used for softening fruits at the start of many of these recipes. It is particularly useful for the long simmering needed to soften citrus fruits for marmalades.

Making chutney

Long, gentle cooking in the slow cooker produces chutneys with a well-developed flavour. As a result, slow cooker chutneys can often be eaten immediately and do not need to be matured before eating. Because the slow cooker allows little evaporation, only chutneys with a relatively low liquid content are suitable. Those whose main ingredients contain a lot of liquid, such as rhubarb, tomatoes and marrows (large zucchini), should be avoided because the juices will not evaporate sufficiently to make a thick, spoonable preserve.

You can use the following fruity apple chutney recipe as a guide to making other chutneys. Vary the ingredients, depending on your preference, seasonal availability and the dried fruits that you have to hand.

MAKES JUST OVER 1.3KG/3LB

225g/8oz onions
675g/1½lb cooking apples
25g/1oz fresh root ginger
3 garlic cloves, crushed
450g/1lb/2 cups soft light brown sugar
175ml/6fl oz/¾ cup cider vinegar
450g/1lb mixed dried fruit, such as
    apricots, peaches, figs, dates, prunes
    or sultanas (golden raisins)
5ml/1 tsp salt

1 Peel and finely chop the onions and place in the ceramic cooking pot. Quarter, core, peel and roughly chop the apples into even-size pieces and add to the onions. Peel the ginger, then finely chop and add to the pot. (If the ginger is tough and fibrous, grate it rather than chopping, squeeze the juices into the pot, then discard the fibres.)

2 Add the garlic, sugar and cider vinegar to the ceramic cooking pot and switch the slow cooker to high.

3 Heat, uncovered, for 30 minutes, then stir until the sugar has completely dissolved. Cover with the lid and cook for 6 hours, stirring occasionally.

4 Towards the end of cooking time, chop the dried fruit into small, even-size pieces and stir into the chutney with the salt. Cover and cook for 2–3 hours, or until the chutney is thick, stirring once or twice towards the end of cooking.

5 Spoon the chutney into hot sterilized jars and seal with vinegar-proof tops. Label and store in a cool dark place. Use within 6 months of making and once opened, store in the refrigerator.

Making fruit curd

Using the slow cooker as a bain-marie is a great way to make fruit curds because the temperature of the water won't get too hot and spoil the preserve. You can use this basic citrus fruit curd recipe as a base for other fruit curds. To make a passion fruit curd, use 30ml/2 tbsp less citrus juice and stir in the seeds and pulp of 2 passion fruits at the end of cooking. If you prefer a richer, firmer preserve, replace some of the beaten egg with 2 egg yolks.

MAKES ABOUT 675G/1½LB

finely grated rind of 3 lemons,
    4 limes or 2 oranges (preferably
    unwaxed or organic)
150ml/¼ pint/⅔ cup lemon, lime
    or orange juice
350g/12oz/1¾ cups caster
    (superfine) sugar
115g/4oz/8 tbsp unsalted (sweet)
    butter, diced
150ml/¼ pint/⅔ cup beaten eggs

1 Pour 5cm/2in hot water into the ceramic cooking pot and switch the slow cooker to high. Put the citrus rind and juice, sugar and butter into a large heatproof bowl, first checking that it will fit in the slow cooker.

2 Put the bowl in the slow cooker and pour enough near-boiling water around the bowl to come just over halfway up the sides. Leave for 15 minutes, stirring occasionally, until the sugar has dissolved and the butter has melted. Remove the bowl from the ceramic cooking pot and leave to cool for a few minutes. Turn the slow cooker to low.

3 Pour the beaten eggs through a sieve (strainer) into the fruit mixture and whisk to combine. Cover the bowl with foil, then return it to the slow cooker.

4 Cook on low for 1–1½ hours, stirring every 15 minutes, until the curd thickens and lightly coats the back of the spoon.

5 Remove the bowl from the slow cooker and pour the curd into small warmed sterilized jars. If you prefer a smooth curd, strain through a sieve before potting.

6 Cover each jar with a waxed disc and cellophane, then label. Store in a cool, dark place or the refrigerator and use within 3 months. Once opened, store in the refrigerator and use within 1 week.

Making marmalade

Although the slow cooker can't be used to bring marmalade to setting point, it is ideal for the long simmering of the peel. This recipe will fit in a 3.4 litre/6 pint/14¼ cup slow cooker, but you can double or halve the quantities as necessary.

MAKES ABOUT 2.75KG/6LB

900g/2lb Seville (Temple) oranges
1.5 litres/2½ pints/6¼ cups
   near-boiling water
juice of 2 lemons
1.8kg/4lb/9 cups sugar

1 Wash and scrub the oranges. Cut them in half, squeeze out the juice and reserve. Remove the pips and membrane from the peel and tie them in a piece of muslin (cheesecloth). Slice the orange peel thinly or thickly, as preferred.

2 Put the peel and muslin bag in the ceramic cooking pot, then pour over the water and lemon juice. Cover the pot with the lid and switch the slow cooker to high. Cook for 4–6 hours, or until the peel is tender. (The peel must be really soft before adding the sugar.)

3 Remove the muslin bag and leave until cool enough to handle. Squeeze the liquid from it into a large, heavy pan. Transfer the rind and cooking liquid from the slow cooker to the pan. Add the orange juice and sugar and heat gently, stirring until the sugar has dissolved.

4 Bring the mixture to the boil and boil rapidly for about 15 minutes until the marmalade reaches 105°C/220°F on a sugar thermometer. (Alternatively, place a spoonful of the marmalade on a chilled saucer and leave to cool for 1 minute. Press gently with your finger and it should wrinkle; if not, continue boiling.)

5 Remove the pan from the heat and skim off any scum using a slotted spoon. Leave to stand for 15 minutes, then stir to distribute the peel evenly. Ladle the marmalade into hot sterilized jars, seal and label. Store in a cool, dark place and use within one year of making.

Making cordial

The slow cooker is the perfect vehicle for infusing flavours such as citrus rind and spices. It brings the liquid very slowly to the boil and maintains it at a constant, low temperature, ensuring that maximum flavour is extracted. It is therefore perfect for making cordials, as well as syrups for fruit compotes. This recipe is for lemon cordial, but you can use the same method to make other flavours. Try using the rind of 2 oranges and the juice of 1 lemon. Alternatively, omit the lemon rind and use 10 scented rose petals, 1 split vanilla pod (bean) and the juice of 1 lemon.

MAKES ABOUT 1.2 LITRES/2 PINTS/5 CUPS

3 large juicy lemons, preferably
   unwaxed or organic
350g/12oz/1¾ cups caster
   (superfine) sugar
sparkling mineral water and ice, to serve

1 Wash the lemons, then thinly pare off the rind, leaving the bitter white pith behind. Put the rind in the cooking pot with the sugar and 1 litre/1¾ pints/4 cups cold water. Cover and switch the slow cooker to high.

2 Heat for 30 minutes, then stir until the sugar has dissolved. Cook for a further 1½ hours, then leave to cool.

3 Halve the lemons and squeeze out the juice. Stir into the syrup, then strain through a stainless steel or plastic sieve. Pour into sterilized bottles, seal and label. Store in the refrigerator for up to 10 days. To serve, dilute to taste with mineral water and serve over ice.

SLOW COOKER SAFETY

The slow cooker is an extremely efficient and safe way to cook food. It is however an electrical appliance, and some basic common-sense safety precautions should be followed. Because slow cooker models vary, always take the time to read the instruction manual supplied by the manufacturer before use.

Cooker care

Looking after your cooker is simple but very important. When you first unwrap and remove your slow cooker from its box, check that it isn't damaged in any way, that the plug (which has hopefully been provided) is attached properly and, if you bought your slow cooker in another country, that the voltage on the rating plate of the appliance corresponds with your house electricity supply. If you are in any doubt, consult a qualified electrician before using the slow cooker.

Before you use the slow cooker for the first time, wash the ceramic cooking pot in warm soapy water and dry it thoroughly. Stand the slow cooker on a heat-resistant surface when in use, making sure that the mains lead is tucked away safely; the slow cooker should not touch anything hot or hang over the edge of the table or work-top in case it falls off accidentally.

Take extra care if you have young children (or curious pets) and position the slow cooker out of reach. After an hour or so of cooking, the slow cooker can become very hot; not just the

Below: Do not submerge the slow cooker in water. If it needs cleaning, make sure it is unplugged and use a damp, soapy sponge.

Above: Protect your hands from the hot cooker and escaping steam with a pair of padded oven gloves.

ceramic cooking pot, but the outer casing and the lid as well. Always use oven gloves when lifting the lid (do this away from you to prevent scalding from steam or drips), and when removing the cooking pot from inside the slow cooker.

Do not switch on the slow cooker if the ceramic cooking pot is empty (the only exception to this would be if the manufacturer recommends preheating). As soon as you have finished cooking, remove the plug from the socket to prevent the slow cooker being switched on accidentally.

Never immerse the outer casing of the slow cooker in water – this would be extremely dangerous, risking electric shock and fatal injury, because the outer casing contains the electrical elements that heat the ceramic cooking pot.

You should never use the outer casing for cooking without the ceramic cooking pot in place. If you need to clean the casing, do so with warm soapy water and a damp cloth, and be absolutely sure that the appliance is unplugged before you put it in contact with water.

Ensuring food safety

Slow cookers cook food slowly using a gentle heat – the precise temperature will vary from model to model but the average is from about 90°C/200°F on the low setting to about 150°C/300°F on the high setting. Bacteria in food is destroyed at a temperature of 74°C/165°F, so as long as the food is cooked

for the appropriate length of time, as stated in the recipe, this temperature will be reached quickly enough to ensure that the food is safe to eat. However, additional factors may affect the slow cooker's ability to reach the desired temperature and you should be aware of the following to ensure food safety:

• Avoid placing the slow cooker near an open window or in a draught.

• Do not lift the lid during cooking time unless instructed to do so in the recipe.

• Do not add ingredients that are frozen or part-frozen to the ceramic cooking pot because they will increase the length of time needed to reach the required cooking temperature, and the timings given in the recipe will not be sufficient.

• Increase the cooking time in extreme cold temperatures, where the kitchen temperature is considerably lower than normal, and check food is cooked before serving, particularly poultry and pork.

Checking meat is cooked

When it comes to food safety, one of the main things to look out for is that meat is properly cooked – in particular, poultry and pork. A meat thermometer is a worthwhile investment if you are planning to cook whole joints of meat and poultry in your slow cooker. It is the most reliable way to ensure that the inside of the meat has reached a high enough temperature to kill any potentially harmful bacteria, without losing its juices and becoming dry and overcooked.

Below: A meat thermometer is easy to use and gives an accurate temperature reading to let you know when meat is safe to eat.

Above: A skewer or the tip of a sharp knife can be inserted into a thick part of a meat joint to check that it is thoroughly cooked

When using a meat thermometer, the tip of the stainless steel probe should be inserted as near the centre of the meat as possible, but not touching any bone. Meat thermometers have different markings for various meats, indicating rare and pinkish lamb and beef, through to medium and well cooked. Pork and poultry must always be cooked thoroughly to avoid the risk of food poisoning as they can pass on harmful bacteria when raw or partially cooked; always err on the side of caution and go for well cooked, rather than risk the meat being underdone and therefore unsafe.

To check that meat is cooked without a thermometer, insert the tip of a thin sharp knife or skewer into the thickest part of the meat joint and hold it there for 20 seconds. For medium to well-cooked lamb or beef, the juices will be almost clear and the knife will feel hot on the back of the hand. When cooking pork or poultry, it is essential that the meat juices should be completely clear. If there is any trace of pink, the meat is not ready to eat and should be cooked for a further 30 minutes; check again with the skewer or knife before serving.

With poultry, you can double check by giving the leg a tug – it should have some give in it and not be resistant. If you are still unsure, make a deep cut where the thigh joins the body; there should be no visible trace of pink meat. If there is, cook the meat for a further 30 minutes, then check again.

FOOD SAFETY TIPS

Basic food safety recommendations should be followed when preparing or using food in the slow cooker.

• Food should always be at room temperature when it is added to the slow cooker, otherwise it will take longer to reach the safe cooking temperature. However, ingredients such as meat and fish should not be left out of the refrigerator for longer than is necessary, so remove from the refrigerator just to take off the chill and keep covered with cling film or plastic wrap.

• Marinating food in the ceramic cooking pot before cooking saves on washing up, but the cooking pot will become cold in the refrigerator, so remove it at least 1 hour before you plan to start cooking.

• Large joints of meat and whole poultry should be cooked at a high temperature for the first 1–2 hours to accelerate the cooking process. Switch the slow cooker to low for the remaining cooking time.

• Avoid lifting the lid of the ceramic cooking during the cooking time, especially in the early stages. It takes 15–20 minutes to recover the lost heat each time the lid is removed, so it will take much longer to reach a safe temperature.

• Don't be tempted to partially cook meat or poultry, then refrigerate for subsequent cooking. Also avoid reheating pre-cooked dishes in the slow cooker.

• Frozen foods should always be thoroughly thawed before being placed in the slow cooker. If added when frozen, they will increase the time the food takes to reach a safe temperature. If adding frozen vegetables towards the end of cooking time, thaw them first under cold running water.

• Soak dried beans, in particular red kidney beans, overnight and then fast-boil them on the stovetop for 10 minutes in a pan of fresh cooking water to destroy toxins before adding to the slow cooker.

ONE-POT COOKING TECHNIQUES

Cooking a dish in a single pot doesn't demand any particular expertise, but mastering a few simple techniques will make for greater efficiency, especially when preparing the ingredients. Many one-pot dishes need very little attention while they are actually cooking, but it is important to follow the instructions in individual recipes as regards stirring.

Stewing, Braising and Casseroling Meat

These are long, slow and moist methods of cooking either in the oven or on top of the stove. The meat is browned first to seal in the natural juices and improve the flavour and colour of the finished dish, then it is simmered slowly at a low temperature in liquid – wine, water, beer or stock.

1 Trim off any excess fat from the meat. For stewing and casseroling, cut the meat into 2.5cm/1in cubes. For braising use thickly cut steaks or cut the meat into thick slices.

2 Toss the meat a few pieces at a time in seasoned flour, then shake off any excess. The flour coating browns to give the casserole a good flavour and also thickens the liquid.

3 Heat 30ml/2 tbsp sunflower oil in a flameproof casserole. Add the meat in batches and cook over a high heat. When the meat is well browned on all sides, use a draining spoon to remove the meat before adding the next batch.

4 Add the sliced or chopped onions and other vegetables to the remaining fat and juices in the casserole and cook, stirring occasionally, for about 5 minutes.

5 Return the meat to the casserole, add herbs and pour in the cooking liquid. Stir to loosen the cooking residue from the base of the pan and then heat until simmering. Simmer gently on the hob or in the oven until the meat is tender. The casserole may be covered for the entire cooking time or uncovered towards the end to allow excess liquid to evaporate.

Pot-roasting Meat

This long, slow method of cooking is ideal for slightly tough joints of meat such as topside of beef, lamb shoulder and shanks, and knuckle of pork.

1 Heat a little sunflower oil in a large flameproof casserole until very hot. Add the meat and cook over a high heat, turning frequently, until browned on all sides. Remove the meat from the pan.

2 Add the onions, leeks and any root vegetables to the pan, then cook, stirring, for a few minutes. Replace the meat on top of the vegetables and pour in a little liquid, such as stock, wine or beer. Cover and cook gently in the oven until the meat is tender.

Casseroling Chicken

Moist cooking methods not only bring out the flavour of poultry but also offer the opportunity for allowing herbs and spices and aromatics to infuse the light meat thoroughly. Whole birds and joints can be casseroled.

1 Brown the poutry pieces or bird all over first. Remove from the pan before softening chopped onion, carrot, celery and other flavouring ingredients in the fat remaining in the pan.

2 Replace the poultry before adding the chosen liquid – stock, wine or canned tomatoes. Season the casserole well, then bring it just to simmering point. Cover it closely and allow it to simmer very gently on top of the stove, or cook in the oven at 180°C/350°F/Gas 4.

COOKING TIMES FOR CASSEROLING CHICKEN
• For a whole bird allow 20 minutes per 450g/1lb, plus 20 minutes.
• Large portions 45–60 minutes.
• Boneless breasts about 30 minutes.
• Chunks or diced poultry 20–40 minutes, depending on their size.

Pan-frying Meat

This is the traditional cooking method for steaks such as sirloin and fillet, and it is also good for veal escalopes (US scallops) and veal chops, lamb chops, cutlets and noisettes, and pork chops, steaks and escalopes.

1 Cook steaks and chops in the minimum of fat, then add flavoured butter when serving, if you like. Dab a little sunflower oil on kitchen paper and use to grease the pan lightly. Heat the pan until it is very hot (almost smoking). Add the steak or chops and cook for 2–4 minutes on each side.

2 Pan-fry other lean cuts of meat in a mixture of butter and oil. Butter burns easily, so heat the oil in the pan first and add the butter just before the meat to avoid this. Make sure that the butter and oil are sizzling before adding the meat. Cook on both sides until browned. Beef and thin cuts of meat such as escalopes will be ready to serve. For some thicker cuts and meat such as pork that needs to be well-cooked, reduce the heat to low once the meat is browned and cook for 10–15 minutes, or until cooked through. Test by piercing the centre of the meat with the point of a sharp knife.

Pan-frying Poultry

This quick cooking method is ideal for chicken breast fillets and portions. Once the meat is cooked, the cooking juices can be made into a tasty sauce, simply stir in a little cream, add some chopped herbs and season to taste.

When frying poultry, remember that it must be cooked through. Escalopes and boneless breasts cook quickly, so are ideal for pan-frying over a high heat, but uneven thicker portions require careful cooking. With larger pieces, reduce the heat to low once the chicken is browned and cook it slowly for up to 30 minutes to ensure that the centre is cooked.

Stir-frying

This is a fast method of cooking tender meat. The meat should be cut into thin slices across the grain, and then cut into fine, long strips. Use a wok or a heavy frying pan.

Heat a little oil in a wok or frying pan until it is smoking hot. Add the meat in batches and stir-fry over a high heat. Remove the cooked meat before adding a fresh batch. When all the meat is cooked, add the other ingredients and stir-fry over a slightly lower heat.

CLAY-POT COOKING TECHNIQUES

Used with care, clay cooking pots last for years, but it is very important to follow the manufacturer's instructions closely. The advice that follows should be read in conjunction with your handbook.

Preparing a Clay Pot

All unglazed clay cooking pots must be soaked in cold water before every use. This is essential because it is the water retained in the clay that provides the moisture required during cooking. Ideally, the soaking time should be about 20 minutes. If it is the first time you have used the pot, leave it to soak for at least 30 minutes.

Place both the pot and its lid in a sink of cold water, inverting the lid on top of the base if necessary. The entire pot and the lid must be submerged. This thorough soaking is recommended before every use. If you are really short of time, you can just hold the pot under cold running water for about 1 minute, but this is not as satisfactory as soaking.

You can use your clay pot for lots of different recipes, but should avoid cooking fish or any highly flavoured dish in it the first time you use it. If you have more than one clay pot, consider keeping separate pots for savoury and sweet dishes.

Partially Glazed Clay Pots

Also available are clay pots that are glazed on the inside, but which have unglazed lids. With this type of pot, only the lid needs to be soaked, and this is done by holding it under running cold water for a few minutes. The ingredients are put into the pot, seasoned, and moistened with stock. The lid is fitted

and the pot is placed in a cold oven, which is then heated to 220°C/425°F/ Gas 7. Steam released from the soaked lid helps to keep the food moist as it bakes. The lid can be removed towards the end of cooking to allow the food to brown, if necessary.

Cooking with a Clay Pot

Most clay pots should only be used in the oven. Unglazed pots are sensitive to sudden changes of temperature, which can cause the pot to crack or break if it is placed directly over the heat.

Some clay pots can be used on top of the stove on a very low heat, but it is recommended that a heat diffuser or flame-tamer is used. These are available from specialist cookware stores.

1 Some recipes suggest sautéing vegetables or meat in a frying pan to brown them before adding them to the clay pot. If you do this, let the browned foods cool slightly before putting them into the cold clay pot.

2 Once the browned foods have been added, it is okay to pour in warm or hand-hot cooking liquids. If what is in the pot is cold, any liquid added should be at room temperature.

USING A HEAT DIFFUSER

If your handbook states that your pot can safely be used on top of the stove you can obviously do so, but always use a heat diffuser between the heat source and the pot.

Some cazuelas can be used on top of the stove with a heat diffuser.

Cooking in an Oven

An unglazed clay pot must always be heated gradually.

Place the clay pot in a cold oven and then heat to the required temperature. It might crack if subjected to a sudden change of temperature.

You will notice that the recipes in this book advise you to place the clay pot, which will be cold, in a cold oven, then set the oven temperature to allow the oven and clay pot to heat slowly.

An electric oven heats up gradually, giving the clay pot time to acclimatize. If, however, you are using a traditional gas oven, the flames may be too fierce for the cold clay pot. You should start by setting the oven temperature to 190°C/375°F/Gas 5. After 5 minutes, increase the temperature to 200°C/400°F/Gas 6. Continue to increase the temperature of the oven gradually, each time raising it to the next setting on your cooker, until the required temperature is reached.

The exact cooking times for recipes containing liquids may vary from oven to oven, as the time taken for the liquid to come to the boil will differ.

Cooking with a Cast-iron Tagine on a Stovetop

In addition to the classic all-earthenware tagines, which can't be used on a stovetop, there is a modern version that has an earthenware lid and cast-iron base. The base can be used on the top of any type of stove, be it gas, electric or wood-burning, to brown ingredients such as onions, vegetables or meat before the other ingredients and liquid are added. The pot is then covered and the tagine or stew is simmered gently on top of the stove or in the oven.

Place the cast-iron tagine base on the stovetop, add a little oil and heat. Add the vegetables or other ingredients and cook over a medium-high heat, stirring occasionally, until browned.

Browning in a Clay Pot

A certain amount of browning will occur during cooking, depending on the cooking temperature, cooking time and type of food. Some recipes suggest removing the lid for a short period of time towards the end of the cooking time to enhance the colour of baked items and roasts, and also to develop a crisper finish. The oven temperature for clay-pot cooking is fairly high, so the browning process will only take a few minutes; keep a close check on the food.

To remove the lid, lift the clay pot out of the oven using oven gloves and place it on a pot stand, wooden board or folded dishtowel. Take care when lifting the lid to avoid any escaping steam.

Adding Liquids to a Clay Pot

Never add boiling liquids – or even very hot liquids – to a cold clay pot or the sudden change in temperature may cause the claypot to crack.

If you need to add liquid to the clay pot during the cooking period, this liquid should be hot. This not only avoids a sudden temperature change, but also ensures that the food isn't cooled too much, which would slow the cooking.

Adding Flavourings

To get the best results, place herb sprigs and spices in among vegetables that are to be roasted or underneath joints of meat. This will ensure that the flavour penetrates as deeply as possible.

Adding Ingredients during Cooking

In some recipes, ingredients that don't need to be cooked for long, such as prawns or cooked ham, are added towards the end of the cooking time.

Remove the pot from the oven using oven gloves and remove the lid. Add the cold food and stir well to ensure that it is distributed evenly, then re-cover the pot and return it to the oven.

Cooking on a Barbecue

Moroccan tagines are sometimes placed on a barbecue, but they should not be too near the heat source. It is best to wait until the coals have all turned grey. Cover the coals with some sand, to make the heat less concentrated, and then allow the tagine to heat up slowly by initially placing it at the edge of the barbecue and gradually moving it to the hottest part.

Using a Clay Pot for Baking

Clay pots can be used for baking cakes, breads and sponge-based desserts. It is, however, best to keep a separate clay pot for sweet foods or, alternatively, use earthenware that is glazed inside.

If you use a clay pot for baking, it is a good idea to line the base of the clay pot with a piece of baking parchment, so that the food doesn't stick to the base and is easy to remove after baking.

SAFETY FIRST

When you remove any type of clay pot from the oven, either to add extra ingredients or to serve the food, protect your hands with oven gloves. Place the pot on a folded towel, wooden board, heatproof mat or pot stand, as sudden contact with a cold surface could cause the pot to crack. Do the same with the lid, when you lift it off.

Clay pots should not be used under the grill (broiler) or in the freezer as the sudden change in temperature could cause the clay pot to crack or break.

Microwave Cooking

Clay pots can be used to cook foods in the microwave oven, as well as in a conventional oven. One of the advantages with using a clay pot for microwave cooking is that, because it is moist from soaking, it will absorb some of the microwave energy. This slows down the cooking process, which is perfect for protecting delicate foods, cooking foods more evenly and pot-roasting less tender cuts of meat, whole chickens or game birds.

Select a clay pot that will fit inside your microwave oven. The smaller, rectangular or round pots are ideal.

Prepare the pot as for oven cooking, by soaking it in water for 20 minutes. When setting the cooking time, refer to your microwave handbook for detailed instructions on using a clay pot, as each appliance is different. If you are adapting an existing microwave recipe, expect the food to take slightly longer to cook in a clay pot. The food is usually cooked on full (100%) power, but it may also be cooked on medium-high (70%) or medium (50%) settings so that the food simmers, rather than boils.

A safety note worth remembering is that because a clay pot is moist and absorbs microwave energy it will become hot; hotter, in fact, than many other types of microwave cookware. Make sure you use oven gloves to lift the clay pot out of the microwave, and always place the pot on a pot stand, wooden board or mat, or folded dishtowel when removing it from the oven, both for your own safety, and to avoid subjecting the pot to severe temperature changes.

ADAPTING RECIPES FOR CLAY-POT COOKING

A wide range of foods can be cooked in a clay pot, and you may wish to try using it for some of your favourite dishes. Find a clay-pot recipe in this book that is similar to the one you want to make, and use it as a blueprint. The main differences in cooking techniques that need to be observed are these:

• When an unglazed or partially glazed clay pot is used, the oven must not be preheated.

• When the pot is put into the cold oven, it is heated gradually until it reaches the required cooking temperature. If the dish contains liquid, it must be heated until it boils. This is likely to be at a higher temperature than when cooking in another type of container, because the pot forms an insulating layer between the heat of the oven and the food. When the liquid boils, the oven temperature may then be reduced, so that the contents of the pot simmer.

• If you are using a gas stove, it is essential that you increase the temperature gradually or the transition from cold to blasting heat may cause the pot to crack.

• You will probably have to extend the cooking time to take into account the fact that the ingredients, including any liquids, are cold when put into the oven, which also starts off cold. When foods are roasted with little or no liquid, however, the cooking time stays about the same because the higher cooking temperature compensates for the insulation of the clay pot.

• Because of the moist environment, food cooked in a clay pot doesn't overcook quickly when the lid is on, however, it is important to check the food frequently if the lid is removed towards the end of cooking to promote browning as the top of the food can easily scorch.

Cleaning and Storing Clay Pots

Before using a clay pot for the first time, brush it thoroughly inside and out to remove any loose clay particles left from the manufacturing process. Rinse the pot after brushing, then drain it. If you intend to cook in it straight away, then soak it thoroughly in cold water first.

After using the pot a few times, you may notice a colour change. This is completely natural and is part of the character of a clay pot. As with a well-seasoned frying pan or wok, this effect is due to a protective layer that builds up with use and enhances the cooking qualities of the pot.

Washing the Pot

1 Wash a clay pot promptly after every use, using a brush and hot water. A soft-bristled brush is fine if the pot is not too dirty, otherwise use a firm-bristled washing-up brush, Add washing-up (dishwashing) liquid to the water if this is recommended in your handbook, as this helps to get rid of stubborn stains. Avoid using abrasive cleaning materials, as these may affect the porous nature of the clay and may impair its cooking qualities.

2 Having washed the pot, rinse it under hot water, then stand it upside down on kitchen paper to drain thoroughly.

Using a Dishwasher

Most glazed earthenware dishes can be put in the dishwasher, but some manufacturers do not recommend washing clay pots that way. Check your manufacturer's handbook.

Removing Food Residue

Sometimes food may bake on to the surface of a clay pot, especially if it has been used for cooking without the cover. Soaking the pot in hot water to which a little washing-up liquid has been added is usually sufficient to release the residue. Leave the pot to soak overnight if the residue is particularly stubborn. Some earthenware dishes can be filled with hot water to remove baked-on food, but do not leave them immersed in hot soapy water.

1 If an unglazed clay pot becomes tainted with residual flavours, soak it overnight in cold water containing bicarbonate of soda (baking soda). If the problem is severe, or if smells still linger, fill the pot with water, add bicarbonate of soda and place it in a cold oven.

2 Set the oven to 180°C/350°F/Gas 4 and leave the clay pot to heat in the oven for about 20 minutes. Increase the temperature of the oven to 200°C/400°F/Gas 6 and heat for another 20 minutes, then increase the oven temperature again to 230°C/450°F/Gas 8 and leave the pot at this temperature for 30 minutes to 1 hour.

3 Carefully lift the pot out of the oven using oven gloves and then discard the contents. Scrub the interior of the pot gently before rinsing it thoroughly with very hot water. Turn the pot and lid upside-down on a rack and leave to dry at room temperature. It is worth following this cleaning procedure after about a hundred uses, to clean the pores of your clay pot. This will allow it to take up water with the same efficiency as when it was brand new.

Storing the Pot

Before you put a clay pot away, make sure that it is not only completely clean but also thoroughly dried.

Invert the lid into the base. This is not only for safety and so that it takes up less room in your storecupboard, but also because placing the lid on the pot as for cooking could encourage moulds and mildew to grow on the inside surface of the pot and lid.

It is for this reason that the pot must also be stored somewhere dry and airy. Do not leave it in a damp place. It is the nature of a clay pot to absorb moisture, so it is important to keep it completely dry during storage. Do not wrap the clay pot or seal it in a plastic bag during storage.

SLOW COOKER SOUPS

The slow cooker truly excels when it comes to soup-making – the long, gentle cooking allows the flavours to develop fully over time, giving rich, flavoursome results. This chapter draws on recipes from around the world – from North African Spiced Soup, Asian-Style Duck Consommé and Galician Broth, to French Onion Soup with Cheese Croûtes, Chicken Soup with Knaidlach and Genoese Minestrone. There are also soups for every occasion – from Spicy Pumpkin Soup for a hearty lunch and Chilled Tomato and Sweet Pepper Soup for a summer lunch party to delicate Greek Avgolemono for an elegant start to a meal.

FRENCH ONION SOUP with CHEESE CROÛTES

Probably the most famous of all onion soups, this hearty, warming dish was traditionally served as a sustaining early morning meal to the porters and workers of Les Halles market in Paris. Use large yellow Spanish onions for the best result.

3 Add the sugar and stir well. Cover again with the lid and folded dish towel and continue cooking on high for 4 hours, stirring two or three times, to ensure the onions are colouring evenly. At the end of this time, they should be a dark golden colour.

4 Sprinkle the flour over the onions and stir to mix. Next, stir in the vinegar followed by the brandy, then slowly blend in the wine. Stir in the stock and thyme and season with salt and pepper. Cook on high for a further 2 hours, or until the onions are very tender.

5 For the croûtes, place the bread slices under a low grill (broiler) and cook until dry and lightly browned. Rub the bread with the cut surface of the garlic and spread with mustard, then sprinkle the grated Gruyère cheese over the slices.

SERVES 4

40g/1½oz/3 tbsp butter
10ml/2 tsp olive oil
1.2kg/2½lb onions, peeled and sliced
5ml/1 tsp caster (superfine) sugar
15ml/1 tbsp plain (all-purpose) flour
15ml/1 tbsp sherry vinegar
30ml/2 tbsp brandy
120ml/4fl oz/½ cup dry white wine
1 litre/1¾ pints/4 cups boiling beef,
    chicken or duck stock
5ml/1 tsp chopped fresh thyme
salt and ground black pepper

For the croûtes
4 slices day-old French stick or baguette,
    about 2.5cm/1in thick
1 garlic clove, halved
5ml/1 tsp French mustard
50g/2oz/½ cup grated Gruyère cheese

1 Put the butter and olive oil in the ceramic cooking pot and heat on high for about 15 minutes until melted.

2 Add the onions to the pot and stir to coat well in the melted butter and oil. Cover with the lid, then place a folded dish towel over the top to retain all the heat and cook for 2 hours, stirring halfway through cooking time.

6 Turn the grill to high and cook the croûtes for 2–3 minutes, until the cheese melts, bubbles and browns. Ladle the soup into warmed bowls and float a Gruyère croûte on top of each. Serve straight away.

Energy 418Kcal/1747kJ; Protein 11.5g; Carbohydrate 51.8g, of which sugars 19.4g; Fat 15.9g, of which saturates 8.2g; Cholesterol 33mg; Calcium 209mg; Fibre 5.3g; Sodium 1195mg.

CARROT and CORIANDER SOUP

Root vegetables, such as carrots, are great for slow cooker soups. Their earthy flavour becomes rich and sweet when cooked slowly over a gentle heat and goes perfectly with robust herbs and spices, and their texture becomes beautifully smooth when puréed.

SERVES 4

450g/1lb carrots, preferably young
   and tender
15ml/1 tbsp sunflower oil
40g/1½oz/3 tbsp butter
1 onion, chopped
1 stick celery, plus 2–3 pale leafy tops
2 small potatoes, peeled
900ml/1½ pints/3¾ cups boiling
   vegetable stock
10ml/2 tsp ground coriander
15ml/1 tbsp chopped fresh coriander
   (cilantro)
150ml/¼ pint/⅔ cup milk
salt and ground black pepper

1 Trim and peel the carrots and cut into chunks. Heat the oil and 25g/1oz/2 tbsp of the butter in a pan and fry the onion over a gentle heat for 3–4 minutes until slightly softened. Do not let it brown.

2 Slice the celery and chop the potatoes, and add them to the onion in the pan. Cook for 2 minutes, then add the carrots and cook for a further 1 minute. Transfer the fried vegetables to the ceramic cooking pot.

3 Pour the boiling vegetable stock over the vegetables, then season with salt and ground black pepper. Cover the pot with the lid and cook on low for 4–5 hours until the vegetables are tender.

4 Reserve 6–8 tiny celery leaves from the leafy tops for the garnish, then finely chop the remaining celery tops. Melt the remaining butter in a large pan and add the ground coriander. Fry for about 1 minute, stirring constantly, until the aromas are released.

5 Reduce the heat under the pan and add the chopped celery tops and fresh coriander. Fry for about 30 seconds, then remove the pan from the heat.

6 Ladle the soup into a food processor or blender and process until smooth, then pour into the pan with the celery tops and coriander. Stir in the milk and heat gently until piping hot. Check the seasoning, then serve garnished with the reserved celery leaves.

Energy 168Kcal/697kJ; Protein 3g; Carbohydrate 11.9g, of which sugars 9.2g; Fat 12.4g, of which saturates 6g; Cholesterol 24mg; Calcium 94mg; Fibre 3.1g; Sodium 758mg.

TOMATO and FRESH BASIL SOUP

Peppery, aromatic basil is the perfect partner for sweet, ripe tomatoes – and it is easy to grow at home in a pot on a sunny kitchen windowsill. Make this soup in late summer when fresh tomatoes are at their best and most flavoursome.

SERVES 4

15ml/1 tbsp olive oil
25g/1oz/2 tbsp butter
1 onion, finely chopped
900g/2lb ripe tomatoes, roughly chopped
1 garlic clove, roughly chopped
about 600ml/1 pint/2½ cups
   vegetable stock
120ml/4fl oz/½ cup dry white wine
30ml/2 tbsp sun-dried tomato paste
30ml/2 tbsp shredded fresh basil
150ml/¼ pint/⅔ cup double
   (heavy) cream
salt and ground black pepper
whole basil leaves, to garnish

1 Heat the oil and butter in a large saucepan until foaming. Add the onion and cook gently for about 5 minutes, stirring, until the onion is softened but not brown, then add the chopped tomatoes and garlic.

2 Add the stock, white wine and sun-dried tomato paste to the pan and stir to combine. Heat until just below boiling point, then carefully pour the mixture into the ceramic cooking pot.

3 Switch the slow cooker to the high or auto setting, cover with the lid and cook for 1 hour. Leave the slow cooker on auto or switch to low and cook for a further 4–6 hours, until tender.

4 Leave the soup to cool for a few minutes, then ladle into a food processor or blender and process until smooth. Press the puréed soup through a sieve (strainer) into a clean pan.

5 Add the shredded basil and the cream to the soup and heat through, stirring. Do not allow the soup to reach boiling point. Check the consistency and add a little more stock if necessary. Season, then pour into warmed bowls and garnish with basil. Serve immediately.

Energy 335Kcal/1387kJ; Protein 3.1g; Carbohydrate 11.7g, of which sugars 10.8g; Fat 28.9g, of which saturates 16.4g; Cholesterol 65mg; Calcium 50mg; Fibre 3g; Sodium 168mg.

CHILLED TOMATO and SWEET PEPPER SOUP

*Inspired by the classic Spanish soup, gazpacho, which is made with raw salad vegetables,
this soup is cooked first and then chilled. Grilling the peppers gives a slightly smoky
flavour, but you can leave out this step to save on preparation time, if you like.*

SERVES 4

2 red (bell) peppers
30ml/2 tbsp olive oil
1 onion, finely chopped
2 garlic cloves, crushed
675g/1½lb ripe, well-flavoured
    tomatoes
120ml/4fl oz/½ cup red wine
450ml/¾ pint/scant 2 cups vegetable
    or chicken stock
2.5ml/½ tsp caster (superfine) sugar
salt and ground black pepper
chopped fresh chives, to garnish

For the croûtons
2 slices white bread, crusts removed
45ml/3 tbsp olive oil

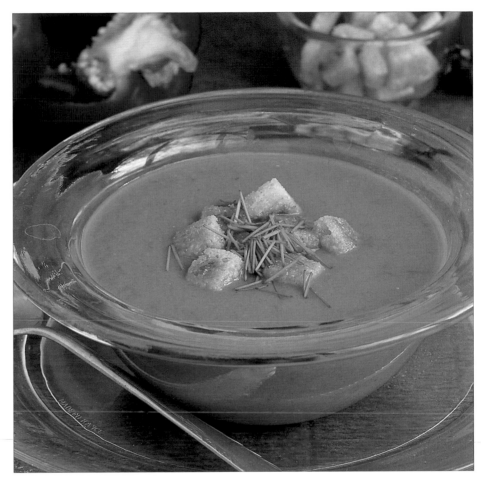

1 Cut each pepper into quarters and remove the core and seeds. Place each quarter, skin side up, on a grill (broiler) rack. Grill (broil) until the skins are blistered and charred, then transfer to a bowl and cover with a plate.

2 Heat the oil in a frying pan. Add the onion and garlic and cook gently for about 10 minutes until soft, stirring occasionally. Meanwhile, remove the skin from the peppers and roughly chop the flesh. Cut the tomatoes into chunks.

3 Transfer the onions to the ceramic cooking pot and add the peppers, tomatoes, wine, stock and sugar. Cover and cook on high for 3–4 hours, or until the vegetables are very tender. Leave the soup to stand for about 10 minutes to cool slightly.

4 Ladle the soup into a food processor or blender and process until smooth. Press through a fine sieve (strainer) into a bowl. Leave to cool before chilling in the refrigerator for at least 3 hours.

5 Meanwhile, make the croûtons. Cut the bread into cubes. Heat the oil in a frying pan, add the bread and fry until golden. Drain well on kitchen paper.

6 Season the soup to taste with salt and pepper, then ladle into chilled bowls. Serve topped with a few croûtons and a sprinkling of chopped chives.

Energy 262Kcal/1090kJ; Protein 3.5g; Carbohydrate 17.6g, of which sugars 11.5g; Fat 18g, of which saturates 2.6g; Cholesterol 0mg; Calcium 47mg; Fibre 3.4g; Sodium 499mg.

SPICY PUMPKIN SOUP

This stunning golden-orange soup has a smooth velvety texture, and a delicate taste, which is subtly spiced with cumin and garlic. Long, slow cooking really gives the flavours time to develop and come together to make a wonderful autumnal dish.

SERVES 4

900g/2lb pumpkin, peeled
   and seeds removed
30ml/2 tbsp olive oil
2 leeks, trimmed and sliced
1 garlic clove, crushed
5ml/1 tsp ground ginger
5ml/1 tsp ground cumin
750ml/1¼ pints/3 cups near-boiling
   chicken stock
salt and ground black pepper
60ml/4 tbsp natural (plain) yogurt, to serve
coriander (cilantro) leaves, to garnish

COOK'S TIP
To save time, reheat the soup on the
stovetop rather than in the slow cooker.

1 Using a sharp knife, cut the pumpkin into large chunks. Place the chunks in the ceramic cooking pot.

2 Heat the oil in a large pan and add the leeks and garlic. Cook gently until softened but not coloured.

3 Add the ginger and cumin to the pan and cook, stirring, for a further minute. Tip the mixture into the ceramic cooking pot, pour over the chicken stock and season with salt and black pepper.

4 Cover the slow cooker with the lid, switch to low and cook for 6–8 hours, or until the pumpkin is very tender.

5 Ladle the soup, in batches if necessary, into a food processor or blender and process until smooth. Return the soup to the rinsed out cooking pot, cover and cook on high for 1 hour, or until piping hot. Serve in warmed individual bowls, with a swirl of natural yogurt and a few coriander leaves.

Energy 89Kcal/372kJ; Protein 2.3g; Carbohydrate 6.2g, of which sugars 4.7g; Fat 6.3g, of which saturates 1.1g; Cholesterol 0mg; Calcium 75mg; Fibre 3.1g; Sodium 127mg.

WILD MUSHROOM SOUP

*This robust, creamy soup is ideal for a simple lunch or supper, served with chunks of
nutty wholegrain bread spread with fresh butter. The rich flavour and colour of the soup
are further enhanced by the addition of dried wild mushrooms and a dash of Madeira.*

SERVES 4

15g/½oz/¼ cup dried wild mushrooms,
   such as morels, ceps or porcini
600ml/1 pint/2½ cups hot chicken
   or vegetable stock
25g/1oz/2 tbsp butter
1 onion, finely chopped
1 garlic clove, crushed
450g/1lb button (white) or other
   cultivated mushrooms, trimmed
   and sliced
15ml/1 tbsp plain (all-purpose) flour
fresh nutmeg
1.5ml/¼ tsp dried thyme
60ml/4 tbsp Madeira or dry sherry
60ml/4 tbsp crème fraîche or
   sour cream
salt and ground black pepper
chopped fresh chives, to garnish

1 Put the dried mushrooms in a sieve
(strainer) and rinse under cold running
water to remove any grit, then place in
the ceramic cooking pot. Pour over half
of the hot chicken or vegetable stock
and cover with the lid. Switch the slow
cooker to the auto or high setting.

2 Place the butter in a large pan and melt
over a medium heat. Add the chopped
onion and cook for 5–7 minutes until
softened and just golden.

3 Add the garlic and fresh mushrooms
to the pan and cook for 5 minutes.
Sprinkle over the flour, then grate some
nutmeg into the mixture and add the
thyme. Cook for 3 minutes more,
stirring all the time, until blended.

4 Stir in the Madeira or sherry and the
remaining stock, and season with salt and
pepper. Bring to the boil, then transfer
to the ceramic cooking pot. Cook for
1 hour, then switch to low or leave on
auto and cook for a further 3–4 hours,
or until the mushrooms are very tender.

5 Ladle the soup into a food processor
or blender and process until smooth.
Strain it back into the pan, pressing it
with the back of a spoon to force the
purée through the sieve.

6 Reheat the soup until piping hot, then
stir in half the crème fraîche or sour
cream. Ladle into warmed bowls, swirl
a little of the remaining crème fraîche
or sour cream on top of each and
sprinkle with chives.

COOK'S TIP

Dried mushrooms have a rich, intense
flavour and are perfect for boosting the
flavour of cultivated mushrooms, which
can often be rather bland.

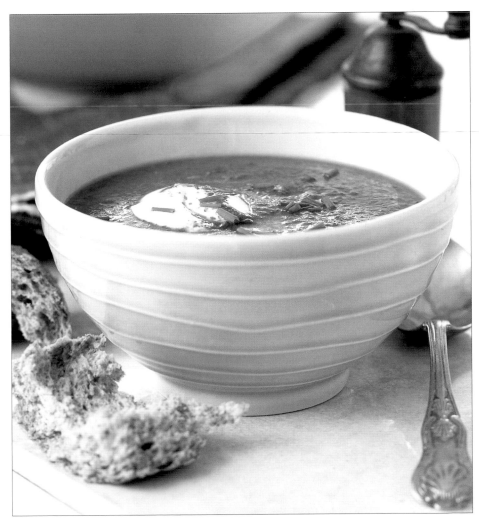

Energy 143Kcal/592kJ; Protein 3.7g; Carbohydrate 8.2g, of which sugars 3.2g; Fat 9g, of which saturates 5.3g; Cholesterol 22mg; Calcium 41mg; Fibre 2g; Sodium 174mg.

GENOESE MINESTRONE

In the Italian city of Genoa, pesto is stirred into minestrone to add extra flavour and colour. This tasty version is packed with vegetables and makes an excellent vegetarian supper dish when served with bread. To save time, you can use ready-made bottled pesto.

SERVES 4

30ml/2 tbsp olive oil
1 onion, finely chopped
2 celery sticks, finely chopped
1 large carrot, finely chopped
1 potato, weighing about 115g/4oz,
    cut into 1cm/½in cubes
1 litre/1¾ pints/4 cups vegetable stock
75g/3oz green beans, cut into 5cm/
    2in pieces
1 courgette (zucchini), thinly sliced
2 Italian plum tomatoes, peeled
    and chopped
200g/7oz can cannellini beans, drained
    and rinsed
¼ Savoy cabbage, shredded
40g/1½oz dried "quick-cook" spaghetti
    or vermicelli, broken into short lengths
salt and ground black pepper

For the pesto
about 20 fresh basil leaves
1 garlic clove
10ml/2 tsp pine nuts
15ml/1 tbsp freshly grated
    Parmesan cheese
15ml/1 tbsp freshly grated Pecorino cheese
30ml/2 tbsp olive oil

1 Heat the olive oil in a pan, then add the chopped onion, celery and carrot and cook, stirring, for about 7 minutes, until the vegetables begin to soften.

2 Transfer the fried vegetables to the ceramic cooking pot. Add the potato cubes and vegetable stock, cover the cooking pot with the lid and cook on high for 1½ hours.

3 Add the green beans, courgette, tomatoes and cannellini beans to the pot. Cover and cook for 1 hour, then stir in the cabbage and pasta and cook for a further 20 minutes.

4 Meanwhile, place all the pesto ingredients in a food processor. Blend to make a smooth sauce, adding 15–45ml/ 1–3 tbsp water through the feeder tube to loosen the mixture if necessary.

5 Stir 30ml/2 tbsp of the pesto sauce into the soup. Check the seasoning, adding more if necessary. Serve hot, in warmed bowls, with the remaining pesto spooned on top of each serving.

Energy 263Kcal/1098kJ; Protein 8.5g; Carbohydrate 25.1g, of which sugars 7g; Fat 14.9g, of which saturates 2.8g; Cholesterol 5mg; Calcium 103mg; Fibre 5.4g; Sodium 1034mg.

GALICIAN BROTH

This classic Galician soup from the north coast of Spain needs long, slow cooking to give the flavours time to develop fully. Traditionally it would be made with young, green leafy turnip tops, but in this version tasty spring greens are used instead.

SERVES 6

450g/1lb gammon, in one piece, soaked
   overnight in cold water
2 bay leaves
2 onions, sliced
10ml/2 tsp paprika
675g/1½lb baking potatoes, cut into
   2.5cm/1in chunks
225g/8oz spring greens (collards)
425g/15oz can haricot (navy) or cannellini
   beans, drained
ground black pepper

COOK'S TIP
Bacon knuckles can be used instead of
the gammon. The bones will give the
stock a delicious flavour. If there is any
broth left over, you can freeze it and use
it as stock for another soup.

1 Drain the gammon and put it in the
ceramic cooking pot with the bay leaves
and onions. Pour over just enough fresh
cold water to cover the gammon. Switch
to high, cover and cook for 1 hour.

2 Skim off any scum, then re-cover and
cook for 3 hours. Check and skim the
broth once or twice if necessary.

3 Using a slotted spoon and a large
fork, carefully lift the gammon out of the
slow cooker and on to a board. Add the
paprika and potatoes to the broth and
cook for 1 hour.

4 Meanwhile, discard the skin and fat
from the gammon and cut the meat into
small chunks. Add it to the slow cooker
and cook for a further 2 hours, or until
the meat and potatoes are tender.

5 Remove the cores from the greens,
then roll up the leaves and cut into thin
shreds. Add to the slow cooker with the
beans and cook for 30 minutes.

6 Remove the bay leaves from the
broth, season with black pepper to taste
and serve piping hot.

Energy 273Kcal/1147kJ; Protein 21.4g; Carbohydrate 33.7g, of which sugars 5.3g; Fat 6.7g, of which saturates 2g; Cholesterol 17mg; Calcium 113mg; Fibre 6.7g; Sodium 974mg.

NORTH AFRICAN SPICED SOUP

The great advantage of cooking soup in the slow cooker is that all the flavours have a chance to develop and mingle. This technique is particularly well suited to richer soups with complex spicing, such as this version of the Moroccan national soup harira.

3 Mix together the cinnamon, turmeric, ginger, cayenne pepper and 30ml/2 tbsp of stock to form a paste, then add to the pot with the carrots, celery and remaining stock. Stir well and season. Cover and cook for 1 hour.

4 Add the chopped tomatoes, potatoes, chickpeas and saffron to the pot. Cook for 4–5 hours until the vegetables are tender. Stir in the coriander and lemon juice, then check the seasoning and adjust if necessary. Ladle into warmed bowls and serve piping hot, with fried wedges of lemon, if you like.

SERVES 6

1 large onion, very finely chopped
1 litre/1¾ pints/4 cups near-boiling
   vegetable stock
5ml/1 tsp ground cinnamon
5ml/1 tsp ground turmeric
15ml/1 tbsp grated fresh root ginger
pinch cayenne pepper
2 carrots, finely diced
2 celery sticks, finely diced
400g/14oz can chopped tomatoes
450g/1lb potatoes, finely diced
400g/14oz can chickpeas, drained
5 strands saffron
30ml/2 tbsp chopped fresh coriander
   (cilantro)
15ml/1 tbsp lemon juice
salt and ground black pepper
fried wedges of lemon, to serve (optional)

1 Place the chopped onion in the ceramic cooking pot and add 600ml/ 1 pint/2½ cups of the nearly-boiling vegetable stock.

2 Switch the slow cooker to high or auto, cover with the lid and cook for about 1 hour, until the onion is soft and translucent.

Energy 166Kcal/705kJ; Protein 7.5g; Carbohydrate 30.3g, of which sugars 7.4g; Fat 2.5g, of which saturates 0.3g; Cholesterol 0mg; Calcium 62mg; Fibre 5.3g; Sodium 335mg.

AVGOLEMONO

This light, delicate soup is a great favourite in Greece and is a fine example of a few carefully chosen ingredients combining to make a delicious dish. It is essential to use a stock that is well flavoured, so use home-made if you can.

SERVES 4

900ml/1½ pints/3¾ cups near-boiling
    chicken stock
50g/2oz/⅓ cup easy-cook (converted)
    white rice
3 egg yolks
30–60ml/2–4 tbsp lemon juice
30ml/2 tbsp finely chopped fresh parsley
salt and ground black pepper
lemon slices and parsley sprigs, to garnish

1 Pour the stock into the ceramic cooking pot. Cover with a lid and cook on high for 30 minutes, or until it reaches boiling point.

2 Stir in the rice, cover and cook for 45 minutes, or until the rice is tender. Season to taste with salt and pepper. Switch off the slow cooker, remove the lid and leave to stand for 5 minutes.

3 Meanwhile, whisk the egg yolks in a bowl, then add about 30ml/2 tbsp of the lemon juice, whisking constantly until the mixture is smooth and bubbly. Add a ladleful of the hot soup to the egg mixture, whisking continuously.

4 Slowly add the egg mixture to the soup in the ceramic cooking pot, whisking all the time. The soup will thicken slightly and turn a pretty yellow.

5 Taste and add more lemon juice and seasoning if necessary. Stir in the parsley and serve immediately, garnished with lemon slices and parsley sprigs.

COOK'S TIP
When adding the egg mixture, you need to be careful not to let the soup curdle. You should avoid whisking the mixture into boiling liquid, so allow the soup to cool very slightly before whisking in the egg mixture in a slow, steady stream. Do not reheat the soup.

Energy 98Kcal/410kJ; Protein 3.3g; Carbohydrate 11.1g, of which sugars 0.3g; Fat 4.8g, of which saturates 1.3g; Cholesterol 151mg; Calcium 26mg; Fibre 0.1g; Sodium 211mg.

CABBAGE, BEETROOT and TOMATO BORSCHT

There are numerous versions of this classic soup, which originates in eastern Europe. Beetroot and soured cream are the traditional ingredients in every borscht, but other ingredients tend to be many and varied. This version has a deliciously sweet and sour taste and can be served piping hot or refreshingly chilled.

SERVES 6

1 onion, chopped
1 carrot, chopped
6 raw or vacuum-packed (cooked, not pickled) beetroot (beets), 4 diced and 2 coarsely grated
400g/14oz can chopped tomatoes
6 new potatoes, cut into bitesize pieces
1 small white cabbage, thinly sliced
600ml/1 pint/2½ cups vegetable stock
45ml/3 tbsp sugar
30–45ml/2–3 tbsp white wine vinegar or cider vinegar
45ml/3 tbsp chopped fresh dill
salt and ground black pepper
sour cream and dill, to garnish
buttered rye bread, to serve

1 Put the onion, carrot, diced beetroot, tomatoes, potatoes and cabbage into the ceramic cooking pot and pour over the vegetable stock. Cover the cooking pot with the lid and cook on high for about 4 hours, or until the vegetables are just tender.

2 Add the grated beetroot, sugar and vinegar to the pot and stir to combine. Cook for a further hour until the beetroot is cooked.

3 Taste the soup, checking for a good sweet/sour balance, and add more sugar and/or vinegar if necessary. Season to taste with plenty of salt and freshly ground black pepper.

4 Just before serving, stir the chopped dill into the soup and ladle into warmed soup bowls. Garnish each serving with a generous spoonful of sour cream and plenty more fresh dill, then serve with thick slices of buttered rye bread.

VARIATIONS

• Borscht is often served cold in summer. To serve chilled, leave it to cool at room temperature, then chill in the refrigerator for at least 4 hours. Ladle into bowls, each containing an ice cube, and top with a large spoonful of soured cream.
• For a different garnish, try scattering finely chopped hard-boiled egg or spring onions (scallions) over the top.

Energy 125Kcal/531kJ; Protein 3.5g; Carbohydrate 27.8g, of which sugars 7g; Fat 0.7g, of which saturates 0.1g; Cholesterol 0mg; Calcium 58mg; Fibre 3.2g; Sodium 357mg.

POTAGE of LENTILS

In this soup, red lentils and vegetables are cooked slowly until very soft, then puréed to give a rich and velvety consistency. On a hot day, serve chilled with extra lemon juice.

SERVES 4

45ml/3 tbsp olive oil
1 onion, chopped
2 celery sticks, chopped
1 carrot, sliced
2 garlic cloves, peeled and chopped
1 potato, peeled and diced
250g/9oz/generous 1 cup red lentils
750ml/1¼ pints/3 cups near-boiling
    vegetable stock
2 bay leaves
1 small lemon
2.5ml/½ tsp ground cumin
cayenne pepper or Tabasco sauce, to taste
salt and ground black pepper
lemon slices and chopped fresh flat leaf
    parsley, to serve

1 Heat the oil in a frying pan. Add the onion and cook, stirring frequently, for 5 minutes, or until beginning to soften. Stir in the celery, carrot, garlic and potato. Cook for a further 3–4 minutes.

2 Tip the fried vegetables into the ceramic cooking pot and switch to high. Add the lentils, vegetable stock, bay leaves and a pared strip of lemon rind and stir briefly to combine.

3 Cover the slow cooker with a lid and cook on auto or high for 1 hour.

4 Leave the cooker on auto or switch to low and cook for a further 5 hours, or until the vegetables and lentils are soft and tender.

5 Remove and discard the bay leaves and lemon rind. Process the soup in a food processor or blender until smooth. Tip the soup back into the cleaned cooking pot, stir in the cumin and cayenne pepper or Tabasco, and season.

6 Cook the soup on high for a further 45 minutes, or until piping hot. Squeeze in lemon juice to taste and check the seasoning. Ladle into warmed bowls and top each portion with lemon slices and a sprinkling of chopped fresh parsley.

Energy 300Kcal/1265kJ; Protein 15.8g; Carbohydrate 40.1g, of which sugars 3.6g; Fat 9.6g, of which saturates 1.3g; Cholesterol 0mg; Calcium 47mg; Fibre 3.9g; Sodium 456mg.

CHICKEN SOUP with KNAIDLACH

This famous Jewish soup is often made using a whole chicken cut into portions and slowly simmered in a huge stockpot. If you have a very large slow cooker you can double the quantities given here, using a small whole chicken; the cooking times will remain the same. The knaidlach are cooked separately, so that the clarity of the soup is retained.

SERVES 4

2 chicken portions, about 275g/10oz each
1 onion
1.2 litres/2 pints/5 cups boiling
   chicken stock
2 carrots, thickly sliced
2 celery sticks, thickly sliced
1 small parsnip, cut into large chunks
small pinch of ground turmeric
30ml/2 tbsp roughly chopped fresh parsley,
   plus extra to garnish
15ml/1 tbsp chopped fresh dill
salt and ground black pepper

For the knaidlach
175g/6oz/¾ cup medium matzo meal
2 eggs, lightly beaten
45ml/3 tbsp vegetable oil
30ml/2 tbsp chopped fresh parsley
½ onion, finely grated
pinch of chicken stock cube (optional)
about 90ml/6 tbsp water
salt and ground black pepper

1 Rinse the chicken pieces and put them in the ceramic cooking pot. Peel the onion, keeping it whole. Cut a small cross in the stem end and add to the pot with the stock, carrots, celery, parsnip, turmeric, salt and pepper.

2 Cover with the lid and cook on high for 1 hour. Skim off the scum that comes to the surface. (Scum will continue to form but it is only the first scum that rises that will detract from the appearance and flavour of the soup.)

3 Cook for a further 3 hours, or until the chicken is tender. Remove the chicken, discard the skin and bones and chop the flesh. Skim the fat off the soup, then return the pieces of chicken. Stir in the parsley and dill and continue cooking while you make the knaidlach.

4 Put the matzo meal, eggs, oil, parsley, onion, chicken stock, if using, and water in a large bowl. Mix together well; it should be the consistency of a thick, soft paste. Cover and chill for 30 minutes, until the mixture has become firm.

5 Bring a pan of water to the boil and have a bowl of cold water next to the stove. Dip two tablespoons into the cold water, then take a spoonful of the matzo batter. With wet hands, roll it into a ball, then slip it into the boiling water and reduce the heat so that the water simmers. Continue with the remaining matzo batter, then cover the pan and cook for 15–20 minutes.

6 Remove the knaidlach from the pan with a slotted spoon and divide between individual serving bowls. Leave them to firm up for a few minutes. Ladle the hot soup over the knaidlach and serve sprinkled with extra chopped parsley.

VARIATIONS
• Instead of knaidlach, the soup can be served over cooked rice or noodles.
• To make knaidlach with a lighter texture, separate the eggs and add the yolks to the matzo mixture. Whisk the whites until stiff, then fold into the batter.

Energy 586Kcal/2451kJ; Protein 38.2g; Carbohydrate 42.6g, of which sugars 6.3g; Fat 30.3g, of which saturates 7.7g; Cholesterol 272mg; Calcium 131mg; Fibre 3.7g; Sodium 802mg.

SPINACH and ROOT VEGETABLE SOUP

This is a typical Russian soup, traditionally prepared when the first vegetables of spring appear. You will need to use a large slow cooker to accommodate the spinach.

SERVES 4

1 small turnip, cut into chunks
2 carrots, diced
1 small parsnip, cut into large dice
1 potato, peeled and diced
1 onion, chopped
1 garlic clove, finely chopped
¼ celeriac bulb, diced
750ml/1¼ pints/3 cups boiling vegetable
   or chicken stock
175g/6oz fresh spinach, roughly chopped
1 small bunch fresh dill, chopped
salt and ground black pepper

For the garnish
2 hard-boiled eggs, sliced lengthways
1 lemon, sliced
30ml/2 tbsp fresh parsley and dill

COOK'S TIP
For best results, use a really good-quality vegetable or chicken stock.

1 Put the turnip, carrots, parsnip, potato, onion, garlic, celeriac and stock into the ceramic cooking pot. Cook on high or auto for 1 hour, then either leave on auto or switch to low and cook for a further 5–6 hours, until the vegetables are soft and tender.

2 Stir the spinach into the cooking pot and cook on high for 45 minutes, or until the spinach is tender but still green and leafy. Season with salt and pepper.

3 Stir in the dill, then ladle the soup into warmed bowls and serve garnished with egg, lemon and a sprinkling of fresh parsley and dill.

Energy 67Kcal/280kJ; Protein 3g; Carbohydrate 11.5g, of which sugars 7g; Fat 1.3g, of which saturates 0.1g; Cholesterol 0mg; Calcium 121mg; Fibre 3.9g; Sodium 499mg.

ASIAN-STYLE DUCK CONSOMMÉ

The Vietnamese community in France has had a profound influence on French cooking.
As a result, you will find many classic French dishes brought together with Asian flavours.

SERVES 4

1 small carrot
1 small leek, halved lengthwise
4 shiitake mushrooms, thinly sliced
soy sauce
2 spring onions (scallions), thinly sliced
finely shredded watercress
    or Chinese cabbage
ground black pepper

For the consommé
1 duck carcass (raw or cooked), plus
    2 legs or any giblets, trimmed of fat
1 large onion, unpeeled, with root
    end trimmed
2 carrots, cut into 2.5cm/1in pieces
1 parsnip, cut into 2.5cm/1in pieces
1 leek, cut into 2.5cm/1in pieces
2 garlic cloves, crushed
15ml/1 tbsp black peppercorns
2.5cm/1in piece fresh root ginger,
    peeled and sliced
4 thyme sprigs or 5ml/1 tsp dried thyme
1 small bunch fresh coriander (cilantro)

1 To make the consommé, put the duck carcass, legs or giblets, onion, carrots, parsnip, leek and garlic in the ceramic cooking pot. Add the peppercorns, ginger, thyme and coriander stalks (reserve the leaves) and enough cold water to cover the bones, leaving at least 4cm/1½in space at the top of the pot.

2 Cover the pot with the lid and cook on high or auto for 2 hours. Skim off any surface scum, then reduce the temperature to low or leave on auto. Cover and cook for a further 4 hours, removing the lid for the last hour.

3 Line a sieve (strainer) with muslin (cheesecloth) and strain the consommé into a bowl, discarding the bones and vegetables. Leave to cool, then chill for several hours or overnight. Skim off any congealed fat and blot the surface with kitchen paper to remove all traces of fat.

4 Cut the carrot and leek into 5cm/2in pieces. Cut each piece lengthways into thin slices, then stack and slice into thin julienne strips. Place the julienne strips in the clean ceramic cooking pot with the sliced shiitake mushrooms.

5 Pour over the consommé and add a few dashes of soy sauce and some ground black pepper. Cover and cook on high for about 45 minutes, or until piping hot, skimming off any foam that rises to the surface with a slotted spoon.

6 Adjust the seasoning and stir in the spring onions and watercress or Chinese cabbage. Ladle into warmed bowls and sprinkle with the fresh coriander leaves.

Energy 96Kcal/406kJ; Protein 7.1g; Carbohydrate 12.1g, of which sugars 7.9g; Fat 2.5g, of which saturates 0.6g; Cholesterol 28mg; Calcium 51mg; Fibre 4g; Sodium 47mg.

HOT and SOUR PRAWN SOUP

This salty, sour, spicy hot Thai soup, known as Tom Yam Kung, *is a real classic. Cooking the stock in the slow cooker maximizes the flavour before the final ingredients are added.*

SERVES 4

450g/1lb raw king prawns (jumbo shrimp), thawed if frozen
900ml/1½ pints/3¾ cups near-boiling light chicken stock or water
3 lemon grass stalks
6 kaffir lime leaves, torn in half
225g/8oz straw mushrooms, drained
45ml/3 tbsp Thai fish sauce
60ml/4 tbsp fresh lime juice
30ml/2 tbsp chopped spring onion (scallion)
15ml/1 tbsp fresh coriander (cilantro) leaves
4 fresh red chillies, seeded and thickly sliced
salt and ground black pepper

1 Peel the prawns, reserving the shells. Using a sharp knife, make a shallow cut along the back of each prawn and use the point of the knife to remove the thin black vein. Place the prawns in a bowl, cover and place in the refrigerator until ready to use.

2 Rinse the reserved prawn shells under cold running water, then put them in the ceramic cooking pot and add the chicken stock or water. Cover with the lid and switch the slow cooker to high.

3 Using a pestle, bruise the bulbous end of the lemon grass stalks. Lift the lid of the ceramic pot and quickly add the lemon grass stalks and half the torn kaffir lime leaves to the stock. Stir well, then re-cover with the lid and cook for about 2 hours until the stock is fragrant and aromatic.

4 Strain the stock into a large bowl and rinse out the ceramic cooking pot. Pour the stock back into the cleaned pot. Add the drained mushrooms and cook on high for 30 minutes.

5 Add the prawns to the soup and cook for a further 10 minutes until the prawns turn pink and are cooked.

6 Stir the fish sauce, lime juice, spring onion, coriander, chillies and remaining lime leaves into the soup. Taste and adjust the seasoning if necessary. The soup should be sour, salty, spicy and hot.

Energy 127Kcal/536kJ; Protein 27g; Carbohydrate 1.4g, of which sugars 1.2g; Fat 1.4g, of which saturates 0.3g; Cholesterol 315mg; Calcium 133mg; Fibre 0.7g; Sodium 2715mg.

ONE-POT, CLAY-POT SOUPS

There's something supremely comforting about hot soup, and when you prepare it yourself, the aroma ensures that the pleasure starts long before you lift the ladle. Nourishing, easy to digest, quick to cook and convenient, soup provides the perfect meal-in-a-bowl at lunchtime or a warming after-school snack, and when served as a first course, it gives guests a real sense of welcome. Mediterranean Leek and Fish Soup with Tomatoes, Italian Farmhouse Soup, Chicken and Leek Soup with Prunes and Barley, Seafood Chowder, and Bean and Pistou Soup are just some of the treats in store.

CATALAN POTATO and BROAD BEAN SOUP

While they are in season fresh broad beans are perfect, but canned or frozen are just as good in this creamy, richly flavoured soup.

SERVES 6

30ml/2 tbsp olive oil
2 onions, chopped
3 large floury potatoes, diced
450g/1lb fresh shelled broad
    (fava) beans
1.75 litres/3 pints/7½ cups vegetable or
    chicken stock
1 bunch coriander (cilantro),
    finely chopped
150ml/¼ pint/⅔ cup single (light) cream
salt and ground black pepper
coriander (cilantro) leaves, to garnish

COOK'S TIP
Broad beans sometimes have a tough outer skin, particularly if they are large. To remove this, first cook the beans briefly in boiling water, then peel off the skin, and add the tender, bright green centre part to the soup.

1 Heat the olive oil in a large pan, add the chopped onions and fry, stirring occasionally with a wooden spoon, for about 5 minutes until they are just softened but not brown.

2 Add the diced potatoes, shelled broad beans (reserving a few for garnishing) and vegetable or chicken stock to the pan. Bring to the boil, then simmer for 5 minutes.

3 Stir in the finely chopped coriander and simmer for a further 10 minutes.

4 Process the soup in batches in a food processor or blender, then return the soup to the rinsed-out pan.

5 Stir in the cream (reserving a little for garnishing), season, and bring to a simmer. Serve garnished with more coriander leaves, beans and cream.

SPANISH POTATO and GARLIC SOUP

Traditionally served in shallow earthenware dishes, this delicious, classic Spanish soup is a great choice for vegetarians.

SERVES 6

30ml/2 tbsp olive oil
1 large onion, finely sliced
4 garlic cloves, crushed
1 large potato, halved and cut
    into thin slices
5ml/1 tsp paprika
400g/14oz can chopped tomatoes, drained
5ml/1 tsp thyme leaves, plus extra chopped
    thyme leaves, to garnish
900ml/1½ pints/3¾ cups vegetable stock
5ml/1 tsp cornflour (cornstarch)
salt and ground black pepper

COOK'S TIP
Paprika is a popular spice in many Spanish dishes. It is made from red peppers that are dried and powdered into a coarse-grained spice. It has a slightly sweet, mild flavour and a rich red colour.

1 Heat the oil in a large, heavy pan, add the onion, garlic, potato and paprika and cook, stirring occasionally, for about 5 minutes, or until the onions have softened, but not browned.

2 Add the chopped tomatoes, thyme leaves and vegetable stock to the pan and simmer for 15–20 minutes until the potatoes have cooked through.

3 In a small bowl, mix the cornflour with a little water to form a smooth paste, then stir into the soup. Bring to the boil, stirring, then simmer for about 5 minutes until the soup has thickened.

4 Using a wooden spoon, break up the potatoes slightly, then season to taste. Serve the soup garnished with the extra chopped thyme leaves.

Catalan Potato and Broad Bean Soup: Energy 236Kcal/990kJ; Protein 9.3g; Carbohydrate 30.3g, of which sugars 4.6g; Fat 9.4g, of which saturates 3.8g; Cholesterol 14mg; Calcium 94mg; Fibre 6.8g; Sodium 30mg.
Spanish Potato and Garlic Soup: Energy 86Kcal/359kJ; Protein 1.5g; Carbohydrate 11.5g, of which sugars 4.4g; Fat 4.1g, of which saturates 0.6g; Cholesterol 0mg; Calcium 15mg; Fibre 1.5g; Sodium 12mg.

LENTIL and PASTA SOUP

This rustic vegetarian soup makes a warming winter meal and goes especially well with Granary or crusty Italian bread.

SERVES 4–6

175g/6oz/¾ cup brown lentils
3 garlic cloves, unpeeled
1 litre/1¾ pints/4 cups water
45ml/3 tbsp olive oil
25g/1oz/2 tbsp butter
1 onion, finely chopped
2 celery sticks, finely chopped
30ml/2 tbsp sun-dried tomato
    purée (paste)
1.75 litres/3 pints/7½ cups vegetable stock
a few fresh marjoram leaves
a few fresh basil leaves
leaves from 1 fresh thyme sprig
50g/2oz/½ cup dried small pasta shapes,
    such as macaroni or tubetti
salt and ground black pepper
tiny fresh herb leaves, to garnish

1 Put the lentils in a large pan. Smash one of the garlic cloves using the blade of a large knife (there's no need to peel it first), then add it to the lentils. Pour in the water and bring to the boil. Simmer for about 20 minutes, or until the lentils are tender. Tip the lentils into a sieve, remove the garlic and set it aside. Rinse the lentils under the cold tap and leave to drain.

2 Heat 30ml/2 tbsp of the oil with half the butter in the pan. Add the onion and celery and cook gently for 5 minutes.

3 Crush the remaining garlic, then peel and mash the reserved garlic. Add to the pan with the remaining oil, the tomato purée and the lentils. Stir, then add the stock, herbs and salt and pepper. Bring to the boil, stirring. Simmer for 30 minutes, stirring occasionally.

4 Add the pasta and bring the soup back to the boil, stirring. Reduce the heat and simmer until the pasta is just tender. Add the remaining butter to the pan and stir until melted. Taste the soup for seasoning, then serve hot in warmed bowls, sprinkled with herb leaves.

Energy 206Kcal/865kJ; Protein 8.1g; Carbohydrate 23.5g, of which sugars 1.7g; Fat 9.5g, of which saturates 3g; Cholesterol 9mg; Calcium 24mg; Fibre 1.9g; Sodium 42mg.

ITALIAN FARMHOUSE SOUP

Root vegetables form the base of this chunky, minestrone-style main meal soup. You can vary the vegetables according to what you have to hand.

SERVES 4

30ml/2 tbsp olive oil

1 onion, roughly chopped

3 carrots, cut into large chunks

175–200g/6–7oz turnips, cut into large chunks

about 175g/6oz swede (rutabaga), cut into large chunks

400g/14oz can chopped Italian tomatoes

15ml/1 tbsp tomato purée (paste)

5ml/1 tsp dried mixed herbs

5ml/1 tsp dried oregano

50g/2oz dried (bell) peppers, washed and thinly sliced (optional)

1.5 litres/2½ pints/6¼ cups vegetable stock or water

50g/2oz/½ cup dried small macaroni or conchiglie

400g/14oz can red kidney beans, rinsed and drained

30ml/2 tbsp chopped fresh flat leaf parsley

salt and ground black pepper

freshly grated Parmesan cheese, to serve

1 Heat the olive oil in a large pan, add the onion and cook over a low heat for about 5 minutes until softened. Add the carrot, turnip and swede chunks, canned chopped tomatoes, tomato purée, dried mixed herbs, dried oregano and dried peppers, if using. Stir in salt and pepper to taste.

2 Pour in the vegetable stock or water and bring to the boil. Stir well, cover the pan, then lower the heat and simmer for 30 minutes, stirring occasionally.

3 Add the pasta to the pan and bring quickly to the boil, stirring. Lower the heat and simmer, uncovered, for about 5 minutes until the pasta is only just tender, or according to the instructions on the packet. Stir frequently.

4 Stir in the kidney beans. Heat through for 2–3 minutes, then remove the pan from the heat and stir in the parsley. Taste the soup for seasoning. Serve hot in warmed soup bowls, with grated Parmesan cheese handed separately.

Energy 248Kcal/1047kJ; Protein 10.2g; Carbohydrate 38.6g, of which sugars 14.9g; Fat 7g, of which saturates 1.1g; Cholesterol 0mg; Calcium 139mg; Fibre 10.6g; Sodium 422mg.

BROCCOLI, ANCHOVY and PASTA SOUP

This wonderfully chunky and flavourful soup is from Puglia in the south of Italy, where anchovies and broccoli are often used together.

SERVES 4

30ml/2 tbsp olive oil
1 small onion, finely chopped
1 garlic clove, finely chopped
¼–⅓ fresh red chilli, seeded and
    finely chopped
2 drained canned anchovies
200ml/7fl oz/scant 1 cup passata (bottled
    strained tomatoes)
45ml/3 tbsp dry white wine
1.2 litres/2 pints/5 cups vegetable or light
    chicken stock
300g/11oz broccoli florets
200g/7oz/1¾ cups dried orecchiette pasta
    or other medium-size pasta shapes
salt and ground black pepper
freshly grated Pecorino cheese, to serve

1 Heat the oil in a large pan. Add the onion, garlic, chilli and anchovies and cook over a low heat, stirring constantly, for 5–6 minutes.

2 Add the passata and wine, with salt and pepper to taste. Bring to the boil, cover, then cook over a low heat, stirring occasionally, for 12–15 minutes.

3 Pour in the stock. Bring to the boil, then add the broccoli and simmer for about 5 minutes. Add the pasta and bring back to the boil, stirring. Simmer, stirring frequently for 7–8 minutes until the pasta is just tender, or according to the packet instructions. Taste for seasoning. Serve hot, in warmed bowls. Hand around grated Pecorino separately.

PASTA SQUARES and PEAS in BROTH

This thick, filling Italian soup, flavoured with pancetta or bacon and prosciutto, is traditionally made with home-made pasta and fresh peas. In this modern, more convenient version, ready-made fresh lasagne sheets are used with frozen peas, to save time.

SERVES 4–6

25g/1oz/2 tbsp butter
50g/2oz pancetta or rindless smoked
    streaky (fatty) bacon, roughly chopped
1 small onion, finely chopped
1 celery stick, finely chopped
400g/14oz/3½ cups frozen peas
5ml/1 tsp tomato purée (paste)
5–10ml/1–2 tsp finely chopped fresh flat
    leaf parsley
1 litre/1¾ pints/4 cups chicken stock
300g/11oz fresh lasagne sheets
about 50g/2oz prosciutto, cut into cubes
salt and ground black pepper
freshly grated Parmesan cheese, to serve

1 Melt the butter in a large pan and add the pancetta or rindless smoked streaky bacon, with the chopped onion and chopped celery. Cook together over a low heat, stirring constantly, for 5 minutes.

2 Add the frozen peas to the pan and cook, stirring, for 3–4 minutes. Stir in the tomato purée and finely chopped parsley, then add the chicken stock, with salt and pepper to taste. Bring to the boil. Cover, lower the heat and simmer the soup for 10 minutes.

3 Meanwhile, using a large, sharp knife and a ruler, cut the lasagne sheets into 2cm/¾in squares.

4 Taste the soup for seasoning. Drop the pasta into the pan, then stir and bring to the boil. Simmer for 2 minutes, or until the pasta is just tender, then stir in the prosciutto. Serve hot with grated Parmesan handed around separately.

COOK'S TIP
Take care when seasoning the soup with salt, because of the saltiness of the pancetta and the prosciutto.

Broccoli, Anchovy and Pasta Soup: Energy 268Kcal/1131kJ; Protein 10.3g; Carbohydrate 41.2g, of which sugars 5.2g; Fat 7.3g, of which saturates 1.1g; Cholesterol 1mg; Calcium 69mg; Fibre 3.9g; Sodium 182mg.
Pasta Squares and Peas in Broth: Energy 175Kcal/730kJ; Protein 9.5g; Carbohydrate 19.7g, of which sugars 2.6g; Fat 7.1g, of which saturates 3.2g; Cholesterol 19mg; Calcium 24mg; Fibre 4g; Sodium 236mg.

CORN and POTATO CHOWDER

This creamy yet chunky soup is rich with the sweet taste of corn. It's excellent served with thick, crusty bread and topped with some grated Cheddar cheese.

2 Heat until the oil and butter are sizzling, then reduce the heat to low. Cover the pan and cook gently for about 10 minutes until the vegetables are just softened, shaking the pan occasionally.

3 Pour in the stock, season with salt and pepper to taste and bring to the boil. Reduce the heat, cover the pan again and simmer gently, stirring occasionally, for about 15 minutes, or until the vegetables are tender.

SERVES 4

1 onion, chopped
1 garlic clove, crushed
1 medium baking potato, chopped
2 celery sticks, sliced
1 green (bell) pepper, seeded and sliced
30ml/2 tbsp sunflower oil
25g/1oz/2 tbsp butter
600ml/1 pint/2½ cups vegetable stock
300ml/½ pint/1¼ cups milk
200g/7oz can flageolet, cannellini or
   haricot (navy) beans
300g/11oz can sweetcorn
good pinch of dried sage
salt and ground black pepper
freshly grated Cheddar cheese, to serve

1 Put the onion, garlic, potato, celery and green pepper into a large, heavy pan with the sunflower oil and butter.

4 Add the milk, canned beans and sweetcorn – including their liquids. Stir in the dried sage and simmer, uncovered, for 5 minutes, then check the seasoning and adjust to taste. Serve hot in bowls, sprinkled with the grated Cheddar cheese.

Energy 275Kcal/1161kJ; Protein 9.6g; Carbohydrate 43.3g, of which sugars 16.5g; Fat 8.3g, of which saturates 1.8g; Cholesterol 4mg; Calcium 141mg; Fibre 5.5g; Sodium 441mg.

BEAN and PISTOU SOUP

This hearty vegetarian soup is a typical Provençal-style soup, richly flavoured with a home-made garlic and fresh basil pistou sauce.

SERVES 4–6

150g/5oz/scant 1 cup dried haricot (navy) beans, soaked overnight in cold water
150g/5oz/scant 1 cup dried flageolet or cannellini beans, soaked overnight in cold water
1 onion, chopped
1.2 litres/2 pints/5 cups hot vegetable stock
2 carrots, roughly chopped
225g/8oz Savoy cabbage, shredded
1 large potato, about 225g/8oz, roughly chopped
225g/8oz French (green) beans, chopped
salt and ground black pepper
basil leaves, to garnish

For the pistou
4 garlic cloves
8 large sprigs basil leaves
90ml/6 tbsp olive oil
60ml/4 tbsp freshly grated Parmesan cheese

1 Soak a bean pot in cold water for 20 minutes then drain. Drain the soaked haricot and flageolet or cannellini beans and place in the bean pot. Add the chopped onion and pour over sufficient cold water to come 5cm/2in above the beans. Cover and place the pot in an unheated oven. Set the oven to 200°C/400°F/Gas 6 and cook for about 1½ hours, or until the beans are tender.

2 Drain the beans and onions. Place half the beans and onions in a food processor or blender and process to a paste. Return the drained beans and the bean paste to the bean pot. Add the hot vegetable stock.

3 Add the chopped carrots, shredded cabbage, chopped potato and French beans to the bean pot. Season with salt and pepper, cover and return the pot to the oven. Reduce the oven temperature to 180°C/350°F/Gas 4 and cook for 1 hour, or until all the vegetables are cooked right through.

4 Meanwhile place the garlic and basil in a mortar and pound with a pestle, then gradually beat in the oil. Stir in the grated Parmesan. Stir half the pistou into the soup and then ladle into warmed soup bowls. Top each bowl of soup with a spoonful of the remaining pistou and serve garnished with basil.

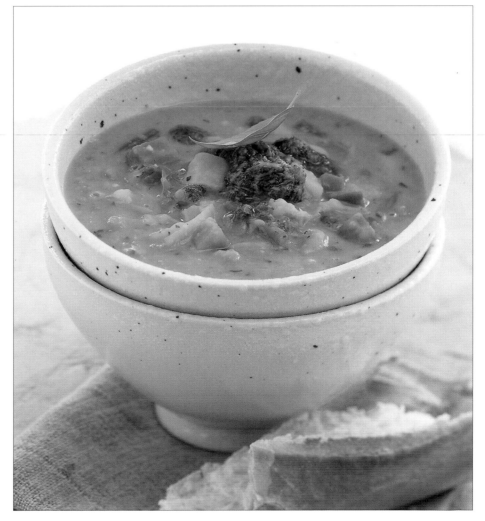

Energy 305Kcal/1281kJ; Protein 17.2g; Carbohydrate 34.6g, of which sugars 7.5g; Fat 11.8g, of which saturates 3.3g; Cholesterol 10mg; Calcium 215mg; Fibre 10.8g; Sodium 133mg.

MEDITERRANEAN SAUSAGE and PESTO SOUP

This hearty soup makes a satisfying one-pot meal that brings the summery flavour of basil to midwinter meals. Thick slices of warm crusty bread make the perfect accompaniment.

SERVES 4

oil, for deep-frying
450g/1lb smoked pork sausages
a handful of fresh basil leaves
15ml/1 tbsp olive oil
1 red onion, chopped
225g/8oz/1 cup red lentils
400g/14oz can chopped tomatoes
   with herbs
1 litre/1¾ pints/4 cups chicken stock
   or water
salt and ground black pepper
60ml/4 tbsp pesto, to serve

COOK'S TIP
The flavour of smoked sausages is very good in this soup, but you could use ordinary fresh sausages if you like. Choose course-textured sausages, such as Toulouse.

1 Heat the oil for deep-frying to 190°C/ 375°F or until a cube of day-old bread browns in about 60 seconds. Slice one of the sausages diagonally and deep-fry for 2–3 minutes, or until brown and crisp. Add the basil leaves and fry for a few seconds until crisp. Lift out the sausage slices and basil leaves using a slotted spoon and drain them on kitchen paper. Strain the oil into a bowl.

2 Heat the olive oil in the pan, add the chopped red onion and cook until softened. Coarsely chop the remaining sausages and add them to the pan. Cook for about 5 minutes, stirring, or until the sausages are cooked.

3 Stir in the lentils, tomatoes and stock or water and bring to the boil. Reduce the heat, cover and simmer for about 20 minutes. Cool the soup slightly before puréeing it in a blender. Return the soup to the rinsed-out pan.

4 Reheat the soup, add seasoning to taste, then ladle into warmed individual soup bowls. Sprinkle the soup with the deep-fried sausage slices and basil and swirl a little pesto through each portion just before serving. Serve with plenty of warm crusty bread.

Energy 738Kcal/3075kJ; Protein 26.2g; Carbohydrate 46.7g, of which sugars 6.9g; Fat 50.9g, of which saturates 15.8g; Cholesterol 53mg; Calcium 86mg; Fibre 4.5g; Sodium 885mg.

MOROCCAN SPICED LAMB SOUP

Classic north African spices – ginger, turmeric and cinnamon – are combined with chickpeas and lamb to make this hearty, warming soup.

SERVES 6

75g/3oz/½ cup chickpeas, soaked overnight
15g/½oz/1 tbsp butter
225g/8oz lamb, cut into cubes
1 onion, chopped
450g/1lb tomatoes, peeled and chopped
a few celery leaves, chopped
30ml/2 tbsp chopped fresh parsley
15ml/1 tbsp chopped fresh
    coriander (cilantro)
2.5ml/½ tsp ground ginger
2.5ml/½ tsp ground turmeric
5ml/1 tsp ground cinnamon
1.75 litres/3 pints/7½ cups water
75g/3oz/scant ½ cup green lentils
75g/3oz vermicelli or soup pasta
2 egg yolks
juice of ½–1 lemon
salt and ground black pepper
fresh coriander (cilantro), to garnish
lemon wedges, to serve

1 Drain the chickpeas, rinse under cold water and set aside. Melt the butter in a large flameproof casserole or pan and fry the lamb and onion for 2–3 minutes, stirring, until the lamb is just browned.

2 Add the chopped tomatoes, celery leaves, herbs and spices and season well with ground black pepper. Cook for about 1 minute, then stir in the water and add the green lentils and the soaked, drained and rinsed chickpeas.

3 Slowly bring to the boil and skim the surface to remove the froth. Boil rapidly for 10 minutes, then reduce the heat and simmer very gently for 2 hours, or until the chickpeas are very tender.

4 Season with salt and pepper, then add the vermicelli or soup pasta to the pan and cook for 5–6 minutes until it is just tender. If the soup is very thick at this stage, add a little more water.

5 Beat the egg yolks with the lemon juice and stir into the simmering soup. Immediately remove the soup from the heat and stir until thickened. Pour into warmed serving bowls and garnish with plenty of fresh coriander. Serve the soup with lemon wedges.

COOK'S TIP
If you have forgotten to soak the chickpeas overnight, place them in a pan with about four times their volume of cold water. Bring very slowly to the boil, then cover the pan, remove it from the heat and leave to stand for 45 minutes before using as described in the recipe.

Energy 248Kcal/1042kJ; Protein 16.3g; Carbohydrate 25.8g, of which sugars 4.1g; Fat 9.5g, of which saturates 4g; Cholesterol 101mg; Calcium 64mg; Fibre 3.6g; Sodium 70mg.

CHINESE CHICKEN and CHILLI SOUP

Ginger and lemon grass add an aromatic note to this tasty, refreshing soup, which can be served as a light lunch or appetizer.

2 Place the Chinese sand pot in an unheated oven. Set the temperature to 200°C/400°F/Gas 6 and cook the soup for 30–40 minutes, or until the stock is simmering and the chicken and vegetables are tender.

3 Add the spring onions and mushrooms, cover and return the pot to the oven for 10 minutes. Meanwhile place the noodles in a large bowl and cover with boiling water – soak for the required time, following the packet instructions.

4 Drain the noodles and divide among four warmed serving bowls. Stir the soy sauce into the soup and season with salt and pepper. Divide the soup between the bowls and serve immediately.

COOK'S TIP
Rice noodles are available in a variety of thicknesses and can be bought in straight lengths or in coils or loops. They are a creamy white colour and very brittle in texture. Rice noodles are pre-cooked so they only require a very short soaking time – check the packet for exact timings. Vermicelli rice noodles are very fine and will only need to be soaked for a few minutes.

SERVES 4

150g/5oz boneless chicken breast portion, cut into thin strips
2.5cm/1in piece fresh root ginger, finely chopped
5cm/2in piece lemon grass stalk, finely chopped
1 red chilli, seeded and thinly sliced
8 baby corn cobs, halved lengthwise
1 large carrot, cut into thin sticks
1 litre/1¾ pints/4 cups hot chicken stock
4 spring onions (scallions), thinly sliced
12 small shiitake mushrooms, sliced
115g/4oz/1 cup vermicelli rice noodles
30ml/2 tbsp soy sauce
salt and ground black pepper

1 Place the chicken strips, chopped ginger, chopped lemon grass and sliced chilli in a Chinese sand pot. Add the halved baby corn and the carrot sticks. Pour over the hot chicken stock and cover the pot.

Energy 168Kcal/707kJ; Protein 13.7g; Carbohydrate 26.1g, of which sugars 3.1g; Fat 1g, of which saturates 0.2g; Cholesterol 26mg; Calcium 25mg; Fibre 1.7g; Sodium 853mg.

CHICKEN and LEEK SOUP with PRUNES and BARLEY

This recipe is based on the traditional Scottish soup, Cock-a-leekie. The unusual combination of leeks and prunes is surprisingly delicious.

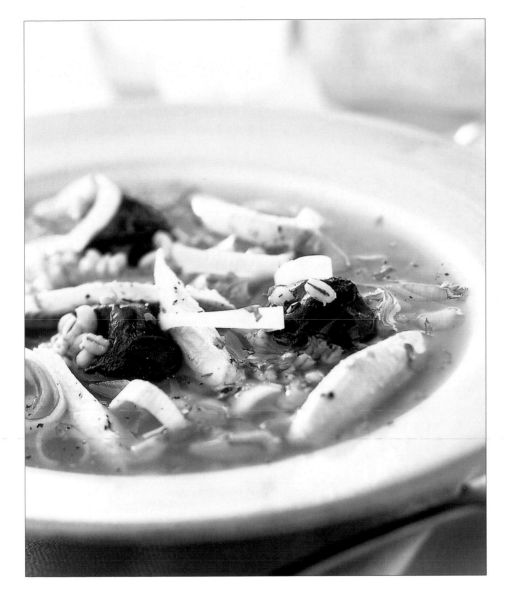

3 Bring the stock to the boil, then reduce the heat and cover the pan. Simmer gently for 1 hour. Skim off any scum when the water first starts to boil and occasionally during simmering.

4 Add the chicken breast portions to the pan and continue to cook for another 30 minutes until they are just cooked. Leave until cool enough to handle, then strain the stock. Reserve the chicken breast portions and the meat from the carcass. Discard all the skin, bones, cooked vegetables and herbs. Skim as much fat as you can from the stock, then return it to the pan.

5 Add the pearl barley to the stock. Bring to the boil over a medium heat, then lower the heat and cook very gently for 15–20 minutes, until the barley is just cooked and tender. Season the soup with 5ml/1 tsp each salt and ground black pepper.

SERVES 6

115g/4oz/⅔ cup pearl barley
1 chicken, weighing about 2kg/4¼lb
900g/2lb leeks
1 fresh bay leaf
a few fresh parsley stalks and
    thyme sprigs
1 large carrot, thickly sliced
2.4 litres/4 pints/10 cups chicken or
    beef stock
400g/14oz ready-to-eat prunes
salt and ground black pepper
chopped fresh parsley, to garnish

1 Rinse the pearl barley thoroughly in a sieve under cold running water, then cook it in a large pan of boiling water for about 10 minutes. Drain the barley, rinse well again and drain thoroughly. Set aside in a cool place.

2 Cut the breast portions off the chicken and set aside, then place the remaining chicken carcass in the pan. Cut half the leeks into 5cm/2in lengths and add them to the pan. Tie the herbs together into a bouquet garni and add to the pan with the carrot and stock.

6 Add the ready-to-eat prunes to the pan, then thinly slice the remaining leeks and add them to the pan. Bring to the boil, then cover the pan and simmer gently for about 10 minutes, or until the leeks are just cooked.

7 Slice the chicken breast portions and then add them to the soup with the remaining chicken meat from the carcass, sliced or cut into neat pieces. Reheat the soup, if necessary, then ladle it into warm, deep soup plates and sprinkle with plenty of chopped parsley to serve.

Energy 273Kcal/1158kJ; Protein 21.7g; Carbohydrate 44.4g, of which sugars 27.2g; Fat 2.1g, of which saturates 0.4g; Cholesterol 47mg; Calcium 70mg; Fibre 7.5g; Sodium 55mg.

BOUILLABAISSE

Perhaps the most famous of all Mediterranean fish soups, this recipe, originating from Marseilles in the south of France, is a rich and colourful mixture of fish and shellfish, flavoured with tomatoes, saffron and orange.

SERVES 4–6

1.3–1.6kg/3–3½lb mixed fish and shellfish, such as red mullet, John Dory, monkfish, large prawns (shrimp) and clams
1.2 litres/2 pints/5 cups water
225g/8oz tomatoes
pinch of saffron threads
90ml/6 tbsp olive oil
1 onion, sliced
1 leek, sliced
1 celery stick, sliced
2 garlic cloves, crushed
bouquet garni
1 strip pared orange rind
2.5ml/½ tsp fennel seeds
15ml/1 tbsp tomato purée (paste)
10ml/2 tsp Pernod
4–6 thick slices French bread
45ml/3 tbsp chopped fresh parsley
salt and ground black pepper

1 Remove the heads, tails and fins from the fish and put in a large pan, with the water. Bring to the boil, and simmer for 15 minutes. Strain, and reserve the liquid.

2 Cut the fish into large chunks. Leave the shellfish in their shells.

3 Scald the tomatoes, then drain and refresh in cold water. Peel and chop them. Soak the saffron in 15–30ml/1–2 tbsp hot water. Heat the oil in the cleaned pan, add the onion, leek and celery and cook until softened. Add the garlic, bouquet garni, orange rind, fennel seeds and tomatoes, then stir in the saffron and liquid and the fish stock. Season with salt and pepper, then bring to the boil and simmer for 30–40 minutes.

4 Add the shellfish and boil for about 6 minutes. Discard any clams that remain closed. Add the fish and cook for a further 6–8 minutes until it flakes easily. Using a slotted spoon, transfer the fish to a warmed serving platter. Keep the liquid boiling and add the tomato purée and Pernod, then check the seasoning. Place a slice of bread in each soup bowl, pour the broth over and serve the fish separately, sprinkled with the parsley.

Energy 338Kcal/1418kJ; Protein 42.2g; Carbohydrate 12.8g, of which sugars 3.8g; Fat 13.2g, of which saturates 1.9g; Cholesterol 100mg; Calcium 55mg; Fibre 1.6g; Sodium 239mg.

MEDITERRANEAN LEEK and FISH SOUP with TOMATOES

This chunky soup, which is almost a stew, makes a robust and wonderfully aromatic meal in a bowl. Serve it with crisp-toasted croûtes spread with a spicy garlic mayonnaise.

SERVES 4

30ml/2 tbsp olive oil
2 large thick leeks, white and green
   parts separated
5ml/1 tsp crushed coriander seeds
good pinch of dried red chilli flakes
300g/11oz small salad potatoes,
   thickly sliced
200g/7oz can chopped tomatoes
600ml/1 pint/2½ cups fish stock
150ml/¼ pint/⅔ cup fruity white wine
1 fresh bay leaf
1 star anise
1 strip pared orange rind
good pinch of saffron threads
450g/1lb white fish fillets, such as sea bass,
   monkfish, cod or haddock, skinned
450g/1lb small squid, cleaned
250g/9oz uncooked peeled
   prawns (shrimp)
30–45ml/2–3 tbsp chopped fresh parsley
salt and ground black pepper

For the garlic croûtes
1 short French loaf, sliced and toasted
spicy garlic mayonnaise

1 Gently heat the olive oil in a pan, then thinly slice the green part of the leeks. Add with the crushed coriander seeds and the dried red chilli flakes, and cook for 5 minutes, stirring occasionally.

2 Add the thickly sliced potatoes and chopped tomatoes and pour in the fish stock and white wine. Add the bay leaf, star anise, pared orange rind and saffron threads to the pan and stir well.

3 Bring to the boil, then reduce the heat and partly cover the pan. Simmer for about 20 minutes until the potatoes are tender. Taste and adjust the seasoning.

4 Cut the fish into chunks. Cut the squid sacs into rectangles and score a criss-cross pattern into them without cutting right through.

5 Add the fish to the soup, cook gently for 4 minutes, then add the prawns and cook for 1 minute. Add the squid and the thinly sliced white part of the leek and cook, stirring occasionally, for 2 minutes.

6 Stir in the chopped parsley and serve with the toasted croûtes topped with spicy garlic mayonnaise.

Energy 383Kcal/1615kJ; Protein 52g; Carbohydrate 17.8g, of which sugars 4.7g; Fat 9.4g, of which saturates 1.6g; Cholesterol 427mg; Calcium 107mg; Fibre 3.2g; Sodium 326mg.

COCONUT and SEAFOOD SOUP with GARLIC CHIVES

The long list of ingredients in this Thai-inspired recipe could mislead you into thinking that this soup is complicated. In fact, it is very easy to put together.

SERVES 4

600ml/1 pint/2½ cups fish stock
5 thin slices fresh root ginger
2 lemon grass stalks, chopped
3 kaffir lime leaves, shredded
25g/1oz garlic chives (1 bunch), chopped
15g/½oz fresh coriander (cilantro)
15ml/1 tbsp vegetable oil
4 shallots, chopped
400ml/14fl oz can coconut milk
30–45ml/2–3 tbsp Thai fish sauce
45–60ml/3–4 tbsp Thai green curry paste
450g/1lb uncooked large prawns (jumbo shrimp), peeled and deveined
450g/1lb prepared squid
a little lime juice (optional)
salt and ground black pepper
60ml/4 tbsp fried shallot slices, to serve

4 Stir in the curry paste and the peeled prawns and cook for 3 minutes. Add the squid, cook for a further 2 minutes. Add the lime juice, if using, and season.

5 Stir in the remaining fish sauce, chopped chives and the chopped coriander leaves. Serve in warmed, shallow bowls sprinkled with fried shallots.

VARIATIONS

• Instead of squid, you could add 400g/ 14oz firm white fish, such as monkfish, cut into small pieces.
• You could also replace the squid with fresh mussels. Steam 675g/1½lb closed mussels in a tightly covered pan for about 3 minutes, or until the shells have opened. Discard any that remain shut, then remove the mussels from their shells.

1 Pour the stock into a pan and add the slices of fresh ginger, the chopped lemon grass and half the lime leaves.

2 Add half the chopped chives to the pan with the coriander stalks. Bring to the boil, then reduce the heat. Cover the pan, then simmer gently for 20 minutes. Strain the stock.

3 Rinse the pan, then add the oil and shallots. Cook over a medium heat for 5–10 minutes, stirring occasionally, until the shallots are just beginning to brown. Stir in the stock, coconut milk, the remaining lime leaves and half the fish sauce. Heat gently until the soup is just simmering and cook over a low heat for 5–10 minutes.

Energy 282Kcal/1185kJ; Protein 37.9g; Carbohydrate 7.7g, of which sugars 6g; Fat 11.3g, of which saturates 1.9g; Cholesterol 473mg; Calcium 156mg; Fibre 0.7g; Sodium 451mg.

CLAM, MUSHROOM and POTATO CHOWDER

The delicate, sweet taste of clams and the soft earthiness of wild mushrooms combine
with potatoes to make this a great meal on its own — fit for any occasion.

SERVES 4

48 clams, scrubbed
50g/2oz/¼ cup unsalted (sweet)
   butter
1 large onion, chopped
1 celery stick, sliced
1 carrot, sliced
225g/8oz assorted wild and
   cultivated mushrooms
225g/8oz floury potatoes,
   thickly sliced
1.2 litres/2 pints/5 cups boiling light
   chicken or vegetable stock
1 thyme sprig
4 parsley stalks
salt and ground black pepper
thyme sprigs, to garnish

1 Place the clams in a large, heavy pan, discarding any that are open. Add 1cm/½in of water to the pan, then cover and bring to the boil. Cook over a medium heat for 6–8 minutes, shaking the pan occasionally, until the clams open (discard any clams that do not open).

2 Drain the clams over a bowl and remove most of the shells, leaving some in the shells as a garnish. Strain the cooking juices into the bowl, add all the clams and set aside.

3 Add the butter, onion, celery and carrot to the pan and cook gently until softened but not coloured. Add the mushrooms and cook for 3–4 minutes until their juices begin to appear. Add the potato slices, the clams and their juices, the stock, thyme and parsley stalks.

4 Bring to the boil, then reduce the heat, cover and simmer for 25 minutes. Season to taste, ladle into soup bowls, and garnish with thyme sprigs.

Energy 203Kcal/848kJ; Protein 10.8g; Carbohydrate 15.8g, of which sugars 5.2g; Fat 11.2g, of which saturates 6.8g; Cholesterol 60mg; Calcium 66mg; Fibre 2.4g; Sodium 696mg.

SEAFOOD CHOWDER

Chowder takes its name from the French word for cauldron – chaudière – the type of pot once traditionally used for soups and stews. Like most chowders, this is a substantial dish, which is good served with crusty bread for a lunch or supper.

SERVES 4–6

200g/7oz/generous I cup drained, canned sweetcorn
600ml/I pint/2½ cups milk
I5g/½oz/I tbsp butter
I small leek, sliced
I small garlic clove, crushed
2 rindless smoked streaky (fatty) bacon rashers (strips), finely chopped
I small green or red (bell) pepper, seeded and diced
I celery stick, chopped
I15g/4oz/generous ½ cup white long grain rice
5ml/I tsp plain (all-purpose) flour
about 450ml/¾ pint/scant 2 cups hot chicken or vegetable stock
4 large scallops
I15g/4oz white fish fillet, such as monkfish, plaice or flounder
I5ml/I tbsp finely chopped fresh flat leaf parsley
good pinch of cayenne pepper
30–45ml/2–3 tbsp single (light) cream (optional)
salt and ground black pepper
crusty bread, to serve

I Place half the drained sweetcorn in a food processor or blender. Add a little of the milk and then process until the mixture is thick and creamy. Set aside.

COOK'S TIP
If you don't have a food processor, then simply chop the sweetcorn finely and transfer to a bowl. Beat in the milk a little at time until the mixture is thick and creamy.

2 Melt the butter in a large, heavy pan. add the leek, garlic and bacon and gently fry for 4–5 minutes until the leek has softened but not browned.

3 Add the diced green or red pepper and the chopped celery and cook over a very gentle heat for 3–4 minutes more, stirring frequently, until the pepper and celery have softened slightly.

4 Stir in the rice and cook for a few minutes, stirring occasionally, until the grains begin to swell, then sprinkle the flour evenly over the top of the rice and vegetables. Cook for about I minute, stirring all the time, then gradually stir in the remaining milk and the hot stock.

VARIATIONS
You can use other shellfish in place of the scallops if you prefer – try fresh or frozen prawns (shrimp), or mussels or clams, which are equally good in or out of their shells. Allow frozen shellfish to thaw at room temperature before adding to the chowder. Undyed, naturally smoked haddock or cod would make a delicious alternative fish.

5 Bring the mixture to the boil over a medium heat, then lower the heat and stir in the creamed sweetcorn mixture, with the whole sweetcorn. Season well.

6 Cover the pan and simmer very gently for about 20 minutes, or until the rice is tender, stirring occasionally. Add a little more chicken or vegetable stock or water to the pan if the mixture thickens too quickly or if the rice begins to stick to the base of the pan.

7 Cut the corals away from the scallops and set them aside, slice the white flesh into 5mm/¼in pieces. Cut the white fish fillet into bitesize chunks.

8 Add the scallops and chunks of fish to the chowder. Stir gently, then cook for 4 minutes.

9 Stir in the scallop corals, chopped parsley and cayenne pepper. Cook for a few minutes more until the scallops are just cooked and heated through, then stir in the cream, if using. Adjust the seasoning and serve the chowder with thick slices of crusty bread.

Energy 263Kcal/1106kJ; Protein 19.2g; Carbohydrate 32.8g, of which sugars 10.4g; Fat 6.5g, of which saturates 3.2g; Cholesterol 40mg; Calcium 149mg; Fibre 1.6g; Sodium 353mg.

SLOW COOKER FIRST COURSES AND LIGHT MEALS

Whether you are planning a light lunch with friends, or a delicate first course for a special dinner party, the slow cooker is perfect for cooking a beautiful dish while giving you the time to concentrate on something else. Among the tasty appetizers here are a pretty Haddock and Smoked Salmon Terrine, Cardamom Chicken Mousselines and Red Lentil and Goat's Cheese Pâté. For a delicious trouble-free lunch there are mouthwatering Baked Eggs with Creamy Leeks, Mushroom and Courgette Lasagne, and a Savoury Nut Loaf which is sensational when served with a spicy fresh tomato sauce.

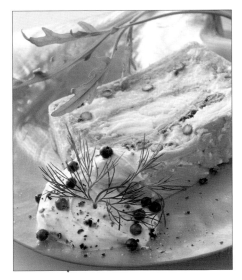

MUSHROOM and BEAN PÂTÉ

This light and tasty pâté is delicious served on wholemeal toast or with crusty French bread and makes an excellent vegetarian appetizer or light lunch served with salad.

SERVES 8

450g/1lb/6 cups mushrooms, sliced
1 onion, finely chopped
2 garlic cloves, crushed
1 red (bell) pepper, seeded and diced
30ml/2 tbsp vegetable stock
30ml/2 tbsp dry white wine
400g/14oz can red kidney beans, rinsed
   and drained
1 egg, beaten
50g/2oz/1 cup fresh wholemeal
   (whole-wheat) breadcrumbs
10ml/2 tsp chopped fresh thyme
10ml/2 tsp chopped fresh rosemary
salt and ground black pepper
salad leaves, fresh herbs and tomato
   wedges, to garnish

VARIATION
To make a lighter, milder-tasting pâté, use cannellini or flageolet beans in place of the kidney beans.

1 Put the mushrooms, onion, garlic, red pepper, vegetable stock and wine in the ceramic cooking pot. Cover and cook on high for about 2 hours, or until the vegetables are almost tender, then set aside for about 10 minutes to cool.

2 Tip the vegetable mixture into a food processor or blender and add the rinsed kidney beans. Process to make a smooth purée, stopping the machine once or twice to scrape down the sides.

3 Lightly grease and line a 900g/2lb loaf tin. Put an inverted saucer or metal pastry ring in the bottom of the ceramic cooking pot. Pour in about 2.5cm/1in of hot water, and switch the slow cooker on to high.

4 Transfer the mushroom mixture to a bowl. Add the egg, breadcrumbs and herbs, and season with salt and pepper. Mix together thoroughly, then spoon the mixture into the prepared tin and cover with cling film (plastic wrap) or foil.

5 Put the tin in the slow cooker and pour in enough boiling water to come just over halfway up the sides of the tin. Cover with the lid and cook on high for 4 hours, or until lightly set.

6 Remove the tin from the ceramic cooking pot and place on a wire rack until completely cool. Refrigerate for several hours, or overnight if preferred. Turn out of the tin, remove the lining paper and serve in slices, garnished with salad leaves, herbs and tomato wedges.

Energy 85Kcal/358kJ; Protein 5.5g; Carbohydrate 12.3g, of which sugars 3.8g; Fat 1.6g, of which saturates 0.4g; Cholesterol 28mg; Calcium 47mg; Fibre 3.7g; Sodium 187mg.

RED LENTIL and GOAT'S CHEESE PÂTÉ

The slightly smoky, earthy flavour of red lentils provides a perfect partner to tangy goat's cheese, making a pâté that will be a hit with vegetarians and non-vegetarians alike.

SERVES 8

225g/8oz/1 cup red lentils
1 shallot, very finely chopped
1 bay leaf
475ml/16fl oz/2 cups near-boiling
   vegetable stock
115g/4oz/½ cup soft goat's cheese
5ml/1 tsp ground cumin
3 eggs, lightly beaten
salt and ground black pepper
melba toast and rocket (arugula) leaves,
   to serve

1 Place the lentils in a sieve (strainer) and rinse well under cold running water. Drain, then tip the lentils into the ceramic cooking pot and add the shallot, bay leaf and hot vegetable stock.

2 Switch the slow cooker to high, cover and cook for 2 hours, or until all the liquid has been absorbed and the lentils are soft and pulpy. Stir once or twice towards the end of cooking time to prevent the lentils sticking to the pot.

3 Turn off the slow cooker. Tip the lentil mixture into a bowl, remove the bay leaf and leave to cool uncovered, so that the steam can evaporate. Meanwhile, wash and dry the ceramic cooking pot.

4 Lightly grease the base of a 900ml/ 1½ pint/3¾ cup loaf tin (pan) with oil and line the base with greaseproof (waxed) paper. Put an upturned saucer or metal pastry ring in the bottom of the ceramic cooking pot and pour in about 2.5cm/1in of hot water. Turn the slow cooker to high.

5 Put the goat's cheese in a bowl with the cumin and beat together until soft and creamy. Gradually mix in the eggs until blended. Stir in the lentil mixture and season well with salt and pepper.

6 Tip the mixture into the prepared tin. Cover with clear film (plastic wrap) or foil. Put the tin in the slow cooker and pour in enough boiling water to come just over halfway up the sides. Cover the slow cooker with the lid and cook for 3–3½ hours, until the pâté is lightly set.

7 Carefully remove the tin from the slow cooker and place on a wire rack to cool completely. Chill in the refrigerator for several hours, or overnight.

8 To serve, turn the pâté out of the tin, peel off the lining paper and cut into slices. Serve with melba toast and rocket.

Energy 136Kcal/573kJ; Protein 9.8g; Carbohydrate 16g, of which sugars 0.9g; Fat 4.1g, of which saturates 2.6g; Cholesterol 13mg; Calcium 34mg; Fibre 1.4g; Sodium 97mg.

CHEESE-STUFFED PEARS

These pears, with their scrumptious creamy topping, make a sublime dish when served with a simple salad. If you don't have a very large slow cooker, choose short squat pears rather than long, tapering ones, so that they will fit in a single layer.

SERVES 4

50g/2oz/¼ cup ricotta cheese
50g/2oz/¼ cup dolcelatte cheese
15ml/1 tbsp honey
½ celery stick, finely sliced
8 green olives, pitted and
    roughly chopped
4 dates, stoned and cut into
    thin strips
pinch of paprika
2 medium barely ripe pears
150ml/¼ pint/⅔ cup apple juice
salad leaves, to serve (optional)

4 Pour the apple juice around the pears, then cover with the lid. Cook on high for 1½–2 hours, or until the fruit is tender. (The cooking time will depend on the ripeness of the pears.)

5 Remove the pears from the slow cooker. If you like, brown them under a hot grill (broiler) for a few minutes. Serve with salad leaves, if you like.

COOK'S TIP
These pears go particularly well with slightly bitter and peppery leaves, such as chicory and rocket. Try them tossed in a walnut oil dressing.

1 Place the ricotta cheese in a bowl and crumble in the dolcelatte. Add the honey, celery, olives, dates and paprika and mix together well until creamy and thoroughly blended.

2 Halve the pears lengthways. Use a melon baller or teaspoon to remove the cores and make a hollow for the filling.

3 Divide the ricotta filling equally between the pears, packing it into the hollow, then arrange the fruit in a single layer in the ceramic cooking pot.

Energy 236Kcal/992kJ; Protein 6.9g; Carbohydrate 35.6g, of which sugars 35.6g; Fat 8.2g, of which saturates 5.0g; Cholesterol 24mg; Calcium 141mg; Fibre 4.1g; Sodium 261mg.

COUNTRY-STYLE TERRINE with LEEKS

Traditionally, this sort of French pork terrine contains pork liver and egg to bind the mixture together. This version uses leeks instead to give a lighter result. In France, cornichons (small dill pickles or gherkins) and mustard are served as accompaniments.

3 Reserve two of the bacon rashers (strips) for the garnish, then finely chop the remaining bacon. Add to the pork mixture along with the leeks, herbs, spices, salt and pepper. Mix together, using a wooden spoon or your fingertips, until thoroughly combined.

4 Lightly grease the base and sides of a 1.2 litre/2 pint/5 cup heatproof dish or loaf tin (pan) with oil and line with greaseproof (waxed) paper. Put an upturned saucer or metal pastry ring in the base of the ceramic cooking pot and pour in 2.5cm/1in of hot water. Turn the slow cooker to high.

5 Spoon the meat mixture into the prepared dish or tin, pressing it into the corners. Tap firmly to settle the mixture, and smooth the top. Arrange the bay leaves and reserved bacon (trimmed to size) on top, then cover with foil.

6 Place the dish or tin in the slow cooker and pour in enough boiling water to come just over halfway up the sides. Cover with the lid and cook for 4–5 hours or until cooked; the juices of the pâté should run clear when pierced with a skewer. Lift out of the ceramic cooking pot and leave to cool in the dish or tin.

7 Put the dish or tin on a tray, then place a foil-covered plate or board (just smaller than the size of the dish or tin) on top of the pâté. Weight the plate or board with two or three large cans or other heavy objects, and chill for several hours, or preferably overnight.

SERVES 8

350g/12oz trimmed leeks
25g/1oz/2 tbsp butter
2 garlic cloves, finely chopped
900g/2lb lean pork leg or shoulder
115g/4oz rinded smoked streaky
   (fatty) bacon
5ml/1 tsp chopped fresh thyme
3 sage leaves, finely chopped
1.5ml/¼ tsp quatre épices (see Cook's Tip)
1.5ml/¼ tsp ground cumin
2.5ml/½ tsp salt
2.5ml/½ tsp ground black pepper
3 bay leaves

COOK'S TIP

Quatre épices is a classic French spice mix containing ground cloves, cinnamon, nutmeg and pepper.

1 Cut the leeks lengthways, wash well and slice thinly. Melt the butter in a large heavy pan, add the leeks, then cover and cook over medium-low heat for about 10 minutes, stirring occasionally. Add the garlic and continue cooking for a further 10 minutes until the leeks are very soft. Set aside to cool.

2 Trim off any excess fat and gristle from the pork, then cut the meat into 2.5cm/1in cubes. Working in two or three batches, put the meat into a food processor fitted with a metal blade; the bowl should be about half-full. Pulse to chop the meat to a coarse purée. Alternatively, pass the meat through the coarse blade of a meat grinder. Transfer the meat to a large mixing bowl and remove any white stringy pieces.

Energy 211Kcal/884kJ; Protein 27.5g; Carbohydrate 1.3g, of which sugars 1g; Fat 10.7g, of which saturates 4.4g; Cholesterol 87mg; Calcium 20mg; Fibre 1.0g; Sodium 395mg.

BAKED EGGS with CREAMY LEEKS

Enjoy these deliciously creamy eggs for a light lunch or supper with toast and a salad.
You can use other vegetables in place of the leeks, such as puréed spinach or ratatouille.

3 Melt the butter in a small frying pan and cook the leeks over a medium heat, stirring frequently, until softened.

4 Add 45ml/3 tbsp of the cream and cook gently for about 5 minutes, or until the leeks are very soft and the cream has thickened a little. Season with salt, black pepper and nutmeg.

5 Spoon the leeks into the ramekins or soufflé dishes, dividing the mixture equally. Using the back of the spoon, make a hollow in the centre of each pile of leeks, then break an egg into the hollow. Spoon 5–10ml/1–2 tsp of the remaining cream over each egg and season lightly with salt and pepper.

6 Cover each dish with clear film (plastic wrap) and place in the slow cooker. If necessary, pour in a little more boiling water to come halfway up the sides of the dishes. Cover and cook for 30 minutes, or until the egg whites are set and the yolks are still soft, or a little longer if you prefer the eggs firmer.

SERVES 4

15g/½oz/1 tbsp butter, plus extra
    for greasing
225g/8oz small leeks, thinly sliced
60–90ml/4–6 tbsp whipping or double
    (heavy) cream
freshly grated nutmeg
4 eggs
salt and ground black pepper

VARIATION
To make herb and cheese eggs, put 15ml/1 tbsp double (heavy) cream in each dish with some chopped herbs. Break in the eggs, add 15ml/1 tbsp double cream and a little grated cheese, then cook as before. This is the perfect recipe for a lazy weekend brunch.

1 Pour about 2.5cm/1in hot water into the ceramic cooking pot and switch the slow cooker to high.

2 Using a pastry brush, lightly butter the base and insides of four 175ml/6fl oz/¾ cup ramekins or individual soufflé dishes.

Energy 239Kcal/990kJ; Protein 8.5g; Carbohydrate 2g, of which sugars 1.6g; Fat 21.9g, of which saturates 11.4g; Cholesterol 266mg; Calcium 58mg; Fibre 1.2g; Sodium 110mg.

SAVOURY NUT LOAF

Ideal as an alternative to the traditional meat roast, this wholesome dish is perfect for special occasions. It is also particularly good served with a spicy fresh tomato sauce.

SERVES 4

30ml/2 tbsp olive oil, plus extra
    for greasing
1 onion, finely chopped
1 leek, finely chopped
2 celery sticks, finely chopped
225g/8oz/3 cups mushrooms, chopped
2 garlic cloves, crushed
425g/15oz can lentils, rinsed and drained
115g/4oz/1 cup mixed nuts, such as
    hazelnuts, cashew nuts and almonds,
    finely chopped
50g/2oz/½ cup plain (all-purpose) flour
50g/2oz/½ cup grated mature (sharp)
    Cheddar cheese
1 egg, beaten
45–60ml/3–4 tbsp chopped fresh
    mixed herbs
salt and ground black pepper
chives and sprigs of fresh flat leaf parsley,
    to garnish

1 Place an upturned saucer or metal pastry ring in the base of the ceramic cooking pot. Pour in about 2.5cm/1in hot water and switch the slow cooker to high.

2 Lightly grease the base and sides of a 900g/2lb loaf tin (pan) or terrine – first making sure it will fit in the slow cooker – and line the base and sides of the tin with baking parchment.

3 Heat the oil in a large pan, add the onion, leek, celery, mushrooms and garlic, then cook for 10 minutes, until the vegetables have softened. Do not let them brown.

4 Remove the pan from the heat, then stir in the lentils, mixed nuts and flour, grated cheese, beaten egg and herbs. Season well with salt and black pepper and mix thoroughly.

5 Spoon the nut mixture into the prepared loaf tin or terrine, pressing right into the corners. Level the surface with a fork, then cover the tin with a piece of foil. Place the loaf tin in the ceramic cooking pot and pour in enough near-boiling water to come just over halfway up the side of the dish.

6 Cover the slow cooker with the lid and cook for 3–4 hours, or until the loaf is firm to the touch.

7 Leave the loaf to cool in the tin for about 15 minutes, then turn out on to a serving plate. Serve the loaf hot or cold, cut into thick slices and garnished with fresh chives and sprigs of flat leaf parsley.

Energy 484Kcal/2019kJ; Protein 23.7g; Carbohydrate 34.1g, of which sugars 5.1g; Fat 29g, of which saturates 5.4g; Cholesterol 69mg; Calcium 238mg; Fibre 8.7g; Sodium 128mg.

PASTA with MUSHROOMS

Slow-cooking a mixture of mushrooms, garlic and sun-dried tomatoes together with white wine and stock makes a rich and well-flavoured pasta sauce. Served with warm ciabatta, this makes a truly excellent vegetarian lunch dish.

SERVES 4

15g/½oz dried porcini mushrooms
120ml/4fl oz/½ cup hot water
2 cloves garlic, finely chopped
2 large pieces drained sun-dried tomato
   in olive oil, sliced into thin strips
120ml/4fl oz/½ cup dry white wine
120ml/4fl oz/½ cup vegetable stock
225g/8oz/2 cups chestnut mushrooms,
   thinly sliced
1 handful fresh flat leaf parsley, roughly
   chopped
450g/1lb/4 cups dried short pasta shapes,
   such as ruote, penne, fusilli or eliche
salt and ground black pepper
rocket and/or fresh flat leaf parsley,
   to garnish

1 Put the dried porcini mushrooms in a large bowl. Pour over the hot water and leave to soak for 15 minutes.

2 While the mushrooms are soaking, put the garlic, tomatoes, wine, stock and chestnut mushrooms into the ceramic cooking pot and switch the slow cooker to high.

3 Tip the porcini mushrooms into a sieve (strainer) set over a bowl, then squeeze them with your hands to release as much liquid as possible. Reserve the soaking liquid. Chop the porcini finely. Add the liquid and the chopped porcini to the ceramic cooking pot, and cover the slow cooker with the lid. Cook on high for 1 hour, stirring halfway through cooking time to make sure that the mushrooms cook evenly.

4 Switch the slow cooker to the low setting and cook for a further 1–2 hours, until the mushrooms are tender.

5 Cook the pasta in boiling salted water for 10 minutes, or according to the instructions on the packet. Drain the pasta and tip it into a warmed large bowl. Stir the chopped parsley into the sauce and season to taste with salt and black pepper. Add the sauce to the pasta and toss well. Serve immediately, garnished with rocket and/or parsley.

VARIATIONS
Fresh wild mushrooms can be used instead of chestnut mushrooms, although they are seasonal and often expensive. A cheaper alternative is to use a box of mixed wild mushrooms, available from good supermarkets and delicatessens.

Energy 420Kcal/1787kJ; Protein 15.1g; Carbohydrate 84.9g, of which sugars 5.1g; Fat 2.6g, of which saturates 0.3g; Cholesterol 0 mg; Calcium 61mg; Fibre 4.8g; Sodium 14mg.

MUSHROOM AND COURGETTE LASAGNE

This is the perfect lasagne for vegetarians. Adding dried porcini to fresh chestnut mushrooms intensifies the flavour. The dish can be made and assembled in the slow cooker early in the day, then left to cook. Serve with crusty Italian bread.

SERVES 6

For the tomato sauce
15g/½oz dried porcini mushrooms
120ml/4fl oz/½ cup hot water
1 onion
1 carrot
1 celery stick
30ml/2 tbsp olive oil
2 x 400g/14oz cans chopped tomatoes
15ml/1 tbsp sun-dried tomato paste
5ml/1 tsp granulated sugar
5ml/1 tsp dried basil or mixed herbs

For the lasagne
30ml/2 tbsp olive oil
50g/2oz/¼ cup butter
450g/1lb courgettes (zucchini), thinly sliced
1 onion, finely chopped
450g/1lb/6 cups chestnut mushrooms,
    thinly sliced
2 garlic cloves, crushed
6–8 non-pre-cook lasagne sheets
50g/2oz/½ cup freshly grated Parmesan
    cheese
salt and ground black pepper
fresh oregano leaves, to garnish
Italian-style bread, to serve (optional)

For the white sauce
40g/1½oz/3 tbsp butter
40g/1½oz/⅓ cup plain (all-purpose) flour
900ml/1½ pints/3¾ cups milk
freshly grated nutmeg

1 Put the dried porcini mushrooms in a bowl. Pour over the hot water and leave to soak for 15 minutes. Tip the porcini and liquid into a sieve (strainer) set over a bowl and squeeze the mushrooms with your hands to release as much liquid as possible. Chop the mushrooms finely and set aside. Strain the soaking liquid through a fine sieve and reserve.

2 Chop the onion, carrot and celery finely. Heat the olive oil in a pan and fry the vegetables until softened. Place in a food processor with the tomatoes, tomato paste, sugar, herbs, porcini and soaking liquid, and blend to a purée.

3 For the lasagne, heat the olive oil and half the butter in a large pan. Add half the courgette slices and season to taste. Cook over a medium heat, turning the courgettes frequently, for 5–8 minutes, until lightly coloured on both sides. Remove from the pan with a slotted spoon and transfer to a bowl. Repeat with the remaining courgettes.

4 Melt the remaining butter in the pan, and cook the onion for 3 minutes, stirring. Add the chestnut mushrooms, chopped porcini and garlic and cook for 5 minutes. Add to the courgettes.

5 For the white sauce, melt the butter in a large pan, then add the flour and cook, stirring, for 1 minute. Turn off the heat and gradually whisk in the milk. Bring to the boil and cook, stirring, until the sauce is smooth and thick. Season with salt, black pepper and nutmeg.

6 Ladle half of the tomato sauce into the ceramic cooking pot and spread out to cover the base. Add half the vegetable mixture, spreading it evenly. Top with about one-third of the white sauce, then about half the lasagne sheets, breaking them to fit the cooking pot. Repeat these layers, then top with the remaining white sauce and sprinkle with grated Parmesan cheese.

7 Cover the ceramic cooking pot with the lid and cook on low for 2–2½ hours or until the lasagne is tender. If you like, brown the top under a medium grill (broiler). Garnish with a sprinkling of fresh oregano leaves, and serve with fresh Italian-style bread.

Energy 421Kcal/1757kJ; Protein 15.5g; Carbohydrate 32.9g, of which sugars 15g; Fat 26.2g, of which saturates 12.4g; Cholesterol 49mg; Calcium 346mg; Fibre 3.8g; Sodium 310mg.

CHICKEN and PISTACHIO PÂTÉ

This easy version of a classic French charcuterie can be made with white chicken breast portions or a mixture of light and dark meat for a more robust flavour. Serve it as an elegant appetizer for a special dinner, or with salad for a light lunch.

SERVES 8

oil, for greasing
800g/1¾lb boneless chicken meat
40g/1½oz/¾ cup fresh white breadcrumbs
120ml/4fl oz/½ cup double (heavy) cream
1 egg white
4 spring onions (scallions) finely chopped
1 garlic clove, finely chopped
75g/3oz cooked ham, cut into small cubes
75g/3oz/½ cup shelled pistachio nuts
30ml/2 tbsp green peppercorns
    in brine, drained
45ml/3 tbsp chopped fresh tarragon
pinch of grated nutmeg
salt and ground black pepper
French bread and salad, to serve

1 Line the base of a 1.2 litre/2 pint/ 5 cup round or oval heatproof dish (such as a soufflé dish) with greaseproof (waxed) paper, then lightly brush the base and sides with oil.

2 Put an upturned saucer or metal pastry ring in the base of the ceramic cooking pot and pour in about 2.5cm/ 1in of hot water. Switch the slow cooker to high.

3 Cut the chicken meat into cubes, then put in a food processor and blend until fairly smooth. (You may need to do this in batches depending on the capacity of your food processor.) Alternatively, pass the meat through the medium blade of a food mill. Remove any white stringy pieces from the minced (ground) meat.

4 Place the breadcrumbs in a large mixing bowl, pour over the cream and leave to soak.

5 Meanwhile, lightly whisk the egg white with a fork, then add it to the soaked breadcrumbs. Add the minced chicken, spring onions, garlic, ham, pistachio nuts, green peppercorns, tarragon, nutmeg, salt and pepper. Using a wooden spoon or your fingers, mix thoroughly.

6 Spoon the mixture into the prepared dish and cover with foil. Place the dish in the ceramic cooking pot and pour a little more boiling water around the dish to come just over halfway up the sides. Cover the slow cooker with the lid and cook for about 4 hours until the pâté is cooked through.

7 To check whether the pâté is cooked, pierce with a skewer or fine knife – the juices should run clear. Carefully lift out of the slow cooker and leave the pâté to cool in the dish. Chill in the refrigerator, preferably overnight.

8 To serve, turn out the pâté on to a serving dish and cut into slices. Serve with crusty French bread and salad.

VARIATIONS
• You can use turkey breast fillet in place of some or all of the chicken, and serve with a tangy cranberry sauce.
• Pale green pistachio nuts look very pretty in this pâté but you can use hazelnuts instead; they are equally good.
• This pâté also makes a perfect dish for a special picnic or a cold buffet. Serve with a delicately flavoured herb mayonnaise.

Energy 321Kcal/1344kJ; Protein 36.6g; Carbohydrate 3.7g, of which sugars 1.2g; Fat 17.9g, of which saturates 7.7g; Cholesterol 125mg; Calcium 37mg; Fibre 0.7g; Sodium 379mg.

CARDAMOM CHICKEN MOUSSELINES

These light chicken mousselines, served with a tangy tomato vinaigrette, make an elegant appetizer. They should be served warm rather than hot, so as soon as they are cooked, turn off the slow cooker and leave to cool for half an hour before eating.

SERVES 6

350g/12oz skinless, boneless
  chicken breast portions
1 shallot, finely chopped
115g/4oz/1 cup full-fat soft cheese
1 egg, lightly beaten
2 egg whites
crushed seeds of 2 cardamom pods
60ml/4 tbsp white wine
150ml/¼ pint/⅔ cup double (heavy) cream
oregano sprigs, to serve

For the tomato vinaigrette
350g/12oz ripe tomatoes
10ml/2 tsp balsamic vinegar
30ml/2 tbsp olive oil
sea salt and ground black pepper

1 Roughly chop the chicken and put in a food processor with the finely chopped shallot. Process until the mixture becomes fairly smooth.

2 Add the soft cheese, beaten egg, egg whites, crushed cardamom seeds and white wine to the chicken mixture and season with salt and ground black pepper. Process again until the ingredients are thoroughly blended.

3 Gradually add the cream, using the pulsing action, until the mixture has a smooth and creamy texture. Transfer the mixture to a bowl, cover with clear film (plastic wrap) and chill in the refrigerator for about 30 minutes.

4 Meanwhile, prepare six 150ml/¼ pint/ ⅔ cup ramekins or dariole moulds, checking first that they will all fit in the slow cooker. Lightly grease the base of each one, then line. Pour about 2cm/¾in hot water into the ceramic cooking pot and switch the cooker to high.

5 Divide the chicken mixture among the prepared dishes and level the tops. Cover each with foil and place in the ceramic cooking pot. Pour in a little more near-boiling water to come half-way up the dishes. Cover and cook for 2½–3 hours, or until the mousselines are firm; a skewer or thin knife inserted into the middle should come out clean.

6 Meanwhile, peel, quarter, seed and finely dice the tomatoes. Place them in a bowl, sprinkle with balsamic vinegar and season with a little salt. Stir well.

7 To serve, unmould the mousselines on to warmed plates. Place small spoonfuls of the tomato vinaigrette around each plate, then drizzle over a little olive oil and grind over a little black pepper. Garnish with sprigs of fresh oregano.

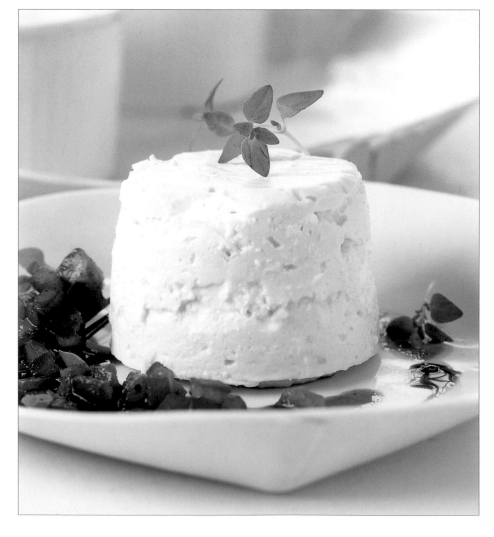

Energy 191Kcal/795kJ; Protein 18.1g; Carbohydrate 2g, of which sugars 2g; Fat 11.6g, of which saturates 5g; Cholesterol 96mg; Calcium 30mg; Fibre 0.7g; Sodium 130mg.

FISH TERRINE

This colourful layered terrine makes a spectacular appetizer or main course on a special occasion. It is particularly good for entertaining because it can be made in advance, chilled until ready to serve, then arranged on plates at the last minute.

SERVES 6

450g/1lb skinless white fish fillets
225g/8oz thinly sliced smoked salmon
2 egg whites, chilled
1.5ml/¼ tsp each salt and ground
    white pepper
pinch of freshly grated nutmeg
250ml/8fl oz/1 cup double (heavy) cream
50g/2oz small tender fresh spinach leaves
lemon mayonnaise, to serve

1 Cut the white fish fillets into 2.5cm/1in pieces, removing any bones. Spread out the fish pieces on a plate, cover with clear film (plastic wrap) and chill in the freezer for 15 minutes until very cold.

2 Lightly oil a 1.2 litre/2 pint/5 cup terrine or loaf tin (pan). Line the base and sides of the tin with the smoked salmon slices, making sure they overlap each other all the way around and letting them hang over the edges of the tin.

3 Remove the white fish from the freezer, then place in a food processor and blend to make a very smooth purée. (You may need to stop the machine and scrape down the sides two or three times as you do this.)

4 Add the egg whites, one at a time, processing after each addition, then add the salt, pepper and nutmeg. With the machine running, pour in the cream and stop as soon as it is blended. (If over-processed the cream will thicken.)

5 Transfer the fish mixture to a large glass bowl. Put the spinach leaves into the food processor and process to make a smooth purée. Add one-third of the fish mixture to the spinach and process briefly until just combined, scraping down the sides once or twice.

6 Pour about 2.5cm/1in of very hot water into the ceramic cooking pot. Place an upturned saucer or metal pastry ring in the base, then turn the slow cooker on to high.

7 Spread half the plain fish mixture in the base of the tin. Spoon the green fish mixture over the top and smooth it level, then cover with the remaining plain mixture. Fold the overhanging pieces of smoked salmon over the top to enclose the mixture. Tap the tin to settle the mixture and remove any air pockets, then cover the tin with a double layer of lightly oiled foil.

8 Put the tin in the slow cooker and pour in enough boiling water to come just over halfway up the sides. Cook for 3–3½ hours, or until a skewer inserted into the terrine comes out clean. Leave the terrine to cool in the tin, then chill in the refrigerator until firm.

9 To serve the terrine, turn out on to a board, remove the lining paper and slice. Arrange the slices on individual plates and serve with lemon mayonnaise.

Energy 340Kcal/1409kJ; Protein 23.2g; Carbohydrate 0.8g, of which sugars 0.8g; Fat 27.1g, of which saturates 14.7g; Cholesterol 110mg; Calcium 50mg; Fibre 0.2g; Sodium 201mg.

HADDOCK and SMOKED SALMON TERRINE

This substantial terrine makes a superb dish for a summer buffet. It is very good served with dill mayonnaise or a tangy mango salsa instead of the crème fraîche or sour cream.

SERVES 6

15ml/1 tbsp sunflower oil, for greasing
350g/12oz smoked salmon
900g/2lb haddock fillets, skinned
2 eggs, lightly beaten
105ml/7 tbsp low-fat crème fraîche
   or sour cream
30ml/2 tbsp drained bottled capers
30ml/2 tbsp drained soft green or pink
   peppercorns
salt and ground white pepper
low-fat crème fraîche or sour cream,
   peppercorns, fresh dill and rocket
   (arugula), to serve

1 Pour about 2.5cm/1in of warm water into the ceramic cooking pot. Place an upturned saucer or metal pastry ring in the base, then turn the slow cooker on to high. Lightly grease a 1 litre/1¾ pint/ 4 cup loaf tin (pan) or terrine. Use some of the smoked salmon slices to line the tin or terrine, letting them hang over the edge. Reserve the remaining salmon.

2 Cut two long slices of the haddock the length of the tin or terrine, and cut the remaining haddock into small pieces. Season with salt and pepper.

3 Combine the eggs, crème fraîche or sour cream, capers and soft peppercorns in a bowl. Season with salt and pepper, then stir in the small pieces of haddock. Spoon half the mixture into the mould and smooth the surface with a spatula.

4 Wrap the long haddock fillets in the reserved smoked salmon. (Don't worry if there isn't enough salmon to cover them completely.) Lay the wrapped haddock fillets on top of the fish mixture in the tin or terrine.

5 Spoon the rest of the fish mixture into the tin or terrine and smooth the surface. Fold the overhanging pieces of smoked salmon over the top and cover tightly with a double thickness of foil.

6 Tap the terrine to settle the contents, then place in the slow cooker and pour in enough boiling water to come just over halfway up the sides. Cook for 3–4 hours, or until a skewer inserted into the terrine comes out clean.

7 Remove the terrine from the slow cooker, but do not remove the foil cover. Place two or three large heavy cans on the foil to weight it, and leave until cold. Chill in the refrigerator for 24 hours.

8 About 1 hour before serving, remove the terrine from the refrigerator, lift off the weights and carefully remove the foil. Gently invert the terrine on to a serving plate and lift off the mould.

9 Cut the terrine into thick slices using a sharp knife. Serve with crème fraîche or sour cream, peppercorns, dill sprigs and rocket leaves.

Energy 316Kcal/1326kJ; Protein 46.1g; Carbohydrate 0.4g, of which sugars 0.4g; Fat 14.5g, of which saturates 6.2g; Cholesterol 170mg; Calcium 653mg; Fibre 0g; Sodium 1228mg.

ONE-POT, CLAY-POT FIRST COURSES AND LIGHT MEALS

When you are cooking a first course, appetizer or snack for family or friends, the most successful dishes are often the simplest, so anything that can be cooked in one pot is a sure winner. Whether you opt for a simple pasta dish such as Spaghetti with Cheese and Black Pepper, a hot and spicy clay-pot treat such as Potato Wedges with Tomato and Chilli Salsa, or Pork Ribs with Ginger and Chilli, or use your wok to make a stunning Sweet-and-sour Pork Stir-fry or Stir-fried Crispy Duck, everyone will be glad you chose the easy option.

  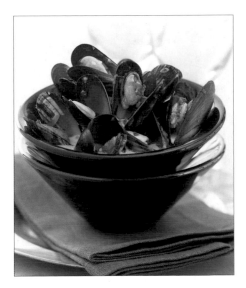

BRAISED BABY LEEKS in RED WINE with AROMATICS

Coriander seeds and oregano lend a Greek flavour to this dish of braised leeks. Serve it as part of a mixed hors d'oeuvre or as a partner for baked white fish.

SERVES 6

12 baby leeks or 6 thick leeks
15ml/1 tbsp coriander seeds,
   lightly crushed
5cm/2in piece of cinnamon stick
120ml/4fl oz/½ cup olive oil
3 fresh bay leaves
2 strips pared orange rind
5–6 fresh or dried oregano sprigs
5ml/1 tsp sugar
150ml/¼ pint/⅔ cup fruity red wine
10ml/2 tsp balsamic or
   sherry vinegar
30ml/2 tbsp coarsely chopped fresh
   oregano or marjoram
salt and ground black pepper

1 If using baby leeks, simply trim the ends, but leave them whole. Cut thick leeks into 5–7.5cm/2–3in lengths.

2 Place the coriander seeds and cinnamon in a pan wide enough to take all the leeks in a single layer. Cook over a medium heat for 2–3 minutes, until the spices give off a fragrant aroma, then stir in the olive oil, bay leaves, orange rind, fresh or dried oregano, sugar, wine and balsamic or sherry vinegar. Bring to the boil and simmer for 5 minutes.

3 Add the leeks to the pan. Bring back to the boil, reduce the heat and cover the pan. Cook the leeks gently for 5 minutes. Uncover and simmer gently for another 5–8 minutes, until the leeks are just tender when tested with the tip of a sharp knife.

4 Use a slotted spoon to transfer the leeks to a serving dish. Boil the pan juices rapidly until reduced to about 75–90ml/5–6 tbsp. Add salt and pepper to taste and pour the liquid over the leeks. Leave to cool.

5 The leeks can be left to stand for several hours. If you chill them, bring them back to room temperature again before serving. Sprinkle the chopped herbs over the leeks just before serving.

COOK'S TIP
Genuine balsamic vinegar from Modena in northern Italy has been produced for over 1,000 years. It has a high sugar content and wonderfully strong bouquet. It is a very dark brown colour and has a deep, rich flavour with hints of herbs and port. Nowadays you can find quite good balsamic vinegar in supermarkets. It is expensive, but the flavour is so rich that you only need to use a little.

Energy 185Kcal/768kJ; Protein 2.9g; Carbohydrate 5.7g, of which sugars 4.5g; Fat 15.1g, of which saturates 2.2g; Cholesterol 0mg; Calcium 52mg; Fibre 3.9g; Sodium 7mg.

POTATO WEDGES with TOMATO and CHILLI SALSA

This is a healthier version of traditionally baked potato skins; the clay pot keeps the potato flesh wonderfully moist and fluffy.

SERVES 4

6 potatoes, about 115g/4oz each
45ml/3 tbsp olive oil
salt and ground black pepper

For the tomato and chilli salsa
4 juicy ripe tomatoes
1 sun-dried tomato in olive
    oil, drained
3 spring onions (scallions)
1–2 red or green chillies, halved
    and seeded
15ml/1 tbsp extra virgin
    olive oil
10ml/2 tsp lemon juice

COOK'S TIP
Varieties of floury potatoes that produce a fluffy texture when baked are best for these wedges. Good types to use include Maris Piper, Désirée, King Edward and Pentland Squire.

1 Soak the clay pot or a potato pot in cold water for 20 minutes, then drain. Scrub the potatoes and dry with kitchen paper. Cut each potato lengthwise into four wedges. Brush with a little of the oil and sprinkle with salt and pepper.

2 Place the potatoes in the clay pot and cover with the lid. Place in an unheated oven, set the temperature to 200°C/400°F/Gas 6 and cook for 55–60 minutes, or until the potatoes are tender.

3 Meanwhile, finely chop the tomatoes, sun-dried tomato, spring onions and chilli and mix together with the olive oil and lemon juice. Cover and leave to stand to allow the flavours to mingle.

4 Uncover the potatoes, brush with the remaining olive oil and bake, uncovered, for a further 15 minutes until slightly golden. Divide the potato wedges and salsa among four serving bowls and plates, and serve immediately.

Energy 238Kcal/1001kJ; Protein 4g; Carbohydrate 30.8g, of which sugars 4.9g; Fat 11.9g, of which saturates 1.8g; Cholesterol 0mg; Calcium 23mg; Fibre 2.6g; Sodium 28mg.

BRAISED VINE LEAVES

This popular eastern Mediterranean dish keeps moist when cooked slowly in a clay pot.

SERVES 4

12 fresh vine leaves
30ml/2 tbsp olive oil
1 small onion, chopped
30ml/2 tbsp pine nuts
1 garlic clove, crushed
115g/4oz cooked long grain rice
2 tomatoes, skinned, seeded and
    finely chopped
15ml/1 tbsp chopped fresh mint
1 lemon, sliced
150ml/¼ pint/⅔ cup dry white wine
200ml/7fl oz/scant 1 cup vegetable stock
salt and ground black pepper
lemon wedges, to serve

1 Soak the clay pot in cold water for 20 minutes, then drain. Blanch the vine leaves in a pan of boiling water for about 2 minutes or until they darken and soften. Rinse the leaves under cold running water and leave to drain.

2 Heat the oil in a frying pan, add the onion and fry for 5–6 minutes, stirring frequently, until softened. Add the pine nuts and crushed garlic and cook, stirring continuously until the onions and pine nuts are a golden brown colour.

3 Stir into the cooked rice, with the tomatoes, mint and seasoning, to taste.

4 Place a spoonful of the rice mixture at the stalk end of each vine leaf. Fold the sides over the filling and roll up tightly.

5 Place the stuffed vine leaves close together, seam side down in the clay pot. Place the lemon slices on top. Pour over the wine and sufficient stock to just cover the lemon slices.

6 Cover with the lid and place in an unheated oven. Set the oven to 200°C/400°F/Gas 6 and cook for 30 minutes. Reduce to 160°C/325°F/Gas 3 and cook for a further 30 minutes. Serve hot or cold, with lemon wedges.

Energy 258Kcal/1072kJ; Protein 4.6g; Carbohydrate 28.8g, of which sugars 5.5g; Fat 11.1g, of which saturates 1.2g; Cholesterol 0mg; Calcium 49mg; Fibre 2.1g; Sodium 11mg.

PAN-FRIED HAM and VEGETABLES with EGGS

A perfect family supper dish, this is very easy to prepare. Serve with plenty of hot, crusty bread: Italian ciabatta is particularly good.

3 Add the courgettes and peppers to the onion and garlic and cook over a medium heat for 3–4 minutes.

4 Stir in the paprika, tomatoes, tomato purée, ham and seasoning. Bring to the boil and simmer gently for 15 minutes.

5 Reduce the heat to low. Make four wells in the tomato mixture, break an egg into each and season. Cook over a gentle heat until the white begins to set.

6 Preheat the grill (broiler). Sprinkle the cheese over the vegetables and grill (broil) for about 5 minutes until the eggs are set. Serve immediately with bread.

SERVES 4

30ml/2 tbsp olive oil
1 onion, roughly chopped
2 garlic cloves, crushed
175g/6oz cooked ham
225g/8oz courgettes (zucchini)
1 red (bell) pepper, seeded and
    thinly sliced
1 yellow (bell) pepper, seeded and
    thinly sliced
10ml/2 tsp paprika
400g/14oz can chopped tomatoes
15ml/1 tbsp sun-dried tomato purée (paste)
4 eggs
115g/4oz/1 cup coarsely grated
    Cheddar cheese
salt and ground black pepper
crusty bread, to serve

1 Heat the olive oil in a deep frying pan. Add the onion and garlic and cook for 4 minutes, stirring frequently, or until just beginning to soften.

2 While the onions and garlic are cooking, cut the ham and courgettes into 5cm/2in long batons. Set the ham aside.

Energy 350Kcal/1457kJ; Protein 24.4g; Carbohydrate 11.4g, of which sugars 10.7g; Fat 22.8g, of which saturates 9.3g; Cholesterol 244mg; Calcium 276mg; Fibre 3.1g; Sodium 817mg.

WILD MUSHROOM and SUN-DRIED TOMATO SOUFFLES

These impressive little soufflés are baked in individual earthenware pots. They are packed with rich, Italian flavours and are remarkably easy to prepare and cook.

SERVES 4

25g/1oz/½ cup dried ceps
40g/1½oz/3 tbsp butter, plus extra
    for greasing
20ml/4 tsp grated Parmesan cheese
40g/1½oz/⅓ cup plain (all-purpose) flour
250ml/8fl oz/1 cup milk
50g/2oz/½ cup grated mature (sharp)
    Cheddar cheese
4 eggs, separated
2 sun-dried tomatoes in oil, drained
    and chopped
15ml/1 tbsp chopped fresh chives
salt and ground black pepper

1 Place the ceps in a bowl, pour over enough warm water to cover and leave to soak for 15 minutes. Grease four individual earthenware soufflé dishes with a little butter. Sprinkle the grated Parmesan cheese into the soufflé dishes and rotate each dish to coat the sides with cheese. Preheat the oven to 190°C/375°F/Gas 5.

2 Melt the 40g/1½oz/3 tbsp of butter in a large pan, remove from the heat and stir in the flour. Cook over a low heat for 1 minute, stirring constantly. Remove the pan from the heat and gradually stir in the milk. Return to the heat and bring to the boil, stirring constantly, until the sauce has thickened.

COOK'S TIP
A variety of different dried mushrooms are available – any can be used instead of the ceps.

3 Remove the sauce from the heat, then stir in the grated Cheddar cheese and plenty of seasoning. Beat in the egg yolks, one at a time, then stir in the chopped sun-dried tomatoes and the chives. Drain the soaked mushrooms, then coarsely chop them and add them to the cheese sauce.

4 Whisk the egg whites until they stand in soft peaks. Mix one spoonful into the sauce then carefully fold in the remainder. Divide the mixture among the soufflé dishes and bake for 25 minutes, or until the soufflés are golden brown on top, well risen and just firm to the touch. Serve immediately – before they sink.

Energy 290Kcal/1207kJ; Protein 14.7g; Carbohydrate 11.6g, of which sugars 3.9g; Fat 20.8g, of which saturates 11.2g; Cholesterol 232mg; Calcium 274mg; Fibre 0.6g; Sodium 305mg.

LINGUINE with ROCKET

This is a first course that you will find in many a fashionable restaurant in Italy. It is very quick and easy to make at home and is worth trying for yourself.

SERVES 4

350g/12oz fresh or dried linguine
120ml/4fl oz/½ cup extra virgin olive oil
1 large bunch rocket (arugula), about
    150g/5oz, stalks removed, shredded
    or torn
75g/3oz/1 cup freshly grated
    Parmesan cheese
salt and ground black pepper

VARIATION

Oil-based pasta sauces such as this one are best served with fine, long pastas such as linguine. Spaghetti, capelli d'angelo, bucatini or fettucine would work just as well in this recipe.

1 Cook the pasta in a large pan of salted boiling water for 8–10 minutes until it is just tender, or according to the instructions on the packet. As soon as the pasta is cooked, drain thoroughly.

2 Heat about 60ml/4 tbsp of the olive oil in the pasta pan, then add the drained pasta, followed by the rocket. Toss over a medium to high heat for 1–2 minutes or until the rocket is just wilted, then remove the pan from the heat.

3 Tip the pasta and rocket into a warmed, large serving bowl. Add half the freshly grated Parmesan cheese and the remaining olive oil. Add a little salt and black pepper to taste.

4 Toss the mixture quickly to mix and serve immediately. Hand round the remaining Parmesan cheese.

COOK'S TIP

Buy rocket by the bunch from the greengrocer. The type sold in small cellophane packets in supermarkets is usually very expensive. Always check when buying rocket that all the leaves are bright green. In hot weather, rocket leaves quickly turn yellow.

Energy 585Kcal/2451kJ; Protein 19g; Carbohydrate 65.4g, of which sugars 3.5g; Fat 29.2g, of which saturates 7.1g; Cholesterol 19mg; Calcium 311mg; Fibre 3.3g; Sodium 260mg.

SPAGHETTI with GARLIC and OIL

This simple Roman pasta dish can be made in less than 15 minutes. Use fresh chillies if you prefer and, since the oil is so important, the very best extra virgin olive oil.

SERVES 4

400g/14oz fresh or dried spaghetti
90ml/6 tbsp extra virgin olive oil
2–4 garlic cloves, crushed
1 dried red chilli
1 small handful fresh flat leaf parsley,
    roughly chopped
salt

COOK'S TIP

Don't use salt when you are preparing the hot oil, garlic and chilli mixture, because the salt will not dissolve sufficiently. This is why plenty of salt is recommended for cooking the pasta.

1 Cook the pasta in a large pan of salted boiling water, according to the packet instructions, until it is just tender, adding plenty of salt to the water (see Cook's Tip).

2 When the pasta is just tender, drain it by tipping it into a large colander, then transfer it to a warmed, large serving bowl. Rinse out the pasta pan and dry.

3 Heat the olive oil in the pan. Add the crushed garlic and the whole dried chilli and stir over a low heat for a minute or two until the garlic is just beginning to brown. Remove the chilli and discard.

4 Pour the hot olive oil and cooked garlic mixture over the pasta, add the roughly chopped fresh flat leaf parsley and toss vigorously until the pasta glistens, then serve immediately.

Energy 495Kcal/2084kJ; Protein 12.4g; Carbohydrate 74.5g, of which sugars 3.6g; Fat 18.5g, of which saturates 2.6g; Cholesterol 0mg; Calcium 50mg; Fibre 3.5g; Sodium 7mg.

SPAGHETTI with BUTTER and HERBS

This is a versatile recipe. You can use just one favourite herb or several — basil, flat leaf parsley, rosemary, thyme, marjoram or sage would all work well.

SERVES 4

400g/14oz fresh or dried spaghetti
    alla chitarra
2 good handfuls mixed fresh herbs,
    plus extra herb leaves and flowers
    to garnish
115g/4oz/½ cup butter, diced
salt and ground black pepper
freshly grated Parmesan cheese, to serve

1 Cook the pasta in a large pan of salted boiling water for 10–12 minutes until just tender or according to the instructions on the packet.

2 Using a large sharp knife, chop the fresh herbs roughly or finely, whichever you prefer.

COOK'S TIP
Square-shaped chitarra spaghetti is the traditional type for this sauce, but you can use any type of long thin pasta, such as ordinary spaghetti or spaghettini, or even linguine.

VARIATION
If you like the flavour of garlic, add one or two crushed cloves to the pan when melting the butter.

3 Drain the pasta in a colander and then return the pasta to the pan. Add the butter and heat until it melts and sizzles, then add the chopped herbs and salt and pepper to taste.

4 Toss the pasta over a medium heat until it is thoroughly coated in the butter and herbs.

5 Serve the pasta immediately in warmed shallow bowls, sprinkled with some extra herb leaves and flowers. Hand around a bowl of freshly grated Parmesan separately.

SPAGHETTI with CHEESE and BLACK PEPPER

This dish is very quick and easy to cook, perfect for a midweek supper. The flavours are very simple, so choose a strong-tasting cheese and a good extra virgin olive oil. Pecorino is traditional in this dish, but Parmesan could also be used.

SERVES 4

400g/14oz fresh or
    dried spaghetti
115g/4oz/1 cup freshly grated
    Pecorino cheese
about 5ml/1 tsp coarsely ground
    black pepper
extra virgin olive oil, to taste
salt

1 Cook the fresh or dried pasta in a large pan of salted boiling water until it is just tender, or according to the instructions on the packet.

2 As soon as the spaghetti is cooked, drain it, leaving it a little moister than usual, then tip the spaghetti straight into a large warmed serving bowl.

3 Add the freshly grated cheese, lots of black pepper, and salt to taste. Toss the pasta well to mix, then moisten with as much olive oil as you like. Serve the pasta immediately.

Spaghetti with Butter and Herbs: Energy 565Kcal/2371kJ; Protein 12.9g; Carbohydrate 75g, of which sugars 4.1g; Fat 25.8g, of which saturates 15.2g; Cholesterol 61mg; Calcium 80mg; Fibre 4.2g; Sodium 186mg.
Spaghetti with Cheese and Black Pepper: Energy 472Kcal/1997kJ; Protein 23.3g; Carbohydrate 74.1g, of which sugars 3.3g; Fat 11.2g, of which saturates 6.1g; Cholesterol 29mg; Calcium 370mg; Fibre 2.9g; Sodium 317mg.

DEVILLED KIDNEYS on BRIOCHE CROUTES

The expression "devilled" dates from the 18th century. It was used to describe dishes or foods that were seasoned with hot spices giving a fiery flavour that was associated with the devil and the heat of hell – in this case, cayenne pepper and Worcestershire sauce provide the "fire".

SERVES 4

8 mini brioche slices
25g/1oz/2 tbsp butter
1 shallot, finely chopped
2 garlic cloves, finely chopped
115g/4oz/1½ cups mushrooms, halved
1.5ml/¼ tsp cayenne pepper
15ml/1 tbsp Worcestershire sauce
8 lamb's kidneys, halved and trimmed
150ml/¼ pint/⅔ cup double (heavy) cream
30ml/2 tbsp chopped fresh parsley,
    to garnish

1 Preheat the grill (broiler) to high and toast the brioche slices until they are a golden brown colour on both sides, and keep warm.

2 Melt the butter in a large frying pan until it is just foaming. Add the finely chopped shallot, finely chopped garlic and halved mushrooms, then cook for about 5 minutes, or until the shallot is just beginning to soften. Stir in the cayenne pepper and the Worcestershire sauce and allow the mixture to simmer for about 1 minute, stirring continuously with a wooden spoon.

3 Add the kidneys to the pan and cook for 3–5 minutes on each side. Finally, stir in the cream and simmer for about 2 minutes, or until the sauce is heated through and slightly thickened.

4 Remove the brioche croûtes from the wire rack and place on warmed plates. Top with the kidneys. Sprinkle with the chopped parsley and serve immediately.

COOK'S TIPS
• If you can't find mini brioches, you can use a large brioche instead. Slice it thickly and stamp out croûtes using a 5cm/2in round cutter.
• If you prefer, the brioche croûtes can be fried rather than toasted. Melt 25g/1oz/ 2 tbsp butter in the frying pan and fry the croûtes until crisp and golden on both sides. Remove from the pan and drain on kitchen paper.

Energy 367Kcal/1526kJ; Protein 12.7g; Carbohydrate 18.6g, of which sugars 2.5g; Fat 27.4g, of which saturates 16.3g; Cholesterol 222mg; Calcium 66mg; Fibre 1g; Sodium 299mg.

PORK RIBS with GINGER and CHILLI

Ginger, garlic and chilli are used to flavour the sweet-and-sour sauce that coats these ribs. Cook the pork ribs in a covered clay pot first to tenderize the meat, then uncover the dish so the ribs become deliciously sticky and brown.

SERVES 4

16–20 small meaty pork ribs, about
   900g/2lb total weight
1 onion, finely chopped
5cm/2in piece fresh root ginger, peeled
   and grated
2 garlic cloves, crushed
2.5–5ml/½–1 tsp chilli powder
60ml/4 tbsp soy sauce
45ml/3 tbsp tomato purée (paste)
45ml/3 tbsp clear honey
30ml/2 tbsp red wine vinegar
45ml/3 tbsp dry sherry
60ml/4 tbsp water
salt and ground black pepper

1 Soak the clay pot in cold water for 20 minutes, then drain. Place the ribs in the clay pot, arranging them evenly.

2 Mix together the onion, ginger, garlic, chilli powder, soy sauce, tomato purée, honey, wine vinegar, sherry and water.

3 Pour the sauce over the ribs and toss to coat them. Cover the clay pot and place in an unheated oven. Set the oven to 220°C/425°F/Gas 7. Cook for 1 hour.

4 Remove the lid, baste the ribs and season with salt and pepper. Cook uncovered for 15–20 minutes, basting the ribs two to three times during the cooking. Serve with steamed rice or baked potatoes.

COOK'S TIPS
• For a stronger flavour, place the ribs in a shallow dish, coat them evenly with the sauce and leave to marinate in a cool place for 1–2 hours before cooking in the clay pot.
• If you cannot get hold of fresh root ginger, ginger in sunflower oil (sold in small jars) is available from major supermarkets. It is in a paste form and can simply be added when the flavour of fresh root ginger is required. Use 10ml/ 2 tsp instead of 5cm/2in of fresh ginger.

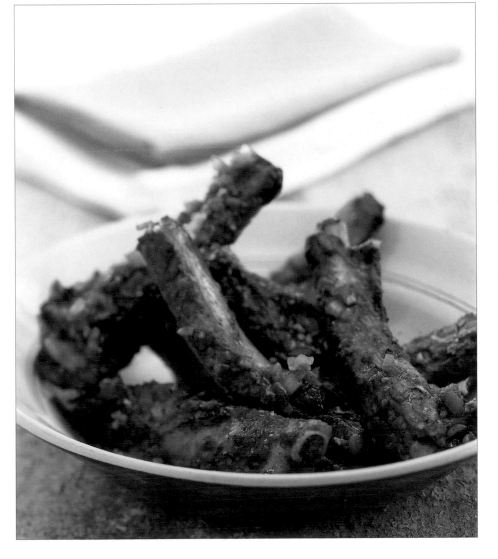

Energy 633Kcal/2637kJ; Protein 42.9g; Carbohydrate 11.5g, of which sugars 11.2g; Fat 45.2g, of which saturates 14.1g; Cholesterol 149mg; Calcium 43mg; Fibre 0.5g; Sodium 250mg.

LAMB'S LIVER and BACON CASSEROLE

The trick when cooking liver is to seal it quickly, then simmer it gently and briefly. Prolonged and/or fierce cooking makes liver hard and grainy. Boiled new potatoes tossed in lots of butter go well with this simple casserole.

SERVES 4

30ml/2 tbsp extra virgin olive oil or
   sunflower oil
225g/8oz rindless unsmoked lean bacon
   rashers (strips), cut into pieces
2 onions, halved and sliced
175g/6oz/2 cups chestnut
   mushrooms, halved
450g/1lb lamb's liver, trimmed
   and sliced
25g/1oz/2 tbsp butter
15ml/1 tbsp soy sauce
30ml/2 tbsp plain (all-purpose) flour
150ml/¼ pint/⅔ cup hot, well-flavoured
   chicken stock
salt and ground black pepper

1 Heat the oil in a frying pan, add the bacon and fry until crisp. Add the sliced onions to the pan and cook for about 10 minutes, stirring frequently, or until softened. Add the mushrooms to the pan and fry for a further 1 minute.

2 Use a slotted spoon to remove the bacon and vegetables from the pan and keep warm. Add the liver to the fat remaining in the pan and cook over a high heat for 3–4 minutes, turning once to seal the slices on both sides. Remove the liver from the pan and keep warm.

3 Melt the butter in the pan, add the soy sauce and flour and blend together. Stir in the stock and bring to the boil, stirring until thickened. Return the liver, bacon and vegetables to the pan and heat through for 1 minute. Season with salt and pepper to taste, and serve immediately with new potatoes and lightly cooked green beans.

Energy 418Kcal/1739kJ; Protein 34.2g; Carbohydrate 9.3g, of which sugars 2.6g; Fat 27.3g, of which saturates 9.5g; Cholesterol 527mg; Calcium 34mg; Fibre 1.3g; Sodium 1257mg.

FILLET of BEEF STROGANOFF

Legend has it that this Russian recipe was devised by Count Paul Stroganov's cook to use beef frozen by the Siberian climate. The only way that it could be prepared was cut into very thin strips. The strips of lean beef were served in a brandy-flavoured cream sauce.

SERVES 8

1.2kg/2½lb beef fillet (tenderloin)
30ml/2 tbsp plain (all-purpose) flour
large pinch each of cayenne pepper
   and paprika
75ml/5 tbsp sunflower oil
1 large onion, chopped
3 garlic cloves, finely chopped
450g/1lb/6½ cups chestnut
   mushrooms, sliced
75ml/5 tbsp brandy
300ml/½ pint/1¼ cups beef stock
   or consommé
300ml/½ pint/1¼ cups sour cream
45ml/3 tbsp chopped fresh flat leaf parsley
salt and ground black pepper

3 Cook the onion and garlic over a low heat, stirring occasionally until the onion has softened. Add the mushrooms and stir-fry over a high heat for 1–2 minutes. Transfer the vegetables and their juices to a dish and set aside.

4 Wipe the pan, then add and heat the remaining oil. Coat a batch of meat with flour, then fry over a high heat until well browned. Remove from the pan, then coat and fry another batch. When the last batch is cooked, replace all the meat and vegetables. Add the brandy and simmer until it has almost evaporated.

1 Thinly slice the beef fillet across the grain, then cut it into fine strips. Season the flour with the cayenne and paprika.

2 Heat half the oil in a large frying pan and add the chopped onion and garlic.

5 Stir in the beef stock or consommé and seasoning and cook for 10–15 minutes, stirring frequently with a wooden spoon, or until the meat is tender and the sauce is thick and glossy. Add the sour cream, stir well and sprinkle with the chopped fresh flat leaf parsley. Serve immediately with plain boiled rice and a simple salad.

COOK'S TIP

If you do not have a very large frying pan, it may be easier to cook this dish in a large, flameproof casserole.

Energy 399Kcal/1659kJ; Protein 34.6g; Carbohydrate 6.5g, of which sugars 3g; Fat 23.9g, of which saturates 9.8g; Cholesterol 114mg; Calcium 56mg; Fibre 1.1g; Sodium 85mg.

SWEET-and-SOUR PORK STIR-FRY

This is a great idea for a quick family lunch. Remember to cut the carrots into thin matchstick strips so that they cook in time.

SERVES 4

450g/1lb pork fillet (tenderloin)
30ml/2 tbsp plain (all-purpose) flour
45ml/3 tbsp oil
1 onion, roughly chopped
1 garlic clove, crushed
1 green (bell) pepper, seeded and sliced
350g/12oz carrots, cut into thin strips
225g/8oz can bamboo shoots, drained
15ml/1 tbsp white wine vinegar
15ml/1 tbsp soft brown sugar
10ml/2 tsp tomato purée (paste)
30ml/2 tbsp light soy sauce
salt and ground black pepper

1 Thinly slice the pork. Season the flour and toss the pork in it to coat.

2 Heat the oil in a wok or large frying pan and cook the pork over a medium heat for about 5 minutes, until golden and cooked through. Remove the pork with a slotted spoon and drain on kitchen paper. You may need to do this in several batches.

3 Add the onion and garlic to the pan and cook for 3 minutes. Stir in the pepper and carrots and stir-fry over a high heat for 6–8 minutes, or until beginning to soften slightly.

4 Return the meat to the pan with the bamboo shoots. Add the remaining ingredients with 120ml/4fl oz/½ cup water and bring to the boil. Simmer gently for 2–3 minutes, or until piping hot. Adjust the seasoning, if necessary, and serve immediately.

VARIATION
Finely sliced strips of skinless chicken breast fillet can be used in this recipe instead of the pork.

Energy 324Kcal/1357kJ; Protein 27.9g; Carbohydrate 23.9g, of which sugars 16.2g; Fat 13.6g, of which saturates 3g; Cholesterol 71mg; Calcium 63mg; Fibre 4.2g; Sodium 646mg.

PORK CHOW MEIN

This is a very speedy dish to cook, but make sure that you prepare all the ingredients before you start to cook. If you don't have a wok, use a very large frying pan instead.

SERVES 4

175g/6oz medium egg noodles
350g/12oz pork fillet (tenderloin)
30ml/2 tbsp sunflower oil
15ml/1 tbsp sesame oil
2 garlic cloves, crushed
8 spring onions (scallions), sliced
1 red (bell) pepper, seeded and
    roughly chopped
1 green (bell) pepper, seeded and
    roughly chopped
30ml/2 tbsp dark soy sauce
45ml/3 tbsp dry sherry
175g/6oz/¾ cup beansprouts
45ml/3 tbsp chopped fresh flat leaf parsley
15ml/1 tbsp toasted sesame seeds

1 Soak the noodles according to the packet instructions, then drain well.

2 Thinly slice the pork fillet. Heat the sunflower oil in a wok or large frying pan and cook the pork over a high heat until golden brown and cooked through.

3 Add the sesame oil to the pan, with the garlic, spring onions and peppers. Cook over a high heat for 3–4 minutes, or until beginning to soften.

4 Reduce the heat slightly, then stir in the soaked noodles, with the dark soy sauce and dry sherry. Stir-fry for about 2 minutes. Add the beansprouts and cook for a further 1–2 minutes. If the noodles begin to stick to the pan, add a splash of water. Stir in the chopped parsley and serve the chow mein sprinkled with the toasted sesame seeds.

Energy 404Kcal/1696kJ; Protein 26.9g; Carbohydrate 40.2g, of which sugars 8.5g; Fat 14.8g, of which saturates 3.3g; Cholesterol 68mg; Calcium 45mg; Fibre 3.7g; Sodium 683mg.

MINTED LAMB STIR-FRY

Lamb and mint have a long-established partnership that works particularly well in this full-flavoured stir-fry. Serve simply, with noodles or rice.

SERVES 2

275g/10oz lamb neck fillet or boneless
   leg steaks
30ml/2 tbsp sunflower oil
10ml/2 tsp sesame oil
1 onion, roughly chopped
2 garlic cloves, crushed
1 red chilli, seeded and
   finely chopped
75g/3oz fine green beans, halved
225g/8oz fresh spinach, shredded
30ml/2 tbsp oyster sauce
30ml/2 tbsp Thai fish sauce (*nam pla*)
15ml/1 tbsp lemon juice
5ml/1 tsp sugar
45ml/3 tbsp chopped fresh mint
salt and ground black pepper
mint sprigs, to garnish
noodles or rice, to serve

1 Trim the lamb of any excess fat and cut into thin slices. Heat the sunflower and sesame oils in a wok or large frying pan and cook the lamb over a high heat until browned. Remove with a slotted spoon and drain on kitchen paper.

2 Add the onion, garlic and chilli to the wok, cook for 2–3 minutes, then add the beans and stir-fry for 3 minutes.

3 Stir in the shredded spinach with the browned meat, oyster sauce, Thai fish sauce, lemon juice and sugar. Stir-fry for a further 3–4 minutes, or until the lamb is cooked through.

4 Sprinkle in the chopped mint and toss lightly, then adjust the seasoning. Serve piping hot, garnished with mint sprigs and accompanied by noodles or rice.

Energy 438Kcal/1819kJ; Protein 31.9g; Carbohydrate 9.3g, of which sugars 8g; Fat 30.6g, of which saturates 9.1g; Cholesterol 105mg; Calcium 229mg; Fibre 3.6g; Sodium 1879mg.

STIR-FRIED CRISPY DUCK

This stir-fry would be delicious wrapped in flour tortillas or steamed Chinese pancakes, with a little extra warm plum sauce.

2 Heat the oil in a wok or large frying pan and cook the duck over a high heat until golden and crisp. Keep stirring to prevent the duck from sticking. Remove the duck with a slotted spoon and drain on kitchen paper. You may need to cook the duck in several batches.

3 Add the spring onions to the pan and cook for 2 minutes. Stir in the cabbage and cook for 5 minutes, or until it is softened and golden.

SERVES 2

275–350g/10–12oz boneless duck breast
30ml/2 tbsp plain (all-purpose) flour
60ml/4 tbsp oil
1 bunch spring onions (scallions), halved
lengthwise and cut into 5cm/2in strips,
plus extra to garnish
275g/10oz/2½ cups finely shredded
green cabbage
225g/8oz can water chestnuts, drained
and sliced
50g/2oz/½ cup unsalted cashew nuts
115g/4oz cucumber, cut into strips
45ml/3 tbsp plum sauce
15ml/1 tbsp light soy sauce
salt and ground black pepper

1 Remove any skin from the duck breast, then trim off a little of the fat. Thinly slice the meat into even-size pieces. Season the flour with plenty of salt and pepper and use it to completely coat each piece of duck.

4 Return the duck to the pan with the water chestnuts, cashews and cucumber. Stir-fry for 2 minutes. Add the plum sauce and soy sauce and season to taste, then heat for 2 minutes. Serve garnished with the sliced spring onions.

Energy 682Kcal/2846kJ; Protein 36.9g; Carbohydrate 41.3g, of which sugars 26.3g; Fat 44.4g, of which saturates 7.5g; Cholesterol 151mg; Calcium 174mg; Fibre 5.8g; Sodium 844mg.

MUSSELS and CLAMS with LEMON GRASS and COCONUT CREAM

Lemon grass has an incomparable flavour and aroma and is widely used in Thai cooking, especially with seafood. If you have difficulty obtaining fresh baby clams for this recipe, then use a few extra mussels instead.

SERVES 6

1.8–2kg/4–4½lb mussels
450g/1lb baby clams
120ml/4fl oz/½ cup dry white wine
1 bunch spring onions (scallions), chopped
2 lemon grass stalks, chopped
6 kaffir lime leaves, chopped
10ml/2 tsp Thai green curry paste
200ml/7fl oz/scant 1 cup coconut cream
30ml/2 tbsp chopped fresh
   coriander (cilantro)
salt and ground black pepper
garlic chives, to garnish

1 Clean the mussels by pulling off the beards, scrubbing the shells well and removing any barnacles. Discard any broken mussels or any that do not close when tapped sharply. Wash the clams.

COOK'S TIP
The kaffir lime tree is native to South-east Asia and both the leaves and fruit rind are used in cooking. Dried kaffir lime leaves, available from supermarkets, can be used in place of fresh – add them at the beginning of the cooking time and remove and discard just before serving.

2 Put the white wine in a large, heavy pan with the spring onions, chopped lemon grass stalks, kaffir lime leaves and Thai green curry paste. Simmer all the ingredients together until the wine has almost evaporated.

3 Add the mussels and clams to the pan, cover tightly and steam the shellfish over a high heat for 5–6 minutes, or until they open.

4 Using a slotted spoon, transfer the cooked mussels and clams to a heated serving bowl and keep hot. At this stage discard any shellfish that remain closed. Strain the cooking liquid into the clean pan and gently simmer until it is reduced to about 250ml/8fl oz/1 cup.

5 Stir in the coconut cream and fresh coriander, with plenty of salt and pepper to taste. Increase the heat and simmer gently until the sauce is piping hot. Pour the sauce over the mussels and clams and serve immediately, garnished with garlic chives.

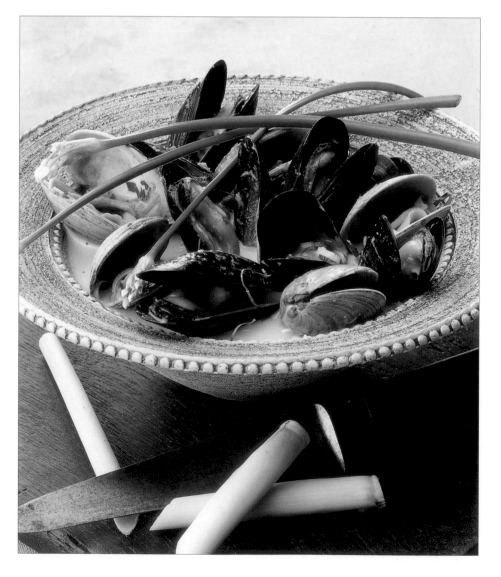

Energy 132Kcal/563kJ; Protein 19.6g; Carbohydrate 3.1g, of which sugars 3g; Fat 3.4g, of which saturates 0.6g; Cholesterol 44mg; Calcium 239mg; Fibre 0.3g; Sodium 288mg.

SAFFRON MUSSELS with WHITE WINE and GARLIC

Mussels are easy to cook in a clay pot and they stay deliciously moist. The saffron adds a lovely pungent flavour as well as its characteristic yellow colour to the creamy sauce.

SERVES 4

few threads of saffron
1kg/2¼lb mussels in their shells
25g/1oz/2 tbsp butter
2 shallots, finely chopped
2 garlic cloves, finely chopped
200ml/7fl oz/scant 1 cup dry white wine
60ml/4 tbsp double (heavy) cream or
   crème fraîche
30ml/2 tbsp chopped fresh parsley
salt and ground black pepper
French bread, to serve

1 Soak a large clay pot in cold water for about 20 minutes, then drain. Put the saffron in a small bowl, add 15ml/1 tbsp boiling water and leave to soak.

2 Scrub the mussels, pull off the beards and discard any open mussels that don't close when tapped. Place all the closed mussels in the soaked clay pot.

3 Melt the butter in a frying pan, add the shallots and garlic and cook gently for 5 minutes, to soften. Stir in the wine and saffron water and bring to the boil. Pour the liquid over the mussels.

4 Cover the clay pot and place in an unheated oven. Set the oven to 220°C/425°F/Gas 7. Cook the mussels for 15 minutes, then remove the pot from the oven and, firmly holding the lid on, shake the pot. Return the pot to the oven and cook for another 10 minutes, or until the mussels have opened.

COOK'S TIP
Saffron is the stigma of a type of crocus. It is an expensive spice and is sold as thin, wiry threads. It has a mild aroma and adds a slightly pungent flavour to both sweet and savoury dishes, and also to buns, cakes and breads. However, the main characteristic of saffron is the distinctive yellow colour it imparts once diluted in a liquid.

5 Using a slotted spoon, transfer the mussels to four warmed serving bowls (discard any that have not opened). Mix the cream or crème fraîche and parsley into the cooking liquid and season to taste. Pour the cooking liquid over the mussels and serve immediately with French bread to soak up the sauce.

Energy 224Kcal/935kJ; Protein 13.5g; Carbohydrate 1.8g, of which sugars 1.4g; Fat 14.7g, of which saturates 8.5g; Cholesterol 64mg; Calcium 164mg; Fibre 0.2g; Sodium 201mg.

PENNE with CREAM and SMOKED SALMON

This modern way of serving pasta is popular all over Italy. The three essential ingredients combine together beautifully, and the dish is very quick and easy to make. Accompany with a green salad, ciabatta bread and some sparkling wine for an easy but impressive meal.

SERVES 4

350g/12oz/3 cups dried penne
115g/4oz thinly sliced
   smoked salmon
2–3 fresh thyme sprigs
25g/1oz/2 tbsp unsalted (sweet)
   butter, diced
150ml/¼ pint/⅔ cup extra-thick single
   (light) cream
salt and ground black pepper

VARIATION
Although penne is the traditional pasta to serve with this sauce, it also goes very well with fresh ravioli stuffed with spinach and ricotta.

COOK'S TIP
This dish can be served as an appetizer or a main course.

1 Cook the dried pasta in a large pan of lightly salted boiling water for 10 minutes until it is just tender or according to the instructions on the packet.

2 Meanwhile, using sharp kitchen scissors, cut the smoked salmon slices into thin strips, about 5mm/¼in wide. Strip the leaves from the thyme sprigs and rinse in cold water.

3 Drain the pasta and return it to the pan. Add the butter and heat gently until melted, then stir in the cream with about one-quarter of the smoked salmon and thyme leaves, then season with pepper. Heat gently for 3–4 minutes, stirring all the time. Check the seasoning. Divide among four warmed bowls, top with the remaining salmon and thyme leaves and serve immediately.

Energy 459Kcal/1936kJ; Protein 19.1g; Carbohydrate 65.7g, of which sugars 3.8g; Fat 15.2g, of which saturates 8.2g; Cholesterol 44mg; Calcium 62mg; Fibre 2.6g; Sodium 592mg.

PRAWNS with BAKED GARLIC and ROASTED TOMATOES

Packed full of wonderful Mediterranean flavours, this simple, gutsy dish makes a marvellous first course for a dinner party.

SERVES 4

4 small garlic bulbs
60–75ml/4–5 tbsp olive oil
500g/1¼lb baby plum tomatoes on
    the vine
16 raw large prawns (jumbo shrimp), in
    their shells
a few sprigs of fresh thyme
salt and ground black pepper
lemon wedges and warm crusty bread,
    to serve

COOK'S TIPS
• If you can't find small garlic bulbs use
one large one and bake it in the oven for
about 50 minutes, or until the cloves are
soft and creamy.
• Spread a little of the baked garlic on the
bread and drizzle with olive oil.

1 Cut a small cross in the top of each
bulb of garlic. Place the bulbs in a garlic
baker, brush with half the olive oil and
sprinkle with a little salt and ground
black pepper.

2 Place the garlic baker in an unheated
oven, set the temperature to 200°C/
400°F/Gas 6 and bake the garlic for
about 40 minutes. The garlic cloves
should be soft and creamy – if not, bake
for a further 10 minutes.

3 Place the tomatoes and prawns in a
shallow earthenware baking dish. Drizzle
over the remaining olive oil, sprinkle with
thyme sprigs and season. Place the dish
in the oven after the garlic has been
cooking for 30 minutes; turn the prawns
after 7 minutes.

4 Arrange the garlic, tomatoes and
prawns on a warmed serving plate and
serve with lemon wedges and plenty of
crusty bread.

Energy 183Kcal/761kJ; Protein 11.7g; Carbohydrate 8g, of which sugars 4.3g; Fat 11.8g, of which saturates 1.8g; Cholesterol 98mg; Calcium 53mg; Fibre 2.3g; Sodium 107mg.

COD and PRAWN GREEN COCONUT CURRY

This quick curry takes just minutes to make. If you can't find green masala curry paste at your local supermarket, simply substitute another variety – the curry will be just as good.

SERVES 4

675g/1½lb cod fillets, skinned
90ml/6 tbsp green masala curry paste
175ml/6fl oz/¾ cup canned coconut
    milk or 200ml/7fl oz/scant 1 cup
    coconut cream
175g/6oz raw or cooked, peeled
    prawns (shrimp)
fresh coriander (cilantro), to garnish
basmati rice, to serve

VARIATION

Any firm fish, such as monkfish, can be used instead of cod. Whole fish steaks can be cooked in the sauce, but allow an extra 5 minutes' cooking time and baste them with the sauce from time to time.

1 Using a sharp knife, cut the skinned cod fillets into 4cm/1½in pieces.

2 Put the green masala curry paste and the coconut milk or cream into a frying pan. Heat to simmering and simmer gently for 5 minutes, stirring occasionally.

3 Add the cod pieces and prawns (if raw) to the cream mixture and cook gently for 5 minutes. If using cooked prawns, then add them after this time and heat through. Garnish the curry with fresh coriander and serve immediately with basmati rice.

Energy 255Kcal/1066kJ; Protein 39g; Carbohydrate 2.4g, of which sugars 2.3g; Fat 9.9g, of which saturates 1.5g; Cholesterol 163mg; Calcium 78mg; Fibre 0.4g; Sodium 235mg.

FISH STEW with LEMON GRASS

Lemon grass and ginger give this delicate stew of fish, prawns, new potatoes and broccoli an appetizing aromatic flavour.

SERVES 4

25g/1oz/2 tbsp butter
175g/6oz onions, chopped
20ml/4 tsp plain (all-purpose) flour
400ml/14fl oz/1⅔ cups light fish stock
150ml/¼ pint/⅔ cup white wine
2.5cm/1in piece fresh root ginger, peeled
    and finely chopped
2 lemon grass stalks, trimmed and
    finely chopped
450g/1lb new potatoes, scrubbed and
    halved if necessary
450g/1lb white fish fillets
175g/6oz large, cooked, peeled
    prawns (shrimp)
275g/10oz small broccoli florets
150ml/¼ pint/⅔ cup double (heavy) cream
60ml/4 tbsp chopped fresh garlic chives
salt and ground black pepper
crusty bread, to serve

3 Remove the skin from the fish fillets and cut the fillets into large chunks. Add the chunks of fish to the pan with the prawns, broccoli and cream. Stir gently.

4 Simmer gently for 5 minutes, taking care not to break up the fish. Adjust the seasoning and sprinkle in the chives. Serve with plenty of crusty bread.

1 Melt the butter in a large pan. Add the onions and cook for 3–4 minutes. Stir in the flour and cook for 1 minute.

2 Stir in the stock, wine, ginger, lemon grass and potatoes. Season and bring to the boil. Cover and cook for 15 minutes, or until the potatoes are almost tender.

Energy 515Kcal/2148kJ; Protein 34.9g; Carbohydrate 27.6g, of which sugars 5.9g; Fat 27.4g, of which saturates 16.2g; Cholesterol 202mg; Calcium 131mg; Fibre 3.7g; Sodium 218mg.

GINGERED SEAFOOD STIR-FRY

This would make a lovely summer supper. Serve with lots of bread to mop up the juices and some chilled dry white wine. It would also be good as a first course for four.

SERVES 2

15ml/1 tbsp sunflower oil
5ml/1 tsp sesame oil
2.5cm/1in piece fresh root ginger, peeled
    and finely chopped
1 bunch spring onions (scallions), sliced
1 red (bell) pepper, seeded and
    finely chopped
115g/4oz small "queen" scallops
8 large, raw prawns (shrimp), peeled
115g/4oz squid rings
15ml/1 tbsp lime juice
15ml/1 tbsp light soy sauce
60ml/4 tbsp coconut milk
salt and ground black pepper
mixed salad leaves and crusty bread,
    to serve

1 Heat the sunflower and sesame oils in a wok or large frying pan and cook the chopped ginger and sliced spring onions for 2–3 minutes, stirring frequently, until golden brown. Add the chopped red pepper and cook, stirring constantly, for a further 3 minutes.

2 Add the scallops, prawns and squid rings to the wok or frying pan and cook over a medium heat for about 3 minutes stirring occasionally with a wooden spoon, until all the seafood is opaque and just cooked through. Add the lime juice and light soy sauce.

3 Pour in the coconut milk and mix well, then simmer the sauce, uncovered, for 2 minutes, until the sauce begins to thicken slightly.

4 Season the stir-fry well. Arrange the mixed salad leaves on two individual serving plates and spoon over the seafood mixture with the juices. Serve the seafood with plenty of crusty bread to mop up the juices.

Energy 284Kcal/1194kJ; Protein 37.6g; Carbohydrate 11.9g, of which sugars 8.8g; Fat 9.9g, of which saturates 1.6g; Cholesterol 303mg; Calcium 120mg; Fibre 2.2g; Sodium 884mg.

TUNA FRITTATA

This is the ultimate meal in a pan – easy to prepare and easy to serve. For a stronger cheese flavour, try a creamy goat's cheese in place of the soft white cheese.

SERVES 2–3

25g/1oz/2 tbsp butter
15ml/1 tbsp olive oil
1 onion, finely chopped
175g/6oz courgettes (zucchini), halved
    lengthwise and sliced
75g/3oz/1¼ cups brown cap (cremini)
    mushrooms, sliced
50g/2oz asparagus tips
4 eggs, beaten
75g/3oz/⅜ cup soft white (farmer's) cheese
    or ricotta cheese
30ml/2 tbsp chopped fresh thyme
200g/7oz can tuna, in olive oil, drained and
    roughly flaked
115g/4oz cooked, peeled
    prawns (shrimp)
salt and ground black pepper

1 Heat the butter and oil in a non-stick frying pan. Add the chopped onion and cook for 3 minutes, then add the sliced courgettes, mushrooms and asparagus tips and cook for a further 10 minutes, or until beginning to soften and brown.

2 Beat together the eggs, soft or ricotta cheese, chopped thyme and plenty of seasoning until they are well combined.

3 Stir the tuna into the pan, add the prawns and season well. Heat through gently. Pour over the egg mixture and cook over a gentle heat for 5 minutes.

4 Push the egg away from the sides to allow the uncooked egg to run on to the pan. Preheat the grill (broiler) to medium and grill (broil) the omelette to set and brown the surface. Serve cut in wedges.

Energy 465Kcal/1935kJ; Protein 39.6g; Carbohydrate 3.9g, of which sugars 2.5g; Fat 32.6g, of which saturates 13g; Cholesterol 435mg; Calcium 174mg; Fibre 1.4g; Sodium 1033mg.

SLOW COOKER FISH AND SHELLFISH

Delicious, healthy and perfectly suited to cooking in a slow cooker, fish and shellfish can be used in a fabulous range of dishes. The gentle heat of this method cooks the delicate flesh to perfection every time. Although large whole fish, such as salmon, are too big for the slow cooker, smaller fish, such as herring and red mullet, fillets, fish steaks and shellfish are perfect. Unlike meat, fish cooks relatively quickly in the slow cooker, so is ideal for combining with rice or pasta. It is incredibly versatile and can be cooked in all manner of ways, to make both light and hearty dishes. Try Salmon Risotto with Cucumber for a light and sophisticated summer dish, or comforting Fish Pie as a winter warmer.

  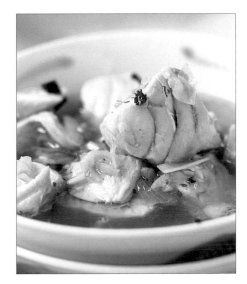

CREAMY ANCHOVY and POTATO BAKE

This classic Scandinavian dish of potatoes, onions and anchovies cooked with cream makes a hearty winter lunch or simple supper, served with a refreshing salad. In Norway and Sweden, it is often served as a hot appetizer.

2 Use half of the butter to grease the base and sides of the ceramic cooking pot, and layer half the potatoes and onions in the base of the dish.

3 Drain the anchovies, reserving 15ml/ 1 tbsp of the oil. Cut the anchovies into thin strips and lay these over the potatoes and onions, then layer the remaining potatoes and onions on top.

4 Combine the single cream and anchovy oil in a small jug (pitcher) and season with a little ground black pepper. Pour the mixture evenly over the potatoes and dot the surface with butter.

5 Cover and cook on high for 3½ hours, or until the potatoes and onions are tender. Brown under a hot grill (broiler), if you like, then drizzle over the double cream and sprinkle with parsley and pepper. Serve with fresh crusty bread.

SERVES 4

1kg/2¼lb maincrop potatoes
2 onions
25g/1oz/2 tbsp butter
2 x 50g/2oz cans anchovy fillets
150ml/¼ pint/⅔ cup single (light) cream
150ml/¼ pint/⅔ cup double (heavy) cream
15ml/1 tbsp chopped fresh parsley
ground black pepper
fresh crusty bread, to serve

COOK'S TIP

This recipe can also be served as an appetizer for six, or as a side dish to accompany a main meal.

1 Peel the potatoes and cut into slices slightly thicker than 1cm/½in. Cut the slices into strips slightly more than 1cm/½in wide. Peel the onions and cut into very thin rings.

Energy 378Kcal/1580kJ; Protein 11.3g; Carbohydrate 37.9g, of which sugars 6.4g; Fat 21.2g, of which saturates 11.4g; Cholesterol 54mg; Calcium 1460mg; Fibre 11.5g; Sodium 133mg.

SALMON RISOTTO with CUCUMBER

A classic risotto is time-consuming to make because the stock needs to be added very gradually and requires constant attention from the cook. Here, the wine and stock are added in one go, making it far easier, yet still giving a delicious, creamy texture.

SERVES 4

25g/1oz/2 tbsp butter
small bunch of spring onions (scallions), finely sliced
½ cucumber, peeled, seeded and chopped
225g/8oz/generous 1 cup easy-cook (converted) Italian rice
750ml/1¼ pints/3 cups boiling vegetable or fish stock
120ml/4fl oz/½ cup white wine
450g/1lb salmon fillet, skinned and diced
45ml/3 tbsp chopped fresh tarragon
salt and ground black pepper

1 Put the butter in the ceramic cooking pot and switch the slow cooker to high. Leave to melt for 15 minutes, then stir in the spring onions and cucumber. Cover and cook for 30 minutes.

2 Add the rice to the pot and stir, then pour in the stock and wine. Cover with the lid and cook for 45 minutes, stirring once halfway through cooking.

3 Stir the diced salmon into the risotto and season with salt and pepper. Cook for a further 15 minutes, or until the rice is tender and the salmon just cooked. Switch off the slow cooker and leave the risotto to stand for 5 minutes.

4 Remove the lid, add the chopped tarragon and mix lightly. Spoon the risotto into individual warmed serving bowls or plates and serve immediately.

COOK'S TIP
Frozen peas can be used instead of cucumber, if you like. These should be defrosted and stirred into the risotto at the same time as the salmon.

Energy 506Kcal/2122kJ; Protein 28.4g; Carbohydrate 51.3g, of which sugars 2.8g; Fat 20g, of which saturates 5.9g; Cholesterol 70mg; Calcium 91mg; Fibre 1.4g; Sodium 266mg.

SPECIAL FISH PIE

Fish pie topped with melting, cheesy breadcrumbs is the ultimate comfort food and is always a firm family favourite. Serve with plenty of lightly steamed green vegetables such as asparagus spears, green beans or sugar snap peas.

SERVES 4

350g/12oz haddock fillet, skinned
30ml/2 tbsp cornflour (cornstarch)
175g/6oz/1 cup drained, canned corn
115g/4oz/1 cup frozen peas, defrosted
115g/4oz peeled cooked prawns (shrimp)
115g/4oz/½ cup cream cheese
150ml/¼ pint/⅔ cup milk
15g/½oz/¼ cup wholemeal (whole-wheat)
   breadcrumbs
50g/2oz/½ cup grated Cheddar cheese
salt and freshly ground black pepper

1 Cut the haddock into bitesize pieces and place in a mixing bowl. Sprinkle with the cornflour and toss thoroughly to coat the pieces evenly.

2 Add the corn, peas and prawns to the coated haddock pieces and mix together well. In a separate mixing bowl, blend together the cream cheese and milk, season with salt and ground black pepper and pour over the fish mixture. Stir well to combine.

3 Spoon the fish mixture into the ceramic cooking pot. Switch the slow cooker to high, cover with the lid and cook for 2 hours.

4 Meanwhile, combine the breadcrumbs and grated cheese. Spoon the mixture evenly over the top of the dish. Remove the ceramic cooking pot from the slow cooker and brown the top under a moderate grill (broiler) for 5 minutes until golden and crisp. Serve hot.

COOK'S TIP
To make a more economical dish, you can leave out the prawns and replace them with the same weight of haddock. Alternatively, to make a more extravagant dish, use more shellfish, replacing some of the haddock with the same weight of scallops and shelled mussels.

Energy 306Kcal/1283kJ; Protein 31.3g; Carbohydrate 12.2g, of which sugars 2.1g; Fat 15.1g, of which saturates 9.2g; Cholesterol 153mg; Calcium 224mg; Fibre 0.6g; Sodium 736mg.

SMOKED TROUT CANNELLONI

This delicious dish makes a great change to the classic meat or spinach and cheese cannelloni that are usually served. You can also buy smoked trout ready-filleted, which can save on preparation time. If you buy fillets you will need only about 225g/8oz.

SERVES 4

25g/1oz/2 tbsp butter, plus extra
    for greasing
1 large onion, finely chopped
400g/14oz can chopped tomatoes
2.5ml/½ tsp dried mixed herbs
1 smoked trout, weighing
    about 400g/14oz
75g/3oz/¾ cup frozen peas, thawed
75g/3oz/1½ cups fresh white breadcrumbs
16 cannelloni tubes
15g/½oz/1½ tbsp freshly grated
    Parmesan cheese
salt and ground black pepper
mixed salad, to serve (optional)

For the sauce
40g/1½oz/3 tbsp butter
40g/1½oz/⅓ cup plain (all-purpose)
    flour
550ml/18fl oz/2½ cups milk
1 bay leaf
freshly grated nutmeg

VARIATION
To make a more economical dish, use
a drained 200g/7oz can of tuna in oil in
place of the trout.

1 Melt the butter in a frying pan, add the onion and cook gently for about 10 minutes until soft, stirring frequently. Stir in the chopped tomatoes and dried herbs and simmer uncovered for a further 10 minutes, or until the sauce is very thick.

2 Meanwhile, skin the smoked trout using a sharp knife. Carefully flake the flesh and discard all the bones. Add the fish to the tomato sauce, then stir in the peas and breadcrumbs and season with plenty of salt and black pepper.

3 Lightly grease the base and halfway up the sides of the ceramic cooking pot. Carefully spoon the trout filling into the cannelloni tubes and arrange the filled tubes in the base of the slow cooker, placing them side by side.

4 To make the sauce, melt the butter in the pan and add the flour. Cook for 1 minute, stirring, then gradually whisk in the milk and add the bay leaf. Cook over a medium heat, whisking constantly until the sauce thickens, then simmer for 2–3 minutes, continuing to stir. Remove the bay leaf and season to taste with salt, pepper and nutmeg.

5 Pour the sauce over the cannelloni and sprinkle with grated Parmesan. Cover and cook on high or auto for 1 hour.

6 Switch the slow cooker to low or leave on auto and cook for 1–1½ hours, or until the cannelloni is tender. If you like, brown the top under a moderate grill (broiler) before serving. Serve with a mixed salad, if using.

Energy 669Kcal/2811kJ; Protein 41.5g; Carbohydrate 74.5g, of which sugars 15.1g; Fat 24.9g, of which saturates 11.9g; Cholesterol 116mg; Calcium 353mg; Fibre 3.1g; Sodium 390mg.

CANNELLONI SORRENTINA-STYLE

There is more than one way of making cannelloni. For this fresh-tasting dish, sheets of cooked lasagne are rolled around a tomato, ricotta and anchovy filling. You can, of course, use traditional cannelloni tubes, if you prefer.

SERVES 4–6

15ml/1 tbsp olive oil, plus extra for
greasing
1 small onion, finely chopped
900g/2lb ripe Italian tomatoes, peeled and
finely chopped
2 garlic cloves, crushed
5ml/1 tsp dried mixed herbs
150ml/¼ pint/⅔ cup vegetable stock
150ml/¼ pint/⅔ cup dry white wine
30ml/2 tbsp sun-dried tomato paste
2.5ml/½ tsp sugar
16 dried lasagne sheets
250g/9oz/generous 1 cup ricotta cheese
130g/4½oz packet mozzarella cheese,
drained and diced
30ml/2 tbsp shredded fresh basil, plus
extra basil leaves to garnish
8 bottled anchovy fillets in olive oil,
drained and halved lengthways
50g/2oz/⅔ cup freshly grated Parmesan
cheese
salt and ground black pepper

1 Heat the oil in a pan; add the onion and cook gently, stirring, for 5 minutes until softened. Transfer to the ceramic cooking pot and switch on to high. Stir in the tomatoes, garlic and herbs. Season with salt and black pepper to taste, then cover the slow cooker with the lid and cook for 1 hour.

2 Ladle about half of the tomato mixture out of the cooking pot, place in a bowl and set aside to cool.

3 Stir the vegetable stock, white wine, tomato paste and sugar into the tomato mixture remaining in the slow cooker. Cover with the lid and cook for a further hour. Turn off the slow cooker.

4 Meanwhile, cook the lasagne sheets in batches in a pan of salted boiling water for 3 minutes or according to the instructions on the packet. Drain the sheets of lasagne. Separate them, and lay them out on a clean dishtowel until needed.

5 Add the ricotta and mozzarella to the tomato mixture in the bowl. Stir in the shredded fresh basil and season to taste with salt and black pepper. Spread a little of the mixture over each lasagne sheet. Place one halved anchovy fillet across the width of each sheet, close to one of the short ends. Starting from the end with the anchovy, roll up each lasagne sheet to form a tube.

6 Transfer the tomato sauce in the slow cooker to a food processor or blender, and purée until smooth. Wash and dry the ceramic cooking pot, then lightly grease the base and halfway up the sides with a little oil.

7 Spoon about a third of the puréed sauce into the ceramic cooking pot, covering the base evenly. Arrange the filled cannelloni seam-side down on top of the sauce. Spoon the remaining sauce over the top.

8 Sprinkle with the Parmesan. Cover the slow cooker with the lid and cook on high or auto for 1 hour, then switch to low or leave on auto and cook for a further hour until the cannelloni is tender. Brown under the grill (broiler), if you like, then serve garnished with basil.

Energy 546Kcal/2293kJ; Protein 25.5g; Carbohydrate 54.3g, of which sugars 9.7g; Fat 24.1g, of which saturates 13.4g; Cholesterol 58mg; Calcium 301mg; Fibre 3.5g; Sodium 282mg.

TUNA LASAGNE

This delicious, comforting dish is perfect for a family supper or casual entertaining, and is incredibly simple to make. Use pre-cooked sheets of lasagne, breaking them into smaller pieces as necessary to fit the shape of your slow cooker.

SERVES 6

65g/2½oz/5 tbsp butter, plus extra
    for greasing
I small onion, finely chopped
I garlic clove, finely chopped
II5g/4oz mushrooms, thinly sliced
40g/1½oz/⅓ cup plain (all-purpose)
    flour
50ml/2fl oz/¼ cup dry white wine
150ml/¼ pint/⅔ cup double (heavy) cream
600ml/1 pint/2½ cups milk
45ml/3 tbsp chopped fresh parsley
2 × 200g/7oz cans tuna in oil
2 canned pimientos, cut into strips
II5g/4oz/1 cup mozzarella cheese, grated
8–12 sheets pre-cooked lasagne
25g/1oz/3 tbsp freshly grated
    Parmesan cheese
salt and ground black pepper
Italian-style bread, such as ciabatta,
    and green salad, to serve

I Lightly grease the base and halfway up the sides of the ceramic cooking pot.

2 Melt 25g/1oz/2 tbsp of the butter in a large pan, add the onion and fry gently for 5 minutes until almost soft but not coloured. Add the garlic and mushrooms and cook for a further 3 minutes, stirring occasionally. Tip the vegetables into a bowl and set aside.

3 Melt the remaining 40g/1½oz/3 tbsp of butter in the pan. Sprinkle over the flour and stir in. Turn off the heat, then gradually blend in the wine, followed by the cream and milk. Gently heat, stirring constantly, until the mixture bubbles and thickens. Stir in the parsley and season well with salt and ground black pepper.

4 Reserve 300ml/½ pint/1¼ cups of the sauce, then stir the mushroom mixture into the remaining sauce.

5 Drain the tuna well and tip into a bowl. Flake the fish with a fork, then gently mix in the pimiento strips, grated mozzarella and a little salt and pepper.

6 Spoon a thin layer of the mushroom sauce over the base of the ceramic cooking pot and cover with 2–3 lasagne sheets, breaking them to fit. Sprinkle half of the tuna mixture over the pasta. Spoon half of the remaining sauce evenly over the top and cover with another layer of lasagne sheets. Repeat, ending with a layer of lasagne. Pour over the reserved plain sauce, then sprinkle with the Parmesan cheese.

7 Cover the slow cooker with the lid and cook on low for 2 hours, or until the lasagne is tender.

8 If you like, brown the top of the lasagne under a medium grill (broiler) and serve with bread and a green salad.

Energy 554Kcal/2315kJ; Protein 32.2g; Carbohydrate 28.9g, of which sugars 7.4g; Fat 34.7g, of which saturates 18.5g; Cholesterol 110mg; Calcium 371mg; Fibre 0.6g; Sodium 616mg.

POACHED FISH in SPICY TOMATO SAUCE

This traditional Jewish dish is known as Samak. It is usually served with flatbreads, such as pitta or matzos, but you can serve it with plain boiled rice or noodles, if you prefer.

SERVES 4

15ml/1 tbsp vegetable or olive oil
1 onion, finely chopped
150ml/¼ pint/⅔ cup passata (bottled
    strained tomatoes)
75ml/2½fl oz/⅓ cup boiling fish
    or vegetable stock
2 garlic cloves, crushed
1 small red chilli, seeded and
    finely chopped
pinch of ground ginger
pinch of curry powder
pinch of ground cumin
pinch of ground turmeric
seeds from 1 cardamom pod
juice of 1 lemon, plus extra if needed
900g/2lb mixed firm white fish fillets
30ml/2 tbsp chopped fresh
    coriander (cilantro)
30ml/2 tbsp chopped fresh parsley
salt and ground black pepper

1 Heat the oil in a frying pan, add the onion and cook gently, stirring, for 10 minutes until soft but not coloured.

2 Transfer the onions to the ceramic cooking pot, then stir in the passata, stock, garlic, chilli, ginger, curry powder, cumin, turmeric, cardamom, lemon juice, salt and pepper. Cover and cook on high or auto for 1½ hours, until the mixture is just simmering.

3 Add the fish to the pot, cover and continue cooking on auto or low for 45 minutes–1 hour, or until the fish is tender. (The flesh should flake easily.)

4 Lift the fish on to warmed serving plates. Stir the fresh herbs into the sauce, then taste and adjust the seasoning, adding more lemon juice, if necessary. Spoon the sauce over the fish and serve immediately.

Energy 224Kcal/942kJ; Protein 42g; Carbohydrate 4.1g, of which sugars 3.1g; Fat 4.4g, of which saturates 0.6g; Cholesterol 104mg; Calcium 34mg; Fibre 0.8g; Sodium 151mg.

COCONUT SALMON

Salmon is quite a robust fish, and responds well to being cooked with this fragrant blend of spices, garlic and chilli. Coconut milk adds a mellow touch and a creamy taste.

SERVES 4

15ml/1 tbsp oil
1 onion, finely chopped
2 fresh green chillies, seeded and chopped
2 garlic cloves, crushed
2.5cm/1in piece fresh root ginger, grated
175ml/6fl oz/¾ cup coconut milk
10ml/2 tsp ground cumin
5ml/1 tsp ground coriander
4 salmon steaks, each about 175g/6oz
10ml/2 tsp chilli powder
2.5ml/½ tsp ground turmeric
15ml/1 tbsp white wine vinegar
1.5ml/¼ tsp salt
fresh coriander (cilantro) sprigs, to garnish
rice tossed with spring onions (scallions),
    to serve

VARIATION
Trout fillets go well with spices and can be used instead of salmon in this dish.

1 Heat the oil in a pan, add the onion, chillies, garlic and ginger and fry for 5-6 minutes, until fairly soft. Place in a food processor with 120ml/4fl oz/½ cup of the coconut milk and blend until smooth.

2 Tip the paste into the ceramic cooking pot. Stir in 5ml/1 tsp of the cumin, the ground coriander and the rest of the coconut milk. Cover and cook on high for 1½ hours.

3 About 20 minutes before the end of cooking time, arrange the salmon steaks in a single layer in a shallow glass dish. Combine the remaining 5ml/1 tsp cumin, the chilli powder, turmeric, vinegar and salt in a bowl to make a paste. Rub the mixture over the salmon steaks and leave to marinate at room temperature while the sauce finishes cooking.

4 Add the salmon steaks to the sauce, arranging them in a single layer and spoon some of the coconut sauce over the top to keep the fish moist while it cooks. Cover with the lid, reduce the temperature to low and cook for 45 minutes–1 hour, or until the salmon is opaque and tender.

5 Transfer the fish to a serving dish, spoon over the sauce and garnish with fresh coriander. Serve with the rice.

Energy 363Kcal/1512kJ; Protein 35.9g; Carbohydrate 5.1g, of which sugars 4.2g; Fat 22.2g, of which saturates 3.8g; Cholesterol 88mg; Calcium 59mg; Fibre 0.5g; Sodium 275mg.

MIXED FISH JAMBALAYA

As with the Spanish paella, the ingredients used to make this classic Creole dish can be varied according to what is available. The name jambalaya is thought to have come from the French word for ham – jambon – and the Creole word for rice – à la ya.

SERVES 4

30ml/2 tbsp oil
6 rashers (strips) rinded smoked streaky (fatty) bacon, chopped
1 onion, chopped
2 sticks celery, sliced
2 garlic cloves, crushed
5ml/1 tsp cayenne pepper
2 bay leaves
5ml/1 tsp dried oregano
2.5ml/½ tsp dried thyme
4 tomatoes, skinned, seeded and chopped
750ml/1¼ pints/3 cups boiling vegetable or fish stock
15ml/1 tbsp tomato purée (paste)
300g/10oz/1½ cups easy-cook (converted) rice
225g/8oz firm white fish, such as haddock, skinned, boned and cubed
115g/4oz cooked prawns (shrimp)
salt and ground black pepper
4 spring onions (scallions) and 4 cooked prawns (shrimp) in their shells, to garnish

1 Heat the oil in a frying pan and cook the bacon over a medium-high heat for 2 minutes. Reduce the heat, add the onion and celery and cook for a further 5–10 minutes, or until soft and beginning to turn brown.

2 Transfer the mixture to the ceramic cooking pot and switch the slow cooker to high. Add the garlic, cayenne pepper, bay leaves, oregano, thyme, tomatoes, boiling stock and tomato purée. Stir well to mix, then cover with the lid and cook for about 1 hour.

3 Sprinkle the rice over the tomato mixture, followed by the cubes of fish. Season with salt and pepper and stir. Re-cover and cook for 45 minutes.

4 Add the prawns and stir, then cook for 15 minutes, or until the fish and rice are tender and most of the liquid has been absorbed. Serve garnished with spring onions and prawns in their shells.

COOK'S TIP

If you like a really hot, spicy bite to your jambalaya, serve with a little hot chilli sauce for sprinkling over at the table.

Energy 243Kcal/1015kJ; Protein 23.2g; Carbohydrate 6.5g, of which sugars 5.4g; Fat 14g, of which saturates 3.4g; Cholesterol 126mg; Calcium 64mg; Fibre 1.6g; Sodium 1303mg.

HOKI BALLS in TOMATO SAUCE

This simple fish dish is ideal for serving to young children because there is no risk of bones. For adults, it can be spiced up with a dash of chilli sauce. It is low in fat and therefore ideal for anyone on a low-fat or low-cholesterol diet.

SERVES 4

400g/14oz can chopped tomatoes
50g/2oz button mushrooms, sliced
450g/1lb hoki or other firm white fish
    fillets, skinned
15g/½oz/¼ cup wholemeal
    (whole-wheat) breadcrumbs
30ml/2 tbsp chopped fresh chives or
    spring onions (scallions)
salt and ground black pepper
chopped fresh chives, to garnish
steamed green vegetables, to serve

COOK'S TIP

If hoki is not available, you can use the same weight of cod, haddock or whiting.

2 Meanwhile, cut the fish into large chunks and place in a food processor. Add the breadcrumbs and the chives or spring onions and season with salt and pepper. Process until the fish is finely chopped, but still has some texture.

3 Divide the mixture into 16 even-size pieces, then roll them into balls with damp hands. Put the fish balls on a plate and chill in the refrigerator until needed.

4 About 30 minutes before the end of the sauce's cooking time, take the fish balls out of the refrigerator and leave them to stand at room temperature.

5 Add the fishballs to the sauce in a single layer. Cook for 1 hour on high, then reduce the temperature to low and cook for a further hour, or until the fish balls are thoroughly cooked. Serve hot, garnished with chives and accompanied by steamed green vegetables.

1 Pour the chopped tomatoes into the ceramic cooking pot, then add the sliced mushrooms and a little salt and ground black pepper. Cover with the lid, switch the slow cooker to high and cook for about 2 hours.

Energy 116Kcal/490kJ; Protein 22.2g; Carbohydrate 4.6g, of which sugars 2.9g; Fat 1.0g, of which saturates 0.1g; Cholesterol 52mg; Calcium 27mg; Fibre 1.0g; Sodium 125mg.

RED MULLET BRAISED on a BED of FENNEL

These pretty pink fish have a wonderful firm flesh and sweet flavour. They are usually cooked whole, but you can remove the heads if there is not enough room in your slow cooker to fit them all in a single layer. Other small whole fish, such as sardines, or fish fillets, such as salmon, cod and hake, can also be cooked in this way.

SERVES 4

10ml/2 tsp fennel seeds
5ml/1 tsp chopped fresh thyme
30ml/2 tbsp chopped fresh parsley
1 clove garlic, crushed
10ml/2 tsp olive oil
4 red mullet, weighing about
   225g/8oz each
lemon wedges, to serve

For the fennel
8 ripe tomatoes
2 fennel bulbs
30ml/2 tbsp olive oil
120ml/4fl oz/½ cup boiling fish
   or vegetable stock
10ml/2 tsp balsamic vinegar
salt and ground black pepper

1 Crush the fennel seeds using a mortar and pestle, then work in the chopped thyme and parsley, garlic and olive oil.

2 Clean and scale the fish and trim off the fins. Use a sharp knife to make deep slashes on each side of the fish.

3 Push the herb paste into the cuts in the fish and spread any excess inside the body cavities. Place the fish on a plate, loosely cover with clear film (plastic wrap) and leave to marinate. On a warm day, it is best to place the marinating fish in the refrigerator and then bring to room temperature about 20 minutes before cooking.

4 Meanwhile, prepare the bed of fennel. Put the tomatoes in a heatproof bowl, add boiling water to cover and leave to stand for 1 minute. Drain and cool under cold running water and peel off the skins. Quarter the tomatoes, seed and cut into small dice.

5 Trim the feathery fronds from the fennel (these can be kept for garnishing), then cut the bulbs into 1cm/½ in slices from the top to the root end.

6 Heat the olive oil in a frying pan and cook the fennel slices over a medium heat for about 10 minutes, or until just starting to colour.

7 Transfer the fennel to the ceramic cooking pot. Add the diced tomatoes, hot stock, balsamic vinegar, salt and pepper, cover with the lid and cook on high for 2 hours.

8 Give the fennel sauce a stir, then place the red mullet on top in a single layer. Cover and cook for 1 hour, or until the fish is cooked through and tender. Serve immediately, with lemon wedges for squeezing over.

COOK'S TIP
Red mullet is highly perishable, so be sure to buy very fresh fish. Look for specimens with bright eyes and skin, and that feel firm. The liver is considered a delicacy, so if your fishmonger will clean them for you, ask for the liver along with the fish.

Energy 194Kcal/816kJ; Protein 26.5g; Carbohydrate 4.2g, of which sugars 4.1g; Fat 8.1g, of which saturates 1.2g; Cholesterol 63mg; Calcium 95mg; Fibre 3.0g; Sodium 239mg.

HADDOCK with SPICY PUY LENTILS

Dark brown Puy lentils have a delicate taste and texture and hold their shape during cooking, which makes them particularly good for slow cooker dishes. Red chilli pepper and ground cumin add a hint of heat and spice without overpowering the flavour of the fish.

SERVES 4

175g/6oz/¾ cup Puy lentils
600ml/1 pint/2½ cups near-boiling
    vegetable stock
30ml/2 tbsp olive oil
1 onion, finely chopped
2 celery sticks, finely chopped
1 red chilli, halved, seeded
    and finely chopped
2.5ml/½ tsp ground cumin
four thick 150g/5oz pieces of haddock
    fillet or steak
10ml/2 tsp lemon juice
25g/1oz/2 tbsp butter, softened
5ml/1 tsp finely grated lemon rind
salt and ground black pepper
lemon wedges, to garnish

1 Put the lentils in a sieve (strainer) and rinse under cold running water. Drain well, then tip into the ceramic cooking pot. Pour over the hot vegetable stock, cover with the lid and switch the slow cooker on to high.

2 Heat the oil in a frying pan, add the onion and cook gently for 8 minutes. Stir in the celery, chilli and cumin, and cook for a further 2 minutes, or until soft but not coloured. Add the mixture to the lentils, stir, re-cover and cook for about 2½ hours.

3 Meanwhile, rinse the haddock pieces and pat dry on kitchen paper. Sprinkle them with the lemon juice. In a clean bowl, beat together the butter, lemon rind, salt and a generous amount of ground black pepper.

4 Put the haddock on top of the lentils, then dot the lemon butter over the top. Cover and cook for 45 minutes–1 hour, or until the fish flakes easily, the lentils are tender and most of the stock has been absorbed. Serve immediately, garnished with the lemon wedges.

COOK'S TIP
Any firm white fish can be cooked in this way. Both cod and swordfish give particularly good results.

Energy 366Kcal/1538kJ; Protein 38.9g; Carbohydrate 25.2g, of which sugars 3.2g; Fat 12.8g, of which saturates 4.3g; Cholesterol 82mg; Calcium 64mg; Fibre 4.7g; Sodium 353mg.

SKATE with TOMATO and OLIVE SAUCE

The classic way of serving skate is with a browned butter sauce, but here it is given a Mediterranean twist with tomatoes, olives, orange and a dash of Pernod. If time allows, soak the skate in salted water for a few hours before cooking, to firm up the flesh.

SERVES 4

15ml/1 tbsp olive oil
1 small onion, finely chopped
2 fresh thyme sprigs
grated rind of ½ orange
15ml/1 tbsp Pernod
400g/14oz can chopped tomatoes
50g/2oz/1 cup stuffed green olives
1.5ml/¼ tsp caster (superfine) sugar
4 small skate wings
plain (all-purpose) flour, for coating
salt and ground black pepper
15ml/1 tbsp basil leaves, to garnish
lime wedges, to serve

COOK'S TIP
Pernod gives this dish a deliciously distinctive taste of aniseed, but for those who don't like the flavour, use 15ml/1 tbsp vermouth instead.

1 Heat the oil in a pan, add the onion and fry gently for 10 minutes. Stir in the thyme and orange rind and cook for 1 minute. Add the Pernod, tomatoes, olives, sugar and a little salt and pepper, and heat until just below boiling point.

2 Tip the mixture into the ceramic pot and switch on to high. Cover with the lid and cook for 1½ hours.

3 Meanwhile, rinse the skate wings under cold water and pat dry on kitchen paper. Sprinkle the flour on a large, flat dish and season well with salt and ground black pepper. Coat each skate wing in the flour, shaking off any excess, then place on top of the tomato sauce.

4 Re-cover the ceramic cooking pot and reduce the temperature to low. Cook for 1½–2 hours, or until the skate is cooked and flakes easily.

5 Place the fish on to warmed serving plates and spoon over the sauce. Sprinkle over the basil leaves and serve with a wedge of lime for squeezing over.

Energy 144Kcal/606kJ; Protein 15.5g; Carbohydrate 8.1g, of which sugars 3.7g; Fat 4.8g, of which saturates 0.7g; Cholesterol 35mg; Calcium 37mg; Fibre 1.4g; Sodium 366mg.

LEMON SOLE and PROSCIUTTO ROULADES

*In this elegant dish, prosciutto and delicately textured lemon sole are rolled around
a subtle herb and lemon stuffing. Serve this dish for a special dinner party with new
potatoes tossed in butter, and lightly steamed asparagus.*

2 Remove most of the fat from the prosciutto. Lay two overlapping slices on a board and place a sole fillet on top, skinned side up.

3 Mix the walnuts, breadcrumbs, parsley, eggs, lemon rind and pepper together and spread a quarter of the mixture over the fish fillet, then press down gently. Starting at the thicker end of the fillet, carefully roll up the fish and ham to enclose the filling.

4 Repeat with the remaining prosciutto, fish and filling, then secure each roll with a cocktail stick (toothpick).

5 Place the fish seam-side down in the ceramic cooking pot. Cover with the lid, then turn the temperature down to low. Cook for 1½–2 hours, or until the fish flakes easily. Remove the cocktail sticks and serve straight away with freshly cooked vegetables.

SERVES 4

10ml/2 tsp unsalted (sweet) butter,
    at room temperature
120ml/4fl oz/½ cup dry white wine
4 large lemon sole fillets, about
    150g/5oz each
8 thin slices of prosciutto, about
    130g/4½oz in total
50g/2oz/½ cup chopped toasted walnuts
75g/3oz/1½ cups fresh white breadcrumbs
30ml/2 tbsp finely chopped fresh parsley
2 eggs, lightly beaten
5ml/1 tsp finely grated lemon rind
ground black pepper
new potatoes and steamed green
    vegetables, to serve

1 Smear the inside of the ceramic cooking pot with the butter. Pour in the wine and switch the slow cooker to high. Skin the fish fillets and check that all the bones have been removed, then pat dry with kitchen paper.

BASQUE-STYLE TUNA

In Spain, this traditional fisherman's stew is known as marmitako. *It used to be cooked at sea on the fishing boats, and takes its name from the cooking pot, known in France as a* marmite. *The rich flavourings go perfectly with the robust taste of chunky tuna.*

SERVES 4

30ml/2 tbsp olive oil
1 onion, finely chopped
1 clove garlic, finely chopped
75ml/2½fl oz/⅓ cup white wine,
    preferably Spanish
150ml/¼ pint/⅔ cup boiling fish
    or vegetable stock
200g/7oz can chopped tomatoes
5ml/1 tsp paprika
2.5ml/½ tsp dried crushed chillies
450g/1lb waxy new potatoes, cut into
    1cm/½in chunks
1 red and 1 yellow (bell) pepper, seeded
    and chopped
1 small sprig of fresh rosemary
1 bay leaf
450g/1lb fresh tuna, cut into 2.5cm/
    1in chunks
salt and ground black pepper
crusty bread, to serve

3 Stir the chunks of tuna into the sauce. Cover and cook for 15–20 minutes, or until the fish is firm and opaque.

4 Remove the rosemary and bay leaf, then ladle the stew into warmed dishes, grind over a little more black pepper and serve with crusty bread.

1 Heat the oil in a large frying pan, add the onion and fry gently for 10 minutes until soft and translucent. Stir in the garlic, followed by the wine, stock, tomatoes, paprika and chillies. Bring to just below boiling point, then carefully pour the mixture into the ceramic cooking pot.

2 Add the chunks of potato, red and yellow pepper, rosemary and bay leaf to the pot and stir to combine. Cover the slow cooker with the lid and cook on high for 2–2½ hours, or until the potatoes are just tender, then season the sauce to taste with salt and a little ground black pepper.

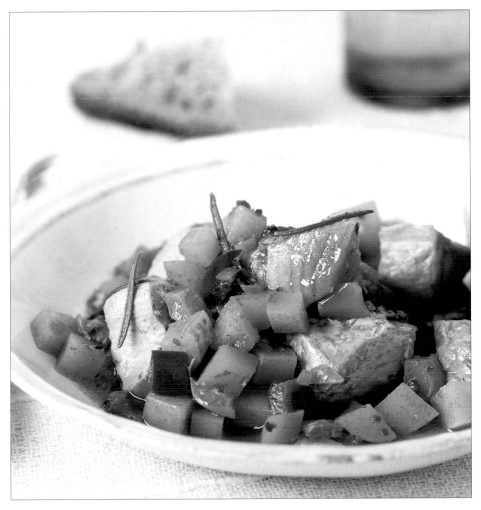

Energy 297Kcal/1256kJ; Protein 30.1g; Carbohydrate 27.5g, of which sugars 9.6g; Fat 6.g, of which saturates 1.2g; Cholesterol 57mg; Calcium 39mg; Fibre 3.2g; Sodium 397mg.

COD with CARAMELIZED ONIONS

After very long slow cooking, sliced onions become caramelized and turn a deep golden colour with a fabulously rich, sweet flavour, which is further enhanced here by the addition of balsamic vinegar. Tangy caper and coriander butter adds a fresh, sharp contrast.

SERVES 4

40g/1½oz/3 tbsp butter
10ml/2 tsp olive oil
1.2kg/2½lb yellow onions, peeled
    and finely sliced
5ml/1 tsp caster (superfine) sugar
30ml/2 tbsp balsamic vinegar
30ml/2 tbsp vegetable stock, white wine
    or water
4 x 150g/5oz thick cod fillets

For the butter
115g/4oz/½ cup butter, softened
30ml/2 tbsp capers, drained and chopped
30ml/2 tbsp chopped fresh
    coriander (cilantro)
salt and ground black pepper

1 Put the butter and oil in the ceramic cooking pot and heat on high for about 15 minutes, until melted.

2 Add the sliced onions and stir to coat well in the butter and oil. Cover the pot with the lid, then place a folded dish towel over the top to retain all the heat. Cook for 2 hours, stirring halfway through cooking time.

3 Sprinkle the sugar over the onions and stir well to mix. Replace the lid and folded dish towel and cook on high for 4 hours, stirring two or three times, to ensure the onions colour evenly. At the end of the cooking time, they should be a dark golden colour.

4 Add the vinegar to the onions and stir in the stock, wine or water. Cover again and cook for 1 hour; the onions should now be fairly tender. Season with a little salt and pepper and stir well. Arrange the cod fillets on top of the onions and cook for a final 45 minutes–1 hour, or until the fish flakes easily.

5 Meanwhile, make the caper and coriander butter. Cream the butter in a small bowl until soft, then beat in the capers, coriander, salt and pepper. Roll up the butter in foil, clear film (plastic wrap) or greaseproof (waxed) paper to form a short log shape, twisting the ends to secure them. Chill in the refrigerator or freezer until firm.

6 To serve, spoon the onions and fish on to warmed serving plates. Slice off discs of the butter and top each piece of fish with one or two slices. Serve immediately, with the butter melting over the hot fish.

Energy 534Kcal/2213kJ; Protein 31.3g; Carbohydrate 25g, of which sugars 18.1g; Fat 35g, of which saturates 20.6g; Cholesterol 152mg; Calcium 96mg; Fibre 4.2g; Sodium 334mg.

SWORDFISH in BARBECUE SAUCE

This is an ideal way to cook any firm fish steaks. The warmly spiced smoky sauce goes particularly well with meaty fish, such as swordfish, shark and tuna. Choose smaller, thicker fish steaks rather than large, thinner ones, so that they will fit in the slow cooker.

SERVES 4

15ml/1 tbsp sunflower oil
1 small onion, very finely chopped
1 garlic clove, crushed
2.5ml/½ tsp chilli powder
15ml/1 tbsp Worcestershire sauce
15ml/1 tbsp soft light brown sugar
15ml/1 tbsp balsamic vinegar
15ml/1 tbsp American mustard
150ml/¼ pint/⅔ cup tomato juice
4 swordfish steaks, about 115g/4oz each
salt and ground black pepper
fresh flat leaf parsley, to garnish
boiled or steamed rice, to serve

1 Heat the oil in a frying pan, add the onion and cook gently for 10 minutes, until soft. Stir in the garlic and chilli powder and cook for a few seconds, then add the Worcestershire sauce, sugar, vinegar, mustard and tomato juice. Heat gently, stirring, until nearly boiling.

2 Pour half the sauce into the ceramic cooking pot. Rinse the swordfish steaks, pat dry on kitchen paper and arrange in a single layer on top of the sauce. Top with the remaining sauce.

3 Cover the slow cooker with a lid and switch on to high. Cook for 2–3 hours, or until the fish is tender and cooked.

4 Carefully transfer the fish to warmed serving plates and spoon the barbecue sauce over the top. Garnish with sprigs of flat-leaf parsley and serve immediately with boiled or steamed rice.

COOK'S TIP
For a really smoky barbecue flavour use a crushed dried chipotle chilli instead of the chilli powder.

Energy 158Kcal/670kJ; Protein 27.3g; Carbohydrate 4.9g, of which sugars 4.5g; Fat 3.5g, of which saturates 0.6g; Cholesterol 59mg; Calcium 21mg; Fibre 0.2g; Sodium 414mg.

SPINACH and NUT STUFFED HERRINGS

It is difficult to cook large whole fish in a slow cooker, but smaller fish, such as sardines and herrings, are ideal. Their slightly oily flesh is perfectly suited to slow cooking, too, because it helps to keep the fish wonderfully moist.

SERVES 4

40g/1½oz/3 tbsp unsalted (sweet) butter
5ml/1 tsp sunflower oil
25g/1oz/¼ cup pine nuts
1 small onion, finely chopped
175g/6oz frozen spinach, thawed
50g/2oz/1 cup white breadcrumbs
25g/1oz/⅓ cup grated Parmesan cheese
pinch of freshly grated nutmeg
75ml/5 tbsp fish or vegetable stock
    or white wine
4 small herrings, heads removed,
    and boned
salt and ground black pepper
lemon wedges, to serve

1 Heat 25g/1oz/2 tbsp of the butter and sunflower oil in a frying pan until melted. Add the pine nuts and gently fry for 3–4 minutes until golden. Lift them from the pan with a slotted spoon, leaving the fat behind, and place in a mixing bowl.

2 Add the finely chopped onion to the pan and cook gently for 10 minutes, stirring frequently, until soft.

3 Meanwhile, place the thawed spinach in a fine sieve (strainer) and press out as much liquid as possible. (Use your hands to squeeze out the liquid, or press firmly with the back of a spoon.)

VARIATIONS
• Other kinds of nuts can be used in place of pine nuts in the stuffing. Try chopped hazelnuts or walnuts instead.
• As an alternative to nuts, add 15ml/1 tbsp chopped dried apricots to the stuffing.

4 Put the onion and spinach in the mixing bowl with the pine nuts and add the breadcrumbs, cheese, nutmeg, salt and pepper. Mix the ingredients with a fork until thoroughly combined.

5 Smear the remaining 15g/½oz/1 tbsp of butter over the base of the ceramic cooking pot and pour in the stock or wine. Cover with the lid and switch the slow cooker on to high.

6 Using a sharp knife, make three shallow cuts down each side of the fish, then spoon the stuffing into the cavities, packing it in quite firmly. Bring the edges of the fish together and secure with wooden cocktail sticks (toothpicks).

7 Arrange the fish on the base of the ceramic cooking pot in a single layer. Cover the pot with the lid and cook for 1½–2½ hours, or until the fish is cooked. (Test the flesh with a fork; it should flake easily when ready.)

8 Carefully lift the stuffed fish out of the slow cooker on to warmed serving plates, and serve with lemon wedges.

COOK'S TIP
This dish is perfect for a simple, tasty supper, but it is great for entertaining, too. Serve with a tasty couscous salad tossed with plenty of herbs and raisins. The sweetness of the dried fruit goes particularly well with the spinach and pine nut stuffing, and complements the rich flavour of the fish.

Energy 351Kcal/1462kJ; Protein 24g; Carbohydrate 7.6g, of which sugars 1.9g; Fat 23.9g, of which saturates 6.9g; Cholesterol 78mg; Calcium 619mg; Fibre 1.5g; Sodium 624mg.

NORTHERN THAI FISH CURRY

Thin, soupy, strongly flavoured curries are typical of the northern region of Thailand. Fragrant lemon grass, zesty galangal and salty Thai fish sauce come together to give this dish its characteristic Thai flavour. Serve with lots of sticky rice to soak up the juices.

5 Add the shallots, garlic, galangal or ginger, lemon grass, chilli flakes, fish sauce and sugar to the pot and stir to combine. Cover with the lid and cook for 2 hours.

6 Add the cubes of salmon to the stock and cook for 15 minutes. Turn off the slow cooker and leave to stand for a further 10–15 minutes, or until the fish is cooked through. Serve immediately.

SERVES 4

450g/1lb salmon fillet
475ml/16fl oz/2 cups near-boiling
   vegetable stock
4 shallots, very finely chopped
1 garlic clove, crushed
2.5cm/1in piece fresh galangal or ginger,
   finely chopped
1 lemon grass stalk, finely chopped
2.5ml/½ tsp dried chilli flakes
15ml/1 tbsp Thai fish sauce
5ml/1 tsp palm sugar or light muscovado
   (brown) sugar

COOK'S TIP

Allow the fish to return to room temperature before adding to the stock, so that the temperature of the liquid doesn't fall below simmering point.

1 Wrap the salmon fillet in clear film (plastic wrap) and place in the freezer for 30–40 minutes to firm up slightly.

2 Unwrap the fish, and carefully remove and discard the skin. Using a sharp knife, cut the fish into 2.5cm/1in cubes and remove any stray bones with your fingers or a pair of tweezers.

3 Place the cubed fish in a bowl, cover with clear film (plastic wrap) and leave to stand at room temperature.

4 Meanwhile, pour the hot vegetable stock into the ceramic cooking pot and switch the slow cooker to high.

Energy 216Kcal/902kJ; Protein 23.2g; Carbohydrate 2.7g, of which sugars 2.2g; Fat 12.6g, of which saturates 2.1g; Cholesterol 56mg; Calcium 30mg; Fibre 0.2g; Sodium 522mg.

GREEN FISH CURRY

Fresh-tasting, spicy curries made with coconut milk are a classic of Thai cuisine. This slow-cooker version of green curry uses desiccated coconut and cream to give a really rich taste and texture, which is offset by the generous use of spices, chilli and fragrant herbs.

SERVES 4

1 onion, chopped
1 large fresh green chilli, halved, seeded and chopped, plus extra slices to garnish
1 garlic clove, crushed
50g/2oz/½ cup cashew nuts
2.5ml/½ tsp fennel seeds
30ml/2 tbsp desiccated (dry unsweetened shredded) coconut
150ml/¼ pint/⅔ cup water
30ml/2 tbsp vegetable oil
1.5ml/¼ tsp cumin seeds
1.5ml/¼ tsp ground coriander
1.5ml/¼ tsp ground cumin
150ml/¼ pint/⅔ cup double (heavy) cream
4 white fish fillets, such as cod or haddock, skinned
1.5ml/¼ tsp ground turmeric
30ml/2 tbsp lime juice
salt
45ml/3 tbsp chopped fresh coriander (cilantro), plus extra to garnish
boiled rice, to serve

1 Place the onion, chilli, garlic, cashew nuts, fennel seeds and desiccated coconut in a food processor with 45ml/ 3 tbsp of the water and blend to make a smooth paste. Alternatively, work the dry ingredients to a paste in a mortar with a pestle, then stir in the water.

2 Heat the oil in a frying pan and fry the cumin seeds for 1 minute, until they give off their aroma. Add the coconut paste and fry for 5 minutes, then stir in the ground coriander, cumin and remaining water. Bring to the boil, then let the mixture bubble for 1 minute.

3 Transfer the mixture to the ceramic cooking pot. Stir in the cream, cover with the lid and switch the slow cooker to high. Cook for 1½ hours.

COOK'S TIP
Do not leave the fish to marinate for longer than 15 minutes because the texture will be spoilt.

4 Towards the end of cooking time, prepare and marinate the fish. Cut the fillets into 5cm/2in chunks and put them in a glass bowl. Combine the turmeric, lime juice and a pinch of salt in a separate bowl and pour it over the fish. Use your hands to rub it into the fish. Cover with clear film (plastic wrap) and leave to marinate for 15 minutes.

5 Stir the fish into the sauce, re-cover and cook for 30 minutes–1 hour, or until the fish flakes easily. Stir in the coriander. Spoon the curry into a warmed bowls. Garnish with chopped coriander and sliced green chilli, and serve with rice.

Energy 511Kcal/2118kJ; Protein 36.1g; Carbohydrate 6.4g, of which sugars 3.9g; Fat 37.9g, of which saturates 18.8g; Cholesterol 132mg; Calcium 50mg; Fibre 2g; Sodium 153mg.

ONE-POT, CLAY-POT FISH AND SHELLFISH

For a healthy, speedy meal with superb flavour, fish and shellfish are the perfect choice. Cooking on top of the stove means you can check the dish frequently, and serve it the moment it is ready. Italian Fish Stew or Seafood Pie with Rösti Topping would make a fine dish for a family meal, Seafood Risotto is a good choice for an impromptu supper with friends, while a more formal dinner would provide the perfect opportunity for trying Octopus and Red Wine Stew, Fillets of Brill in Red Wine Sauce or a colourful Seafood Paella.

ITALIAN FISH STEW

Italians are renowned for enjoying good food and this stew is a veritable feast of fish and shellfish in a delicious tomato broth – ideal for a family lunch.

SERVES 4

30ml/2 tbsp olive oil
1 onion, thinly sliced
a few saffron threads
5ml/1 tsp dried thyme
large pinch of cayenne pepper
2 garlic cloves, finely chopped
2 x 400g/14oz cans tomatoes, drained
   and chopped
175ml/6fl oz/¾ cup dry white wine
2 litres/3½ pints/8 cups hot fish stock
350g/12oz white, skinless fish fillets, such
   as haddock or cod, cut into pieces
450g/1lb monkfish, cut into pieces
450g/1lb mussels, scrubbed
225g/8oz small squid, cleaned and cut
   into rings
30ml/2 tbsp chopped fresh basil
   or parsley
salt and ground black pepper
thickly sliced bread, to serve

1 Heat the olive oil in a large, heavy pan. Add the onion, saffron threads, thyme, cayenne pepper and salt, to taste. Stir well and cook over a low heat for 10 minutes, until the onion is soft. Add the garlic and cook for 1 minute more.

2 Stir in the chopped tomatoes, dry white wine and hot fish stock. Bring to the boil and boil for 1 minute, then reduce the heat and simmer gently for 15 minutes.

COOK'S TIP
Cayenne pepper has quite a hot, spicy flavour and was originally made from a type of chilli from the Cayenne region of French Guiana. It should be used sparingly.

3 Add the fish pieces to the tomato mixture in the pan and stir gently. Simmer the stew over a low heat for a further 3 minutes.

4 Add the mussels and squid rings and simmer for about 2 minutes, until the mussels open. Discard any that remain closed. Stir in the basil or parsley and season to taste. Ladle into warmed soup bowls and serve with bread.

Energy 337Kcal/1423kJ; Protein 49.8g; Carbohydrate 8.3g, of which sugars 7.3g; Fat 8.8g, of which saturates 1.5g; Cholesterol 196mg; Calcium 112mg; Fibre 2.2g; Sodium 226mg.

OCTOPUS and RED WINE STEW

Fresh octopus can be quite tricky to prepare so unless you're happy to clean and prepare it for this traditional Greek dish, buy one that's ready for cooking.

SERVES 4

900g/2lb prepared octopus
450g/1lb onions, sliced
2 bay leaves
450g/1lb ripe tomatoes
60ml/4 tbsp olive oil
4 garlic cloves, crushed
5ml/1 tsp sugar
15ml/1 tbsp chopped fresh oregano
    or rosemary
30ml/2 tbsp chopped fresh parsley
150ml/¼ pint/⅔ cup red wine
30ml/2 tbsp red wine vinegar
chopped fresh herbs, to garnish
warm bread and pine nuts, to serve

COOK'S TIP
The octopus, along with cuttlefish and squid, is a member of the mollusc family – their main shared characteristic is that they have no shell. Octopus can be very tough, so it needs long, slow cooking to tenderize it.

1 Put the octopus in a large pan of gently simmering water with one-quarter of the onions and the bay leaves. Cover the pan and cook gently for 1 hour.

2 While the octopus is cooking, plunge the tomatoes into boiling water for 30 seconds, then refresh in cold water. Peel away the skins and chop roughly.

3 Drain the octopus and, using a small sharp knife, cut it into bitesize pieces. Discard the head.

4 Heat the oil in the pan and fry the octopus, the remaining onions and the garlic for 3 minutes. Add the tomatoes, sugar, herbs, wine and vinegar and cook, stirring, for 5 minutes.

5 Cover the pan and cook over the lowest possible heat for about 1½ hours until the red wine and tomato sauce is thickened and the octopus is tender. To serve, garnish with fresh herbs and serve with plenty of warm bread, and pine nuts to scatter on top.

Energy 371Kcal/1556kJ; Protein 42.5g; Carbohydrate 12.5g, of which sugars 9.9g; Fat 14.5g, of which saturates 2.4g; Cholesterol 108mg; Calcium 113mg; Fibre 2.7g; Sodium 16mg.

GOAN FISH CASSEROLE

The cooking of Goa is a mixture of Portuguese and Indian; the addition of tamarind gives a slightly sour note to the spicy coconut sauce.

SERVES 4

7.5ml/1½ tsp ground turmeric
5ml/1 tsp salt
450g/1lb monkfish fillet, cut into eight pieces
15ml/1 tbsp lemon juice
5ml/1 tsp cumin seeds
5ml/1 tsp coriander seeds
5ml/1 tsp black peppercorns
1 garlic clove, chopped
5cm/2in piece fresh root ginger, finely chopped
25g/1oz tamarind paste
150ml/¼ pint/⅔ cup hot water
30ml/2 tbsp vegetable oil
2 onions, halved and sliced lengthways
400ml/14fl oz/1⅔ cups coconut milk
4 mild green chillies, seeded and cut into thin strips
16 large raw prawns (shrimp), peeled
30ml/2 tbsp chopped fresh coriander (cilantro) leaves, to garnish

1 Mix together the ground turmeric and salt in a small bowl. Place the monkfish in a shallow dish and sprinkle over the lemon juice, then rub the turmeric and salt mixture over the fish fillets to coat them completely. Cover and chill until ready to cook.

COOK'S TIP
Tamarind, which is also known as Indian date, is a popular spice throughout India, South-east Asia and the Caribbean. It has little smell, but the distinctive sour, yet fruity taste makes up for this. It is often used in curries and spicy dishes and is available from Indian and South-east Asian stores and some large supermarkets.

2 Put the cumin seeds, coriander seeds and black peppercorns in a blender or small food processor and blend to a powder. Add the garlic and ginger and process for a few seconds more.

3 Preheat the oven to 200°C/400°F/ Gas 6. Mix the tamarind paste with the hot water and set aside.

4 Heat the oil in a frying pan, add the onions and cook for 5–6 minutes, until softened and golden. Transfer the onions to a shallow earthenware dish.

VARIATION
You may use any firm white fish fillets such as cod, halibut or hake instead of the monkfish in this casserole.

5 Add the fish fillets to the oil remaining in the frying pan, and fry briefly over a high heat, turning them to seal on all sides. Remove the fish from the pan and place on top of the onions.

6 Add the ground spice mixture to the frying pan and cook over a medium heat, stirring constantly, for 1–2 minutes. Stir in the tamarind liquid, coconut milk and chilli strips and bring to the boil. Pour the sauce into the earthenware dish to coat the fish completely.

7 Cover the earthenware dish and cook the fish casserole in the oven for about 10 minutes. Add the prawns, pushing them into the liquid, then cover the dish again and return it to the oven for 5 minutes, or until the prawns turn pink. Do not overcook them or they will toughen. Check the seasoning, sprinkle with coriander leaves and serve.

Energy 220Kcal/926kJ; Protein 28g; Carbohydrate 12.8g, of which sugars 10.5g; Fat 6.8g, of which saturates 1g; Cholesterol 113mg; Calcium 103mg; Fibre 1.4g; Sodium 720mg.

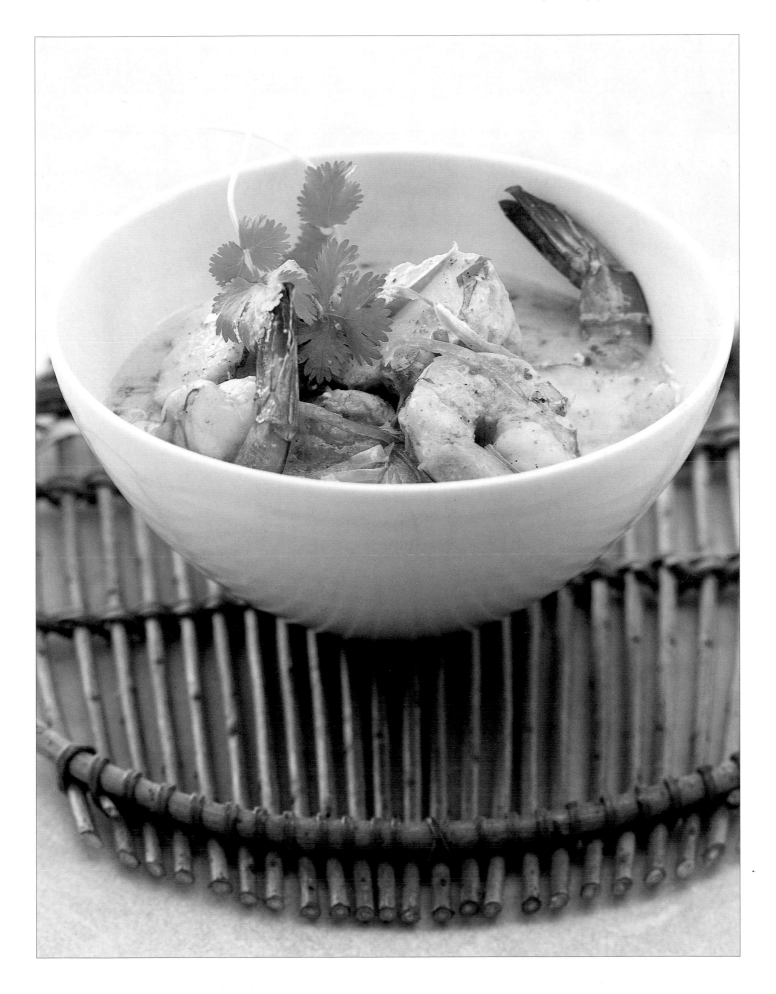

MOROCCAN FISH TAGINE

This spicy, aromatic dish proves just how exciting an ingredient fish can be. Serve it with couscous, which you can steam in the traditional way in a colander on top of the tagine.

SERVES 8

1.3kg/3lb firm fish fillets, skinned and cut
    into 5cm/2in chunks
60ml/4 tbsp olive oil
1 large aubergine (eggplant), cut into
    1cm/½in cubes
2 courgettes (zucchini), cut into
    1cm/½in cubes
4 onions, chopped
400g/14oz can chopped tomatoes
400ml/14fl oz/1⅔ cups passata (bottled
    strained tomatoes)
200ml/7fl oz/scant 1 cup fish stock
1 preserved lemon, chopped
90g/3½oz/scant 1 cup olives
60ml/4 tbsp chopped fresh coriander
    (cilantro), plus extra coriander leaves
    to garnish
salt and ground black pepper

For the harissa
3 large fresh red chillies, seeded
    and chopped
3 garlic cloves, peeled
15ml/1 tbsp ground coriander
30ml/2 tbsp ground cumin
5ml/1 tsp ground cinnamon
grated rind of 1 lemon
30ml/2 tbsp sunflower oil

1 Make the harissa. Whizz everything in a food processor to a smooth paste.

2 Put the fish in a wide bowl and add 30ml/2 tbsp of the harissa. Toss to coat, cover and chill for at least 1 hour.

COOK'S TIP
To make the fish go further, add 225g/8oz/ 1¼ cups cooked chickpeas to the tagine.

3 Heat half the olive oil in a shallow heavy pan. Add the aubergine cubes and fry for about 10 minutes, or until they are golden brown. Add the courgettes and fry for a further 2 minutes. Remove the vegetables from the pan using a slotted spoon and set aside.

4 Add the remaining olive oil to the pan, add the onions and cook over a low heat for about 10 minutes until golden brown. Stir in the remaining harissa and cook for 5 minutes, stirring occasionally.

5 Add the vegetables and combine with the onions, then stir in the chopped tomatoes, the passata and fish stock. Bring to the boil, then lower the heat and simmer for about 20 minutes.

6 Stir the fish chunks and preserved lemon into the pan. Add the olives and stir gently. Cover and simmer over a low heat for about 15–20 minutes. Season to taste. Stir in the chopped coriander. Serve with couscous, if you like, and garnish with coriander leaves.

Energy 263Kcal/1099kJ; Protein 32.3g; Carbohydrate 8.3g, of which sugars 7g; Fat 11.3g, of which saturates 1.7g; Cholesterol 75mg; Calcium 57mg; Fibre 3.2g; Sodium 360mg.

FISH PLAKI

Greece has so much coastline, it's no wonder that fish is so popular there. Generally, it is treated simply, but in this recipe the fish is cooked with onions and tomatoes.

SERVES 6

300ml/½ pint/1¼ cups olive oil
2 onions, thinly sliced
3 large, well-flavoured tomatoes,
   roughly chopped
3 garlic cloves, thinly sliced
5ml/1 tsp sugar
5ml/1 tsp chopped fresh dill
5ml/1 tsp chopped fresh mint
5ml/1 tsp chopped fresh celery leaves
15ml/1 tbsp chopped fresh flat
   leaf parsley
300ml/½ pint/1¼ cups water
6 hake or cod steaks
juice of 1 lemon
salt and ground black pepper
extra fresh dill, mint or parsley sprigs,
   to garnish

1 Heat the oil in large heavy sauté pan or flameproof casserole. Add the onions and cook, stirring, until pale golden, then add the tomatoes, garlic, sugar, dill, mint, celery leaves and parsley with the water. Season with salt and pepper, then simmer, uncovered, for 25 minutes, until the liquid has reduced by one-third.

2 Add the fish steaks and cook gently for 10–12 minutes until the fish is just cooked. Remove the pan or casserole from the heat and add the lemon juice. Cover and leave to stand for 20 minutes before serving. Arrange the cod in a dish and pour the sauce over. Garnish with herbs and serve warm or cold.

Energy 455Kcal/1885kJ; Protein 29g; Carbohydrate 6.5g, of which sugars 5.3g; Fat 34.9g, of which saturates 5g; Cholesterol 69mg; Calcium 64mg; Fibre 2.2g; Sodium 103mg.

SEAFOOD PIE with RÖSTI TOPPING

In this variation of a classic fish pie, a mixture of white fish and shellfish are combined with a creamy herb-flavoured sauce and finished with a grated potato topping.

SERVES 4

750g/1lb 10oz potatoes, unpeeled
and scrubbed
50g/2oz/¼ cup butter, melted
350g/12oz cod or haddock fillets, skinned
and cut into bitesize pieces
115g/4oz cooked, peeled prawns (shrimp)
115g/4oz cooked, shelled mussels
8–12 shelled queen scallops
50g/2oz/¼ cup butter
1 onion, finely chopped
50g/2oz/½ cup plain (all-purpose) flour
200ml/7fl oz/scant 1 cup dry white wine
300ml/½ pint/1¼ cups fish or
vegetable stock
105ml/7 tbsp double (heavy) cream
30ml/2 tbsp chopped fresh dill, plus extra
sprigs to garnish
15ml/1 tbsp chopped fresh parsley
60ml/4 tbsp freshly grated
Parmesan cheese
salt and ground black pepper

1 Place the potatoes in a large pan. Cover with cold water and bring to the boil. Cook for 10–15 minutes, or until they are only just tender.

VARIATIONS
• For a speedy version of these individual pies, buy ready-prepared potato rösti and sprinkle it evenly over the fish and sauce as in step 6.
• To make an alternative topping, cook the potatoes until soft, drain and mash with a little milk and butter. Spoon the mashed potato over the fish and sauce and top with cheese as in step 6.
• Add 30ml/2 tbsp chopped capers to the sauce at the end of step 5.

2 Drain the potatoes well, and set aside until they are cool enough to handle. Peel and coarsely grate the par-boiled potatoes into a large mixing bowl. Stir in the melted butter and season well with salt and pepper.

3 Preheat the oven to 220°C/425°F/ Gas 7. Divide the pieces of cod or haddock and the prawns, mussels and scallops among four individual 19cm/ 7½in rectangular earthenware dishes.

4 Melt the butter in a large pan, add the onion and cook for 6–8 minutes, stirring occasionally with a wooden spoon, or until softened and light golden. Sprinkle in the flour and stir thoroughly with a wooden spoon until well blended.

5 Remove the pan from the heat and gradually pour in the wine and stock, stirring constantly until smooth. Bring to the boil, stirring constantly, then stir in the cream, dill and parsley and season to taste. Pour the sauce over the fish.

6 Sprinkle the grated potato evenly over the fish and sauce in the dishes and top with the grated Parmesan cheese. Bake for 25 minutes, or until the topping is crisp and golden and the fish is cooked. Serve hot, garnished with dill.

COOK'S TIP
Choose waxy potatoes for this dish and cook until barely tender. Floury potatoes are too soft and will break up, so if you only have floury potatoes, opt for the mashed potato option (see Variations).

Energy 770Kcal/3215kJ; Protein 47.3g; Carbohydrate 44.5g, of which sugars 4.5g; Fat 42.4g, of which saturates 25.5g; Cholesterol 236mg; Calcium 298mg; Fibre 2.7g; Sodium 626mg.

SHELLFISH TAGINE

*The distinctive mixture of spices and chillies used in this tagine is known as charmoula –
a classic Moroccan marinade for fish, meat and vegetable dishes.*

SERVES 4

60ml/4 tbsp olive oil
4 garlic cloves, sliced
1–2 green chillies, seeded and chopped
a large handful of flat leaf parsley,
　　roughly chopped
5ml/1 tsp coriander seeds
2.5ml/½ tsp ground allspice
6 cardamom pods, split open
2.5ml/½ tsp ground turmeric
15ml/1 tbsp lemon juice
350g/12oz scorpion fish, red mullet or red
　　snapper fillets, cut into large chunks
225g/8oz squid, cleaned and cut into rings
1 onion, chopped
4 tomatoes, seeded and chopped
300ml/½ pint/1¼ cups warm fish or
　　vegetable stock
225g/8oz large, raw prawns (shrimp)
15ml/1 tbsp chopped fresh
　　coriander (cilantro)
salt and ground black pepper
lemon wedges, to garnish
couscous or rice and crusty bread,
　　to serve

1 Place the olive oil, garlic, chillies, parsley, coriander seeds, allspice and cardamom pods in a mortar and pound to a smooth paste using a pestle. Stir in the ground turmeric, salt, pepper and lemon juice.

VARIATIONS

Scorpion fish is the traditional choice for this dish and red mullet or snapper makes a good, authentic alternative, but there's no reason why you shouldn't substitute other fish – try red bream, porgy or even halved cod or hake steaks.

2 Place the chunks of fish in a large glass or china bowl with the squid rings, add the spice paste and toss together. Cover and leave the fish to marinate in the refrigerator for about 2 hours, or longer, if time allows.

3 Place the chopped onion, seeded and chopped tomatoes and fish or vegetable stock in a tagine (see Cook's Tip) and cover. Place the tagine in an unheated oven and set the oven to 200°C/400°F/ Gas 6. Cook the vegetables for 20 minutes.

4 Remove the fish from the marinade, then drain well. Set aside the squid and any excess marinade, then place the fish in the tagine with the vegetables. Cover and cook in the oven for 5 minutes.

5 Add the prawns, squid rings and the remaining marinade to the tagine and stir to combine. Cover the tagine and return it to the oven for 5–10 minutes, or until all the fish, prawns and squid are cooked right through.

6 Taste the sauce and season to taste with salt and pepper if necessary, then stir in the chopped coriander. Serve immediately, garnished with lemon wedges. Serve the tagine with couscous or rice and crusty bread to soak up the juices.

COOK'S TIPS

• A tagine is a traditional Moroccan stew and it is also the name given to the shallow earthenware cooking dish with a tall, conical, earthenware lid in which the stew is traditionally cooked. A shallow, earthenware baking dish or a soaked, shallow clay pot can be used in place of a tagine.
• To ensure that the fish fillets have no tiny bones left in the flesh after filleting, lay the fillets on a board, skin-side down, and run your hand gently over the surface of the flesh. Pull out any bones that you find using a pair of tweezers.

Energy 301Kcal/1261kJ; Protein 37.2g; Carbohydrate 7.1g, of which sugars 5.5g; Fat 14g, of which saturates 2.2g; Cholesterol 269mg; Calcium 128mg; Fibre 2.2g; Sodium 251mg.

FISH with SPINACH and LIME

Fresh herbs and hot spices are combined to make the charmoula marinade that is used to flavour this delicious Moroccan-style dish. Crusty bread makes a good accompaniment.

SERVES 4

675g/1½lb white fish, such as haddock, cod, sea bass or monkfish
sunflower oil, for frying
500g/1¼lb potatoes, sliced
1 onion, chopped
1–2 garlic cloves, crushed
5 tomatoes, peeled and chopped
375g/13oz fresh spinach, chopped
lime wedges, to garnish

For the charmoula
6 spring onions (scallions), chopped
10ml/2 tsp fresh thyme
60ml/4 tbsp chopped flat leaf parsley
30ml/2 tbsp chopped fresh
    coriander (cilantro)
10ml/2 tsp paprika
generous pinch of cayenne pepper
60ml/4 tbsp olive oil
grated rind of 1 lime and 60ml/4 tbsp
    lime juice
salt

1 Cut the white fish into large even-size pieces, discarding any skin and bones. Place the fish in a large shallow dish.

2 Blend together the ingredients for the charmoula. Season with salt. Pour over the fish, stir to mix and leave in a cool place, covered with clear film (plastic wrap), to marinate for 2–4 hours.

3 Heat about 5mm/¼in oil in a large heavy pan, add the potato slices and cook, turning them occasionally, until they are cooked right through and golden brown. Drain the fried potatoes on kitchen paper.

4 Pour off all but 15ml/1 tbsp of the oil from the pan and add the onion, garlic and tomatoes. Cook over a gentle heat for 5–6 minutes, stirring occasionally, until the onion is soft. Place the potatoes on top and then add the spinach.

5 Place the marinated fish pieces on top of the chopped spinach in the pan and pour over all of the marinade. Cover the pan tightly and cook for 15–18 minutes. After about 8 minutes of the cooking time, carefully stir the contents of the pan with a wooden spoon, so that the pieces of fish at the top are distributed throughout the dish.

6 Cover the pan again and continue cooking, but check occasionally – the dish is cooked once the fish is just tender and opaque and the spinach has wilted. Serve the dish hot, with wedges of lime and plenty of warm crusty bread, if you like.

Energy 433Kcal/1810kJ; Protein 37.3g; Carbohydrate 28.9g, of which sugars 9.4g; Fat 19.3g, of which saturates 2.8g; Cholesterol 78mg; Calcium 206mg; Fibre 5.2g; Sodium 260mg.

FISH with FREGOLA

This Sardinian speciality is a cross between a soup and a stew. Serve it with crusty Italian country bread to mop up the juices.

SERVES 4–6

75ml/5 tbsp olive oil
4 garlic cloves, finely chopped
½ small fresh red chilli, seeded and
    finely chopped
1 large handful fresh flat leaf parsley,
    roughly chopped
1 red snapper, about 450g/1lb, cleaned,
    with head and tail removed
1 grey mullet or porgy, about 500g/1¼lb,
    cleaned, with head and tail removed
350–450g/12oz–1lb thick cod fillet
400g/14oz can chopped plum tomatoes
175g/6oz/1½ cups dried fregola
250ml/8fl oz/1 cup water
salt and ground black pepper

1 Heat 30ml/2 tbsp of the olive oil in a large flameproof casserole. Add the chopped garlic and chilli, with about half the chopped fresh parsley. Fry over a medium heat, stirring occasionally, for about 5 minutes.

2 Cut all of the fish into large chunks – including the skin and the bones in the case of the snapper and mullet – and add the pieces to the casserole. Sprinkle with a further 30ml/2 tbsp of the olive oil and fry for a few minutes more.

3 Add the tomatoes, then fill the empty can with water and add to the pan. Bring to the boil. Season to taste, lower the heat and cook for 10 minutes.

4 Add the fregola and simmer for about 5 minutes, then add the water and the remaining oil. Simmer for 15 minutes until the fregola is just tender.

5 If the sauce becomes too thick, add more water, then taste for seasoning. Serve hot, in warmed bowls, sprinkled with the remaining parsley.

VARIATION
Any white fish fillet can be used instead of cod in this dish. Monkfish, haddock, hake or plaice could all be used.

COOK'S TIPS
• Fregola is a tiny pasta shape from Sardinia. If you can't get it, use a tiny soup pasta (*pastina*), such as *corallini* or *semi de melone*.
• You can make the basic fish sauce several hours in advance or even the day before, bringing it to the boil and adding the fregola just before serving.

Energy 300Kcal/1256kJ; Protein 29.6g; Carbohydrate 17.3g, of which sugars 2.3g; Fat 12.9g, of which saturates 1.7g; Cholesterol 44mg; Calcium 79mg; Fibre 1.1g; Sodium 126mg.

SEAFOOD PAELLA

There are as many versions of paella as there are regions of Spain. Those from near the coast contain a lot of seafood, while inland versions add chicken or pork. Here the only meat is the chorizo — essential for an authentic flavour.

SERVES 4

45ml/3 tbsp olive oil
1 large onion, chopped
2 fat garlic cloves, chopped
150g/5oz chorizo, sliced
300g/11oz small squid, cleaned
1 red (bell) pepper, seeded and sliced
4 tomatoes, peeled, seeded and diced,
    or 200g/7oz can tomatoes
about 500ml/17fl oz/generous 2 cups
    chicken stock
105ml/7 tbsp dry white wine
200g/7oz/1 cup short grain Spanish rice
    or risotto rice
a large pinch of saffron threads
150g/5oz/1¼ cups fresh or frozen peas
12 large cooked prawns (shrimp), in the
    shell, or 8 langoustines
450g/1lb mussels, scrubbed
450g/1lb clams, scrubbed
salt and ground black pepper

1 Heat the olive oil in a large sauté pan or a paella pan, add the onion and garlic and fry until the onion is translucent. Add the chorizo and fry until golden.

2 If the squid are very small, you can leave them whole; otherwise cut the bodies into rings and the tentacles into pieces. Add the squid to the pan and sauté over a high heat for 2 minutes, stirring occasionally.

3 Stir in the pepper slices and the seeded and diced tomatoes and simmer gently for 5 minutes, until the pepper slices are tender. Pour in the stock and wine, stir well and bring to the boil.

4 Stir in the rice and saffron and season to taste with salt and pepper. Spread the contents of the pan in an even layer over the base. Bring the liquid back to the boil, then lower the heat and simmer gently for 10 minutes.

5 Add the peas, prawns or langoustines, mussels and clams, stirring them gently into the rice. Cook gently for another 15–20 minutes, until the rice is tender and all the mussels and clams have opened. If any remain closed, discard them. If the paella seems dry, add a little more stock. Gently stir everything together and serve piping hot.

Energy 613Kcal/2566kJ; Protein 43.1g; Carbohydrate 57.7g, of which sugars 10g; Fat 21.8g, of which saturates 5.4g; Cholesterol 313mg; Calcium 246mg; Fibre 4.4g; Sodium 639mg.

SEAFOOD RISOTTO

Creamy, saffron-flavoured rice makes the perfect foil for shellfish. Ready-prepared, frozen seafood mixtures, which include prawns, squid and mussels, are ideal for making this quick and easy dish – remember to thaw them before cooking.

SERVES 4

1 litre/1¾ pints/4 cups hot fish or
   shellfish stock
50g/2oz/¼ cup unsalted (sweet) butter
2 shallots, chopped
2 garlic cloves, chopped
350g/12oz/1¾ cups risotto rice
150ml/¼ pint/⅔ cup dry white wine
2.5ml/½ tsp powdered saffron, or a
   pinch of saffron threads
400g/14oz mixed prepared seafood,
   thawed if frozen
30ml/2 tbsp freshly grated
   Parmesan cheese
30ml/2 tbsp chopped fresh flat leaf parsley,
   to garnish
salt and ground black pepper

1 Pour the fish or shellfish stock into a large, heavy pan. Bring it to the boil, then pour it into a large, heatproof jug (pitcher) or bowl and keep warm.

2 Melt the butter in the rinsed-out pan pan, add the shallots and garlic and cook over a low heat for 3–5 minutes, stirring occasionally, until the shallots are soft but not coloured. Add the rice, stir well to coat the grains completely with butter, then pour in the dry white wine. Cook over a medium heat, stirring occasionally, until the wine has been absorbed by the rice.

COOK'S TIP

It is essential to use proper risotto rice, such as arborio or carnaroli for this dish, it has a wonderfully creamy texture when cooked but still retains a "bite".

3 Add a ladleful of hot stock and the saffron, and cook, stirring continuously, until the liquid has been absorbed. Add the seafood and stir well. Continue to add hot stock a ladleful at a time, waiting until each quantity has been absorbed before adding more. Stir the mixture for about 20 minutes in all until the rice is swollen and creamy, but still with a little bite in the middle.

VARIATION

Use peeled prawns (shrimp), or cubes of fish such as cod or salmon in place of the mixed prepared seafood.

4 Vigorously mix in the freshly grated Parmesan cheese and season to taste, then sprinkle over the chopped parsley and serve immediately.

Energy 547Kcal/2284kJ; Protein 27.3g; Carbohydrate 71.3g, of which sugars 1.2g; Fat 13.8g, of which saturates 8.2g; Cholesterol 229mg; Calcium 195mg; Fibre 0.2g; Sodium 350mg.

BAKED SEA BREAM with TOMATOES

John Dory, halibut or sea bass can all be cooked this way. If you prefer to use filleted fish, choose a chunky fillet, such as cod, and roast it skin-side up. Roasting the tomatoes brings out their sweetness, which contrasts beautifully with the flavour of the fish.

SERVES 4–6

8 ripe tomatoes
10ml/2 tsp sugar
200ml/7fl oz/scant 1 cup olive oil
450g/1lb new potatoes
1 lemon, sliced
1 bay leaf
1 fresh thyme sprig
8 fresh basil leaves
1 sea bream, about 900g–1kg/2–2¼lb,
　cleaned and scaled
150ml/¼ pint/⅔ cup dry white wine
30ml/2 tbsp fresh white breadcrumbs
2 garlic cloves, crushed
15ml/1 tbsp finely chopped fresh parsley
salt and ground black pepper
fresh flat parsley or basil leaves, chopped,
　to garnish

1 Preheat the oven to 240°C/475°F/ Gas 9. Cut the tomatoes in half lengthwise and arrange them in a single layer in a baking dish, cut-side up. Sprinkle with sugar, salt and pepper and drizzle over a little of the olive oil. Roast for 30–40 minutes, until lightly browned. Remove the tomatoes from the dish and set aside.

2 Meanwhile, cut the potatoes into 1cm/½in slices. Place in a large pan of salted water and par-boil for 5 minutes. Drain and set aside.

3 Grease the baking dish with a little more of the oil. Arrange the potatoes in a single layer with the lemon slices over; sprinkle on the herbs. Season and drizzle with half the remaining oil. Lay the fish on top and season. Pour over the wine and the rest of the oil. Arrange the tomatoes around the fish.

4 Mix together the breadcrumbs, garlic and parsley; sprinkle over the fish. Bake for 30 minutes. Garnish with chopped parsley or basil.

Energy 440Kcal/1840kJ; Protein 26g; Carbohydrate 21.5g, of which sugars 6.6g; Fat 26.7g, of which saturates 3.4g; Cholesterol 51mg; Calcium 76mg; Fibre 2g; Sodium 205mg.

FILLETS of BRILL in RED WINE SAUCE

Forget the old maxim that red wine and fish do not go well together. The robust sauce adds colour and richness to this excellent dish, which is more than elegant enough for a dinner party. Halibut and John Dory are also good cooked this way.

SERVES 4

4 fillets of brill, about 175–200g/6–7oz
    each, skinned
150g/5oz/10 tbsp chilled butter, diced, plus
    extra for greasing
115g/4oz shallots, thinly sliced
200ml/7fl oz/scant 1 cup robust red wine
200ml/7fl oz/scant 1 cup fish stock
salt and ground black and white pepper
fresh flat leaf parsley leaves or chervil,
    to garnish

1 Preheat the oven to 180°C/350°F/ Gas 4. Season the fish fillets on both sides with salt and ground black pepper. Generously butter a shallow flameproof dish, which is large enough to take all the brill fillets in a single layer. Spread the shallots in an even layer in the dish and lay the fish fillets on top. Season well with salt and ground black pepper.

2 Pour in the red wine and fish stock, cover the dish with a lid or foil and then bring the liquid to just below boiling point. Transfer the dish to the oven and bake for 6–8 minutes, or until the brill is just cooked.

3 Using a fish slice (metal spatula), lift the fish and shallots on to a serving dish, cover with foil and keep hot.

4 Transfer the dish to the stove and bring the cooking liquid to the boil over a high heat. Cook it until it has reduced by half. Lower the heat and whisk in the chilled butter, one piece at a time, to make a smooth, shiny sauce. Season with salt and ground white pepper, set the sauce aside and keep hot.

5 Divide the shallots among four warmed plates and lay the brill fillets on top. Pour the sauce over and around the fish and garnish with the fresh flat leaf parsley or chervil.

Energy 515Kcal/2142kJ; Protein 35.6g; Carbohydrate 2.6g, of which sugars 1.9g; Fat 36.7g, of which saturates 19.5g; Cholesterol 156mg; Calcium 98mg; Fibre 0.4g; Sodium 452mg.

MONKFISH with ROCKET PESTO, PEPPERS and ONIONS

Colourful Mediterranean vegetables complement richly flavoured monkfish layered with pesto sauce in this impressive-looking clay pot dish.

SERVES 4

900g/2lb monkfish tail
50g/2oz rocket (arugula)
30ml/2 tbsp pine nuts
1 garlic clove, chopped
25g/1oz/⅓ cup freshly grated
    Parmesan cheese
90ml/6 tbsp olive oil
45ml/3 tbsp lemon juice
2 red (bell) peppers, halved
2 yellow (bell) peppers, halved
1 red onion, cut into wedges
2 courgettes (zucchini), cut into
    2.5cm/1in slices
4 fresh rosemary sprigs
salt and ground black pepper

3 Place the rocket, pine nuts, chopped garlic, freshly grated Parmesan cheese, 45ml/3 tbsp of the olive oil and 15ml/ 1 tbsp of the lemon juice in a food processor or blender and process to form a smooth paste.

1 Remove any skin or membrane from the monkfish. Using a large, sharp knife cut along one side of the central bone, as close to the bone as possible and then remove the fish fillet. Repeat on the other side. Set aside.

2 Soak a fish clay pot in cold water for 20 minutes, then drain and set aside.

VARIATIONS
• Salmon tail fillets, or thick fillets of cod or haddock could be used in place of the monkfish. Remove the skin from the fish and run your hand along the other side to check for any hidden bones and, if necessary, remove these with tweezers.
• Rocket makes an interestingly peppery pesto, but other leafy herbs can be used to make this sauce. Basil is the classic choice, but flat leaf parsley is also good.

4 Lay one fish fillet out flat, cut-side up and spread with the pesto. Place the remaining fillet on top, cut-side down, on top of the layer of pesto. Tie the fish with string at regular intervals to seal together. Sprinkle with plenty of salt and pepper to season and set aside.

5 Cut each pepper half into three lengthwise. Remove the core and seeds.

6 Place the pieces of pepper in the clay pot with the onion wedges and slices of courgette. In a small bowl, mix together 15ml/1 tbsp of the olive oil and the remaining lemon juice and sprinkle over the vegetables. Mix well and season with salt and plenty of black pepper.

7 Tuck the fresh rosemary sprigs in among the vegetables. Cover the clay pot and place in an unheated oven. Set the temperature to 220°C/425°F/Gas 7 and cook the vegetables for 20 minutes.

8 Remove the clay pot from the oven, place the monkfish parcel in the centre of the vegetables and brush it with 15ml/1 tbsp of the olive oil. Sprinkle the remaining oil over the vegetables. Cover the pot again, then return the pot to the oven and cook for 20–25 minutes more, or until the monkfish is cooked through and turns opaque.

9 To serve, cut the fish into thick slices, removing the string, if you prefer, and serve with the cooked vegetables.

Energy 477Kcal/1991kJ; Protein 47g; Carbohydrate 14.7g, of which sugars 13.7g; Fat 25.8g, of which saturates 4.5g; Cholesterol 42mg; Calcium 160mg; Fibre 4.3g; Sodium 139mg.

BAKED MONKFISH with POTATOES and GARLIC

This simple supper dish can be made with other fish. Sauce tartare or a thick vinaigrette flavoured with chopped gherkins and hard-boiled egg are delicious accompaniments.

3 Pour the main batch of stock over the potatoes and bake, uncovered, stirring once or twice, for about 50 minutes, or until the potatoes are just tender.

4 Nestle the monkfish tail into the potatoes and season well with salt and ground black pepper. Mix the 45ml/ 3 tbsp stock with the wine and use to baste the monkfish two or three times during cooking. Bake the monkfish and potatoes for 10–15 minutes.

5 Finely chop the remaining garlic. Melt the remaining butter and toss it with the fresh breadcrumbs, chopped garlic, most of the chopped parsley and seasoning. Spread the crumb mixture over the monkfish, pressing it down gently with the back of a spoon.

6 Drizzle the olive oil over the crumb-covered fish, then return the dish to the oven and bake for a final 10–15 minutes, or until the breadcrumbs are crisp and golden brown and all the liquid has been absorbed. Sprinkle the remaining chopped parsley on to the potatoes and fish and serve immediately.

SERVES 4

50g/2oz/¼ cup butter
2 onions, thickly sliced
1kg/2¼lb waxy potatoes, peeled and cut into small chunks
4 garlic cloves
a few fresh thyme sprigs
2–3 fresh bay leaves
450ml/¾ pint/scant 2 cups vegetable or fish stock, plus 45ml/3 tbsp
900g/2lb monkfish tail in one piece, membrane removed
30–45ml/2–3 tbsp white wine
50g/2oz/1 cup fresh white breadcrumbs
15g/½oz fresh flat leaf parsley, finely chopped
15ml/1 tbsp olive oil
salt and ground black pepper

1 Preheat the oven to 190°C/375°F/ Gas 5. Melt half the butter in a shallow flameproof dish and cook the onions for 5 minutes until soft. Stir in the potatoes.

2 Slice two of the garlic cloves and add them to the dish with the thyme and bay leaves, and season with salt and pepper.

Energy 529Kcal/2230kJ; Protein 45.8g; Carbohydrate 54g, of which sugars 6.5g; Fat 15g, of which saturates 7.4g; Cholesterol 63mg; Calcium 67mg; Fibre 3.5g; Sodium 245mg.

JANSSON'S TEMPTATION

A traditional Swedish favourite, this rich gratin is utterly moreish. As food writer Jane Grigson pointed out, the name probably does not refer to a specific Jansson but means "everyone's temptation" as Jansson is a common Swedish surname.

SERVES 4–6

50g/2oz/¼ cup butter
900g/2lb potatoes
2 large, sweet onions, sliced
2 × 50g/2oz cans anchovies in olive
   oil, drained
450ml/¾ pint/scant 2 cups whipping cream
   or half and half double (heavy) and
   single (light) cream
a little milk (optional)
salt and ground black pepper

1 Preheat the oven to 200°C/400°F/ Gas 6. Use 15g/½oz/1 tbsp of the butter to grease a shallow 1.5 litre/2½ pint/ 6¼ cup earthenware baking dish.

2 Using a small sharp knife, carefully cut the potatoes into thin slices, then cut the slices into fine matchstick strips.

3 Toss the potato strips with salt and ground black pepper and sprinkle half of them in the base of the prepared ovenproof dish.

COOK'S TIPS
• It is important to cover the gratin with foil for the first half of the cooking time so that the potatoes don't brown or dry out too much.
• If using whole, salted anchovies or Swedish salted sprats (US small whitebait or smelts) they will need to be boned. If they are very salty, soak in a little milk for about 30 minutes before using.
• Serve with small glasses of chilled schnapps and cold beer for an authentic Swedish flavour.

4 Lay half of the onions on top of the potatoes, season with black pepper and dot with butter. Lay the anchovies on top of the onions, then add the rest of the sliced onions and top with the remaining potatoes.

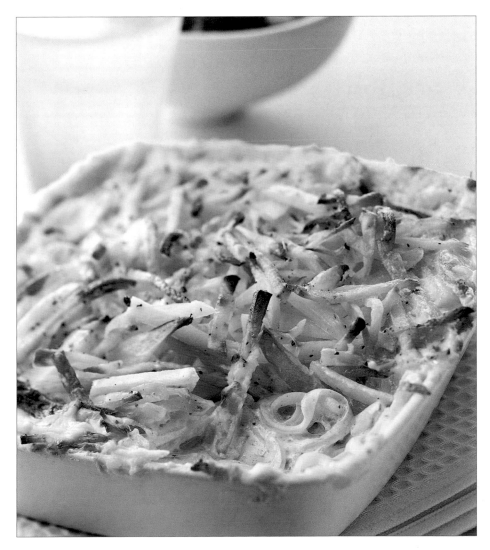

5 Mix the cream with 30ml/2 tbsp cold water and pour this mixture over the potatoes and onions in the dish. Add a little milk, if necessary, to bring the liquid to just below the top of the final layer of potato matchstick strips.

6 Dot the potatoes with the remaining butter, then cover the dish with foil and bake for 1 hour.

7 Reduce the oven temperature to 180°C/350°F/Gas 4 and remove the foil from the top of the dish. Bake for a further 40–50 minutes, or until the potatoes are tender when tested with a knife and brown in colour.

Energy 509Kcal/2111kJ; Protein 9.1g; Carbohydrate 31.5g, of which sugars 7.8g; Fat 39.3g, of which saturates 23.7g; Cholesterol 107mg; Calcium 121mg; Fibre 2.4g; Sodium 743mg.

BAKED SARDINES with CAPER and TOMATO STUFFING

Sardines are often a popular choice for cooking on the barbecue but you can enjoy these delicious Mediterranean-style baked sardines all year round.

SERVES 4

16 fresh sardines, cleaned
8–12 cherry tomatoes, on the vine, sliced
45ml/3 tbsp capers, chopped
½ small red onion, very finely chopped
60ml/4 tbsp olive oil
grated rind and juice 1 lemon
45ml/3 tbsp chopped fresh parsley
15ml/1 tbsp chopped fresh basil
basil sprigs and lemon wedges,
    to garnish
crusty bread, to serve

COOK'S TIP
Removing the bones before cooking, as in step 1 of this recipe, makes the sardines easier to eat.

1 Remove the backbone from the sardines by placing slit side down on a chopping board. Using your fingers, push firmly along the length of the backbone to loosen it from the flesh. Turn the sardine over and pull out the bone; cut the ends with a sharp knife to release it. Repeat with the remaining sardines.

2 Place the tomato slices inside each sardine; they may stick out slightly, depending on the size of the fish. Mix the capers and red onion together and place on top of the tomatoes.

3 Preheat the oven to 200°C/400°F/ Gas 6. Lay the sardines in a single layer in a large earthenware dish.

4 Mix together the olive oil, lemon rind and juice, parsley and basil and drizzle over the sardines. Bake the sardines for about 10 minutes, or until the fish flesh flakes easily. Garnish with basil and lemon wedges and serve with plenty of crusty bread to mop up the sauce.

Energy 214Kcal/887kJ; Protein 13.3g; Carbohydrate 3.4g, of which sugars 3g; Fat 16.4g, of which saturates 3.1g; Cholesterol 0mg; Calcium 89mg; Fibre 1.3g; Sodium 78mg.

SALMON BAKED with POTATOES and THYME

This is clay-pot cooking at its most sophisticated – a mouthwatering combination of potatoes and onions braised in thyme-flavoured stock and topped with perfectly tender pepper-crusted salmon fillets.

SERVES 4

675g/1½lb waxy potatoes, thinly sliced
1 onion, thinly sliced
10ml/2 tsp fresh thyme leaves
450ml/¾ pint/scant 2 cups vegetable or
    fish stock
40g/1½oz/3 tbsp butter,
    finely diced
4 skinless salmon fillets, about
    150g/5oz each
30ml/2 tbsp olive oil
15ml/1 tbsp black peppercorns,
    roughly crushed
salt and ground black pepper
fresh thyme, to garnish
mangetouts (snow peas) or sugar snap
    peas, to serve

1 Soak a fish clay pot in cold water for 20 minutes, then drain.

2 Layer the potato and onion slices in the clay pot, seasoning each layer and sprinkling with thyme. Pour over the stock, dot with butter, cover and place in an unheated oven.

3 Set the oven to 190°C/375°F/Gas 5. Bake the potatoes for 40 minutes then remove the lid and bake for a further 20 minutes, or until they are almost cooked.

4 Meanwhile brush the salmon fillets with olive oil and coat with crushed black peppercorns, pressing them in, if necessary, with the back of a spoon. Place the salmon on top of the potatoes, cover and cook for 15 minutes, or until the salmon is opaque, removing the lid for the last 5 minutes. Serve garnished with fresh thyme sprigs and with mangetouts or sugar snap peas to accompany.

Energy 517Kcal/2160kJ; Protein 33.4g; Carbohydrate 28.4g, of which sugars 3.1g; Fat 30.8g, of which saturates 9g; Cholesterol 96mg; Calcium 47mg; Fibre 1.9g; Sodium 147mg.

BAKED SEA BASS with LEMON GRASS and RED ONIONS

Moist, tender sea bass is flavoured with a combination of traditional Thai ingredients in this simple but mouthwatering clay pot dish.

SERVES 2–3

1 sea bass, about 675g/1½lb, cleaned
    and scaled
30ml/2 tbsp olive oil
2 lemon grass stalks, finely sliced
1 red onion, finely shredded
1 chilli, seeded and finely chopped
5cm/2in piece fresh root ginger,
    finely shredded
45ml/3 tbsp chopped fresh
    coriander (cilantro)
rind and juice of 2 limes
30ml/2 tbsp light soy sauce
salt and ground black pepper

COOK'S TIP
This recipe will taste delicious using a variety of fish, such as red or grey mullet, red snapper, salmon or tilapia. Depending on the weight of the fish you may need to use two smaller fish rather than one whole one.

1 Soak a fish clay pot in cold water for 20 minutes, then drain. Make four to five diagonal slashes on both sides of the fish. Repeat the slashes on one side in the opposite direction to give an attractive cross-hatched effect. Rub the sea bass inside and out with salt, pepper and 15ml/1 tbsp of the olive oil.

2 Mix together the Thai ingredients – the lemon grass, red onion, chilli, ginger, coriander and lime rind.

3 Place a little of the lemon grass and red onion mixture in the base of the clay pot, then lay the fish on top. Sprinkle the remaining mixture over the fish, then sprinkle over the lime juice, soy sauce and the remaining olive oil. Cover and place in an unheated oven.

4 Set the oven to 220°C/425°F/Gas 7 and cook the fish for 30–40 minutes, or until the flesh flakes easily when tested with a knife. Serve immediately.

Energy 298Kcal/1248kJ; Protein 43.7g; Carbohydrate 1.6g, of which sugars 1.1g; Fat 13g, of which saturates 1.9g; Cholesterol 180mg; Calcium 298mg; Fibre 0.3g; Sodium 156mg.

SWORDFISH STEAKS with MANGO and AVOCADO SALSA

Meaty swordfish steaks, marinated in a tangy mix of lime juice, coriander and chilli, served with a vibrant fruity salsa.

SERVES 4

4 swordfish steaks, about 150g/5oz each
lime wedges and shredded spring onions
   (scallions), to garnish

For the marinade
rind and juice of 2 limes
2 garlic cloves, crushed
1 red chilli, seeded and finely chopped
30ml/2 tbsp olive oil
30ml/2 tbsp chopped fresh
   coriander (cilantro)
salt and ground black pepper

For the salsa
1 mango
4 spring onions (scallions), thinly sliced
1 red chilli, seeded and finely chopped
30ml/2 tbsp chopped fresh dill or
   coriander (cilantro)
30ml/2 tbsp lime juice
30ml/2 tbsp olive oil
1 ripe avocado

1 Place the swordfish steaks in a shallow non-metallic dish. Mix together the marinade ingredients and pour over the swordfish. Cover and leave to marinate in the refrigerator for 2 hours, or longer if time allows.

2 Soak a fish clay pot in cold water for 20 minutes, then drain. To prepare the salsa, peel the mango and slice the flesh off the stone (pit). Cut the flesh into rough dice. Add the spring onions, chilli, dill or coriander, lime juice and olive oil. Toss the ingredients together, cover and set aside to allow the flavours to blend.

3 Place the swordfish steaks in the clay pot and pour over the marinade. Cover and place in an unheated oven. Set the oven to 220°C/425°F/Gas 7 and bake for 15–20 minutes, or until the fish is cooked. The time will vary depending on the thickness of the steaks.

4 To complete the salsa, using a sharp knife, cut the avocado in half, remove the stone (pit), then roughly dice the flesh. Stir it into the prepared salsa ingredients and mix well. Serve the swordfish steaks with a mound of salsa, garnished with lime wedges and shredded spring onions.

Energy 311Kcal/1297kJ; Protein 29g; Carbohydrate 5.5g, of which sugars 5.3g; Fat 19.4g, of which saturates 3.3g; Cholesterol 69mg; Calcium 30mg; Fibre 1.3g; Sodium 212mg.

SLOW COOKER POULTRY AND GAME

The slow cooker is perfect for making all manner of stews, casseroles and curries, and this chapter is packed with fantastic, healthy recipe ideas using poultry and game as the basis. Chicken is always a firm favourite, and the versatility of the slow cooker means that there is something here for everyone. In addition, there are plenty of other poultry and game dishes to whet the appetite, using turkey, guinea fowl and rabbit. All of these recipes draw their inspiration from favourite cuisines around the world, giving a wonderful choice of dishes for every occasion. Try Mexican Drunken Chicken, Indian Chicken Korma, Creole Jambalaya or French Duck Stew.

TURKEY and TOMATO HOT-POT

Often reserved for festive meals, turkey makes a great choice for any occasion. Here the meat is shaped into balls and simmered with rice in a richly flavoured tomato sauce.

SERVES 4

white bread loaf, unsliced
30ml/2 tbsp milk
1 garlic clove, crushed
2.5ml/½ tsp caraway seeds
225g/8oz minced (ground) turkey
1 egg white
350ml/12fl oz/1½ cups near-boiling
　chicken stock
400g/14oz can chopped tomatoes
15ml/1 tbsp tomato purée (paste)
90g/3½oz/½ cup easy-cook
　(converted) rice
salt and ground black pepper
15ml/1 tbsp chopped fresh basil, to garnish
courgette (zucchini) ribbons, to serve

1 Using a serrated knife, remove the crusts and cut the bread into cubes.

2 Place the bread in a mixing bowl and sprinkle with the milk, then leave to soak for about 5 minutes.

3 Add the garlic clove, caraway seeds, turkey, and salt and pepper to the bread and mix together well.

4 Whisk the egg white until stiff, then fold, half at a time, into the turkey mixture. Chill in the refrigerator.

5 Pour the stock into the ceramic cooking pot. Add the tomatoes and tomato purée, then switch to high, cover with the lid and cook for 1 hour.

6 Meanwhile, shape the turkey mixture into 16 small balls. Stir the rice into the tomato mixture, then add the turkey balls. Cook on high for a further hour, or until the turkey balls and rice are cooked. Serve with the courgettes.

Energy 187Kcal/797kJ; Protein 18.2g; Carbohydrate 26.6g, of which sugars 3.9g; Fat 1.7g, of which saturates 0.5g; Cholesterol 32mg; Calcium 44mg; Fibre 1g; Sodium 212mg.

LAYERED CHICKEN and MUSHROOM BAKE

*This rich, creamy dish makes a hearty winter supper. The thick sauce combines with
juices from the mushrooms and chicken during cooking to make a well-flavoured gravy.*

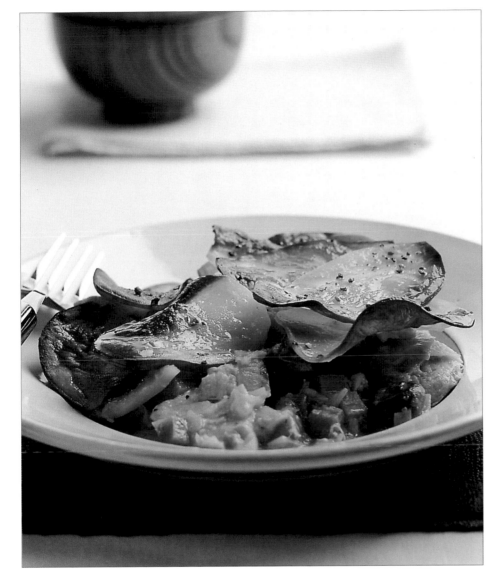

2 Add 25g/1oz/2 tbsp of the butter to
the pan and heat gently until melted.
Stir in the leek and fry gently for about
minutes. Sprinkle the flour over the
leeks, then turn off the heat and
gradually blend in the milk until smooth.
Slowly bring the mixture to the boil,
stirring all the time, until thickened.

3 Remove the pan from the heat and
stir in the Worcestershire sauce, if using,
mustard, diced carrot, mushrooms and
chicken. Season generously.

4 Arrange enough potato slices to cover
the base of the ceramic cooking pot.
Spoon one-third of the chicken mixture
over the top, then cover with another
layer of potatoes. Repeat layering,
finishing with a layer of potatoes. Dot
the remaining butter on top.

5 Cover and cook on high for 4 hours,
or until the potatoes are cooked and
tender when pierced with a skewer.
If you like, place the dish under a
moderate grill (broiler) for 5 minutes
to brown, then serve.

SERVES 4

15ml/1 tbsp olive oil
4 large chicken breast portions,
   cut into chunks
40g/1½oz/3 tbsp butter
1 leek, finely sliced into rings
25g/1oz/¼ cup plain (all-purpose) flour
550ml/18fl oz/2½ cups milk
5ml/1 tsp Worcestershire sauce (optional)
5ml/1 tsp wholegrain mustard
1 carrot, finely diced
225g/8oz/3 cups button (white)
   mushrooms, thinly sliced
900g/2lb potatoes, thinly sliced
salt and ground black pepper

1 Heat the olive oil in a large pan. Add
the chicken and fry gently until beginning
to brown. Remove the chicken from the
pan using a slotted spoon, leaving any
juices behind. Set aside.

Energy 461Kcal/1943kJ; Protein 42.4g; Carbohydrate 43.8g, of which sugars 5.2g; Fat 14.1g, of which saturates 6.4g; Cholesterol 126.3mg; Calcium 49mg; Fibre 4.3g; Sodium 351mg.

APRICOT and ALMOND STUFFED CHICKEN

Couscous makes a delicious and simple base for this sweet-and-sour stuffing flavoured with dried apricots and crunchy toasted almonds. A couple of spoonfuls of orange jelly marmalade adds tanginess to the sauce, as well as thickening it slightly.

SERVES 4

50g/2oz/¼ cup dried apricots
150ml/¼ pint/⅔ cup orange juice
4 skinned boneless chicken breast portions
50g/2oz/⅓ cup instant couscous
150ml/¼ pint/⅔ cup boiling chicken stock
25g/1oz/¼ cup chopped toasted almonds
1.5ml/¼ tsp dried tarragon
1 egg yolk
30ml/2 tbsp orange jelly marmalade
salt and ground black pepper
boiled or steamed basmati and wild rice,
   to serve

1 Put the dried apricots in a small bowl and pour over the orange juice. Leave to soak at room temperature while you prepare the remaining ingredients.

2 Using a sharp knife, cut a deep pocket horizontally in each chicken breast portion, taking care not to cut all the way through. Put the chicken portions between two sheets of oiled baking parchment or clear film (plastic wrap), then gently beat with a rolling pin or mallet until slightly thinner.

3 Put the couscous in a bowl and spoon over 50ml/2fl oz/¼ cup of the stock. Leave to stand for 2–3 minutes, or until all the stock has been absorbed.

4 Drain the apricots, reserving the juice, then stir them into the couscous along with the chopped almonds and tarragon. Season with salt and black pepper, then stir in just enough egg yolk to bind the mixture together.

5 Divide the stuffing equally between the chicken portions, packing it firmly into the pockets, then securing with wooden cocktail sticks (toothpicks). Place the stuffed chicken portions in the base of the ceramic cooking pot.

6 Stir the orange marmalade into the remaining hot stock until dissolved, then stir in the orange juice. Season with salt and pepper and pour over the chicken. Cover the pot and cook on high for 3–5 hours, or until the chicken is cooked through and tender.

7 Remove the chicken from the sauce and keep warm. Tip the sauce into a wide pan and boil rapidly until reduced by half. Carve the chicken into slices on the diagonal and arrange on serving plates. Spoon over the sauce and serve immediately with basmati and wild rice.

COOK'S TIP
Sautéed spinach or steamed green vegetables make a great accompaniment to this dish. They go particularly well with the sweet, fruity stuffing.

Energy 379Kcal/1604kJ; Protein 40.2g; Carbohydrate 38g, of which sugars 27g; Fat 8.5g, of which saturates 1.3g; Cholesterol 155mg; Calcium 61mg; Fibre 1.6g; Sodium 117mg.

HEN in a POT with PARSLEY SAUCE

Although harder to find nowadays, a boiling fowl will feed a family well. A large chicken could replace the boiling fowl. Serve with potatoes boiled in their jackets and cabbage.

SERVES 6

1.6–1.8kg/3½–4lb boiling fowl or
    whole chicken
½ lemon, sliced
small bunch of parsley and thyme
675g/1½lb carrots, cut into large chunks
12 shallots or small onions, left whole

For the sauce
50g/2oz/½ cup butter
50g/2oz/½ cup plain (all-purpose) flour
15ml/1 tbsp lemon juice
60ml/4 tbsp chopped flat leaf parsley
150ml/½ pint/⅔ cup milk
salt and ground black pepper
sprigs of flat leaf parsley, to garnish

VARIATION
A small joint of ham or bacon can also be added to the pot if available. Soak it overnight in cold water before cooking and do not add any extra salt without tasting first. A boiling fowl with a small joint of bacon, weighing 900g–lkg/2–2¼lb in total, should feed 8–10 people. Red cabbage makes a tasty accompaniment.

1 Remove any trussing string and loose pieces of fat from inside the boiling fowl or chicken, then rinse under cold water and place in the ceramic cooking pot. Add the lemon, parsley and thyme, carrots and onions and season well.

2 Pour in near-boiling water to just cover the fowl and vegetables. Cover with the lid, switch the slow cooker to high and cook for 1 hour.

3 Skim off any scum and fat using a slotted spoon. Re-cover the pot and cook for 2–2½ hours, or until the fowl is cooked and tender. Using a slotted spoon, lift the fowl on to a warmed serving dish, arrange the vegetables around it and keep warm.

4 Strain the cooking liquid into a pan and boil uncovered to reduce by a third. Strain and leave to settle for 2 minutes, then skim the fat off the surface.

5 Melt the butter in a saucepan, add the flour and cook, stirring, for 1 minute. Gradually stir in the stock (there should be about 600ml/1 pint/2½ cups) and bring to the boil.

6 Add the lemon juice, parsley and milk to the pan. Season with salt and ground black pepper and simmer the sauce for another 1–2 minutes.

7 To serve, pour a little of the sauce over the fowl and add the carrots and onions, then garnish with a few sprigs of fresh parsley, and take to the table for carving. Pour the rest of the sauce into a warmed sauceboat and serve separately.

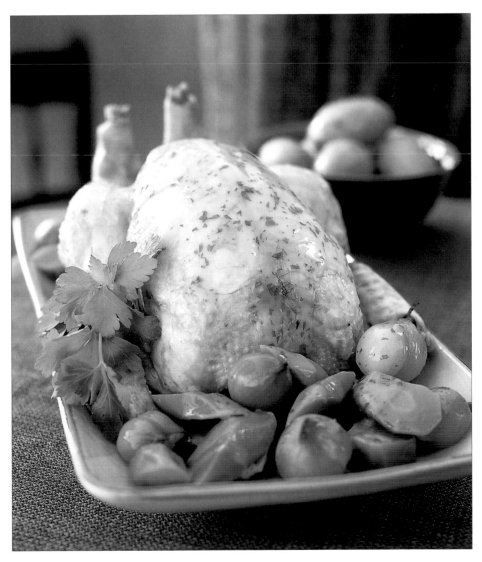

Energy 509Kcal/2114kJ; Protein 36.2g; Carbohydrate 20.1g, of which sugars 12.2g; Fat 32g, of which saturates 11.4g; Cholesterol 195mg; Calcium 109mg; Fibre 4g; Sodium 214mg

CHICKEN FRICASSÉE

Traditionally made with chicken, rabbit or veal, this fricassée dish has a wonderfully rich and flavoursome sauce that is further enhanced with cream and fresh herbs. The meat is first seared in fat, then braised in stock with vegetables until tender. It is a perfect dish for entertaining because you can prepare it in advance and then simply leave it to simmer while you enjoy the company of your guests.

SERVES 4

20 small even-size button (pearl) onions or
   shallots
1.2–1.3kg/2½–3lb chicken, cut into pieces
25g/1oz/2 tbsp butter
30ml/2 tbsp sunflower oil
45ml/3 tbsp plain (all-purpose) flour
250ml/8fl oz/1 cup dry white wine
600ml/1 pint/2½ cups boiling chicken stock
1 bouquet garni
5ml/1 tsp lemon juice
225g/8oz/3 cups button (white) mushrooms
75ml/2½fl oz/⅓ cup double (heavy) cream
45ml/3 tbsp chopped fresh parsley
salt and ground black pepper
mashed potatoes and steamed seasonal
   vegetables, to serve

1 Put the onions or shallots in a bowl, add just enough boiling water to cover them, and leave to soak.

2 Meanwhile, rinse the chicken pieces well in cold water, and pat dry with kitchen paper.

3 Melt half the butter with the oil in a large frying pan. Add the chicken pieces and cook, turning occasionally, until lightly browned all over. Using a slotted spoon or tongs, transfer the chicken pieces to the ceramic cooking pot, leaving the juices behind.

4 Stir the flour into the pan juices, then blend in the wine. Stir in the stock and add the bouquet garni and the lemon juice. Bring the mixture to the boil, stirring all the time, until the sauce has thickened. Season well and pour over the chicken. Cover the pot with the lid and switch the slow cooker to high.

5 Drain and peel the onions or shallots. (Soaking them in boiling water loosens the skins, making them easy to peel.) Trim the stalks from the mushrooms.

6 Clean the frying pan, then add the remaining butter and heat gently until melted. Add the mushrooms and onions or shallots and cook for 5 minutes, turning frequently until they are lightly browned. Tip into the ceramic cooking pot with the chicken.

7 Re-cover the slow cooker with the lid and cook on high for 3–4 hours, or until the chicken is cooked and tender. (To test that the chicken is cooked through, pierce the thickest part of one of the portions with a skewer or thin knife; the juices should run clear.)

8 Using a slotted spoon, remove the chicken and vegetables to a warmed serving dish. Add the cream and 30ml/ 2 tbsp of the parsley to the sauce and whisk to combine. Check the seasoning and adjust if necessary, then pour the sauce over the chicken and vegetables.

9 Sprinkle the fricassée with the remaining parsley and serve with mashed potatoes and seasonal vegetables.

COOK'S TIP
A classic bouquet garni is made up of parsley stalks, a sprig of thyme and a bay leaf. You can tie these together with a piece of string, or tie the herbs in a small square of muslin (cheesecloth). Some people like to add rosemary as well.

Energy 613Kcal/2563kJ; Protein 53.1g; Carbohydrate 36.4g, of which sugars 17.9g; Fat 25g, of which saturates 11.1g; Cholesterol 196mg; Calcium 128mg; Fibre 5.3g; Sodium 396mg.

SPRING CHICKEN SLOW-BRAISED in SMOKY BACON SAUCE

Sweet, succulent and tangy with the flavour of apples and aromatic thyme, this delicious stew makes a great alternative to the classic roast. Baby spring chickens are also known as poussin and can weigh 350–500g/12oz–1¼lb. Be sure to buy large ones because the smaller birds are only big enough for a single serving.

SERVES 4

2 large spring chickens
25g/1oz/2 tbsp unsalted
    (sweet) butter
10ml/2 tsp sunflower oil
115g/4oz chopped bacon pieces
    or smoked streaky (fatty) bacon
2 leeks, washed and sliced
175g/6oz/2¼ cup small button (white)
    mushrooms, trimmed
120ml/4fl oz/½ cup apple juice,
    plus a further 15ml/1 tbsp
120ml/4fl oz/½ cup chicken stock
30ml/2 tbsp clear honey
10ml/2 tsp chopped fresh thyme
    or 2.5ml/½ tsp dried
225g/8oz crisp red apples
10ml/2 tsp cornflour (cornstarch)
salt and ground black pepper
creamy mashed potatoes and
    pan-fried or steamed baby leeks,
    to serve

3 Add the chopped bacon to the pan and cook for about 5 minutes, stirring occasionally, until beginning to brown.

4 Using a slotted spoon transfer the bacon to the ceramic cooking pot, leaving all the fat and juices behind.

5 Add the leeks and mushrooms to the pan and cook for a few minutes until they begin to soften and the mushrooms begin to release their juices.

1 Using a sharp, heavy knife or a meat cleaver, carefully split the spring chickens in half to make four portions. Rinse the portions well under cold running water, then pat dry using kitchen paper.

2 Heat the butter and sunflower oil in a large pan and add the spring chicken portions. Fry, turning the pieces over, until lightly browned on all sides. Transfer the chicken portions to the ceramic cooking pot, leaving the cooking fat in the pan.

6 Pour 120ml/4fl oz/½ cup apple juice and the chicken stock into the pan, then stir in the honey and thyme. Season well with salt and ground black pepper.

7 Bring the mixture almost to boiling point, then pour over the chicken and bacon. Cover the ceramic cooking pot with the lid, switch the slow cooker to high and cook for 2 hours.

8 Quarter, core and thickly slice the apples. Add them to the cooking pot, submerging them in the liquid to stop them turning brown. Cook for a further 2 hours, or until the chicken and vegetables are cooked and tender.

9 Remove the chicken from the cooking pot, place on a plate and keep warm.

10 Blend the cornflour with the 15ml/1 tbsp apple juice and stir into the cooking liquid until thickened. Taste and adjust the seasoning, if necessary.

11 Serve the chicken on warmed plates with sauce poured over the top. Accompany with mashed potatoes and pan-fried or steamed baby leeks.

COOK'S TIP
Always check that chicken is thoroughly cooked before serving to avoid any risk of salmonella. To test, pierce the thickest part of the meat with a skewer or thin knife; the juices should run clear.

Energy 465Kcal/1945kJ; Protein 32.8g; Carbohydrate 25.9g, of which sugars 20.7g; Fat 26.3g, of which saturates 9.5g; Cholesterol 172mg; Calcium 40mg; Fibre 3.3g; Sodium 632mg.

TARRAGON CHICKEN in CIDER

Aromatic tarragon has a distinctive flavour that goes wonderfully with both cream and chicken. This recipe is truly effortless, yet provides an elegant dish for entertaining or a special family meal. Serve with sautéed potatoes and a green vegetable.

SERVES 4

350g/12oz small button (pearl) onions
15ml/1 tbsp sunflower oil
4 garlic cloves, peeled
4 boneless chicken breast portions,
  skin on
350ml/12fl oz/1½ cups dry (hard) cider
1 bay leaf
200g/7oz/scant 1 cup crème fraîche
  or sour cream
30ml/2 tbsp chopped fresh tarragon
15ml/1 tbsp chopped fresh parsley
salt and ground black pepper

1 Put the button onions in a heatproof bowl and pour over enough boiling water to cover. Leave to stand for at least 10 minutes, then drain and peel off the skins. (They should come off very easily after soaking.)

2 Heat the oil in a frying pan, add the onions and cook gently for 10 minutes, or until lightly browned, turning them frequently. Add the garlic and cook for a further 2–3 minutes. Using a slotted spoon, transfer the onions and garlic to the ceramic cooking pot.

3 Place the chicken breast portions in the frying pan and cook for 3–4 minutes, turning once or twice until lightly browned on both sides. Transfer the chicken to the ceramic cooking pot.

4 Pour the cider into the pan, add the bay leaf and a little salt and pepper, and bring to the boil.

5 Pour the hot cider and bay leaf over the chicken. Cover the ceramic cooking pot with the lid and cook on low for 4–5 hours, or until the chicken and onions are cooked and very tender. Lift out the chicken breasts. Set aside while you finish preparing the cider sauce.

COOK'S TIP
When preparing and cooking poultry, always be sure to wash utensils, surfaces and hands afterwards to avoid risk of contamination or food poisoning. Use a plastic or glass chopping board when cutting all poultry, meat or fish because they are easier to wash and much more hygienic. Wooden boards are absorbent and should therefore be avoided.

6 Stir the crème fraîche or sour cream and the herbs into the sauce. Return the chicken breasts to the pot and cook for a further 30 minutes on high, or until piping hot. Serve the chicken immediately, with lightly sautéed potatoes and a green vegetable, such as cabbage.

VARIATIONS
• Guinea fowl and pheasant portions can also be cooked in this way. Try using white wine in place of the cider and serve with creamy mashed potatoes and steamed baby carrots drizzled with a little melted butter.
• Try using 1 or 2 sprigs of fresh thyme in place of the tarragon. It gives a very different flavour but is equally good. Serve with rice and roasted tomatoes.

Energy 520Kcal/2167kJ; Protein 36.9g; Carbohydrate 12.1g, of which sugars 9.2g; Fat 33.9g, of which saturates 12.9g; Cholesterol 184mg; Calcium 90mg; Fibre 1.5g; Sodium 138mg.

CHICKEN with CHIPOTLE SAUCE

Spicy-hot and deliciously rich and smoky, this dish of chicken cooked in a rich chilli sauce is great served with rice for a tasty, healthy supper. The purée can be prepared ahead of time, making this recipe ideal for casual entertaining.

SERVES 6

6 chipotle chillies
200ml/7fl oz/scant 1 cup boiling water
about 200ml/7fl oz/scant 1 cup chicken
    stock
45ml/3 tbsp vegetable oil
3 onions
6 boneless chicken breast portions
salt and ground black pepper
fresh oregano, to garnish

COOK'S TIP
Spicy-hot, wrinkled, dark red chipotle chillies are smoke-dried jalepeños and have a really rich taste. To really bring out their flavour, they need long, slow cooking – making them perfect for slow cooker casseroles.

1 Put the dried chillies in a bowl and cover with the boiling water. Leave to stand for about 30 minutes until very soft. Drain, reserving the soaking water in a measuring jug (pitcher). Cut off the stalk from each chilli, then slit the chilli lengthways and scrape out the seeds with a small, sharp knife.

2 Chop the chillies roughly and put in a food processor or blender. Add enough chicken stock to the soaking water to make it up to 400ml/14fl oz/1⅔ cups, then pour into the food processor or blender. Process until smooth.

3 Heat the oil in a frying pan. Halve and slice the onions and add them to the pan. Cook, stirring, over a medium heat for 5 minutes, or until soft but not coloured.

4 Transfer the onions to the ceramic cooking pot and switch to high. Sprinkle the onion slices with a little salt and ground black pepper.

5 Remove the skin from the chicken breast portions and trim off any pieces of fat. Arrange in a single layer on top of the onion slices. Sprinkle with a little salt and several grindings of black pepper.

6 Pour the chilli purée over the chicken, making sure that each piece is evenly coated. Cover with the lid and cook for 3–4 hours, or until the chicken is cooked through but still moist and tender. Garnish with fresh oregano and serve.

Energy 235Kcal/989kJ; Protein 36.9g; Carbohydrate 5.9g, of which sugars 4.2g; Fat 7.3g, of which saturates 1.1g; Cholesterol 105mg; Calcium 26mg; Fibre 1.1g; Sodium 92mg.

DRUNKEN CHICKEN

Flavoured with a mixture of sherry and tequila, this rich, fruity casserole makes a great meal for any occasion. Serve with bowls of steamed or plain boiled rice to soak up the juices, or with warmed flour tortillas to scoop up the chicken and sauce.

SERVES 4

150g/5oz/1 cup raisins
120ml/4fl oz/½ cup sherry
115g/4oz/1 cup plain (all-purpose) flour
2.5ml/½ tsp salt
2.5ml/½ tsp ground black pepper
45ml/3 tbsp vegetable oil
8 skinless chicken thighs
1 onion, halved and thinly sliced
2 garlic cloves, crushed
2 tart eating apples
115g/4oz/1 cup flaked (sliced) almonds
1 slightly under-ripe plantain, peeled
    and sliced
300ml/½ pint/1¼ cups boiling
    chicken stock
120ml/4fl oz/½ cup tequila
chopped fresh herbs, to garnish

1 Put the raisins in a bowl and add the sherry. Set aside to soak.

2 Meanwhile, combine the flour, salt and pepper and spread the mixture out on a large plate. Heat 30ml/2 tbsp of the oil in a large frying pan. Coat each chicken thigh in the seasoned flour, then fry, turning, until browned all over. Drain well on kitchen paper.

3 Heat the remaining oil in the pan, add the onion and fry for 5 minutes, or until soft and beginning to brown. Stir in the garlic, then remove the pan from the heat. Tip the onions and garlic into the ceramic cooking pot and switch the slow cooker to high.

4 Peel, core and dice the apples. Add them to the ceramic cooking pot, then sprinkle with the almonds, plantain slices and raisins. Pour in the sherry, chicken stock and tequila and stir to combine.

5 Add the chicken pieces to the fruit and vegetable mixture, pressing them down into the stock so that they are completely covered. Cover with the lid and cook for 3 hours, or until the chicken thighs are very tender.

6 Check the chicken is cooked: pierce the thickest part with a sharp knife or skewer; the juices should run clear. Cook for a little longer, if necessary.

7 Taste the sauce and add a little more salt and ground black pepper if necessary. Serve the chicken piping hot, sprinkled with chopped fresh herbs.

Energy 529Kcal/2227kJ; Protein 23.1g; Carbohydrate 63.7g, of which sugars 34.1g; Fat 11.5g, of which saturates 1.8g; Cholesterol 94.5mg; Calcium 76mg; Fibre 2.9g; Sodium 401mg.

CARIBBEAN PEANUT CHICKEN

Peanut butter adds a delicious richness and depth of flavour to this spicy rice dish.
It is a classic ingredient used in many slow-cooked Caribbean curries and stews.

3 Meanwhile, heat the remaining oil in a frying pan, add the onion and fry for 10 minutes until soft. Transfer to the ceramic cooking pot and switch the slow cooker to high. Add the chopped tomatoes and chilli and stir to combine.

4 Put the peanut butter into a bowl, then blend in the stock, adding a little at a time. Pour the mixture into the ceramic cooking pot, season and stir. Cover with the lid and cook for 1 hour.

5 About 30 minutes before the end of cooking time, remove the chicken from the refrigerator and leave it to come to room temperature.

6 Add the chicken and the marinade to the ceramic cooking pot and stir to mix. Re-cover and cook for 1 hour.

7 Sprinkle the rice over the casserole, then stir to mix. Cover and cook for a final 45 minutes–1 hour, or until the chicken and rice are cooked and tender. Serve straight away, garnished with lemon or lime wedges for squeezing over, and sprigs of fresh parsley.

SERVES 4

4 skinless, boneless chicken
    breast portions
45ml/3 tbsp groundnut (peanut) or
    sunflower oil
1 garlic clove, crushed
5ml/1 tsp chopped fresh thyme
15ml/1 tbsp curry powder
juice of half a lemon
1 onion, finely chopped
2 tomatoes, peeled, seeded and chopped
1 fresh green chilli, seeded and sliced
60ml/4 tbsp smooth peanut butter
750ml/1¼ pints/3 cups boiling
    chicken stock
300g/10oz/1½ cups easy-cook (converted)
    white rice
salt and ground black pepper
lemon or lime wedges and sprigs of fresh
    flat leaf parsley, to garnish

1 Cut the chicken breast portions into thin strips. In a bowl, mix together 15ml/1 tbsp of the oil with the garlic, thyme, curry powder and lemon juice.

2 Add the chicken strips to the ingredients in the bowl and stir well to combine. Cover with clear film (plastic wrap) and leave to marinate in the refrigerator for 1½–2 hours.

Energy 635Kcal/2677kJ; Protein 45.8g; Carbohydrate 70.7g, of which sugars 4.4g; Fat 20.8g, of which saturates 4.1g; Cholesterol 105mg; Calcium 65mg; Fibre 2.1g; Sodium 354mg.

JAMAICAN JERK CHICKEN

The word "jerk" refers to the herb and spice seasoning traditionally used to marinate
meat in Jamaica. It was originally used only for pork, but jerked chicken is just as good.

SERVES 4

8 chicken pieces, such as thighs and legs
15ml/1 tbsp sunflower oil
15g/½ oz/1 tbsp unsalted (sweet) butter

For the sauce
1 bunch of spring onions (scallions),
   trimmed and finely chopped
2 garlic cloves, crushed
1 hot red chilli pepper, halved, seeded
   and finely chopped
5ml/1 tsp ground allspice
2.5ml/½ tsp ground cinnamon
5ml/1 tsp dried thyme
1.5ml/¼ tsp freshly grated nutmeg
10ml/2 tsp demerara sugar
15ml/1 tbsp plain (all-purpose) flour
300ml/½ pint/1¼ cups chicken stock
15ml/1 tbsp red or white wine vinegar
15ml/1 tbsp lime juice
10ml/2 tsp tomato purée (paste)
salt and ground black pepper
salad leaves or rice, to serve

VARIATION
For jerked pork, sauté 4 pork loin steaks
(each about 90g/3½oz) in oil for 30 seconds
on each side. Make the jerk sauce as above,
using vegetable instead of chicken stock.
Cook in the same way as the chicken recipe
above, and serve with plain boiled rice and
chargrilled pineapple wedges.

1 Wipe the chicken pieces, then pat dry
on kitchen paper. Heat the oil and butter
in a frying pan until melted, then add the
chicken, in batches if necessary, and cook
until browned on all sides. Remove with
a slotted spoon, leaving the fat in the
pan, and transfer to the ceramic cooking
pot. Switch the slow cooker to high.

2 Add the spring onions, garlic and chilli
to the frying pan and cook gently for
4–5 minutes, or until softened, stirring
frequently. Stir in the allspice, cinnamon,
thyme, nutmeg and sugar. Sprinkle in the
flour and stir to mix, then gradually add
the chicken stock, stirring until the
mixture bubbles and thickens. Remove
the pan from the heat.

3 Stir the vinegar, lime juice, tomato
purée and some salt and ground black
pepper into the sauce. Pour over the
chicken pieces, cover with a lid and cook
on high for 3–4 hours, or until the
chicken is cooked and very tender.

4 Remove the chicken from the sauce
and place on a serving dish. Taste the
sauce and adjust the seasoning, then
serve separately, with salad leaves or
rice as an accompaniment.

COOK'S TIP
There are many recipes for jerk seasoning,
but all include chillies, allspice and thyme.
The spicy sauce not only flavours the
meat, it also tenderizes it.

Energy 189Kcal/794kJ; Protein 21g; Carbohydrate 7g, of which sugars 3.1g; Fat 8.8g, of which saturates 3.1g; Cholesterol 107mg; Calcium 24mg; Fibre 0.5g; Sodium 238mg.

SPICY CHICKEN JAMBALAYA

This classic Creole dish is great for a family supper, served with a simple salad. Spicy red Spanish chorizo sausage gives the stew a real flavour boost. It is available from most large supermarkets, or from specialist Mediterranean stores and delicatessens.

SERVES 6

225g/8oz skinless, boneless chicken
   breast portions
175g/6oz piece raw smoked gammon
   or bacon
30ml/2 tbsp olive oil
1 large onion, peeled and chopped
2 garlic cloves, crushed
2 sticks celery, diced
5ml/1 tsp chopped fresh thyme or
   2.5ml/½ tsp dried thyme
5ml/1 tsp mild chilli powder
2.5ml/½ tsp ground ginger
10ml/2 tsp tomato purée (paste)
2 dashes of Tabasco sauce
750ml/1¼ pints/3 cups boiling
   chicken stock
300g/10oz/1½ cups easy-cook
   (converted) rice
115g/4oz chorizo sausage (cooked), sliced
30ml/2 tbsp chopped fresh flat leaf parsley,
   plus extra, to garnish
salt and ground black pepper

1 Cut the chicken into 2.5cm/1in cubes and season with salt and pepper. Trim any fat off the gammon or bacon, then cut the meat into 1cm/½in cubes.

2 Heat 15ml/1 tbsp of the olive oil in a pan, add the onion and fry gently for about 5 minutes, until beginning to colour. Stir in the garlic, celery, thyme, chilli powder and ginger and cook for about 1 minute. Transfer the mixture to the ceramic cooking pot and turn the slow cooker to high.

3 Heat the remaining 15ml/1 tbsp olive oil in the pan, add the chicken pieces and fry briefly until lightly browned. Add the chicken to the ceramic cooking pot with the gammon or bacon cubes.

4 Add the tomato purée and Tabasco sauce to the stock and whisk together. Pour into the slow cooker, cover with the lid and cook on high for 1½ hours.

5 Sprinkle the rice into the pot and stir to mix. Cover and cook on high for 45 minutes–1 hour, or until the rice is almost tender and most of the stock has been absorbed. Check towards the end of cooking time and add a little extra hot stock or water if the mixture is dry.

6 Stir in the chorizo and cook on high for a further 15 minutes, or until heated through. Stir in the chopped parsley, then taste and adjust the seasoning. Turn off the slow cooker and leave to stand for 10 minutes. Stir with a fork to fluff up the rice, then serve garnished with chopped fresh parsley.

Energy 384Kcal/1617kJ; Protein 21.2g; Carbohydrate 48.6g, of which sugars 2.9g; Fat 13g, of which saturates 3.6g; Cholesterol 43mg; Calcium 57mg; Fibre 1.1g; Sodium 630mg.

DOROWAT

The long-simmered stews eaten in Ethiopia are known as wats *and are traditionally served with a pancake-like flatbread called* injera. *Hard-boiled eggs are added to the sauce towards the end of cooking, so that they soak up the flavour of the spices.*

SERVES 4

30ml/2 tbsp vegetable oil
2 large onions, chopped
3 garlic cloves, chopped
2.5cm/1in piece peeled and finely
    chopped fresh root ginger
175ml/6fl oz/¾ cup chicken
    or vegetable stock
250ml/8fl oz/1 cup passata (bottled
    strained tomatoes) or 400g/14oz
    can chopped tomatoes
seeds from 5 cardamom pods
2.5ml/½ tsp ground turmeric
large pinch of ground cinnamon
large pinch of ground cloves
large pinch of grated nutmeg
1.3kg/3lb chicken, cut into 8–12 portions
4 hard-boiled eggs
cayenne pepper or hot paprika, to taste
salt and ground black pepper
roughly chopped fresh coriander (cilantro)
    and onion rings, to garnish
flatbread or rice, to serve

1 Heat the oil in a large pan, add the onions and cook for 10 minutes until softened. Add the garlic and ginger and cook for 1–2 minutes.

2 Add the stock and the passata or chopped tomatoes to the pan. Bring to the boil and cook, stirring frequently, for about 10 minutes, or until the mixture has thickened, then season.

COOK'S TIP
Check the sauce just before you add the hard-boiled eggs. If it seems too thick, add a little more stock.

3 Transfer the mixture to the ceramic cooking pot and stir in the cardamom, turmeric, cinnamon, cloves and nutmeg. Add the chicken in a single layer, pushing the pieces down into the sauce.

4 Cover with the lid and cook on high for 3 hours. Remove the shells from the eggs, then prick the eggs a few times with a fork or very fine skewer. Add to the sauce and cook for 30–45 minutes, or until the chicken is cooked through and tender. Season to taste with cayenne pepper or hot paprika. Garnish with coriander and onion rings and serve with flatbread or rice.

Energy 388Kcal/1629kJ; Protein 54.6g; Carbohydrate 13g, of which sugars 9.6g; Fat 13.4g, of which saturates 2.8g; Cholesterol 13mg; Calcium 81mg; Fibre 2.5g; Sodium 311mg.

FRAGRANT CHICKEN CURRY

Lentils are used to thicken the sauce in this mild, fragrant curry, and fresh coriander gives the dish a really distinctive, fresh taste. The generous quantities of spinach mean that you won't need an additional vegetable dish to balance the meal.

2 Add the chicken to the lentil mixture, pressing it down in a single layer. Cover and cook on high for 3 hours, or until the chicken is just tender.

3 Add the spinach to the pot, pressing it down into the hot liquid. Cover and cook for a further 30 minutes until wilted. Stir in the chopped coriander.

4 Season the curry with salt and pepper to taste, then serve garnished with fresh coriander sprigs and accompanied with basmati rice and poppadums.

COOK'S TIP

You will need a large slow cooker to accommodate all the spinach in this recipe. It will shrink down during cooking, but the initial volume is large. If you have a small slow cooker, use thawed, well-drained frozen spinach instead.

SERVES 4

75g/3oz/scant ½ cup red lentils
30ml/2 tbsp mild curry powder
10ml/2 tsp ground coriander
5ml/1 tsp cumin seeds
350ml/12fl oz/1½ cups boiling vegetable
    or chicken stock
8 chicken thighs, skinned
225g/8oz fresh shredded spinach
15ml/1 tbsp chopped fresh
    coriander (cilantro)
salt and ground black pepper
sprigs of fresh coriander,
    to garnish
white or brown basmati rice
    and poppadums, to serve

1 Place the lentils in a sieve (strainer) and rinse under cold running water. Drain well, then put in the ceramic cooking pot with the curry powder, ground coriander, cumin seeds and stock. Cover and cook on high for 2 hours.

Energy 591Kcal/2490kJ; Protein 75.5g; Carbohydrate 38.2g, of which sugars 3.9g; Fat 16.1g, of which saturates 3.9g; Cholesterol 171mg; Calcium 426mg; Fibre 9.4g; Sodium 880mg.

CHICKEN in a CASHEW NUT SAUCE

The Moguls had a profound impact on the Indian cuisine, and the resulting style of cooking is known as Mughlai food. One of their legacies is the use of nut paste, which is used here to give the curry a rich yet delicately flavoured sauce.

SERVES 4

1 large onion, roughly chopped
1 clove garlic, crushed
15ml/1 tbsp tomato purée (paste)
50g/2oz/½ cup cashew nuts
7.5ml/1½ tsp garam masala
5ml/1 tsp chilli powder
1.5ml/¼ tsp ground turmeric
5ml/1 tsp salt
15ml/1 tbsp lemon juice
15ml/1 tbsp natural (plain) yogurt
30ml/2 tbsp vegetable oil
450g/1lb chicken breast fillets, skinned
  and cubed
175g/6oz/2¼ cups button (white)
  mushrooms
15ml/1 tbsp sultanas (golden raisins)
300ml/½ pint/1¼ cups chicken
  or vegetable stock
30ml/2 tbsp chopped fresh coriander
  (cilantro), plus extra to garnish
rice and fruit chutney, to serve

1 Put the onion, garlic, tomato purée, cashew nuts, garam masala, chilli powder, turmeric, salt, lemon juice and yogurt in a food processor and process to a paste.

2 Heat the oil in a large frying pan or wok and fry the cubes of chicken for a few minutes, or until just beginning to brown. Using a slotted spoon, transfer the chicken to the ceramic cooking pot, leaving the oil in the pan.

3 Add the spice paste and mushrooms to the pan, lower the heat and fry gently, stirring frequently, for 3–4 minutes. Tip the mixture into the ceramic pot.

4 Add the sultanas to the pot and stir in the chicken or vegetable stock. Cover with the lid and switch the slow cooker to high. Cook for 3–4 hours, stirring halfway through the cooking time. The chicken should be cooked through and very tender, and the sauce fairly thick.

5 Stir the chopped coriander into the sauce, then taste and add a little more salt and pepper, if necessary. Serve the curry from the ceramic cooking pot, or transfer to a warmed serving dish, and garnish with a sprinkling of chopped fresh coriander. Serve with rice and a fruit chutney, such as mango.

Energy 239Kcal/1006kJ; Protein 31.6g; Carbohydrate 10.7g, of which sugars 7.6g; Fat 8.1g, of which saturates 1.7g; Cholesterol 78.9mg; Calcium 39mg; Fibre 1.9g; Sodium 696mg.

CHICKEN KORMA

The use of ground almonds to thicken the sauce gives this mild, fragrant curry a beautifully creamy texture. Its mild taste makes it particularly popular with children.

SERVES 4

75g/3oz/¾ cup flaked (sliced) almonds
15ml/1 tbsp ghee or butter
675g/1½lb skinless, boneless chicken
    breast portions, cut into bitesize
    pieces
about 15ml/1 tbsp sunflower oil
1 onion, chopped
4 green cardamom pods
2 garlic cloves, crushed
10ml/2 tsp ground cumin
5ml/1 tsp ground coriander
pinch of ground turmeric
1 cinnamon stick
good pinch of chilli powder
250ml/8fl oz/1 cup coconut milk
120ml/4fl oz/½ cup boiling chicken stock
5ml/1 tsp tomato purée (paste) (optional)
75ml/5 tbsp single (light) cream
15–30ml/1–2 tbsp fresh lime
    or lemon juice
10ml/2 tsp grated lime or lemon rind
5ml/1 tsp garam masala
salt and ground black pepper
saffron rice and poppadums, to serve

1 Dry-fry the flaked almonds in a frying pan until pale golden. Transfer about two-thirds of the almonds to a plate and continue to dry-fry the remainder until they are slightly deeper in colour. Put the darker almonds on a separate plate and set them aside to use for the garnish. Leave the paler almonds to cool, then grind them until fine in a spice grinder or coffee mill used for the purpose.

2 Heat the ghee or butter in the frying pan and gently fry the chicken pieces until evenly brown. Transfer to a plate.

3 Add a little sunflower oil to the fat in the pan, if necessary, then fry the onion for 8 minutes. Stir in the cardamom pods and garlic and fry for a further 2 minutes, until the onion is soft and just starting to colour.

4 Add the ground almonds, cumin, coriander, turmeric, cinnamon stick and chilli powder to the frying pan and cook for about 1 minute. Transfer the mixture to the ceramic cooking pot and switch the slow cooker to high.

5 Add the coconut milk, stock and tomato purée, if using, to the pot and stir in. Add the chicken and season with salt and pepper. Cover with the lid and cook on high for 3 hours, or until the chicken is cooked and very tender.

6 Stir the cream, citrus juice and rind and the garam masala into the curry and cook on high for 30 minutes. Check the seasoning, garnish with the reserved almonds, and serve immediately with saffron rice and poppadums.

Energy 410Kcal/1714kJ; Protein 45.7g; Carbohydrate 7.8g, of which sugars 6.4g; Fat 22g, of which saturates 6g; Cholesterol 136mg; Calcium 98mg; Fibre 1.9g; Sodium 202mg.

CHICKEN and SPLIT PEA KORESH

A traditional Persian Koresh – a thick saucy stew served with rice – is usually made with lamb, but here chicken is used to create a lighter, lower-fat dish.

SERVES 4

50g/2oz/¼ cup green split peas
45ml/3 tbsp olive oil
1 large onion, finely chopped
450g/1lb boneless chicken thighs
350ml/12fl oz/1½ cups boiling
　chicken stock
5ml/1 tsp ground turmeric
2.5ml/½ tsp ground cinnamon
1.5ml/¼ tsp grated nutmeg
30ml/2 tbsp dried mint
2 aubergines (eggplant), diced
8 ripe tomatoes, diced
2 garlic cloves, crushed
salt and ground black pepper
fresh mint, to garnish
plain boiled rice, to serve

1 Put the split peas in a large bowl. Pour in cold water to cover and leave to soak for at least 6 hours or overnight.

2 Tip the split peas into a sieve (strainer) and drain well. Place in a large pan, cover with fresh cold water and bring to the boil. Boil rapidly for 10 minutes, then rinse, drain and set aside.

3 Heat 15ml/1 tbsp of the oil in a pan, add the onion and cook for about 5 minutes. Add the chicken and cook until golden on all sides, then transfer to the ceramic cooking pot. Add the split peas, hot chicken stock, turmeric, cinnamon, nutmeg and mint and season well with salt and black pepper.

4 Cover the pot with the lid and cook on high or auto for 1 hour. Switch the slow cooker to low or leave on auto and cook for a further 3 hours, or until the chicken is just cooked and the split peas are nearly tender.

5 Heat the remaining 30ml/2 tbsp of oil in a frying pan, add the diced aubergines and cook for about 5 minutes until lightly browned. Add the tomatoes and garlic and cook for a further 2 minutes.

6 Transfer the aubergines to the ceramic cooking pot, stir to combine, then cook for about 1 hour. Sprinkle with fresh mint leaves to garnish and serve with plain boiled rice.

Energy 298Kcal/1251kJ; Protein 29.1g; Carbohydrate 18.5g, of which sugars 10.2g; Fat 12.5g, of which saturates 2.3g; Cholesterol 118mg; Calcium 48mg; Fibre 4.5g; Sodium 206mg.

BRAISED GUINEA FOWL with RED CABBAGE

The slightly gamey flavour of guinea fowl is complemented perfectly by the sweet, fruity flavour of red cabbage, braised in apple juice and scented with juniper berries.

SERVES 4

15ml/1 tbsp unsalted (sweet) butter
½ red cabbage, weighing
    about 450g/1lb
1.3kg/3lb oven-ready guinea
    fowl, jointed
15ml/1 tbsp sunflower oil
3 shallots, very finely chopped
15ml/1 tbsp plain (all-purpose) flour
120ml/4fl oz/½ cup chicken stock
150ml/¼ pint/⅔ cup apple juice
15ml/1 tbsp soft light brown sugar
15ml/1 tbsp red wine vinegar
4 juniper berries, lightly crushed
salt and ground black pepper

VARIATIONS
• Other mild-tasting poultry or game such as chicken or pheasant can be used in place of the guinea fowl, if preferred.
• Add to the fruity flavour of the cabbage by adding 15ml/1tbsp sultanas (golden raisins) to the pot before cooking.

1 Use half the butter to grease the ceramic cooking pot. Cut the cabbage into wedges, removing any tough outer leaves and the central core. Shred the cabbage finely, then place in the ceramic cooking pot, packing it down tightly.

2 Rinse the guinea fowl portions and pat dry with kitchen paper. Heat the remaining butter and the oil in a pan and brown the guinea fowl on all sides. Lift from the pan, leaving the fat behind, and place on top of the red cabbage.

3 Add the shallots to the frying pan and cook gently for 5 minutes. Sprinkle with the flour, cook for a few seconds, then gradually stir in the stock followed by the apple juice. Bring to the boil, stirring continuously, until thickened. Remove from the heat, stir in the sugar, vinegar and juniper berries, and season.

4 Pour the sauce over the guinea fowl, cover and cook on high for 4 hours, or until the meat and cabbage are tender. Check the seasoning and serve.

Energy 456Kcal/1907kJ; Protein 44.5g; Carbohydrate 20g, of which sugars 15g; Fat 22.5g, of which saturates 6.7g; Cholesterol 225mg; Calcium 96mg; Fibre 3.1g; Sodium 15mg.

GUINEA FOWL and SPRING VEGETABLE STEW

Resembling a well-flavoured chicken stew, this tasty dish of guinea fowl cooked with
spring vegetables and flavoured with mustard and herbs is a sure winner.

SERVES 4

1.6kg/3½lb guinea fowl
45ml/3 tbsp plain (all-purpose) flour
45ml/3 tbsp olive oil
115g/4oz pancetta, cut into tiny cubes
1 onion, chopped
3 cloves garlic, chopped
200ml/7fl oz/scant 1 cup white wine
225g/8oz baby carrots
225g/8oz baby turnips
6 baby leeks, cut into 7.5cm/3in lengths
sprig of fresh thyme
1 bay leaf
10ml/2 tsp Dijon mustard
150ml/¼ pint/⅔ cup boiling chicken
    or vegetable stock
225g/8oz shelled peas
30ml/2 tbsp chopped fresh parsley
15ml/1 tbsp chopped fresh mint
salt and ground black pepper

1 Joint the guinea fowl into eight pieces. Wipe or lightly rinse them, then pat dry on kitchen paper. Season the flour with salt and pepper and toss the guinea fowl portions in it. Set aside any leftover flour.

2 Heat 30ml/2 tbsp of the oil in a large frying pan, add the pancetta and fry over a medium heat until lightly browned, stirring occasionally. Using a slotted spoon, transfer the pancetta to the ceramic cooking pot, leaving any fat and juices in the frying pan.

3 Add the guinea fowl portions to the pan and fry, turning, until browned on all sides. Arrange the guinea fowl portions in a single layer in the cooking pot on top of the pancetta.

4 Add the remaining 15ml/1 tbsp oil to the frying pan, add the onion and cook for 3–4 minutes, until just beginning to soften. Add the garlic and cook for about 1 minute, then stir in the reserved flour. Gradually stir in the wine and bring to the boil. Pour over the guinea fowl.

5 Add the carrots, turnips and leeks to the cooking pot with the thyme and bay leaf. Blend the mustard with the stock, season with salt and pepper and pour over. Cover with the lid and cook on high for 3–4 hours, or until the guinea fowl and vegetables are tender.

6 Add the peas to the stew and cook for a further 45 minutes. Taste and adjust the seasoning, then stir in most of the fresh herbs. Divide the stew among four warmed serving plates, sprinkle the remaining fresh herbs over the top and serve immediately.

COOK'S TIPS
• To save time on preparation, ask your butcher to joint the guinea fowl for you.
• Rabbit has a delicate flavour that goes well with the tender spring vegetables and herbs used in this stew. Try using eight rabbit joints in place of the guinea fowl.

Energy 581Kcal/2425kJ; Protein 50.5g; Carbohydrate 29.1g, of which sugars 11.2g; Fat 26.5g, of which saturates 7.4g; Cholesterol 224mg; Calcium 109mg; Fibre 6.9g; Sodium 668mg.

DUCK STEW with OLIVES

This method of cooking duck with olives, onions and wine has its roots in Provence in France. The sweetness brought out by slow-cooking the onions balances the saltiness of the olives beautifully. Simple, creamy mashed potatoes make a perfect accompaniment.

SERVES 4

4 duck quarters or breast portions
225g/8oz baby (pearl) onions, peeled
2.5ml/½ tsp caster (superfine) sugar
30ml/2 tbsp plain (all-purpose) flour
250ml/8fl oz/1 cup dry red wine
250ml/8fl oz/1 cup duck or chicken stock
1 bouquet garni
115g/4oz/1 cup pitted green or black
   olives, or a combination
salt and ground black pepper

1 Put the duck skin side down in a large frying pan and cook for 10–12 minutes, turning to colour evenly, until browned on both sides. Lift out with a slotted spoon and place skin side up in the ceramic cooking pot. Switch the slow cooker to high.

2 Pour off most of the fat from the pan, leaving about 15ml/1 tbsp behind. Add the onions and cook over a medium-low heat until beginning to colour. Sprinkle over the sugar and cook for 5 minutes until golden, stirring frequently. Sprinkle with the flour and cook, uncovered, for 2 minutes, stirring frequently.

3 Gradually stir the red wine into the onions, followed by the stock. Bring to the boil, then pour over the duck. Add the bouquet garni to the pot, cover with the lid and cook on high for 1 hour.

4 Turn the slow cooker to low and cook for a further 4–5 hours, or until the duck and onions are very tender.

5 Put the olives in a heatproof bowl and pour over very hot water to cover. Leave to stand for about 1 minute, then drain thoroughly. Add the olives to the casserole, re-cover with the lid and cook for a further 30 minutes.

6 Transfer the duck, onions and olives to a warm serving dish or individual plates. Skim all the fat from the cooking liquid and discard the bouquet garni. Season the sauce to taste with black pepper and a little salt, if needed, then spoon over the duck and serve immediately.

COOK'S TIPS
• Taste the stew before adding more salt; if the olives were salty, the stew will not need any more.
• The skin may be removed from the duck before cooking, if you prefer, and the duck pieces cooked in 15ml/1 tbsp oil for a few minutes to brown them.

Energy 414Kcal/1736kJ; Protein 47.3g; Carbohydrate 8.2g, of which sugars 2.3g; Fat 18.5g, of which saturates 5.2g; Cholesterol 257mg; Calcium 67mg; Fibre 1.6g; Sodium 917mg.

PAPPARDELLE with RABBIT

This rich-tasting dish comes from northern Italy, where rabbit sauces are very popular. It is ideal for entertaining as the sauce can be kept warm in the slow cooker until needed.

SERVES 4

15g/½oz dried porcini mushrooms
150ml/¼ pint/⅔ cup warm water
1 small onion
½ carrot
½ celery stick
2 bay leaves
25g/1oz/2 tbsp butter or 15ml/1 tbsp
    olive oil
40g/1½oz pancetta or rindless streaky
    (fatty) bacon, chopped
15ml/1 tbsp roughly chopped fresh flat leaf
    parsley, plus extra to garnish
250g/9oz boneless rabbit meat
60ml/4 tbsp dry white wine
200g/7oz can chopped Italian plum
    tomatoes or 200ml/7fl oz/scant 1 cup
    passata (bottled strained tomatoes)
300g/11oz fresh or dried pappardelle
salt and ground black pepper

1 Put the dried mushrooms in a bowl, pour over the warm water and leave to soak for 15 minutes. Finely chop the vegetables, either in a food processor or by hand. Make a tear in each bay leaf, so that they will release their flavour when added to the sauce.

2 Heat the butter or oil in a large frying pan until just sizzling. Add the chopped vegetables, pancetta or bacon and the parsley and cook for about 5 minutes.

3 Add the rabbit pieces and fry on both sides for 3–4 minutes. Transfer the mixture to the ceramic cooking pot and switch to the high or auto setting. Add the wine and tomatoes or passata.

4 While the mixture is starting to heat through, drain the mushrooms and strain the soaking liquid into the slow cooker through a fine sieve (strainer). Chop the mushrooms and add to the mixture, with the bay leaves. Season to taste with salt and black pepper. Stir well, cover with the lid and cook for 1 hour. Reduce the setting to low or leave on auto, and cook for a further 2 hours, or until the meat is tender.

5 Lift out the rabbit pieces, cut them into bite-size chunks and stir them back into the sauce. Remove and discard the bay leaves. Taste the sauce and season, as necessary. The sauce is now ready to serve, but can be kept hot in the slow cooker for 1–2 hours.

6 About 10 minutes before serving, cook the pasta according to the instructions on the packet. Drain the pasta, add to the sauce and toss well to mix. Serve immediately, sprinkled with fresh parsley.

VARIATION
If you prefer, or if rabbit is not available, this dish can be made with chicken instead.

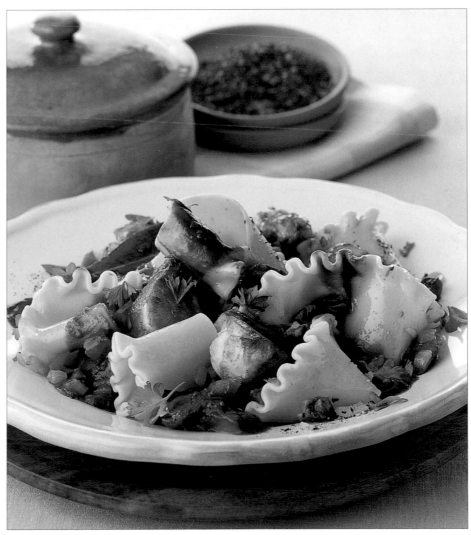

Energy 393Kcal/1653kJ; Protein 23g; Carbohydrate 46g, of which sugars 4.9g; Fat 13.3g, of which saturates 5g; Cholesterol 46mg; Calcium 80mg; Fibre 1.1g; Sodium 128mg.

RABBIT CASSEROLE with JUNIPER

*Because rabbit is such a lean meat, casseroling is an ideal way to cook it, helping to keep
it really moist and juicy. Using a well-flavoured marinade improves both the taste and
texture of the meat. Chicken leg portions make an excellent alternative to rabbit if you
prefer. Serve with steamed new potatoes and whole baby carrots.*

SERVES 4

900g/2lb prepared rabbit pieces
1 onion, roughly chopped
2 garlic cloves, crushed
1 bay leaf
350ml/12fl oz/1½ cups fruity red wine
2 sprigs of fresh thyme
1 sprig of fresh rosemary
15ml/1 tbsp juniper berries
30ml/2 tbsp olive oil
15g/½oz dried porcini mushrooms
30ml/2 tbsp chopped fresh parsley
25g/1oz/2 tbsp chilled butter
salt and ground black pepper

1 Put the rabbit pieces in a glass or
ceramic dish with the onion, garlic, bay
leaf and wine. Bruise the thyme and
rosemary to release their flavour and
lightly crush the juniper berries and add
them to the dish. Toss to combine.
Cover and marinate in the refrigerator
for at least 4 hours or overnight, turning
the pieces once or twice, if possible.

2 Remove the rabbit from the marinade,
reserving the marinade, and pat dry with
kitchen paper. Heat the oil in a frying
pan, add the rabbit pieces and fry
for 3–5 minutes, turning to brown all
over. Transfer the meat to the ceramic
cooking pot.

3 Pour the marinade into the frying pan
and bring to boiling point. Pour over the
rabbit, cover the ceramic cooking pot
with the lid and switch the slow cooker
to high. Cook for about 1 hour.

4 Meanwhile, put the mushrooms in a
heatproof bowl and pour over 150ml/
¼ pint/⅔ cup boiling water. Leave to
soak for 1 hour, then drain, reserving
the soaking liquid, and finely chop the
mushrooms. Put the mushrooms in
a small bowl and cover with clear film
(plastic wrap) to keep them moist.

5 Pour the soaking liquid from the
mushrooms into the ceramic cooking
pot. Cook for a further 2 hours. Lift out
the rabbit pieces with a slotted spoon
and strain the cooking liquid, discarding
the vegetables, herbs and juniper berries.
Wipe the ceramic cooking pot clean,
then return the rabbit and cooking
liquid. Add the mushrooms and season.

6 Cover and cook for a further hour,
or until the meat and mushrooms are
cooked and tender. Stir in the chopped
parsley, then lift out the rabbit pieces
and arrange on a warmed serving dish.
Cut the chilled butter into small cubes
and whisk it into the sauce, one or two
pieces at a time, to thicken. Spoon the
sauce over the rabbit and serve.

Energy 356Kcal/1483kJ; Protein 32g; Carbohydrate 3.2g, of which sugars 2.3g; Fat 17.5g, of which saturates 6.3g; Cholesterol 163mg; Calcium 30mg; Fibre 0.6g; Sodium 66mg.

HARE POT PIES

The full, gamey flavour of hare is perfect for this dish, but boneless rabbit, venison, pheasant or any other game meat can be used instead. The meat filling is cooked in the slow cooker until tender and succulent – this can be done the day before if you like – before being topped with pastry and finished in the oven.

3 Heat the remaining oil in the pan and fry the hare in batches until well browned. When all the meat has been cooked, return it to the pan. Sprinkle over the flour and cook, stirring, for a few seconds, then gradually stir in the Madeira and stock and bring to the boil.

4 Transfer the hare mixture to the ceramic cooking pot and cook for 1 hour. Switch the slow cooker to low or leave on auto and cook for a further 5–6 hours, until the meat and vegetables are tender. Stir in the chopped parsley, then set aside to cool.

5 To make the pies, preheat the oven to 220°C/425°F/Gas 7. Spoon the hare mixture into four individual pie dishes. Cut the pastry into quarters and roll out on a lightly floured work surface to make the pie covers. Make the pieces larger than the dishes. Trim off any excess pastry and use the trimmings to line the rim of each dish.

6 Dampen the pastry rims with cold water and cover with the pastry lids. Pinch the edges together to seal in the filling. Brush each pie with beaten egg yolk and make a small hole in the top of each one to allow steam to escape.

7 Stand the pies on a baking tray and bake for 25 minutes, or until the pastry is well risen and dark golden. If the pastry is browning too quickly, cover with foil after 15 minutes to prevent it from overbrowning.

SERVES 4

45ml/3 tbsp olive oil
1 leek, sliced
225g/8oz parsnips, sliced
225g/8oz carrots, sliced
1 fennel bulb, sliced
675g/1½lb boneless hare, diced
30ml/2 tbsp plain (all-purpose) flour
60ml/4 tbsp Madeira
300ml/½ pint/1¼ cups game
   or chicken stock
45ml/3 tbsp chopped fresh parsley
450g/1lb puff pastry, thawed
   if frozen
beaten egg yolk, to glaze

VARIATION
You can make one large single pie, instead of four individual ones, if you like.

1 Heat 30ml/2 tbsp of the oil in a large pan. Add the leek, parsnips, carrots and fennel and cook for about 10 minutes, stirring frequently, until softened.

2 Using a slotted spoon, transfer the vegetables to the ceramic cooking pot. Cover with the lid and switch the slow cooker to the high or auto setting.

Energy 906Kcal/3784kJ; Protein 45g; Carbohydrate 60.4g, of which sugars 10g; Fat 53.7g, of which saturates 15.9g; Cholesterol 107mg; Calcium 180mg; Fibre 7.6g; Sodium 553mg.

ONE-POT, CLAY-POT POULTRY AND GAME

This chapter lifts the lid on delicious main courses using chicken, duck, pheasant, grouse, guinea fowl, pigeon, venison and rabbit. All are made effortlessly on top of the stove or in a free-standing electric cooker. You'll be reminded of old favourites like Coq au Vin, Chicken Casserole with Winter Vegetables and Hunter's Chicken, and invited to try some exciting new flavours, such as Guinea Fowl with Beans and Curly Kale, Mediterranean Duck with Harissa and Saffron, or Grouse with Orchard Fruit Stuffing. For a great experience you'll be sure to repeat, try Spicy Venison Casserole.

CHICKEN with CHICKPEAS and ALMONDS

The almonds in this tasty Moroccan-style recipe are pre-cooked until soft, adding an interesting texture and flavour to the chicken.

SERVES 4

75g/3oz/½ cup blanched almonds
75g/3oz/½ cup chickpeas, soaked overnight
   and drained
4 part-boned chicken breast portions, skinned
50g/2oz/4 tbsp butter
2.5ml/½ tsp saffron threads
2 Spanish onions, finely sliced
900ml/1½ pints/3¾ cups chicken stock
1 small cinnamon stick
60ml/4 tbsp chopped fresh flat leaf
   parsley, plus extra to garnish
lemon juice, to taste
salt and ground black pepper

1 Place the blanched almonds and the soaked and drained chickpeas in a large flameproof casserole of water and bring to the boil. Boil for 10 minutes, then reduce the heat. Simmer for 1–1½ hours until the chickpeas are soft. Drain the chickpeas and almonds and set aside.

2 Place the skinned chicken pieces in the casserole, together with the butter, half of the saffron, and salt and plenty of black pepper. Heat gently, stirring, until the butter has melted.

3 Add the onions and stock, bring to the boil, then add the reserved cooked almonds, chickpeas and cinnamon stick. Cover with a tightly fitting lid and cook very gently for 45–60 minutes until the chicken is completely tender.

4 Transfer the cooked chicken to a serving plate and keep warm. Bring the sauce to the boil and cook over a high heat until it is well reduced, stirring frequently with a wooden spoon.

5 Add the chopped parsley and remaining saffron to the casserole and cook for a further 2–3 minutes. Sharpen the sauce with a little lemon juice, then pour the sauce over the chicken and serve, garnished with extra fresh parsley.

CHICKEN with TOMATOES and HONEY

A thick tomato and honey sauce coats chicken pieces in this subtly spiced dish.

SERVES 4

30ml/2 tbsp sunflower oil
25g/1oz/2 tbsp butter
4 chicken quarters
1 onion, grated or very finely chopped
1 garlic clove, crushed
5ml/1 tsp ground cinnamon
good pinch of ground ginger
1.3–1.6kg/3–3½lb tomatoes, peeled,
   cored and roughly chopped
30ml/2 tbsp clear honey
50g/2oz/⅓ cup blanched almonds
15ml/1 tbsp sesame seeds
salt and ground black pepper
chopped flat leaf parsley, to garnish

1 Place the oil and butter in a large, flameproof casserole. Add the chicken and cook over a medium heat for about 3 minutes until it is lightly browned.

2 Add the grated or chopped onion, garlic, cinnamon, ginger, tomatoes and plenty of seasoning, and heat gently until the tomatoes begin to bubble.

3 Lower the heat and then cover the casserole. Simmer very gently for about 1 hour, stirring and turning the chicken occasionally, or until it is completely cooked through.

4 Lift out the chicken pieces and transfer them to a plate. Increase the heat and cook the tomato sauce until it is reduced to a thick purée, stirring frequently. Stir in the honey, cook for 1 minute, then return the chicken pieces to the pan and cook for 2–3 minutes to heat through.

5 Transfer the chicken and sauce to a warmed serving dish and sprinkle with the blanched almonds and sesame seeds. Serve hot, garnished with parsley.

COOK'S TIP
To blanch whole almonds, place them in a strainer and lower it into boiling water. Cook the almonds for 2–3 minutes, then remove the strainer from the water. Pinch the softened almond skin between your thumb and finger to squeeze it off.

Chicken with Chickpeas and Almonds: Energy 463Kcal/1935kJ; Protein 45.2g; Carbohydrate 18.6g, of which sugars 7g; Fat 23.6g, of which saturates 7.9g; Cholesterol 132mg; Calcium 110mg; Fibre 4.8g; Sodium 179mg.
Chicken with Tomatoes and Honey: Energy 579Kcal/2413kJ; Protein 33.7g; Carbohydrate 20.7g, of which sugars 19.2g; Fat 40.8g, of which saturates 10.5g; Cholesterol 178mg; Calcium 103mg; Fibre 5.2g; Sodium 192mg.

HUNTER'S CHICKEN

This traditional dish sometimes has strips of green pepper in the sauce instead of the mushrooms. Creamed potato or polenta makes a good accompaniment.

2 Heat the oil and butter in a large, flameproof casserole until foaming. Add the chicken portions and sauté over a medium heat for 5 minutes, or until golden brown. Remove the pieces and drain on kitchen paper.

3 Add the sliced onion and chopped porcini mushrooms to the pan. Cook gently, stirring frequently, for about 3 minutes until the onion has softened but not browned. Stir in the chopped tomatoes, red wine and reserved mushroom soaking liquid, then add the crushed garlic and chopped rosemary, with salt and pepper to taste. Bring to the boil, stirring constantly.

4 Return the chicken to the casserole and turn to coat with the sauce. Cover with a tightly fitting lid and simmer gently for 30 minutes.

SERVES 4

15g/½oz/¼ cup dried porcini mushrooms
30ml/2 tbsp olive oil
15g/½oz/1 tbsp butter
4 chicken portions, on the bone, skinned
1 large onion, thinly sliced
400g/14oz can chopped tomatoes
150ml/¼ pint/⅔ cup red wine
1 garlic clove, crushed
leaves of 1 fresh rosemary sprig,
    finely chopped
115g/4oz/1¾ cups fresh field (portabello)
    mushrooms, thinly sliced
salt and ground black pepper
fresh rosemary sprigs, to garnish

1 Put the porcini in a bowl, add 250ml/ 8fl oz/1 cup warm water and soak for 20 minutes. Squeeze the porcini over the bowl, strain the liquid and reserve. Finely chop the porcini.

5 Add the fresh mushrooms to the casserole and stir well to mix into the sauce. Continue simmering gently for 10 minutes, or until the chicken is tender. Taste for seasoning. Serve hot, with creamed potato or polenta, if you like. Garnish with the rosemary sprigs.

Energy 310Kcal/1299kJ; Protein 38.2g; Carbohydrate 9.2g, of which sugars 7.5g; Fat 10.8g, of which saturates 3.3g; Cholesterol 113mg; Calcium 38mg; Fibre 2.4g; Sodium 128mg.

SEVILLE CHICKEN

Oranges and almonds are a favourite ingredient in southern Spain, especially around
Seville, where the orange and almond trees are a familiar and wonderful sight.

SERVES 4

1 orange
8 chicken thighs
plain (all-purpose) flour, seasoned with
    salt and pepper
45ml/3 tbsp olive oil
1 large Spanish (Bermuda) onion,
    roughly chopped
2 garlic cloves, crushed
1 red (bell) pepper, seeded and sliced
1 yellow (bell) pepper, seeded and sliced
115g/4oz chorizo, sliced
50g/2oz/½ cup flaked (sliced) almonds
225g/8oz/generous 1 cup brown
    basmati rice
about 600ml/1 pint/2½ cups chicken
    or vegetable stock
400g/14oz can chopped tomatoes
175ml/6fl oz/¾ cup white wine
generous pinch of dried thyme
salt and ground black pepper
fresh thyme sprigs, to garnish

3 Add the chorizo, stir-fry for a few
minutes, then sprinkle over the almonds
and rice. Cook, stirring, for 1–2 minutes.

4 Pour in the chicken or vegetable stock,
chopped tomatoes and white wine, then
add the reserved orange peel and the
dried thyme. Season well. Bring the
sauce to simmering point, stirring, then
return the chicken to the pan.

5 Cover tightly and cook over a very
low heat for 1–1¼ hours until the rice
and chicken are tender. Just before
serving, add the orange segments and
juice, and allow to cook briefly to heat
through. Season to taste, garnish with
sprigs of fresh thyme and serve.

1 Pare a thin strip of peel from the
orange using a vegetable peeler and set
it aside. Peel the orange, then cut it into
even segments, working over a bowl to
catch any excess juice. Dust the chicken
thighs with plenty of seasoned flour.

2 Heat the olive oil in a large frying pan
and fry the chicken pieces on both sides
until nicely brown. Transfer the browned
chicken to a plate. Add the chopped
onion and crushed garlic to the pan and
fry for 4–5 minutes until the onion
begins to brown. Add the sliced red
and yellow peppers to the pan and fry,
stirring occasionally with a wooden
spoon, until they are slightly softened.

Energy 861Kcal/3598kJ; Protein 65.3g; Carbohydrate 67.1g, of which sugars 17.1g; Fat 34g, of which saturates 5.6g; Cholesterol 155mg; Calcium 172mg; Fibre 6.3g; Sodium 453mg.

MUSTARD BAKED CHICKEN

In this recipe, a mild, aromatic wholegrain mustard makes a tasty way of cooking chicken. Speciality mustards are freely available in delicatessens and wholefood shops. Serve with new potatoes and peas or mangetouts.

SERVES 4–6

8–12 chicken joints, or 1 medium chicken,
    about 1kg/2¼lb, jointed
juice of ½ lemon
15–30ml/2–3 tbsp whiskey mustard
10ml/2 tsp chopped fresh tarragon
sea salt and ground black pepper

VARIATION
A whole chicken can also be baked this way. Allow about 1½ hours in an oven preset to 180°C/350°F/Gas 4. When cooked, the juices will run clear without any trace of blood.

1 Preheat the oven to 190°C/375°F/ Gas 5. Put the chicken joints into a large shallow baking dish in a single layer and sprinkle the lemon juice over the chicken to flavour the skin. Season well with sea salt and black pepper.

2 Spread the mustard over the joints and sprinkle with the chopped tarragon. Bake in the preheated oven for 20–30 minutes or until thoroughly cooked, depending on the size of the chicken pieces. Serve immediately.

Per portion Energy 426Kcal/1768kJ; Protein 40.3g; Carbohydrate 0g, of which sugars 0g; Fat 29.3g, of which saturates 8.1g; Cholesterol 215mg; Calcium 13mg; Fibre 0g; Sodium 146mg

ROAST FARMYARD DUCK with APPLES and CIDER

Sharp fruit flavours offset the richness of duck: orange is the classic, but cooking apples are used here with dry cider. Serve with a selection of vegetables, including roast potatoes and, perhaps, some red cabbage.

SERVES 4

2kg/4½lb oven-ready duck or duckling
300ml/½ pint/1¼ cups dry (hard) cider
60ml/4 tbsp double (heavy) cream
sea salt and ground black pepper

For the stuffing
75g/3oz/6 tbsp butter
115g/4oz/2 cups fresh white
   breadcrumbs
450g/1lb cooking apples, peeled, cored
   and diced
15ml/1 tbsp sugar, or to taste
freshly grated nutmeg

1 Preheat the oven to 200°C/400°F/ Gas 6. To make the stuffing, melt the butter in a pan and gently fry the breadcrumbs until golden brown. Add the apples to the breadcrumbs with salt, pepper, the sugar and a pinch of nutmeg. Mix together well.

2 Wipe the duck out with a clean, damp cloth, and remove any obvious excess fat (including the flaps just inside the vent). Rub the skin with salt. Stuff the duck with the prepared mixture, then secure the vent with a small skewer.

COOK'S TIP
The giblets aren't required for this recipe, but you can remove the liver and set it aside to use in a warm salad. The remaining giblets can be used later, with the duck carcass, to make a delicious stock for soup.

3 Weigh the stuffed duck and calculate the cooking time, allowing 20 minutes per 450g/1lb. Prick the skin all over with a fork to allow the fat to run out during the cooking time, then lay it on top of a wire rack in a roasting pan, sprinkle with freshly ground black pepper and put it into the preheated oven to roast.

4 About 20 minutes before the end of the estimated cooking time, remove the duck from the oven and pour off all the fat that has accumulated under the rack (reserve it for frying). Slide the duck off the rack into the roasting pan and pour the cider over it. Return to the oven and finish cooking, basting occasionally.

5 When the duck is cooked, remove it from the pan and keep warm while you make the sauce. Set the roasting pan over a medium heat and boil the cider to reduce it by half. Stir in the cream, heat through and season. Meanwhile, remove the stuffing from the duck. Carve the duck into slices or quarter it using poultry shears. Serve with a portion of stuffing and the cider sauce.

Energy 572Kcal/2397kJ; Protein 31.5g; Carbohydrate 34.6g, of which sugars 13.1g; Fat 33.1g, of which saturates 17.8g; Cholesterol 211mg; Calcium 74mg; Fibre 2.4g; Sodium 498mg

OVEN-ROASTED CHICKEN with MEDITERRANEAN VEGETABLES

This is a delicious – and trouble-free – alternative to a traditional roast chicken. The recipe also works very well with guinea fowl.

SERVES 4

1.8–2.25kg/4–5lb roasting chicken
150ml/¼ pint/⅔ cup extra virgin olive oil
½ lemon
a few sprigs of fresh thyme
450g/1lb small new potatoes
1 aubergine (eggplant), cut into
    2.5cm/1in cubes
1 red or yellow (bell) pepper, seeded
    and quartered
1 fennel bulb, trimmed and quartered
8 large garlic cloves, unpeeled
coarse salt and ground black pepper

1 Preheat the oven to 200°C/400°F/ Gas 6. Rub the chicken all over with olive oil and season with pepper. Place the lemon half inside the bird, with a sprig or two of thyme. Put the chicken breast side down in a large roasting pan. Roast for about 30 minutes.

2 Remove the chicken from the oven and season with salt. Turn the chicken right side up, and baste with the juices from the pan.

3 Arrange the potatoes around the chicken and roll them in the cooking juices until they are thoroughly coated. Return the roasting pan to the oven, to continue roasting.

4 After 30 minutes, add the aubergine, red pepper, fennel and garlic cloves to the pan. Drizzle the vegetables with the remaining oil, and season to taste with salt and pepper.

5 Add the remaining sprigs of thyme to the roasting pan, tucking the sprigs in among the vegetables. Return the chicken and vegetables to the oven and cook for 30–50 minutes more, basting and turning the vegetables occasionally during cooking.

6 To find out if the chicken is cooked, push the tip of a small sharp knife between the thigh and breast – if the juices run clear, rather than pink, it is done. The vegetables should be tender and beginning to brown. Serve the chicken and vegetables from the pan.

Energy 798Kcal/3310kJ; Protein 43.3g; Carbohydrate 23.7g, of which sugars 6.1g; Fat 59.3g, of which saturates 13.5g; Cholesterol 208mg; Calcium 45mg; Fibre 4.2g; Sodium 183mg.

CHICKEN with FORTY CLOVES of GARLIC

This dish does not have to be mathematically exact, so do not worry if you have 35 or even 50 cloves of garlic – the important thing is that there should be lots. The smell that emanates from the oven as the chicken and garlic cook is indescribably delicious.

SERVES 4–5

5–6 whole heads of garlic
15g/½oz/1 tbsp butter
45ml/3 tbsp olive oil
1.8–2kg/4–4½lb chicken
150g/5oz/1¼ cups plain (all-purpose) flour,
    plus 5ml/1 tsp
75ml/5 tbsp white port, Pineau
    de Charentes or other white,
    fortified wine
2–3 fresh tarragon or rosemary sprigs
30ml/2 tbsp crème fraîche (optional)
a few drops of lemon juice (optional)
salt and ground black pepper

1 Separate three of the heads of garlic into cloves and peel them. Remove the first layer of papery skin from the remaining heads of garlic and cut off the tops to expose the cloves, if you like, or leave them whole. Preheat the oven to 180°C/350°F/Gas 4.

2 Heat the butter and 15ml/1 tbsp of the olive oil in a flameproof casserole that is just large enough to take the chicken and garlic. Add the chicken and cook over a medium heat, turning it frequently, for 10–15 minutes, until it is browned all over.

3 Sprinkle in 5ml/1 tsp flour and cook for 1 minute. Add the port or wine. Tuck in the whole heads of garlic and the peeled cloves with the sprigs of tarragon or rosemary. Pour over the remaining oil and season to taste with salt and pepper.

4 Mix the main batch of flour with sufficient water to make a firm dough. Roll it out into a long sausage and press it around the rim of the casserole, then press on the lid, folding the dough up and over it to create a tight seal. Cook in the oven for 1½ hours.

5 To serve, lift off the lid to break the seal and remove the chicken and whole garlic to a serving platter and keep warm. Remove and discard the herb sprigs, then place the casserole on the stove top and whisk the remaining ingredients to combine the garlic cloves with the juices. Add the crème fraîche, if using, and a little lemon juice to taste, if using. Process the sauce in a food processor or blender until smooth. Reheat the garlic sauce in a clean pan if necessary and serve it with the chicken.

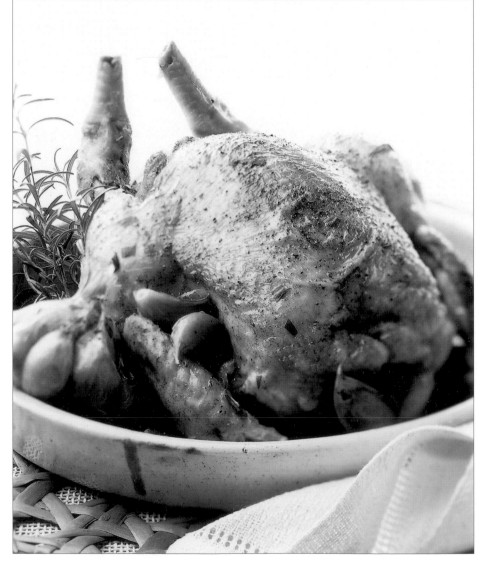

Energy 616Kcal/2565kJ; Protein 37.7g; Carbohydrate 31.6g, of which sugars 2.9g; Fat 36.5g, of which saturates 10.4g; Cholesterol 173mg; Calcium 64mg; Fibre 2.6g; Sodium 151mg.

CHICKEN BAKED with SHALLOTS, GARLIC and FENNEL

This is a very simple and delicious way to cook chicken. If you have time, leave the chicken to marinate for a few hours for the best flavour.

SERVES 4

1.6–1.8kg/3½–4lb chicken, cut into
   8 pieces, or 8 chicken joints
250g/9oz shallots, peeled
1 head of garlic, separated into cloves
   and peeled
60ml/4 tbsp extra virgin olive oil
45ml/3 tbsp tarragon vinegar
45ml/3 tbsp white wine or
   vermouth (optional)
5ml/1 tsp fennel seeds, crushed
2 bulbs fennel, cut into wedges, feathery
   tops reserved
150ml/¼ pint/⅔ cup double (heavy) cream
5ml/1 tsp redcurrant jelly
15ml/1 tbsp tarragon mustard
a little sugar (optional)
30ml/2 tbsp chopped fresh flat leaf parsley
salt and ground black pepper

1 Place the chicken pieces, shallots and all but one of the garlic cloves in a large, shallow flameproof dish. Add the olive oil, tarragon vinegar, white wine or vermouth, if using, and the crushed fennel seeds. Season to taste with plenty of ground black pepper, then set aside and leave to marinate in a cool place for 2–3 hours.

2 Preheat the oven to 190°C/375°F/ Gas 5. Add the wedges of fennel to the chicken, then season with salt and stir well to mix. Transfer the chicken to the oven and cook for 50–60 minutes, stirring once or twice, until the chicken is thoroughly cooked. The chicken juices should run clear, not pink, when the thick thigh meat is pierced with a skewer or a small sharp knife.

3 Transfer the chicken and vegetables to a serving dish and keep them warm. Skim off some of the fat and bring the cooking juices to the boil, then pour in the cream. Stir, scraping up all the juices. Whisk in the redcurrant jelly followed by the mustard. Check the seasoning, adding a little sugar, if necessary.

4 Finely chop the remaining garlic clove with the feathery fennel tops and mix them with the parsley. Pour the sauce over the chicken and then sprinkle the chopped garlic and herb mixture over the top. Serve immediately with rice or baked potatoes.

COOK'S TIPS
• If possible, use the fresh, new season's garlic for this dish, as it is plump, moist and full of flavour. Purple-skinned garlic is considered by many cooks to have the best flavour.
• The cut surfaces of fennel will quickly discolour, so do not prepare it too far in advance of using it. If you must prepare it beforehand, then put the wedges into a bowl of cold water acidulated with a little lemon juice.

Energy 743Kcal/3075kJ; Protein 43.1g; Carbohydrate 5.7g, of which sugars 5.6g; Fat 60.9g, of which saturates 22.2g; Cholesterol 266mg; Calcium 96mg; Fibre 3.9g; Sodium 176mg.

STOVED CHICKEN

"Stovies" were originally potatoes slowly cooked on the stove with onions and dripping or butter until falling to pieces. This version includes a delicious layer of bacon and chicken.

2 Heat the butter and oil in a large, heavy frying pan, add the chopped bacon and chicken pieces and cook, turning occasionally, until brown on all sides. Using a slotted spoon, transfer the chicken and bacon to the earthenware dish. Reserve the fat in the pan.

3 Sprinkle the remaining chopped thyme over the chicken, season with salt and pepper, then cover with the remaining onion slices, followed by a neat, overlapping layer of the remaining potato slices. Season the top layer of potatoes with more salt and ground black pepper.

4 Pour the chicken stock into the casserole, add the bay leaf and brush the potatoes with the reserved fat from the frying pan. Cover tightly with foil and bake for about 2 hours, or until the chicken is cooked and tender.

SERVES 4

1kg/2¼lb baking potatoes, cut into
   5mm/¼in slices
butter, for greasing
2 large onions, thinly sliced
15ml/1 tbsp chopped fresh thyme
25g/1oz/2 tbsp butter
15ml/1 tbsp vegetable oil
2 large bacon rashers (strips), chopped
4 large chicken portions, halved
600ml/1 pint/2½ cups chicken stock
1 bay leaf
salt and ground black pepper

COOK'S TIP
Instead of chicken portions, choose eight chicken thighs or chicken drumsticks.

1 Preheat the oven to 150°C/300°F/ Gas 2. Arrange a thick layer of half the potato slices in a large lightly greased, earthenware baking dish, then cover with half the onions. Sprinkle with half of the thyme, and season with salt and pepper to taste.

5 Preheat the grill (broiler) to medium-hot, then remove the foil from the earthenware dish and place the dish under the grill. Cook until the slices of potato are beginning to turn golden brown and crisp. Remove the bay leaf and serve immediately.

Energy 500Kcal/2107kJ; Protein 50g; Carbohydrate 48.2g, of which sugars 8.9g; Fat 13.2g, of which saturates 5.4g; Cholesterol 144mg; Calcium 51mg; Fibre 3.9g; Sodium 405mg.

POT-ROAST CHICKEN with LEMON and GARLIC

This is a rustic dish that is easy to prepare. Lardons are thick strips of bacon fat; if you can't get them, use fatty bacon instead. Serve with thick bread to mop up the juices.

SERVES 4

30ml/2 tbsp olive oil
25g/1oz/2 tbsp butter
175g/6oz/1 cup smoked lardons, or
    roughly chopped streaky (fatty) bacon
8 garlic cloves, peeled
4 onions, quartered
10ml/2 tsp plain (all-purpose) flour
600ml/1 pint/2½ cups chicken stock
2 lemons, thickly sliced
45ml/3 tbsp chopped fresh thyme
1 chicken, about 1.3–1.6kg/3–3½lb
2 × 400g/14oz cans flageolet, cannellini
    or haricot (navy) beans, drained
    and rinsed
salt and ground black pepper

3 Bring the sauce to the boil, stirring constantly until thickened, then place the chicken on top. Season well. Transfer the casserole to the oven. Cook for 1 hour, basting the chicken once or twice during cooking to ensure it stays moist.

4 Baste the chicken again. Stir the beans into the casserole and return it to the oven for a further 30 minutes, or until the chicken is cooked through and tender. Carve the chicken into thick slices and serve with the beans.

1 Preheat the oven to 190°C/375°F/ Gas 5. Heat the oil and butter in a flameproof casserole that is large enough to hold the chicken with a little room around the sides. Add the lardons and cook until golden. Remove with a slotted spoon and drain on kitchen paper.

2 Add the garlic and onions and brown over a high heat. Stir in the flour, then the stock. Return the lardons to the pan with the lemon, thyme and seasoning.

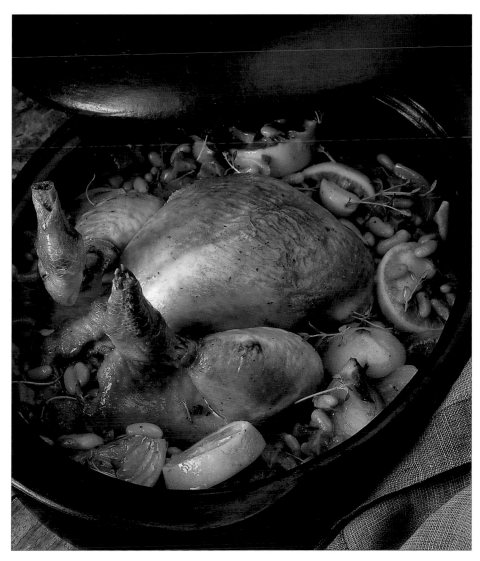

Energy 887Kcal/3696kJ; Protein 62.5g; Carbohydrate 45.5g, of which sugars 12.9g; Fat 51.7g, of which saturates 16g; Cholesterol 256mg; Calcium 187mg; Fibre 13.9g; Sodium 1519mg.

POUSSINS and NEW POTATO POT-ROAST

Pot roasts are traditionally associated with the colder months, but this delicious version is a simple summer dish that makes the most of new season potatoes.

SERVES 4

2 poussins, about 500g/1¼lb each
25g/1oz/2 tbsp butter
15ml/1 tbsp clear honey
500g/1¼lb small new potatoes
1 red onion, halved lengthwise and cut
   into thin wedges
4–5 small rosemary sprigs
2 bay leaves
1 lemon, cut into wedges
450ml/¾ pint/scant 2 cups hot
   chicken stock
salt and ground black pepper

1 Soak a clay chicken brick in cold water for 20 minutes, then drain. Cut the poussins in half, along the breast bone.

2 Melt the butter, mix it together with the honey and brush over the poussins. Season with salt and pepper.

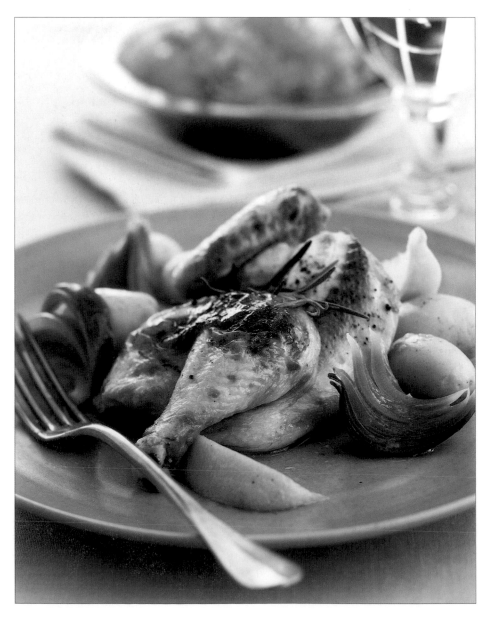

3 Place the small new potatoes and onion wedges in the base of the chicken brick. Tuck the rosemary sprigs, bay leaves and lemon wedges in among the vegetables. Pour over the hot chicken stock (see Cook's Tip).

4 Place the halved poussins on top of the vegetables. Cover the chicken brick and place it in an unheated oven. Set the oven to 200°C/400°F/Gas 6 and cook for 55–60 minutes, or until the poussin juices run clear and the vegetables are tender. Uncover the chicken brick for the last 10 minutes of cooking to add more colour to the poussins, if necessary.

COOK'S TIPS
• Make sure the stock is hot, but not boiling when it is added to the chicken brick otherwise the chicken brick may crack.
• A poussin is a baby chicken – usually around 4–6 weeks old. Poussins can be cooked by grilling (broiling), roasting or pot-roasting, but are especially tender and moist cooked in a chicken brick.

Energy 443Kcal/1852kJ; Protein 30.1g; Carbohydrate 24.2g, of which sugars 5.4g; Fat 25.8g, of which saturates 8.9g; Cholesterol 158mg; Calcium 23mg; Fibre 1.5g; Sodium 153mg.

CORN-FED CHICKEN with WINTER VEGETABLES

Chicken cooked in a clay pot remains beautifully moist and tender. Flavoured with lemon, parsley and tarragon, serve this as an alternative to a traditional Sunday roast.

SERVES 4

3 large carrots, cut into batons
1 celery heart, thickly sliced
2 red onions, quartered
a few sprigs of fresh thyme
1.6kg/3½lb corn-fed chicken
40g/1½oz/3 tbsp butter, softened
15ml/1 tbsp chopped fresh parsley
15ml/1 tbsp chopped fresh tarragon
1 small lemon, halved
300ml/½ pint/1¼ cups dry white wine or
    chicken stock
salt and ground black pepper

COOK'S TIP
Cook some potatoes in the oven at the same time to accompany the pot roast – baked potatoes or roast potatoes both go well with this main course. Or, if you prefer, serve the pot-roast with creamy mashed potatoes.

1 Soak a chicken brick or large clay pot in cold water for 20 minutes, then drain. Place the carrots, celery, red onions and thyme in the pot.

2 Wash the chicken and dry thoroughly. Mix together the butter, parsley and tarragon. Ease up the breast skin of the chicken and spread the butter under it, taking care not to puncture the skin. Place the lemon halves inside the chicken.

3 Rub the chicken with seasoning and nestle on top of the vegetables. Add the wine or chicken stock and cover. Place the chicken brick or pot in an unheated oven. Set the oven temperature to 200°C/400°F/Gas 6 and cook for about 1¾ hours, or until the chicken is cooked.

4 Remove the lid from the brick or pot and cook for a further 10 minutes, or until the chicken is golden brown.

Energy 717Kcal/2975kJ; Protein 47.3g; Carbohydrate 13.8g, of which sugars 12.3g; Fat 47.4g, of which saturates 16.6g; Cholesterol 261mg; Calcium 89mg; Fibre 4.1g; Sodium 314mg.

CHICKEN GUMBO with OKRA, HAM, TOMATOES and PRAWNS

This classic Creole dish is really a very hearty soup, but is usually served over rice as a delicious and filling main course, like a stew.

SERVES 4

30ml/2 tbsp olive oil
1 onion, chopped
225g/8oz skinless, boneless chicken
　breast portions, cut into
　small chunks
25g/1oz/¼ cup plain (all-purpose) flour
5ml/1 tsp paprika
30ml/2 tbsp tomato purée (paste)
600ml/1 pint/2½ cups well-flavoured
　chicken stock
400g/14oz can chopped tomatoes
　with herbs
a few drops of Tabasco
175g/6oz okra
1 red, orange or yellow (bell) pepper,
　seeded and chopped
2 celery sticks, sliced
225g/8oz/1⅓ cups diced lean
　cooked ham
225g/8oz large prawns (shrimp), peeled,
　deveined and heads removed, but with
　tails intact
salt and ground black pepper
boiled rice, to serve

1 Soak a large clay pot or chicken brick in cold water for 20 minutes, then drain. Heat the oil in a large frying pan, add the chopped onion and cook over a medium heat for about 5 minutes, stirring occasionally, until softened and lightly golden.

2 Add the chicken chunks to the pan and sauté for 1–2 minutes, to seal. Stir in the flour, paprika and tomato purée and cook, stirring constantly, for 1–2 minutes.

3 Gradually add the stock, stirring constantly, then bring the sauce to the boil, stirring. Add the chopped tomatoes, then remove the pan from the heat. Add a few drops of Tabasco and season with salt and pepper.

4 Cut the okra pods in half if they are large, then add them to the clay pot or chicken brick with the chopped red, orange or yellow pepper and the sliced celery. Add the chicken and tomato mixture and stir well to mix.

5 Cover the clay pot or chicken brick and place it in an unheated oven. Set the oven to 200°C/400°F/Gas 6 and cook for 30 minutes.

6 Remove the clay pot or chicken brick from the oven, then add the diced ham and the prawns and stir well to combine. Cover the pot or brick and return it to the oven for about 10 minutes, or until the ham is heated through and the prawns are just cooked. To serve, spoon some freshly boiled rice into four warmed, individual serving plates or bowls and ladle over the gumbo.

VARIATIONS
Replace the cooked ham with crab meat or cooked and shelled mussels or, for a special occasion, replace the peeled prawns with crayfish and replace the ham with cooked and shelled oysters.

COOK'S TIPS
• Okra is a favourite ingredient in the southern states of the USA and in African and Caribbean cooking. When buying, look for firm, bright green pods that are less than 10cm/4in long. Larger pods may be slightly tough and fibrous. When cooked, okra produces a rather viscous substance that thickens the liquid in which it is cooked – an essential part of many traditional okra recipes.
• If you don't have a bottle of Tabasco sauce to hand, add about 2.5ml/½ tsp chilli powder, or a finely chopped fresh or dried chilli. Remove the seeds from the chilli if you would prefer the gumbo to be only medium-hot.

Energy 290Kcal/1221kJ; Protein 37.3g; Carbohydrate 15g, of which sugars 9.6g; Fat 9.4g, of which saturates 1.9g; Cholesterol 182mg; Calcium 153mg; Fibre 4.2g; Sodium 858mg.

CHICKEN and PRAWN JAMBALAYA

This colourful mixture of rice, peppers and tomatoes with chicken, gammon and prawns is flavoured with garlic and fresh herbs and a few dashes of fiery Tabasco sauce. It's an ideal dish for big family gatherings and celebrations.

SERVES 10

2 chickens, each about 1.3–1.6kg/3–3½lb
450g/1lb piece raw smoked gammon
  (smoked or cured ham)
50g/2oz/⅓ cup lard or
  bacon fat
50g/2oz/½ cup plain (all-purpose) flour
3 onions, finely sliced
2 green (bell) peppers, seeded and sliced
675g/1½lb tomatoes, peeled and chopped
2–3 garlic cloves, crushed
10ml/2 tsp chopped fresh thyme or
  5ml/1 tsp dried thyme
24 raw Mediterranean prawns (jumbo
  shrimp), peeled with tails intact
500g/1¼lb/2½ cups white long grain rice
1.2 litres/2 pints/5 cups water
2–3 dashes Tabasco sauce
45ml/3 tbsp chopped fresh flat leaf parsley,
  plus tiny fresh parsley sprigs to garnish
salt and ground black pepper

4 Add the diced gammon, onions, green peppers, tomatoes, garlic and thyme and stir well to mix. Cook, stirring regularly, for about 10 minutes, then add the prawns and mix lightly.

5 Stir the rice into the frying pan and pour in the water. Season well with salt, black pepper and Tabasco sauce. Bring to the boil, then cook gently, stirring occasionally, until the rice is tender and all the liquid has been fully absorbed. Add a little extra boiling water if the rice looks like drying out before it is cooked. Check the seasoning and add salt, pepper and more Tabasco if necessary.

6 Mix the chopped fresh flat leaf parsley into the finished dish, garnish with tiny sprigs of flat leaf parsley and serve the jambalaya immediately with plenty of crusty bread.

1 Cut each chicken into ten pieces and season the pieces well with salt and pepper. Dice the gammon, discarding the rind and fat.

2 Melt the lard or bacon fat in a large, heavy frying pan. Add the chicken pieces in several batches, cook them until they are golden brown all over, then lift them out with a slotted spoon and set them aside.

3 Reduce the heat. Sprinkle the flour into the fat in the pan and stir with a wooden spoon until the roux turns a golden brown colour. Return the chicken pieces to the pan.

Energy 740Kcal/3079kJ; Protein 50.6g; Carbohydrate 52.9g, of which sugars 7.7g; Fat 36.1g, of which saturates 11.1g; Cholesterol 240mg; Calcium 79mg; Fibre 2.2g; Sodium 593mg.

RISOTTO with CHICKEN

This is a classic risotto combination of creamy rice and tender cubes of chicken, flavoured with aromatic saffron, prosciutto, white wine and Parmesan cheese.

SERVES 6

30ml/2 tbsp olive oil
225g/8oz skinless, boneless chicken breast
    portions, cut into 2.5cm/1in cubes
1 onion, finely chopped
1 garlic clove, finely chopped
450g/1lb/2¼ cups risotto rice
120ml/4fl oz/½ cup dry white wine
1.5ml/¼ tsp saffron threads
1.75 litres/3 pints/7½ cups simmering
    chicken stock
50g/2oz prosciutto, cut into
    thin strips
25g/1oz/2 tbsp butter, diced
25g/1oz/⅓ cup freshly grated Parmesan
    cheese, plus extra to serve
salt and ground black pepper
sprigs of flat leaf parsley, to garnish

1 Heat the olive oil in a large frying pan over a medium-high heat. Add the cubes of chicken and cook, stirring occasionally with a wooden spoon, until they start to turn white.

2 Reduce the heat to low and add the chopped onion and garlic. Cook, stirring occasionally, until the onion is soft. Stir in the risotto rice, then sauté for 2 minutes, stirring constantly, until all the rice grains are coated in oil.

3 Add the dry white wine to the rice mixture and cook, stirring constantly, until the wine has been absorbed. Add the saffron threads to the simmering stock and stir well, then add ladlefuls of hot stock to the rice mixture, allowing each ladleful to be fully absorbed before adding the next.

4 When the rice is about three-quarters cooked, add the strips of prosciutto and stir well. Continue cooking, stirring occasionally, until the rice is just tender and the risotto is creamy.

5 Add the butter and the Parmesan and stir in well. Season with salt and pepper to taste. Serve the risotto hot, sprinkled with a little more Parmesan, and garnish with flat leaf parsley.

Energy 418Kcal/1744kJ; Protein 17.9g; Carbohydrate 60.9g, of which sugars 0.8g; Fat 9.5g, of which saturates 3.8g; Cholesterol 44mg; Calcium 72mg; Fibre 0.1g; Sodium 194mg.

CHICKEN PIRI-PIRI

This is a classic Portuguese dish, based on a hot sauce made from Angolan chillies. It is popular wherever there are Portuguese communities, and is often served in South Africa.

SERVES 4

4 chicken breast portions
30–45ml/2–3 tbsp olive oil
1 large onion, finely sliced
2 carrots, cut into thin strips
1 large parsnip or 2 small parsnips,
 cut into thin strips
1 red (bell) pepper, seeded and sliced
1 yellow (bell) pepper, seeded
 and sliced
1 litre/1¾ pints/4 cups chicken or
 vegetable stock
3 tomatoes, peeled, seeded and chopped
generous dash of piri-piri sauce
15ml/1 tbsp tomato purée (paste)
½ cinnamon stick
1 fresh thyme sprig, plus extra fresh thyme
 to garnish
1 bay leaf
275g/10oz/1½ cups white long grain rice
15ml/1 tbsp lime or lemon juice
salt and ground black pepper

1 Preheat the oven to 180°C/350°F/ Gas 4. Rub the chicken skin with a little salt and ground black pepper. Heat 30ml/2 tbsp of the olive oil in a large frying pan, add the chicken portions and cook, turning occasionally until browned on all sides. Transfer to a plate using a metal spatula.

2 Add some more oil to the pan if necessary, add the sliced onion and fry for 2–3 minutes until slightly softened. Add the carrot and parsnip strips and the pepper slices and stir-fry for a few minutes more. Cover the pan and cook for 4–5 minutes until all the vegetables are quite soft.

3 Pour in the chicken or vegetable stock, then add the tomatoes, piri-piri sauce, tomato purée and cinnamon stick. Stir in the thyme and bay leaf. Season to taste and bring to the boil. Using a ladle, spoon off 300ml/½ pint/1¼ cups of the liquid and set aside in a small pan.

4 Put the rice in the base of a large earthenware dish. Using a slotted spoon, scoop the vegetables out of the frying pan and spread them over the rice. Arrange the chicken pieces on top. Pour over the spicy chicken stock from the frying pan, cover tightly and cook in the oven for about 45 minutes, until both the rice and chicken are completely tender.

5 Meanwhile, heat the reserved chicken stock, adding a few more drops of piri-piri sauce and the lime or lemon juice.

6 To serve, spoon the piri-piri chicken and rice on to warmed serving plates. Serve the remaining sauce separately or poured over the chicken.

Energy 557Kcal/2337kJ; Protein 44.3g; Carbohydrate 75.4g, of which sugars 15.5g; Fat 8.8g, of which saturates 1.5g; Cholesterol 105mg; Calcium 73mg; Fibre 5.8g; Sodium 122mg.

CHICKEN BIRYANI

Easy to make and very tasty, this is the ideal one-pot dish for a family supper.

SERVES 4

10 green cardamom pods
275g/10oz/1½ cups basmati rice, soaked
    and drained
2.5ml/½ tsp salt
2–3 cloves
5cm/2in cinnamon stick
45ml/3 tbsp vegetable oil
3 onions, sliced
4 chicken breast portions, each about
    175g/6oz, cubed
1.5ml/¼ tsp ground cloves
5ml/1 tsp ground cumin
5ml/1 tsp ground coriander
2.5ml/½ tsp ground black pepper
3 garlic cloves, chopped
5ml/1 tsp finely chopped fresh root ginger
juice of 1 lemon
4 tomatoes, sliced
30ml/2 tbsp chopped fresh
    coriander (cilantro)
150ml/¼ pint/⅔ cup natural (plain) yogurt
4–5 saffron threads, soaked in 10ml/2 tsp
    hot milk
150ml/¼ pint/⅔ cup water
toasted flaked (sliced) almonds and fresh
    coriander (cilantro) sprigs, to garnish
natural (plain) yogurt, to serve

1 Preheat the oven to 190°C/375°F/
Gas 5. Remove the seeds from half the
cardamom pods and grind them finely, using
a mortar and pestle. Set the seeds aside.

2 Bring a flameproof casserole of water
to the boil and add the soaked and
drained basmati rice, then stir in the salt,
the remaining whole cardamom pods,
whole cloves and cinnamon stick. Boil
the rice for 2 minutes, then drain,
leaving the whole spices in the rice.

3 Heat the oil in the flameproof
casserole and fry the onions for about
8 minutes, until softened and browned.
Add the cubed chicken and the ground
spices, including the ground cardamom
seeds. Mix well, then add the chopped
garlic, ginger and lemon juice. Stir-fry the
mixture together for 5 minutes.

4 Arrange the sliced tomatoes on top.
Sprinkle on the coriander, spoon the
yogurt on top and cover with the rice.

5 Drizzle the saffron milk over the rice
and add the water. Cover and bake for
1 hour. Garnish with almonds and
coriander and serve with extra yogurt.

Energy 563Kcal/2359kJ; Protein 45.4g; Carbohydrate 70g, of which sugars 12.5g; Fat 11.3g, of which saturates 1.7g; Cholesterol 105mg; Calcium 152mg; Fibre 3.2g; Sodium 138mg.

CHICKEN CASSEROLE with WINTER VEGETABLES

A casserole of wonderfully tender chicken, root vegetables and lentils, finished with crème fraîche, mustard and tarragon.

SERVES 4

350g/12oz onions
350g/12oz leeks
225g/8oz carrots
450g/1lb swede (rutabaga)
30ml/2 tbsp oil
4 chicken portions, about 900g/2lb
   total weight
115g/4oz/½ cup green lentils
475ml/16fl oz/2 cups chicken stock
300ml/½ pint/1¼ cups apple juice
10ml/2 tsp cornflour (cornstarch)
45ml/3 tbsp crème fraîche
10ml/2 tsp wholegrain mustard
30ml/2 tbsp chopped fresh tarragon
salt and ground black pepper
fresh tarragon sprigs, to garnish

1 Preheat the oven to 190°C/375°F/ Gas 5. Prepare the onions, leeks, carrots and swede and roughly chop them.

COOK'S TIP
Chop the vegetables into similarly sized pieces so that they cook evenly.

2 Heat the oil in a large flameproof casserole. Season the chicken portions with plenty of salt and pepper and brown them in the hot oil until golden. Drain on kitchen paper.

3 Add the onions to the casserole and cook for 5 minutes, stirring, until they begin to soften and colour. Add the leeks, carrots, swede and lentils to the casserole and stir over a medium heat for 2 minutes.

4 Return the chicken to the pan, then add the stock, apple juice and seasoning. Bring to the boil and cover tightly. Cook in the oven for 50–60 minutes, or until the chicken and lentils are tender.

5 Place the casserole on the stove-top over a medium heat. In a small bowl, blend the cornflour with about 30ml/ 2 tbsp water to make a smooth paste and add to the casserole with the crème fraîche, wholegrain mustard and chopped tarragon. Adjust the seasoning, then simmer gently for about 2 minutes, stirring, until thickened slightly, before serving, garnished with tarragon sprigs.

Energy 477Kcal/2010kJ; Protein 46.8g; Carbohydrate 45.7g, of which sugars 24.9g; Fat 13.2g, of which saturates 4.5g; Cholesterol 118mg; Calcium 151mg; Fibre 8.1g; Sodium 141mg.

COQ au VIN

This French country casserole was traditionally made with an old boiling bird, marinated overnight in red wine, then simmered gently until tender. Modern recipes use tender roasting birds to save time and because boiling fowl are not readily available.

SERVES 6

45ml/3 tbsp light olive oil
12 shallots
225g/8oz rindless streaky (fatty) bacon
    rashers (strips), chopped
3 garlic cloves, finely chopped
225g/8oz small mushrooms, halved
6 boneless chicken thighs
3 boneless chicken breast
    portions, halved
1 bottle red wine
salt and ground black pepper
45ml/3 tbsp chopped fresh parsley,
    to garnish

For the bouquet garni
3 sprigs each parsley, thyme and sage
1 bay leaf
4 peppercorns

For the beurre manié
25g/1oz/2 tbsp butter, softened
25g/1oz/¼ cup plain (all-purpose) flour

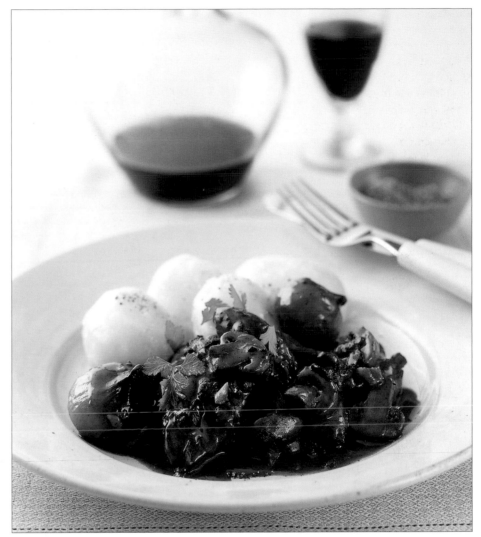

1 Heat the oil in a large, flameproof casserole and cook the shallots for about 5 minutes, or until golden. Increase the heat, then add the chopped bacon, garlic and mushrooms and cook for a further 10 minutes, stirring frequently.

2 Use a slotted spoon to transfer the cooked ingredients to a plate, then brown the chicken portions in the oil remaining in the pan, turning them until they are golden brown all over. Return the cooked shallots, garlic, mushrooms and bacon to the casserole and pour in the red wine.

3 Tie the ingredients for the bouquet garni in a bundle in a small piece of muslin (cheesecloth) and add to the casserole. Bring to the boil, reduce the heat and cover the casserole with a tightly fitting lid, then simmer for 30–40 minutes.

4 To make the beurre manié, cream the butter and flour together in a small bowl using your fingers or a spoon to make a smooth paste.

5 Add small lumps of the beurre manié paste to the bubbling casserole, stirring well until each piece has melted into the liquid before adding the next. When all the paste has been added, bring the casserole back to the boil and simmer for 5 minutes.

6 Season the casserole to taste with salt and pepper and serve garnished with chopped fresh parsley and accompanied by boiled potatoes.

Energy 538Kcal/2240kJ; Protein 43.5g; Carbohydrate 7g, of which sugars 2.8g; Fat 28.2g, of which saturates 8.9g; Cholesterol 170mg; Calcium 50mg; Fibre 1.1g; Sodium 610mg.

MEDITERRANEAN DUCK with HARISSA and SAFFRON

Harissa is a fiery chilli sauce from north Africa. Mixed with cinnamon, saffron and preserved lemon, it gives this colourful casserole an unforgettable flavour.

SERVES 4

15ml/1 tbsp olive oil
1.8–2kg/4–4½lb duck, quartered
1 large onion, thinly sliced
1 garlic clove, crushed
2.5ml/½ tsp ground cumin
400ml/14fl oz/1⅔ cups duck or
    chicken stock
juice of ½ lemon
5–10ml/1–2 tsp harissa
1 cinnamon stick
5ml/1 tsp saffron threads
50g/2oz/⅓ cup black olives
50g/2oz/⅓ cup green olives
peel of 1 preserved lemon, rinsed, drained
    and cut into fine strips
2–3 lemon slices
30ml/2 tbsp chopped fresh coriander
    (cilantro), plus extra leaves
    to garnish
salt and ground black pepper

1 Heat the oil in a flameproof casserole. Add the duck quarters and cook until browned all over. Remove the duck with a slotted spoon and set aside. Add the onion and garlic to the oil remaining in the casserole and cook for 5 minutes until soft. Add the ground cumin and cook, stirring, for 2 minutes.

COOK'S TIP
The term "duck" refers to birds over two months old. The rich flavour of duck is best appreciated when a duck reaches its full-grown size. Look for a duck with a supple, waxy skin with a dry appearance. It should have a long body with tender, meaty breasts.

2 Pour in the stock and lemon juice, then add the harissa, cinnamon and saffron. Bring to the boil. Return the duck to the casserole and add the olives, preserved lemon peel and lemon slices. Season with salt and pepper.

3 Lower the heat, partially cover the casserole and simmer gently for about 45 minutes, or until the duck is cooked through. Discard the cinnamon stick. Stir in the chopped coriander and garnish with the coriander leaves.

Energy 262Kcal/1095kJ; Protein 26.6g; Carbohydrate 8.3g, of which sugars 5.9g; Fat 34g, of which saturates 13.5g; Cholesterol 135mg; Calcium 79mg; Fibre 2.8g; Sodium 709mg.

BRAISED SAUSAGES with ONIONS, CELERIAC and APPLE

This richly flavoured casserole is comfort food at its best – serve with mashed potatoes and a glass or two of full-bodied red wine on a cold winter night.

SERVES 4

45ml/3 tbsp sunflower oil
450g/1lb duck or venison sausages
2 onions, sliced
15ml/1 tbsp plain (all-purpose) flour
400ml/14fl oz/1⅔ cups dry (hard) cider
350g/12oz celeriac, cut into
   large chunks
15ml/1 tbsp Worcestershire sauce
15ml/1 tbsp chopped fresh sage
2 small tart cooking apples, cored
   and sliced
salt and ground black pepper

1 Preheat the oven to 180°C/350°F/ Gas 4. Heat the oil in a frying pan, add the sausages and fry until evenly browned, about 5 minutes. Transfer to an earthenware casserole dish.

2 Drain off any excess oil from the pan to leave 15ml/1 tbsp. Add the onions and sauté for a few minutes until golden.

3 Stir in the flour, then gradually add the cider and bring to the boil, stirring. Add the celeriac and cook for 2 minutes. Stir in the Worcestershire sauce and sage. Season well with salt and black pepper.

4 Pour the cider and celeriac mixture over the sausages, then cover and cook in the oven for 30 minutes. Add the apples and cook for 10–15 minutes, or until the apples are just tender.

VARIATION
You can use good-quality pork and herb sausages instead, if you like.

Energy 538Kcal/2240kJ; Protein 43.5g; Carbohydrate 7g, of which sugars 2.8g; Fat 28.2g, of which saturates 8.9g; Cholesterol 170mg; Calcium 50mg; Fibre 1.1g; Sodium 610mg.

CASSOULET

Based on the traditional French dish, this recipe is full of delicious flavours and makes a welcoming and warming meal.

SERVES 6

3–4 boneless duck breast portions, about 450g/1lb total weight
225g/8oz thick-cut streaky (fatty) pork or unsmoked streaky (fatty) bacon rashers (strips)
450g/1lb Toulouse or garlic sausages
45ml/3 tbsp vegetable oil
450g/1lb onions, chopped
2 garlic cloves, crushed
2 × 425g/15oz cans cannellini beans, rinsed and drained
225g/8oz carrots, roughly chopped
400g/14oz can chopped tomatoes
15ml/1 tbsp tomato purée (paste)
bouquet garni
30ml/2 tbsp chopped fresh thyme or 15ml/1 tbsp dried
475ml/16fl oz/2 cups well-flavoured chicken stock
115g/4oz/2 cups fresh white or wholemeal (whole-wheat) breadcrumbs
salt and ground black pepper
fresh thyme sprigs, to garnish
warm crusty bread, to serve

1 Preheat the oven to 160°C/325°F/Gas 3. Cut the duck portions and pork or bacon rashers into large pieces. Twist the sausages to shorten them and then cut them into short lengths.

COOK'S TIP

Cannellini beans are large white beans with a nutty flavour. They are especially popular in Italy, particularly in Tuscany, where they are included in a variety of pasta and soup dishes. Cannellini beans are sometimes referred to as white kidney beans or fazola beans.

2 Heat the oil in a large flameproof casserole. Cook the meat in batches, until well browned. Remove from the pan with a slotted spoon and drain on kitchen paper.

3 Add the onions and garlic to the pan and cook for 3–4 minutes, or until beginning to soften, stirring frequently.

4 Stir in the beans, carrots, tomatoes, tomato purée, bouquet garni, thyme and seasoning. Return the meat to the casserole and mix until well combined.

VARIATION

Canned butter (lima) beans or borlotti beans can be used in this recipe instead of the cannellini beans.

5 Add enough of the stock just to cover the meat and beans. (The cassoulet shouldn't be swimming in juices; if the mixture becomes too dry during the cooking time, add a little more stock or water.) Bring to the boil. Cover the casserole tightly and cook in the oven for 1 hour.

6 Remove the cassoulet from the oven and add a little more stock or water, if necessary. Remove the bouquet garni.

7 Sprinkle the breadcrumbs in an even layer over the top of the cassoulet and return to the oven, uncovered, for a further 40 minutes, or until the meat is tender and the top crisp and lightly brown. Garnish with fresh thyme sprigs and serve hot with plenty of warm crusty bread to mop up the juices.

Energy 739Kcal/3085kJ; Protein 40.2g; Carbohydrate 49.6g, of which sugars 11.6g; Fat 44.8g, of which saturates 14.2g; Cholesterol 142mg; Calcium 118mg; Fibre 9.4g; Sodium 1848mg.

PIGEONS in STOUT

Pigeons are usually sold in breast portions, as the edible meat is mainly on the breast. The flesh is dark and, like most small birds, dry, so casseroling them in stout is an ideal cooking method. When buying the pigeon breasts, ask your poulterer for the carcasses for stock, if possible. Serve with spiced rice and a watercress or rocket salad.

SERVES 6

175g/6oz thick streaky (fatty) bacon
2 medium onions, finely chopped
2 or 3 garlic cloves, crushed
seasoned flour, for coating
50g/2oz/¼ cup butter
15ml/1 tbsp olive oil
6 pigeon breasts
30ml/2 tbsp Irish whiskey (optional)
600ml/1 pint/2½ cups chicken stock
300ml/½ pint/1¼ cups stout
175g/6oz button (white) mushrooms
beurre manié, if needed (see Cook's tip)
15–30ml/1–2 tbsp rowan jelly
sea salt and ground black pepper

1 Preheat the oven to 150°C/300°F/ Gas 2. Trim the streaky bacon and cut it into strips. Cook gently in a large, flameproof casserole until the fat runs out, then add the two chopped onions and crushed garlic and continue cooking until they are soft. Remove from the casserole and set aside.

2 Coat the breast portions thickly with seasoned flour. Add the butter and oil to the pan, heat until the butter is foaming, then add the meat and brown well on all sides. Pour in the Irish whiskey, if using. Carefully set it alight and shake the pan until the flames go out – this improves the flavour.

3 Stir in the stock, stout and the mushrooms, and bring slowly to the boil. Cover closely and cook in the preheated oven for 1½–2 hours, or until the pigeons are tender.

4 Remove from the oven and lift the pigeons on to a serving dish. Thicken the gravy, if necessary, by adding small pieces of beurre manié, stirring until the sauce thickens. Stir in rowan jelly to taste and adjust the seasoning. Serve the pigeons with the gravy while hot.

COOK'S TIP
To make beurre manié mix together 15g/½oz/1 tbsp of butter with 15ml/ 1 tbsp flour. Add small pieces of the mixture to the boiling gravy or sauce and stir until thickened.

Energy 436Kcal/1817kJ; Protein 38.7g; Carbohydrate 6.7g, of which sugars 5.3g; Fat 27.2g, of which saturates 6.2g; Cholesterol 33mg; Calcium 48mg; Fibre 1.7g; Sodium 639mg

MARINATED PIGEON in RED WINE

The time taken to marinate and cook this casserole is well rewarded by the fabulous rich flavour of the finished dish. Stir-fried green cabbage and celeriac purée are delicious accompaniments to this casserole.

SERVES 4

4 pigeons (US squabs), about 225g/
    8oz each
30ml/2 tbsp olive oil
1 onion, coarsely chopped
225g/8oz/3¼ cups chestnut
    mushrooms, sliced
15ml/1 tbsp plain (all-purpose) flour
300ml/½ pint/1¼ cups game stock
30ml/2 tbsp chopped fresh parsley
salt and ground black pepper
flat leaf parsley, to garnish

For the marinade
15ml/1 tbsp light olive oil
1 onion, chopped
1 carrot, peeled and chopped
1 celery stick, chopped
3 garlic cloves, sliced
6 allspice berries, bruised
2 bay leaves
8 black peppercorns, bruised
150ml/¼ pint/⅔ cup red wine vinegar
150ml/¼ pint/⅔ cup red wine
45ml/3 tbsp redcurrant jelly

2 Preheat the oven to 150°C/300°F/ Gas 2. Heat the oil in a large, flameproof casserole and cook the onion and mushrooms for about 5 minutes, or until the onion has softened.

3 Meanwhile, drain the pigeons and strain the marinade into a jug (pitcher), then set both aside separately.

4 Sprinkle the flour over the pigeons and add them to the casserole, breast-sides down. Pour in the marinade and stock, and add the chopped parsley and seasoning. Cover and cook for 2½ hours.

5 Check the seasoning, then serve the pigeons on warmed plates and ladle the sauce over them. Garnish with parsley.

1 Mix together all the ingredients for the marinade in a large bowl. Add the pigeons and turn them in the marinade, then cover the bowl and chill for about 12 hours, turning the pigeons frequently.

VARIATIONS
If you are unable to buy pigeon, this recipe works equally well with chicken or rabbit. Buy portions and make deep slashes in the flesh so that the marinade soaks into, and flavours right to, the centre of the pieces of meat.

Energy 428Kcal/1785kJ; Protein 32.8g; Carbohydrate 16.7g, of which sugars 12.4g; Fat 23.3g, of which saturates 1.3g; Cholesterol 0mg; Calcium 51mg; Fibre 2g; Sodium 135mg.

GUINEA FOWL with BEANS and CURLY KALE

Cooking lean poultry such as guinea fowl, chicken or turkey in a clay pot or chicken brick gives a delicious, moist result. Here the guinea fowl is cooked atop a colourful bed of herb-flavoured beans and vegetables.

2 Remove the shallots, garlic and celery with a slotted spoon and place in the chicken brick. Stir in the tomatoes and beans. Tuck in the thyme and bay leaves.

3 Put the guinea fowl in the frying pan and brown on all sides, then pour in the wine and stock and bring to the boil. Lift the bird out of the pan, place it on top of the vegetables in the chicken brick and then pour the liquid over the top. Cover and place in an unheated oven and set to 200°C/400°F/Gas 6. Cook for 1 hour.

4 Add the curly kale to the chicken brick, nestling it among the beans. Cover and cook for 10–15 minutes, or until the guinea fowl is tender. Season the bean mixture and serve.

COOK'S TIP

Guinea fowl and quail were both originally classified as game birds but nowadays farmed varieties are sold, making them available in the stores all year round.

VARIATION

Use chard, spring greens (collards) or Savoy cabbage in place of curly kale.

SERVES 4

1.3kg/3lb guinea fowl
45ml/3 tbsp olive oil
4 shallots, chopped
1 garlic clove, crushed
3 celery sticks, sliced
400g/14oz can chopped tomatoes
2 × 400g/14oz cans mixed
   beans, drained
5 fresh thyme sprigs
2 bay leaves
150ml/¼ pint/⅔ cup dry white wine
300ml/½ pint/1¼ cups well-flavoured
   chicken stock
175g/6oz curly kale
salt and ground black pepper

1 Soak a clay chicken brick in cold water for 20 minutes, then drain. Rub the guinea fowl with 15ml/1 tbsp of the olive oil and season. Place the remaining oil in a frying pan, add the shallots, garlic and celery and sauté for 4–5 minutes.

Energy 617Kcal/2585kJ; Protein 53.1g; Carbohydrate 32.9g, of which sugars 8.7g; Fat 28.6g, of which saturates 1.5g; Cholesterol 0mg; Calcium 98mg; Fibre 11.6g; Sodium 1017mg.

BRAISED PHEASANT with WILD MUSHROOMS, CHESTNUTS and BACON

Pheasant at the end of their season are not suitable for roasting, so consider this tasty casserole enriched with wild mushrooms and chestnuts. Allow two birds for four people.

SERVES 4

2 mature pheasants
50g/2oz/¼ cup butter
75ml/5 tbsp brandy
12 baby (pearl) onions, peeled
1 celery stick, chopped
50g/2oz unsmoked rindless bacon,
    cut into strips
45ml/3 tbsp plain (all-purpose) flour
550ml/18fl oz/2¼ cups chicken
    stock, boiling
175g/6oz peeled, cooked chestnuts
350g/12oz/4 cups fresh ceps, trimmed and
    sliced, or 15g/½oz/¼ cup dried porcini
    mushrooms, soaked in warm water for
    20 minutes
15ml/1 tbsp lemon juice
salt and ground black pepper
watercress sprigs, to garnish

2 Wipe out the casserole and melt the remaining butter. Add the onions, celery and bacon and brown lightly. Stir in the flour. Remove from the heat.

3 Stir in the stock gradually so that it is completely absorbed by the flour. Add the chestnuts, mushrooms, the pheasants and their juices. Bring back to a gentle simmer, then cover and cook in the oven for 1½ hours.

4 Transfer the cooked pheasants and vegetables to a warmed serving plate. Bring the sauce back to the boil, add the lemon juice and season to taste. Pour the sauce into a jug (pitcher) or gravy boat and garnish the birds with watercress.

COOK'S TIP
Cooking and peeling fresh chestnuts can be hard work, so look out for ready-peeled canned or vacuum-packed varieties.

1 Preheat the oven to 160°C/325°F/ Gas 3. Season the pheasants with salt and pepper. Melt half of the butter in a large flameproof casserole and brown the pheasants over a medium heat. Transfer the pheasants to a shallow dish and pour off the cooking fat. Return the casserole to the heat and brown the sediment. Add the brandy, stir well to loosen the sediment using a flat wooden spoon, then pour all the cooking juices over the pheasant.

COOK'S TIP
When buying pheasant choose birds that look fresh. They should be plump and firm, with supple skin. Game birds have a strong odour but they should never smell unpleasant or "off".

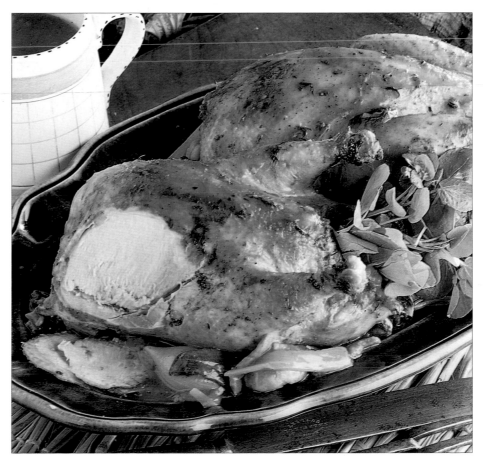

Energy 883Kcal/3699kJ; Protein 86.8g; Carbohydrate 32.3g, of which sugars 6.9g; Fat 41.6g, of which saturates 15.8g; Cholesterol 35mg; Calcium 205mg; Fibre 2.9g; Sodium 920mg.

GROUSE with ORCHARD FRUIT STUFFING

Tart apples, plums and pears make a fabulous orchard fruit stuffing that complements the rich gamey flavour of grouse perfectly.

SERVES 2

juice of ½ lemon
2 young grouse
50g/2oz/¼ cup butter
4 Swiss chard leaves
50ml/2fl oz/¼ cup Marsala
salt and ground black pepper

For the stuffing
2 shallots, finely chopped
1 tart cooking apple, peeled, cored
   and chopped
1 pear, peeled, cored and chopped
2 plums, halved, stoned (pitted)
   and chopped
large pinch of mixed (apple pie) spice

1 Sprinkle the lemon juice over the grouse and season well. Melt half the butter in a flameproof casserole, add the grouse and cook for 10 minutes, or until browned. Use tongs to remove the grouse from the casserole and set aside.

2 Add the shallots to the fat remaining in the casserole and cook until softened but not coloured. Add the apple, pear, plums and mixed spice, and cook for about 5 minutes, or until the fruits are just beginning to soften. Remove the casserole from the heat and spoon the hot fruit mixture into the body cavities of the birds.

3 Truss the birds neatly with string. Smear the remaining butter over the birds and wrap them in the chard leaves, then replace them in the casserole.

4 Pour in the Marsala and heat until simmering. Cover tightly and simmer for 20 minutes, or until the birds are tender, taking care not to overcook them. Leave to rest in a warm place for about 10 minutes before serving.

COOK'S TIP
There isn't a lot of liquid in the casserole for cooking the birds – they are steamed rather than boiled, so it is very important that the casserole has a heavy base and a tight-fitting lid, otherwise the liquid may evaporate and the chard will burn on the base of the pan.

Energy 508Kcal/2121kJ; Protein 46.9g; Carbohydrate 19.5g, of which sugars 18.7g; Fat 24.3g, of which saturates 13.8g; Cholesterol 53mg; Calcium 185mg; Fibre 4.2g; Sodium 406mg.

SPICY VENISON CASSEROLE

Being low in fat but high in flavour, venison is an excellent choice for healthy, yet rich, casseroles. Cranberries and orange bring a festive fruitiness to this spicy recipe. Serve with small baked potatoes and green vegetables.

SERVES 4

15ml/1 tbsp olive oil
1 onion, chopped
2 celery sticks, sliced
10ml/2 tsp ground allspice
15ml/1 tbsp plain (all-purpose) flour
675g/1½lb stewing venison, cubed
225g/8oz fresh or frozen cranberries
grated rind and juice of 1 orange
900ml/1½ pints/3¾ cups beef or
    venison stock
salt and ground black pepper

1 Heat the oil in a flameproof casserole. Add the onion and celery and fry for about 5 minutes, or until softened.

2 Meanwhile, mix the ground allspice with the flour and either spread the mixture out on a large plate or place in a large plastic bag. Toss a few pieces of venison at a time (to prevent them becoming soggy) in the flour mixture until they are all lightly coated. Spread the floured venison out on a large plate until ready to cook.

3 When the onion and celery are just softened, remove them from the casserole using a slotted spoon and set aside. Add the venison pieces to the casserole in batches and cook until well browned and sealed on all sides.

COOK'S TIP

Freshly made stock is always best, but if you are short of time, look for cartons or tubs of fresh stock in the chilled food cabinets of large supermarkets.

4 Add the cranberries and the orange rind and juice to the casserole along with the stock, and stir well. Return the vegetables and the browned venison to the casserole and heat until simmering. Cover tightly and reduce the heat.

5 Simmer for about 45 minutes, or until the venison is tender, stirring occasionally. Season the venison casserole to taste with salt and pepper before serving.

VARIATIONS

Farmed venison is increasingly easy to find and is available from good butchers and many large supermarkets. It makes a rich and flavourful stew, but lean pork or braising steak could be used in place of the venison, if you prefer. You could also replace the cranberries with pitted and halved ready-to-eat prunes and, for extra flavour, use either ale or stout instead of about half the stock.

Energy 242Kcal/1025kJ; Protein 38.3g; Carbohydrate 10.4g, of which sugars 7.1g; Fat 6.6g, of which saturates 1.8g; Cholesterol 84mg; Calcium 27mg; Fibre 1.4g; Sodium 105mg.

VENISON SAUSAGES with RED WINE GRAVY

Strongly flavoured, meaty sausages are delicious with a robust red wine gravy flavoured with assertive shiitake mushrooms. Serve with soft polenta, mashed potatoes or plenty of thickly sliced crusty bread to mop up the delicious gravy.

SERVES 4

15ml/1 tbsp sunflower oil (optional)
12 venison or wild boar sausages
2 leeks, sliced
2 plump garlic cloves, sliced
225g/8oz/3 cups shiitake
   mushrooms, quartered
15ml/1 tbsp plain (all-purpose) flour
600ml/1 pint/2½ cups red wine
30ml/2 tbsp chopped mixed fresh herbs,
   such as flat leaf parsley and marjoram
salt and ground black pepper

1 Pour the sunflower oil, if using, into a large frying pan, add the venison or wild boar sausages and cook over a medium heat for 15–20 minutes, turning frequently.

2 Add the leeks, garlic and mushrooms and mix well. Cook the vegetables for 10–15 minutes, or until the leeks are soft and beginning to brown.

3 Sprinkle in the flour and gradually pour in the red wine, stirring with a wooden spoon and pushing the sausages around to mix the flour and the liquid smoothly with the leeks.

4 Bring slowly to the boil, reduce the heat and simmer for 10–15 minutes, stirring occasionally, or until the gravy is smooth and glossy. Season the gravy with salt and pepper to taste and then sprinkle the mixed herbs over the sausages. Serve immediately with polenta or mashed potatoes.

COOK'S TIP
Shiitake mushrooms have a slightly floury-looking medium to dark grey-brown cap. They have a firm and meaty texture that becomes silky when cooked. The stalks can be tough so discard if necessary.

Energy 246Kcal/1026kJ; Protein 7.8g; Carbohydrate 11.7g, of which sugars 2.9g; Fat 7.8g, of which saturates 3g; Cholesterol 15mg; Calcium 71mg; Fibre 3g; Sodium 447mg.

CASSEROLED VENISON with STOUT

Venison, both wild and (more usually) farmed, is now widely available. It is popular on restaurant menus and, increasingly, available for home cooks from butchers and the better supermarkets. Serve with boiled or baked potatoes and red cabbage.

SERVES 6

900g/2lb stewing venison, such as shoulder
45ml/3 tbsp seasoned flour
30ml/2 tbsp olive oil
2 or 3 large onions, sliced
5 or 6 juniper berries, crushed
3 allspice berries
rind of ½ lemon or orange
25g/1oz/2 tbsp butter
about 300ml/½ pint/1¼ cups chicken or
   beef stock
150ml/¼ pint/⅔ cup red wine vinegar or
   cider vinegar
300ml/½ pint/1¼ cups stout or red wine
salt and ground black pepper

1 Preheat the oven to 180°C/350°F/ Gas 4. Cut the meat into 5cm/2in cubes. Toss the meat in the seasoned flour. Shake off and reserve the excess flour.

2 Heat the olive oil in a heavy frying pan and fry the meat in it until well browned all over. Lift out the pieces with a slotted spoon and put them into a casserole.

3 Add the onions to the casserole with the juniper berries and allspice, a little salt and black pepper and the lemon or orange rind.

4 Melt the butter in the pan in which the meat was browned, add the reserved flour, and stir and cook for 1 minute. Mix the stock, vinegar and stout or red wine together and gradually add to the pan, stirring until it boils and thickens.

5 Pour the sauce over the meat in the casserole, cover closely and cook in the oven for 1 hour. Reduce the temperature to 150°C/300°F/Gas 2 and cook for a further 2 hours, or until the venison is tender. Check the casserole occasionally and add a little extra stock or water if required. Serve piping hot.

COOK'S TIP
Venison is not difficult to cook but, like other game, it is lean, so marinating, basting and braising all help to offset any tendency to dryness.

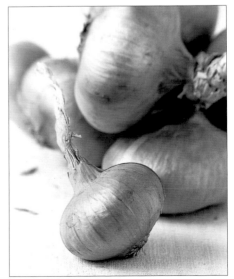

Energy 294Kcal/1233kJ; Protein 34.7g; Carbohydrate 9.3g, of which sugars 4.9g; Fat 10.6g, of which saturates 3.9g; Cholesterol 84mg; Calcium 37mg; Fibre 1.3g; Sodium 114mg

BRAISED RABBIT

Rabbit now features frequently on restaurant menus. It is delicious served with potatoes boiled in their skins and a lightly cooked green vegetable.

SERVES 4–6

1 rabbit, prepared and jointed by
   the butcher
30ml/2 tbsp seasoned flour
30ml/2 tbsp olive oil or vegetable oil
25g/1oz/2 tbsp butter
115g/4oz streaky (fatty) bacon
1 onion, roughly chopped
2 or 3 carrots, sliced
1 or 2 celery sticks, trimmed and sliced
300ml/½ pint/1¼ cups chicken stock
300ml/½ pint/1¼ cups dry (hard) cider
   or stout
a small bunch of parsley leaves, chopped
salt and ground black pepper

1 Soak the joints in cold salted water for at least two hours, then pat them dry with kitchen paper and toss them in seasoned flour. Preheat the oven to 200°C/400°F/Gas 6.

2 Heat the oil and butter together in a heavy flameproof casserole. Shake off (and reserve) any excess flour from the rabbit joints and brown them on all sides. Lift out and set aside.

3 Add the bacon to the casserole and cook for a few minutes, then remove and set aside with the rabbit. Add the vegetables to the casserole and cook gently until just colouring, then sprinkle over any remaining seasoned flour to absorb the fats in the casserole. Stir over a low heat for 1 minute, to cook the flour. Add the stock and cider or stout, stirring, to make a smooth sauce.

4 Return the rabbit and bacon to the casserole, and add half of the chopped parsley and a light seasoning of salt and pepper. Mix gently together, then cover with a lid and put into the preheated oven. Cook for 15–20 minutes, then reduce the temperature to 150°C/300°F/Gas 2 for about 1½ hours, or until the rabbit is tender. Add the remaining parsley and serve.

COOK'S TIP
Buy rabbit whole or jointed, from butchers and good supermarkets.
To make Rabbit Pie, prepare as above then allow to cool. Remove the meat from the bones, and then return the meat to the casserole, taste for seasoning and turn into a suitable pie dish, ensuring that the meat is covered by the sauce. (Add a sliced hard-boiled egg and a few quartered button (white) mushrooms, if you like.) Cover with shortcrust or rough-puff pastry and cook in the oven heated to 200°C/400°F/Gas 6 for about 30 minutes, or until the filling is hot and the pastry is golden brown and cooked through.

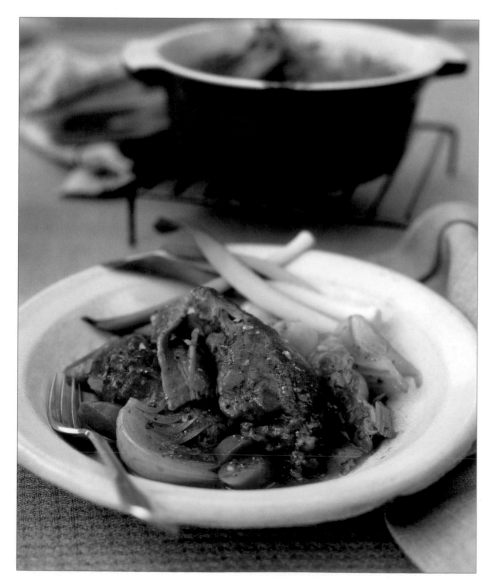

Energy 368Kcal/1535kJ; Protein 32.9g; Carbohydrate 10.5g, of which sugars 5.8g; Fat 19.7g, of which saturates 8g; Cholesterol 133mg; Calcium 88mg; Fibre 1.4g; Sodium 567mg

RABBIT with RED WINE and PRUNES

This is a favourite French dish and is often found on the menus of small country restaurants. It has a wonderfully rich flovour and the prunes add a delicious sweetness to the sauce. Serve with crisp, golden sautéed potatoes.

SERVES 4

8 rabbit portions
30ml/2 tbsp vegetable oil
2 onions, finely chopped
2 garlic cloves, finely chopped
60ml/4 tbsp Armagnac or brandy
300ml/½ pint/1¼ cups dry red wine
5ml/1 tsp soft light brown sugar
16 ready-to-eat prunes
150ml/¼ pint/⅔ cup double (heavy) cream
salt and ground black pepper

VARIATIONS
• Chicken can also be cooked in this way. Use 4 chicken drumsticks and 4 thighs in place of the rabbit portions.
• The prunes can be replaced with ready-to-eat dried apricots if you prefer – these go well with the rabbit and particularly well with chicken.

I Season the rabbit portions liberally with salt and pepper. Heat the vegetable oil in a large, flameproof casserole and fry the rabbit portions in batches until they are golden brown on all sides.

2 Remove the browned rabbit portions from the casserole, add the chopped onion and garlic, and cook, stirring occasionally, until the onion is softened.

3 Return the rabbit to the casserole, add the Armagnac or brandy and ignite it. When the flames have died down, pour in the wine. Stir in the sugar and prunes, cover and simmer for 30 minutes.

4 Remove the rabbit from the casserole and keep warm. Add the cream to the sauce and simmer for 3–5 minutes, then season to taste and serve immediately.

Energy 543Kcal/2259kJ; Protein 29.3g; Carbohydrate 19.4g, of which sugars 18.2g; Fat 29.9g, of which saturates 15.3g; Cholesterol 156mg; Calcium 99mg; Fibre 3g; Sodium 81mg.

SLOW COOKER MEAT

Slow cooking is suitable for all kinds of meat, but it works its magic best on less tender cuts, helping to improve and enhance their flavour and texture. Although beef and pork are great for robust dishes, such as Beef and Mushroom Pudding, they can also be used to make lighter modern meals, like Spicy Pork Casserole with Dried Fruit. Most lamb cuts are naturally tender and succulent and the slow cooker ensures they stay that way – try Moroccan Lamb with Honey and Prunes for a delicious meal. Whatever meat you choose and whether you are looking for a simple supper or an impressive dinner, you will find plenty of recipes here for delicious pot roasts, braised dishes, casseroles and stews.

STEAK and KIDNEY PIE with MUSTARD GRAVY

Peppery mustard gravy flavoured with bay leaves and parsley complements the tasty chunks of succulent beef and kidney in this classic pie. Cooking the puff pastry topping separately from the filling ensures it remains perfectly crisp – and is a perfect technique to use when making the pie using a slow cooker.

SERVES 4

675g/1½lb stewing steak
225g/8oz ox or lamb's kidney
45ml/3 tbsp oil
15g/½oz/1 tbsp unsalted (sweet) butter
2 onions, chopped
30ml/2 tbsp plain (all-purpose) flour
300ml/½ pint/1¼ cups beef stock
15ml/1 tbsp tomato purée (paste)
10ml/2 tsp English mustard
2 bay leaves
375g/13oz puff pastry
beaten egg, to glaze
15ml/1 tbsp chopped fresh parsley
salt and ground black pepper
creamed potatoes and green vegetables,
    to serve

1 Using a sharp knife, cut the stewing steak into 2.5cm/1in cubes. Remove all fat and skin from the kidney and cut into cubes or thick slices.

2 Heat 30ml/2 tbsp of the oil in a frying pan and brown the beef on all sides. Remove from the pan with a slotted spoon and place in the ceramic cooking pot. Switch the slow cooker on to high.

3 Add the kidney to the frying pan and brown for 1–2 minutes before adding to the beef. Add the remaining oil and the butter to the pan, add the onions and cook for 5 minutes, until just beginning to colour. Sprinkle with the flour and stir in, then remove the pan from the heat.

4 Gradually stir the stock into the pan, followed by the tomato purée and mustard. Return to the heat and bring to the boil, stirring constantly, until thickened. Pour the gravy over the meat, then add the bay leaves and season. Stir well and cover with the lid. Reduce the cooker to low and cook for 5–7 hours, or until the meat is very tender.

VARIATION
To make a richer version, use half the quantity of stock and add 150ml/¼ pint/ ⅔ cup stout or red wine.

5 While the beef is cooking, roll out the pastry and, using a dinner plate as a guide, cut out a 25cm/10in round. Transfer the pastry round to a baking sheet lined with baking parchment.

6 Using a sharp knife, mark the pastry into quarters, cutting almost but not quite through it. Decorate with pastry trimmings, then flute the edge. Cover with clear film (plastic wrap) and place in the refrigerator until ready to cook.

7 Towards the end of the beef's cooking time, preheat the oven to 200°C/400°F/ Gas 6. Brush the pastry all over with beaten egg to glaze, then bake for about 25 minutes, or until well risen, golden-brown and crisp.

8 To serve, stir the chopped parsley into the steak and kidney stew and spoon on to warmed serving plates. Cut the baked pie crust into four, using the markings as a guide, and top each portion of stew with a wedge of pastry. Serve immediately with rich, creamed potatoes and green vegetables.

Energy 637Kcal/2652kJ; Protein 18.7g; Carbohydrate 46.2g, of which sugars 5.2g; Fat 43.4g, of which saturates 13.1g; Cholesterol 259mg; Calcium 99mg; Fibre 2.7g; Sodium 578mg.

PROVENÇAL BEEF STEW

Known in France as daube de boeuf à la Provençal, *after the earthernware pot it was originally cooked in, this deliciously rich, fruity stew makes a perfect winter supper dish. Serve with mashed or boiled new potatoes and green vegetables.*

SERVES 4

45ml/3 tbsp olive oil
115g/4oz lean salt pork or
   thick-cut bacon, diced
900g/2lb stewing steak cut into
   4cm/1½in pieces
1 large onion, chopped
2 carrots, sliced
2 ripe tomatoes, peeled, seeded
   and chopped
10ml/2 tsp tomato purée (paste)
2 garlic cloves, very finely chopped
250ml/8fl oz/1 cup fruity red wine
150ml/¼ pint/⅔ cup beef stock
1 bouquet garni
1 small onion, studded with 2 cloves
grated zest and juice of ½ unwaxed orange
15ml/1 tbsp chopped fresh parsley
salt and ground black pepper

1 Heat 15ml/1 tbsp of the oil in a large heavy frying pan, then add the salt pork or bacon and cook over a medium heat for 4–5 minutes, stirring frequently, until browned and the fat is rendered.

2 Using a slotted spoon, transfer the pork or bacon to the ceramic cooking pot and switch the slow cooker to high.

3 Working in batches, add the beef to the pan in a single layer (do not overcrowd the pan, or the meat will stew in its own juices and not brown). Cook for 6–8 minutes until browned, turning to colour all sides.

4 Transfer the beef to the ceramic cooking pot and continue browning the rest of the meat in the same way, adding more oil when needed.

5 Pour the wine and stock over the beef in the ceramic cooking pot, then add the bouquet garni and the onion. Add the remaining oil and the onion to the frying pan and cook gently for 5 minutes. Stir in the carrots and cook for a further 5 minutes, until softened. Stir in the tomatoes, tomato purée and garlic, then transfer to the ceramic cooking pot.

6 Cover with the lid and switch the slow cooker to low. Cook for 5–7 hours, or until the beef and vegetables are very tender. Uncover and skim off any fat. Season, discard the bouquet garni and clove-studded onion, and stir in the orange zest and juice and the parsley.

Energy 547Kcal/2286kJ; Protein 55.8g; Carbohydrate 8.7g, of which sugars 7.2g; Fat 27.8g, of which saturates 8.9g; Cholesterol 170mg; Calcium 43mg; Fibre 2g; Sodium 682mg.

BRAISED BEEF in a RICH PEANUT SAUCE

Like many dishes brought to the Philippines by the Spanish, this slow-cooking Estofado, renamed by the Philippinos as Kari Kari, retains much of its original charm. Peanuts are used to thicken the juices, yielding a rich, sweet, glossy sauce.

SERVES 4

900g/2lb stewing (braising) chuck,
   shin or blade steak
45ml/3 tbsp vegetable oil
2 onions, chopped
2 cloves garlic, crushed
5ml/1 tsp paprika
pinch of ground turmeric
225g/8oz celeriac or swede (rutabaga),
   peeled and cut into 2cm/¾in dice
425ml/15fl oz/1¾ cups boiling beef stock
15ml/1 tbsp fish or anchovy sauce
30ml/2 tbsp tamarind sauce (optional)
10ml/2 tsp soft light brown sugar
1 bay leaf
1 sprig thyme
30ml/2 tbsp smooth peanut butter
45ml/3 tbsp easy-cook (converted)
   white rice
5ml/1 tsp white wine vinegar
salt and ground black pepper

1 Using a sharp knife, cut the beef into 2.5cm/1in cubes. Heat 30ml/2 tbsp of the oil in a pan and fry the beef, turning until well browned all over.

2 Transfer the meat and any juices to the ceramic cooking pot and switch the slow cooker to high.

3 Add the remaining 15ml/1 tbsp oil to the frying pan, add the onions and fry gently for 10 minutes until softened.

4 Add the garlic, paprika and turmeric to the pan and cook for 1 minute. Transfer the mixture to the ceramic pot and add the celeriac or swede.

5 Pour in the stock, fish or anchovy sauce and taramind sauce, if using, and add the sugar, bay leaf and thyme. Cover with the lid, then reduce the heat to low and cook for 4 hours, or until the beef and vegetables are just tender.

6 Turn the slow cooker up to high, then remove about 60ml/4 tbsp of the cooking juices to a bowl and blend with the peanut butter. Stir the mixture into the casserole, sprinkle with the rice, and stir again to combine.

7 Cover the pot and cook for about 45 minutes, or until the rice is cooked and the sauce has thickened slightly. Stir in the wine vinegar and season to taste.

COOK'S TIP
This stew makes a meal in itself so needs no accompaniments. However, a simple green salad served on the side makes a refreshing palate cleanser.

Energy 577Kcal/2408kJ; Protein 48.9g; Carbohydrate 14.1g, of which sugars 8.9g; Fat 36.8g, of which saturates 12.2g; Cholesterol 141mg; Calcium 70mg; Fibre 2.4g; Sodium 561mg.

BEEF and MUSHROOM PUDDING

*Based on a great British classic, this steamed savoury pudding has a light herb pastry
crust made with a mixture of suet and butter for both taste and colour. A mouthwatering
mixture of dried porcini and chestnut mushrooms gives the filling an intense flavour.*

SERVES 4

25g/1oz/½ cup dried porcini mushrooms
475ml/16fl oz/2 cups near-boiling
   beef stock
675g/1½lb stewing (braising) steak
60ml/4 tbsp plain (all-purpose) flour
45ml/3 tbsp sunflower oil
1 large onion, finely chopped
225g/8oz chestnut or flat mushrooms,
   thickly sliced
1 bay leaf
15ml/1 tbsp Worcestershire sauce
75ml/2½fl oz/⅓ cup port or red wine
salt and ground black pepper

For the pastry
275g/10oz/2½ cups self-raising
   (self-rising) flour
2.5ml/½ tsp baking powder
2.5ml/½ tsp salt
15ml/1 tbsp each chopped parsley
   and fresh thyme
75g/3oz/1½ cups beef or vegetable suet
   (chilled, grated shortening)
50g/2oz/¼ cup butter, frozen and grated
1 egg, lightly beaten
about 150ml/¼ pint/⅔ cup cold water

1 Put the dried mushrooms in a bowl
and pour over the stock. Leave to soak
for about 20 minutes.

2 Meanwhile, trim the meat and cut
into 2cm/¾in pieces. Place the flour in
a bowl, season, then add the meat and
toss to coat. Heat the oil in a frying
pan and fry the meat in batches until
browned on all sides. Transfer to the
ceramic cooking pot.

3 Add the onion to the pan and cook
gently for 10 minutes, or until softened.
Transfer to the ceramic cooking pot,
then add the chestnut mushrooms and
the bay leaf.

4 In a bowl or jug (pitcher), combine
the Worcestershire sauce with the port
or wine, then pour into the ceramic
cooking pot. Drain the soaked porcini
mushrooms, pouring the stock into the
pot, then chop them and add to the pot.

5 Stir the ingredients together, then
cover with the lid and cook on high or
auto for 1 hour. Reduce the heat to low
and cook for a further 5–6 hours, or
until the meat and onions are tender.
Remove the bay leaf, then leave the
mixture to cool completely.

6 To make the pastry, butter a deep
1.7 litre/3 pint/7½ cup heatproof
pudding basin. Sift the flour, baking
powder and salt into a mixing bowl and
stir in the herbs followed by the suet
and butter. Make a well in the centre,
add the egg and enough cold water
to mix, and gather into a soft dough.

7 Lightly knead the dough for a few
seconds on a floured surface until
smooth. Cut off a quarter of the dough
and wrap in clear film (plastic wrap).
Shape the rest into a ball and roll out
into a round large enough to line the
basin or bowl. Lift up the pastry and
carefully place in the basin, pressing it
against the sides and allowing the excess
to fall over the sides. Roll out the
reserved pastry to make a round large
enough to use as a lid for the pudding.

8 Spoon in the cooled filling and enough
of the gravy to come to within 1cm/½in
of the rim. (Reserve the remaining gravy
to serve with the pudding.) Brush the
top edge of the pastry with water and
place the lid on top. Press the edges
together to seal and trim off any excess.

9 Cover the pudding basin with a
pleated, double thickness layer of baking
parchment and secure under the rim
using string. Cover with pleated foil to
allow the pudding to rise.

10 Put an inverted saucer or metal
pastry ring in the base of the cleaned
ceramic cooking pot and place the
pudding basin on top. Pour in enough
near-boiling water to come just over
halfway up the sides of the basin. Cover
with the lid and cook on high for 3 hours.

11 Carefully remove the pudding from
the slow cooker, then take off the foil,
string and greaseproof paper. Loosen the
edges of the pudding and invert on to a
warmed serving plate.

Energy 1061Kcal/4444kJ; Protein 70g; Carbohydrate 75.1g, of which sugars 4.8g; Fat 54.3g, of which saturates 24.5g; Cholesterol 265mg; Calcium 319mg; Fibre 4.4g; Sodium 941mg.

BRAISED BEEF with HORSERADISH

This dark rich beef with a spicy kick makes an ideal alternative to a meat roast. The meat slowly tenderizes in the slow cooker and all the flavours blend together beautifully. It is also a great dish for entertaining because it can be prepared in advance and then simply left to simmer on its own until you are ready to serve.

SERVES 4

30ml/2 tbsp plain (all-purpose) flour
4 × 175g/6oz braising steaks
30ml/2 tbsp sunflower oil
12 small shallots, peeled and halved
1 garlic clove, crushed
1.5ml/¼ tsp ground ginger
5ml/1 tsp curry powder
10ml/2 tsp dark muscovado (molasses)
   sugar
475ml/16fl oz/2 cups near-boiling beef stock
15ml/1 tbsp Worcestershire sauce
30ml/2 tbsp creamed horseradish
225g/8oz baby carrots, trimmed
1 bay leaf
salt and ground black pepper
30ml/2 tbsp chopped fresh chives,
   to garnish
roast vegetables, to serve

1 Place the flour in a large, flat dish and season with salt and black pepper. Toss the steaks in the flour to coat.

2 Heat the oil in a pan and quickly brown the steaks on both sides. Transfer them to the ceramic cooking pot.

3 Add the halved shallots to the pan and cook gently for 10 minutes, or until golden and beginning to soften. Stir in the garlic, ginger and curry powder and cook for 1 minute more, then remove the pan from the heat.

4 Tip the shallot mixture into the ceramic cooking pot, spreading it over the meat, and sprinkle with the sugar.

5 Pour the beef stock over the shallots and meat, then add the Worcestershire sauce, horseradish, baby carrots and bay leaf. Stir to combine, then season with salt and black pepper. Cover with the lid and cook on high or auto for 1 hour.

6 Reduce the slow cooker to low, or leave on auto, and continue to cook the stew for a further 5–6 hours, or until the beef and vegetables are very tender.

7 Remove the bay leaf from the stew and sprinkle with the chopped chives before serving with roast vegetables.

COOK'S TIPS
• Choose a medium curry powder for flavouring the stew. There is already plenty of bite from the horseradish, so you don't want to overpower the meat flavours entirely with a very strong, spicy curry powder.
• To give the stew a really robust flavour, replace 175ml/6fl oz/¾ cup of the stock with red wine.
• The sweet flavour of roasted parsnips and butternut squash goes particularly well with the spicy bite of horseradish. Cook plenty of roast potatoes too – they are the perfect accompaniment to braised beef, and are great for mopping up the delicious gravy.

Energy 478Kcal/2010kJ; Protein 62.5g; Carbohydrate 17.7g, of which sugars 9.6g; Fat 18.1g, of which saturates 7.4g; Cholesterol 176mg; Calcium 65mg; Fibre 2.5g; Sodium 423mg.

HUNGARIAN CHOLENT

A traditional Sabbath dish of the Ashkenazi Jews, cholent is a long-simmered dish of beans, grains, meat and vegetables. The addition of whole boiled eggs is a classic feature. Don't forget to start soaking the beans the day before; they need at least 8 hours.

3 Meanwhile, heat the oil in a pan, add the onion and cook gently for about 10 minutes, or until soft. Transfer the onions to the ceramic cooking pot.

4 Add the garlic, beans, barley, paprika, cayenne pepper, celery, tomatoes, carrots, turnip, potatoes, beef and stock to the onions and stir to combine.

5 Cover the pot with the lid and cook on low for 5–6 hours, or until the meat and vegetables are tender. Add the rice, stir, and season with salt and pepper.

6 Rinse the eggs in tepid water, then lower them, one at a time, into the hot stock. Cover and cook for a further 45 minutes, or until the rice is cooked. Serve hot, making sure each portion contains a whole egg.

SERVES 4

250g/9oz/1⅓ cups dried haricot (navy) beans
30ml/2 tbsp olive oil
1 onion, chopped
4 garlic cloves, finely chopped
50g/2oz pearl barley
15ml/1 tbsp ground paprika
pinch of cayenne pepper
1 celery stick, chopped
400g/14oz can chopped tomatoes
3 carrots, sliced
1 small turnip, diced
2 baking potatoes, peeled and cut into chunks
675g/1½lb mixture of beef brisket, stewing beef and smoked beef, cut into cubes
1 litre/1¾ pints/4 cups boiling beef stock
30ml/2 tbsp easy-cook (converted) white rice
4 eggs, at room temperature
salt and ground black pepper

1 Place the beans in a large bowl. Pour over plenty of cold water to cover and leave to soak for at least 8 hours, or overnight if you like.

2 Drain the beans well, then place them in a large pan, cover with fresh cold water and bring to the boil. Boil them steadily for about 10 minutes, skimming off any froth that rises to the surface, then drain well and set aside.

Energy 860Kcal/3607kJ; Protein 58.9g; Carbohydrate 74.2g, of which sugars 13.7g; Fat 38.8g, of which saturates 12.7g; Cholesterol 341mg; Calcium 164mg; Fibre 10.9g; Sodium 639mg.

SPICED BEEF

This is a classic Irish dish, although it is a modern version of the traditional recipe, as it omits the initial pickling stage and takes only three or four days to cure in comparison with ten days for the older method. Serve on thinly sliced brown bread, with chutney.

SERVES 6

15ml/1 tbsp coarsely ground
  black pepper
10ml/2 tsp ground ginger
15ml/1 tbsp juniper berries, crushed
15ml/1 tbsp coriander seeds, crushed
5ml/1 tsp ground cloves
15ml/1 tbsp ground allspice
45ml/3 tbsp soft dark brown sugar
2 bay leaves, crushed
1 small onion, finely chopped
1.8kg/4lb corned beef, silverside or tail end
300ml/½ pint/1¼ cups Guinness
fruit chutney and brown bread, to serve

COOK'S TIP
• As a first course, serve the beef thinly sliced with home-made brown bread and a fruit chutney, such as apple and sultana.
• Spiced beef is excellent as finger food for parties, sliced thinly and served with sour cream lightly flavoured with horseradish and black pepper.

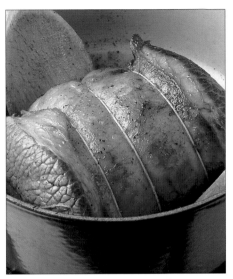

3 When the joint is cooked, leave it to cool in the cooking liquid. Wrap in foil and keep in the refrigerator until required, then slice thinly to serve. It will keep for about 1 week.

1 First, spice the beef: blend the pepper, spices and sugar thoroughly, then mix in the bay leaves and onion. Rub the mixture into the meat, then put it into a suitable lidded container and refrigerate for 3–4 days, turning and rubbing with the mixture daily.

2 Put the meat into the ceramic cooking pot and barely cover with cold water. Cover with the lid and switch on to auto or high. Cook for 3 hours, then leave on auto or reduce to low and cook for a further 3–4 hours, until the meat is very tender. For the last hour add the Guinness.

Energy 309Kcal/1301kJ; Protein 53.6g; Carbohydrate 2g, of which sugars 2g; Fat 9.7g, of which saturates 3.6g; Cholesterol 137mg; Calcium 15mg; Fibre 0g; Sodium 140mg

HOT and SOUR PORK

This has all the flavour of a stir-fry without the hassle of last-minute cooking. Using lean pork fillet and reducing the temperature to low after an hour means that the meat remains wonderfully moist and tender, while the vegetables retain their crunchy texture.

SERVES 4

15ml/1 tbsp dried Chinese mushrooms
150ml/¼ pint/⅔ cup boiling
   vegetable stock
350g/12oz pork fillet
115g/4oz baby corn kernels
1 green (bell) pepper
225g/8oz pineapple chunks
   in natural juice
20ml/4 tsp cornflour (cornstarch)
15ml/1 tbsp sunflower oil
115g/4oz water chestnuts
2.5cm/1 in piece root ginger, grated
1 red chilli, seeded and finely chopped
5ml/1 tsp Chinese five-spice powder
15ml/1 tbsp sherry vinegar
15ml/1 tbsp dark soy sauce
15ml/1 tbsp hoisin sauce
plain boiled or fried rice, to serve

1 Put the mushrooms in a heatproof bowl, then pour over the hot stock and leave to soak for 15–20 minutes.

2 Trim away any visible fat from the pork and cut into 1cm/½ in slices. Slice the baby corn kernels lengthways. Halve, seed and slice the green pepper. Drain the pineapple chunks, reserving the juice. Drain the mushrooms, reserving the stock, and slice any large ones.

3 In a bowl, blend the cornflour with a little of the reserved pineapple juice, then slowly stir in the remainder.

4 Heat the oil in a non-stick frying pan. Add the pork and sear for 30 seconds on each side, or until lightly browned. Transfer to the ceramic cooking pot and add the vegetables, pineapple chunks and water chestnuts.

5 In a bowl, combine the ginger, chilli and five-spice powder with the vinegar, soy sauce, hoisin sauce and reserved stock. Pour in the pineapple juice mixture, then tip into the frying pan and bring to the boil, stirring constantly. As soon as the mixture thickens, pour over the pork and vegetables.

6 Cover with the lid and switch the slow cooker to high. Cook for 1 hour, then reduce the temperature to low and cook for 1–2 hours, or until the pork is cooked and the vegetables retain some crispness. Serve with rice.

Energy 358Kcal/1509kJ; Protein 19.9g; Carbohydrate 49.4g, of which sugars 36.3g; Fat 10.3g, of which saturates 2.8g; Cholesterol 60.4mg; Calcium 43mg; Fibre 2.7g; Sodium 405mg.

BOSTON BAKED BEANS

The slow cooker was actually invented for making baked beans. Molasses gives the beans a very rich flavour and dark colour, but you can replace it with maple syrup if you prefer.

SERVES 8

450g/1lb/2½ cups dried haricot
    (navy) beans
4 whole cloves
2 onions, peeled
1 bay leaf
90ml/6 tbsp tomato ketchup
30ml/2 tbsp molasses
30ml/2 tbsp dark brown sugar
15ml/1tbsp Dijon-style mustard
475ml/16fl oz/2 cups unsalted
    vegetable stock
225g/8oz piece of salt pork
salt and ground black pepper

1 Rinse the beans, then place in a large bowl. Cover with cold water and leave to soak for at least 8 hours or overnight.

2 Drain and rinse the beans. Place them in a large pan, cover with plenty of cold water and bring to the boil. Boil gently for about 10 minutes, then drain and tip into the ceramic cooking pot.

3 Stick 2 cloves in each of the onions. Add them to the pot with the bay leaf, burying them in the beans.

4 In a bowl, blend together the ketchup, molasses, sugar, mustard and stock, and pour over the beans. Add more stock, or water, if necessary, so that the beans are almost covered with liquid. Cover with the lid and switch the slow cooker to low. Cook for 3 hours.

5 Towards the end of the cooking time, place the salt pork in a pan of boiling water and cook for 3 minutes.

6 Using a sharp knife, score the pork rind in deep 1.5cm/½in cuts. Add the salt pork to the ceramic cooking pot, pushing it down just below the surface of the beans, skin side up. Cover the pot with the lid and cook for a further 5–6 hours, until the beans are tender.

7 Remove the pork from the beans and set aside until cool enough to handle, Using a sharp knife, slice off the rind and fat and finely slice the meat.

8 Using a spoon, skim off any fat from the top of the beans, then stir in the pieces of meat. Season to taste with salt and black pepper, and serve hot.

COOK'S TIPS
• Be sure to taste the beans before adding any more salt. The salt pork will have already added plenty, so you may only need to season with black pepper.
• To make a vegetarian version of these beans, simply leave out the salt pork. They are just as good cooked without.

Energy 228Kcal/968kJ; Protein 13.4g; Carbohydrate 43.9g, of which sugars 19.4g; Fat 1g, of which saturates 0.1g; Cholesterol 0mg; Calcium 140mg; Fibre 9.5g; Sodium 334mg.

ITALIAN PORK SAUSAGE STEW

This hearty casserole, made with spicy sausages and haricot beans, is flavoured with fragrant fresh herbs and dry Italian wine. Serve with Italian bread for mopping up the delicious juices. Remember to leave time for the beans to soak before cooking.

SERVES 4

225g/8oz/1¼ cups dried haricot
   (navy) beans
2 sprigs fresh thyme
30ml/2 tsp olive oil
450g/1lb fresh Italian pork sausages
1 onion, finely chopped
2 sticks celery, finely diced
300ml/½ pint/1¼ cups dry red or white
   wine, preferably Italian
1 sprig of fresh rosemary
1 bay leaf
300ml/½ pint/1¼ cups boiling
   vegetable stock
200g/7oz can chopped tomatoes
¼ head dark green cabbage such as cavolo
   nero or Savoy, finely shredded
salt and ground black pepper
chopped fresh thyme, to garnish
crusty Italian bread, to serve

1 Put the haricot beans in a large bowl and cover with cold water. Leave to soak for at least 8 hours, or overnight.

2 Drain the beans and place in a pan with the thyme sprigs and at least twice their volume of cold water. Bring to the boil and boil steadily for 10 minutes, then drain and place in the ceramic cooking pot, discarding the thyme.

3 Meanwhile, heat the oil in a pan and cook the sausages until browned all over. Transfer to the ceramic cooking pot and tip away all but 15ml/1 tbsp of the fat in the frying pan.

4 Add the onion and celery to the pan and cook gently for 5 minutes until softened but not coloured. Add the wine, rosemary and bay leaf and bring to the boil. Pour over the sausages, add the stock and season with salt and pepper. Cover with the lid, switch the slow cooker to high and cook for 5–6 hours, until the beans are tender.

5 Stir the chopped tomatoes and the shredded cabbage into the stew. Cover and cook for 30–45 minutes, or until the cabbage is tender but not overcooked. Divide between warmed plates, garnish with a little chopped fresh thyme and serve with crusty Italian bread.

COOK'S TIP
The tomatoes are added towards the end of cooking because their acidity would prevent the beans from becoming tender if added earlier.

Energy 620Kcal/2593kJ; Protein 28.4g; Carbohydrate 47.4g, of which sugars 9.9g; Fat 30.9g, of which saturates 10.8g; Cholesterol 67.5mg; Calcium 205mg; Fibre 7.6g; Sodium 1139mg.

PORK and POTATO HOT-POT

Long, slow cooking makes the pork chops meltingly tender and allows the potato slices to soak up all the delicious juices from the meat. Perfect for a family meal or casual supper with friends, simply serve with lightly cooked green vegetables.

SERVES 4

25g/1oz/2 tbsp butter
15ml/1 tbsp oil
1 large onion, very thinly sliced
1 garlic clove, crushed
225g/8oz/generous 3 cups button (white)
    mushrooms, sliced
1.5ml/¼ tsp dried mixed herbs
900g/2lb potatoes, thinly sliced
4 thick pork chops
750ml/1¼ pints/3 cups vegetable
    or chicken stock
salt and ground black pepper

1 Use 15g/½oz/1 tbsp of the butter to grease the base and halfway up the sides of the ceramic cooking pot.

2 Heat the oil in a frying pan, add the sliced onion and cook gently for about 5 minutes, until softened and translucent.

3 Add the garlic and mushrooms to the pan and cook for a further 5 minutes until softened. Remove the pan from the heat and stir in the mixed herbs.

4 Spoon half the mushroom mixture into the base of the ceramic cooking pot, then arrange half the potato slices on top and season with salt and ground black pepper.

5 Using a sharp knife, trim as much fat as possible from the pork chops, then place them on top of the potatoes in a single layer. Pour about half the stock over the top to cover the potatoes and prevent them discolouring.

6 Repeat the layers of the mushroom mixture and potatoes, finishing with a layer of neatly overlapping potatoes. Pour over the remaining stock; it should just cover the potatoes, so use a little more or less if necessary. Dot the remaining butter on top of the potatoes and cover with the lid.

7 Cook the stew on high for 4–5 hours, or until the potatoes and meat are tender when pierced with a thin skewer. If you like, place the hot-pot under a medium grill (broiler) for 5–10 minutes to brown before serving.

Energy 511Kcal/2132kJ; Protein 17.9g; Carbohydrate 41.5g, of which sugars 6.5g; Fat 31.5g, of which saturates 12.1g; Cholesterol 67mg; Calcium 40mg; Fibre 3.7g; Sodium 529mg.

POTATO and SAUSAGE CASSEROLE

There are many variations of this traditional Irish supper dish, known as Irish coddle, but the basic ingredients are the same wherever you go – potatoes, sausages and bacon.

SERVES 4

15ml/1 tbsp vegetable oil
8 large pork sausages
4 bacon rashers (slices), cut into 2.5cm/
   1in pieces
1 large onion, chopped
2 garlic cloves, crushed
4 large baking potatoes, peeled
   and thinly sliced
1.5ml/¼ tsp fresh sage
300ml/½ pint/1¼ cups vegetable stock
salt and ground black pepper

COOK'S TIPS
• For an authentic Irish feel, serve this delicious, hearty casserole with braised green cabbage.
• Choose good-quality sausages because it will make all the difference to the final result. Many Irish artisan butchers export quality Irish sausages, so it is well worth keeping an eye out for them.

1 Heat the oil in a frying pan. Gently fry the sausages for about 5 minutes, turning frequently until they are golden but not cooked through. Remove from the frying pan and set aside. Tip away all but about 10ml/2 tsp of fat from the pan.

2 Add the bacon to the pan and fry for 2 minutes. Add the onion and fry for about 8 minutes, stirring frequently until golden. Add the garlic and fry for a further 1 minute, then turn off the heat.

3 Arrange half the potato slices in the base of the ceramic cooking pot. Spoon the bacon and onion mixture on top. Season well with salt and ground black pepper, and sprinkle with the fresh sage. Cover with the remaining potato slices.

4 Pour the stock over the potatoes and top with the sausages. Cover with the lid and cook on high for 3–4 hours, or until the potatoes are tender and the sausages cooked through. Serve hot.

Energy 717Kcal/2984kJ; Protein 20.5g; Carbohydrate 49.9g, of which sugars 6.1g; Fat 49.8g, of which saturates 18.1g; Cholesterol 78.1mg; Calcium 73mg; Fibre 4g; Sodium 1322mg.

PORK FILLETS with PRUNE STUFFING

The sweet flavour and rich texture of dried fruit, such as prunes, goes particularly well
with pork. If you want to ring the changes, dried apricots or figs can be used instead.

SERVES 4

15g/½oz/1 tbsp butter
1 shallot, very finely chopped
1 stick celery, very finely chopped
finely grated rind of ½ orange
115g/4oz/½ cup (about 12) stoned
    (pitted), ready-to-eat prunes, chopped
25g/1oz/½ cup fresh white breadcrumbs
30ml/2 tbsp chopped fresh parsley
pinch of grated nutmeg
two 225g/8oz pork fillets, trimmed
6 slices Parma ham or prosciutto
15ml/1 tbsp olive oil
150ml/¼ pint/⅔ cup dry white wine
salt and ground black pepper
mashed root vegetables and wilted pak
    choi (bok choy), to serve

1 Melt the butter in a frying pan, add
the shallot and celery, and fry gently
until soft. Tip into a bowl and stir in the
orange rind, prunes, breadcrumbs, parsley
and nutmeg. Season and leave to cool.

2 Slice down the length of each fillet,
cutting three-quarters of the way through.

3 Open out each pork fillet and lay it
out on a board. Cover the meat with a
piece of oiled clear film (plastic wrap),
then gently bash with a rolling pin until
the meat is about 5mm/¼in thick.

4 Arrange 3 slices of the ham on a
board and place one pork fillet on top.
Repeat with the remaining ham and fillet.

5 Divide the prune and breadcrumb
stuffing between the pork fillets, then
fold over to enclose the filling.

6 Wrap the ham around one stuffed
pork fillet, and secure with one or two
wooden cocktail sticks (toothpicks).
Repeat with the remaining ham and fillet.

7 Heat the oil in the clean frying pan
and quickly brown the wrapped pork
fillets all over, taking care not to dislodge
the cocktail sticks, before transferring
them to the ceramic cooking pot.

8 Pour the white wine into the frying
pan and bring almost to the boil, then
pour over the pork.

9 Cover the ceramic cooking pot with
the slow cooker lid and cook on high
for 1 hour, then reduce the temperature
to low and cook for a further 2–3 hours,
or until the pork is cooked completely
through and tender.

10 Remove the cocktail sticks from
the meat and cut the pork into slices.
Arrange on warmed plates and spoon
over some of the cooking juices. Serve
with mashed root vegetables and wilted
pak choi leaves.

Energy 245Kcal/1027kJ; Protein 17.3g; Carbohydrate 14.6g, of which sugars 11.3g; Fat 10.8g, of which saturates 4g; Cholesterol 59mg; Calcium 34mg; Fibre 2g; Sodium 378mg.

SPICY PORK CASSEROLE with DRIED FRUIT

Inspired by the South American mole – a paste of chilli, shallots and nuts – this casserole is thickened and flavoured with a similar mixture, which really brings out the taste of the onions, meat and sweet dried fruit. Part of the mole is added at the end of cooking to retain its fresh flavour. Serve the casserole with rice and a green salad.

SERVES 6

25ml/1½ tbsp plain (all-purpose) flour
1kg/2¼lb shoulder or leg of pork,
   cut into 4cm/1½in cubes
30ml/2 tbsp olive oil
450ml/¾ pint/scant 2 cups fruity
   white wine
150ml/¼ pint/⅔ cup vegetable stock
   or water
115g/4oz/1½ cups ready-to-eat prunes
115g/4oz/1½ cups ready-to-eat dried
   apricots
grated rind and juice of 1 small orange
pinch of muscovado sugar
30ml/2 tbsp chopped fresh parsley
1 fresh green or red chilli, seeded
   and finely chopped
salt and ground black pepper
plain boiled rice, to serve

For the *mole*
3 ancho chillies and 2 pasilla chillies
   (or other varieties of large,
   medium-hot dried red chillies)
30ml/2 tbsp olive oil
2 large onions, finely chopped
3 garlic cloves, chopped
1 fresh green chilli, seeded and
   chopped
10ml/2 tsp ground coriander
5ml/1 tsp mild Spanish paprika
   or pimenton
50g/2oz/½ cup blanched almonds,
   toasted
15ml/1 tbsp chopped fresh oregano
   or 2.5ml/½ tsp dried oregano

1 Make the *mole* paste first. Toast the dried chillies in a dry frying pan over a low heat for 1–2 minutes, stirring, until they are aromatic. Remove the chillies from the heat, place in a small bowl and pour over warm water to cover. Leave to soak for about 30 minutes.

2 Drain the chillies, reserving the soaking water, then remove and discard the woody stalks and seeds.

3 Heat the oil in a frying pan and fry the onions over a low heat for about 10 minutes until soft. Remove two-thirds of the onions from the pan and set aside. Add the garlic, fresh green chilli and ground coriander to the pan and cook for a further 5 minutes.

4 Transfer the onion mixture to a food processor and add the drained chillies, paprika or pimenton, almonds and oregano. Process the mixture, adding 45–60ml/3–4 tbsp of the chilli soaking liquid to make a workable paste.

5 Place the flour in a shallow dish and season with salt and black pepper. Add the pork and toss well to coat.

6 Wipe the frying pan clean with kitchen paper and heat the olive oil. Fry the pork in two batches over a high heat for 5–6 minutes, stirring frequently, until it is sealed on all sides. Transfer the pork to the ceramic cooking pot with a slotted spoon and switch the slow cooker to high.

7 Add the reserved fried onions to the pan. Pour in the wine and stock or water and simmer for 1 minute. Stir in half the *mole* paste, bring back to the boil and bubble for a few seconds before pouring over the pork. Stir to mix, then cover with the lid and cook for 2 hours.

8 Stir the fruit, orange juice and sugar into the stew. Switch the slow cooker to low and cook for a further 2–3 hours, or until the pork is very tender.

9 Stir in the remaining *mole* paste and cook for 30 minutes. Serve sprinkled with orange rind, parsley and fresh chilli.

Energy 477Kcal/1999kJ; Protein 40.7g; Carbohydrate 25.6g, of which sugars 21g; Fat 19.1g, of which saturates 3.8g; Cholesterol 105mg; Calcium 86mg; Fibre 4.1g; Sodium 149mg.

CIDER-GLAZED GAMMON

This is a classic buffet centrepiece, which is ideal for Christmas or Thanksgiving. A fresh cranberry sauce provides the perfect foil to the richness of the meat and can be made in the slow cooker the day before if you want to serve the gammon hot, rather than cold. Soaking smoked gammon overnight helps to remove the excess salts.

SERVES 8

2kg/4½lb middle gammon joint, soaked overnight, if smoked
2 small onions
about 30 whole cloves
3 bay leaves
10 black peppercorns
150ml/¼ pint/⅔ cup medium-dry (hard) cider
45ml/3 tbsp soft light brown sugar

For the cranberry sauce
350g/12oz/3 cups cranberries
175g/6oz/scant 1 cup caster (superfine) sugar
grated rind and juice of 2 clementines
30ml/2 tbsp port

1 Drain the gammon joint, if soaked overnight, then place it in the ceramic cooking pot. Stud the onions with 6 of the cloves and add to the cooking pot with the bay leaves and peppercorns.

2 Pour over enough cold water to just cover the gammon. Switch the slow cooker to high, cover with the lid and cook for 1 hour. Skim off any scum from the surface, re-cover and cook for a further 4–5 hours. Check once during cooking and skim the surface, if necessary.

COOK'S TIP
The gammon should remain barely covered with water during cooking. There should be little evaporation from the slow cooker, but if necessary, top up with a small amount of boiling water.

3 Carefully lift the gammon joint out of the slow cooker using large forks or slotted spoons, and place it in a roasting tin (pan) or ovenproof dish. Leave to stand for about 15 minutes until cool enough to handle.

4 Meanwhile, make the glaze. Pour the cider into a small pan, add the soft brown sugar and heat gently, stirring, until dissolved. Simmer for 5 minutes to make a sticky glaze, then remove from the heat and leave to cool for a few minutes so that it thickens slightly.

5 Preheat the oven to 220°C/425°F/ Gas 7. Using a pair of scissors, snip the string off the gammon then carefully slice off the rind, leaving a thin, even layer of fat over the meat.

6 Using a sharp knife, score the fat into a neat diamond pattern. Press a clove into the centre of each diamond, then spoon over the glaze. Bake for about 25 minutes, or until the fat is brown, glistening and crisp. Remove from the oven and set aside until ready to serve.

7 Meanwhile, make the cranberry sauce. Wash the ceramic cooking pot, then add all the ingredients for the cranberry sauce to it. Switch the slow cooker to high and cook uncovered for 20 minutes, stirring continuously, until the sugar has dissolved completely.

8 Cover the pot with the lid and cook on high for 1½–2 hours, or until the cranberries are tender. Transfer the sauce to a jug (pitcher) or bowl, or keep warm in the slow cooker until ready to serve with the gammon. (The sauce can be served hot or cold.)

COOK'S TIPS
• If serving hot, cover the gammon with foil and leave to rest for 15 minutes before carving.
• If you prefer, serve the ham with redcurrant sauce or jelly. You can also use honey in place of the soft brown sugar for the glaze, if you like.

Energy 404Kcal/1689kJ; Protein 44.1g; Carbohydrate 15.2g, of which sugars 14.8g; Fat 18.8g, of which saturates 6.3g; Cholesterol 57mg; Calcium 25mg; Fibre 1g; Sodium 220mg.

VEAL STEW with TOMATOES

This classic French dish is traditionally made with lean and mildly flavoured veal.
Pork fillet makes an excellent, and economical, alternative.

SERVES 4

30ml/2 tbsp plain (all-purpose) flour
675g/1½lb boneless veal shoulder,
    trimmed and cut into cubes
30ml/2 tbsp sunflower oil
4 shallots, very finely chopped
300ml/½ pint/1¼ cups boiling vegetable
    or chicken stock
150ml/¼ pint/⅔ cup dry white wine
15ml/1 tbsp tomato purée (paste)
225g/8oz tomatoes, peeled, seeded
    and chopped
115g/4oz mushrooms, quartered
grated zest and juice of 1 small
    unwaxed orange
bouquet garni
salt and ground black pepper
30ml/2 tbsp chopped fresh parsley,
    to garnish

1 Put the flour in a small plastic bag and season with salt and pepper. Drop the pieces of meat into the bag a few at a time and shake to coat with the flour.

2 Heat 15ml/1 tbsp of the oil in a pan, add the shallots and cook gently for 5 minutes. Transfer to the ceramic cooking pot and switch to high or auto.

3 Add the remaining 15ml/1 tbsp oil to the pan and fry the meat in batches until well browned on all sides, then transfer to the ceramic cooking pot.

4 Pour the stock and white wine into the pan. Add the tomato purée and bring to the boil, stirring. Pour the sauce over the meat. Add the tomatoes, mushrooms, orange zest and juice, and bouquet garni to the pot and stir briefly to mix the ingredients. Cover with the lid and cook for about 1 hour.

5 Reduce the temperature to low or leave on auto and cook for 3–4 hours, or until the meat and mushrooms are very tender. Remove the bouquet garni, check the seasoning and add more salt and ground black pepper if necessary. Garnish with fresh parsley and serve.

Energy 323Kcal/1358kJ; Protein 38.2g; Carbohydrate 13.8g, of which sugars 5.4g; Fat 10.6g, of which saturates 2.3g; Cholesterol 141mg; Calcium 47mg; Fibre 1.7g; Sodium 314mg.

GREEK MEATBALLS in RICH TOMATO SAUCE

There are many versions of these sausage-shaped meatballs, known as yiouvarlakia or soudzoukakia. These are made with lamb, but beef makes an excellent alternative.

SERVES 4

50g/2oz/1 cup fresh white breadcrumbs
1 egg, lightly beaten
finely grated rind of ½ small orange
2.5ml/½ tsp dried oregano
450g/1lb minced (ground) lamb
1 small onion, peeled and grated
2 cloves garlic, crushed
15ml/1 tbsp plain (all-purpose) flour
30ml/2 tbsp olive oil
salt and ground black pepper
flat leaf parsley, to garnish

For the sauce
1 onion, very finely chopped
400g/14oz can chopped tomatoes
150ml/¼ pint/⅔ cup hot lamb or beef
   stock
1 bay leaf

1 Put the breadcrumbs, beaten egg, orange rind and oregano in a bowl and stir together. Add the lamb, onion and garlic and season with salt and pepper. Mix together until thoroughly combined.

2 Using dampened hands, so that the mixture doesn't stick, press the meat mixture into small sausage-shapes, about 5cm/2in long, and roll them in flour. Place in the refrigerator for 30 minutes to firm up slightly.

COOK'S TIP
Serve these meatballs with a refreshing salad and plenty of fresh, country-style crusty bread for mopping up the juices. Alternatively, serve with pitta bread so that guests can stuff the breads with meatballs and fresh green salad.

3 Heat the oil in a large frying pan and add the meatballs, working in batches if necessary. Cook for 5–8 minutes, turning the meatballs, until evenly browned all over. Transfer to a plate and set aside, leaving the fat and juices in the pan.

4 To make the sauce, add the onion to the pan and cook for 3–4 minutes, until beginning to soften. Pour in the chopped tomatoes, bring to the boil and cook gently for 1 minute.

5 Transfer the sauce to the ceramic cooking pot and stir in the stock. Add the bay leaf and season with salt and ground black pepper.

6 Arrange the meatballs in a single layer in the sauce. Cover with the lid and cook on high or auto for 1 hour. Reduce the temperature to low or leave on auto and cook for a further 4–5 hours. Serve garnished with sprigs of fresh parsley.

Energy 363Kcal/1515kJ; Protein 26.1g; Carbohydrate 15g, of which sugars 5.3g; Fat 22.5g, of which saturates 8.3g; Cholesterol 141mg; Calcium 68mg; Fibre 1.5g; Sodium 239mg.

LANCASHIRE HOT-POT

This dish is traditionally made without browning the lamb or vegetables, and relies on long, slow cooking to develop the flavour. You can brown the top under the grill, if you like.

SERVES 4

8 middle neck or loin lamb chops, about 900g/2lb in total weight
900g/2lb potatoes, thinly sliced
2 onions, peeled and sliced
2 carrots, peeled and sliced
1 stick celery, trimmed and sliced
1 leek, peeled and sliced
225g/8oz/generous 3 cups button (white) mushrooms, sliced
5ml/1 tsp dried mixed herbs
small sprig of rosemary
475ml/16fl oz/2 cups lamb or beef stock
15g/½oz/1 tbsp butter, melted
salt and ground black pepper

3 Pour the meat stock into the ceramic cooking pot, then cover with the lid and switch the slow cooker to high or auto. Cook for 1 hour, then reduce the temperature to low or leave on auto and cook for 6–8 hours or until tender.

4 Brush the top layer of potatoes with melted butter. Place under a preheated grill (broiler) and cook for 5 minutes, or until the potatoes are lightly browned. Serve immediately.

1 Trim the lamb chops of excess fat. Place a layer of sliced potatoes in the base of the ceramic cooking pot, and top with some sliced vegetables and a sprinkling of dried herbs, salt and black pepper. Place four of the chops on top.

2 Repeat the layers of sliced potato, vegetables, dried herbs and meat, tucking the rosemary sprig down the side of the pot. Continue layering up the remaining vegetables, finishing with a neat layer of potatoes on the top.

Energy 850Kcal/3544kJ; Protein 44.7g; Carbohydrate 45.3g, of which sugars 10.1g; Fat 55.8g, of which saturates 26.5g; Cholesterol 186mg; Calcium 72mg; Fibre 4.3g; Sodium 274mg.

LAMB PIE with MUSTARD THATCH

Here, a traditional shepherd's pie is given a contemporary twist with a tangy topping
of mashed potato flavoured with peppery mustard. Serve with vegetables.

SERVES 4

450g/1lb lean minced (ground) lamb
1 onion, very finely chopped
2 celery sticks, thinly sliced
2 carrots, finely diced
15ml/1 tbsp cornflour (cornstarch)
    blended into 150ml/¼ pint/⅔ cup
    lamb stock
15ml/1 tbsp Worcestershire sauce
30ml/2 tbsp chopped fresh rosemary,
    or 10ml/2 tsp dried
800g/1¾lb floury potatoes, diced
60ml/4 tbsp milk
15ml/1 tbsp wholegrain mustard
25g/1oz/2 tbsp butter
salt and ground black pepper

1 Heat a non-stick frying pan, then add
the lamb, breaking it up with a wooden
spoon, and cook until lightly browned all
over. Add the onion, celery and carrots
to the pan and cook for 2–3 minutes,
stirring frequently.

2 Stir the stock and cornflour mixture
into the pan. Bring to the boil, stirring
constantly, then remove from the heat.
Stir in the Worcestershire sauce and
rosemary, and season well with salt
and ground black pepper.

3 Transfer the mixture to the ceramic
cooking pot and switch the slow cooker
to high. Cover and cook for 3 hours.

4 Towards the end of the cooking time,
cook the potatoes in a large pan of
boiling salted water until tender. Drain
well, mash, and stir in the milk, mustard
and butter. Season to taste.

5 Spoon the mashed potatoes on top
of the lamb, spreading the mixture out
evenly. Cook for a further 45 minutes.
Brown the topping under a pre-heated
grill (broiler) for a few minutes, if you
like, then serve immediately.

Energy 458Kcal/1920kJ; Protein 26.5g; Carbohydrate 42.2g, of which sugars 8.1g; Fat 21.5g, of which saturates 10.6g; Cholesterol 101mg; Calcium 84mg; Fibre 3.5g; Sodium 264mg.

MOUSSAKA

This classic Greek dish topped with a light egg and cheese sauce is delicious in summer or winter, served with a crisp leafy salad. Try to find small, sweet aubergines with firm, shiny skins because they have much the best flavour. For an authentic touch, look out for Kefolotiri cheese in delicatessens and specialist food stores – although if you can't find it, Cheddar cheese will give equally good results.

SERVES 6

900g/2lb small or medium aubergines
    (eggplant), thinly sliced
60ml/4 tbsp olive oil
1 onion, finely chopped
2 garlic cloves, crushed
450g/1lb lean minced (ground) lamb
400g/14oz can chopped tomatoes
5ml/1 tsp dried oregano
pinch of ground cinnamon
salt and ground black pepper

For the topping
50g/2oz/¼ cup butter
50g/2oz/½ cup plain (all-purpose) flour
600ml/1 pint/2½ cups milk
pinch of freshly grated nutmeg
75g/3oz/¾ cup grated Kefolotiri or
    mature Cheddar cheese
1 egg yolk
30ml/2 tbsp fresh white breadcrumbs

1 Layer the aubergine slices in a sieve (strainer) or colander, sprinkling each layer with salt. Place the sieve over a bowl and leave to drain for 20 minutes. Rinse the aubergine slices thoroughly under cold running water and pat dry with kitchen paper.

VARIATION
You can use courgettes (zucchini) in place of the aubergines, if you prefer. Simply slice the courgettes, brush with olive oil and grill as before. There is no need to salt the courgette slices.

2 Lightly brush the aubergine slices with about half the oil, then arrange the slices in a single layer on a baking sheet. Place the baking sheet under a medium grill (broiler) and cook, turning once, until the aubergine slices are softened and golden brown on both sides.

3 Arrange half the aubergine slices in the bottom of the ceramic cooking pot and switch the slow cooker to high. Set aside the remaining slices.

4 Heat the remaining olive oil in a heavy pan, add the onion and fry gently for about 10 minutes, or until softened. Add the garlic and lamb and cook, stirring and breaking up the meat with a wooden spoon, until the meat is evenly browned.

5 Stir the tomatoes, oregano and cinnamon into the meat mixture, season generously with salt and ground black pepper and slowly bring to the boil over a gentle heat.

6 Spoon the lamb mixture into the slow cooker, covering the aubergine slices. Arrange the remaining aubergine slices on top, cover and cook for 2 hours.

7 Meanwhile, make the cheese topping. Melt the butter in a pan, stir in the flour and cook for one minute. Gradually stir in the milk, bring to the boil over a low heat, stirring constantly, and cook until thick and creamy. Lower the heat and simmer for 1 minute. Remove from the heat, season, then stir in the nutmeg and two-thirds of the cheese.

8 Leave the sauce to cool for 5 minutes, then beat in the egg yolk. Pour the sauce over the aubergine slices. Cover and cook for a further 2 hours, or until the topping is lightly set.

9 Sprinkle the remaining cheese and the breadcrumbs over the top and cook under a grill (broiler) for 3–4 minutes, or until golden brown. Leave to stand for 5–10 minutes before serving.

Energy 444Kcal/1850kJ; Protein 24.1g; Carbohydrate 1.5g, of which sugars 11.2g; Fat 31g, of which saturates 14g; Cholesterol 93.5mg; Calcium 268mg; Fibre 4.1g; Sodium 266mg.

MOROCCAN LAMB with HONEY and PRUNES

This classic dish of the Moroccan Jews is eaten at Rosh Hashanah – the Jewish New Year – when sweet foods are served in anticipation of a sweet new year to come.

SERVES 6

130g/4½oz/generous ½ cup stoned (pitted) prunes
350ml/12fl oz/1½ cups hot tea
1kg/2¼lb stewing or braising lamb, such as shoulder
30ml/2 tbsp olive oil
1 onion, chopped
2.5ml/½ tsp ground ginger
2.5ml/½ tsp curry powder
pinch of freshly grated nutmeg
10ml/2 tsp ground cinnamon
1.5ml/¼ tsp saffron threads
30ml/2 tbsp hot water
75ml/5 tbsp clear honey
200ml/7fl oz/scant 1 cup near-boiling lamb or beef stock
salt and ground black pepper
115g/4oz/1 cup blanched almonds, toasted
30ml/2 tbsp chopped fresh coriander (cilantro) and 3 hard-boiled eggs, cut into wedges, to garnish

3 Drain the prunes, adding the soaking liquid to the lamb. Cover the prunes.

4 Soak the saffron in the hot water for 1 minute, then add to the cooking pot with the honey and stock. Cover with the lid and cook on high or auto for 1 hour. Reduce the temperature to low and cook for a further 5–7 hours, or until the lamb is very tender.

5 Add the prunes to the cooking pot and stir to mix. Cook for 30 minutes, or until warmed through. Serve sprinkled with the toasted almonds and chopped coriander, and topped with the wedges of hard-boiled egg.

1 Put the prunes in a heatproof bowl, then pour over the tea and leave to soak. Meanwhile, trim the lamb and cut into chunky pieces, no larger than 2.5cm/ 1in. Heat the oil in a frying pan and sauté the lamb in batches for 5 minutes, stirring frequently, until well-browned. Remove with a slotted spoon and transfer to the ceramic cooking pot.

2 Add the onion to the frying pan and cook for 5 minutes, until starting to soften. Stir in the ginger, curry powder, nutmeg, cinnamon, salt and a large pinch of black pepper, and cook for 1 minute. Add to the ceramic cooking pot with the meat and their juices.

Energy 490Kcal/2051kJ; Protein 43.6g; Carbohydrate 23.8g, of which sugars 23.4g; Fat 25.2g, of which saturates 10.3g; Cholesterol 279mg; Calcium 41mg; Fibre 1.4g; Sodium 197mg.

LAMB in DILL SAUCE

In this recipe, the lamb is cooked with vegetables to make a clear well-flavoured broth, which is then thickened with an egg and cream mixture to make a smooth delicate sauce.

SERVES 6

1.3kg/3lb lean boneless lamb
1 small onion, trimmed and quartered
1 carrot, peeled and thickly sliced
1 bay leaf
4 sprigs of fresh dill, plus 45ml/3 tbsp
   chopped
1 thinly pared strip of lemon rind
750ml/1¼ pints/3 cups near-boiling lamb
   or vegetable stock
225g/8oz small shallots
15ml/1 tbsp olive oil
15g/½oz/1 tbsp unsalted (sweet) butter
15ml/1 tbsp plain (all-purpose) flour
115g/4oz frozen petits pois, defrosted
1 egg yolk
75ml/2½fl oz/⅓ cup single (light) cream, at
   room temperature
salt and ground black pepper
new potatoes and carrots, to serve

1 Trim the lamb and cut into 2.5cm/1in pieces. Place in the ceramic cooking pot with the onion, carrot, bay leaf, sprigs of dill and lemon rind. Pour over the stock, cover and cook on high for 1 hour. Skim off any scum, then re-cover and cook for a further 2 hours on high or 4 hours on low, until the lamb is fairly tender.

2 Meanwhile, put the shallots in a heatproof bowl and pour over enough boiling water to cover. Leave to cool, then drain and peel off the skins.

3 Remove the meat from the pot. Strain the stock, discarding the vegetables and herbs. Clean the pot. Return the meat and half the stock (reserving the rest), cover and switch to high.

4 Heat the oil and butter in a pan, add the shallots and cook gently, stirring, for 10–15 minutes, or until browned and tender. Turn off the heat, then transfer the shallots to the cooking pot, using a slotted spoon.

5 Sprinkle the flour over the fat remaining in the pan, then stir in the reserved stock, a little at a time. Bring to the boil, stirring all the time until thickened, then stir into the lamb and shallot mixture. Stir in the peas and season with salt and pepper. Cook on high for 30 minutes until piping hot.

6 Blend the egg yolk and the cream together, then stir in a few spoonfuls of the hot stock. Add to the casserole in a thin stream, stirring until slightly thickened. Stir in the chopped dill and serve immediately, with steamed new potatoes and carrots.

Energy 631Kcal/2629kJ; Protein 60.9g; Carbohydrate 7g, of which sugars 3.5g; Fat 40g, of which saturates 17.5g; Cholesterol 249mg; Calcium 123mg; Fibre 1.9g; Sodium 566mg.

TUSCAN POT-ROASTED SHOULDER of LAMB

This delicious boned and rolled shoulder of lamb, studded with rosemary sprigs and garlic, then cooked on a bed of vegetables, makes a perfect alternative to a traditional meat roast. Check that the lamb will fit comfortably in the slow cooker before you start.

SERVES 6

15ml/1 tbsp olive oil
1.3kg/3lb lamb shoulder, trimmed, boned and tied
3 large garlic cloves
12 small fresh rosemary sprigs
115g/4oz lean rinded smoked bacon, chopped
1 onion, chopped
3 carrots, finely chopped
3 celery sticks, finely chopped
1 leek, finely chopped
150ml/1/4 pint/2/3 cup red wine
300ml/1/2 pint/11/4 cups lamb or vegetable stock
400g/14oz can chopped tomatoes
3 sprigs of fresh thyme
2 bay leaves
400g/14oz can flageolet (small cannellini) beans, drained and rinsed
salt and ground black pepper
potatoes or warm crusty bread, to serve

1 Heat the oil in a large frying pan and brown the lamb on all sides. Remove from the pan and leave to stand until it is cool enough to handle.

2 Meanwhile, cut the garlic cloves into quarters. When the lamb is cool enough, make twelve deep incisions all over the meat. Push a piece of garlic and a small sprig of rosemary into each incision.

COOK'S TIP
Lamb can be quite a fatty meat, so ask your butcher to trim off as much excess fat as possible from the joint, before boning, rolling and tying it.

3 Add the bacon, onion, carrot, celery and leek to the pan and cook for about 10 minutes until soft, then transfer to the ceramic cooking pot. Stir the red wine into the cooking pot.

4 Add the stock and chopped tomatoes to the pot and season with salt and pepper. Add the thyme and bay leaves, submerging them in the liquid. Place the lamb on top, cover with the lid and cook on high for 4 hours.

5 Lift the lamb out of the pot and stir the beans into the vegetable mixture. Return the lamb, re-cover and cook for a further 1–2 hours, or until the lamb is cooked and tender.

6 Remove the lamb from the ceramic cooking pot using slotted spoons, cover with foil to keep warm, and leave to rest for 10 minutes.

7 Remove the string from the lamb and carve the meat into thick slices. Remove the thyme and bay leaves from the vegetable and bean mixture and carefully skim off any fat from the surface. Spoon the vegetables on to warmed serving plates and arrange the sliced lamb on top. Serve with potatoes or warm bread.

VARIATIONS
• Flageolet beans have a delicate yet distinctive flavour that goes particularly well in this dish. However, you can use other mildly flavoured beans instead, such as butter beans or cannellini beans.
• Try using 15ml/1 tsp fresh oregano in place of the thyme, if you prefer. This classic Italian herb tastes just as good.

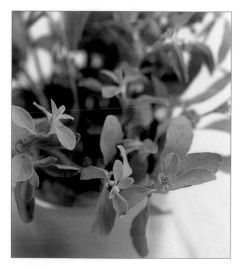

Energy 710Kcal/2958kJ; Protein 60.2g; Carbohydrate 13.7g, of which sugars 4.8g; Fat 44.6g, of which saturates 19.4g; Cholesterol 229mg; Calcium 58mg; Fibre 4.7g; Sodium 864mg.

LAMB and CARROT CASSEROLE with BARLEY

Barley and carrots make natural partners for lamb and mutton. In this convenient casserole the barley extends the meat and adds to the flavour and texture as well as thickening the sauce. This warming dish is comfort food at its very best.

SERVES 6

675g/1½lb stewing (braising) lamb
15ml/1 tbsp vegetable oil
2 onions
675g/1½lb carrots, thickly sliced
4–6 celery sticks, sliced
45ml/3 tbsp pearl barley, rinsed
600ml/1 pint/2½ cups near-boiling lamb or
   vegetable stock
5ml/1 tsp fresh thyme leaves or pinch of
   dried mixed herbs
salt and ground black pepper
spring cabbage and jacket potatoes,
   to serve

1 Trim all excess fat from the lamb, then cut the meat into 3cm/1¼in pieces. Heat the oil in a frying pan, add the lamb and fry until browned. Remove from with a slotted spoon and set aside.

2 Slice the onions and add to the pan. Fry gently for 5 minutes until golden. Add the carrots and celery and cook for a further 3–4 minutes or until beginning to soften. Transfer the vegetables to the ceramic cooking pot and switch the slow cooker to high.

3 Sprinkle the pearl barley over the vegetables in the cooking pot, then arrange the lamb pieces meat on top.

4 Lightly season with salt and ground black pepper, then scatter with the herbs. Pour the stock over the meat, so that all of the meat is covered.

5 Cover the slow cooker with the lid and cook on auto or high for 2 hours. Lift the lid and, using a large spoon, skim off any scum that has risen to the surface of the casserole.

6 Re-cover the pot and leave on auto or switch to low and cook for a further 4–6 hours or until the meat, vegetables and barley are tender. Serve with spring cabbage and jacket potatoes.

Energy 304Kcal/1263kJ; Protein 23.2g; Carbohydrate 13g, of which sugars 11.3g; Fat 18g, of which saturates 7.5g; Cholesterol 84mg; Calcium 53mg; Fibre 3.6g; Sodium 110mg

LAMB STEWED with TOMATOES and GARLIC

This simple rustic stew comes from the plateau of Puglia in Italy, where sheep graze beside the vineyards. Serve simply, with fresh crusty bread and a green leaf salad.

SERVES 4

1.2kg/2½lb stewing (braising) lamb
30ml/2 tbsp plain (all-purpose) flour, seasoned with ground black pepper
60ml/4 tbsp olive oil
2 large cloves garlic, finely chopped
1 sprig fresh rosemary
150ml/¼ pint/⅔ cup dry white wine
150ml/¼ pint/⅔ cup lamb or beef stock
2.5ml/½ tsp salt
450g/1lb fresh tomatoes, peeled and chopped, or 400g/14oz can chopped tomatoes
salt and ground black pepper

4 Season with salt and pepper and stir in the tomatoes. Cover the cooking pot with the lid and switch the slow cooker to high or auto. Cook for 1 hour.

5 Reduce the heat to low or leave on auto and cook for a further 6–8 hours, or until the lamb is tender. Taste and adjust the seasoning before serving.

VARIATION

For Lamb with Butternut Squash, sauté 675g/1½lb cubed lamb fillet in 15ml/1 tbsp oil, then transfer to the ceramic cooking pot. Fry 1 chopped onion and 2 crushed garlic cloves until soft, and add to the lamb with 1 cubed butternut squash, 400g/14oz can chopped tomatoes, 150ml/¼ pint/⅔ cup lamb stock and 5ml/1 tsp dried marjoram. Cover and cook on low for 5–6 hours.

1 Trim all fat and gristle from the lamb and cut into 2.5cm/1in cubes. Toss in the flour to coat. Set aside the excess flour.

2 Heat the oil in a pan and fry the lamb, in two batches for 5 minutes, stirring, until browned. Lift out the lamb and transfer to the ceramic cooking pot.

3 Add the garlic and cook for a few seconds before adding the rosemary, wine and stock. Bring almost to the boil, stirring, to remove any meat sediment from the pan. Pour over the lamb.

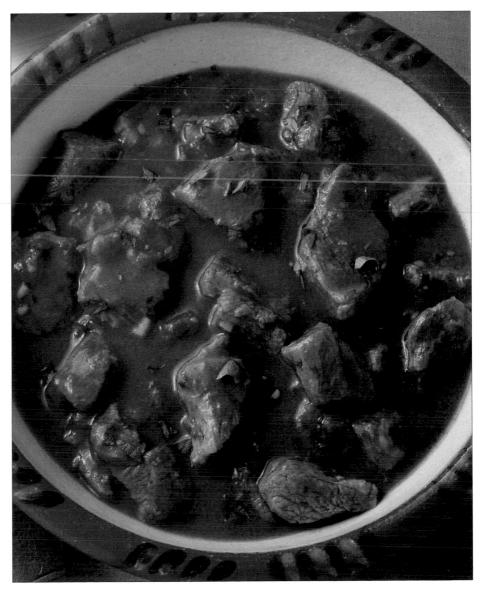

Energy 636Kcal/2656kJ; Protein 62.4g; Carbohydrate 11.5g, of which sugars 3.9g; Fat 35.5g, of which saturates 12.2g; Cholesterol 222mg; Calcium 62mg; Fibre 1.4g; Sodium 508mg.

ONE-POT, CLAY-POT MEAT

Nothing quite matches the flavour of meat that has simmered in the oven for hours with tasty root vegetables and aromatic herbs, especially when a little beer or wine has been poured into the pot, as in Pot-roast Beef with Guinness, Pork cooked in Cider with Parsley Dumplings, or Osso Bucco with Risotto Milanese. Equally delicious are sustaining stews, such as Boeuf Bourguignon and Braised Lamb with Apricots and Herb Dumplings. For sophisticated entertaining, why not try Calf's Liver with Slow-cooked Onions, Marsala and Sage, or Noisettes of Pork with Creamy Calvados and Apple Sauce?

CITRUS BEEF CURRY

This superbly aromatic Thai-style curry is not too hot but full of flavour. For a special meal, it goes perfectly with fried noodles.

SERVES 4

450g/1lb rump (round) steak
30ml/2 tbsp sunflower oil
30ml/2 tbsp medium curry paste
2 bay leaves
400ml/14fl oz/1⅔ cups coconut milk
300ml/½ pint/1¼ cups beef stock
30ml/2 tbsp lemon juice
45ml/3 tbsp Thai fish sauce
   (*nam pla*)
15ml/1 tbsp sugar
115g/4oz baby (pearl) onions, peeled but
   left whole
225g/8oz new potatoes, halved
115g/4oz/1 cup unsalted roasted peanuts,
   roughly chopped
115g/4oz fine green beans, halved
1 red (bell) pepper, seeded and
   thinly sliced
unsalted roasted peanuts, to
   garnish (optional)

1 Trim any fat off the beef and cut the beef into 5cm/2in strips.

2 Heat the sunflower oil in a large, heavy pan, add the curry paste and cook over a medium heat for 30 seconds, stirring constantly.

3 Add the beef and cook, stirring, for 2 minutes until it is beginning to brown and is thoroughly coated with the spices.

4 Stir in the bay leaves, coconut milk, stock, lemon juice, fish sauce and sugar, and bring to the boil, stirring.

5 Add the onions and potatoes, then bring back to the boil, reduce the heat and simmer, uncovered, for 5 minutes.

6 Stir in the peanuts, beans and pepper and simmer for a further 10 minutes, or until the beef and potatoes are tender. Serve in shallow bowls, with a spoon and fork, to enjoy all the rich and creamy juices. Sprinkle with extra unsalted roasted peanuts, if you like.

Energy 476Kcal/1990kJ; Protein 33.8g; Carbohydrate 27.5g, of which sugars 16.3g; Fat 26.4g, of which saturates 6.6g; Cholesterol 69mg; Calcium 77mg; Fibre 4.1g; Sodium 169mg.

IRISH STEW

Simple and delicious, this is the quintessential Irish main course. Traditionally, mutton chops are used, but as they are harder to find these days you can use lamb instead.

SERVES 4

1.3kg/3lb boneless lamb chops, cut into
  large chunks
15ml/1 tbsp vegetable oil
3 onions
4 large carrots
900ml/1 ½ pints/3¾ cups water
4 large potatoes, cut into
  large chunks
1 large fresh thyme sprig
15g/½oz/1 tbsp unsalted
  (sweet) butter
15ml/1 tbsp chopped fresh parsley
salt and ground black pepper

1 Trim any fat from the lamb. Heat the oil in a large, flameproof casserole and brown the meat on all sides. Remove from the casserole.

2 Cut the onions into quarters and thickly slice the carrots. Add them to the casserole and cook for 5 minutes, stirring, or until the onions are browned. Return the meat to the pan with the water. Bring to the boil, reduce the heat, cover and simmer for 1 hour.

3 Add the potatoes to the pan with the thyme and cook for a further 1 hour.

4 Leave the stew to settle for a few minutes. Remove the fat from the liquid with a spoon, then stir in the butter and the parsley. Season well before serving.

Energy 898Kcal/3763kJ; Protein 70.4g; Carbohydrate 60g, of which sugars 19.1g; Fat 43.6g, of which saturates 19.5g; Cholesterol 255mg; Calcium 104mg; Fibre 7g; Sodium 359mg.

POT-ROAST BEEF with GUINNESS

This heart-warming, rich pot-roast is ideal for a winter supper. Brisket of beef has the best flavour but this dish works equally well with rolled silverside or topside.

SERVES 6

30ml/2 tbsp vegetable oil
900g/2lb rolled brisket of beef
275g/10oz onions, roughly chopped
2 celery sticks, thickly sliced
450g/1lb carrots, cut into large chunks
675g/1½lb potatoes, peeled and cut into large chunks
30ml/2 tbsp plain (all-purpose) flour
475ml/16fl oz/2 cups beef stock
300ml/½ pint/1¼ cups Guinness
1 bay leaf
45ml/3 tbsp chopped fresh thyme
5ml/1 tsp soft light brown sugar
30ml/2 tbsp wholegrain mustard
15ml/1 tbsp tomato purée (paste)
salt and ground black pepper

1 Preheat the oven to 180°C/350°F/ Gas 4. Heat the oil in a large flameproof casserole and brown the meat all over until golden.

3 Add the celery, carrot and potato to the casserole and cook over a medium heat for 2–3 minutes, or until they are just beginning to colour.

5 Add the bay leaf, thyme, sugar, mustard, tomato purée and plenty of seasoning. Place the meat on top, cover tightly and transfer to the oven.

2 Remove the meat from the pan and drain it on a double layer of kitchen paper. Add the chopped onions to the pan and cook for about 4 minutes, or until they are just beginning to soften and turn brown, stirring all the time.

4 Stir in the flour and cook for a further 1 minute stirring continuously. Pour in the beef stock and the Guinness and stir until well combined. Bring the sauce to the boil, stirring continuously with a wooden spoon.

6 Cook for about 2½ hours, or until the vegetables and meat are tender. Adjust the seasoning and add another pinch of sugar, if necessary. To serve, remove the meat and carve into thick slices. Serve with the vegetables and plenty of gravy.

Energy 402Kcal/1691kJ; Protein 35.5g; Carbohydrate 33.8g, of which sugars 11.9g; Fat 13.6g, of which saturates 4.4g; Cholesterol 81mg; Calcium 58mg; Fibre 4g; Sodium 142mg.

CLAY-POT BEEF with RED PEPPERS

Using a clay pot to cook lean meat keeps it moist and juicy. Here it is cooked with sweet
peppers and onion in a rich red wine sauce.

SERVES 6

1.2kg/2½lb top rump (round) steak
   or silverside (pot roast) of beef,
   neatly tied
2 garlic cloves
30ml/2 tbsp sunflower oil
1 large onion, chopped
300ml/½ pint/1¼ cups beef stock
15ml/1 tbsp tomato purée (paste)
150ml/¼ pint/⅔ cup red wine
bouquet garni
4 sweet romano red (bell) peppers, halved
   lengthwise and seeded
15ml/1 tbsp butter, softened
15ml/1 tbsp plain (all-purpose) flour
salt and ground black pepper

1 Soak the clay pot in cold water for 20 minutes, then drain. Using a sharp knife, make about 20 small incisions in the beef. Cut the garlic cloves into thin slivers and insert into the cuts.

2 Season the beef with salt and pepper. Heat the sunflower oil in a large frying pan, add the beef and cook, stirring frequently with a wooden spoon until browned on all sides. Remove the beef from the pan and set aside.

3 Add the onion to the frying pan and fry gently for 5–8 minutes, stirring occasionally, until light golden. Transfer the onion to the clay pot.

4 Place the beef on top of the onion in the clay pot, then mix together the beef stock, tomato purée and wine and pour over the beef.

5 Add the bouquet garni to the pot, then cover the pot and place it in an unheated oven. Set the oven to 200°C/400°F/Gas 6 and cook for 1 hour. Uncover, baste the meat and add the pepper halves, arranging them around the meat. Cook uncovered for a further 45 minutes until the beef is tender, basting occasionally.

6 To serve, transfer the beef to a large warmed serving dish with the peppers and onion. Drain the juices from the clay pot into a pan and heat gently.

7 Blend together the butter and flour to make a smooth paste, then gradually add small pieces of the paste to the sauce, whisking until well blended. Bring the sauce to the boil and simmer gently for about 1 minute, whisking all the time, until the sauce is thickened slightly. Pour into a sauce boat and serve with the beef and vegetables.

VARIATIONS
Romano peppers are an elongated variety that are available in large supermarkets. If you can't find them, use ordinary bell-shaped peppers instead – the dish will be just as good. If you prefer, use green, orange or yellow peppers in place of red.

COOK'S TIPS
• The butter and flour paste used in step 7 to thicken the sauce is known as a beurre manié. The paste is always made from equal quantities of plain flour and softened butter. It is used for thickening casseroles, sauces and occasionally soups.
• A bouquet garni is a selection of aromatic herbs used to flavour soups, stocks or casseroles. The most widely used herbs include thyme, parsley, rosemary and bay leaves. Fresh herbs can be tied together with string or dried herbs can be wrapped in a small muslin (cheesecloth) square and secured with string. Ready-made bouquet garnis of dried herbs are sold in many supermarkets.

Energy 420Kcal/1760kJ; Protein 44.7g; Carbohydrate 15.5g, of which sugars 11.7g; Fat 18.6g, of which saturates 6.9g; Cholesterol 113mg; Calcium 42mg; Fibre 3g; Sodium 154mg.

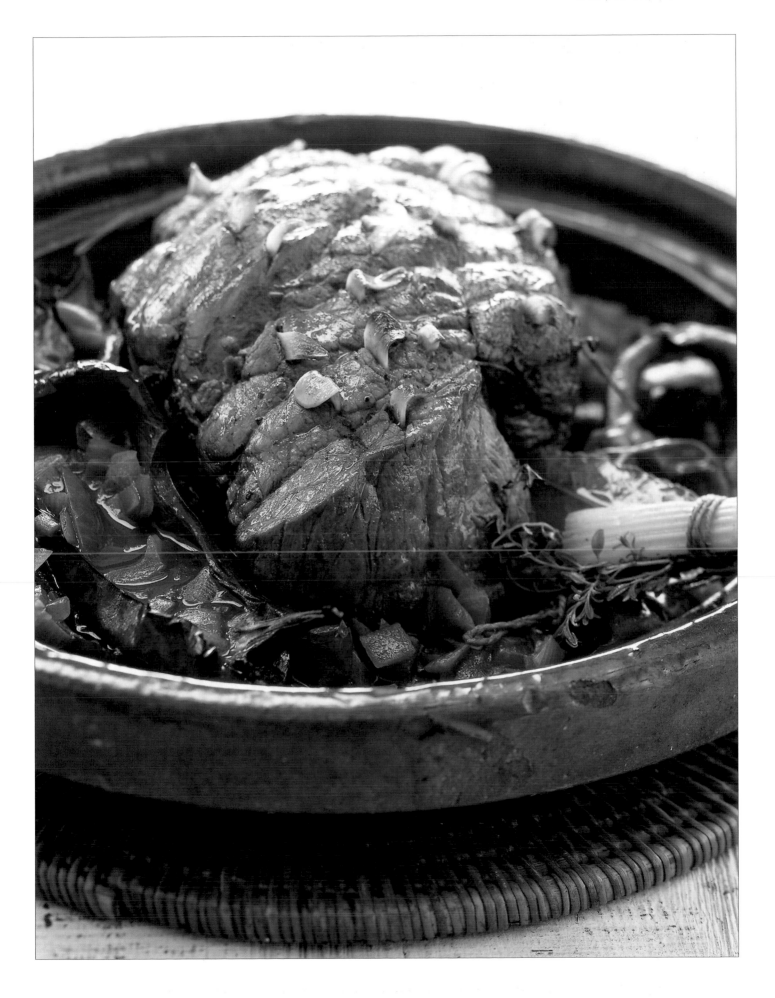

BEEF CARBONADE

This rich, dark stew of beef cooked slowly with lots of onions, garlic and beer is a classic casserole from the north of France and neighbouring Belgium.

SERVES 6

45ml/3 tbsp vegetable oil or beef dripping
3 onions, sliced
45ml/3 tbsp plain (all-purpose) flour
2.5ml/½ tsp mustard powder
1kg/2¼lb stewing beef (shin, shank or
    chuck), cut into large cubes
2–3 garlic cloves, finely chopped
300ml/½ pint/1¼ cups dark beer or ale
150ml/¼ pint/⅔ cup water
5ml/1 tsp dark brown sugar
1 fresh thyme sprig
1 fresh bay leaf
1 celery stick
salt and ground black pepper

For the topping
50g/2oz/¼ cup butter
1 garlic clove, crushed
15ml/1 tbsp Dijon mustard
45ml/3 tbsp chopped fresh parsley
6–12 slices of French baguette

1 Preheat the oven to 160°C/325°F/ Gas 3. Heat 30ml/2 tbsp of the oil or dripping in a pan and cook the onions over a low heat until softened. Remove from the pan and set aside.

2 Meanwhile, mix together the flour and mustard and season. Toss the beef in the flour. Add the remaining oil or dripping to the pan and heat over a high heat. Brown the beef all over, then transfer it to a deep, earthenware baking dish.

3 Reduce the heat and return the onions to the pan. Add the garlic, cook briefly, then add the beer or ale, water and sugar. Tie the thyme and bay leaf together and add to the pan with the celery. Bring to the boil, stirring, then season with salt and pepper.

4 Pour the sauce over the beef and mix well. Cover tightly, then place in the oven and cook for 2½ hours. Check the beef once or twice to make sure that it is not too dry, adding a little extra water, if necessary. Test for tenderness, allowing an extra 30–40 minutes' cooking time if necessary.

5 To make the topping, beat together the butter, crushed garlic, Dijon mustard and 30ml/2 tbsp of the chopped fresh parsley. Spread the flavoured butter thickly over the bread. Increase the oven temperature to 190°C/375°F/Gas 5. Taste and season the stew, then arrange the prepared bread slices, buttered side uppermost, on top. Bake for 20 minutes, or until the bread is browned and crisp. Sprinkle the remaining chopped fresh parsley over the top to garnish and serve immediately.

Energy 532Kcal/2234kJ; Protein 41.1g; Carbohydrate 40g, of which sugars 10.7g; Fat 21.8g, of which saturates 9.1g; Cholesterol 108mg; Calcium 102mg; Fibre 2.7g; Sodium 409mg.

BOEUF BOURGUIGNON

The classic French dish of beef cooked in Burgundy style, with red wine, small pieces of bacon, shallots and mushrooms, is baked for several hours at a low temperature.

SERVES 6

175g/6oz rindless streaky (fatty) bacon
    rashers (strips), chopped
900g/2lb lean braising steak, such as top
    rump (round) steak
30ml/2 tbsp plain (all-purpose) flour
45ml/3 tbsp sunflower oil
25g/1oz/2 tbsp butter
12 shallots
2 garlic cloves, crushed
175g/6oz/2⅓ cups mushrooms, sliced
450ml/¾ pint/scant 2 cups robust
    red wine
150ml/¼ pint/⅔ cup beef stock
    or consommé
1 bay leaf
2 sprigs each of fresh thyme, parsley
    and marjoram
salt and ground black pepper

1 Preheat the oven to 160°C/325°F/
Gas 3. Heat a large flameproof casserole,
then add the bacon and cook, stirring
occasionally, until the pieces are crisp
and golden brown.

2 Meanwhile, cut the beef into 2.5cm/
1in cubes. Season the flour and use to
coat the meat. Use a slotted spoon to
remove the bacon from the casserole
and set aside. Add and heat the oil, then
brown the beef in batches and set aside
with the bacon.

COOK'S TIP
Beef consommé, which can be used as an
alternative to beef stock in this recipe, is
a clear, light soup. It is sold in cans, or in
cartons as a fresh soup. Fresh beef stock
is also available in cartons.

3 Add the butter to the fat remaining
in the casserole. Cook the shallots and
garlic until they are just beginning to
colour, then add the mushrooms and
cook for a further 5 minutes. Return the
bacon and beef to the casserole, and stir
in the wine and stock or consommé. Tie
the herbs together into a bouquet garni
and add to the casserole.

4 Cover and cook in the oven for
1½ hours, or until the meat is tender,
stirring once or twice during the cooking
time. Season to taste and serve the
casserole with creamy mashed root
vegetables, such as celeriac and potatoes.

COOK'S TIP
Boeuf Bourguignon freezes very well.
Transfer the mixture to a dish so that it
cools quickly, then pour it into a rigid
plastic container. Push all the cubes of
meat down into the sauce or they will
dry out. Freeze for up to 2 months. Thaw
overnight in the refrigerator, then transfer
to a flameproof casserole and add 150ml/
¼ pint/⅔ cup water. Stir well, then bring
to the boil, stirring occasionally, and
simmer steadily for at least 10 minutes,
or until the meat is piping hot.

Energy 459Kcal/1913kJ; Protein 39g; Carbohydrate 8.1g, of which sugars 3.1g; Fat 24.7g, of which saturates 8.9g; Cholesterol 122mg; Calcium 37mg; Fibre 1.2g; Sodium 497mg.

BEEF HOTPOT with HERB DUMPLINGS

Tender chunks of beef braised in beer, flavoured with shallots and mushrooms and finished with parsley- and thyme-flavoured dumplings.

SERVES 4

20g/¾oz/⅓ cup dried porcini mushrooms
60ml/4 tbsp warm water
40g/1½oz/3 tbsp butter
30ml/2 tbsp sunflower oil
115g/4oz/⅔ cup lardons or cubed pancetta
900g/2lb lean braising steak, cut
   into chunks
45ml/3 tbsp plain (all-purpose) flour
450ml/¾ pint/scant 2 cups beer
450ml/¾ pint/scant 2 cups beef stock
bouquet garni
8 shallots
175g/6oz/2 cups button (white) mushrooms
salt and ground black pepper
sprigs of thyme, to garnish

For the herb dumplings
115g/4oz/1 cup self-raising
   (self-rising) flour
50g/2oz/scant ½ cup shredded suet
2.5ml/½ tsp salt
2.5ml/½ tsp mustard powder
15ml/1 tbsp chopped fresh parsley
15ml/1 tbsp chopped fresh thyme

1 Soak a clay pot in cold water for 20 minutes, then drain. Place the porcini mushrooms in a bowl, add the warm water and leave to soak. In a frying pan, melt half the butter with half the oil, add the lardons or pancetta and quickly brown. Remove with a slotted spoon and transfer to the clay pot.

2 Add the beef to the frying pan and brown in batches, then, using a slotted spoon, transfer to the clay pot. Sprinkle the flour into the fat remaining in the frying pan and stir well.

3 Stir the beer and stock into the flour and bring to the boil, stirring constantly. Strain the mushroom soaking liquid and add to the frying pan along with the porcini. Season well. Pour the sauce over the meat in the clay pot, then add the bouquet garni. Cover the pot and place in an unheated oven. Set the oven to 200°C/400°F/Gas 6. Cook for 30 minutes, then reduce the oven temperature to 160°C/325°F/Gas 3 and cook for a further 1 hour.

4 Heat the remaining butter and oil in a frying pan and cook the shallots until golden. Remove and set aside. Add the button mushrooms and sauté for 2–3 minutes. Stir the shallots and mushrooms into the pot and cook for 30 minutes.

5 In a bowl, mix together the dumpling ingredients with sufficient cold water to bind to a soft, sticky dough. Divide into 12 small balls and place on top of the hotpot. Cover and cook for 25 minutes.

Energy 527Kcal/2194kJ; Protein 10.3g; Carbohydrate 39.1g, of which sugars 6.4g; Fat 35.5g, of which saturates 14.9g; Cholesterol 50mg; Calcium 169mg; Fibre 3.1g; Sodium 789mg.

SLOW-BAKED BEEF with a POTATO CRUST

This recipe makes the most of braising beef by marinating it in red wine and topping it with a cheesy grated potato crust that bakes to a golden, crunchy consistency.

SERVES 4

675g/1½lb stewing beef, diced
300ml/½ pint/1¼ cups red wine
3 juniper berries, crushed
pared strip of orange peel
30ml/2 tbsp olive oil
2 onions, cut into chunks
2 carrots, cut into chunks
1 garlic clove, crushed
225g/8oz/3 cups button
    (white) mushrooms
150ml/¼ pint/⅔ cup beef stock
30ml/2 tbsp cornflour (cornstarch)
salt and ground black pepper

For the crust
450g/1lb potatoes, grated
15ml/1 tbsp olive oil
30ml/2 tbsp creamed horseradish
50g/2oz/½ cup grated mature (sharp)
    Cheddar cheese
salt and ground black pepper

1 Place the diced beef in a non-metallic bowl. Add the wine, juniper berries and orange peel and season with pepper. Mix the ingredients together, then cover and leave to marinate for at least 4 hours or overnight if possible.

COOK'S TIP
Use a large-holed, coarse grater on the food processor for the potatoes. They will hold their shape better while being blanched than if you use a finer blade.

2 Preheat the oven to 160°C/325°F/ Gas 3. Drain the diced stewing beef, reserving the marinade.

3 Heat the oil in a large flameproof casserole and fry the meat in batches for 5 minutes to brown and seal. Add the onions, carrots and garlic and cook for 5 minutes. Stir in the mushrooms, red wine marinade and beef stock.

4 Mix the cornflour with water to make a smooth paste and stir into the beef mixture. Season, cover and cook in the oven for 1½ hours.

5 Prepare the crust about 45 minutes before the end of the cooking time for the beef. Start by blanching the grated potatoes in boiling water for 5 minutes. Drain well and then squeeze out all the extra liquid.

6 Stir in the olive oil, horseradish, grated cheese and seasoning, then sprinkle the mixture evenly over the surface of the beef. Increase the oven temperature to 200°C/400°F/Gas 6 and cook for a further 30 minutes until the potato crust is crisp and lightly browned.

Energy 641Kcal/2678kJ; Protein 45.9g; Carbohydrate 36.6g, of which sugars 10.8g; Fat 29.6g, of which saturates 10.6g; Cholesterol 111mg; Calcium 152mg; Fibre 4.2g; Sodium 306mg.

CALFS' LIVER with SLOW-COOKED ONIONS, MARSALA and SAGE

Liver and onions are an international favourite, from British liver with onion gravy to the famous Venetian dish of Fegato alla Veneziana. Inspired by Italian cooking, this dish is good served with polenta, either soft or set and grilled.

3 Add the remaining oil to the pan and fry the remaining sage leaves for about 30 seconds, then leave them to drain on kitchen paper.

4 Add the remaining butter and extra oil to the pan and increase the heat to high. Season the flour, then dip the liver in it and fry quickly for about 2 minutes on each side until browned, but still pink in the middle. Use a slotted spoon or metal spatula to transfer the liver to warm plates and keep warm.

5 Immediately add the Marsala to the pan and let it bubble fiercely until reduced to a few tablespoons of sticky glaze. Distribute the onions over the liver and spoon over the Marsala juices. Sprinkle with the fried sage leaves and extra parsley and serve immediately.

VARIATION

Chicken liver and onion bruschetta
Cook the onions as above, replacing the sage with 5ml/1 tsp chopped fresh thyme. Fry 400g/14oz chicken livers in 25g/1oz/ 2 tbsp butter and 15ml/1 tbsp olive oil until browned but still pink in the centre. Flame the chicken livers with 45ml/3 tbsp cognac, and add 150g/5oz seeded, skinned grapes (optional). Heat the grapes through, then toss them into the cooked onions. Heap the mixture on to thick slices of toasted country bread rubbed with oil and garlic or on to thick slices of grilled (broiled) polenta. Serve sprinkled with chopped fresh parsley.

SERVES 4

45ml/3 tbsp olive oil, plus extra for
    shallow frying
25g/1oz/2 tbsp butter
500g/1¼lb mild onions, thinly sliced
small bunch of fresh sage leaves
30ml/2 tbsp chopped fresh parsley, plus a
    little extra to garnish
2.5ml/½ tsp sugar
15ml/1 tbsp balsamic vinegar
30ml/2 tbsp plain (all-purpose) flour
675g/1½lb calfs' liver, thinly sliced
150ml/¼ pint/⅔ cup Marsala
salt and ground black pepper

1 Heat half the oil with half the butter in a large, wide, heavy pan and cook the onions, covered, over a very gentle heat for 30 minutes. Stir once or twice.

2 Chop five of the sage leaves and add them to the pan with the chopped parsley, a pinch of salt, the sugar and balsamic vinegar. Cook, uncovered and stirring frequently with a wooden spoon, until the onions are very tender and a golden brown colour. Taste for seasoning and add salt and pepper as necessary. Tip the onions into a heatproof dish and keep warm.

Energy 427Kcal/1777kJ; Protein 32.5g; Carbohydrate 14.9g, of which sugars 12.1g; Fat 22.1g, of which saturates 6.5g; Cholesterol 638mg; Calcium 44mg; Fibre 1.8g; Sodium 163mg.

BLACK BEAN CHILLI CON CARNE

Fresh green and dried red chillies add plenty of fire to this classic Tex-Mex dish of tender beef cooked in a spicy tomato sauce.

SERVES 6

225g/8oz/1¼ cups dried black beans
500g/1¼lb braising steak
30ml/2 tbsp vegetable oil
2 onions, chopped
1 garlic clove, crushed
1 fresh green chilli, seeded and
   finely chopped
15ml/1 tbsp paprika
10ml/2 tsp ground cumin
10ml/2 tsp ground coriander
400g/14oz can chopped tomatoes
300ml/½ pint/1¼ cups beef stock
1 dried red chilli, crumbled
5ml/1 tsp hot pepper sauce
1 fresh red (bell) pepper, seeded and chopped
salt
fresh coriander (cilantro), to garnish
boiled rice, to serve

1 Put the beans in a large pan. Add enough cold water to cover them, bring to the boil and boil vigorously for about 10 minutes. Drain, tip into a clean bowl, cover with cold water and leave to soak for about 8 hours or overnight.

2 Preheat the oven to 150°C/300°F/ Gas 2. Cut the braising steak into small dice. Heat the vegetable oil in a large, flameproof casserole. Add the chopped onion, crushed garlic and chopped green chilli and cook them gently for 5 minutes until soft, using a slotted spoon to transfer the mixture to a plate.

3 Increase the heat to high, add the meat to the casserole and brown on all sides, then stir in the paprika, ground cumin and ground coriander.

4 Add the tomatoes, beef stock, dried chilli and hot pepper sauce. Drain the beans and add them to the casserole, with enough water to cover. Bring to simmering point, cover and cook in the oven for 2 hours. Stir occasionally and add extra water, if necessary.

5 Season the casserole with salt and add the chopped red pepper. Replace the lid, return the casserole to the oven and cook for 30 minutes more, or until the meat and beans are tender. Sprinkle over the fresh coriander and serve with rice.

COOK'S TIP
Red kidney beans are traditionally used in chilli con carne, but in this recipe black beans are used instead. They are the same shape and size as red kidney beans but have a shiny black skin. They are also known as Mexican or Spanish black beans.

VARIATION
Use minced (ground) beef in place of the braising steak.

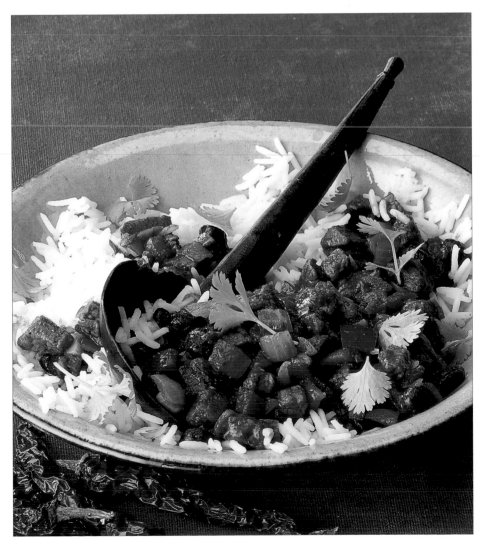

Energy 289Kcal/1216kJ; Protein 27.3g; Carbohydrate 24.7g, of which sugars 7.8g; Fat 9.7g, of which saturates 2.8g; Cholesterol 45mg; Calcium 61mg; Fibre 7.8g; Sodium 65mg.

NOISETTES of PORK with CREAMY CALVADOS and APPLE SAUCE

This dish gives the impression of being far more difficult to prepare than it really is, so it is ideal as part of a formal menu to impress guests. Buttered gnocchi or griddled polenta and red cabbage are suitable accompaniments.

SERVES 4

30ml/2 tbsp plain (all-purpose) flour
4 noisettes of pork, about 175g/6oz each,
   firmly tied
25g/1oz/2 tbsp butter
4 baby leeks, finely sliced
5ml/1 tsp mustard seeds,
   coarsely crushed
30ml/2 tbsp Calvados
150ml/¼ pint/⅔ cup dry white wine
2 eating apples, peeled, cored
   and sliced
150ml/¼ pint/⅔ cup double (heavy) cream
30ml/2 tbsp chopped fresh flat
   leaf parsley
salt and ground black pepper

1 Place the flour in a bowl and add plenty of seasoning. Turn the noisettes in the flour mixture to coat them lightly.

2 Melt the butter in a heavy frying pan and cook the noisettes until golden on both sides. Remove from the pan and set aside.

3 Add the leeks to the fat remaining in the pan and cook for 5 minutes. Stir in the mustard seeds and pour in the Calvados, then carefully ignite it to burn off the alcohol. When the flames have died down pour in the wine and replace the pork. Cook gently for 10 minutes, turning the pork frequently.

4 Add the sliced apples to the pan and pour in the cream. Simmer for about 5 minutes, or until the apples are tender and the sauce is thick and creamy. Taste for seasoning, then stir in the chopped fresh parsley and serve immediately.

Energy 553Kcal/2304kJ; Protein 40.6g; Carbohydrate 14.3g, of which sugars 6.1g; Fat 32.9g, of which saturates 18.3g; Cholesterol 175mg; Calcium 72mg; Fibre 2.8g; Sodium 173mg.

PANCETTA and BROAD BEAN RISOTTO

This delicious risotto makes a healthy and filling meal, when served with a mixed green salad. Use smoked bacon instead of pancetta, if you like.

SERVES 4

225g/8oz frozen baby broad (fava) beans
15ml/1 tbsp olive oil
1 onion, chopped
2 garlic cloves, finely chopped
175g/6oz smoked pancetta, diced
350g/12oz/1¾ cups risotto rice
1.2 litres/2 pints/5 cups chicken stock
30ml/2 tbsp chopped fresh mixed herbs,
    such as parsley, thyme and oregano
salt and ground black pepper
coarsely chopped fresh parsley, to garnish
shavings of Parmesan cheese, to serve
    (see Cook's Tip)

1 First, cook the broad beans in a large flameproof casserole of lightly salted boiling water for about 3 minutes until tender. Drain and set aside.

2 Heat the olive oil in the casserole. Add the chopped onion, chopped garlic and diced pancetta and cook gently for about 5 minutes, stirring occasionally.

3 Add the rice to the pan and cook for 1 minute, stirring. Add 300ml/½ pint/1¼ cups of the stock and simmer, stirring frequently until it has been absorbed.

4 Continue adding the stock, a ladleful at a time, stirring frequently until the rice is just tender and creamy, and almost all of the liquid has been absorbed. This will take 30–35 minutes. It may not be necessary to add all the stock.

5 Stir the beans, mixed herbs and seasoning into the risotto. Heat gently, then serve garnished with the chopped fresh parsley and sprinkled with shavings of Parmesan cheese.

COOK'S TIP
To make thin Parmesan cheese shavings, take a rectangular block or long wedge of Parmesan and firmly scrape a vegetable peeler down the side of the cheese to make shavings. The swivel-bladed type of peeler is best for this job.

Energy 511Kcal/2132kJ; Protein 18g; Carbohydrate 77.6g, of which sugars 1.6g; Fat 13.9g, of which saturates 4g; Cholesterol 28mg; Calcium 55mg; Fibre 3.9g; Sodium 556mg.

POT-ROAST LOIN of PORK with APPLE

Roasted pork loin with crisp crackling and a lightly spiced apple and raisin stuffing makes a wonderful Sunday-lunch main course.

SERVES 6–8

1.8kg/4lb boned loin of pork
300ml/½ pint/1¼ cups dry (hard) cider
150ml/¼ pint/⅔ cup sour cream
7.5ml/1½ tsp salt

For the stuffing
25g/1oz/2 tbsp butter
1 small onion, chopped
50g/2oz/1 cup fresh white breadcrumbs
2 apples, cored, peeled and chopped
50g/2oz/scant ½ cup raisins
finely grated rind of 1 orange
pinch of ground cloves
salt and ground black pepper

1 Preheat the oven to 220°C/425°F/ Gas 7. To make the stuffing, melt the butter in a frying pan and gently fry the onion for 10 minutes until soft. Stir in the remaining stuffing ingredients.

2 Put the pork, rind side down, on a board. Make a horizontal cut between the meat and outer layer of fat, cutting to within 2.5cm/1in of the edges to make a pocket.

3 Push the prepared stuffing into the pocket. Roll up the pork lengthwise and tie firmly with string. Score the rind at 2cm/¾in intervals with a sharp knife.

4 Pour the cider and sour cream into a large casserole. Stir to combine, then add the pork, rind-side down. Transfer to the oven and cook, uncovered, for 30 minutes.

5 Turn the joint over, so that the rind is on top. Baste with the juices, then sprinkle the rind with salt. Cook for a further 1 hour, basting after 30 minutes. Reduce the oven temperature to 180°C/ 350°F/Gas 4. Cook for 1½ hours, then remove the casserole from the oven and leave the joint to stand for 20 minutes before carving.

COOK'S TIP
Do not baste during the final 1½ hours of roasting, so the crackling becomes crisp.

Energy 398Kcal/1667kJ; Protein 49.7g; Carbohydrate 13g, of which sugars 8.2g; Fat 15.5g, of which saturates 7.1g; Cholesterol 160mg; Calcium 50mg; Fibre 0.7g; Sodium 239mg.

BRAZILIAN PORK and RICE CASSEROLE

We tend to associate Brazil with beef recipes, but there are also some excellent pork recipes, including this hearty dish of marinated pork, vegetables and rice.

SERVES 4–6

500g/1¼lb lean pork, such as fillet
    (tenderloin), cut into strips
60ml/4 tbsp vegetable oil
1 onion, chopped
1 garlic clove, crushed
1 green (bell) pepper, cut into pieces
about 300ml/½ pint/1¼ cups chicken or
    vegetable stock
225g/8oz/generous 1 cup white long
    grain rice
150ml/¼ pint/⅔ cup single (light) cream
150g/5oz/1½ cups freshly grated
    Parmesan cheese
salt and ground black pepper

For the marinade
120ml/4fl oz/½ cup dry white wine
30ml/2 tbsp lemon juice
1 onion, chopped
4 juniper berries, lightly crushed
3 cloves
1 fresh red chilli, seeded and finely sliced

1 Mix the marinade ingredients in a shallow dish, add the pork strips and leave to marinate for 3–4 hours, stirring occasionally. Transfer the pork to a plate using a slotted spoon and pat dry. Strain the marinade and set aside.

2 Heat the oil in a heavy pan, add the pork strips and fry for a few minutes until evenly brown. Transfer to a plate using a slotted spoon.

3 Add the chopped onion and the garlic to the pan and fry for 3–4 minutes. Stir in the pieces of pepper and cook for 3–4 minutes more, then return the pork strips to the pan. Pour in the reserved marinade and the stock. Bring to the boil and season with salt and pepper, then lower the heat, cover the pan and simmer gently for 10 minutes, or until the meat is nearly tender.

VARIATION
Strips of chicken breast meat can be used in this recipe instead of the lean pork fillet.

4 Preheat the oven to 160°C/325°F/ Gas 3. Cook the rice in plenty of lightly salted boiling water for 8 minutes or until three-quarters cooked. Drain well. Spread half the rice over the base of a buttered, earthenware dish. Using a slotted spoon, make a neat layer of meat and vegetables on top, then spread over the remaining rice.

5 Stir the cream and 30ml/2 tbsp of the grated Parmesan into the liquid in which the pork was cooked. Tip into a jug (pitcher) and then carefully pour the cream mixture over the rice and sprinkle with the remaining Parmesan. Cover with foil and bake for 20 minutes, then remove the foil and cook for 5 minutes more, until the top is lightly brown.

Energy 490Kcal/2040kJ; Protein 31.7g; Carbohydrate 33.3g, of which sugars 3g; Fat 23.9g, of which saturates 10.2g; Cholesterol 91mg; Calcium 342mg; Fibre 0.6g; Sodium 340mg.

PORK COOKED in CIDER with PARSLEY DUMPLINGS

Pork and fruit are a perfect combination. If you don't want to make dumplings, serve creamy mashed potatoes with the stew.

SERVES 6

115g/4oz/½ cup pitted prunes, roughly chopped
115g/4oz/½ cup ready-to-eat dried apricots, roughly chopped
300ml/½ pint/1¼ cups dry (hard) cider
30ml/2 tbsp plain (all-purpose) flour
675g/1½lb lean boneless pork, cut into cubes
30ml/2 tbsp vegetable oil
350g/12oz onions, roughly chopped
2 garlic cloves, crushed
6 celery sticks, roughly chopped
475ml/16fl oz/2 cups stock
12 juniper berries, lightly crushed
30ml/2 tbsp chopped fresh thyme
425g/15oz can black-eyed beans (peas), drained
salt and ground black pepper

For the dumplings
115g/4oz/1 cup self-raising (self-rising) flour
50g/2oz/scant ½ cup vegetable suet
45ml/3 tbsp chopped fresh parsley
90ml/6 tbsp water

I Preheat the oven to 180°C/350°F/ Gas 4. Place the roughly chopped prunes and apricots in a small bowl. Pour over the cider and leave to soak for at least 20 minutes.

VARIATION
This recipe can also be made with lean lamb – leg steaks or diced shoulder would be ideal cuts to choose. Omit the juniper berries, try cannellini beans in place of the black-eyed beans and use red onions rather than brown ones.

2 Season the flour, then toss the pork in the flour to coat. Reserve any leftover flour. Heat the oil in a large flameproof casserole. Brown the meat in batches, adding a little more oil if necessary. Remove the meat with a slotted spoon and drain on kitchen paper.

3 Add the onions, garlic and celery to the casserole and cook for 5 minutes. Add any reserved flour and cook for a further 1 minute.

4 Blend in the stock until smooth. Add the cider and fruit, juniper berries, thyme and plenty of seasoning. Bring to the boil, add the pork, cover tightly and then cook in the oven for 50 minutes.

5 Just before the end of the cooking time prepare the dumplings. Sift the flour into a large bowl, add a pinch of salt, then stir in the suet and chopped fresh parsley. Add the water gradually and mix all the ingredients together to form a smooth, slightly sticky dough.

6 Remove the casserole from the oven, then stir in the black-eyed beans and adjust the seasoning. Divide the dumpling mixture into six, form into rough rounds and place on top of the stew. Return the casserole to the oven, then cover and cook for a further 20–25 minutes, or until the dumplings are cooked and the pork is tender.

COOK'S TIP
Black-eyed beans or peas, as they are called in America, are also sometimes referred to as cowpeas. They are a medium-size cream-coloured bean with a distinctive black spot or "eye" on the inner curve. They have a smooth, creamy texture and a subtle flavour. Black-eyed beans are a popular addition to soups and casseroles and are widely used in southern American cuisines.

Energy 468Kcal/1968kJ; Protein 32.6g; Carbohydrate 46.9g, of which sugars 21g; Fat 16.5g, of which saturates 5.9g; Cholesterol 71mg; Calcium 174mg; Fibre 8.2g; Sodium 437mg.

PORK TENDERLOIN with SPINACH and PUY LENTILS

Lean pork tenderloin, wrapped in spinach and cooked in a clay pot on a bed of tiny French green lentils, flavoured with coconut.

SERVES 4

500–675g/1¼–1½lb pork tenderloin
15ml/1 tbsp sunflower oil
15g/½oz/1 tbsp butter
8–12 large spinach leaves
1 onion, chopped
1 garlic clove, finely chopped
2.5cm/1in piece fresh root ginger,
   finely grated
1 red chilli, finely chopped (optional)
250g/9oz/generous 1 cup Puy lentils
750ml/1¼ pints/3 cups chicken or
   vegetable stock
200ml/7fl oz/scant 1 cup coconut cream
salt and ground black pepper

3 Meanwhile, add the spinach leaves to a large pan of boiling water and cook for 1 minute, or until just wilted. Drain immediately in a colander and refresh under cold running water. Drain well.

6 Add the lentils to the onion mixture in the frying pan and then stir in the chicken or vegetable stock. Bring to the boil, then boil rapidly for 10 minutes. Remove the pan from the heat and stir in the coconut cream until well blended. Transfer the onion and lentil mixture to the clay pot and arrange the pork tenderloins on top.

1 Soak a small clay pot in cold water for about 15 minutes, then drain. Cut the pork tenderloin widthwise into two equal pieces. Season the pork well with salt and ground black pepper.

4 Lay the spinach leaves on the work surface, overlapping them slightly to form a rectangle. Place the pork on top and wrap the leaves around the pork to enclose it completely.

7 Cover the clay pot and place it in an unheated oven. Set the oven to 190°C/375°F/Gas 5 and cook for 45 minutes, or until the lentils and pork are cooked.

8 To serve, remove the spinach-wrapped pork tenderloins from the clay pot using a slotted spoon or tongs and cut the pork into thick slices. Stir the lentils and spoon them, with some of the cooking juices, on to warmed, individual plates and top each portion with a few of the pork slices.

VARIATIONS
• Wrap the pork in slices of prosciutto, instead of the spinach leaves, and tie in place with string or secure with wooden cocktail sticks (toothpicks).
• Use 4 large chicken or duck breast portions in place of the pork tenderloin. Check the chicken or duck after about 30 minutes cooking time. Cut the breast portions into thick, diagonal slices to serve. The chicken would also be good wrapped with prosciutto.

2 Heat the sunflower oil and butter in a heavy frying pan, add the pork tenderloin and cook over a high heat until browned on all sides. Remove the meat from the pan using a metal spatula and set aside.

5 Add the onion to the oil in the frying pan and cook for about 5 minutes, stirring occasionally, until softened. Add the chopped garlic, grated ginger and finely chopped chilli, if using, and fry for a further 1 minute.

Energy 399Kcal/1683kJ; Protein 42.3g; Carbohydrate 39.1g, of which sugars 5g; Fat 9.2g, of which saturates 4g; Cholesterol 87mg; Calcium 81mg; Fibre 3.5g; Sodium 206mg.

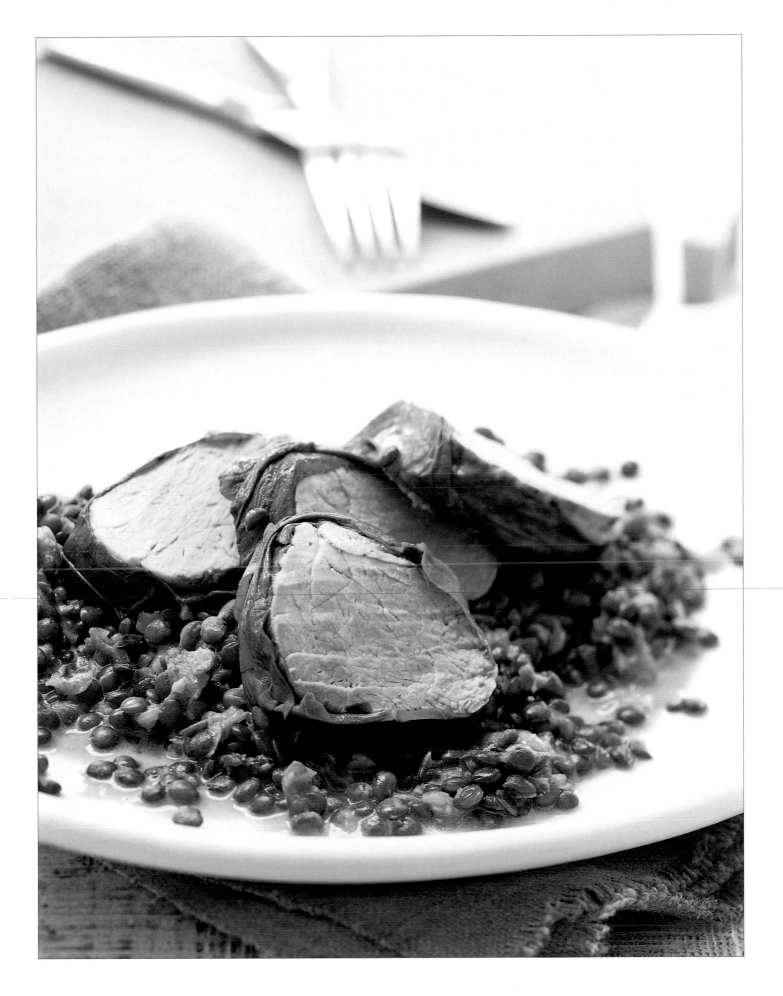

SAUSAGE, BACON and POTATO CASSEROLE

This simple supper dish will become a firm favourite with all the family. Warming and nourishing, it is perfect for those long winter evenings by the fire.

2 Heat the oil in a frying pan, then add the bacon and fry for 2 minutes, stirring. Add the onions and fry for 5–6 minutes until golden. Add the garlic and fry for 1 minute, then remove the mixture from the pan and set aside.

3 Fry the sausages in the same pan for 5–6 minutes until golden brown.

4 Arrange the potatoes in the base of the prepared dish. Spoon the bacon and onion mixture on top. Season with the salt and pepper and sprinkle with the fresh sage. Pour on the stock and top with the sausages. Cover and bake for about 1 hour, or until the potatoes and sausages are tender. Serve hot with crusty bread.

SERVES 4

15ml/1 tbsp vegetable oil
4 bacon rashers (strips), cut into
    2.5cm/1in pieces
2 large onions, chopped
2 garlic cloves, crushed
8 large pork sausages
4 large baking potatoes, peeled and
    thinly sliced
1.5ml/¼ tsp fresh sage
300ml/½ pint/1¼ cups vegetable stock
salt and ground black pepper
crusty bread, to serve

1 Preheat the oven to 180°C/350°F/ Gas 4. Lightly grease a large, shallow earthenware baking dish and set aside.

Energy 526Kcal/2201kJ; Protein 19.6g; Carbohydrate 53.4g, of which sugars 7.5g; Fat 27.4g, of which saturates 9.7g; Cholesterol 56mg; Calcium 71mg; Fibre 3.8g; Sodium 1214mg.

TOAD-in-the-HOLE

This is one of those dishes that is classic comfort food – perfect for lifting the spirits on cold days. Use only the best sausages for this grown-up version, which includes chives.

SERVES 4–6

175g/6oz/1½ cups plain (all-purpose) flour
30ml/2 tbsp chopped fresh chives (optional)
2 eggs
300ml/½ pint/1¼ cups milk
50g/2oz/⅓ cup white vegetable fat
    or lard
450g/1lb Cumberland sausages or good-
    quality pork sausages
salt and ground black pepper

VARIATION

For a young children's supper, make small individual toad-in-the-holes: omit the chopped fresh chives from the batter and cook small cocktail sausages in patty tins (muffin pans) until golden. Add the batter and cook for 10–15 minutes, or until puffed and golden brown.

1 Preheat the oven to 220°C/425°F/ Gas 7. Sift the flour into a bowl with a pinch of salt and pepper. Make a well in the centre of the flour. Whisk the chives, if using, with the eggs and milk, then pour this into the well in the flour. Gradually whisk the flour into the liquid to make a smooth batter. Cover and leave to stand for at least 30 minutes.

2 Put the vegetable fat or lard into a small roasting pan and place in the oven for 3–5 minutes until very hot. Add the sausages and cook for 15 minutes. Turn the sausages twice during cooking.

3 Pour the batter over the sausages and cook for about 20 minutes, or until the batter is risen and golden. Serve immediately.

Energy 448Kcal/1871kJ; Protein 15.6g; Carbohydrate 33.1g, of which sugars 4.9g; Fat 29.2g, of which saturates 11.7g; Cholesterol 111mg; Calcium 188mg; Fibre 1.7g; Sodium 692mg.

ROAST LAMB with BEANS and GREEN PEPPERCORNS

Roasting the lamb slowly on a bed of beans results in a dish that combines meltingly tender meat with vegetables all in one pot.

SERVES 6

8–10 garlic cloves, peeled
1.8–2kg/4–4½lb leg of lamb
30ml/2 tbsp olive oil
400g/14oz spinach leaves
400g/14oz can flageolet, cannellini or
   haricot (navy) beans, drained
400g/14oz can butter (lima) beans, drained
2 large, fresh rosemary sprigs, plus extra
   to garnish
15–30ml/1–2 tbsp drained, bottled
   green peppercorns

1 Preheat the oven to 150°C/300°F/ Gas 2. Set four garlic cloves aside and slice the rest lengthwise into three or four pieces. Make shallow slits in the skin of the lamb and insert a piece of garlic in each.

2 Heat the olive oil in a heavy, shallow flameproof casserole or a roasting pan that is large enough to hold the leg of lamb. Add the reserved garlic cloves and the fresh spinach leaves to the casserole or pan and cook over a medium heat, stirring occasionally, for 4–5 minutes, or until the spinach is wilted.

3 Add the beans and tuck the rosemary sprigs and peppercorns among them. Place the lamb on top, then cover the casserole or roasting pan with foil or a lid. Roast the lamb for 3–4 hours until it is cooked to your taste. Serve the lamb and beans hot, garnished with the remaining fresh rosemary sprigs.

Energy 705Kcal/2945kJ; Protein 74.3g; Carbohydrate 22.2g, of which sugars 4.2g; Fat 35.9g, of which saturates 15.4g; Cholesterol 246mg; Calcium 186mg; Fibre 8.7g; Sodium 775mg.

MIDDLE-EASTERN ROAST LAMB and POTATOES

When the Eastern aroma of the garlic and saffron come wafting out of the oven, this deliciously garlicky lamb won't last very long.

SERVES 6–8

2.75kg/6lb leg of lamb
4 garlic cloves, halved
60ml/4 tbsp olive oil
juice of 1 lemon
2–3 saffron threads, soaked in
    15ml/1 tbsp boiling water
5ml/1 tsp mixed dried herbs, oregano
    or marjoram
450g/1lb small baking potatoes,
    thickly sliced
2 large or 4 small onions,
    thickly sliced
salt and ground black pepper
fresh thyme, to garnish

1 Make eight evenly-spaced incisions in the leg of lamb, press the halved garlic cloves into the slits and place the lamb in a large non-metallic dish.

2 Mix together the olive oil, lemon juice, saffron mixture and herbs. Rub over the lamb and marinate for 2 hours.

3 Preheat the oven to 180°C/350°F/ Gas 4. Layer the potato and onion slices in a large roasting pan. Lift the lamb out of the marinade and place it on top of the sliced potato and onions, fat side up and season well with plenty of salt and ground black pepper.

4 Pour the marinade over the lamb, then roast for 2 hours, basting occasionally. Remove from the oven and cover with foil, then rest for 10 minutes before carving. Garnish with thyme.

Energy 719Kcal/2997kJ; Protein 74.4g; Carbohydrate 13g, of which sugars 3.5g; Fat 41.2g, of which saturates 17.7g; Cholesterol 282mg; Calcium 33mg; Fibre 1.3g; Sodium 169mg.

LAMB SHANKS with BEANS and HERBS

A hearty winter meal, the lamb shanks are slowly cooked in a clay pot until tender on a bed of tasty beans and vegetables.

SERVES 4

175g/6oz/1 cup dried cannellini beans,
    soaked overnight in cold water
150ml/¼ pint/⅔ cup water
45ml/3 tbsp olive oil
4 large lamb shanks, about 225g/8oz each
1 large onion, chopped
450g/1lb carrots, cut into thick chunks
2 celery sticks, cut into thick chunks
450g/1lb tomatoes, quartered
250ml/8fl oz/1 cup vegetable stock
4 fresh rosemary sprigs
2 bay leaves
salt and ground black pepper

1 Soak a large clay pot in cold water for 20 minutes, then drain. Drain and rinse the cannellini beans and place in a large pan of unsalted boiling water and boil rapidly for 10 minutes, then drain.

2 Place the 150ml/¼ pint/⅔ cup water in the soaked clay pot and then add the drained cannellini beans.

3 Heat 30ml/2 tbsp of the olive oil in a large frying pan, add the lamb shanks and cook over a high heat, turning the lamb shanks occasionally until brown on all sides. Remove the lamb shanks with a slotted spoon and set aside.

4 Add the remaining oil to the pan, then add the onion and sauté for 5 minutes, until soft and translucent.

5 Add the carrots and celery to the pan and cook for 2–3 minutes. Stir in the quartered tomatoes and vegetable stock and mix well. Transfer the vegetable mixture to the clay pot and season well with salt and pepper, then add the fresh rosemary and bay leaves and stir again to combine.

6 Place the lamb shanks on top of the beans and vegetables. Cover the clay pot and place it in an unheated oven. Set the oven to 220°C/425°F/Gas 7 and cook for about 30 minutes, or until the liquid is bubbling.

7 Reduce the oven temperature to 160°C/325°F/Gas 3 and cook for about 1½ hours, or until the meat is tender. Check the seasoning and serve on warmed plates, placing each lamb shank on a bed of beans and vegetables.

COOK'S TIP

Lamb shanks are small joints cut from the lower end of the leg. One shank is an ideal-sized portion for one. Until recently you would have had to order them from the butcher, but they are now becoming increasingly available from larger supermarkets. To obtain a tender result, shanks should be cooked for a long time at a low heat.

VARIATIONS

• Dried butter (lima) beans or the smaller haricot (navy) beans can be used in place of the cannellini beans.
• If you prefer, two 400g/14oz cans cannellini beans can be used in this dish – simply place the drained beans in the soaked clay pot with the water and continue from step 3.
• A variety of other root vegetables would work well in this recipe – try chopped swede (rutabaga), sweet potatoes, butternut squash, parsnips or celeriac instead of the carrots. In spring, a mixture of baby turnips and baby carrots would also be good.

Energy 743Kcal/3121kJ; Protein 79.2g; Carbohydrate 39.7g, of which sugars 18.7g; Fat 30.9g, of which saturates 10.1g; Cholesterol 225mg; Calcium 127mg; Fibre 12.3g; Sodium 200mg.

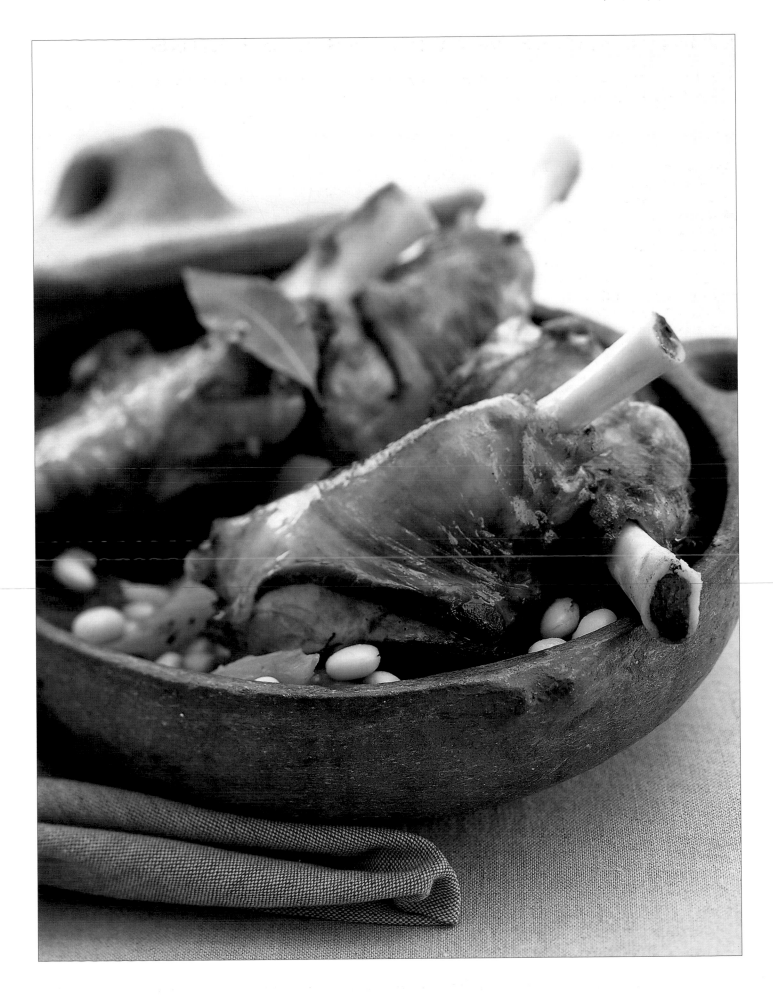

SPICED LAMB with TOMATOES and PEPPERS

Select lean tender lamb from the leg for this lightly spiced curry with juicy peppers and wedges of onion. Serve warm naan bread to mop up the tomato-rich juices.

3 Cut two of the onions into wedges (six from each onion) and add to the oil remaining in the pan. Fry the onions over a medium heat for 10 minutes, or until they are beginning to colour. Add the peppers and cook for 5 minutes. Use a slotted spoon to remove the vegetables from the pan and set aside.

4 Meanwhile, chop the remaining onion. Add it to the oil remaining in the pan with the chopped garlic, chilli and ginger, and cook for 4–5 minutes, stirring frequently, until the onion has softened.

5 Stir in the curry paste and canned tomatoes with the reserved yogurt. Return the lamb to the pan, season and stir well. Bring to the boil, then reduce the heat and simmer for 30 minutes.

SERVES 6

1.5kg/3¼lb lean boneless lamb, cubed
250ml/8fl oz/1 cup natural (plain) yogurt
30ml/2 tbsp sunflower oil
3 onions
2 red (bell) peppers, seeded and cut
    into chunks
3 garlic cloves, finely chopped
1 red chilli, seeded and chopped
2.5cm/1in piece fresh root ginger, peeled
    and chopped
30ml/2 tbsp mild curry paste
2 × 400g/14oz cans chopped tomatoes
large pinch of saffron threads
800g/1¾lb plum tomatoes, halved, seeded
    and cut into chunks
salt and ground black pepper
chopped fresh coriander (cilantro),
    to garnish

1 Mix the lamb with the yogurt in a bowl. Cover and chill for about 1 hour.

2 Heat the oil in a large pan. Drain the lamb and reserve the yogurt, then cook the lamb in batches until it is golden on all sides – this will take about 15 minutes in total. Remove the lamb from the pan using a slotted spoon and set aside.

6 Pound the saffron to a powder in a mortar, then stir in a little boiling water to dissolve the saffron. Add this liquid to the curry and stir well. Return the onion and pepper mixture to the pan, then stir in the fresh tomatoes. Bring the curry back to simmering point and cook for 15 minutes. Garnish with chopped fresh coriander to serve.

Energy 559Kcal/2343kJ; Protein 54.4g; Carbohydrate 20.5g, of which sugars 18.8g; Fat 29.6g, of which saturates 13.5g; Cholesterol 191mg; Calcium 139mg; Fibre 4.6g; Sodium 278mg.

BRAISED SHOULDER of LAMB with PEARL BARLEY and BABY VEGETABLES

In this wonderful, slow-cooked stew, the pearl barley absorbs all the rich meat juices and stock to become full-flavoured and nutty in texture when cooked.

SERVES 4

60ml/4 tbsp olive oil
1 large onion, chopped
2 garlic cloves, chopped
2 celery sticks, sliced
a little plain (all-purpose) flour
675g/1½lb boned shoulder of lamb, cut
    into cubes
900ml–1 litre/1½–1¾ pints/3¾–4 cups
    lamb stock
115g/4oz/⅔ cup pearl barley
225g/8oz baby carrots
225g/8oz baby turnips
salt and ground black pepper
30ml/2 tbsp chopped fresh marjoram,
    to garnish

1 Heat 45ml/3 tbsp of the oil in a flameproof casserole. Cook the onion and garlic until softened, add the celery, then cook until the vegetables brown.

2 Season the flour and toss the lamb in it. Use a slotted spoon to remove the vegetables from the casserole.

3 Add and heat the remaining oil with the juices in the casserole. Brown the lamb in batches until golden. When all the meat is browned, return it to the casserole with the onion mixture. Stir in 900ml/1½ pints/3¾ cups of the stock. Add the pearl barley. Cover, then bring to the boil, reduce the heat and simmer for 1 hour, or until the pearl barley and lamb are tender.

4 Add the baby carrots and turnips to the casserole for the final 15 minutes of cooking. Stir the meat occasionally during cooking and add the remaining stock, if necessary. Stir in seasoning to taste, and serve piping hot, garnished with marjoram. Warm, crusty bread would make a good accompaniment.

Energy 565Kcal/2364kJ; Protein 37.2g; Carbohydrate 37.2g, of which sugars 11g; Fat 30.9g, of which saturates 10.4g; Cholesterol 128mg; Calcium 85mg; Fibre 3.9g; Sodium 180mg.

BRAISED LAMB with APRICOTS and HERB DUMPLINGS

A rich and fruity lamb casserole, topped with light, herby dumplings, which is delicious served with baked potatoes and broccoli.

SERVES 6

30ml/2 tbsp sunflower oil
675g/1½lb lean lamb fillet, cut into
   2.5cm/1in cubes
350g/12oz baby (pearl) onions, peeled
1 garlic clove, crushed
225g/8oz/3 cups button
   (white) mushrooms
175g/6oz/¾ cup small ready-to-eat
   dried apricots
about 250ml/8fl oz/1 cup well-flavoured
   lamb or beef stock
250ml/8fl oz/1 cup red wine
15ml/1 tbsp tomato purée (paste)
salt and ground black pepper
fresh herb sprigs, to garnish

For the dumplings
115g/4oz/1 cup self-raising
   (self-rising) flour
50g/2oz/scant ½ cup shredded
   vegetable suet
15–30ml/1–2 tbsp chopped fresh
   mixed herbs

1 Preheat the oven to 160°C/325°F/ Gas 3. Heat the oil in a large, flameproof casserole, add the lamb and cook over a high heat until browned all over, stirring occasionally. Remove the meat from the casserole using a slotted spoon, then set aside and keep warm.

2 Reduce the heat slightly, then add the baby onions, crushed garlic and whole mushrooms to the oil remaining in the casserole and cook them gently for about 5 minutes, stirring occasionally with a wooden spoon.

3 Return the meat to the casserole, then add the dried apricots, stock, wine and tomato purée. Season to taste with salt and pepper and stir to mix.

4 Bring to the boil, stirring, then remove the casserole from the heat and cover. Transfer the casserole to the oven and cook for 1½–2 hours until the lamb is cooked and tender, stirring once or twice during the cooking time and adding a little extra stock, if necessary.

5 Meanwhile, make the dumplings. Place the flour, suet, herbs and seasoning in a bowl and stir to mix. Add enough cold water to make a soft, elastic dough. Divide the dough into small, marble-size pieces and, using lightly floured hands, roll each piece into a small ball.

6 Remove the lid from the casserole and place the dumplings on top of the braised lamb and vegetables.

7 Increase the oven temperature to 190°C/375°F/Gas 5. Return the casserole to the oven and cook for a further 20–25 minutes until the herb dumplings are cooked. Serve, garnished with the fresh herb sprigs.

VARIATIONS
Use lean beef or pork in place of the lamb and substitute shallots for the baby onions, if you prefer.

Energy 499Kcal/2091kJ; Protein 28.5g; Carbohydrate 36.7g, of which sugars 20.2g; Fat 24.4g, of which saturates 10.1g; Cholesterol 86mg; Calcium 132mg; Fibre 4.8g; Sodium 277mg.

ITALIAN LAMB MEATBALLS with CHILLI TOMATO SAUCE

Serve these piquant Italian-style meatballs with pasta and a leafy salad. Sprinkle with a little grated Parmesan cheese for that extra Italian touch.

SERVES 4

450g/1lb lean minced (ground) lamb
1 large onion, grated
1 garlic clove, crushed
50g/2oz/1 cup fresh white breadcrumbs
15ml/1 tbsp chopped fresh parsley
1 small egg, lightly beaten
30ml/2 tbsp olive oil
salt and ground black pepper
60ml/4 tbsp finely grated Parmesan cheese
    and rocket (arugula) leaves, to serve

For the sauce

1 onion, finely chopped
400g/14oz can chopped tomatoes
200ml/7fl oz/scant 1 cup passata (bottled
    strained tomatoes)
5ml/1 tsp granulated sugar
2 green chillies, seeded and finely chopped
30ml/2 tbsp chopped fresh oregano
salt and ground black pepper

1 Soak a small clay pot in cold water for 15 minutes, then drain. Place the minced lamb, onion, garlic, breadcrumbs, parsley and seasoning in a bowl and mix well. Add the beaten egg and mix to bind the meatball mixture together.

2 Shape the mixture into 20 small even-size balls. Heat the olive oil in a frying pan, add the meatballs and cook over a high heat, stirring occasionally, until they are browned all over.

VARIATIONS

Minced (ground) beef or sausage meat (bulk sausage) can be used in place of the minced lamb in this dish.

3 Meanwhile, to make the sauce, mix together the chopped onion, tomatoes, passata, sugar, seeded and chopped chillies and oregano. Season well and pour the sauce into the clay pot.

4 Place the meatballs in the sauce, then cover and place in an unheated oven. Set the oven to 200°C/400°F/Gas 6 and cook for 1 hour, stirring after 30 minutes. Serve with Parmesan cheese and rocket.

Energy 443Kcal/1853kJ; Protein 33.1g; Carbohydrate 22.5g, of which sugars 11.1g; Fat 25.3g, of which saturates 10.3g; Cholesterol 148mg; Calcium 246mg; Fibre 3g; Sodium 389mg.

FRAGRANT LAMB CURRY
with CARDAMOM-SPICED RICE

Wonderfully aromatic, this Indian-style lamb biriani, with the meat and rice cooked together, is a delicious meal in itself.

SERVES 4

1 large onion, quartered
2 garlic cloves
1 small green chilli, halved and seeded
5cm/2in piece fresh root ginger
15ml/1 tbsp ghee
15ml/1 tbsp vegetable oil
675 g/1½lb boned shoulder or leg of lamb,
    cut into chunks
15ml/1 tbsp ground coriander
10ml/2 tsp ground cumin
1 cinnamon stick, broken into 3 pieces
150ml/¼ pint/⅔ cup thick natural
    (plain) yogurt
150ml/¼ pint/⅔ cup water
75g/3oz/⅓ cup ready-to-eat dried apricots,
    cut into chunks
salt and ground black pepper

For the rice
250g/9oz/1¼ cups basmati rice
6 cardamom pods, split open
25g/1oz/2 tbsp butter, cut into small pieces
45ml/3 tbsp toasted cashew nuts or flaked
    (sliced) almonds

For the garnish
1 onion, sliced and fried until golden
a few sprigs of fresh coriander (cilantro)

1 Soak a large clay pot or chicken brick in cold water for 20 minutes, then drain. Place the onion, garlic, chilli and ginger in a food processor or blender and process with 15ml/1 tbsp water, to a smooth paste.

COOK'S TIP
Serve a cooling yogurt raita and a fresh fruit chutney or relish as an accompaniment.

2 Heat the ghee and vegetable oil in a heavy frying pan. Fry the lamb chunks in batches over a high heat until golden brown. Remove from the pan using a slotted spoon and set aside.

3 Add the onion paste to the remaining oil left in the frying pan, stir in the ground coriander and cumin, add the cinnamon stick pieces and fry for 1–2 minutes, stirring constantly with a wooden spoon.

4 Return the meat to the frying pan, then gradually add the yogurt, a spoonful at a time, stirring well between each addition with a wooden spoon. Season the meat well with plenty of salt and pepper and stir in the water.

5 Transfer the contents of the frying pan to the prepared clay pot, cover with the lid and place in an unheated oven. Set the oven to 180°C/350°F/Gas 4 and cook for 45 minutes.

6 Meanwhile prepare the basmati rice. Place it in a bowl, cover with cold water and leave to soak for 20 minutes. Drain the rice and place it in a large pan of boiling salted water, bring back to the boil and cook for 10 minutes. Drain and stir in the split cardamom pods.

7 Remove the clay pot from the oven and stir in the chopped ready-to-eat apricots. Pile the cooked rice on top of the lamb and dot with the butter. Drizzle over 60ml/4 tbsp water, then sprinkle the cashew nuts or flaked almonds on top. Cover the pot, reduce the oven temperature to 150°C/300°F/Gas 2 and cook the meat and rice for 30 minutes.

8 Remove the lid from the pot and fluff up the rice with a fork. Spoon into warmed individual bowls, then sprinkle over the fried onion slices and garnish with the sprigs of fresh coriander.

Energy 769Kcal/3208kJ; Protein 43.6g; Carbohydrate 67.6g, of which sugars 14.5g; Fat 36.2g, of which saturates 15g; Cholesterol 142mg; Calcium 134mg; Fibre 2.6g; Sodium 252mg.

LAMB and CARROT CASSEROLE with BARLEY

Barley and carrots make natural partners for lamb and mutton. In this convenient casserole the barley ekes out the meat and adds to the flavour and texture as well as thickening the sauce. The dish is comfort food at its best. Serve with boiled or baked potatoes and a green vegetable, such as spring cabbage.

SERVES 6

675g/1½lb stewing lamb
15ml/1 tbsp oil
2 onions, sliced
675g/1½lb carrots, thickly sliced
4–6 celery sticks, sliced
45ml/3 tbsp pearl barley, rinsed
stock or water
salt and ground black pepper
chopped fresh parsley, to garnish

1 Trim the lamb and cut it into bitesize pieces. Heat the oil in a flameproof casserole and brown the lamb.

2 Add the vegetables to the casserole and fry them briefly with the meat. Add the barley and enough stock or water to cover, and season to taste.

3 Cover the casserole and simmer gently or cook in a slow oven, 150°C/300°F/Gas 2 for 1–1½ hours until the meat is tender. Add extra stock or water during cooking if necessary. Serve garnished with the chopped fresh parsley.

COOK'S TIP
Tougher cuts of meat cook more evenly if they are cut into small, even-size cubes; 2.5cm/1in is ideal. They should be slightly larger than the vegetables being cooked in the stew because these will take a little longer to cook than the meat. Although excess fat should be removed, some marbling is useful for keeping the meat moist. Any excess fat can be skimmed off after cooking.

Energy 304Kcal/1263kJ; Protein 23.2g; Carbohydrate 13g, of which sugars 11.3g; Fat 18g, of which saturates 7.5g; Cholesterol 84mg; Calcium 53mg; Fibre 3.6g; Sodium 110mg

LAMB and PUMPKIN COUSCOUS

Pumpkin is a very popular Moroccan ingredient and this is a traditional couscous recipe, with echoes of the very early vegetable couscous dishes made by the Berbers.

2 Cut the lamb into bitesize pieces and place in the pan with the sliced onions, and add the saffron, ginger, turmeric, pepper and salt. Pour in the water and stir well, then slowly bring to the boil. Cover the pan and simmer for about 1 hour until the meat is tender.

3 Peel or scrape the carrots and cut them into large chunks. Cut the pumpkin into 2.5cm/1in cubes, discarding the skin, seeds and pith.

4 Stir the carrots, pumpkin and raisins into the meat mixture with the chickpeas, cover the pan and simmer for 30–35 minutes more, stirring occasionally, until the vegetables and meat are completely tender.

5 Meanwhile, prepare the couscous according to the instructions on the packet and steam on top of the stew, then fork lightly to fluff up. Spoon the couscous on to a warmed serving plate, add the stew and stir the stew into the couscous. Extra gravy can be served separately. Sprinkle some tiny sprigs of fresh parsley over the top and serve immediately.

SERVES 4–6

75g/3oz/½ cup chickpeas, soaked overnight and drained
675g/1½lb lean lamb
2 large onions, sliced
pinch of saffron threads
1.5ml/¼ tsp ground ginger
2.5ml/½ tsp ground turmeric
5ml/1 tsp ground black pepper
1.2 litres/2 pints/5 cups water
450g/1lb carrots
675g/1½lb pumpkin
75g/3oz/⅔ cup raisins
400g/14oz/2¼ cups couscous
salt
sprigs of fresh parsley, to garnish

1 Place the chickpeas in a large pan of boiling water. Boil for 10 minutes, then reduce the heat and cook for 1–1½ hours until tender. Place in cold water and remove the skins by rubbing with your fingers. Discard the skins and drain.

Energy 725Kcal/3034kJ; Protein 34.8g; Carbohydrate 115.4g, of which sugars 69.5g; Fat 16.6g, of which saturates 6.8g; Cholesterol 86mg; Calcium 282mg; Fibre 21.5g; Sodium 297mg.

OSSO BUCCO with RISOTTO MILANESE

Two one-pot dishes in one recipe, both so utterly delicious that it seemed churlish to omit them from this collection. Osso Bucco is a traditional Milanese veal stew and is classically accompanied by this saffron-scented risotto.

SERVES 4

50g/2oz/¼ cup butter
15ml/1 tbsp olive oil
1 large onion, chopped
1 leek, finely chopped
45ml/3 tbsp plain (all-purpose) flour
4 large portions of veal shin, hind cut
600ml/1 pint/2½ cups dry white wine
salt and ground black pepper

For the risotto
25g/1oz/2 tbsp butter
1 onion, finely chopped
350g/12oz/1¾ cups risotto rice
1 litre/1¾ pints/4 cups chicken stock
2.5ml/½ tsp saffron threads
60ml/4 tbsp white wine
50g/2oz/⅔ cup freshly grated
   Parmesan cheese

For the gremolata
grated rind of 1 lemon
30ml/2 tbsp chopped fresh parsley
1 garlic clove, finely chopped

1 Heat the butter and oil until sizzling in a large heavy frying pan. Add the onion and leek, and cook gently for about 5 minutes. Season the flour and toss the veal in it, then add to the pan and cook over a high heat until it browns.

2 Gradually stir in the wine and heat until simmering. Cover the pan and simmer for 1½ hours, stirring occasionally. Use a slotted spoon to transfer the veal to a warmed serving dish, then boil the sauce over a high heat until it is reduced and thickened to the required consistency.

3 Make the risotto about 30 minutes before the end of the cooking time for the stew. Melt the butter in a large pan and cook the onion until softened.

4 Stir in the rice to coat all the grains in butter. Add a ladleful of boiling chicken stock and mix well. Continue adding the boiling stock a ladleful at a time, allowing each portion to be completely absorbed before adding the next.

5 Pound the saffron threads in a mortar, then stir in the wine. Add the saffron-scented wine to the risotto and cook for a final 5 minutes. Remove the pan from the heat and stir in the Parmesan.

6 Mix the lemon rind, chopped parsley and garlic together for the gremolata. Spoon some risotto on to each plate, then add some veal. Sprinkle each with a little gremolata and serve immediately.

Energy 899Kcal/3754kJ; Protein 46.3g; Carbohydrate 90.6g, of which sugars 7.1g; Fat 27.4g, of which saturates 14.2g; Cholesterol 178mg; Calcium 249mg; Fibre 2.4g; Sodium 427mg.

OSTRICH STEW with SWEET POTATOES and CHICKPEAS

Lean and firm, ostrich meat marries well with the soft-textured sweet potatoes and chickpeas in this quick and easy, rich-flavoured stew.

SERVES 4

45ml/3 tbsp olive oil
1 large onion, chopped
2 garlic cloves, finely chopped
675g/1½lb ostrich fillet, cut into
    short strips
450g/1lb sweet potatoes, peeled
    and diced
2 × 400g/14oz cans chopped tomatoes
400g/14oz can chickpeas, drained
salt and ground black pepper
fresh oregano, to garnish

COOK'S TIP
Steamed couscous is a quick and easy accompaniment to this healthy stew, but it would also be good served with rice, or simply some warm, crusty bread.

1 Heat half the oil in a flameproof casserole. Add the chopped onion and garlic, and cook for about 5 minutes, or until softened but not coloured, stirring occasionally. Remove from the casserole using a slotted spoon and set aside. Add the remaining oil to the casserole and heat.

2 Fry the meat in batches over a high heat until browned. When the last batch is cooked, replace the meat and onions and stir in the potatoes, tomatoes and chickpeas. Bring to the boil, reduce the heat and simmer for 25 minutes, or until the meat is tender. Season and serve, garnished with the fresh oregano.

Energy 639Kcal/2682kJ; Protein 49g; Carbohydrate 51.2g, of which sugars 16.5g; Fat 27.9g, of which saturates 8.2g; Cholesterol 98mg; Calcium 108mg; Fibre 9.7g; Sodium 393mg.

SLOW COOKER VEGETARIAN AND SIDE DISHES

Just because you follow a vegetarian diet doesn't mean you need to miss out on fabulous-tasting food. This chapter makes use of all kinds of wonderful vegetables, beans and grains to make fabulous slow-cooked main meals that will appeal just as much to meat eaters as they do to vegetarians. Try rich and creamy Rosemary Risotto with Borlotti Beans, or aromatic Vegetable Kashmiri for a hearty main meal. Or if you are looking for a special side dish why not try Potato, Onion and Garlic Gratin, or Spicy Tamarind Chickpeas. Whatever you are in the mood for, you are sure to find the perfect meat-free recipe in this chapter.

MUSHROOM and FENNEL HOT-POT

Hearty and richly flavoured, this tasty stew makes a marvellous vegetarian main dish, but it can also be served as an accompaniment to meat dishes. Dried mushrooms swell up a great deal after soaking, so a little goes a long way in terms of both flavour and quantity.

SERVES 4

25g/1oz/½ cup dried shiitake mushrooms
1 small head of fennel
30ml/2 tbsp olive oil
12 shallots, peeled
225g/8oz/3 cups button (white)
　　mushrooms, trimmed and halved
250ml/8fl oz/1 cup dry (hard) cider
25g/1oz/½ cup sun-dried tomatoes
30ml/2 tbsp/½ cup sun-dried
　　tomato paste
1 bay leaf
salt and ground black pepper
chopped fresh parsley,
　　to garnish

1 Place the dried shiitake mushrooms in a heatproof bowl. Pour over just enough hot water to cover them and leave to soak for about 15 minutes. Meanwhile, trim and slice the fennel.

2 Heat the oil in a heavy pan. Add the shallots and fennel, then sauté for about 10 minutes over a medium heat, until the vegetables are softened and just beginning to brown. Add the button mushrooms to the pan and cook for a further 2–3 minutes, stirring occasionally.

3 Transfer the vegetable mixture to the ceramic cooking pot. Drain the shiitake mushrooms, adding 30ml/2 tbsp of the soaking liquid to the cooking pot. Chop them and add them to the pot.

4 Pour the cider into the pot and stir in the sun-dried tomatoes and tomato paste. Add the bay leaf. Cover with the lid and cook on high for 3–4 hours, or until the vegetables are tender.

5 Remove the bay leaf and season to taste with salt and black pepper. Serve sprinkled with plenty of chopped parsley.

Energy 94Kcal/394kJ; Protein 2.1g; Carbohydrate 4.2g, of which sugars 4g; Fat 6g, of which saturates 0.9g; Cholesterol 0mg; Calcium 28mg; Fibre 2.4g; Sodium 17mg.

SWEET and SOUR MIXED-BEAN HOT-POT

This impressive-looking dish, topped with sliced potatoes, is incredibly easy, making the most of dried and canned ingredients from the kitchen cupboard and combining them with a deliciously rich and tangy tomato sauce.

SERVES 6

40g/1½oz/3 tbsp butter
4 shallots, peeled and finely chopped
40g/1½oz/⅓ cup plain (all-purpose)
    or wholemeal (whole-wheat) flour
300ml/½ pint/1¼ cups passata (bottled
    strained tomatoes)
120ml/4fl oz/½ cup unsweetened
    apple juice
60ml/4 tbsp soft light brown sugar
60ml/4 tbsp tomato ketchup
60ml/4 tbsp dry sherry
60ml/4 tbsp cider vinegar
60ml/4 tbsp light soy sauce
400g/14oz can butter beans
400g/14oz can flageolet (small cannellini)
    beans
400g/14oz can chickpeas
175g/6oz green beans, cut into 2.5cm/
    1in lengths
225g/8oz/3 cups mushrooms, sliced
450g/1lb unpeeled potatoes
15ml/1 tbsp olive oil
15ml/1 tbsp chopped fresh thyme
15ml/1 tbsp fresh marjoram
salt and ground black pepper
fresh herbs, to garnish

1 Melt the butter in a pan, add the shallots and fry gently for 5–6 minutes, until softened. Add the flour and cook for 1 minute, stirring all the time, then gradually stir in the passata.

2 Add the apple juice, sugar, tomato ketchup, sherry, vinegar and light soy sauce to the pan and stir in. Bring the mixture to the boil, stirring constantly until it thickens.

VARIATIONS
• You can vary the proportions and types of beans used, depending on what you have in the store cupboard (pantry). Kidney beans and borlotti beans would work well and can be either interchanged with any of the beans used here, or combined with them.
• Try using mangetout or sugar snap peas in place of the green beans, if you prefer.

3 Rinse the beans and chickpeas and drain well. Place them in the ceramic cooking pot with the green beans and mushrooms and pour over the sauce. Stir well, then cover with the lid and cook on high for 3 hours.

4 Meanwhile, thinly slice the potatoes and par-boil them for 4 minutes. Drain well, then toss them in the oil so that they are lightly coated all over.

5 Stir the fresh herbs into the bean mixture and season with salt and pepper. Arrange the potato slices on top of the beans, overlapping them slightly so that they completely cover them. Cover the pot and cook for a further 2 hours, or until the potatoes are tender.

6 Place the ceramic cooking pot under a medium grill (broiler) and cook for 4–5 minutes to brown the potato topping. Serve garnished with herbs.

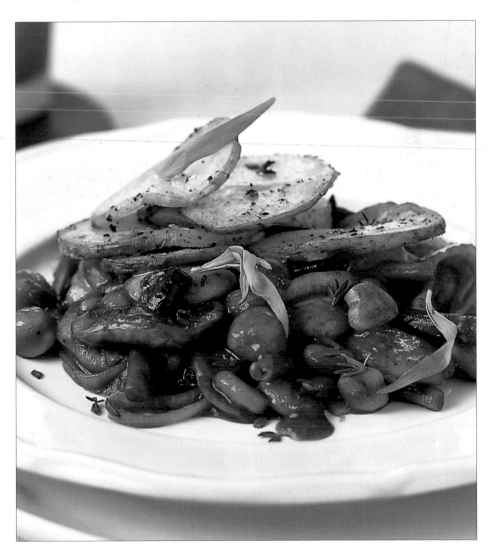

Energy 483Kcal/2042kJ; Protein 18.5g; Carbohydrate 73.3g, of which sugars 24.8g; Fat 13.8g, of which saturates 4.5g; Cholesterol 14mg; Calcium 134mg; Fibre 10.9g; Sodium 826mg.

ROOT VEGETABLE CASSEROLE
with CARAWAY DUMPLINGS

*Stirring soft cheese into the cooking juices gives this incredibly easy casserole a
wonderfully creamy richness, while thickening and flavouring it at the same time.
Light courgette dumplings spiced with caraway complete the meal.*

SERVES 3

300ml/½ pint/1¼ cups dry (hard) cider
175ml/6fl oz/¾ cup boiling vegetable stock
2 leeks
2 carrots
2 small parsnips
225g/8oz potatoes
1 sweet potato, weighing about 175g/6oz
1 bay leaf
7.5ml/1½ tsp cornflour (cornstarch)
115g/4oz full-fat soft cheese with garlic
    and herbs
salt and ground black pepper

For the dumplings
115g/4oz/1 cup self-raising
    (self-rising) flour
5ml/1 tsp caraway seeds
50g/2oz/½ cup shredded vegetable suet
    (chilled, grated shortening)
1 courgette (zucchini), grated
about 75ml/5 tbsp cold water

1 Reserve 15ml/1 tbsp of the cider and
pour the rest into the ceramic cooking
pot with the stock. Cover with the lid
and switch the slow cooker to high.

2 Meanwhile, prepare the vegetables.
Trim the leeks and cut into 2cm/¾in
slices. Peel the carrots, parsnips,
potatoes and sweet potato and cut
into 2cm/¾in chunks.

3 Add the vegetables to the ceramic
cooking pot with the bay leaf. Cover
with the lid and cook for 3 hours.

4 In a small bowl, blend the cornflour
with the reserved cider. Add the cheese
and mix together until combined, then
gradually blend in a few spoonfuls of the
cooking liquid. Pour over the vegetables
and stir until thoroughly mixed. Season
with salt and black pepper. Cover and
cook for a further 1–2 hours, or until
the vegetables are almost tender.

5 Towards the end of the cooking time,
make the dumplings. Sift the flour into a
bowl and stir in the caraway seeds, suet,
courgettes, salt and black pepper. Stir
in the water, adding a little more if
necessary, to make a soft dough. With
floured hands, shape the mixture into
12 dumplings, about the size of walnuts.

6 Carefully place the dumplings on top
of the casserole, cover with the lid and
cook for a further hour, or until the
vegetables and dumplings are cooked.
Adjust the seasoning and serve in
warmed deep soup plates.

VARIATION
To make a non-vegetarian version of this
dish, add some fried chopped bacon or
pancetta to the pot with the vegetables.

Energy 616Kcal/2584kJ; Protein 11.9g; Carbohydrate 74.9g, of which sugars 17.1g; Fat 28.9g, of which saturates 15.9g; Cholesterol 35mg; Calcium 256mg; Fibre 9.5g; Sodium 369mg.

SPICY-HOT MIXED-BEAN CHILLI with CORNBREAD TOPPING

Inspired by traditional Texan cooking, this chilli combines Tex-mex with classic Texan cornbread. The delicious topping offers the starch component of the dish, making this dish a filling one-pot meal with no need for accompaniments.

SERVES 4

115g/4oz/generous ½ cup dried red
    kidney beans
115g/4oz/generous ½ cup dried
    black-eyed beans
1 bay leaf
15ml/1 tbsp vegetable oil
1 large onion, finely chopped
1 garlic clove, crushed
5ml/1 tsp ground cumin
5ml/1 tsp chilli powder
5ml/1 tsp mild paprika
2.5ml/½ tsp dried marjoram
450g/1lb mixed vegetables such
    as potatoes, carrots, aubergines
    (eggplant), parsnips and celery
1 vegetable stock cube
400g/14oz can chopped tomatoes
15ml/1 tbsp tomato purée (paste)
salt and ground black pepper

For the cornbread topping
250g/9oz/2¼ cups fine cornmeal
30ml/2 tbsp wholemeal
    (whole-wheat) flour
7.5ml/1½ tsp baking powder
1 egg, plus 1 egg yolk lightly beaten
300ml/½ pint/1¼ cups milk

1 Put the dried beans in a large bowl and pour over at least twice their volume of cold water. Leave to soak for at least 6 hours, or overnight.

2 Drain the beans and rinse well, then place in a pan with 600ml/1 pint/ 2½ cups of cold water and the bay leaf. Bring to the boil and boil rapidly for 10 minutes. Turn off the heat, leave to cool for a few minutes, then tip into the ceramic cooking pot and switch the slow cooker to high.

3 Heat the oil in a pan, add the onion and cook for 7–8 minutes. Add the garlic, cumin, chilli powder, paprika and marjoram and cook for 1 minute. Tip into the ceramic cooking pot and stir.

4 Prepare the vegetables, peeling or trimming them as necessary, then cut into 2cm/¾ in chunks.

5 Add the vegetables to the mixture, making sure that those that may discolour, such as potatoes and parsnips, are submerged. It doesn't matter if the other vegetables are not completely covered. Cover with the lid and cook for 3 hours, or until the beans are tender.

6 Add the stock cube and chopped tomatoes to the cooking pot, then stir in the tomato purée and season with salt and ground black pepper. Replace the lid and cook for a further 30 minutes until the mixture is at boiling point.

7 To make the topping, combine the cornmeal, flour, baking powder and a pinch of salt in a bowl. Make a well in the centre and add the egg, egg yolk and milk. Mix, then spoon over the bean mixture. Cover and cook for 1 hour, or until the topping is firm and cooked.

Energy 613Kcal/2595kJ; Protein 29.6g; Carbohydrate 97.4g, of which sugars 15.8g; Fat 14.5g, of which saturates 3.4g; Cholesterol 112mg; Calcium 257mg; Fibre 13.4g; Sodium 413mg.

SWEET PUMPKIN and PEANUT CURRY

Rich, sweet, spicy and fragrant, the flavours of this delicious Thai-style curry really come together with long, slow cooking. Serve with rice or noodles for a substantial supper dish.

3 Add the lime leaves, galangal, pumpkin and sweet potatoes to the cooking pot. Pour the stock and 150ml/¼ pint/⅔ cup of the coconut milk over the vegetables, and stir to combine. Cover with the lid and cook on high for 1½ hours.

4 Stir the mushrooms, soy sauce and Thai fish sauce into the curry, then add the chopped peanuts and pour in the remaining coconut milk. Cover and cook on high for a further 3 hours, or until the vegetables are very tender.

5 Spoon the curry into warmed serving bowls, garnish with the pumpkin seeds and chillies, and serve immediately.

SERVES 4

30ml/2 tbsp vegetable oil
4 garlic cloves, crushed
4 shallots, finely chopped
30ml/2 tbsp yellow curry paste
400ml/14fl oz/1⅔ cups near-boiling
   vegetable stock
300ml/½ pint/1¼ cups coconut milk
2 kaffir lime leaves, torn
15ml/1 tbsp chopped fresh galangal
450g/1lb pumpkin, peeled, seeded
   and diced
225g/8oz sweet potatoes, diced
90g/3½oz/1½ cups chestnut
   mushrooms, sliced
15ml/1 tbsp soy sauce
30ml/2 tbsp Thai fish sauce
90g/3½ oz/scant 1 cup peanuts, roasted
   and chopped
50g/2oz/⅓ cup pumpkin seeds, toasted,
   and fresh green chilli flowers, to garnish

1 Heat the oil in a frying pan. Add the garlic and shallots and cook over a medium heat, stirring occasionally, for 10 minutes, until softened and beginning to turn golden.

2 Add the yellow curry paste to the pan and stir-fry over a medium heat for 30 seconds, until fragrant. Tip the mixture into the ceramic cooking pot.

COOK'S TIP
Fresh chilli flowers make an impressive garnish for a special occasion dinner, and will make the curry look authentically Thai. To make chilli flowers, hold each chilli by the stem and slit the chilli in half lengthways, keeping the stem end intact. Continue slitting the chilli in the same way to make thin strips. Put the chillies in a bowl of iced water and leave for several hours to curl up like flower petals.

Energy 337Kcal/1404kJ; Protein 10.3g; Carbohydrate 21.7g, of which sugars 10.8g; Fat 23.8g, of which saturates 4g; Cholesterol 0mg; Calcium 168mg; Fibre 5.1g; Sodium 554mg.

VEGETABLE KASHMIRI

Delicious vegetables cooked in a spicy and aromatic yogurt sauce make a lovely vegetarian main meal. You can use any combination of your favourite vegetables.

SERVES 4

10ml/2 tsp cumin seeds
8 black peppercorns
2 green cardamom pods, seeds only
5cm/2in cinnamon stick
2.5ml/½ tsp grated nutmeg
45ml/3 tbsp vegetable oil
1 fresh green chilli, seeded and chopped
2.5cm/1in piece of fresh root ginger, grated
5ml/1 tsp chilli powder
2.5ml/½ tsp salt
2 large potatoes, cut into 2.5cm/
    1in chunks
225g/8oz cauliflower florets
400ml/14fl oz/1⅔ cups boiling
    vegetable stock
150ml/¼ pint/⅔ cup Greek (US strained
    plain) yogurt
225g/8oz okra, thickly sliced
toasted flaked (sliced) almonds and
    sprigs of fresh coriander (cilantro),
    to garnish

4 In a bowl, stir a few spoonfuls of the hot stock into the yogurt, then pour over the vegetable mixture, and stir until thoroughly combined.

5 Add the okra to the pot, stir, cover and cook for a further 1½–2 hours, or until all the vegetables are very tender.

6 Serve the curry straight from the ceramic cooking pot, or spoon into a warmed serving dish. Sprinkle with toasted almonds and fresh coriander sprigs to garnish.

1 Put the cumin seeds, peppercorns, cardamom seeds, cinnamon stick and nutmeg in a mortar or spice grinder, and grind to a fine powder.

2 Heat the oil in a frying pan, add the chilli and ginger and fry for 2 minutes, stirring all the time. Add the chilli powder, salt and ground spice mixture, and fry gently for 2–3 minutes, stirring constantly to prevent the spices from sticking to the pan.

3 Transfer the mixture to the ceramic cooking pot and stir in the potatoes and cauliflower. Pour in the stock, cover with the lid, and cook on high for 2 hours.

Energy 294Kcal/1231kJ; Protein 9g; Carbohydrate 35.5g, of which sugars 7g; Fat 13.8g, of which saturates 4g; Cholesterol 6mg; Calcium 161mg; Fibre 5.1g; Sodium 427mg.

VEGETABLE and CASHEW NUT BIRYANI

Full of the flavours of India, this hearty supper dish is great for chilly winter evenings.
The nuts add protein, and the combination of aubergines and parsnips is delicious.

SERVES 4

1 small aubergine (eggplant), sliced
3 onions
2 garlic cloves
2.5cm/1in piece of fresh root
    ginger, peeled
about 60ml/4 tbsp sunflower oil
3 parsnips, chopped into 2cm/¾in pieces
5ml/1 tsp ground cumin
5ml/1 tsp ground coriander
2.5ml/½ tsp chilli powder
750ml/1¼ pints/3 cups boiling
    vegetable stock
1 red (bell) pepper, seeded and sliced
275g/10oz/generous 1½ cups easy-cook
    (converted) basmati or white rice
175g/6oz/1½ cup unsalted cashew nuts
40g/1½oz/¼ cup sultanas (golden raisins)
salt and ground black pepper
2 hard-boiled eggs, quartered, and sprigs
    of fresh coriander to garnish

1 Layer the aubergine slices in a strainer or colander, lightly sprinkle with salt and leave to drain for 30 minutes. Rinse thoroughly under cold running water, pat dry and cut into bitesize pieces.

2 Roughly chop one of the onions and place in a food processor with the garlic and ginger. Add 45ml/3 tbsp cold water and process to a smooth paste.

3 Finely slice the remaining onions. Heat 30ml/2 tbsp of the oil in a large frying pan, add the onions and fry gently for 10–15 minutes until they are soft and golden. Add the aubergine and parsnips and cook for 3–4 minutes to soften. Transfer to the ceramic cooking pot.

4 Add 15ml/1 tbsp oil to the pan, add the onion paste and cook, stirring, for 3–4 minutes. Stir in the cumin, coriander and chilli powder and cook for 1 minute.

5 Gradually stir one-third of the stock into the pan, then transfer the mixture to the ceramic cooking pot and switch the slow cooker to high. Add the remaining stock and the pepper, then season and cover with the lid. Cook for 2–3 hours, or until the vegetables are almost tender.

6 Spoon the rice in a layer over the vegetables, then re-cover and cook for 45 minutes–1 hour until the rice is tender and most of the stock has been absorbed. If the rice becomes too dry, add an extra 30ml/2 tbsp stock.

7 Meanwhile, heat the remaining 15ml/ 1 tbsp of oil in a clean frying pan, add the cashew nuts and stir-fry for about 2 minutes. Add the sultanas and fry for a few seconds until they swell up. Remove the pan from the heat and drain the nuts and sultanas on kitchen paper.

8 Add half the cashew nuts and sultanas to the vegetable rice and gently fold in using a fork. Turn off the slow cooker, cover with the lid and leave the biryani to stand for 5 minutes to finish cooking.

9 Spoon the vegetable biryani on to a warmed serving dish and scatter with the remaining nuts and sultanas. Garnish with quartered eggs and fresh coriander, and serve immediately.

Energy 801Kcal/3360kJ; Protein 18.7g; Carbohydrate 103.4g, of which sugars 25.7g; Fat 37.6g, of which saturates 6.7g; Cholesterol 0mg; Calcium 129mg; Fibre 9.2g; Sodium 230mg.

PILAFF with SAFFRON and PICKLED WALNUTS

Fragrant saffron gives this lovely rice dish a warm, spiced flavour and glorious colour. The pickled walnuts, which are available in large supermarkets and delicatessens, have a strong, really distinctive flavour that goes well with the spices, pine nuts and dried fruit.

SERVES 4

5ml/1 tsp saffron strands
50g/2oz/½ cup pine nuts
45ml/3 tbsp olive oil
1 large onion, finely chopped
3 garlic cloves, crushed
1.5ml/¼ tsp ground allspice
4cm/1½in piece fresh root ginger, grated
750ml/1¼ pints/3 cups boiling
    vegetable stock
300g/10oz/generous 1½ cups easy-cook
    (converted) rice
50g/2oz/½ cup pickled walnuts, drained
    and roughly chopped
40g/1½oz/¼ cup raisins
45ml/3 tbsp roughly chopped fresh parsley
    or coriander (cilantro)
salt and ground black pepper
parsley or coriander (cilantro) leaves,
    to garnish
natural (plain) yogurt, to serve

1 Put the saffron strands in a heatproof bowl with 15ml/1 tbsp boiling water and leave to stand.

2 Meanwhile, heat a large frying pan and dry-fry the pine nuts until golden. Set them aside until needed.

COOK'S TIP
Saffron is the most expensive spice in the world because the stigmas of the saffron crocus have to be hand-picked. Ground turmeric makes a cheaper alternative and gives a similar golden yellow colour and warm flavour and aroma. Simply leave out step 1 and stir in 2.5ml/½ tsp ground turmeric with the allspice and the ginger.

3 Heat the oil in a pan, add the onion and fry gently for 8 minutes. Stir in the garlic, allspice and ginger and cook for 2 minutes, stirring constantly. Transfer the mixture to the ceramic cooking pot.

4 Pour the boiling vegetable stock into the cooking pot and stir to combine, then cover with the lid and switch the slow cooker to high. Cook for 1 hour.

5 Sprinkle the rice into the cooking pot, then stir to mix thoroughly. Re-cover with the lid and cook for 1 hour, or until the rice is almost tender and most of the stock has been absorbed. Add a little extra boiling stock or water to the pot if the mixture is already becoming dry.

6 Stir the saffron and soaking liquid into the rice, then add the pine nuts, pickled walnuts, raisins and parsley or coriander and stir well to combine. Season to taste with salt and ground black pepper.

7 Re-cover the ceramic cooking pot with the lid and cook for a further 15 minutes, until the rice is very tender and all the ingredients are completely warmed through. Garnish with fresh parsley or coriander leaves and provide a bowl of natural yogurt on the side for guests to serve themselves.

VARIATION
For a spicy mushroom pilaff, cook 3 sliced shallots in 15ml/1 tbsp oil until soft. Stir in 2.5ml/½ tsp ground turmeric and 5ml/ 1 tsp each cumin and coriander. Transfer to the ceramic cooking pot. Add 750ml/ 1¼ pints/3 cups hot vegetable stock. Cover with the lid and cook on high for 30 minutes. Stir in 300g/10oz/ generous 1½ cups easy-cook (converted) rice and cook for 30 minutes. Fry 225g/8oz mixed mushrooms in 25g/1oz butter until soft, then stir into the ceramic cooking pot and season to taste. Cook for a further 30 minutes, then serve.

Energy 585Kcal/2456kJ; Protein 10.2g; Carbohydrate 77.1g, of which sugars 11.1g; Fat 28.5g, of which saturates 3.1g; Cholesterol 0mg; Calcium 72mg; Fibre 2g; Sodium 222mg.

ROSEMARY RISOTTO with BORLOTTI BEANS

Using easy-cook Italian rice means that all the wine and stock can be added at the same time, rather than ladleful by ladleful, as with a traditional risotto. The gentle, constant heat of the slow cooker produces a delicious risotto that is still thick and creamy.

SERVES 3

400g/14oz can borlotti beans
15g/½oz/1 tbsp butter
15ml/1 tbsp olive oil
1 onion, finely chopped
2 garlic cloves, crushed
120ml/4fl oz/½ cup dry white wine
225g/8oz/generous 1 cup easy-cook (converted) Italian rice
750ml/1¼ pints/3 cups boiling vegetable stock
60ml/4 tbsp mascarpone cheese
5ml/1 tsp chopped fresh rosemary
65g/2½oz/¾ cup freshly grated Parmesan cheese, plus extra to serve (optional)
salt and ground black pepper

1 Drain the borlotti beans in a sieve, rinse well under cold running water and drain again. Place about two-thirds of the beans in a food processor or blender and process to a coarse purée. Tip the remaining beans into a bowl and set aside for later.

2 Heat the butter and oil in a pan, add the onion and garlic and fry gently for 7–8 minutes until soft. Transfer the mixture to the ceramic cooking pot and stir in the wine and bean purée. Cover with the lid and cook on high for 1 hour.

3 Add the rice to the pot, then stir in the stock. Re-cover with the lid and cook for about 45 minutes, stirring once halfway through cooking. The rice should be almost tender and most of the stock should have been absorbed.

4 Stir the reserved beans, mascarpone and rosemary into the risotto. Cover again with the lid and cook for a further 15 minutes, until the rice is tender but still has a little bite.

5 Stir the Parmesan cheese into the risotto and season to taste with salt and ground black pepper. Turn off the slow cooker, cover and leave to stand for about 5 minutes, so that the risotto absorbs the flavours fully and the rice completes cooking.

6 Spoon the rice into warmed serving bowls and serve immediately, sprinkled with extra Parmesan, if you like.

VARIATIONS
• Try using different herbs to vary the flavour. Fresh thyme or marjoram would make a good alternative to rosemary.
• To make a lower-fat version of this dish, use Quark cheese in place of the mascarpone. It offers the same creamy texture with much less fat.

Energy 651Kcal/2740kJ; Protein 25g; Carbohydrate 87g, of which sugars 4.6g; Fat 22.2g, of which saturates 10.5g; Cholesterol 41.9mg; Calcium 357mg; Fibre 7.1g; Sodium 1462mg.

COUSCOUS-STUFFED SWEET PEPPERS

The peppers are softened in boiling water before filling to ensure really tender results.
Choose red, yellow or orange peppers for this dish, but avoid green ones because they
tend to discolour after a couple of hours of cooking and do not have such a sweet taste.

SERVES 4

4 (bell) peppers
75g/3oz/½ cup instant couscous
75ml/2½fl oz/⅓ cup boiling
   vegetable stock
15ml/1 tbsp olive oil
10ml/2 tsp white wine vinegar
50g/2oz dried apricots, finely chopped
75g/3oz feta cheese, cut into tiny cubes
3 ripe tomatoes, skinned, seeded
   and chopped
45ml/3 tbsp toasted pine nuts
30ml/2 tbsp chopped fresh parsley
salt and ground black pepper
flat leaf parsley, to garnish

1 Halve the peppers lengthways, then
remove the core and seeds. Place the
peppers in a large heatproof bowl and
pour over boiling water to cover. Leave
to stand for about 3 minutes, then drain
thoroughly and set aside.

2 Meanwhile, put the couscous in a
small bowl and pour over the stock.
Leave to stand for about 5 minutes until
all the water has been absorbed.

3 Using a fork, fluff up the couscous,
then stir in the oil, vinegar, apricots, feta
cheese, tomatoes, pine nuts and parsley,
and season to taste with salt and ground
black pepper.

COOK'S TIP
Be sure to taste the stuffing before adding
any more salt. Feta cheese can be very
salty already, so you may not need to
add any extra.

4 Fill the peppers with the couscous
mixture, gently packing it down using
the back of a spoon.

5 Place the peppers, filling side up,
in the ceramic cooking pot, then
pour 150ml/¼ pint/⅔ cup near-boiling
water around them.

6 Cover with the lid, switch the slow
cooker to high and cook for 2–3 hours,
or until the peppers are tender. Brown
under a hot grill (broiler) for 2 minutes
and serve garnished with fresh parsley.

Energy 303Kcal/1266kJ; Protein 33.7g; Carbohydrate 33.6g, of which sugars 17g; Fat 15.8g, of which saturates 3.9g; Cholesterol 13mg; Calcium 105mg; Fibre 4.3g; Sodium 285mg.

PARSNIPS and CHICKPEAS in GARLIC, ONION, CHILLI and GINGER PASTE

The sweet flavour of parsnips goes very well with the spices in this Indian-style vegetable stew. It makes an ideal meal for vegetarians, because chickpeas are high in protein. Complete the meal with warm Indian breads, such as chapati or naan.

SERVES 4

5 garlic cloves, finely chopped
1 small onion, chopped
5cm/2in piece fresh root ginger, chopped
2 green chillies, seeded and finely chopped
75ml/5 tbsp cold water
60ml/4 tbsp groundnut (peanut) oil
5ml/1 tsp cumin seeds
10ml/2 tsp coriander seeds
5ml/1 tsp ground turmeric
2.5ml/½ tsp chilli powder or mild paprika
50g/2oz/½ cup cashew nuts, toasted and ground
225g/8oz tomatoes, peeled and chopped
400g/14oz can chickpeas, drained and rinsed
900g/2lb parsnips, cut into 2cm/¾in chunks
350ml/12 fl oz/1½ cups boiling vegetable stock
juice of 1 lime, to taste
salt and ground black pepper
chopped fresh coriander (cilantro) leaves, toasted cashew nuts and natural (plain) yogurt, to serve

1 Reserve 10ml/2 tsp of the garlic, then place the remainder in a food processor or blender with the onion, ginger and half the chilli. Add the water and process to make a smooth paste.

2 Heat the oil in a large frying pan, add the cumin seeds and cook for about 30 seconds. Stir in the coriander seeds, turmeric, chilli powder or paprika and the ground cashew nuts. Add the ginger and chilli paste and cook, stirring frequently, until the paste bubbles and the water begins to evaporate.

COOK'S TIPS
• Buy spices in small quantities and store them in a cool, dark place. Try to use them within a few months because they quickly lose their flavour.
• Frying spices before adding to the cooking pot intensifies their taste.

3 Add the tomatoes to the pan and cook for 1 minute. Transfer the mixture to the ceramic cooking pot and switch the slow cooker to high.

4 Add the chickpeas and parsnips to the pot and stir to coat in the spicy tomato mixture, then stir in the stock and season with salt and pepper. Cover with the lid and cook on high for 4 hours, or until the parsnips are tender.

5 Stir half the lime juice, the reserved garlic and green chilli into the stew. Re-cover and cook for 30 minutes more, then taste and add more lime juice if needed. Spoon on to plates and sprinkle with fresh coriander leaves and toasted cashew nuts. Serve immediately with a generous spoonful of natural yogurt.

Energy 453Kcal/1899kJ; Protein 14.8g; Carbohydrate 50.1g, of which sugars 16.6g; Fat 23g, of which saturates 4.3g; Cholesterol 0mg; Calcium 148mg; Fibre 15.8g; Sodium 394mg.

ONIONS STUFFED with GOAT'S CHEESE and SUN-DRIED TOMATOES

Long, slow cooking is the best way to get maximum flavour from onions, so the slow cooker is the natural choice for these delicious stuffed onions. Serve with a rice or cracked wheat pilaff to make a great vegetarian main course.

SERVES 4

2 large onions
30ml/2 tbsp olive oil (or use oil from
    the sun-dried tomatoes)
150g/5oz/⅔ cup firm goat's cheese,
    crumbled or cubed
50g/2oz/1 cup fresh white breadcrumbs
8 sun-dried tomatoes in olive oil, drained
    and chopped
1 garlic clove, finely chopped
2.5ml/½ tsp fresh thyme
30ml/2 tbsp chopped fresh parsley
1 small egg, beaten
45ml/3 tbsp pine nuts
150ml/¼ pint/⅔ cup near-boiling
    vegetable stock
salt and ground black pepper
chopped fresh parsley, to garnish

1 Bring a large pan of water to the boil. Add the whole onions in their skins and boil for 10 minutes.

4 Divide the stuffing among the onions and cover each one with a piece of oiled foil. Brush the base of the ceramic cooking pot with 15ml/1 tbsp of the oil, then pour in the stock. Arrange the onions in the base of the cooking pot, cover with the lid and cook on high for 4 hours, or until the onions are very tender but still hold their shape.

5 Carefully remove the onions from the slow cooker and transfer them to a grill (broiler) pan. Remove the foil and drizzle the tops with the remaining 10ml/1 tsp oil. Brown under a medium grill for 3–4 minutes, taking care not to burn the nuts. Serve immediately, garnished with fresh chopped parsley.

VARIATIONS
• Try using feta cheese in place of the goat's cheese and add chopped fresh mint, currants and pitted black olives in place of the other flavourings.
• Alternatively, use 175g/6oz Roquefort or Gorgonzola in place of the goat's cheese and add about 75g/3oz/¾ cup chopped walnuts and 115g/4oz/1 cup very finely chopped celery in place of the sun-dried tomatoes and pine nuts.

2 Drain the onions and leave until cool enough to handle, then cut each onion in half horizontally and peel. Using a teaspoon, remove the centre of each onion, leaving a thick shell.

3 Very finely chop the flesh from one of the scooped-out onion halves and place in a bowl. Stir in 5ml/1 tsp of the olive oil or oil from the sun-dried tomatoes, then add the goat's cheese, breadcrumbs, sun-dried tomatoes, garlic, thyme, parsley, egg and pine nuts. Season with salt and pepper and mix well.

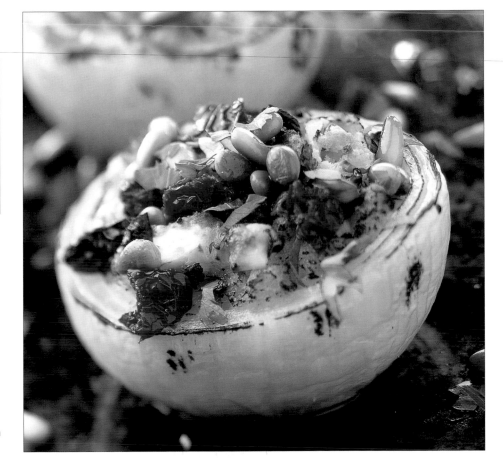

Energy 330Kcal/1370kJ; Protein 13.8g; Carbohydrate 14.3g, of which sugars 11.3g; Fat 24.7g, of which saturates 8.4g; Cholesterol 83.7mg; Calcium 98mg; Fibre 1.9g; Sodium 349mg.

ORANGE CANDIED SWEET POTATOES

Candied sweet potatoes are the classic accompaniment to a traditional Thanksgiving dinner. For a really fresh, festive look, serve with extra orange segments.

SERVES 8

900g/2lb sweet potatoes
150ml/¼ pint/⅔ cup orange juice
30ml/2 tbsp maple syrup
5ml/1 tsp freshly grated ginger
2.5ml/½ tsp ground cinnamon
2.5ml/½ tsp ground cardamom
5ml/1 tsp salt
ground black pepper
orange segments, to serve (optional)

VARIATION
You can serve this rich vegetable dish as a purée if you prefer (but omit the orange segments). Transfer the cooked candied sweet potatoes to a food processor, adding a little of the sauce, and blend until smooth. You may need to add a little more of the sauce to make a soft, creamy, spoonable purée.

I Peel the potatoes and cut them into 2cm/¾in cubes. Put them in a large heatproof bowl and pour over just enough boiling water to cover. Leave to stand for 5 minutes.

2 Meanwhile, put the orange juice, maple syrup, spices and salt in the ceramic cooking pot and stir to mix. Switch the slow cooker to high.

3 Drain the sweet potato cubes and add to the ceramic cooking pot. Gently stir to coat in the spicy orange mixture. Cover and cook for 4–5 hours, until tender, stirring twice during cooking.

4 Stir the orange segments, if using, into the sweet potatoes, and season to taste with pepper. Serve immediately.

Energy 53Kcal/226kJ; Protein 2.9g; Carbohydrate 13.7g, of which sugars 11.8g; Fat 0g, of which saturates 0g; Cholesterol 0mg; Calcium 5mg; Fibre 0.2g; Sodium 158mg.

POTATO, ONION and GARLIC GRATIN

This tasty side dish makes the perfect accompaniment to roasts, stews and grilled meat or fish. Cooking the potatoes in stock with onions and garlic gives them a really rich flavour.

3 Pour just enough of the stock into the pot to cover the potatoes. Cover with the lid and cook on low for 8–10 hours, or on high for 4–5 hours, until the potatoes are tender.

4 If you like, brown the potatoes under a hot grill (broiler) for 3–4 minutes. Serve sprinkled with a little salt and ground black pepper.

VARIATIONS

• To make this dish more substantial, sprinkle 115g/4oz/1 cup of grated Gruyère cheese over the top of the cooked potatoes and brown under a preheated grill (broiler) for 3–4 minutes until golden-brown and bubbling.
• Alternatively, crumble 165g/5½oz/scant 1 cup soft goat's cheese on the gratin 30 minutes before the end of cooking.
• To vary the flavour, try using chopped rosemary or sage in place of the thyme, or use crushed juniper berries instead.

SERVES 4

40g/1½oz/3 tbsp butter
1 large onion, finely sliced into rings
2–4 garlic cloves, finely chopped
2.5ml/½ tsp dried thyme
900g/2lb waxy potatoes, very finely sliced
450ml/¾ pint/scant 2 cups boiling
   vegetable stock
sea salt and ground black pepper

1 Grease the inside of the ceramic cooking pot with 15g/½oz/1 tbsp of the butter. Spoon a thin layer of onions on to the base of the cooking pot, then sprinkle over a little of the chopped garlic, thyme, salt and pepper.

2 Carefully arrange an overlapping layer of potato slices on top of the onion mixture in the ceramic cooking pot. Continue to layer the ingredients in the pot until all the onions, garlic, herbs and potatoes are used up, finishing with a layer of sliced potatoes.

Energy 260Kcal/1092kJ; Protein 5.1g; Carbohydrate 41.9g, of which sugars 6.4g; Fat 9.1g, of which saturates 5.4g; Cholesterol 21mg; Calcium 31mg; Fibre 3.3g; Sodium 171mg.

BROWN RICE with LIME and LEMON GRASS

It is unusual to find brown rice given the Thai treatment, but the nutty flavour of the grains is enhanced by the fragrance of limes and lemon grass in this delicious dish.

3 Heat the oil in a large pan. Add the onion and cook over a low heat for 5 minutes. Stir in the ginger, coriander and cumin seeds, lemon grass and lime rind and cook for 2–3 minutes. Tip the mixture into the ceramic cooking pot.

4 Pour the stock into the pot, briefly stir to combine, then cover with the lid and switch the slow cooker to high. Cook for 1 hour.

5 Rinse the rice in cold water until the water runs clear, then drain and add to the ceramic cooking pot. Cook for 45 minutes–1½ hours, or until the rice is tender and has absorbed the stock.

6 Stir the fresh coriander into the rice and season with salt and pepper. Fluff up the grains with a fork and serve garnished with strips of spring onions and toasted coconut, and lime wedges.

SERVES 4

2 limes
1 lemon grass stalk
15ml/1 tbsp sunflower oil
1 onion, chopped
2.5cm/1in piece fresh root ginger, peeled and very finely chopped
7.5ml/1½ tsp coriander seeds
7.5ml/1½ tsp cumin seeds
750ml/1¼ pints/3 cups boiling vegetable stock
275g/10oz/1½ cups easy-cook (converted) brown rice
60ml/4 tbsp chopped fresh coriander (cilantro)
salt and ground black pepper
spring onions (scallion), toasted coconut strips and lime wedges, to garnish

1 Using a cannelle knife (zester) or fine grater, pare the rind from the limes, taking care not to remove any of the bitter white pith. Set the rind aside.

2 Cut off the lower portion of the lemon grass stalk, discarding the papery top end of the stalk. Finely chop the lemon grass and set aside.

Energy 308Kcal/1304kJ; Protein 5.6g; Carbohydrate 64g, of which sugars 5.1g; Fat 5.1g, of which saturates 0.9g; Cholesterol 0mg; Calcium 17mg; Fibre 2g; Sodium 129mg.

SPICY TAMARIND CHICKPEAS

Chickpeas make a good base for many vegetarian dishes. Here, they are tossed with sharp tamarind and spices to make a deliciously light vegetarian lunch or side dish.

SERVES 4

225g/8oz/1¼ cups dried chickpeas
50g/2oz tamarind pulp
45ml/3 tbsp vegetable oil
2.5ml/½ tsp cumin seeds
1 onion, very finely chopped
2 garlic cloves, crushed
2.5cm/1in piece of fresh root ginger,
　peeled and grated
1 fresh green chilli, finely chopped
5ml/1 tsp ground cumin
5ml/1 tsp ground coriander
1.5ml/¼ tsp ground turmeric
2.5ml/½ tsp salt
225g/8oz tomatoes, skinned
　and finely chopped
2.5ml/½ tsp garam masala
chopped fresh chillies and chopped
　onion, to garnish

1 Put the chickpeas in a large bowl and pour over cold water to cover. Leave to soak for at least 8 hours, or overnight.

2 Drain the chickpeas and put in a pan with at least double the volume of cold water. (Do not add salt to the water because this will toughen the chickpeas and spoil the final dish.)

3 Bring the water to the boil and boil vigorously for at least 10 minutes. Skim off any scum, then drain the chickpeas and tip into the ceramic cooking pot.

4 Pour 750ml/1¼ pints/3 cups of near-boiling water over the chickpeas and switch the slow cooker to high. Cover with the lid and cook for 4–5 hours, or until the chickpeas are just tender.

5 Towards the end of the cooking time, put the tamarind in a bowl and break up with a fork. Pour over 120ml/4fl oz/ ½ cup of boiling water and leave to soak for about 15 minutes.

6 Tip the tamarind into a sieve (strainer) and discard the water. Rub the pulp through, discarding any stones and fibre.

7 Heat the oil in a large pan, add the cumin seeds and fry for 2 minutes, until they splutter. Add the onion, garlic and ginger and fry for 5 minutes. Add the cumin, coriander, turmeric, chilli and salt and fry for 3–4 minutes. Add the tomatoes, garam masala and tamarind pulp and bring to the boil.

8 Stir the tamarind mixture into the chickpeas, cover and cook for a further 1 hour. Either serve straight from the ceramic cooking pot, or spoon into a warmed serving dish and garnish with chopped chilli and onion.

COOK'S TIP

To save time, make double the quantity of tamarind pulp and freeze in ice-cube trays. It will keep for up to 2 months.

Energy 277Kcal/1164kJ; Protein 12.8g; Carbohydrate 32.6g, of which sugars 5.3g; Fat 11.5g, of which saturates 1.3g; Cholesterol 0mg; Calcium 103mg; Fibre 7.1g; Sodium 274mg.

COCONUT, TOMATO and LENTIL DHAL with TOASTED ALMONDS

Richly flavoured and utterly moreish, this lentil dish makes a filling supper served with warm naan bread and plain yogurt. Split red lentils give the dish a vibrant colour, but you could use larger yellow split peas instead, although they will take a little longer to cook.

SERVES 4

30ml/2 tbsp vegetable oil
1 large onion, very finely chopped
3 garlic cloves, chopped
1 carrot, diced
10ml/2 tsp cumin seeds
10ml/2 tsp yellow mustard seeds
2.5cm/1in piece fresh root ginger, grated
10ml/2 tsp ground turmeric
5ml/1 tsp mild chilli powder
5ml/1 tsp garam masala
225g/8oz/1 cup split red lentils
400ml/14fl oz/1⅔ cup boiling
    vegetable stock
400ml/14fl oz/1⅔ cups coconut milk
5 tomatoes, peeled, seeded and chopped
juice of 2 limes
60ml/4 tbsp chopped fresh coriander
    (cilantro)
salt and ground black pepper
25g/1oz/¼ cup flaked (sliced) almonds,
    toasted, to garnish

1 Heat the oil in a pan. Add the onion and cook for 5 minutes, until softened, stirring occasionally.

2 Add the garlic, carrot, cumin, mustard seeds and ginger to the pan. Cook for 3–4 minutes, stirring, until the seeds begin to pop, the aromas are released and the carrot softens slightly.

COOK'S TIP
This dish reheats well, so it is worth making a double batch and freezing half. Thaw, then add a little water and reheat.

3 Add the ground turmeric, chilli powder and garam masala to the pan and cook, stirring, for 1 minute, or until the flavours begin to mingle.

4 Tip the mixture into the ceramic cooking pot. Add the lentils, stock, coconut milk and tomatoes and season with salt and pepper. Stir well and cover the pot with the lid.

5 Cook on high for 2 hours, or until the lentils are soft, stirring halfway through the cooking time to prevent the lentils sticking. Stir the lime juice and 45ml/ 3 tbsp of fresh coriander into the dhal.

6 Check the seasoning and cook for a further 30 minutes. To serve, sprinkle with the remaining fresh coriander and the toasted almonds.

Energy 335Kcal/1421kJ; Protein 16.6g; Carbohydrate 46.3g, of which sugars 14.3g; Fat 10.6g, of which saturates 1.4g; Cholesterol 0mg; Calcium 99mg; Fibre 5.5g; Sodium 230mg.

SPICED INDIAN RICE with SPINACH, TOMATOES and CASHEW NUTS

This all-in-one rice dish makes a delicious, nutritious vegetarian meal but can also be served as an accompaniment to a spicy meat curry. Ghee, the clarified butter used in much Indian cooking, is available in cans from large supermarkets and Asian stores.

SERVES 4

30ml/2 tbsp sunflower oil
15ml/1 tbsp ghee or unsalted
   (sweet) butter
1 onion, finely chopped
2 garlic cloves, crushed
3 tomatoes, peeled, seeded and chopped
275g/10oz/1½ cups easy-cook (converted)
   brown rice
5ml/1 tsp each ground coriander
   and ground cumin, or 10ml/2 tsp
   dhana jeera powder
2 carrots, coarsely grated
750ml/1¼ pints/3 cups boiling
   vegetable stock
175g/6oz baby spinach leaves, washed
50g/2oz/½ cup unsalted cashew nuts,
   toasted
salt and ground black pepper

1 Heat the oil and ghee or butter in a heavy-based pan, add the onion and fry gently for 6–7 minutes, until soft. Add the garlic and chopped tomatoes and cook for a further 2 minutes.

2 Rinse the rice in a sieve (strainer) under cold water, drain well and tip into the pan. Add the coriander and cumin or dhana jeera powder and stir for a few seconds. Turn off the heat and transfer the mixture to the ceramic cooking pot.

3 Stir in the carrots, then pour in the stock, season with salt and pepper and stir to mix. Switch the slow cooker on to high. Cover and cook for 1 hour.

4 Lay the spinach on the surface of the rice, replace the lid and cook for a further 30–40 minutes, or until the spinach has wilted and the rice is cooked and tender.

5 Stir the spinach into the rice and check the seasoning, adding a little more salt and pepper if necessary. Sprinkle the cashew nuts over the rice and serve.

COOK'S TIP
If baby spinach leaves are unavailable, use larger fresh spinach leaves instead. Remove any tough stalks and chop the leaves roughly before adding to the rice.

Energy 473Kcal/1989kJ; Protein 10.1g; Carbohydrate 72.1g, of which sugars 9.2g; Fat 18g, of which saturates 4.5g; Cholesterol 8mg; Calcium 111mg; Fibre 4.8g; Sodium 349mg.

ONE-POT, CLAY-POT VEGETARIAN AND SIDE DISHES

Coming home to a delectable slow-cooked dish is always a delight. You open the door to delicious, tantalizing smells, take a few moments to assemble plates and cutlery, and tuck in. On occasions like these, a vegetarian dish such as Truffade is the ideal choice. If you have a clay pot, try Clay-pot Risotto with Spinach and Saffron, or Vegetable Paella. There are also stove-top recipes you'll make time and time again because they are so simple. Pan Haggerty, for instance, owes its excellent flavour to three simple ingredients: potatoes, Cheddar cheese and chives. Vegetable Korma is very adaptable, and Fettucine with Butter and Parmesan is as easy as its name suggests.

RATATOUILLE

A highly versatile vegetable stew from Provence. Ratatouille is delicious hot or cold, on its own or with eggs, pasta, fish or meat – particularly roast lamb.

2 Heat a little of the oil in a large, heavy pan and fry the onions for 5 minutes. Add the peppers and fry for a further 2 minutes. Drain. Add the aubergine and more oil and fry gently for 5 minutes. Add the remaining oil and courgettes and fry for 3 minutes. Drain.

3 Add the garlic and tomatoes to the pan with the bay leaves and thyme and a little salt and pepper. Cook gently until the tomatoes have softened and are turning pulpy.

4 Return all the vegetables to the pan and cook gently, stirring frequently, for about 15 minutes, until they are fairly pulpy but have retained a little texture. Season with more salt and pepper to taste if required.

COOK'S TIPS

• There are no specific quantities for the vegetables when making ratatouille so you can, to a large extent, vary the quantities and types of vegetables depending on what you have in the refrigerator.
• If the tomatoes are a little tasteless, add 30–45ml/2–3 tbsp tomato purée (paste) and a pinch of sugar to the mixture along with the tomatoes.
• Aubergines no longer need to be salted to draw out the bitter juices, however, this salting process does help prevent the aubergines from soaking up too much oil during frying. So, if you have the time, it is worth sprinkling the aubergine chunks with salt and leaving them in a colander in the sink for about 30 minutes to drain. Rinse them well and pat dry with kitchen paper before frying.

SERVES 6

900g/2lb ripe, well-flavoured tomatoes
120ml/4fl oz/½ cup olive oil
2 onions, thinly sliced
2 red (bell) peppers, seeded and
    cut into chunks
1 yellow or orange (bell) pepper,
    seeded and cut into chunks
1 large aubergine (eggplant),
    cut into chunks
2 courgettes (zucchini), cut
    into thick slices
4 garlic cloves, crushed
2 bay leaves
15ml/1 tbsp chopped fresh thyme
salt and ground black pepper

1 To skin the tomatoes plunge them into a bowl of boiling water for about 30 seconds, remove them using a slotted spoon and then refresh in cold water. Peel away the skins and roughly chop the tomato flesh.

Energy 204Kcal/848kJ; Protein 4.3g; Carbohydrate 13.3g, of which sugars 12.5g; Fat 15.2g, of which saturates 2.3g; Cholesterol 0mg; Calcium 49mg; Fibre 4.5g; Sodium 64mg.

VEGETABLE KORMA

The blending of spices is an ancient art in India. Here the aim is to produce a subtle, aromatic curry rather than an assault on the senses.

SERVES 4

50g/2oz/¼ cup butter
2 onions, sliced
2 garlic cloves, crushed
2.5cm/1in piece fresh root ginger, grated
5ml/1 tsp ground cumin
15ml/1 tbsp ground coriander
6 cardamom pods
5cm/2in piece of cinnamon stick
5ml/1 tsp ground turmeric
1 fresh red chilli, seeded and
   finely chopped
1 potato, peeled and cut into
   2.5cm/1in cubes
1 small aubergine (eggplant), chopped
115g/4oz/1½ cups mushrooms,
   thickly sliced
175ml/6fl oz/¾ cup water
115g/4oz/1 cup green beans, cut into
   2.5cm/1in lengths
60ml/4 tbsp natural (plain) yogurt
150ml/¼ pint/⅔ cup double (heavy) cream
5ml/1 tsp garam masala
salt and ground black pepper
fresh coriander (cilantro) sprigs, to garnish
boiled rice and poppadums, to serve

1 Melt the butter in a heavy pan. Add the onions and cook for 5 minutes until soft. Add the garlic and ginger and cook for 2 minutes, then stir in the cumin, coriander, cardamom pods, cinnamon stick, turmeric and finely chopped chilli. Cook, stirring constantly, for 30 seconds.

VARIATION

All kinds of vegetables and pulses can be used for this korma; try broccoli, carrots, cauliflower, peas, canned or fresh beans and canned chickpeas.

2 Add the potato cubes, aubergine and mushrooms and the water. Cover the pan, bring to the boil, then lower the heat and simmer for 15 minutes. Add the beans and cook, uncovered, for 5 minutes. With a slotted spoon, remove the vegetables to a warmed serving dish and keep hot.

3 Allow the cooking liquid to bubble up until it has reduced a little. Season with salt and pepper, then stir in the yogurt, cream and garam masala. Pour the sauce over the vegetables and garnish with fresh coriander. Serve with boiled rice and poppadums.

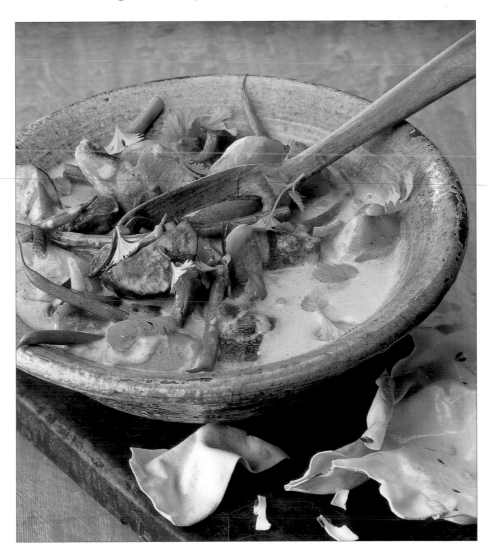

Energy 381Kcal/1577kJ; Protein 5.1g; Carbohydrate 20.9g, of which sugars 9.9g; Fat 31.4g, of which saturates 19.3g; Cholesterol 78mg; Calcium 95mg; Fibre 3.9g; Sodium 108mg.

TOFU and VEGETABLE THAI CURRY

Traditional Thai ingredients – chillies, galangal, lemon grass and kaffir lime leaves – give this curry a wonderfully fragrant aroma.

SERVES 4

175g/6oz tofu, drained
45ml/3 tbsp dark soy sauce
15ml/1 tbsp sesame oil
5ml/1 tsp chilli sauce
2.5cm/1in piece fresh root ginger,
    finely grated
225g/8oz cauliflower
225g/8oz broccoli
30ml/2 tbsp vegetable oil
1 onion, sliced
400ml/14fl oz/1⅔ cups coconut milk
150ml/¼ pint/⅔ cup water
1 red (bell) pepper, seeded
    and chopped
175g/6oz green beans, halved
115g/4oz/1½ cups shiitake or button
    (white) mushrooms, halved
shredded spring onions (scallions),
    to garnish
boiled jasmine rice or noodles,
    to serve

For the curry paste
2 chillies, seeded and chopped
1 lemon grass stalk, chopped
2.5cm/1in piece fresh galangal, chopped
2 kaffir lime leaves
10ml/2 tsp ground coriander
a few sprigs fresh coriander (cilantro),
    including the stalks

1 Cut the drained tofu into 2.5cm/1in cubes and place in an ovenproof dish. Mix together the soy sauce, sesame oil, chilli sauce and ginger and pour over the tofu. Toss gently to coat all the cubes evenly, then leave to marinate for at least 2 hours or overnight if possible, turning and basting the tofu occasionally.

2 To make the curry paste, place the chopped chillies, lemon grass, galangal, kaffir lime leaves, ground coriander and fresh coriander in a food processor and process for a few seconds until well blended. Add 45ml/3 tbsp water and process to a thick paste.

3 Preheat the oven to 190°C/375°F/ Gas 5. Using a large sharp knife, cut the cauliflower and broccoli into small florets and cut any stalks into thin slices.

4 Heat the vegetable oil in a frying pan, add the sliced onion and gently fry for about 8 minutes, or until soft and lightly browned. Stir in the prepared curry paste and the coconut milk. Add the water and bring to the boil.

5 Stir in the red pepper, green beans, cauliflower and broccoli. Transfer to a Chinese sand pot or earthenware casserole. Cover and place in the oven.

6 Stir the tofu and marinade, then place the dish in the top of the oven and cook for 30 minutes, then stir them into the curry with the mushrooms. Reduce the oven temperature to 180°C/350°F/Gas 4 and cook for about 15 minutes, or until the vegetables are tender. Garnish with spring onions and serve with boiled jasmine rice or noodles.

COOK'S TIP

Tofu or beancurd is made from soya beans and is sold in blocks. It is a creamy white colour and has a solid gel-like texture. Tofu has a bland flavour and its absorbent nature means that it takes on the flavours of marinades or any other food that it is cooked with.

Energy 212Kcal/883kJ; Protein 10.7g; Carbohydrate 16.2g, of which sugars 13.8g; Fat 12g, of which saturates 1.8g; Cholesterol 0mg; Calcium 329mg; Fibre 5.2g; Sodium 126mg.

MIXED BEAN and AUBERGINE TAGINE with MINT YOGURT

In this traditional-style Moroccan dish, the mixed beans and aubergine provide both texture and flavour, which are enhanced by the herbs and chillies.

SERVES 4

115g/4oz/generous ½ cup dried red kidney beans, soaked overnight in cold water and drained
115g/4oz/generous ½ cup dried black-eyed beans (peas) or cannellini beans, soaked overnight in cold water and drained
600ml/1 pint/2½ cups water
2 bay leaves
2 celery sticks, each cut into 4 batons
75ml/5 tbsp olive oil
1 aubergine (eggplant), about 350g/12oz, cut into chunks
1 onion, thinly sliced
3 garlic cloves, crushed
1–2 fresh red chillies, seeded and finely chopped
30ml/2 tbsp tomato purée (paste)
5ml/1 tsp paprika
2 large tomatoes, roughly chopped
300ml/½ pint/1¼ cups vegetable stock
15ml/1 tbsp each chopped fresh mint, parsley and coriander (cilantro)
salt and ground black pepper
fresh herb sprigs, to garnish

For the mint yogurt
150ml/¼ pint/⅔ cup natural (plain) yogurt
30ml/2 tbsp chopped fresh mint
2 spring onions (scallions), chopped

1 Place the soaked and drained kidney beans in a large pan of unsalted boiling water. Bring back to the boil and boil rapidly for 10 minutes, then drain. Place the soaked and drained black-eyed or cannellini beans in a separate large pan of boiling unsalted water and boil rapidly for 10 minutes, then drain.

2 Place the 600ml/1 pint/2½ cups of water in a soaked bean pot or a large tagine, add the bay leaves, celery and beans. Cover and place in an unheated oven. Set the oven to 190°C/375°F/Gas 5. Cook for 1–1½ hours or until the beans are tender. Drain.

3 Heat 60ml/4 tbsp of the oil in a large frying pan or cast iron tagine base. Add the aubergine and cook, stirring for 4–5 minutes, until evenly browned. Remove and set aside.

4 Add the remaining oil to the tagine base or frying pan, then add the onion and cook, stirring, for 4–5 minutes, until softened. Add the garlic and chillies and cook for a further 5 minutes, stirring frequently, until the onion is golden.

VARIATIONS
• Use 10–15ml/2–3 tsp harissa paste or chilli sauce instead of fresh chillies.
• A mixture of courgettes (zucchini) and red and yellow (bell) peppers can be used instead of the aubergines. Cut them into small chunks and fry them in the oil as in step 3 above.

5 Reduce the oven temperature to 160°C/325°F/Gas 3. Add the tomato purée and paprika and cook, stirring, for 1–2 minutes. Add the tomatoes, browned aubergine, drained red kidney and black-eyed or cannellini beans and stock. Season with salt and pepper.

6 Cover the iron tagine base with the earthenware lid or, if using a frying pan, transfer the contents to a clay tagine. Place in the oven and cook for 1 hour.

7 Meanwhile, mix together the yogurt, mint and spring onions and place in a small serving dish. To serve, add the mint, parsley and coriander to the tagine and lightly mix through the vegetables. Season to taste. Garnish with fresh herb sprigs and serve with the mint yogurt.

COOK'S TIP
The cooking time for the dried beans will vary depending on the age of the beans. Older beans will take longer to cook until tender. The tagine will happily keep warm once it's ready, so if you are serving this to guests, it is a good idea to allow extra time for the beans to become tender.

Energy 328Kcal/1377kJ; Protein 14.9g; Carbohydrate 35.2g, of which sugars 9.3g; Fat 15.3g, of which saturates 2.2g; Cholesterol 0mg; Calcium 96mg; Fibre 12.8g; Sodium 28mg.

MOROCCAN BRAISED CHICKPEAS

This sweet and spicy vegetarian dish is a real treat. Serve it hot as a main course with rice or couscous or serve cold as a salad, drizzled with olive oil and lemon juice.

SERVES 4

250g/9oz/1½ cups dried chickpeas, soaked
    overnight in cold water
30ml/2 tbsp olive oil
2 onions, cut into wedges
10ml/2 tsp ground cumin
1.5ml/¼ tsp ground turmeric
1.5ml/¼ tsp cayenne pepper
15ml/1 tbsp ground coriander
5ml/1 tsp ground cinnamon
300ml/½ pint/1¼ cups vegetable stock
2 carrots, sliced
115g/4oz/½ cup ready-to-eat dried
    apricots, halved
50g/2oz/scant ½ cup raisins
25g/1oz/¼ cup flaked (sliced) almonds
30ml/2 tbsp chopped fresh
    coriander (cilantro)
30ml/2 tbsp chopped fresh flat leaf parsley
salt and ground black pepper

3 Meanwhile, place the olive oil and onions in a frying pan and cook for about 6 minutes, or until softened. Add the cumin, turmeric, cayenne, coriander and cinnamon and cook for 2–3 minutes. Stir in the stock, carrots, apricots, raisins and almonds and bring to the boil.

4 Drain the chickpeas, add the spicy vegetable mixture and stir. Cover and return to the oven for 30 minutes.

5 Season with salt and pepper, lightly stir in half the fresh coriander and parsley and serve sprinkled with the remainder.

1 Soak a bean clay pot in cold water for 20 minutes, then drain. Place the chickpeas in a pan with plenty of cold water. Bring to the boil and boil rapidly for 10 minutes, then place the chickpeas in the bean pot, cover with lukewarm water and cover.

2 Place in an unheated oven and set the temperature to 200°C/400°F/Gas 6. Cook for 1 hour, then reduce the oven temperature to 160°C/325°/Gas 3. Cook for another hour, or until the chickpeas are tender.

COOK'S TIP
The cooking time for the chickpeas will vary depending on their age – if old, they could take a further 30 minutes.

Energy 403Kcal/1696kJ; Protein 17.1g; Carbohydrate 58.5g, of which sugars 27.1g; Fat 12.8g, of which saturates 1.4g; Cholesterol 0mg; Calcium 167mg; Fibre 10.9g; Sodium 45mg.

JAMAICAN BLACK BEAN POT

Molasses imparts a rich treacly flavour to the spicy sauce, which incorporates a stunning mix of black beans, vibrant red and yellow peppers and orange butternut squash.

SERVES 4

225g/8oz/1¼ cups dried black beans
1 bay leaf
30ml/2 tbsp vegetable oil
1 large onion, chopped
1 garlic clove, chopped
5ml/1 tsp mustard powder
15ml/1 tbsp molasses or black treacle
30ml/2 tbsp soft dark brown sugar
5ml/1 tsp dried thyme
2.5ml/½ tsp dried chilli flakes
5ml/1 tsp vegetable bouillon powder
1 red (bell) pepper, seeded and diced
1 yellow (bell) pepper, seeded
    and diced
675g/1½lb butternut squash or pumpkin,
    seeded and cut into 1cm/½in dice
salt and ground black pepper
sprigs of thyme, to garnish
cornbread or plain boiled rice, to serve

1 Soak the beans overnight in plenty of water, then drain and rinse well. Place in a large pan, cover with fresh water and add the bay leaf. Bring to the boil, then boil rapidly for 10 minutes. Reduce the heat, cover the pan, and simmer for about 30 minutes until tender. Drain, reserving the cooking water. Preheat the oven to 180°C/350°F/Gas 4.

COOK'S TIPS
• To prepare squash or pumpkin, cut it in half using a large sharp knife, then cut off the skin. Remove the seeds using a spoon and cut the flesh into chunks. Choose firm specimens that are blemish-free.
• If you don't have bouillon powder, then dissolve half a stock (bouillon) cube in the bean cooking water.

2 Heat the vegetable oil in a flameproof casserole, add the onion and garlic and sauté for about 5 minutes until softened, stirring occasionally. Stir in the mustard powder, molasses or treacle, sugar, dried thyme, chilli flakes and seasoning. Cook for about 1 minute, stirring, then stir in the black beans.

3 Add enough water to the reserved liquid to make 400ml/14fl oz/1⅔ cups, mix in the bouillon powder and pour into the casserole. Bake for 25 minutes.

4 Add the peppers and the squash or pumpkin and mix well. Cover, then bake for 45 minutes. Garnish with thyme.

Energy 297Kcal/1252kJ; Protein 15.1g; Carbohydrate 45.9g, of which sugars 20.3g; Fat 7.1g, of which saturates 1g; Cholesterol 0mg; Calcium 129mg; Fibre 12.6g; Sodium 16mg.

OKRA and TOMATO TAGINE

A spicy vegetarian dish that is delicious served either with other vegetable dishes or as a side dish to accompany a meat tagine.

SERVES 4

350g/12oz small okra
5–6 tomatoes
2 small onions
2 garlic cloves, crushed
1 green chilli, seeded
5ml/1 tsp paprika
a small handful of fresh coriander
    (cilantro) leaves
30ml/2 tbsp vegetable oil
juice of 1 lemon
120ml/4fl oz/½ cup water

1 Preheat the oven to 190°C/350°F/ Gas 5. Trim the okra, then cut the pods into 1cm/½in lengths. Set aside.

2 Peel the tomatoes, remove the seeds, then chop roughly. Set aside. Chop one of the onions, place in a food processor with the garlic, spices and 60ml/4 tbsp water and blend to form a paste.

3 Thinly slice the second onion. Heat the oil in a flameproof casserole or pan and fry the onion for 5–6 minutes until it turns golden brown. Transfer to a plate with a slotted spoon.

4 Reduce the heat and pour the onion and coriander paste over the onions. Cook for 1–2 minutes, stirring frequently, then add the okra, tomatoes and lemon juice. Pour in the water and stir well to mix. Cover tightly and transfer to the oven. Bake for about 15 minutes until the okra is tender.

5 Transfer the tagine to a serving dish, sprinkle with the fried onion rings and serve immediately.

VARIATION
Canned, chopped tomatoes can be used instead of the fresh tomatoes in this recipe – simply add the contents of a 200g/7oz can with the okra in step 4.

Energy 115Kcal/482kJ; Protein 4.2g; Carbohydrate 9.6g, of which sugars 8.5g; Fat 7g, of which saturates 1.2g; Cholesterol 0mg; Calcium 182mg; Fibre 6g; Sodium 26mg.

PAN HAGGERTY

Use a firm-fleshed potato, such as Romano or Maris Piper, which will hold its shape when cooked. For a change, try adding chopped ham or salami between the layers.

SERVES 2

1 large onion
450g/1lb potatoes
30ml/2 tbsp olive oil
25g/1oz/2 tbsp butter
2 garlic cloves, crushed
115g/4oz/1 cup grated mature (sharp)
  Cheddar cheese
45ml/3 tbsp chopped fresh chives, plus
  extra to garnish
salt and ground black pepper

1 Halve and thinly slice the onion. Peel and thinly slice the potatoes.

2 Heat the oil and butter in a large heavy or non-stick frying pan. Remove from the heat and cover the base with a layer of potatoes, followed by layers of onion slices, garlic, cheese, chives and plenty of seasoning.

VARIATIONS
• Other hard cheeses such as Red Leicester or Monterey Jack work well in this recipe.
• For a slightly sweeter flavour and extra colour, use 1 sliced red onion in place of the brown-skinned variety.

3 Continue layering, ending with grated cheese. Cover with a lid or foil and cook the pan haggerty over a gentle heat on the stove top for about 30 minutes, or until the potatoes and onion are tender when tested with a knife.

4 Preheat the grill (broiler) to hot. Uncover the pan, cover the pan handle with foil to protect it, if necessary, and brown the top under the grill. Serve the pan haggerty straight from the pan, sprinkled with extra chives to garnish.

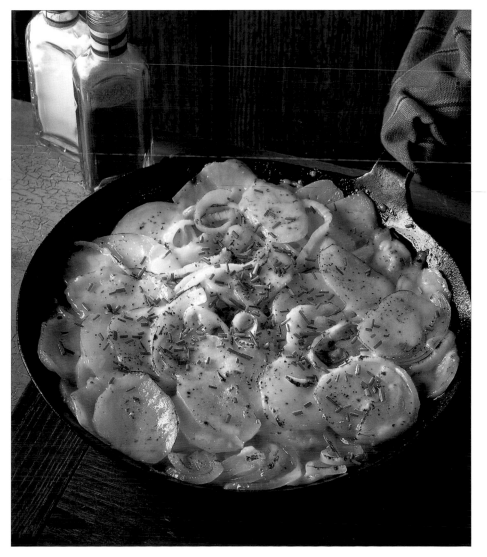

Energy 542Kcal/2257kJ; Protein 19.6g; Carbohydrate 42.2g, of which sugars 7.2g; Fat 33.9g, of which saturates 15g; Cholesterol 60mg; Calcium 429mg; Fibre 3.3g; Sodium 413mg.

MEDITERRANEAN BAKED VEGETABLES

This colourful selection of vegetables is baked in a shallow clay pot, known as a tian *in Provence where it is also the name given to the food baked in it.*

SERVES 4–6

75ml/5 tbsp olive oil
2 onions, halved and sliced
1 garlic clove, crushed
15ml/1 tbsp finely chopped
    fresh sage
4 large, well-flavoured
    tomatoes, quartered
3 courgettes (zucchini),
    thickly sliced
2 small yellow (bell) peppers, quartered
    and seeded
2 small red (bell) peppers, quartered
    and seeded
60ml/4 tbsp fresh white or wholemeal
    (whole-wheat) breadcrumbs
60ml/4 tbsp freshly grated
    Parmesan cheese
8–10 pitted black olives
salt and ground black pepper
sage leaves, to garnish

1 Heat 30ml/2 tbsp of the olive oil in a frying pan, add the onions and cook, stirring occasionally, until softened. Add the garlic and continue cooking until the onions are really soft and golden. Stir in the sage and season well.

2 Transfer the onions to a large oval *tian* or earthenware baking dish. Spread them evenly, then arrange the tomatoes, courgettes and peppers on top.

3 Preheat the oven to 200°F/400°C/ Gas 6. Drizzle the remaining oil over the mixed vegetables and season well. Bake for 30 minutes.

4 Sprinkle the fresh breadcrumbs and Parmesan cheese over the vegetables and arrange the olives on top. Return to the oven for a further 10–15 minutes, or until the vegetables are tender. Serve garnished with the sage leaves.

Energy 260Kcal/1083kJ; Protein 9.5g; Carbohydrate 24.9g, of which sugars 15.4g; Fat 14.2g, of which saturates 3.7g; Cholesterol 10mg; Calcium 192mg; Fibre 4.9g; Sodium 275mg.

FIELD MUSHROOMS with HAZELNUTS

Large mushrooms, full of texture and flavour, are topped with crunchy hazelnut pieces and fresh parsley and garlic-flavoured olive oil.

SERVES 4

2 garlic cloves
grated rind of 1 lemon
90ml/6 tbsp olive oil
8 large field (portabello) mushrooms
50g/2oz/½ cup hazelnuts, coarsely chopped
30ml/2 tbsp chopped fresh parsley
salt and ground black pepper

1 Crush the garlic cloves with a little salt using a mortar and pestle or on a chopping board. Place the crushed garlic in a small bowl and stir in the grated lemon rind and the olive oil. If time allows, leave the mixture to stand to enable the flavours to infuse.

2 Preheat the oven to 200°C/400°F/ Gas 6. Arrange the mushrooms, stalk side up, in a single layer in an ovenproof earthenware dish. Drizzle over about 60ml/4 tbsp of the oil mixture and bake for 10 minutes.

3 Remove the mushrooms from the oven and baste them with the remaining oil mixture, then sprinkle the chopped hazelnuts evenly over the top. Bake for a further 10–15 minutes, or until the mushrooms are tender. Season with salt and pepper and sprinkle with chopped parsley. Serve immediately.

COOK'S TIP
Almost any unsalted nuts can be used in place of the hazelnuts in this recipe – try pine nuts, cashew nuts, almonds or walnuts. Nuts can go rancid quickly so, for the freshest flavour, either buy nuts in small quantities or buy them in shells and remove the shells just before use.

Energy 255Kcal/1052kJ; Protein 5.2g; Carbohydrate 1.7g, of which sugars 1g; Fat 25.4g, of which saturates 3.1g; Cholesterol 0mg; Calcium 43mg; Fibre 3.1g; Sodium 12mg.

ROASTED SQUASH with RICE STUFFING

Gem squash has a sweet, subtle taste that contrasts well with the olives and sun-dried tomatoes in this recipe. The rice adds substance without changing any of the flavour.

SERVES 4 AS A FIRST COURSE

4 whole gem squashes
225g/8oz cooked white long grain rice
    (about 90g/3½oz/½ cup raw weight)
75g/3oz sun-dried tomatoes in oil, drained
    and chopped
50g/2oz/½ cup pitted black olives, chopped
60ml/4 tbsp soft goat's cheese
30ml/2 tbsp olive oil
15ml/1 tbsp chopped fresh basil leaves,
    plus basil sprigs, to serve
yogurt and mint dressing and green salad,
    to serve

1 Preheat the oven to 180°C/350°F/ Gas 4. Using a sharp knife, trim the base of each squash, slice off the top of each and scoop out and discard the seeds.

2 Mix the rice, tomatoes, olives, cheese, half the oil and the basil in a bowl.

3 Oil a shallow baking dish with the remaining oil, just large enough to hold the squash side by side. Divide the rice mixture among the squash and place them in the dish.

4 Cover with foil and bake for about 45 minutes until the squash are tender when pierced with a skewer. Garnish with basil sprigs and serve with a yogurt and mint dressing and a green salad.

VARIATION
Try ricotta cheese or cream cheese with garlic and herbs in place of the soft goat's cheese in this recipe.

Energy 208Kcal/870kJ; Protein 6.3g; Carbohydrate 23.1g, of which sugars 4.6g; Fat 10.6g, of which saturates 3.9g; Cholesterol 14mg; Calcium 97mg; Fibre 2.5g; Sodium 93mg.

CHEESE-TOPPED ROAST BABY VEGETABLES

A simple way of serving baby vegetables that really brings out their flavour.

SERVES 4

1kg/2¼lb mixed baby vegetables, such as
    aubergines (eggplant), onions or
    shallots, courgettes (zucchini), corn
    cobs and mushrooms
1 red (bell) pepper, seeded and cut into
    large pieces
1–2 garlic cloves, finely chopped
15–30ml/1–2 tbsp olive oil
30ml/2 tbsp chopped fresh mixed herbs
225g/8oz cherry tomatoes
115g/4oz/1 cup coarsely grated
    mozzarella cheese
salt and ground black pepper
black olives, to serve (optional)

1 Preheat the oven to 220°C/425°F/Gas 7.
Cut the vegetables in half lengthwise.

2 Place the halved baby vegetables and
pepper pieces in an ovenproof dish with
the finely chopped garlic and plenty of salt
and ground black pepper. Drizzle the oil
over and toss the vegetables to coat them.
Bake the vegetables for 20 minutes, or
until they are tinged brown at the edges,
stirring once during the cooking time.

3 Remove the ovenproof dish from the
oven and stir in the chopped fresh mixed
herbs. Sprinkle the cherry tomatoes over
the surface and top with the coarsely
grated mozzarella cheese. Return to the
oven and bake for 5–10 minutes more
until the cheese has melted and is
bubbling. Serve immediately with black
olives, if you like.

COOK'S TIP

This dish can also be made with a mixture
of regular-sized vegetables. Simply chop
them into bitesize pieces and continue
from Step 2.

VARIATION

Use 2–3 sprigs of fresh rosemary in place
of the chopped fresh mixed herbs.

Energy 212Kcal/883kJ; Protein 9.2g; Carbohydrate 24.3g, of which sugars 18.4g; Fat 9.4g, of which saturates 4.5g; Cholesterol 17mg; Calcium 174mg; Fibre 4.8g; Sodium 128mg.

POTATOES and PARSNIPS BAKED with GARLIC and CREAM

As the potatoes and parsnips cook, they gradually absorb the garlic-flavoured cream, while the cheese browns to a crispy finish.

SERVES 4–6

3 large potatoes, total weight about
   675g/1½lb
350g/12oz small to medium parsnips
200ml/7fl oz/scant 1 cup single
   (light) cream
105ml/7 tbsp milk
2 garlic cloves, crushed
butter, for greasing
about 5ml/1 tsp freshly grated nutmeg
75g/3oz/¾ cup coarsely grated
   Gruyère cheese
salt and ground black pepper

3 Lightly grease a 25cm/10in rectangular earthenware baking dish. Preheat the oven to 180°C/350°F/Gas 4.

6 Remove the dish from the oven and remove the foil or parchment from the dish. Sprinkle the grated Gruyère cheese over the vegetables in an even layer.

7 Return the dish to the oven and bake uncovered for a further 20–30 minutes, or until the potatoes and parsnips are tender (see Cook's Tip) and the topping is golden brown.

COOK'S TIPS

• If you have one, use a mandolin or a food processor fitted with a slicing blade to thinly and evenly slice the potatoes and parsnips for this gratin.
• At the end of the cooking time, to test if the vegetables are tender, insert a sharp knife through the middle of the potatoes and parsnips. The knife should slide in easily and the vegetables feel soft.

VARIATIONS

• Use sweet potatoes in place of some or all of the ordinary potatoes – choose orange-fleshed ones for a pretty colour contrast with the parsnips. Other root vegetables such as Jerusalem artichokes and carrots would also work well.
• Other hard cheeses would be equally good in this recipe – try Cheddar or Red Leicester, or go for the even more strongly flavoured Parmesan or Pecorino.

1 Peel the potatoes and parsnips and cut them into thin slices using a sharp knife. Place them in a large pan of salted boiling water and cook for 5 minutes. Drain and leave to cool slightly.

4 Arrange the potatoes and parsnips in layers in the greased earthenware dish, sprinkling each layer with a little freshly grated nutmeg and plenty of salt and ground black pepper.

2 Meanwhile, pour the cream and milk into a heavy pan, add the crushed garlic and bring to the boil over a medium heat. Remove the pan from the heat and leave to stand at room temperature for about 10 minutes to allow the flavour of the garlic to infuse into the cream and milk mixture.

5 Pour the garlic-flavoured cream and milk mixture into the dish and then press the sliced potatoes and parsnips down into the liquid. The liquid should come to just underneath the top layer of vegetables. Cover the dish with a piece of lightly buttered foil or baking parchment and bake for 45 minutes.

Energy 241Kcal/1009kJ; Protein 7.8g; Carbohydrate 27g, of which sugars 6.4g; Fat 11.7g, of which saturates 7.2g; Cholesterol 31mg; Calcium 174mg; Fibre 3.8g; Sodium 126mg.

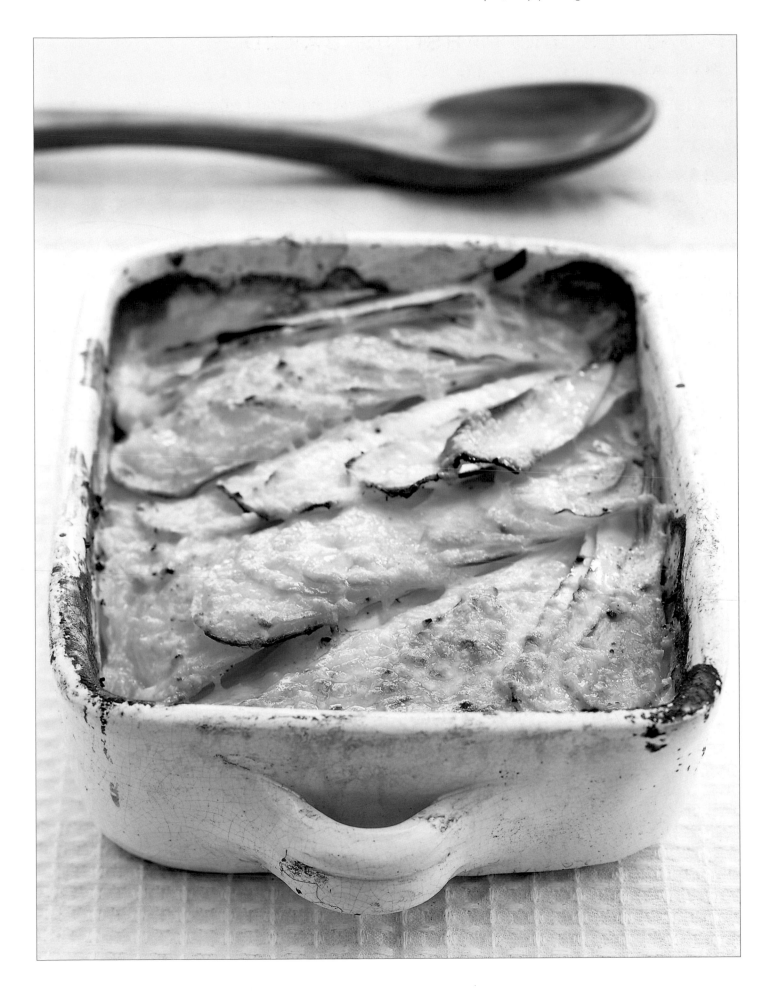

NEW POTATOES and VEGETABLES BAKED TURKISH-STYLE

Here's a meal in a pot that's suitable for feeding large numbers of people. It's lightly spiced and has plenty of garlic — who could refuse?

SERVES 4

60ml/4 tbsp olive oil
1 large onion, chopped
2 aubergines (eggplant), cut into
    small cubes
4 courgettes (zucchini), cut into
    small chunks
1 green (bell) pepper, seeded
    and chopped
1 red or yellow (bell) pepper,
    seeded and chopped
115g/4oz/1 cup fresh or frozen peas
115g/4oz green beans
450g/1lb new or salad potatoes, cubed
2.5ml/½ tsp ground cinnamon
2.5ml/½ tsp ground cumin
5ml/1 tsp paprika
4–5 tomatoes, skinned
400g/14oz can chopped tomatoes
30ml/2 tbsp chopped fresh parsley
3–4 garlic cloves, crushed
350ml/12fl oz/1½ cups vegetable stock
salt and ground black pepper
black olives and fresh parsley,
    to garnish

1 Preheat the oven to 190°C/375°F/ Gas 5. Heat 45ml/3 tbsp of the oil in a large frying pan, add the onion and fry until golden.

2 Add the aubergine and sauté for about 3 minutes, then add the courgette, chopped peppers, peas, beans and cubed potatoes, together with the cinnamon, cumin, paprika and seasoning. Continue to cook for a further 3 minutes, stirring the mixture constantly. Transfer the vegetables to an ovenproof dish.

3 Halve the fresh tomatoes, remove the seeds using a teaspoon and then chop the tomato flesh. Mix the tomato flesh with the canned tomatoes, chopped parsley, crushed garlic and the remaining olive oil in a bowl.

4 Pour the vegetable stock over the aubergine and pepper mixture and then spoon the prepared tomato mixture evenly over the top. Cover the dish with foil and bake for 30–45 minutes. Serve hot, garnished with olives and parsley.

Energy 332Kcal/1387kJ; Protein 11.4g; Carbohydrate 42.5g, of which sugars 21.6g; Fat 14g, of which saturates 2.4g; Cholesterol 0mg; Calcium 110mg; Fibre 10.1g; Sodium 41mg.

MEDITERRANEAN VEGETABLES BAKED in GOLDEN BATTER

Crunchy golden batter surrounds these vegetables, making them delicious and filling. Serve with salad as a light lunch, or with grilled sausages for a more substantial meal.

SERVES 6

1 small aubergine (eggplant), trimmed,
   halved and thickly sliced
1 egg
115g/4oz/1 cup plain (all-purpose) flour
300ml/½ pint/1¼ cups milk
30ml/2 tbsp fresh thyme leaves, or
   10ml/2 tsp dried
1 red onion
2 large courgettes (zucchini)
1 red (bell) pepper
1 yellow (bell) pepper
60–75ml/4–5 tbsp sunflower oil
30ml/2 tbsp freshly grated
   Parmesan cheese
salt and ground black pepper
fresh herbs, to garnish

1 Place the aubergine in a colander or sieve, sprinkle generously with salt and leave for 10 minutes. Drain, rinse well and pat dry on kitchen paper.

2 Meanwhile, beat the egg in a bowl, then gradually beat in the flour and a little milk to make a smooth thick paste. Gradually blend in the rest of the milk, add the thyme leaves and seasoning to taste and stir until smooth. Leave the batter in a cool place until required. Preheat the oven to 220°C/425°F/Gas 7.

COOK'S TIP
As with Yorkshire pudding, it is essential to get the fat in the dish really hot before adding the batter, which should sizzle slightly as it goes in. If the fat is not hot enough, the batter will not rise well. Use a dish that is not too deep.

3 Cut the onion into quarters, slice the courgettes and seed and quarter the peppers. Put the oil in a shallow baking tray or roasting pan and heat in the oven. Add the prepared vegetables, toss them in the oil to coat thoroughly and return the pan to the oven for 20 minutes.

4 Give the batter another whisk, then pour it over the vegetables and return to the oven for about 30 minutes. When the batter is puffed up and golden, reduce the heat to 190°C/375°F/Gas 5 for about 10 minutes, or until the edges are crisp. Sprinkle with Parmesan and herbs.

Energy 231Kcal/966kJ; Protein 8.9g; Carbohydrate 24.1g, of which sugars 8.9g; Fat 11.7g, of which saturates 2.9g; Cholesterol 40mg; Calcium 181mg; Fibre 3.3g; Sodium 93mg.

TRUFFADE

Baked until meltingly soft, this warming cheese and potato supper is the perfect slow
bake to come home to. In France, where it originated, it would be made with a Tomme or
Cantal cheese – look for them in good cheese stores.

SERVES 4–6

a little sunflower oil or melted butter
1 large onion, thinly sliced
675g/1½lb baking potatoes, very
    thinly sliced
150g/5oz/1¼ cups grated hard cheese,
    such as Tomme, Cantal or mature
    (sharp) Cheddar
freshly grated nutmeg
salt and ground black pepper
mixed salad leaves, to serve

VARIATION
In France, they make a non-vegetarian
version of this dish, which is cooked with
finely diced fatty bacon (lardons) and
the cheese is chopped, not grated. The
ingredients are mixed and cooked slowly
in a little lard in a heavy frying pan on top
of the stove.

1 Preheat the oven to 180°C/350°F/
Gas 4. Lightly grease the base of a
shallow baking dish or roasting pan with
the oil or melted butter.

2 Arrange a layer of sliced onion over
the base of the dish, then add a layer of
sliced potatoes and about half of the
grated cheese. Finish with the remaining
onions and a layer of sliced potatoes.

3 Brush the top layer of potatoes with
oil or melted butter and season with
nutmeg, salt and pepper.

4 Sprinkle the remaining grated cheese
over the top and bake for about 1 hour,
or until the vegetables are tender and
the top is golden brown. Leave the dish
to stand for about 5 minutes, then serve
cut in wedges with a salad.

POTATOES BAKED with TOMATOES

This simple, hearty dish from the south of Italy is best made in the summer when
fresh, ripe tomatoes are in season and bursting with flavour.

SERVES 6

90ml/6 tbsp olive oil
2 large red or yellow onions, thinly sliced
1kg/2¼lb baking potatoes, thinly sliced
450g/1lb well-flavoured tomatoes, sliced,
    with their juice
115g/4oz/1 cup freshly grated Parmesan or
    Cheddar cheese
a few fresh basil leaves
50ml/2fl oz/¼ cup water
salt and ground black pepper

1 Preheat the oven to 180°C/350°F/
Gas 4. Brush a large baking dish
generously with 30ml/2 tbsp of the oil.

2 Arrange a layer of some of the thinly
sliced onions in the base of the prepared
dish, followed by a layer of the potatoes
and tomatoes.

3 Drizzle a little of the olive oil over
the potatoes and tomatoes, and sprinkle
with some of the grated cheese. Season
generously with plenty of salt and
ground black pepper.

4 Continue to layer the vegetables in
the dish until they are used up, ending
with an overlapping layer of potatoes
and tomatoes.

5 Reserve a sprig of fresh basil for the
garnish, tear the remaining leaves into
small pieces, and add them here and
there among the vegetables. Sprinkle the
top with the remaining grated cheese
and drizzle with the rest of the oil. Pour
the water evenly over the vegetables and
cheese, then bake for about 1 hour, or
until the vegetables are tender.

6 Check towards the end of the cooking
time and, if the top begins to brown
too much, place a sheet of foil, baking
parchment or a flat baking tray on top
of the dish. Garnish with the remaining
basil, once it is cooked, and serve hot.

VARIATION
If you can't get hold of really flavoursome
tomatoes, a 400g/14oz can of chopped
plum tomatoes can be used instead.

Truffade: Energy 117Kcal/494kJ; Protein 3.2g; Carbohydrate 20.8g, of which sugars 3.4g; Fat 2.9g, of which saturates 1.7g; Cholesterol 7mg; Calcium 40mg; Fibre 1.6g; Sodium 48mg.
Potatoes Baked with Tomatoes: Energy 339Kcal/1418kJ; Protein 11.7g; Carbohydrate 34.4g, of which sugars 8.2g; Fat 18.1g, of which saturates 5.8g; Cholesterol 19mg; Calcium 262mg; Fibre 3.4g; Sodium 236mg.

BAKED SCALLOPED POTATOES with FETA CHEESE and OLIVES

Thinly sliced potatoes are cooked with Greek feta cheese and black and green olives and olive oil. This dish is a good one to serve with toasted pitta bread.

SERVES 4

4–6 large, unpeeled potatoes, total weight
    about 900g/2lb
150ml/¼ pint/⅔ cup extra virgin
    olive oil
leaves from a sprig of rosemary
275g/10oz/2½ cups feta cheese,
    coarsely crumbled
115g/4oz/1 cup pitted mixed black and
    green olives
300ml/½ pint/1¼ cups hot vegetable stock
salt and ground black pepper
toasted pitta bread, to serve

1 Preheat the oven to 200°C/400°F/ Gas 6. Bring a large pan of salted water to the boil and cook the potatoes for 15 minutes until only just tender.

2 Drain the potatoes and set them aside until they are cool enough to handle. Carefully remove the peel from the potatoes using a small sharp knife and then cut them into thin slices.

3 Brush the base and sides of a 1.5 litre/ 2½ pint/6¼ cup rectangular ovenproof dish with some of the olive oil.

COOK'S TIP
Cooking the potatoes with their skins on not only helps to preserve their vitamin content, but will also ensure that the potatoes cook more evenly. If you prefer, peel them before they are cooked.

4 Arrange half the potatoes in the dish in an even layer. Top with half of the rosemary, cheese and olives and season with salt and pepper. Arrange the rest of the potatoes in an even layer on top.

5 Add the remaining rosemary leaves, crumbled cheese and olives, and drizzle with the remaining olive oil. Pour the hot vegetable stock over the top and season the top layer with salt and plenty of ground black pepper.

6 Bake for 35 minutes, covering the dish loosely with foil after about 20 minutes to prevent the potatoes from getting too brown. Serve hot, straight from the dish with the toasted pitta bread.

VARIATION
Thinly sliced sun-dried tomatoes would make a delicious addition.

Energy 584Kcal/2429kJ; Protein 14.8g; Carbohydrate 37.3g, of which sugars 4g; Fat 42.7g, of which saturates 13.7g; Cholesterol 48mg; Calcium 279mg; Fibre 3.1g; Sodium 1662mg.

TOMATO, FETA CHEESE and OLIVE TARTS

These upside-down tartlets are filled with vegetables and chunks of salty cheese. They
make the perfect first course, or may be served with salad leaves for a lunchtime snack.

SERVES 4

25g/1oz sun-dried aubergine
   (eggplant) slices
300ml/½ pint/1¼ cups boiling water
45ml/3 tbsp sunflower oil
1 onion, thinly sliced
150g/5oz/2 cups button (white)
   mushrooms, sliced
1 garlic clove, crushed
12–16 cherry tomatoes, halved
8 black or green olives, pitted
   and chopped
115g/4oz/1 cup feta cheese, crumbled
350g/12oz ready-made puff pastry
salt and ground black pepper

1 Preheat the oven to 200°C/400°F/
Gas 6. Place the aubergine slices in a
shallow dish. Pour over the boiling water
and leave to soak for 10 minutes. Rinse
in cold water, drain and dry on kitchen
paper. Cut the aubergine slices in half or
quarters, depending on their size.

2 Heat 30ml/2 tbsp of the sunflower oil
in a frying pan and fry the onion over a
medium heat for 4–5 minutes. Add the
mushrooms and cook for 3–4 minutes,
or until the onions are light golden.
Remove and set aside.

3 Heat the remaining oil in the frying
pan, add the aubergine slices and garlic
and lightly fry for 1–2 minutes. Lightly oil
four individual cazuelas. Mix the halved
tomatoes with the onions, mushrooms,
aubergines, olives and feta cheese and
divide among the cazuelas. Season well.

4 Roll out the pastry thinly into an
oblong, then cut out four rounds, each
slightly larger than the diameter of the
cazuelas. Place the pastry on top of the
vegetable and cheese mixture, tucking
the overlap down inside the dish.

5 Bake for 20 minutes, or until the
pastry is risen and golden. Cool slightly
then invert on to individual warmed
serving plates to serve.

COOK'S TIP
Choose cherry tomatoes on the vine for
the very best flavour.

Energy 506Kcal/2105kJ; Protein 11.1g; Carbohydrate 35.9g, of which sugars 4.1g; Fat 37.2g, of which saturates 5.2g; Cholesterol 20mg; Calcium 175mg; Fibre 1.6g; Sodium 989mg.

FRITTATA with LEEK, RED PEPPER and SPINACH

Apart from the fact that Italian frittata does not usually contain potato and is generally slightly softer in texture, it is not hugely different from Spanish tortilla. This combination of sweet leek, red pepper and spinach is delicious with the egg.

3 Add the spinach and cover the pan. Allow the spinach to wilt in the steam for 3–4 minutes, then stir to mix it into the vegetables, adding the pine nuts.

4 Beat the eggs with salt, pepper, the remaining cumin, basil and parsley. Add to the pan and cook over a gentle heat until the base of the omelette sets and turns golden brown. Pull the edges of the omelette away from the sides of the pan as it cooks and tilt the pan so that the uncooked egg runs underneath.

5 Preheat the grill (broiler). Flash the frittata under the hot grill to set the egg on top, but do not let it become too brown. Cut the frittata into wedges and serve warm, garnished with watercress and sprinkled with Parmesan, if using.

SERVES 3–4

30ml/2 tbsp olive oil
1 large red (bell) pepper, seeded and diced
2.5–5ml/½–1 tsp ground cumin
3 leeks (about 450g/1lb), thinly sliced
150g/5oz baby spinach leaves
45ml/3 tbsp pine nuts, toasted
5 large (US extra large) eggs
15ml/1 tbsp chopped fresh basil
15ml/1 tbsp chopped fresh flat leaf parsley
salt and ground black pepper
watercress, to garnish
50g/2oz/⅔ cup freshly grated Parmesan
    cheese, to serve (optional)

1 Heat a heavy, non-stick frying pan and add the olive oil. Add the diced red pepper and cook over a medium heat, stirring occasionally, for 6–8 minutes, until the pepper is soft and beginning to brown. Add 2.5ml/½ tsp of the ground cumin, mix well and cook for another 1–2 minutes.

2 Stir in the thinly sliced leeks, then partly cover the pan and cook gently for about 5 minutes, or until the leeks have softened and collapsed. Season the cooked vegetables with plenty of salt and ground black pepper.

VARIATION
A delicious way to serve frittata is to pack it into a slightly hollowed-out loaf and then drizzle it with olive oil. Wrap tightly in clear film (plastic wrap) and stand for 1–2 hours before cutting into slices.

Energy 267Kcal/1107kJ; Protein 12.7g; Carbohydrate 7.1g, of which sugars 6.2g; Fat 21.2g, of which saturates 3.4g; Cholesterol 238mg; Calcium 131mg; Fibre 4.2g; Sodium 144mg.

LENTIL FRITTATA

Throughout the Mediterranean a variety of thick, vegetable omelettes are cooked. This tasty supper dish combines green lentils, red onions, broccoli and cherry tomatoes.

SERVES 4–6

75g/3oz/scant ½ cup green lentils
225g/8oz small broccoli florets
2 red onions, halved and thickly sliced
30ml/2 tbsp olive oil
8 eggs
45ml/3 tbsp milk or water
45ml/3 tbsp chopped mixed herbs, such as
    oregano, parsley, tarragon and chives,
    plus extra sprigs to garnish
175g/6oz cherry tomatoes, halved
salt and ground black pepper

I Place the lentils in a pan, cover with cold water and bring to the boil, reduce the heat and simmer for 25 minutes until tender. Add the broccoli, return to the boil and cook for 1 minute.

VARIATIONS
Add about 50g/2oz/⅔ cup freshly grated Parmesan cheese or 115g/4oz/1 cup diced mozzarella cheese to the egg mixture.

2 Meanwhile place the onion slices and olive oil in a shallow earthenware dish or cazuela about 23–25cm/9–10in in diameter and place in an unheated oven. Set the oven to 200°C/400°F/Gas 6 and cook for 25 minutes.

3 In a bowl, whisk together the eggs, milk or water, a pinch of salt and plenty of black pepper. Stir in the herbs. Drain the lentils and broccoli and stir into the onions. Add the cherry tomatoes. Stir gently to combine.

4 Pour the egg mixture evenly over the vegetables. Reduce the oven to 190°C/375°F/Gas 5. Return the dish to the oven and cook for 10 minutes, then push the mixture into the centre of the dish using a spatula, allowing the raw mixture in the centre to flow to the edges.

5 Return the dish to the oven and cook the frittata for a further 15 minutes, or until it is just set. Garnish with sprigs of fresh herbs and serve warm, cut into thick wedges.

Energy 200Kcal/836kJ; Protein 13.6g; Carbohydrate 11.3g, of which sugars 3.6g; Fat 11.7g, of which saturates 2.7g; Cholesterol 254mg; Calcium 76mg; Fibre 2.4g; Sodium 105mg.

BULGUR WHEAT, ASPARAGUS and BROAD BEAN PILAFF

Nutty-textured bulgur wheat is usually simply soaked in boiling water until it is softened, but it can be cooked like rice to make a pilaff. Here it is combined with broad beans, herbs and lemon and orange rinds, which add a fresh, springtime flavour.

SERVES 4

250g/9oz/1½ cups bulgur wheat
750–900ml/1¼–1½ pints/3–3¾ cups warm
   vegetable stock
225g/8oz asparagus spears
225g/8oz/2 cups frozen broad (fava)
   beans, thawed
8 spring onions (scallions), chopped
15ml/1 tbsp grated lemon rind
15ml/1 tbsp grated orange rind
40g/1½oz/3 tbsp butter, cut into
   small pieces
60ml/4 tbsp chopped fresh flat leaf parsley
30ml/2 tbsp chopped fresh dill, plus extra
   sprigs to garnish
salt and ground black pepper

1 If using a clay pot, soak in cold water for 20 minutes, then drain. Place the bulgur wheat in the clay pot or in a shallow, ovenproof earthenware dish and pour over 600ml/1 pint/2½ cups of the stock. Season with salt and pepper.

VARIATIONS
• Try using fresh green beans and either fresh or frozen peas in place of the asparagus and broad beans and, instead of using dill, stir in plenty of chopped fresh mint along with the parsley.
• If you'd like to add a little extra colour to the pilaff, then stir in some finely shredded red (bell) pepper, or some peeled and seeded wedges of tomato.
• To make a richer pilaff, stir in some finely grated Parmesan cheese along with the butter in step 6.

2 Cut the asparagus spears into 2.5cm/ 1in lengths, discarding any hard, woody ends from the stems. Add the asparagus pieces to the clay pot or dish and gently stir these into the bulgur wheat.

3 Cover the clay pot or dish tightly and place in an unheated oven. Set the oven to 200°C/400°F/Gas 6 and then cook the bulgur wheat and asparagus for 20 minutes.

4 Meanwhile pop the broad beans out of their shells and then stir the beans into the bulgur pilaff after it has cooked for about 20 minutes, adding a little more stock at the same time. Re-cover the clay pot or dish and return the dish to the oven for about 10 minutes.

COOK'S TIP
If your clay pot or earthenware dish doesn't have its own lid, then cover the pot or dish with foil, crimping it around the edge to seal. Or, if the top of the dish is completely flat, then you can simply place a flat, heavy baking sheet on top.

5 Stir in the spring onions, grated lemon and orange rind. Add a little more stock, if necessary. Cover and return to the oven for 5 minutes.

6 Dot the pieces of butter over the top of the pilaff and leave to stand, covered, for 5 minutes.

7 Add the chopped parsley and dill to the pilaff and stir well with a fork, to fluff up the bulgur wheat and distribute the herbs evenly. Check the seasoning and add salt and plenty of black pepper. Serve the pilaff hot, garnished with sprigs of fresh dill.

Energy 285Kcal/1188kJ; Protein 10.5g; Carbohydrate 40.8g, of which sugars 2.7g; Fat 9.8g, of which saturates 5.4g; Cholesterol 21mg; Calcium 93mg; Fibre 5.5g; Sodium 71mg.

BASMATI RICE and NUT PILAFF

Vegetarians will love this simple pilaff. Add wild or cultivated mushrooms, if you like.

SERVES 4

15–30ml/1–2 tbsp sunflower oil
1 onion, chopped
1 garlic clove, crushed
1 large carrot, coarsely grated
225g/8oz/generous 1 cup basmati
    rice, soaked
5ml/1 tsp cumin seeds
10ml/2 tsp ground coriander
10ml/2 tsp black mustard seeds (optional)
4 green cardamom pods
450ml/¾ pint/scant 2 cups vegetable
    stock or water
1 bay leaf
75g/3oz/½ cup shelled walnuts and/or
    unsalted cashew nuts
salt and ground black pepper
fresh parsley or coriander (cilantro)
    sprigs, to garnish

1 Heat the oil in a large frying pan. Add the onion, garlic and carrot and cook for 3–4 minutes, stirring occasionally.

2 Drain the rice and add it to the pan with the cumin seeds, ground coriander, black mustard seeds, if using, and the green cardamom pods. Cook for about 1 minute, stirring to coat the grains in oil.

3 Pour in the vegetable stock or water, add the bay leaf and season well with salt and pepper. Bring to the boil, then lower the heat, cover and simmer very gently for 10–12 minutes.

4 Remove the frying pan from the heat without lifting the lid. Leave to stand in a warm place for about 5 minutes, then check the rice. If it is cooked, there will be small steam holes on the surface of the rice. Remove the bay leaf and the cardamom pods.

5 Stir the walnuts and/or cashew nuts into the rice mixture. Taste to check the seasoning and add more salt and pepper if necessary. Spoon into warmed individual bowls or on to a large platter, garnish with the sprigs of fresh parsley or coriander and serve immediately.

COOK'S TIPS
• Use whichever nuts you prefer in this pilaff – even unsalted peanuts taste good – although almonds, brazil nuts, cashew nuts or pistachio nuts add a slightly more exotic flavour.
• If you don't have basmati rice, then use any other long grain rice. Thai jasmine rice has a particularly good flavour.

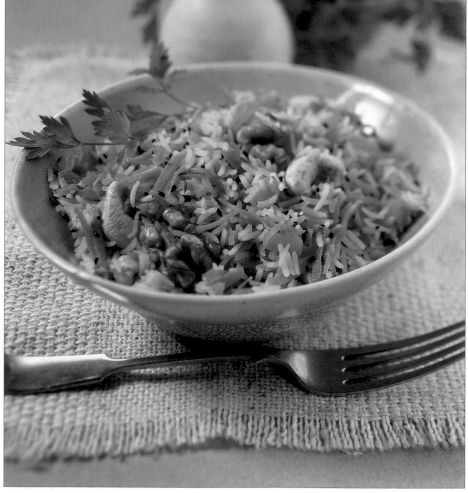

Energy 370Kcal/1538kJ; Protein 7.3g; Carbohydrate 48.7g, of which sugars 3.2g; Fat 16g, of which saturates 1.4g; Cholesterol 0mg; Calcium 38mg; Fibre 1.5g; Sodium 8mg.

VEGETABLE COUSCOUS with SAFFRON and HARISSA

This spicy, north African dish makes an excellent main meal, or serve as part of a vegetarian buffet.

SERVES 4

45ml/3 tbsp olive oil
1 onion, chopped
2 garlic cloves, crushed
5ml/1 tsp ground cumin
5ml/1 tsp paprika
400g/14oz can chopped tomatoes
300ml/½ pint/1¼ cups vegetable stock
1 cinnamon stick
generous pinch of saffron threads
4 baby aubergines (eggplant), quartered
8 baby courgettes (zucchini), trimmed
8 baby carrots
225g/8oz/1⅓ cups couscous
425g/15oz can chickpeas, drained
175g/6oz/¾ cup pitted prunes
45ml/3 tbsp chopped fresh parsley
45ml/3 tbsp chopped fresh coriander
10–15ml/2–3 tsp harissa
salt

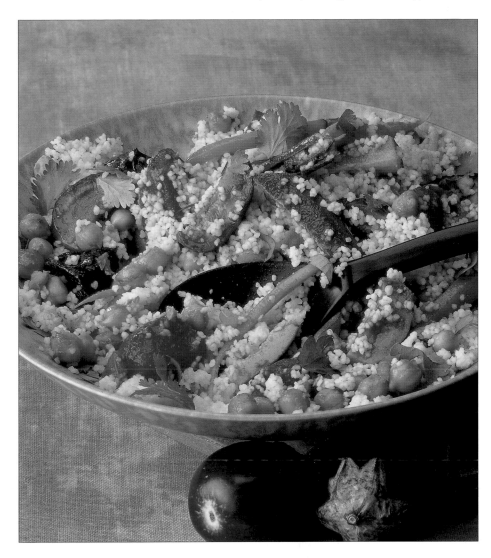

1 Heat the olive oil in a large pan. Add the onion and garlic and cook gently for 5 minutes until soft. Add the cumin and paprika and cook, stirring, for 1 minute.

2 Add the tomatoes, stock, cinnamon stick, saffron, aubergines, courgettes and carrots, and season with salt. Bring to the boil, cover, lower the heat and cook gently for 20 minutes until the vegetables are just tender.

3 Line a steamer or colander with a double thickness of muslin (cheesecloth). Soak the couscous according to the instructions on the packet.

COOK'S TIPS
• Couscous is made from durum wheat and has a similar appearance to semolina. It has a very mild flavour and takes on the flavour of any ingredients it is mixed with. Most couscous is sold pre-cooked and only needs to be re-hydrated in boiling water or according to packet instructions.
• Harissa is a spicy paste made from red chillies, coriander, caraway, garlic, salt and olive oil. Its bright red/orange colour is an indicator of its fiery flavour. It is sold in cans, jars and tubes.

4 Add the chickpeas and prunes to the vegetables, stir and cook for 5 minutes.

5 Spread the couscous in the prepared steamer. Place the steamer on top of the vegetables, cover and cook for 5 minutes until the couscous is hot.

6 Stir the herbs into the vegetables. Heap the couscous on to a serving dish. Using a slotted spoon, remove the vegetables from the frying pan and add to the couscous. Spoon over a little sauce and toss gently. Stir the harissa into the remaining sauce and serve separately.

Energy 463Kcal/1942kJ; Protein 16.2g; Carbohydrate 73.4g, of which sugars 26.9g; Fat 13.5g, of which saturates 1.9g; Cholesterol 0mg; Calcium 152mg; Fibre 12.7g; Sodium 267mg.

VEGETABLE PAELLA

*A colourful assortment of vegetables is cooked slowly with rice to make this tasty –
slightly spicy – vegetarian meal.*

SERVES 4

1 large aubergine (eggplant)
45ml/3 tbsp extra virgin olive or
   sunflower oil
2 onions, quartered and sliced
2 garlic cloves, crushed
300g/11oz/1½ cups short grain Spanish or
   risotto rice
1.2–1.5 litres/2–2½ pints/5–6¼ cups
   vegetable stock
1 red (bell) pepper, halved, seeded
   and sliced
1 yellow (bell) pepper, halved, seeded
   and sliced
200g/7oz fine green beans, halved
115g/4oz/scant 2 cups chestnut
   mushrooms, quartered, or brown
   cap (cremini) or button (white)
   mushrooms, halved
1 dried chilli, crushed
115g/4oz/1 cup frozen peas
salt and ground black pepper
fresh coriander (cilantro) leaves,
   to garnish

1 Soak a clay pot or Chinese sand pot
in cold water for 20 minutes, then drain.
Cut the aubergine in half lengthwise,
then cut it crosswise into thin slices.

COOK'S TIP

Although nowadays aubergines don't need
to be salted to remove the bitter flavour
they used to have, salting them does
ensure that they absorb less oil when
they are fried. So, if you have the time,
layer the slices in a colander and sprinkle
each layer with salt. Leave the slices to
drain for about 30 minutes, then rinse
thoroughly and pat dry before frying.

2 Heat 30ml/2 tbsp of the oil in a large
frying pan, add the aubergine slices and
quickly sauté until slightly golden.
Transfer to the clay pot.

3 Add the remaining oil, add the onion
and cook, stirring occasionally, for a few
minutes until golden.

4 Add the garlic and rice and cook for
1–2 minutes, stirring, until the rice
becomes transparent. Pour in 900ml/
1½ pints/3¾ cups of the stock into the
clay pot, then add the rice mixture.

5 Add the peppers, halved green beans,
mushrooms, crushed chilli and seasoning.
Stir to mix, then cover the pot and place
in an unheated oven.

6 Set the oven to 200°C/400°F/Gas 6
and cook for 1 hour, or until the rice is
almost tender. After 40 minutes, remove
the pot from the oven and add a little
more stock to moisten the paella. Stir
well, re-cover and return to the oven.

7 Add the peas and a little more stock
to the paella and cook for a further
10 minutes. Adjust the seasoning and
sprinkle over the coriander. Lightly stir
through and then serve.

VARIATIONS

• Almost any roughly chopped or sliced
vegetables can be used in this dish.
Broccoli, carrots, cauliflower, courgettes
(zucchini) and okra are all suitable – or
try using frozen sweetcorn in place of all
or some of the peas.
• For a tomato-flavoured paella, use a
400g/14oz can chopped tomatoes in place
of 350ml/12floz/1½ cups of the stock.

Energy 458Kcal/1911kJ; Protein 11.8g; Carbohydrate 80g, of which sugars 14.3g; Fat 10.3g, of which saturates 1.5g; Cholesterol 0mg; Calcium 80mg; Fibre 7.1g; Sodium 10mg.

CLAY-POT RISOTTO with SPINACH and SAFFRON

Rice cooks to perfection in the moist environment of a clay pot. This risotto can be made without the constant checking required when cooked on top of the stove.

SERVES 4

a few saffron threads
30ml/2 tbsp boiling water
15ml/1 tbsp olive oil
50g/2oz/¼ cup butter
1 onion, finely chopped
350g/12oz/1¾ cups risotto rice
900ml/1½ pints/3¾ cups warm
    vegetable stock
150ml/¼ pint/⅔ cup dry white wine
225g/8oz baby spinach leaves
300ml/½ pint/1¼ cups hot vegetable stock
40g/1½oz/¼ cup shelled walnuts, chopped
75g/3oz Parmesan cheese, very
    finely shaved
salt and ground black pepper

1 Soak a large clay pot in cold water for 20 minutes, then drain. Meanwhile, place the saffron in a bowl, cover with the boiling water and leave to infuse (steep).

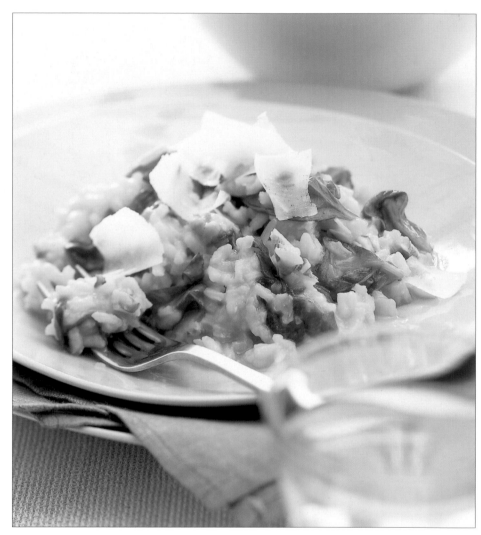

2 Heat the oil and half the butter in a large, heavy pan. Add the finely chopped onion and cook gently for 5 minutes, or until soft, stirring occasionally. Add the rice and stir over the heat for about 3 minutes until the grains are thoroughly coated in oil and butter.

COOK'S TIP
Risotto rice is short grain rice that is widely used in Italy to make a variety of different types of risotto. Arborio rice is the most widely available type, but you may also find carnaroli and vialone nano. When cooked, risotto rice has a creamy consistency but the grains retain a slight "bite" to their texture.

3 Pour the warm stock into the clay pot, add the saffron water, wine and the rice mixture and stir together. Cover and place in an unheated oven. Set the oven to 190°C/375°F/Gas 5 and cook for 50 minutes, stirring after 30 minutes.

4 Stir in the spinach, add the stock, then cover and cook for 10 minutes, or until the rice is tender. Stir in the walnuts, the remaining butter and half the Parmesan cheese. Season and serve sprinkled with the remaining Parmesan cheese.

Energy 630Kcal/2618kJ; Protein 17.2g; Carbohydrate 72.6g, of which sugars 2.3g; Fat 26.9g, of which saturates 11.4g; Cholesterol 45mg; Calcium 356mg; Fibre 1.8g; Sodium 362mg.

TAGLIATELLE BAKED with MUSHROOMS, GORGONZOLA and WALNUTS

This rich, creamy dish is perfect served as a lunch or supper dish with a mixed leaf salad.

2 Meanwhile, place the tagliatelle in a large pan of boiling salted water and cook according to packet instructions or until just tender.

3 Remove the mushrooms and leeks and set aside. Crumble the Gorgonzola cheese into the frying pan and stir over a gentle heat, until melted. Stir in the creams and the dry vermouth or white wine and season to taste.

SERVES 4

25g/1oz/2 tbsp butter
15ml/1 tbsp vegetable oil
350g/12oz/4 cups chestnut mushrooms, quartered, or brown cap (crimini) mushrooms, halved
2 leeks, thinly sliced
400g/14oz mixed spinach and plain tagliatelle
175g/6oz Gorgonzola cheese
150ml/¼ pint/⅔ cup double (heavy) cream
200ml/7fl oz/scant 1 cup thick single (light) cream
90ml/6 tbsp dry vermouth or white wine
50g/2oz/½ cup walnuts, finely chopped
75g/3oz/1 cup grated Parmesan cheese
salt and ground black pepper

1 Preheat the oven to 200°C/400°F/Gas 6. Melt the butter with the oil in a large sauté pan or deep frying pan, add the quartered chestnut mushrooms or halved brown cap mushrooms and the thinly sliced leeks and stir-fry the vegetables together for 4–5 minutes.

4 Drain the pasta and divide it among four individual cazuelas or other shallow ovenproof earthenware dishes. Top with the mushrooms and leeks, spreading them over the pasta. Pour over the sauce, sprinkle the chopped walnuts and Parmesan cheese on top and bake for about 15 minutes, or until the cheese is golden brown and bubbling.

VARIATION
Any type of pasta shapes can be used in this bake in place of the tagliatelle. However, other long ribbon pastas, such as linguine and bucatini, and hollow tube pastas that scoop up the sauce, such as macaroni, penne or rigatoni, will work particularly well.

Energy 1050Kcal/4384kJ; Protein 35.3g; Carbohydrate 79.9g, of which sugars 8.2g; Fat 65.3g, of which saturates 34g; Cholesterol 137mg; Calcium 559mg; Fibre 6.5g; Sodium 808mg.

SPAGHETTI with ROCKET PESTO

This is the pesto for real rocket lovers. It is sharp and peppery, and delicious for a summer pasta meal with a glass of chilled dry white wine.

SERVES 4

4 garlic cloves
90ml/6 tbsp pine nuts
2 large handfuls of rocket (arugula), total
   weight about 150g/5oz, stalks removed
50g/2oz/⅔ cup freshly grated
   Parmesan cheese
50g/2oz/⅔ cup freshly grated
   Pecorino cheese
90ml/6 tbsp extra virgin olive oil
400g/14oz fresh or dried spaghetti
salt and ground black pepper
freshly grated Parmesan and Pecorino
   cheese, to serve

1 Put the garlic and pine nuts in a food processor or blender and process until finely chopped. Add the rocket, grated Parmesan and Pecorino, and olive oil.

2 Add salt and pepper, to taste and process for 5 seconds. Stop and scrape down the side of the bowl, then process for 5–10 seconds more until a smooth paste is formed.

3 Cook the spaghetti in a large pan of boiling salted water until just tender, or according to the packet instructions.

4 Spoon the pesto into a large mixing bowl. Just before the pasta is ready, add one or two ladlefuls of the cooking water to the pesto and stir well to mix.

5 Drain the pasta, tip it into the bowl of pesto and toss well to mix. Serve immediately, with the grated cheeses handed separately.

VARIATION
To temper the flavour of the rocket and make the pesto milder, add 115g/4oz/ ½ cup ricotta or mascarpone cheese to the pesto in step 4 and mix well before adding the water.

Energy 621Kcal/2610kJ; Protein 26.1g; Carbohydrate 75.6g, of which sugars 4.8g; Fat 25.9g, of which saturates 6.4g; Cholesterol 25mg; Calcium 392mg; Fibre 4.2g; Sodium 362mg.

PASTA SHELLS with TOMATOES and RICOTTA

Nothing could be more simple than hot pasta tossed with fresh ripe tomatoes, ricotta cheese and sweet basil. Serve it on hot summer days – it is surprisingly refreshing.

SERVES 4–6

350g/12oz/3 cups dried conchiglie
130g/4½oz/generous ½ cup ricotta cheese
6 ripe plum tomatoes, diced
2 garlic cloves, crushed
a handful of fresh basil leaves, shredded,
    plus extra basil leaves to garnish
60ml/4 tbsp extra virgin olive oil
salt and ground black pepper

1 Cook the pasta in boiling salted water according to the packet instructions.

VARIATIONS
• Use diced mozzarella instead of ricotta.
• An avocado is the ideal ingredient for adding extra colour and flavour to this pasta dish. Halve, stone (pit) and peel, then dice the flesh. Toss it with the hot pasta at the last minute.

2 Meanwhile, put the ricotta cheese in a large mixing bowl and mash with a fork until soft and creamy.

3 Add the diced tomatoes (see Cook's Tip), crushed garlic and shredded basil to the softened ricotta cheese, with salt and pepper to taste, and mix well. Add the olive oil and whisk thoroughly. Taste for seasoning.

4 Drain the cooked pasta, tip it into the ricotta and tomato mixture and toss well to mix. Garnish with basil leaves and serve immediately, sprinkled with black pepper.

COOK'S TIP
If you like, skin the tomatoes before you dice them by plunging them into boiling water for 30 seconds and then refresh in cold water before peeling.

Energy 318Kcal/1342kJ; Protein 9.6g; Carbohydrate 46.5g, of which sugars 5.2g; Fat 11.8g, of which saturates 3.2g; Cholesterol 9mg; Calcium 21mg; Fibre 2.5g; Sodium 9mg.

BUCKWHEAT NOODLES with CABBAGE, POTATOES and CHEESE

This is a very unusual pasta dish from Valtellina in the Italian Alps. The pale brown buckwheat noodles called pizzoccheri are unique to this area.

SERVES 6

400g/14oz Savoy cabbage, cut into
   1cm/½in strips
2 potatoes, total weight about 200g/7oz,
   cut into 5mm/¼in slices
400g/14oz dried pizzoccheri
   (buckwheat noodles)
75g/3oz/6 tbsp butter
1 generous bunch fresh sage
   leaves, shredded
2 garlic cloves
200g/7oz Fontina cheese, rind removed
   and thinly sliced
30–45ml/2–3 tbsp freshly grated
   Parmesan cheese, plus extra to serve
salt and ground black pepper

COOK'S TIPS
• Look for packets of dried pizzoccheri pasta in Italian delicatessens.
• Fontina is an Italian mountain cheese with a sweet, nutty taste. If you cannot get it, look for Taleggio, Gruyère or Emmenthal – they are all similar cheeses.

1 Bring a very large pan of salted water to the boil. Add the cabbage strips and potato slices and boil for 5 minutes.

2 Add the pasta to the pan, stir well and let the water return to the boil over a high heat. Lower the heat and simmer for about 15 minutes, or according to the instructions on the packet, until the pasta is just tender.

3 Drain the pasta and vegetables and set aside. Melt the butter in the pan. Add the sage and whole garlic cloves and fry over a low to medium heat until the garlic is golden and sizzling. Lift the garlic out of the pan and discard it. Set the sage and garlic butter aside.

4 Pour one-quarter of the pasta and vegetable mixture into a warmed large bowl and arrange about one-third of the Fontina slices on top. Repeat these layers until all the ingredients have been used, then sprinkle with the grated Parmesan. Pour the sage and garlic butter over the top and serve immediately, with extra grated Parmesan handed separately.

VARIATION
You could use chard or spinach instead of the cabbage. Spinach will need much less cooking, so add it to the pan about 5 minutes before the end of the cooking time in step 2.

FETTUCINE with BUTTER and PARMESAN

Very few ingredients are needed to make up this incredibly simple dish. It comes from northern Italy, where butter and cheeses are the most popular ingredients for serving with pasta. This dish is especially popular with children.

SERVES 4

400g/14oz fresh or dried fettucine
50g/2oz/¼ cup unsalted (sweet)
   butter, cubed
115g/4oz/1¼ cups freshly grated
   Parmesan cheese
salt and ground black pepper

VARIATIONS
• Other long pastas would be just as good in this recipe; try spaghetti, linguine or tagliatelle. Spinach or tomato flavoured versions would also work well.
• Try freshly grated Pecorino cheese instead of the Parmesan.

1 Cook the pasta in a large pan of salted boiling water until just tender, or according to the instructions on the packet. Drain thoroughly, then tip the pasta into a large warmed bowl.

2 Add the cubes of butter and the grated Parmesan, one-third at a time, tossing the pasta after each addition until it is evenly coated. Season to taste and serve immediately.

Buckwheat Noodles: Energy 469Kcal/1958kJ; Protein 17.9g; Carbohydrate 70.7g, of which sugars 4.4g; Fat 13.9g, of which saturates 8.3g; Cholesterol 37mg; Calcium 351mg; Fibre 3.5g; Sodium 308mg.
Fettucine with Butter and Parmesan: Energy 565Kcal/2379kJ; Protein 23.4g; Carbohydrate 74.2g, of which sugars 3.4g; Fat 21.5g, of which saturates 12.6g; Cholesterol 55mg; Calcium 372mg; Fibre 2.9g; Sodium 392mg.

PASTA TWISTS with PESTO

Bottled pesto is a useful stand-by, but if you have a food processor or blender, it is very easy to make a delicious home-made version.

SERVES 4

50g/2oz fresh basil leaves, plus extra fresh
    basil leaves, to garnish
2–4 garlic cloves
60ml/4 tbsp pine nuts
120ml/4fl oz/½ cup extra virgin
    olive oil
115g/4oz/1¼ cups freshly grated Parmesan
    cheese, plus extra to serve
25g/1oz/¼ cup freshly grated
    Pecorino cheese
400g/14oz/3½ cups dried pasta
    twists (fusilli)
salt and ground black pepper

1 Put the basil, garlic and pine nuts in a food processor. Add 60ml/4 tbsp of the oil. Process until chopped, then stop the machine and scrape the bowl.

2 Turn the machine on again and slowly add the remaining olive oil in a thin, steady stream through the feeder tube. You may need to stop the machine and scrape down the sides of the bowl once or twice to make sure that everything is evenly mixed.

3 Scrape the mixture into a large bowl and beat in the cheeses with a wooden spoon. Taste and add salt and ground black pepper if necessary.

4 Cook the pasta in a large pan of salted boiling water for 10 minutes, or according to the instructions on the packet, until just tender. Drain the pasta well, then add it to the bowl of pesto and toss well. Serve immediately, garnished with the extra fresh basil leaves. Hand around the extra shaved Parmesan separately.

COOK'S TIP
Fresh pesto can be made up to 2–3 days in advance. To store it, transfer the pesto to a small bowl and pour a thin film of olive oil over the surface. Cover the bowl tightly with clear film (plastic wrap) and keep it in the refrigerator.

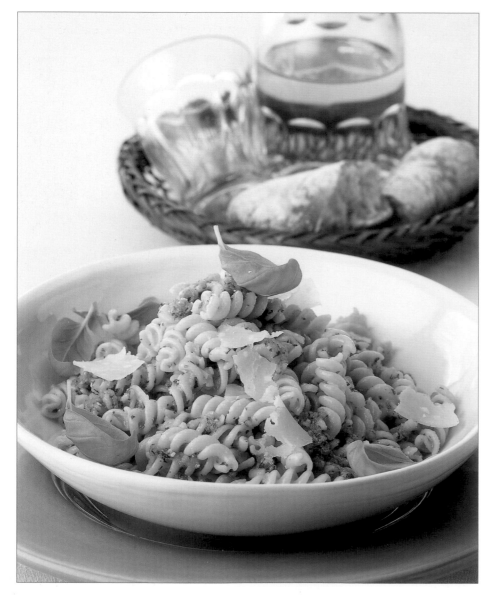

Energy 799Kcal/3343kJ; Protein 28.3g; Carbohydrate 75g, of which sugars 4.2g; Fat 44.9g, of which saturates 11.1g; Cholesterol 35mg; Calcium 472mg; Fibre 3.8g; Sodium 389mg.

PASTA with CHEESE and CREAM

The Italian name for this dish – Mezzanotte – means middle of the night, which is when this rich and filling dish is eaten – after a night on the tiles. When you arrive home hungry from a party, it's just the thing to sober you up!

SERVES 4

400g/14oz/3½ cups dried rigatoni
3 egg yolks
105ml/7 tbsp grated Parmesan cheese
200g/7oz/scant 1 cup ricotta cheese
60ml/4 tbsp double (heavy) cream
nutmeg
40g/1½oz/3 tbsp butter
salt and ground black pepper

1 Cook the pasta according to the instructions on the packet.

2 Meanwhile, mix the egg yolks, grated Parmesan and ricotta together in a bowl. Add the cream and mix with a fork.

3 Grate in nutmeg to taste, then season with plenty of black pepper and a little salt. Drain the pasta thoroughly when cooked. Return the clean pan to the heat. Melt the butter, add the drained pasta and toss over a medium heat.

4 Turn off the heat under the pan and add the ricotta mixture. Stir well with a large spoon for 10–15 seconds, or until all the pasta is coated in sauce. Serve immediately, in warmed individual bowls with plenty of ground black pepper.

Energy 670Kcal/2816kJ; Protein 29.2g; Carbohydrate 75.7g, of which sugars 4.9g; Fat 30g, of which saturates 16.5g; Cholesterol 220mg; Calcium 359mg; Fibre 2.9g; Sodium 357mg.

GLOBE ARTICHOKE SALAD

Globe artichokes are grown widely in country gardens – as much for their architectural qualities in the garden as for the table. This salad makes a versatile first course, and is equally good served hot or cold.

SERVES 4

4 artichokes
juice of 1 lemon
900ml/1½ pints/3¾ cups home-made
  vegetable stock and water mixed
2 garlic cloves, chopped
1 small bunch parsley
6 whole peppercorns
15ml/1 tbsp olive oil, plus extra
  for drizzling

1 To prepare the artichokes: trim the stalks of the artichokes close to the base, cut the very tips off the leaves and then divide them into quarters. Remove the inedible hairy choke (the central part), carefully scraping the hairs away from the heart at the base of the artichoke.

2 Squeeze a little of the lemon juice over the cut surfaces of the artichokes to prevent discoloration.

3 Put the artichokes into a pan and cover with the stock and water, garlic, parsley, peppercorns and olive oil. Cover with a lid and cook gently for 1 hour, or until the artichokes are tender. They are ready when the leaves will come away easily when pulled.

4 Remove the artichokes with a slotted spoon and keep them warm if serving hot. Boil the cooking liquor hard without the lid, to reduce by half, and then strain.

5 To serve, arrange the artichokes in small serving dishes and pour over the reduced juices. Drizzle over a little extra olive oil and lemon juice. Provide finger bowls and a large bowl for the leaves. To eat, pull a leaf away from the artichoke and scrape the fleshy part at the base with your teeth. Discard the remainder of the leaves and then eat the heart at the base.

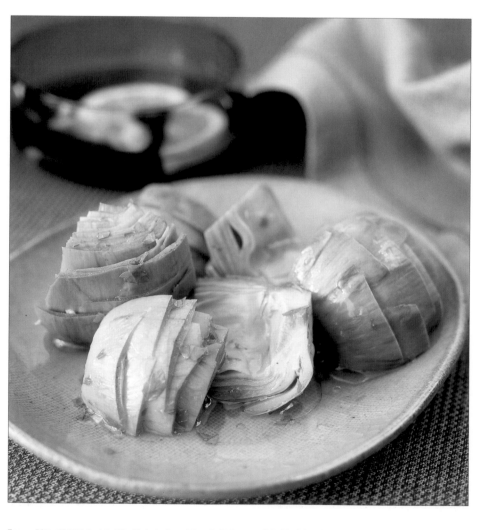

VARIATION
The fleshy bases of the leaves and the artichoke heart or "fond" can be nibbled warm or cold with a dip such as hollandaise sauce or a vinaigrette. Serve with finger bowls and a large dish for the debris.

Energy 59Kcal/245kJ; Protein 0.7g; Carbohydrate 7.8g, of which sugars 7.3g; Fat 3.1g, of which saturates 0.5g; Cholesterol 0mg; Calcium 25mg; Fibre 2.4g; Sodium 61mg

BEETROOT with LEMON DRESSING

Beetroot is often grown in large kitchen gardens attached to country houses, where it also features on menus in the summer. It is widely enjoyed and often used fresh rather than in the pickled form more familiar in other northern European countries.

SERVES 4

450g/1lb evenly-sized raw beetroot (beets)
grated rind and juice of ½ lemon
about 150ml/¼ pint/⅔ cup extra virgin
    olive oil (or a mixture of olive and
    sunflower oil, blended to taste)
sea salt and ground black pepper
chopped fresh chives, to garnish (optional)

COOK'S TIP

To avoid the beetroots "bleeding" during cooking, twist off the tops rather than cutting them with a knife.

1 Twist off the tops from the beetroot (see Cook's tip), and cook in a large pan of salted boiling water for about 30 minutes, or until the beetroot is tender. Pinch the skin between two fingers: when cooked, the skin will come away easily. Drain the beetroot and allow it to cool.

2 Peel when cool and slice into wedges into a bowl. Add the lemon rind and juice, and the oil; season to taste. Mix gently in the dressing and serve.

VARIATION

Serve as a side dish or a first course, adding a few chopped chives, if you like.

Energy 265Kcal/1097kJ; Protein 1.9g; Carbohydrate 8.6g, of which sugars 7.9g; Fat 25.1g, of which saturates 3.6g; Cholesterol 0mg; Calcium 23mg; Fibre 2.2g; Sodium 74mg

CAULIFLOWER with TOMATOES and CUMIN

This makes an excellent side dish to serve with grilled meat or fish.

SERVES 4

30ml/2 tbsp sunflower or olive oil
1 onion, chopped
1 garlic clove, crushed
1 small cauliflower, broken into florets
5ml/1 tsp cumin seeds
good pinch of ground ginger
4 tomatoes, peeled, seeded
   and quartered
175ml/6fl oz/¾ cup water
15–30ml/1–2 tbsp lemon juice (optional)
salt and ground black pepper
30ml/2 tbsp chopped fresh coriander
   (cilantro) (optional)

VARIATIONS
• Use a 200g/7oz can of chopped
tomatoes instead of the fresh tomatoes.
• Broccoli florets can be used in place of
the cauliflower, if you prefer.

1 Heat the oil in a flameproof casserole, add the onion and garlic and stir-fry for 2–3 minutes until the onion is softened. Add the cauliflower and stir-fry for a further 2–3 minutes until the cauliflower is flecked with brown. Add the cumin seeds and ginger, and fry briskly for 1 minute, then add the peeled, seeded and quartered tomatoes, the water and some salt and pepper to taste.

2 Bring to the boil, then reduce the heat, cover with a plate or with foil and simmer for 6–7 minutes, or until the cauliflower is just tender.

3 Stir in a little lemon juice to sharpen the flavour, if you like, and adjust the seasoning if necessary. Sprinkle over the chopped fresh coriander, if using, and serve immediately.

ROAST VEGETABLES with FRESH HERBS and CHILLI SAUCE

Oven roasting brings out all the flavours of these classic Mediterranean vegetables. Serve them hot with grilled or roast meat or fish.

SERVES 4

2–3 courgettes (zucchini)
1 large onion
1 red (bell) pepper
16 cherry tomatoes
2 garlic cloves, chopped
pinch of cumin seeds
5ml/1 tsp fresh thyme or 4–5 torn
   basil leaves
60ml/4 tbsp olive oil
juice of ½ lemon
5–10ml/1–2 tsp harissa
fresh thyme sprigs, to garnish

COOK'S TIP
Harissa is a spicy paste made from a base of beetroot (beets) and carrots and flavoured with chillies, coriander seeds, caraway, garlic, salt and olive oil. It is a popular ingredient in northern African cooking and is sold in small pots – look out for its distinctive orangey red colour.

1 Preheat the oven to 220°C/425°F/ Gas 7. Trim the courgettes and then cut them into long thin strips. Cut the onion into thin wedges and cut the pepper into fairly large chunks, discarding the seeds and core.

VARIATION
Other vegetables would work well in this dish. Add wedges of red and yellow (bell) peppers in place of one of the courgettes, or add chunks of aubergine (eggplant).

2 Place the vegetables in a large roasting pan, add the tomatoes, chopped garlic, cumin seeds and thyme or basil. Sprinkle with the olive oil and toss to coat. Cook in the oven for 25–30 minutes until the vegetables are very soft and slightly charred at the edges.

3 Blend the lemon juice with the harissa and stir into the roasted vegetables just before serving, garnished with the fresh thyme sprigs.

Cauliflower with Tomatoes and Cumin: Energy 106Kcal/441kJ; Protein 4.5g; Carbohydrate 7.3g, of which sugars 6.5g; Fat 6.7g, of which saturates 1g; Cholesterol 0mg; Calcium 32mg; Fibre 3g; Sodium 19mg.
Roast Vegetables with Fresh Herbs: Energy 154Kcal/635kJ; Protein 3.7g; Carbohydrate 8.2g, of which sugars 7.6g; Fat 12g, of which saturates 1.8g; Cholesterol 0mg; Calcium 48mg; Fibre 2.8g; Sodium 8mg.

ROASTED TOMATOES and GARLIC

These are so simple to prepare yet taste absolutely wonderful. Use a large, shallow earthenware dish that will allow the tomatoes to sear and char in a very hot oven.

SERVES 4

8 well-flavoured tomatoes (see Cook's
    Tip), halved
12 garlic cloves, unpeeled
60ml/4 tbsp extra virgin olive oil
3–4 bay leaves
salt and ground black pepper
45ml/3 tbsp fresh oregano leaves,
    to garnish

COOK'S TIP
If possible use ripe plum tomatoes for
this recipe as they not only keep their
shape and their delicious flavour, but also
do not fall apart when roasted at such a
high temperature. Leave the stalks on the
tomatoes, if you like.

1 Preheat the oven to 230°C/450°F/
Gas 8. Select a large, shallow ovenproof
dish that will hold all the tomato halves
snugly in a single layer. Arrange the
tomatoes in the dish and tuck the whole,
unpeeled garlic cloves evenly in among
the tomatoes.

2 Brush the tomatoes with the oil, add
the bay leaves and sprinkle black pepper
over the top. Bake for about 45 minutes,
or until the tomatoes have softened and
are sizzling in the dish. Season with salt
and more black pepper, if needed.
Garnish with oregano leaves and serve.

Energy 138Kcal/571kJ; Protein 2g; Carbohydrate 6.6g, of which sugars 5.6g; Fat 11.7g, of which saturates 1.8g; Cholesterol 0mg; Calcium 36mg; Fibre 2.5g; Sodium 19mg.

SLOW-COOKED SPICED ONIONS

Onions marinated and baked in a spicy sauce are delicious with grilled or roasted meats.
Choose a good, extra virgin olive oil for a rich, peppery flavour.

SERVES 4

675g/1½lb Spanish or red onions
90ml/6 tbsp olive or sunflower oil or a
    mixture of both
pinch of saffron threads
2.5ml/½ tsp ground ginger
5ml/1 tsp ground black pepper
5ml/1 tsp ground cinnamon
15ml/1 tbsp sugar

1 Slice the onions very thinly and place them in a shallow dish. Blend together the olive and/or sunflower oil, saffron, ground ginger, black pepper, cinnamon and sugar, and pour over the onions. Stir gently to mix, then set the onions aside for about 2 hours.

2 Preheat the oven to 160°C/325°F/Gas 3 and pour the onions and the marinade into a casserole or ovenproof dish.

COOK'S TIP
Onions grown in warmer climates are milder than those from cooler regions. Consequently Spanish onions have a mild, sweet flavour. Their skins are a rich golden colour and they are one of the largest varieties available.

3 Fold a large piece of foil into three and place over the top of the casserole or ovenproof dish, securing it with a lid.

4 Cook in the oven for 45 minutes, or until the onions are very soft, then increase the oven temperature to 200°C/400°F/Gas 6. Remove the lid and foil and cook for a further 5–10 minutes, or until the onions are lightly glazed. Serve immediately.

COOK'S TIP
When slicing onions, chop off the neck and just a little of the base to help the onion stay together. Score a line down the side of the onion and peel away the outer skin and first layer of flesh.

Energy 224Kcal/926kJ; Protein 2.1g; Carbohydrate 17.3g, of which sugars 13.4g; Fat 16.9g, of which saturates 2.4g; Cholesterol 0mg; Calcium 60mg; Fibre 2.4g; Sodium 6mg.

OVEN-ROASTED RED ONIONS

The wonderful taste of these sweet red onions is enhanced still further with the powerful flavours of fresh rosemary and juniper berries, and the added tangy sweetness from the balsamic vinegar.

SERVES 4

4 large or 8 small red onions
45ml/3 tbsp olive oil
6 juniper berries, crushed
8 small rosemary sprigs
30ml/2 tbsp balsamic vinegar
salt and ground black pepper

VARIATION
Add a similar quantity of long, thin potato wedges to the onion. Use a larger dish so that the vegetables are still in one layer.

COOK'S TIP
To help hold back the tears during preparation, chill the onions first for about 30 minutes and then remove the root end last. The root contains the largest concentration of the sulphuric compounds that make the eyes water.

1 Soak a clay onion baker in cold water for 15 minutes, then drain. If the base of the baker is glazed, only the lid will need to be soaked.

2 Trim the roots from the onions and remove the skins, if you like. Cut the onions from the tip to the root, cutting the large onions into quarters and the small onions in half.

3 Rub the onions with olive oil, salt and pepper and the juniper berries. Place the onions in the baker, inserting the rosemary in among the onions. Pour the remaining olive oil and vinegar over.

4 Cover and place in an unheated oven. Set the oven to 200°C/400°F/Gas 6 and cook for 40 minutes. Remove the lid and cook for a further 10 minutes.

Energy 128Kcal/530kJ; Protein 1.8g; Carbohydrate 11.9g, of which sugars 8.4g; Fat 8.6g, of which saturates 1.2g; Cholesterol 0mg; Calcium 38mg; Fibre 2.1g; Sodium 5mg.

ROASTED SWEET POTATOES, ONIONS and BEETROOT in COCONUT and GINGER PASTE

Sweet potatoes and beetroot take on a wonderful sweetness when roasted, and are delicious with savoury onions and aromatic coconut, ginger and garlic paste.

SERVES 4

30ml/2 tbsp groundnut (peanut) or mild
    olive oil
450g/1lb sweet potatoes, peeled and cut
    into thick strips or chunks
4 beetroot (beets), cooked, peeled and cut
    into wedges
450g/1lb small onions, halved
5ml/1 tsp coriander seeds, lightly crushed
3–4 small whole fresh red chillies
salt and ground black pepper
chopped fresh coriander (cilantro), to garnish

For the paste

2 large garlic cloves, chopped
1–2 green chillies, seeded and chopped
15ml/1 tbsp chopped fresh root ginger
45ml/3 tbsp chopped fresh coriander (cilantro)
75ml/5 tbsp coconut milk
30ml/2 tbsp groundnut (peanut) or mild
    olive oil
grated rind of ½ lime
2.5ml/½ tsp soft light brown sugar

1 To make the paste, process the garlic, chillies, ginger, coriander and coconut milk in a food processor or blender.

2 Tip the spicy paste into a small bowl and beat in the oil, grated lime rind and light brown sugar. Preheat the oven to 200°C/400°F/Gas 6.

3 Heat the oil in a large roasting pan in the oven for 5 minutes. Add the sweet potatoes, beetroot, onions and coriander seeds, tossing them in the hot oil. Roast the vegetables for 10 minutes.

4 Stir in the spicy paste and the whole red chillies. Season the vegetables well with salt and pepper, and shake the roasting pan to toss the vegetables and coat them thoroughly with the paste.

5 Return the vegetables to the oven and cook for a further 25–35 minutes, or until both the sweet potatoes and onions are fully cooked and tender. During cooking, stir the mixture two or three times with a wooden spoon to prevent the coconut and ginger paste from sticking to the roasting pan. Serve the vegetables immediately, sprinkled with a little chopped fresh coriander.

COOK'S TIP
Try to buy orange-fleshed sweet potatoes for this dish – they not only look more attractive than white-fleshed ones in this dish, they are also more nutritious.

Energy 272Kcal/1143kJ; Protein 4.4g; Carbohydrate 39.8g, of which sugars 19.2g; Fat 11.8g, of which saturates 1.7g; Cholesterol 0mg; Calcium 98mg; Fibre 6.3g; Sodium 122mg.

COURGETTES in TOMATO SAUCE

This rich-flavoured Mediterranean dish can be served hot or cold, either as a side dish or as part of a tapas meal. Cut the courgettes into fairly thick slices, so that they retain their texture and stay slightly crunchy.

SERVES 4

15ml/1 tbsp olive oil
1 onion, chopped
1 garlic clove, chopped
4 courgettes (zucchini), thickly sliced
400g/14oz can chopped tomatoes, drained
2 tomatoes, peeled, seeded and chopped
5ml/1 tsp vegetable bouillon powder
15ml/1 tbsp tomato purée (paste)
salt and ground black pepper

VARIATION
Add 1 or 2 sliced and seeded red, green or yellow (bell) peppers with the courgettes in step 1.

1 Heat the olive oil in a heavy pan, add the chopped onion and garlic and sauté for about 5 minutes, or until the onion is softened, stirring occasionally. Add the thickly sliced courgettes and cook for a further 5 minutes.

2 Add the canned and fresh tomatoes, bouillon powder and tomato purée. Stir well, then simmer for 10–15 minutes until the sauce is thickened and the courgettes are just tender. Season to taste and serve.

BAKED FENNEL with a CRUMB CRUST

The delicate aniseed flavour of baked fennel makes it a very good accompaniment to all kinds of dishes, from pasta and risotto to roast chicken.

SERVES 4

3 fennel bulbs, cut lengthwise into quarters
30ml/2 tbsp olive oil
1 garlic clove, chopped
50g/2oz/1 cup day-old wholemeal (whole wheat) breadcrumbs
30ml/2 tbsp chopped fresh flat leaf parsley
salt and ground black pepper
a few fronds of fennel leaves, to garnish (optional)

COOK'S TIPS
• When buying fennel, look for compact, unblemished white-green bulbs. The leaves should look fresh and green. Tougher specimens will have bulbs that spread at the top.
• Fennel has a distinctive liquorice flavour, which particularly complements fish dishes. All parts of the plant are edible including the bulb, the celery-like stalks and the feathery leaves.

1 Cook the fennel in a pan of boiling salted water for 10 minutes. Preheat the oven to 190°C/375°F/Gas 5.

2 Drain the fennel and place in a large earthenware baking dish or baking tray, then brush with half of the olive oil.

VARIATION
To make a cheese-topped version, add 60ml/4 tbsp finely grated strong-flavoured cheese, such as mature (sharp) Cheddar, Red Leicester or Parmesan, to the breadcrumb mixture in step 3.

3 In a small bowl, mix together the chopped garlic, wholemeal breadcrumbs and chopped fresh flat leaf parsley, then stir in the rest of the olive oil. Sprinkle the mixture evenly over the fennel, then season well with salt and pepper.

4 Bake the fennel for about 30 minutes, or until it is tender and the breadcrumb topping is crisp and golden brown. Serve the baked fennel hot, garnished with a few fronds of fennel leaves, if you like.

Courgettes in Tomato Sauce: Energy 92Kcal/382kJ; Protein 4.8g; Carbohydrate 9.4g, of which sugars 8.9g; Fat 4g, of which saturates 0.8g; Cholesterol 0mg; Calcium 64mg; Fibre 3.5g; Sodium 16mg.
Baked Fennel with a Crumb Crust: Energy 114Kcal/477kJ; Protein 3g; Carbohydrate 12.6g, of which sugars 3.1g; Fat 6.1g, of which saturates 0.8g; Cholesterol 0mg; Calcium 67mg; Fibre 4.3g; Sodium 114mg.

BRAISED LETTUCE and PEAS with MINT

Based on the traditional French way of braising peas with lettuce in butter, this dish is delicious with simply cooked fish or roast or grilled duck.

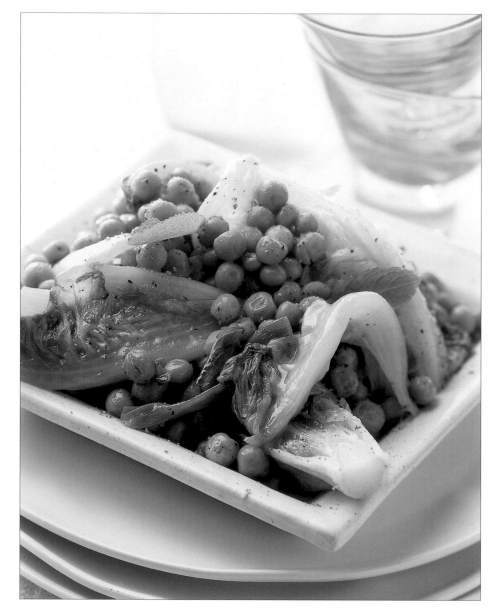

2 Toss the vegetables in the butter, then sprinkle in the sugar, 2.5ml/½ tsp salt and plenty of black pepper. Cover, then cook very gently for 5 minutes, stirring once.

3 Add the peas and mint sprigs to the pan. Toss the peas in the buttery juices, then pour in the light stock or water.

4 Cover the pan and cook over a gentle heat for a further 5 minutes until the peas are almost tender, then remove the lid from the pan. Increase the heat to high and cook, stirring occasionally, until the cooking liquid has reduced to a few tablespoons.

5 Stir in the remaining butter and adjust the seasoning. Transfer to a warmed serving dish and garnish with the extra mint. Serve immediately.

VARIATIONS
• Braise about 250g/9oz baby carrots with the lettuce.
• Use 1 lettuce, shredding it coarsely, and omit the fresh mint. Towards the end of cooking, stir in about 150g/5oz rocket (arugula) – preferably the slightly stronger-flavoured, wild variety – and cook briefly until just wilted.
• Fry 115g/4oz chopped smoked bacon or pancetta with 1 small chopped red or white onion in the butter. Use 1 bunch of spring onions and omit the mint. Stir in some chopped fresh flat leaf parsley before serving. This version is also very good with small, white summer turnips, braised with the lettuce.

SERVES 4

50g/2oz/¼ cup butter
4 Little Gem (Bibb) lettuces,
   halved lengthwise
2 bunches spring onions (scallions)
5ml/1 tsp sugar
400g/14oz shelled peas (about
   1kg/2¼lb in pods)
a few sprigs of mint, plus extra fresh mint
   to garnish
120ml/4fl oz/½ cup light vegetable or
   chicken stock or water
salt and ground black pepper

1 Melt half the butter in a wide, heavy pan over a low heat. Add the lettuces and spring onions.

Energy 164Kcal/680kJ; Protein 9.2g; Carbohydrate 9.8g, of which sugars 3.4g; Fat 10.1g, of which saturates 3.2g; Cholesterol 27mg; Calcium 69mg; Fibre 3.7g; Sodium 64mg.

BRAISED LEEKS with CARROTS

Sweet carrots and leeks go well together and are good finished with a little chopped mint,
chervil or parsley. This is a good accompaniment to roast beef, lamb or chicken.

SERVES 4

65g/2½oz/5 tbsp butter
675g/1½lb carrots, thickly sliced
2 fresh bay leaves
75ml/5 tbsp water
675g/1½lb leeks, cut into 5cm/2in lengths
120ml/4fl oz/½ cup white wine
30ml/2 tbsp chopped fresh mint, chervil
　or parsley
a pinch of sugar
salt and ground black pepper

1 Melt 25g/1oz/2 tbsp of the butter in a wide, heavy pan and cook the carrots without allowing them to brown, for about 5 minutes. Add the bay leaves, seasoning, sugar and the water. Bring to the boil, cover and cook for 10 minutes, or until the carrots are just tender.

2 Uncover the pan and boil until the juices have evaporated, leaving the carrots moist and glazed. Remove the carrots from the pan and set aside.

3 Melt 25g/1oz/2 tbsp of the remaining butter in the pan. Add the leeks and fry them over a low heat for 4–5 minutes, without allowing them to brown.

4 Add seasoning, a good pinch of sugar, the wine and half the chopped herbs. Heat until simmering, then cover and cook gently for 5–8 minutes, until the leeks are tender, but not collapsed.

5 Uncover the leeks and turn them in the buttery juices. Increase the heat and then boil the liquid rapidly until it is reduced to a few tablespoons.

6 Add the carrots to the leeks and reheat them gently, stirring occasionally, then add the remaining butter. Adjust the seasoning, if necessary. Transfer to a warmed serving dish and serve sprinkled with the remaining chopped herbs.

VARIATION
Braised leeks in tarragon cream
Cook 900g/2lb leeks, cut into 5cm/2in lengths, in 40g/1½oz/3 tbsp butter as step 3. Season with salt and pepper, add a pinch of sugar, 45ml/3 tbsp tarragon vinegar, 6 fresh tarragon sprigs or 5ml/1 tsp dried tarragon and 60ml/4 tbsp white wine. Cover and cook as step 4. Add 150ml/¼ pint/⅔ cup double (heavy) cream and allow to bubble and thicken. Adjust the seasoning and serve sprinkled with plenty of finely chopped fresh tarragon leaves. A spoonful of tarragon-flavoured mustard is good stirred into these creamy leeks. Serve with fish or chicken dishes.

Energy 240Kcal/994kJ; Protein 4.1g; Carbohydrate 18.7g, of which sugars 16.7g; Fat 14.8g, of which saturates 8.8g; Cholesterol 35mg; Calcium 103mg; Fibre 8.1g; Sodium 148mg.

BRAISED RED CABBAGE with BEETROOT

The moist, gentle cooking of the clay pot finishes this vegetable dish to perfection.
Serve with casseroles and roast meats — it is especially delicious with roast pork.

SERVES 6–8

675g/1½lb red cabbage
1 Spanish onion, thinly sliced
30ml/2 tbsp olive oil
30ml/2 tbsp light muscovado (brown) sugar
2 tart eating apples, peeled, cored
   and sliced
300ml/½ pint/1¼ cups vegetable stock
60ml/4 tbsp red wine vinegar
375g/13oz raw beetroot (beet), peeled
   and coarsely grated
salt and ground black pepper

COOK'S TIP
When buying cabbage, choose one that
is firm and heavy for its size. The leaves
should look healthy – avoid any with
curling leaves or blemishes. These
guidelines apply to any type of cabbage –
red, green or white.

1 Soak a large clay pot or bean pot in
cold water for 20 minutes, then drain.
Finely shred the red cabbage and place
in the clay pot.

2 Place the onion and olive oil in a
frying pan and sauté until soft and
transparent. Stir in the sugar and fry the
onion gently until it is caramelized and
golden. Take care not to overcook.

3 Stir in the apple slices, vegetable stock
and wine vinegar, then transfer to the
clay pot. Season with salt and pepper.

4 Cover and place in an unheated oven.
Set the oven temperature to 190°C/
375°F/Gas 5 and cook for 1 hour. Stir in
the beetroot, re-cover the pot and cook
for a further 20–30 minutes, or until the
cabbage and beetroot are tender.

Energy 99Kcal/415kJ; Protein 2.5g; Carbohydrate 16.2g, of which sugars 15g; Fat 3.1g, of which saturates 0.4g; Cholesterol 0mg; Calcium 63mg; Fibre 3.5g; Sodium 39mg.

SPINACH BRAISED with SWEET POTATOES

Sweet potatoes make an interesting alternative to the ordinary variety. Here the garlic and ginger subtly complement the flavours of the potatoes and spinach.

SERVES 4

30ml/2 tbsp sunflower oil
1 onion, chopped
1 garlic clove, finely chopped
2.5cm/1in piece fresh root ginger, peeled and grated
2.5ml/½ tsp cayenne pepper
675g/1½lb sweet potatoes
150ml/¼ pint/⅔ cup vegetable or chicken stock
225g/8oz spinach
45ml/3 tbsp pine nuts, toasted
salt and ground black pepper

1 Soak a clay potato pot in cold water for 20 minutes, then drain. Heat the oil in a large frying pan, add the onion, garlic, ginger and cayenne pepper and fry gently, stirring occasionally, for about 8 minutes, or until the onion is softened.

2 Peel the sweet potatoes and cut them into 2.5cm/1in chunks. Add the chunks to the frying pan and stir to coat them in the oil and spices.

COOK'S TIP
To toast pine nuts, heat a heavy frying pan and add the nuts, cook them for 3–4 minutes or until they turn a golden brown colour, stirring occasionally. Watch the nuts carefully – they will scorch and burn quickly if toasted for too long.

VARIATIONS
• Add a drained, 400g/14oz can chickpeas to the potato mixture after 30 minutes cooking and stir well.
• Use baby new potatoes in place of the sweet potatoes.

3 Transfer the potato mixture to the clay pot and add the stock. Cover the pot and place in an unheated oven. Set the oven to 220°C/425°F/Gas 7 and cook for 50–60 minutes, or until the potatoes are just tender, stirring halfway through cooking.

4 Wash the spinach and shred roughly. Stir into the potatoes with the toasted pine nuts, re-cover the clay pot and cook for a further 5 minutes in the oven. Remove from the oven and leave to stand for 5 minutes. Adjust the seasoning and serve immediately.

Energy 293Kcal/1231kJ; Protein 5.4g; Carbohydrate 38.5g, of which sugars 11.8g; Fat 14.2g, of which saturates 1.4g; Cholesterol 0mg; Calcium 141mg; Fibre 5.7g; Sodium 147mg.

ROOT VEGETABLE GRATIN with INDIAN SPICES

*Subtly spiced with curry powder, turmeric, coriander and mild chilli powder, this rich gratin
is substantial enough to serve on its own for lunch or supper. It also makes a good
accompaniment to a vegetable or bean curry.*

2 Preheat the oven to 180°C/350°F/
Gas 4. Heat half the butter in a heavy
pan, add the curry powder, ground
turmeric and coriander and half the chilli
powder. Cook for 2 minutes, then leave
to cool slightly. Drain the vegetables,
then pat them dry with kitchen paper.
Place in a bowl, add the spice mixture
and the shallots and mix well.

3 Arrange the vegetables in a shallow
baking dish, seasoning well with salt and
pepper between the layers. Mix together
the cream and milk, pour the mixture
over the vegetables, then sprinkle the
remaining chilli powder on top.

4 Cover the dish with baking parchment
and bake for 45 minutes. Remove the
baking parchment, dot the vegetables
with the remaining butter and bake for
a further 50 minutes, or until the top is
golden brown. Serve the gratin garnished
with chopped parsley.

SERVES 4

2 large potatoes, about 450g/1lb
   total weight
2 sweet potatoes, about 275g/10oz
   total weight
175g/6oz celeriac
15ml/1 tbsp unsalted (sweet) butter
5ml/1 tsp curry powder
5ml/1 tsp ground turmeric
2.5ml/½ tsp ground coriander
5ml/1 tsp mild chilli powder
3 shallots, chopped
150ml/¼ pint/⅔ cup single (light) cream
150ml/¼ pint/⅔ cup milk
salt and ground black pepper
chopped fresh flat leaf parsley, to garnish

1 Cut the potatoes, sweet potatoes and
celeriac into thin, even slices using a
sharp knife or the slicing attachment on
a food processor. Immediately place the
vegetables in a bowl of cold water to
prevent them from discolouring.

COOK'S TIP
The cream adds a delicious richness to
this gratin; use semi-skimmed (low-fat)
milk, if you prefer a lighter meal.

Energy 268Kcal/1129kJ; Protein 5.8g; Carbohydrate 37.7g, of which sugars 9.8g; Fat 11.6g, of which saturates 7.1g; Cholesterol 31mg; Calcium 127mg; Fibre 3.6g; Sodium 117mg.

LEEKS in CREAM SAUCE

This versatile vegetable makes a great winter standby and leeks find their way into many dishes, including casseroles and soups. Simple buttered leeks are underrated as a side dish, and this recipe makes a tasty accompaniment for plain grilled food, such as chops or chicken, or it can be served as a light lunch or supper on its own.

SERVES 4–6

4 large or 8 medium leeks
300ml/½ pint/1¼ cups milk
8 streaky (fatty) rashers (strips) of bacon, trimmed and sliced (optional)
1 egg, lightly beaten
150ml/¼ pint/⅔ cup single (light) cream
15ml/1 tbsp mild Irish mustard
75g/3oz/¾ cup grated cheese (optional)
salt and ground black pepper

1 Slice the leeks into fairly large chunks. Put them into a pan with the milk. Season and bring to the boil. Reduce the heat and simmer for 15–20 minutes, or until tender. Drain well and turn the leeks into a buttered shallow baking dish, reserving the cooking liquor.

2 Meanwhile, if using the bacon, put it into a frying pan and cook gently to allow the fat to run, then turn up the heat a little and cook for a few minutes until it crisps up. Remove from the pan with a slotted spoon and sprinkle the bacon over the leeks.

3 Rinse the pan used for the leeks. Blend the beaten egg, single cream and Irish mustard together and mix it with the reserved cooking liquor. Return to the pan and heat gently without boiling, allowing the sauce to thicken a little. Taste and adjust the seasoning with salt and freshly ground black pepper. Pour the sauce over the leeks and bacon.

4 Sprinkle with grated cheese, if using, and brown for a few minutes under a hot grill (broiler). (Alternatively, the leeks may served immediately without browning.) Serve with plain grilled meat or poultry, if you like.

VARIATION
The bacon may be grilled and served separately, if you prefer.

Energy 238Kcal/993kJ; Protein 18.6g; Carbohydrate 9g, of which sugars 7.9g; Fat 14.4g, of which saturates 7.3g; Cholesterol 90mg; Calcium 172mg; Fibre 3.5g; Sodium 830mg

GRIDDLE POTATOES

This attractive dish has traditionally been cooked with leftover cooked potatoes that have been boiled in their skins. It makes a tasty accompaniment to grilled meat or fish or would be served as a light meal with glasses of milk or buttermilk.

SERVES 4–6

2 onions, peeled and chopped
450–675g/1lb–1½lb whole cooked
  potatoes, boiled in their skins
a mixture of butter and oil, for
  shallow frying
salt and ground black pepper

1 Put the onions in a large pan and scald them briefly in boiling water. Refresh under cold water and drain well. Peel and slice the potatoes.

2 Put a mixture of butter and oil into a large, heavy frying pan and heat well.

3 When the fat is hot, fry the onion until tender. Add the potato slices and brown them together, turning the potato slices to brown as evenly as possible on both sides. Transfer to a warmed serving dish and season with salt and pepper. Serve very hot.

Energy 163Kcal/681kJ; Protein 3.4g; Carbohydrate 26.4g, of which sugars 5g; Fat 5.5g, of which saturates 3.3g; Cholesterol 13mg; Calcium 26mg; Fibre 2.6g; Sodium 49mg

ROASTED POTATOES with GARLIC and RED ONIONS

These mouthwatering potatoes are a fine accompaniment to just about anything. The key is to use small firm potatoes; the smaller they are cut, the quicker they will cook.

SERVES 4

675g/1½lb small firm potatoes
25g/1oz/2 tbsp butter
30ml/2 tbsp olive oil
2 large or 4 small red onions, cut
    into wedges
8 garlic cloves, unpeeled
30ml/2 tbsp chopped fresh rosemary or
    10ml/2 tsp dried
salt and ground black pepper

COOK'S TIP
Choose waxy or new potatoes that will hold their shape for this dish. You can peel them, or simply scrub them well and leave the skins on.

1 Preheat the oven to 230°C/450°F/ Gas 8. Peel and quarter the potatoes, rinse them and pat dry on kitchen paper.

2 Put the butter and oil in a roasting pan and heat in the oven. When the butter has melted and is foaming, add the potatoes, onion wedges and garlic cloves to the roasting pan.

3 Sprinkle over the rosemary, toss well then spread out the vegetables.

4 Place the pan in the oven and roast for about 25 minutes until the potatoes are golden and tender when tested with a fork. Shake the pan from time to time to redistribute the vegetables. When cooked, season with salt and pepper.

Energy 254Kcal/1063kJ; Protein 4.5g; Carbohydrate 35.4g, of which sugars 8.1g; Fat 11.5g, of which saturates 4.2g; Cholesterol 13mg; Calcium 59mg; Fibre 3.7g; Sodium 63mg.

POTATO GRATIN

Potatoes, layered with mustard butter and baked until golden, are perfect to serve with a green salad, or as an accompaniment to a vegetable or nut roast.

SERVES 4

4 large potatoes, about 900g/2lb
   total weight
30ml/2 tbsp butter
15ml/1 tbsp olive oil
2 large garlic cloves, crushed
30ml/2 tbsp Dijon mustard
15ml/1 tbsp lemon juice
15ml/1 tbsp fresh thyme leaves, plus
   extra to garnish
50ml/2fl oz/¼ cup vegetable stock
salt and ground black pepper

1 Thinly slice the potatoes using a knife, mandolin or a slicing attachment on a food processor. Place the potato slices in a bowl of cold water to prevent them from discolouring.

2 Preheat the oven to 200°C/400°F/ Gas 6. Heat the butter and oil in a deep, flameproof frying pan. Add the garlic and cook gently for 2–3 minutes until light golden, stirring constantly. Stir in the mustard, lemon juice and thyme. Remove from the heat and pour the mixture into a jug (pitcher).

3 Drain the potatoes and pat dry with kitchen paper. Place a layer of potatoes in the frying pan, season and pour over one-third of the butter mixture. Arrange another layer of potatoes on top, pour over half of the remaining butter mixture and season. Arrange a final layer of potatoes on top, pour over the remainder of butter mixture and the stock. Season and sprinkle with the reserved thyme.

4 Cover the potatoes with baking parchment and bake for 1 hour, then remove the paper, return to the oven and cook for 15 minutes, or until golden.

VARIATION
Any root vegetables can be used: try sweet potatoes, parsnips or turnips.

Energy 238Kcal/1002kJ; Protein 3.9g; Carbohydrate 36.3g, of which sugars 3g; Fat 9.6g, of which saturates 4.5g; Cholesterol 16mg; Calcium 15mg; Fibre 2.3g; Sodium 70mg.

NEW POTATOES with THYME and LEMON

These potatoes are the perfect accompaniment to meat or poultry. You can even use old potatoes, cut into chunks, ideal for serving as an alternative with a traditional roast.

SERVES 4

675g/1½lb small new potatoes
4 garlic cloves, sliced
8 thyme sprigs
4 strips finely pared lemon rind
75ml/5 tbsp olive oil
coarsely ground black pepper
coarse sea salt

COOK'S TIPS
• Thyme is an aromatic, woody herb that goes particularly well with lemon. It has a strong aroma and pungent flavour and grows wild in most warm climates. Thyme is often associated with dishes from the Mediterranean.
• You could easily make this dish with older potatoes – simply peel them, if you like, then cut them into even-size chunks or wedges before adding them to the pot.

1 Soak a clay potato pot in cold water for 20 minutes, then drain. Scrub the new potatoes and rinse thoroughly in cold water. Place the potatoes in the pot.

2 Add the sliced garlic cloves, thyme sprigs and pared lemon rind to the pot, tucking them in among the potatoes. Sprinkle over plenty of coarsely ground black pepper and coarse sea salt.

3 Drizzle over the olive oil. Cover with the lid and place in an unheated oven. Set the oven to 200°C/400°F/Gas 6 and cook for 1 hour, or until just tender.

4 If wished, remove the lid and bake for a further 15–20 minutes, until slightly golden. If you prefer to keep the skins soft, remove the potatoes from the oven and leave to stand for 10 minutes.

Energy 242Kcal/1011kJ; Protein 2.9g; Carbohydrate 27.2g, of which sugars 2.2g; Fat 14.3g, of which saturates 2.1g; Cholesterol 0mg; Calcium 10mg; Fibre 1.7g; Sodium 19mg.

POTATOES BAKED with FENNEL, ONIONS, GARLIC and SAFFRON

Potatoes, fennel and onions flavoured with garlic, saffron and spices make a sophisticated and attractive accompaniment to fish or chicken or egg-based main-course dishes.

SERVES 4–6

500g/1¼lb small waxy potatoes, cut into chunks or wedges
good pinch of saffron threads (12–15 threads)
1 head of garlic, separated into individual cloves
12 small red or yellow onions, peeled but left whole
3 fennel bulbs, cut into wedges, feathery tops reserved for garnish (optional)
4–6 fresh bay leaves
6–9 fresh thyme sprigs
175ml/6fl oz/¾ cup fish, chicken or vegetable stock
30ml/2 tbsp sherry or balsamic vinegar
2.5ml/½ tsp sugar
5ml/1 tsp fennel seeds, lightly crushed
2.5ml/½ tsp paprika
45ml/3 tbsp olive oil
salt and ground black pepper

1 Boil the potato chunks or wedges in a pan of boiling salted water for 8–10 minutes. Drain. Preheat the oven to 190°C/375°F/Gas 5. Soak the saffron threads in 30ml/2 tbsp warm water for 10 minutes.

2 Peel and finely chop two of the garlic cloves and set aside. Place the potato chunks or wedges, whole red or yellow onions, remaining unpeeled garlic cloves, fennel wedges, fresh bay leaves and fresh thyme sprigs in a large roasting pan or dish. Mix together the stock and the saffron and its soaking liquid in a jug (pitcher) or measuring cup.

3 Add the vinegar and sugar to the stock mixture, then pour the liquid over the vegetables. Stir in the fennel seeds, paprika, chopped garlic and oil, and season with salt and pepper.

4 Cook the vegetables in the oven for 1–1¼ hours, stirring occasionally, until they are just tender. Chop the reserved fennel tops, if using, and sprinkle them over the vegetables to garnish. Season the vegetables with more salt and pepper and serve immediately .

COOK'S TIP
Sherry vinegar has a rich, mellow flavour and it makes a good addition to a variety of sauces and dressings. It can be used simply to add extra piquancy to a dish. Try sprinkling a little over oven-roasted vegetables or add a teaspoon or two to soups, sauces or stews.

Energy 162Kcal/676kJ; Protein 4.4g; Carbohydrate 23.6g, of which sugars 7.1g; Fat 6.2g, of which saturates 0.9g; Cholesterol 0mg; Calcium 49mg; Fibre 4.9g; Sodium 23mg.

LENTIL DHAL with ROASTED GARLIC and WHOLE SPICES

This spicy lentil dhal makes a sustaining and comforting meal when served with rice or Indian breads and any dry-spiced dish, particularly a cauliflower or potato dish. It's a bit of a cheat to have in a one-pot cookbook, since there's a spicy garnish that needs to be cooked – in a small frying pan – at the end.

SERVES 4–6

40g/1½oz/3 tbsp butter or ghee
1 onion, chopped
2 green chillies, seeded and chopped
15ml/1 tbsp chopped fresh root ginger
225g/8oz/1 cup yellow or red lentils
900ml/1½ pints/3¾ cups water
45ml/3 tbsp roasted garlic purée
5ml/1 tsp ground cumin
5ml/1 tsp ground coriander
200g/7oz tomatoes, peeled and diced
a little lemon juice
salt and ground black pepper
30–45ml/2–3 tbsp coriander (cilantro) sprigs, to garnish

For the spicy garnish
30ml/2 tbsp groundnut (peanut) oil
4–5 shallots, sliced
2 garlic cloves, thinly sliced
15g/½oz/1 tbsp butter or ghee
5ml/1 tsp cumin seeds
5ml/1 tsp mustard seeds
3–4 small dried red chillies
8–10 fresh curry leaves

1 First begin the spicy garnish. Heat the oil in a large, heavy pan. Add the shallots and fry them over a medium heat, stirring occasionally, until they are crisp and browned. Add the garlic and cook, stirring frequently, for a moment or two until the garlic colours slightly. Use a slotted spoon to remove the mixture from the pan and set aside.

COOK'S TIP
Ghee is type of clarified butter that has had all the milk solids removed by heating – it was originally made to extend the keeping qualities of butter in India. It is the main cooking fat used in Indian cooking. Because the milk solids have been removed, ghee has a high smoking point and can therefore be cooked at higher temperatures than ordinary butter. Look for it in Indian and Asian stores.

2 Melt the butter or ghee in the pan and cook the onion, chillies and ginger for 10 minutes, until golden.

3 Stir in the lentils and water, then bring to the boil, reduce the heat and part-cover the pan. Simmer, stirring occasionally, for 50–60 minutes, until similar to a very thick soup.

4 Stir in the roasted garlic purée, cumin and ground coriander, then season with salt and pepper to taste. Cook for a further 10–15 minutes, uncovered, stirring frequently.

5 Stir in the tomatoes and then adjust the seasoning, adding a little lemon juice to taste if necessary.

6 To make the spicy garnish: melt the butter or ghee in a frying pan. Add the cumin and mustard seeds and fry until the mustard seeds pop. Stir in the chillies, curry leaves and the shallot mixture, then immediately swirl the mixture into the cooked dhal. Garnish with coriander, spicy fried shallots and garlic and serve.

Energy 233Kcal/978kJ; Protein 9.5g; Carbohydrate 23.8g, of which sugars 3.1g; Fat 11.8g, of which saturates 5.3g; Cholesterol 20mg; Calcium 28mg; Fibre 2.5g; Sodium 73mg.

RICE with DILL and BROAD BEANS

This is a favourite rice dish in Iran. The combination of broad beans, plenty of fresh dill and warm spices works very well, and the saffron rice adds a splash of bright colour.

SERVES 4

275g/10oz/1½ cups basmati rice,
  soaked in cold water and drained
750ml/1¼ pints/3 cups water
40g/1½oz/3 tbsp butter
175g/6oz/1½ cups frozen baby broad (fava)
  beans, thawed and peeled
90ml/6 tbsp finely chopped fresh dill, plus
  fresh dill sprigs to garnish
5ml/1 tsp ground cinnamon
5ml/1 tsp ground cumin
2–3 saffron threads, soaked in
  15ml/1 tbsp boiling water
salt

1 Tip the rice into a large pan with the water. Add a little salt. Bring to the boil, then simmer very gently for 5 minutes. Drain, rinse in warm water and drain again.

2 Melt the butter in the rinsed-out pan. Pour two-thirds of the melted butter into a bowl and set aside. Spoon enough rice into the pan to cover the base. Add one-quarter of the beans and a little dill.

3 Spread over another layer of rice, then a layer of beans and dill. Repeat the layers until all the beans and dill have been used, ending with a layer of rice. Cook over a gentle heat for 8 minutes until nearly tender.

4 Pour the reserved melted butter evenly over the rice, then sprinkle the ground cinnamon and cumin over the top. Cover the pan with a clean dishtowel or cloth and a tight-fitting lid, lifting the corners of the towel or cloth back over the lid. Cook over a low heat for 25–30 minutes.

5 Spoon about 45ml/3 tbsp of the cooked rice into the bowl of saffron water and then mix the rice and liquid together. Spoon the remaining rice mixture on to a large serving plate and spoon the saffron rice on one side to garnish. Serve immediately, decorated with fresh sprigs of dill.

Energy 364Kcal/1521kJ; Protein 9.3g; Carbohydrate 60.7g, of which sugars 1.2g; Fat 9.1g, of which saturates 5.3g; Cholesterol 21mg; Calcium 84mg; Fibre 4g; Sodium 72mg.

BASMATI RICE with VEGETABLES

Serve this tasty dish with roast chicken, grilled lamb cutlets or pan-fried fish. Add the vegetables near the end of cooking so that they remain crisp.

2 Heat the oil in a large pan and fry the onion for a few minutes over a medium heat until it starts to soften.

3 Add the rice to the pan and fry for about 10 minutes, stirring constantly to prevent the rice sticking to the base of the pan. Stir in the crushed garlic.

4 Pour in the water or stock and stir well. Bring to the boil, then lower the heat. Cover and simmer for 10 minutes.

SERVES 4

350g/12oz/1¾ cups basmati rice
45ml/3 tbsp vegetable oil
1 onion, chopped
2 garlic cloves, crushed
750ml/1¼ pints/3 cups water or
    vegetable stock
115g/4oz/⅔ cup fresh or drained canned
    sweetcorn kernels
1 red or green (bell) pepper, seeded
    and chopped
1 large carrot, grated
fresh chervil sprigs, to garnish

1 Rinse the rice in a sieve under cold water, then leave to drain thoroughly for about 15 minutes.

5 Sprinkle the corn over the rice, spread the chopped pepper on top and sprinkle over the grated carrot. Cover tightly and steam over a low heat until the rice is tender, then mix with a fork. Pile on to a serving plate and garnish with chervil.

Energy 449Kcal/1877kJ; Protein 8.1g; Carbohydrate 83g, of which sugars 7.7g; Fat 9.3g, of which saturates 1.1g; Cholesterol 0mg; Calcium 30mg; Fibre 1.8g; Sodium 85mg.

SAFFRON RICE with ONION and CARDAMOM

This delightfully fragrant, buttery pilaff is wonderful with both Indian and Middle-eastern dishes, especially ones featuring fish, shellfish, chicken or lamb.

2 Toast the saffron threads in a dry, heavy frying pan over a low heat for about 2 minutes, then place in a small bowl and add 30ml/2 tbsp warm water. Leave to soak for 10–15 minutes.

3 Melt the butter in the pan, then cook the onion with the cardamom pods very gently for 8–10 minutes, until soft and buttery yellow.

4 Add the drained rice to the pan and stir well to coat the grains in the butter. Add the salt and bay leaves, followed by the stock and saffron with its liquid. Bring the rice to the boil, stir, then reduce the heat to very low and cover tightly. Cook the rice for 10–12 minutes, until it has absorbed all the liquid.

5 Lay a clean, folded dishtowel over the pan under the lid and press on the lid to wedge it firmly in place. Leave the rice to stand for 10–15 minutes to continue cooking in its own heat.

6 Fluff up the grains of cooked rice with a fork. Tip it into a warmed serving dish and serve immediately as an accompaniment to a spicy main course.

SERVES 4

350g/12oz/1¾ cups basmati rice
good pinch of saffron threads (about 15 threads)
25g/1oz/2 tbsp butter
1 onion, finely chopped
6 green cardamom pods, lightly crushed
5ml/1 tsp salt
2–3 fresh bay leaves
600ml/1 pint/2½ cups well-flavoured chicken or vegetable stock or water

1 Put the rice into a sieve and rinse well under cold running water. Tip it into a bowl, add cold water to cover and set aside to soak for 30–40 minutes. Drain in the sieve.

COOK'S TIP
After boiling, when all the liquid has been absorbed, basmati rice is set aside to finish cooking in its own heat and become tender. Wedging a folded dishtowel under the pan lid ensures the heat is not lost and the steam is absorbed.

Energy 366Kcal/1528kJ; Protein 6.7g; Carbohydrate 71.1g, of which sugars 0.9g; Fat 5.6g, of which saturates 3.3g; Cholesterol 13mg; Calcium 22mg; Fibre 0.2g; Sodium 38mg.

GARLIC CHIVE RICE with MUSHROOMS

Rice is readily infused with the pungent aroma and taste of garlic chives, creating a dish with an excellent flavour. Serve with vegetarian dishes, fish or chicken.

SERVES 4

60ml/4 tbsp groundnut (peanut) oil
250g/9oz mixed mushrooms,
   thickly sliced
25g/1oz garlic chives, chopped
350g/12oz/1¾ cups long grain rice
1 small onion, finely chopped
2 green chillies, seeded and finely chopped
15g/½oz fresh coriander (cilantro)
600ml/1 pint/2½ cups vegetable or
   mushroom stock
5ml/1 tsp salt
50g/2oz toasted cashew nuts
ground black pepper

1 Heat half the oil in a large frying pan and cook the thickly sliced mushrooms for 5–6 minutes, stirring occasionally, until they are tender and browned.

2 Add half of the garlic chives to the pan and cook for 1–2 minutes. Remove from the pan using a slotted spoon and set aside. Wash and drain the rice.

3 Add the remaining oil to the frying pan, add the chopped onion and chillies and cook over a gentle heat, stirring occasionally, for 10–12 minutes, until the onions have softened.

4 Set half the remaining garlic chives aside. Cut the stalks off the coriander and set the leaves aside. Purée the remaining chives and the coriander stalks with the stock in a food processor or blender.

COOK'S TIP
You'll find garlic chives in Asian and Thai food stores.

5 Add the rice to the onions and fry over a low heat, stirring frequently, for 4–5 minutes until the onion is softened. Pour in the stock mixture, then stir in the salt and plenty of black pepper.

6 Bring to the boil, stir and reduce the heat to very low. Cover tightly and cook for 15–20 minutes, until the rice has absorbed all the liquid. Lay a clean, folded dishtowel over the pan under the lid and press on the lid to wedge it firmly in place. Leave to stand in a warm place for 10 minutes, allowing the towel to absorb the steam while the rice becomes completely tender.

7 Add the cooked mushroom and chive mixture to the rice and mix well. Stir in the chopped fresh coriander leaves, then adjust the seasoning. Serve immediately, sprinkled with the toasted cashew nuts.

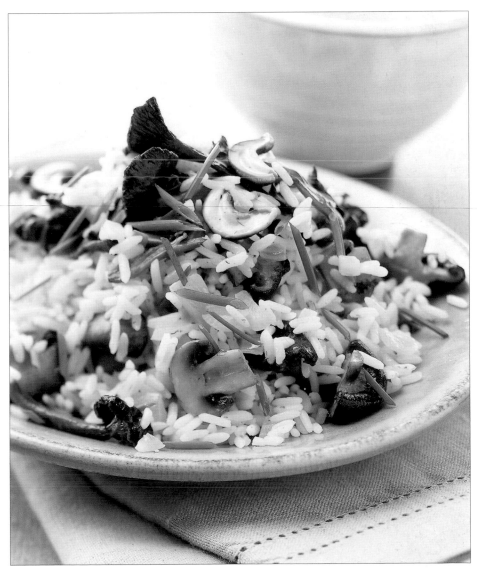

Energy 504Kcal/2100kJ; Protein 10.4g; Carbohydrate 73.8g, of which sugars 1.8g; Fat 18.2g, of which saturates 2.6g; Cholesterol 0mg; Calcium 41mg; Fibre 1.6g; Sodium 533mg.

SLOW COOKER DESSERTS AND CAKES

From baked custards and poached fruit to steamed puddings and luscious cakes, this tempting chapter is perfect for anyone with a sweet tooth. Try old-fashioned favourites such as Poached Pears in Red Wine, Baked Stuffed Apples and Tapioca Pudding, or indulge yourself with a really wicked treat such as Chocolate Chip and Banana Pudding. When you are looking for a little something to enjoy mid-afternoon with a cup of tea or coffee, try any one of the fabulous cakes – Frosted Carrot and Parsnip Cake, Chocolate Cheesecake Brownies or Moist Golden Ginger Cake. One mouthful of any of these delights and you will be in heaven.

COCONUT CUSTARD

This classic Thai dessert, made with rich, creamy coconut milk, is often served
with a selection of fresh fruit. Mangoes and tamarillos go particularly well.

2 Strain the mixture into a jug (pitcher), then pour into four individual heatproof glasses, ramekins or one single ovenproof dish. Cover the containers with clear film (plastic wrap).

3 Place the dishes in the slow cooker and, if necessary, pour a little more boiling water around them to reach just over halfway up their sides.

4 Cover the ceramic cooking pot with the lid, then cook for 3 hours, or until the custards are lightly set. Test with a fine skewer or cocktail stick (toothpick); it should come out clean.

5 Carefully lift the dishes out of the slow cooker and leave to cool. Once cool, chill in the refrigerator until ready to serve. Decorate the custards with a light dusting of icing sugar, and serve with sliced fruit.

SERVES 4

4 eggs
75g/3oz/generous ⅓ cup soft light brown
    sugar
250ml/8fl oz/1 cup coconut milk
5ml/1 tsp vanilla, rose or jasmine extract
icing (confectioners') sugar, to decorate
sliced fresh fruit, to serve

COOK'S TIP
Line the bases of individual ramekins with rounds of baking parchment, then lightly oil the sides. After cooking and chilling, run a knife around the insides of the custards and turn out on to individual dessert plates.

1 Pour about 2.5cm/1in of hot water into the base of the ceramic cooking pot and switch the slow cooker on to low. Whisk the eggs and sugar in a bowl until smooth. Gradually add the coconut milk and flavoured extract, and whisk well.

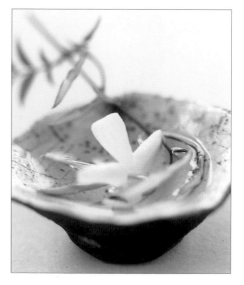

Energy 175Kcal/738kJ; Protein 7.5g; Carbohydrate 22.7g, of which sugars 22.7g; Fat 6.7g, of which saturates 2g; Cholesterol 227mg; Calcium 57mg; Fibre 0g; Sodium 151mg.

TAPIOCA PUDDING

Another Thai-style dessert, this version of the classic tapioca pudding is made from large pearl tapioca and coconut milk and is served warm. It is very good served with lychees.

SERVES 4

115g/4oz/⅔ cup large pearl tapioca
475ml/16fl oz/2 cups very hot water
115g/4oz/generous ½ cup caster
    (superfine) sugar
pinch of salt
250ml/8fl oz/1 cup coconut milk
250g/9oz prepared tropical fruits
shredded lime rind and shaved fresh
    coconut, to decorate (optional)

COOK'S TIP
This dish includes a lot of sugar – as it would in Thailand – but you may prefer to reduce the sugar according to taste.

1 Put the tapioca in a bowl and pour over enough warm water to cover generously. Leave the tapioca to soak for 1 hour until the grains swell, then drain well and set aside.

2 Pour the measured water into the ceramic cooking pot and switch the slow cooker to high. Add the sugar and salt and stir until dissolved. Cover with the lid and heat for about 30 minutes, until the water reaches boiling point.

3 Add the tapioca and coconut milk and stir well. Cover and cook for a further 1–1½ hours, or until the tapioca grains become transparent.

4 Spoon into one large dish or four individual bowls and serve warm with tropical fruits, decorated with the lime rind and coconut shavings, if using.

Energy 273Kcal/1164kJ; Protein 2.7g; Carbohydrate 66.7g, of which sugars 41.9g; Fat 1.3g, of which saturates 0.4g; Cholesterol 0mg; Calcium 43mg; Fibre 1.7g; Sodium 73mg.

POACHED PEARS in RED WINE

The pears take on a red blush from the wine and make a very pretty dessert. It works best in a small slow cooker, which ensures that the pears stay submerged during cooking.

SERVES 4

1 bottle fruity red wine
150g/5oz/¾ cup caster (superfine) sugar
45ml/3 tbsp clear honey
1 cinnamon stick
1 vanilla pod (bean), split lengthwise
large strip of lemon or orange rind
2 whole cloves
2 black peppercorns
4 firm ripe pears
juice of ½ lemon
mint leaves, to garnish
whipped cream or sour cream, to serve

1 Pour the red wine into the ceramic cooking pot. Add the sugar, honey, cinnamon stick, vanilla pod, lemon or orange rind, cloves and peppercorns. Cover with the lid and cook on high for 30 minutes, stirring occasionally.

2 Meanwhile, peel the pears using a vegetable peeler, leaving the stem intact. Take a very thin slice off the base of each pear so it will stand square and upright. As each pear is peeled, toss it in the lemon juice to prevent the flesh browning when exposed to the air.

3 Place the pears in the spiced wine mixture. Cover with the lid and cook for 2–4 hours, turning the pears occasionally, until they are just tender; be careful not to overcook them.

COOK'S TIP
The cooking time will depend on the size and ripeness of the pears. Small, ripe pears will cook quickly; large, hard pears will take longer.

4 Transfer the pears to a bowl using a slotted spoon. Continue to cook the wine mixture uncovered for a further hour, until reduced and thickened a little, then turn off the slow cooker and leave to cool. Alternatively, to save time, pour the cooking liquor into a pan and boil briskly for 10–15 minutes.

5 Strain the cooled liquid over the pears and chill for at least 3 hours. Place the pears in four individual serving dishes and spoon a little of the wine syrup over each one. Garnish with fresh mint and serve with whipped or sour cream.

Energy 87Kcal/367kJ; Protein 0.5g; Carbohydrate 16.6g, of which sugars 16.6g; Fat 0.2g, of which saturates 0g; Cholesterol 0mg; Calcium 19mg; Fibre 3.3g; Sodium 7mg.

WINTER FRUIT POACHED in MULLED WINE

Poaching fresh apples and pears with dried apricots and figs in a spicy wine syrup makes
a delicious winter dessert. Serve on its own or with a generous spoonful of thick cream.

SERVES 4

300ml/½ pint/1¼ cups fruity red wine
300ml/½ pint/1¼ cups fresh apple
   or orange juice
thinly pared strip of orange or
   lemon peel
45ml/3 tbsp clear honey
1 small cinnamon stick
4 whole cloves
4 cardamom pods, split
2 pears, such as Comice or William
8 ready-to-eat figs
12 ready-to-eat dried unsulphured apricots
2 eating apples, peeled, cored and thickly
   sliced

1 Pour the wine and apple or orange
juice into the ceramic cooking pot. Add
the citrus peel, honey, cinnamon stick,
cloves and cardamom pods. Cover with
the lid and cook on high for 1 hour.

2 Peel, core and halve the pears,
keeping the stalk intact if possible. Place
in the slow cooker with the figs and
apricots. Cook for 1 hour. Gently turn
the pears, then add the sliced apples
and cook for a further 1½–2 hours,
or until all the fruit is tender.

3 Using a slotted spoon, carefully
remove the fruit from the cooking pot
and place in a serving dish. Set aside
while you finish making the syrup.

4 Strain the syrup into a pan, discarding
the spices, then bring to the boil. Boil
vigorously for about 10 minutes, until
reduced by about one-third. Pour over
the fruit and serve hot or cold.

COOK'S TIP
Choose tart, well-tasting apples such as
Cox's Orange Pippin, Braeburn or Granny
Smith. They stand up particularly well
against the sweet dried fruits and spicy,
robust red wine syrup.

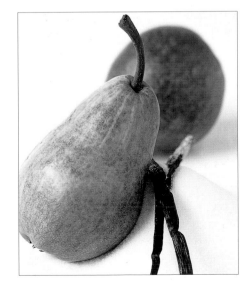

Energy 347Kcal/1476kJ; Protein 5g; Carbohydrate 78.1g, of which sugars 78.1g; Fat 1.9g, of which saturates 0g; Cholesterol 0mg; Calcium 284mg; Fibre 11.4g; Sodium 72mg.

BAKED STUFFED APPLES

Using Italian amaretti to stuff the apples gives a lovely almondy flavour, while dried cranberries and glacé fruit add sweetness and colour. Make sure that you choose a variety of apple that will remain firm during the long cooking time.

3 Add the nuts and dried cranberries or sour cherries and glacé fruit to the bowl and mix well, then set aside the filling while you prepare the apples.

4 Wash and dry the apples. Remove the cores using an apple corer, then carefully enlarge each core cavity to twice its size, using the corer to shave out more flesh. Using a sharp knife, score each apple around its equator.

5 Divide the filling among the apples, packing it into the hole, then piling it on top. Stand the apples in the cooking pot and cover with the lid. Reduce the temperature to low and cook for 4 hours, or until tender. Transfer the apples to warmed serving plates and spoon the sauce over the top. Serve with cream, crème fraîche or vanilla ice cream.

SERVES 4

75g/3oz/6 tbsp butter, softened
45ml/3 tbsp orange or apple juice
75g/3oz/scant ½ cup light muscovado (brown) sugar
grated rind and juice of ½ orange
1.5ml/¼ tsp ground cinnamon
30ml/2 tbsp crushed amaretti
25g/1oz/¼ cup pecan nuts, chopped
25g/1oz/¼ cup dried cranberries or sour cherries
25g/1oz/¼ cup luxury mixed glacé (candied) fruit, chopped
4 large cooking apples, such as Bramleys
cream, crème fraîche or vanilla ice cream, to serve

1 Grease the ceramic cooking pot with 15g/½oz/1 tbsp of the butter, then pour in the fruit juice and switch to high.

2 Put the remaining butter, the sugar, orange rind and juice, cinnamon and amaretti crumbs in a bowl and mix well.

COOK'S TIP
The cooking time will depend on the type and size of apples used.

Energy 347Kcal/1457kJ; Protein 1.6g; Carbohydrate 42.4g, of which sugars 41.3g; Fat 20.3g, of which saturates 10.3g; Cholesterol 40mg; Calcium 27mg; Fibre 3g; Sodium 131mg.

PAPAYA COOKED with GINGER

Spicy ginger enhances the delicate flavour of papaya perfectly. This recipe is excellent for busy people because it takes no more than 10 minutes to prepare and can then just be left to cook gently. Be careful not to overcook papaya or the flesh will become watery.

SERVES 4

150ml/¼ pint/⅔ cup hot water
45ml/3 tbsp raisins
shredded finely pared rind and juice
    of 1 lime
2 ripe papayas
2 pieces stem ginger in syrup, drained,
    plus 15ml/1 tbsp syrup from the jar
8 amaretti or other dessert biscuits
    (cookies), coarsely crushed
25g/1oz/¼ cup pistachio nuts, chopped
15ml/1 tbsp light muscovado
    (brown) sugar
60ml/4 tbsp crème fraîche, plus extra
    to serve

VARIATION
Try using chopped almonds and Greek (US strained plain) yogurt in place of the pistachio nuts and crème fraîche.

1 Pour the water into the base of the ceramic cooking pot and switch the slow cooker to high. Put the raisins in a small bowl and pour over the lime juice. Stir to combine, then leave to soak for at least 5 minutes, while preparing the remaining ingredients.

2 Cut the papayas in half and scoop out and discard their seeds using a teaspoon.

3 Finely chop the stem ginger and combine with the biscuits, raisins and lime juice, lime rind, two-thirds of the nuts, the sugar and crème fraîche.

4 Fill the papayas with the mixture and place in the cooking pot. Cover and cook for 1–1½ hours. Drizzle with the ginger syrup, sprinkle with the remaining nuts and serve with crème fraîche.

Energy 302Kcal/1272kJ; Protein 4.1g; Carbohydrate 45.6g, of which sugars 36.6g; Fat 12.8g, of which saturates 5.7g; Cholesterol 17mg; Calcium 70mg; Fibre 5.7g; Sodium 136mg.

VERMONT BAKED MAPLE CUSTARD

Maple syrup has a really distinctive flavour and gives these little baked custards a wonderfully rich taste. Try to find pure maple syrup – it will make all the difference.

SERVES 6

3 eggs
120ml/4fl oz/½ cup maple syrup
250ml/8fl oz/1 cup warm milk
150ml/¼ pint/⅔ cup warm single
   (light) cream
5ml/1 tsp vanilla extract
whole nutmeg, to grate

COOK'S TIP
Warming the milk and cream until tepid will help the custard cook and set more quickly. You can do this in a pan on the stovetop, or more simply, pour the milk and cream into a heatproof bowl or jug (pitcher) and place in the slow cooker filled with near-boiling water to a depth of about 5cm/2in. Switch the slow cooker to high and leave for 30 minutes. Remove the milk, then turn the slow cooker to low and use the hot water in the ceramic cooking pot to cook the custards.

1 Beat the eggs in a large bowl, then whisk in the maple syrup, followed by the warm milk, cream and the vanilla extract. Grate in a little nutmeg.

2 Strain the custard mixture into six individual ramekins – first checking that the dishes will all fit inside the ceramic cooking pot in a single layer. Carefully cover each ramekin with a piece of kitchen foil, then place them in the ceramic cooking pot.

3 Pour very hot water around the dishes to come three-quarters of the way up their sides. Cover with the lid and cook on low for 2½–3 hours, or until set. To test, insert a skewer in the middle; it should come out clean.

4 Transfer the custards to a wire rack. Leave for 5 minutes and serve warm, or leave to cool completely, then chill. Remove from the refrigerator about 30 minutes before serving.

Energy 174Kcal/735kJ; Protein 8.6g; Carbohydrate 24.5g, of which sugars 18.7g; Fat 5.3g, of which saturates 1.6g; Cholesterol 116mg; Calcium 97mg; Fibre 9.1g; Sodium 120mg.

PETITS POTS de CRÈME au MOCHA

The name of these classic French baked custards comes from the baking cups, called pots de crème. The addition of coffee gives the dessert an even richer, more indulgent flavour.

SERVES 4

5ml/1 tsp instant coffee powder
15ml/1 tbsp soft light brown sugar
300ml/½ pint/1¼ cups milk
150ml/¼ pint/⅔ cup double (heavy) cream
115g/4oz plain (semisweet) chocolate
15ml/1 tbsp coffee liqueur (optional)
4 egg yolks
whipped cream and candied cake
  decorations, to decorate (optional)

1 Put the instant coffee and sugar in a pan and stir in the milk and cream. Bring to the boil over a medium heat, stirring constantly, until the coffee and sugar have dissolved completely.

2 Remove the pan from the heat and add the chocolate. Stir until the chocolate has melted, then stir in the coffee liqueur, if using.

3 In a bowl, whisk the egg yolks, then slowly whisk in the chocolate mixture until well blended. Strain the custard mixture into a large jug (pitcher) and divide equally among *pots de crème* or ramekins – first checking that they will all fit inside the ceramic cooking pot.

4 Cover each *pot de crème* or ramekin with a piece of foil, then transfer to the ceramic cooking pot. Pour enough hot water around the dishes to come just over halfway up their sides. Cover the slow cooker with the lid and cook on high for 2½–3 hours, or until they are just set and a knife inserted into the middle comes out clean.

5 Carefully remove the pots from the cooker and leave to cool. Cover and chill until ready to serve, then decorate with whipped cream and candied cake decorations, if you like.

Energy 443Kcal/1840kJ; Protein 8.3g; Carbohydrate 23.7g, of which sugars 23.7g; Fat 35.7g, of which saturates 20.2g; Cholesterol 264mg; Calcium 196mg; Fibre 0.2g; Sodium 74mg.

HOT BANANAS with RUM and RAISINS

These sticky, sweet baked bananas are utterly moreish and make a great dessert all year round. The rich sauce becomes almost toffee-like during cooking, and is irresistible.

3 Add the bananas to the melted butter and sugar mixture, cover with the lid and cook for about 30 minutes, or until the fruit is almost tender, turning over the bananas halfway through cooking time.

4 Sprinkle the nutmeg and cinnamon over the bananas, then pour in the rum and raisins. Stir very gently to mix, then re-cover and cook for 10 minutes.

5 Carefully lift the bananas out of the ceramic cooking pot and arrange on a serving dish or individual plates. Spoon over the sauce, then sprinkle with almonds, if using. Serve hot with whipped cream or vanilla ice cream.

COOK'S TIP

Choose almost-ripe bananas with even-coloured skins. Over-ripe bananas will not hold their shape during cooking, and will give mushy results.

SERVES 4

30ml/2 tbsp seedless raisins
45ml/3 tbsp dark rum
40g/1½oz/3 tbsp unsalted (sweet) butter
50g/2oz/¼ cup soft light brown sugar
4 slightly under-ripe bananas, peeled and halved lengthways
1.5ml/¼ tsp grated nutmeg
1.5ml/¼ tsp ground cinnamon
25g/1oz/¼ cup flaked (sliced) almonds, toasted (optional)
whipped cream or vanilla ice cream, to serve

1 Put the raisins in a bowl and spoon over 30ml/2 tbsp of the rum. Set aside and leave to soak.

2 Cut the butter into small cubes and place in the ceramic cooking pot with the sugar and remaining 15ml/1 tbsp rum. Switch the slow cooker to high and leave uncovered for 15 minutes, until the butter and sugar have melted.

VARIATION

If you don't like the taste of rum, try using an orange liqueur, such as Cointreau, instead. It makes a very good alternative and is a little less overpowering.

Energy 323Kcal/1355kJ; Protein 3g; Carbohydrate 47.1g, of which sugars 44.7g; Fat 12.1g, of which saturates 5.6g; Cholesterol 21mg; Calcium 33mg; Fibre 1.9g; Sodium 72mg.

CHOCOLATE CHIP and BANANA PUDDING

*Rich, dense and sticky, this steamed pudding served with a glossy chocolate sauce is
a great winter dessert. For an extra treat, serve with a scoop of vanilla ice cream.*

SERVES 4

200g/7oz/1¾ cups self-raising
   (self-rising) flour
75g/3oz/6 tbsp unsalted (sweet) butter
2 ripe bananas
75g/3oz/6 tbsp caster (superfine) sugar
50ml/2fl oz/1¼ cups milk
1 egg, lightly beaten
75g/3oz/⅔ cup chocolate chips or
   chopped unsweetened chocolate

For the chocolate sauce
90g/3½oz/½ cup caster (superfine) sugar
50ml/2fl oz/¼ cup water
175g/6oz/1¼ cups plain (semisweet)
   chocolate chips or chopped
   unsweetened chocolate
25g/1oz/2 tbsp unsalted (sweet) butter
30ml/2 tbsp brandy or orange juice

1 Grease and line the base of a 1 litre/
1¾ pint/4 cup pudding basin with baking
parchment. Put an inverted saucer in the
bottom of the ceramic cooking pot and
pour in about 2.5cm/1in of hot water.
Turn the slow cooker to high.

2 Sift the flour into a large mixing bowl
and rub in the butter until the mixture
resembles coarse breadcrumbs. In a
separate bowl, mash the bananas, then
stir into the flour and butter mixture.
Add the sugar and mix well.

3 In a clean bowl, whisk together the
milk and egg, then beat into the banana
mixture. Stir in the chocolate chips or
chopped chocolate and spoon into the
prepared pudding basin. Cover with
a double thickness of buttered foil and
place in the ceramic cooking pot. Pour
enough boiling water around the basin
to come just over halfway up the sides.

4 Cover the slow cooker and cook on
high for 3–4 hours, or until the pudding
is well risen and a skewer inserted in the
middle comes out clean. Turn off the
slow cooker and leave the pudding in
the water while you make the sauce.

5 Put the sugar and water in a heavy
pan and heat gently, stirring occasionally
with a wooden spoon, until all the sugar
has dissolved. Remove from the heat,
add the chocolate and stir until melted,
then add the butter in the same way.
Stir in the brandy or orange juice.

6 Remove the pudding from the slow
cooker and run a knife around the inside
of the basin to loosen it. Turn it out on
to a warmed serving dish and serve hot,
with the sauce poured over.

Energy 926Kcal/3890kJ; Protein 11.1g; Carbohydrate 131.9g, of which sugars 93.2g; Fat 41.1g, of which saturates 24.6g; Cholesterol 118mg; Calcium 266mg; Fibre 3.3g; Sodium 378mg.

STICKY COFFEE and PEAR PUDDING

This dark and moist fruity pudding is complemented with a tangy citrus-flavoured cream. It is delicious served hot, but is equally good cold; serve at room temperature rather than chilled to enjoy its rich flavour and wonderful texture at their best.

SERVES 6

115g/4oz/½ cup butter, softened, plus extra for greasing
30ml/2 tbsp ground coffee
15ml/1 tbsp near-boiling water
50g/2oz/½ cup toasted skinned hazelnuts
4 small ripe pears
juice of ½ orange
115g/4oz/generous ½ cup golden caster (superfine) sugar, plus 15ml/1 tbsp for baking
2 eggs, beaten
50g/2oz/½ cup self-raising (self-rising) flour
45ml/3 tbsp maple syrup
fine strips of orange rind, to decorate

For the orange cream
300ml/½ pint/1¼ cups whipping cream
15ml/1 tbsp icing (confectioners') sugar, sifted
finely grated rind of ½ orange

1 Pour about 2.5cm/1in of hot water into the ceramic cooking pot. Place an upturned saucer or metal pastry ring in the base, then turn on to high. Grease and line the base of a deep 18cm/7in fixed-base cake tin (pan) or soufflé dish.

COOK'S TIPS
• If you can't find ready-toasted skinned hazelnuts, prepare your own. Toast the nuts under a hot grill (broiler) for about 3 minutes, turning frequently until well browned. Leave to cool and rub off the skins before grinding.
• Many supermarkets and specialist food stores sell flavoured coffees. Try using a hazelnut-flavoured coffee for this dessert.

2 Put the ground coffee in a small bowl and pour the water over. Leave to infuse for 4 minutes, then strain through a fine sieve. Place the hazelnuts in a coffee grinder and grind until fine.

3 Peel, halve and core the pears. Thinly slice across the pear halves part of the way through, then brush them all over with the orange juice.

4 Beat the butter and the larger quantity of caster sugar together in a bowl until very light and fluffy. Gradually beat in the eggs. Sift the flour, then fold into the mixture in the bowl. Add the hazelnuts and coffee. Spoon the mixture into the tin or soufflé dish, and level the surface.

5 Pat the pears dry on kitchen paper and arrange in a circle in the sponge mixture, flat side down. Brush them with some of the maple syrup, then sprinkle with the 15ml/1 tbsp caster sugar.

6 Cover the top of the tin or soufflé dish with kitchen foil and place in the ceramic cooking pot. Pour enough boiling water around the tin or dish to come slightly more than halfway up the sides. Cover with a lid and cook for 3–3½ hours, until firm and well risen.

7 Meanwhile, make the orange cream. Whip the cream, icing sugar and orange rind until soft peaks form. Spoon into a serving dish and chill until needed.

8 Leave the sponge to cool in the tin for about 10 minutes, then turn over on to a serving plate. Lightly brush with the remaining maple syrup, then decorate with orange rind and serve with the orange cream.

Energy 852Kcal/3571kJ; Protein 12.5g; Carbohydrate 107g, of which sugars 45g; Fat 44.5g, of which saturates 23.8g; Cholesterol 169mg; Calcium 362mg; Fibre 5.3g; Sodium 493mg.

STEAMED CHOCOLATE and FRUIT PUDDINGS

Drenched in a rich chocolate syrup, this wickedly indulgent steamed pudding makes a great alternative to a traditional Christmas pudding – although it is a fabulous treat at any time of year, the addition of cranberries gives it an unmistakably festive flavour.

SERVES 4

vegetable oil, for greasing
1 apple
25g/1oz/¼ cup cranberries, thawed
   if frozen
175g/6oz/¾ cup soft dark brown sugar
115g/4oz/½ cup soft margarine
2 eggs, lightly beaten
50g/2oz/½ cup self-raising (self-rising)
   flour, sifted
45ml/3 tbsp (unsweetened) cocoa powder

For the syrup
115g/4oz plain (semisweet) chocolate,
   chopped
30ml/2 tbsp clear honey
15g/½oz/1 tbsp unsalted (sweet) butter
2.5ml/½ tsp vanilla extract

1 Pour 2.5cm/1in of hot water into the cooking pot and switch the slow cooker to high. Grease four pudding basins with oil, then line with baking parchment.

2 Peel and core the apple, then dice the flesh. Place in a mixing bowl, then add the cranberries and 15ml/1 tbsp of the sugar. Mix well, then divide the fruit mixture among the prepared basins, gently patting it down into the base of each one.

3 Place the remaining sugar in a clean mixing bowl and add the margarine, eggs, flour and cocoa. Beat together with a wooden spoon until combined and smooth and creamy.

4 Spoon the mixture into the pudding basins and cover each with a double thickness of greased foil. Place the puddings in the ceramic cooking pot and pour in enough very hot water to come about two-thirds up the sides.

5 Cover with a lid and cook on high for 1½–2 hours, or until the puddings are well-risen and firm to the touch. Carefully remove from the slow cooker and leave to stand for 10 minutes.

6 Meanwhile, make the chocolate syrup. Put the chocolate, honey, butter and vanilla extract in a heatproof bowl and place in the hot water in the slow cooker. Leave for 10 minutes, until the butter has melted, then stir until smooth.

7 Run a knife around the edge of the puddings to loosen, then turn over on to warmed individual plates. Serve immediately with the chocolate syrup.

Energy 739Kcal/3094kJ; Protein 9.1g; Carbohydrate 88.3g, of which sugars 77.2g; Fat 41.3g, of which saturates 14.4g; Cholesterol 124mg; Calcium 103mg; Fibre 3.1g; Sodium 438mg.

HOT DATE PUDDINGS with TOFFEE SAUCE

Fresh dates make this pudding less rich than the classic dried date version, but it still makes an utterly indulgent dessert. Ideally, peel the dates because their skins can be tough. Squeeze them between your thumb and forefinger, and the skins will slip off.

3 Put the dates in a heatproof bowl, pour over the boiling water and mash well with a potato masher to make a fairly smooth paste.

4 Sift the flour and bicarbonate of soda over the creamed butter and sugar mixture, and fold in. Add the date paste and gently fold in.

5 Spoon the mixture into the greased moulds or tins. Cover each with a piece of foil. Place in the ceramic cooking pot and pour enough boiling water around the puddings to come just over halfway up the sides. Cover with the lid and cook on high for 1½–2 hours, or until well risen and firm. Remove the puddings from the slow cooker.

6 Meanwhile, make the sauce. Put the butter, sugar, cream and brandy in a pan and heat very gently, stirring occasionally, until the mixture is smooth. Increase the heat and boil for 1 minute.

7 Turn the warm puddings out on to individual dessert plates. Spoon sauce over each one and serve immediately.

SERVES 6

50g/2oz/¼ cup butter, softened
75g/3oz/½ cup light muscovado (brown) sugar
2 eggs, beaten
175g/6oz/generous 1 cup fresh dates, peeled, stoned (pitted) and chopped
75ml/5 tbsp boiling water
115g/4oz/1 cup self-raising (self-rising) flour
2.5ml/½ tsp bicarbonate of soda (baking soda)

For the sauce
50g/2oz/¼ cup butter, at room temperature
75g/3oz/½ cup light muscovado (brown) sugar
60ml/4 tbsp double (heavy) cream
30ml/2 tbsp brandy

1 Grease six individual pudding moulds or tins (pans) – first making sure that they will all fit in the slow cooker. Pour enough very hot water into the ceramic cooking pot to reach a depth of 2cm/¾in. Switch the slow cooker to high.

2 Put the butter and sugar in a mixing bowl and beat until pale and fluffy. Gradually beat in the eggs.

Energy 462Kcal/1932kJ; Protein 5.1g; Carbohydrate 50.3g, of which sugars 35.9g; Fat 26.9g, of which saturates 16g; Cholesterol 138mg; Calcium 109mg; Fibre 1.1g; Sodium 244mg.

FRESH FRUIT BREAD and BUTTER PUDDING

Fresh currants add a tart touch to this scrumptious hot pudding. For the best results, use a wide, shallow dish rather than a narrow, deep one, but make sure it fits comfortably in the slow cooker. Serve drenched with a generous splash of fresh cream.

SERVES 4

40g/1½oz/3 tbsp butter, softened, plus extra for greasing
6 medium-thick slices of day-old bread, crusts removed
115g/4oz/1 cup prepared redcurrants and raspberries
3 eggs, beaten
50g/2oz/¼ cup golden caster (superfine) sugar
300ml/½ pint/1¼ cups creamy milk
5ml/1 tsp vanilla extract
freshly grated nutmeg
30ml/2 tbsp demerara sugar
single (light) cream, to serve

1 Generously butter a 1 litre/1¾ pints/ 4 cup round or oval baking dish – first checking that it fits in your slow cooker.

2 Pour about 2.5cm/1in of very hot water into the ceramic cooking pot. Place an upturned saucer or metal pastry ring in the base and switch the cooker to high.

3 Spread the slices of bread generously with the butter, then use a long serrated knife to cut them in half diagonally.

VARIATIONS
• Try using slices of Italian panettone in place of the white bread. It gives a particularly rich, indulgent result.
• Use fresh blueberries or blackcurrants in place of the fruit used here.
• When fresh berries and currants are unavailable, use chopped ready-to-eat dried apricots instead.

4 Arrange the buttered bread triangles in the dish in neat layers, overlapping the slices, with the buttered side facing up.

5 Scatter the fresh currants and berries over the bread and between the slices, ensuring that there is an even quantity of fruit throughout the pudding.

6 Place the eggs and caster sugar in a large mixing bowl and briefly beat together. Gradually whisk in the milk, vanilla extract and a large pinch of freshly grated nutmeg until well mixed.

COOK'S TIP
Always buy whole nutmegs. Once grated, the spice loses its flavour quickly.

7 Place the baking dish in the ceramic cooking pot, then slowly pour the egg and milk mixture over the bread, pushing the bread slices down to submerge them and making sure they are thoroughly soaked. Sprinkle the demerara sugar and a little nutmeg over the top, then cover the dish with foil.

8 Pour near-boiling water around the dish, so that the water level comes just over halfway up the sides of the dish. Cover with the lid and cook on high for 3–4 hours, or until a skewer inserted into the centre comes out clean.

9 Carefully remove the dish from the slow cooker and, if you like, briefly brown the top of the pudding under a hot grill (broiler). Cool slightly, then serve with the single cream.

Energy 405Kcal/1700kJ; Protein 12.6g; Carbohydrate 53.7g, of which sugars 30.7g; Fat 16.9g, of which saturates 8.6g; Cholesterol 202mg; Calcium 234mg; Fibre 2.1g; Sodium 405mg.

RICH CHOCOLATE CAKE

This rich, dense steamed chocolate cake filled with a decadently creamy buttercream makes a perfect teatime treat. Serve with a big cup of strong coffee.

SERVES 8

115g/4oz plain (semisweet) chocolate,
    chopped into small pieces
45ml/3 tbsp milk
150g/5oz/10 tbsp butter, at room
    temperature
200g/7oz/scant 1 cup soft light
    brown sugar
3 eggs, lightly beaten
200g/7oz/1¾ cups self-raising
    (self-rising) flour
15ml/1 tbsp (unsweetened) cocoa powder
icing (confectioners') sugar and
    (unsweetened) cocoa powder,
    for dusting

For the chocolate buttercream
75g/3oz/6 tbsp butter, at room
    temperature
115g/4oz/1 cup icing (confectioners') sugar
15ml/1 tbsp (unsweetened) cocoa powder
2.5ml/½ tsp vanilla extract

1 Grease and line a deep 18cm/7in fixed-base cake tin (pan) or soufflé dish with baking parchment. Pour about 5cm/2in very hot water into the ceramic cooking pot, then turn the slow cooker to high.

2 Put the chocolate and milk into a heatproof bowl and place in the cooking pot. Leave for about 10 minutes, until the chocolate softens, then stir until smooth. Remove and leave to cool for a few minutes.

3 Meanwhile, place the butter and sugar in a mixing bowl and beat together until light and fluffy. Beat in the eggs, a little at a time, then stir in the chocolate mixture until well mixed.

4 Sift the flour and cocoa over the chocolate mixture and fold in until evenly mixed. Spoon into the prepared tin or dish and cover the top with a piece of foil. Put a saucer in the bottom of the ceramic cooking pot, then rest the tin on top. If necessary, pour in more boiling water to come just over halfway up the sides of the tin.

5 Cover the slow cooker with the lid and cook for 3–3½ hours, or until firm to the touch and a fine skewer inserted into the middle comes out clean. Carefully lift the tin out of the cooking pot and leave to stand on a wire rack for 10 minutes. Turn out and leave to cool. Remove the lining paper.

6 To make the buttercream, put the butter in a large bowl and beat until very soft. Sift over the icing sugar and cocoa powder, then stir together. Add the vanilla extract and beat until the buttercream is light and fluffy.

7 Very carefully, cut the cake in half horizontally and spread a thick, even layer of the buttercream on one of the cut halves. Sandwich the cakes back together, then dust with a mixture of icing sugar and cocoa and serve.

Energy 564Kcal/2363kJ; Protein 6.6g; Carbohydrate 70g, of which sugars 51g; Fat 30.5g, of which saturates 18.2g; Cholesterol 146mg; Calcium 129mg; Fibre 1.5g; Sodium 321mg.

CHOCOLATE CHIP WALNUT CAKE

The tangy flavour of orange works well in this chocolate and nut loaf. It can be finished simply with a generous dusting of icing sugar, or as here with a zesty orange topping.

SERVES 8

115g/4oz/1 cup plain (all-purpose) flour
25g/1oz/¼ cup cornflour (cornstarch)
5ml/1 tsp baking powder
115g/4oz/½ cup butter, at room temperature
115g/4oz/½ cup golden caster (superfine) sugar
2 eggs, lightly beaten
75g/3oz/½ cup plain (semisweet), milk or white chocolate chips
50g/2oz/½ cup chopped walnuts
finely grated rind of ½ orange

For the topping
115g/4oz/1 cup icing (confectioners') sugar, sifted, plus 5ml/1 tsp for dusting
20–30ml/4 tsp–2 tbsp freshly squeezed orange juice
walnut halves, to decorate

1 Grease and line a 450g/1lb loaf tin (pan), with a capacity of 900ml/1½ pints/3¾ cups, with baking parchment. Place a metal pastry ring or upturned saucer in the base of the ceramic cooking pot and pour in about 2.5cm/1in very hot water. Switch the slow cooker to high.

2 Sift the flour, cornflour and baking powder together twice, so that the dry ingredients are well mixed and aerated, then set aside.

3 Place the butter in a large mixing bowl and beat until creamy. Add the golden caster sugar and continue beating until light and fluffy. Add the eggs a little at a time, beating well after each addition.

4 Gently fold about half of the sifted flour mixture into the creamed butter and sugar mixture, then add the rest with the chocolate chips, walnuts and orange rind. Fold in until just blended, taking care not to overmix.

5 Spoon the mixture into the prepared loaf tin and loosely cover with a piece of foil, allowing some space at the top for the cake to rise as it cooks.

6 Put the loaf tin on the pastry ring or saucer inside the ceramic cooking pot. Pour enough boiling water around the loaf tin to come two-thirds of the way up the sides.

7 Cover the slow cooker with a lid and cook for 2½–3 hours, or until a fine skewer pushed into the centre of the cake comes out clean. Carefully remove the cake from the slow cooker and stand it on a wire rack for 10 minutes, then turn out and leave to cool on the rack.

8 To decorate the cake, place the 115g/4oz/1 cup icing sugar in a mixing bowl. Stir in 20ml/4 tsp of the orange juice, adding a little more if needed to make the consistency of thick cream. Drizzle the mixture over the cake, then decorate with walnut halves dusted with the 5ml/1 tsp icing sugar. Leave the topping to set before serving.

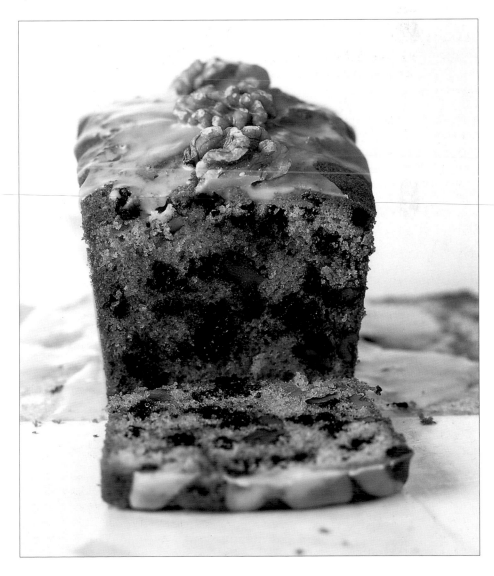

Energy 395Kcal/1655kJ; Protein 4.7g; Carbohydrate 51g, of which sugars 36.9g; Fat 20.5g, of which saturates 9.9g; Cholesterol 87mg; Calcium 49mg; Fibre 0.9g; Sodium 171mg.

FROSTED CARROT and PARSNIP CAKE

A delicious twist on the classic plain carrot cake, this version is wonderfully light and crumbly. The grated vegetables help to keep it moist, and account for its excellent keeping qualities. Cooked meringue spread over the top makes a change from the usual cream cheese topping, and makes a stunning contrast to the wholesome, crumbly cake.

SERVES 8

oil, for greasing
1 orange or lemon
10ml/2 tsp caster (superfine) sugar
175g/6oz/¾ cup butter or margarine
175g/6oz/¾ cup soft light brown sugar
3 eggs, lightly beaten
175g/6oz carrots and parsnips, grated
50g/2oz/⅓ cup sultanas
    (golden raisins)
115g/4oz/1 cup self-raising
    (self-rising) flour
50g/2oz/½ cup self-raising (self-rising)
    wholemeal (whole-wheat) flour
5ml/1 tsp baking powder

For the topping
50g/2oz/¼ cup caster (superfine) sugar
1 egg white
pinch of salt

1 Put an upturned saucer or metal pastry cutter in the base of the ceramic cooking pot and pour in about 2.5cm/1in hot water. Turn the slow cooker to high. Lightly grease a deep 18cm/7in round fixed-based cake tin (pan) or soufflé dish with oil and line the base with baking parchment.

2 Finely grate the orange or lemon rind, taking care not to take off any of the white pith. Selecting the longest shreds, put about half the rind in a bowl and mix with the caster sugar. Arrange the sugar-coated rind on a sheet of greaseproof (waxed) paper and leave in a warm place to dry.

3 Put the butter or margarine and brown sugar in a large mixing bowl and beat together until pale and fluffy. Add the eggs a little at a time, beating well after each addition. Stir in the unsugared orange or lemon rind, grated carrots and parsnips and sultanas.

4 Sift the flours and baking powder together, adding any bran left in the sieve (strainer), then gradually fold into the carrot and parsnip mixture.

5 Transfer the mixture to the prepared tin and level the surface. Cover loosely with greased foil, then place in the ceramic cooking pot, on top of the saucer or pastry cutter. Pour sufficient boiling water around the tin to come just over halfway up the sides.

6 Cover the slow cooker with the lid and cook for 3–5 hours, or until a skewer inserted in the centre of the cake comes out clean. Carefully lift the tin out of the slow cooker and leave to stand for 5 minutes. Turn the cake out on to a wire rack and leave until cool.

7 To make the topping, place the caster sugar in a bowl over the near-simmering water in the slow cooker. Squeeze the juice from the orange or lemon and add 30ml/2 tbsp of the juice to the sugar. Stir over the heat until the sugar dissolves. Remove from the heat, add the egg white and salt, and whisk for 1 minute with an electric beater.

8 Return the bowl to the heat and whisk for about 6 minutes until the mixture becomes stiff and glossy, holding a good shape. Remove from the heat and allow to cool for about 5 minutes, whisking frequently.

9 Swirl the meringue topping over the cake and leave for 1 hour to firm up. To serve, sprinkle with the sugared orange or lemon rind.

VARIATION
If you do not like parsnips, you can make this cake with just carrots, or replace the parsnips with the same weight of grated courgettes (zucchini). Add a pinch of cinnamon and nutmeg to the mixture.

Energy 410Kcal/1718kJ; Protein 5.9g; Carbohydrate 53g, of which sugars 38.2g; Fat 20.8g, of which saturates 12.2g; Cholesterol 132mg; Calcium 98mg; Fibre 1.9g; Sodium 290mg.

CHOCOLATE CHEESECAKE BROWNIES

A very dense chocolate brownie mixture is swirled with creamy cheese to give a marbled effect. Cut into small squares for little mouthfuls of absolute heaven.

MAKES 9

50g/2oz dark (bittersweet) chocolate
   (minimum 70 per cent cocoa solids),
   chopped
50g/2oz/¼ cup unsalted (sweet) butter
65g/2½oz/5 tbsp light muscovado
   (brown) sugar
1 egg, beaten
25g/1oz/¼ cup plain (all-purpose) flour

For the cheesecake mixture
115g/4oz/½ cup full-fat cream cheese
25g/1oz/2 tbsp caster (superfine) sugar
5ml/1 tsp vanilla extract
½ beaten egg

1 Line the base and sides of a 15cm/6in square fixed-base cake tin (pan) with baking parchment. Pour about 5cm/2in of very hot water into the ceramic cooking pot and switch to high.

2 Put the chocolate and butter in a heatproof bowl and place in the slow cooker. Leave to stand for 10 minutes.

3 Meanwhile, make the cheesecake mixture. Put the cream cheese, sugar and vanilla extract in a clean mixing bowl and beat together. Gradually beat in the egg until the mixture is very smooth and creamy. Set aside.

4 Stir the chocolate and butter mixture until completely melted and smooth, then remove the bowl from the slow cooker. Add the muscovado sugar and stir to combine. Place an upturned saucer or metal pastry ring in the base of the ceramic cooking pot.

5 Add the beaten egg to the melted chocolate mixture a little at a time, and beat well until thoroughly mixed, then sift over the flour and gently fold in.

6 Spoon the chocolate mixture into the base of the tin. Drop small spoonfuls of the cheesecake mixture on top. Using a skewer, swirl the mixtures together.

7 Cover the tin with foil and place in the slow cooker. Pour in more boiling water around the tin to come just over halfway up the sides. Cook for 2 hours, or until just set in the centre. Remove the tin from the slow cooker and place on a wire rack to cool. Cut into squares.

Energy 174Kcal/727kJ; Protein 2.9g; Carbohydrate 16.2g, of which sugars 14g; Fat 11.3g, of which saturates 6.8g; Cholesterol 65mg; Calcium 25mg; Fibre 0.2g; Sodium 86mg.

LIGHT FRUIT CAKE

This incredibly easy all-in-one fruit cake has a crumbly texture. The combination of wholemeal flour and long slow cooking ensures that it stays beautifully moist.

SERVES 12

2 eggs
130g/4½oz/generous ½ cup butter,
    at room temperature
225g/8oz/1 cup light muscovado
    (brown) sugar
150g/5oz/1¼ cups self-raising
    (self-rising) flour
150g/5oz/1¼ cups wholemeal
    (whole-wheat) self-raising
    (self-rising) flour
pinch of salt
5ml/1 tsp mixed (apple pie) spice
450g/1lb/2½ cups luxury mixed
    dried fruit

1 Line the base and sides of a deep 18cm/7in round or 15cm/6in square fixed-base cake tin (pan) with baking parchment. Place an upturned saucer or metal pastry ring in the base of the ceramic cooking pot, then pour in about 2.5cm/1in of very hot water. Switch the slow cooker to high.

2 Crack the eggs into a large mixing bowl. Add the butter and sugar, then sift over the flours, salt and spice, adding any bran left in the sieve (strainer). Stir together with a wooden spoon until mixed, then add the dried fruit and beat for 2 minutes until the mixture is smooth and glossy.

COOK'S TIP
Choose a good-quality brand of luxury dried fruits. It should contain a good mix of currants, sultanas (golden raisins), mixed peel and glacé (candied) cherries, as well as other dried fruits.

3 Spoon the mixture into the prepared cake tin and level the surface. Cover the tin with a piece of buttered foil.

4 Put the tin in the slow cooker and pour in enough boiling water to come just over halfway up the sides of the tin. Cover with the lid and cook for 4–5 hours, or until a skewer inserted into the middle of the cake comes out clean.

5 Remove the cake from the slow cooker and place on a wire rack. Leave the cake to cool in the tin for about 15 minutes, then turn out and leave to cool completely. To store, wrap the cake in greaseproof (waxed) paper and then foil, and keep in a cool place.

Energy 351Kcal/1482kJ; Protein 4.9g; Carbohydrate 63g, of which sugars 46g; Fat 10.6g, of which saturates 6g; Cholesterol 60.8mg; Calcium 78.6mg; Fibre 2.3g; Sodium 148mg.

MARBLED SPICE CAKE

This cake can be baked in a fluted ring-shaped cake mould called a kugelhupf *or* gugelhupf, *which originates from Germany and Austria, or in a plain ring-shaped cake tin. The marbled effect looks particularly good when the cake is baked in a ring like this.*

SERVES 8

75g/3oz/6 tbsp butter, at room
   temperature, plus extra for greasing
130g/4½oz/generous 1 cup plain
   (all-purpose) flour, plus extra for
   dusting
115g/4oz/½ cup soft light brown sugar
2 eggs
few drops of vanilla extract
7.5ml/1½ tsp baking powder
45ml/3 tbsp milk
30ml/2 tbsp malt extract or black treacle
5ml/1 tsp mixed (apple pie) spice
2.5ml/½ tsp ground ginger
75g/3oz/¾ cup icing (confectioners') sugar,
   sifted, to decorate

1 Grease and flour a 1.2 litre/2 pint/
5 cup *kugelhupf* mould or ring-shaped
cake tin (pan). Put an inverted saucer
or large metal pastry cutter in the base
of the slow cooker and pour in about
5cm/2in hot water. Switch the slow
cooker to high.

2 Put the butter and sugar in a bowl
and beat together until light and fluffy.

3 In a separate bowl, beat together the
eggs and vanilla extract, then gradually
beat into the butter and sugar mixture,
adding a little at a time and beating well
after each addition.

COOK'S TIP
To make a marbled chocolate and vanilla
cake, stir 15ml/1 tbsp chocolate essence
into the cake mixture, in place of the
malt extract or treacle and spices.

4 Sift together the flour and baking
powder to combine, then fold the flour
into the butter and sugar mixture, adding
a little of the milk between each addition
until evenly combined.

5 Spoon about one-third of the mixture
into a small bowl and stir in the malt
extract or treacle, mixed spice and
ginger until just combined.

6 Drop a large spoonful of the light
mixture into the cake tin, followed by a
spoonful of the dark mixture. Continue
alternating spoonfuls of the light and
dark mixtures until all the mixture has
been used. Run a knife or skewer through
the mixtures to give a marbled effect.

7 Cover the tin with foil and place in
the ceramic cooking pot. Pour a little
more boiling water around the tin to
come just over halfway up the sides.
Cover the slow cooker with the lid and
cook for 3–4 hours. To test if it is done,
insert a skewer into the middle of the
cake; it should come out clean.

8 Carefully lift the cake out of the slow
cooker and leave in the tin for about
10 minutes before turning out on to
a wire rack to cool.

9 To decorate, place the icing sugar in
a bowl and add just enough warm water
to make a smooth icing (frosting) with
the consistency of single (light) cream.
Quickly drizzle the mixture over the
cake, then leave to set before serving
the cake in thick slices.

Energy 215Kcal/902kJ; Protein 2.8g; Carbohydrate 33g, of which sugars 20.3g; Fat 8.8g, of which saturates 5.2g; Cholesterol 49mg; Calcium 84mg; Fibre 0.5g; Sodium 172mg.

BLUEBERRY MUFFIN PUDDING

You can't cook traditional muffins in a slow cooker but this delicious alternative will satisfy your cravings. It's especially good served barely warm with custard or crème fraîche. Take the eggs and buttermilk out of the refrigerator at least an hour before you start mixing.

SERVES 4

75g/3oz/6 tbsp butter, plus extra
   for greasing
75g/3oz/6 tbsp soft light brown sugar
105ml/7 tbsp buttermilk, at room
   temperature
2 eggs, lightly beaten, at room temperature
225g/8oz/2 cups self raising
   (self-rising) flour
pinch of salt
5ml/1 tsp ground cinnamon
150g/5oz/¼ cup fresh blueberries
10ml/2 tsp demerara (raw) sugar,
   for sprinkling
custard or crème fraîche, to serve

1 Place an upturned saucer or metal pastry ring in the base of the slow cooker. Pour in about 5cm/2in of very hot water, then switch the slow cooker to high. Lightly grease a 1.5 litre/2½ pint/6¼ cup heatproof dish with butter – first making sure that it will fit the inside of your slow cooker.

2 Put the butter and sugar in a heatproof jug (pitcher) and place in the ceramic cooking pot. Leave uncovered for 20 minutes, stirring, until melted.

3 Remove the jug from the slow cooker and leave to cool until tepid, then stir in the buttermilk followed by the beaten egg, until well mixed.

COOK'S TIP
Because less liquid evaporates from the pudding in a slow cooker, the mixture is thicker than a conventional muffin batter.

4 Sift the flour, salt and cinnamon into a mixing bowl. Stir in the blueberries, then make a hollow in the middle. Pour in the buttermilk mixture and quickly stir until just combined. Do not overmix.

5 Spoon the mixture into the prepared dish, then sprinkle the top with the demerara sugar. Cover with a piece of buttered foil and place in the ceramic cooking pot. Pour in a little more boiling water around the dish, if necessary, to come halfway up the sides.

6 Cover the slow cooker with the lid and cook for 3–4 hours, until a skewer inserted in the middle comes out clean. Remove from the slow cooker and let the pudding cool slightly before serving with custard or crème fraîche.

Energy 499Kcal/2101kJ; Protein 10.1g; Carbohydrate 76.2g, of which sugars 34.4g; Fat 19.2g, of which saturates 10.7g; Cholesterol 153mg; Calcium 262mg; Fibre 2.2g; Sodium 367mg.

PUMPKIN and BANANA CAKE

Rather like a cross between a carrot cake and banana bread, this luscious cake is an excellent way of using some of the scooped-out pumpkin flesh after making Hallowe'en lanterns. A cream cheese topping provides a delicious contrast with the dense moist cake.

SERVES 12

225g/8oz/2 cups self-raising
   (self-rising) flour
7.5ml/1½ tsp baking powder
2.5ml/½ tsp ground cinnamon
2.5ml/½ tsp ground ginger
pinch of salt
125g/5oz/10 tbsp soft light brown sugar
75g/3oz/¾ cup pecans or walnuts,
   chopped
115g/4oz pumpkin flesh, coarsely grated
2 small bananas, peeled and mashed
2 eggs, lightly beaten
150ml/¼ pint/⅔ cup sunflower oil

For the topping
50g/2oz/¼ cup butter, at room
   temperature
150g/5oz/⅔ cup soft cheese
1.5ml/¼ tsp vanilla extract
115g/4oz/1 cup icing (confectioners') sugar
pecan halves, to decorate

1 Line the base and sides of a deep 20cm/8in round fixed-base cake tin (pan) or soufflé dish with baking parchment. Place an upturned saucer or metal pastry ring in the base of the ceramic cooking pot, then pour in about 2.5cm/1in of very hot water. Switch the slow cooker to high.

2 Sift the flour, baking powder, cinnamon, ginger and salt into a large mixing bowl to combine. Stir in the sugar, chopped pecans or walnuts and grated pumpkin until thoroughly mixed. Make a slight hollow in the middle of the dry ingredients.

3 In a separate bowl, combine the bananas, eggs and sunflower oil, then stir into the dry ingredients. Turn into the prepared tin and level the surface.

4 Cover the tin with a piece of buttered foil and place in the slow cooker. Pour in sufficient boiling water to come just over halfway up the sides of the tin.

5 Cover the pot with the lid and cook on high for 4–4½ hours, or until the cake is firm and a skewer inserted into the middle comes out clean.

6 Carefully remove the cake from the slow cooker and stand the tin on a wire rack to cool for 15 minutes. Turn out and leave to cool completely, then peel off the lining paper.

7 To make the topping, put the butter, soft cheese and vanilla extract in a bowl and beat until blended and smooth. Sift in the icing sugar and beat again until smooth and creamy. Thickly spread the topping over the top of the cake and decorate with pecan halves. Chill in the refrigerator for at least 1 hour before serving, to allow the topping to harden.

Energy 374Kcal/1567kJ; Protein 5.1g; Carbohydrate 43.2g, of which sugars 28.7g; Fat 21.3g, of which saturates 6.5g; Cholesterol 58mg; Calcium 101.7mg; Fibre 1g; Sodium 203mg.

MOIST GOLDEN GINGER CAKE

This is the ultimate ginger cake: instead of the traditional black treacle, a mixture of golden syrup and malt extract gives a really sticky, moist texture. Because of the long slow cooking, the cake matures sufficiently to eat straight away. However, the flavour improves and the texture becomes stickier if it is wrapped and kept for a day or two.

SERVES 10

175g/6oz/generous ¾ cup light muscovado (brown) sugar
115g/4oz/½ cup butter
150g/5oz/⅔ cup golden (light corn) syrup
25g/1oz malt extract
175g/6oz/1½ cups self-raising (self-rising) flour
50g/2oz/½ cup plain (all-purpose) flour
10ml/2 tsp ground ginger
pinch of salt
1 egg, lightly beaten
120ml/4fl oz/½ cup milk, at room temperature
2.5ml/½ tsp bicarbonate of soda (baking soda)

1 Line the base of a deep 18cm/7in round fixed-base cake tin (pan) or soufflé dish with baking parchment. Pour 5cm/2in of very hot water into the ceramic cooking pot. Switch to high.

2 Place the sugar, butter, golden syrup and malt extract in a heatproof bowl that will fit inside the slow cooker. Place in the ceramic cooking pot and leave for 15 minutes, or until melted.

3 Remove the bowl from the slow cooker and stir until smooth. Place an upturned saucer or metal pastry ring in the base of the ceramic cooking pot.

4 Sift the flours, ginger and salt into a separate mixing bowl. Pour the melted butter and sugar mixture into the flour and beat until smooth. Stir in the beaten egg until well mixed.

VARIATION

To turn this moist cake into a tempting treat for kids, try decorating it with plain lemon icing (frosting) and scattering with multi-coloured sugar sprinkles. To make the icing, put 75g/3oz/¾ cup icing sugar in a bowl and stir in just enough lemon juice to make a smooth icing with the consistency of single (light) cream. Drizzle over the cake and scatter with sprinkles.

5 Pour the milk in a jug (pitcher) and stir in the bicarbonate of soda. Pour the mixture into the ginger cake mixture and stir until combined.

6 Pour the cake mixture into the prepared cake tin or soufflé dish, cover with foil and place in the cooking pot.

7 Pour a little more boiling water around the tin or dish to come just over halfway up the sides. Cover with the lid and cook for 5–6 hours, or until firm and a fine skewer inserted into the middle of the cake comes out clean.

8 Remove the cake from the slow cooker and place the tin or dish on a wire cooling rack. Leave to cool for 15 minutes, then turn out and leave to cool completely before serving in slices.

COOK'S TIP

Because this cake improves with keeping, it is the perfect choice when you are expecting guests because you can make it several days in advance.

Energy 289Kcal/1216kJ; Protein 3.4g; Carbohydrate 48g, of which sugars 31.1g; Fat 10.6g, of which saturates 6.4g; Cholesterol 48mg; Calcium 98mg; Fibre 0.7g; Sodium 211mg.

ONE-POT, CLAY-POT DESSERTS AND CAKES

The clever cook who saves time and effort by mastering one-pot and clay-pot cooking deserves a sweet reward, and what better way to celebrate success than with Baked Maple and Pecan Croissant Pudding or Honey-baked Figs – cooked in a clay pot, of course – served with Hazelnut Ice Cream. Black Cherry Clafoutis is another treat or, for pots of pleasure, try sweet and tangy Citrus and Caramel Custards, which are baked in individual cazuelas, or elegant and impressive Plum Charlottes with Foamy Kirsch Sauce. There are also classic tarts and pies to bake including Tarte Tatin and scrumptious Apple Pie.

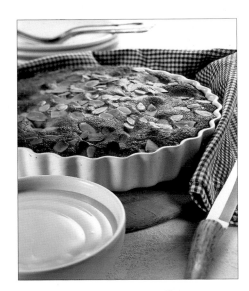

PLUM CHARLOTTES with FOAMY KIRSCH SAUCE

These individual puddings, cooked in mini earthenware dishes, conceal a fresh plum filling and are served on a pool of light, frothy Kirsch-flavoured sauce.

SERVES 4

115g/4oz/½ cup butter, melted
50g/2oz/4 tbsp demerara (raw) sugar
450g/1lb ripe plums, stoned (pitted) and
   thickly sliced
25g/1oz/2 tbsp caster (superfine) sugar
30ml/2 tbsp water
1.5ml/¼ tsp ground cinnamon
25g/1oz/¼ cup ground almonds
8–10 large slices of white bread

For the Kirsch sauce
3 egg yolks
40g/1½oz/3 tbsp caster
   (superfine) sugar
30ml/2 tbsp Kirsch

2 Place the stoned plum slices in a pan with the caster sugar, water and ground cinnamon and cook gently for 5 minutes, or until the plums have softened slightly. Leave them to cool, then stir in the ground almonds.

5 Divide the plum mixture among the lined dishes. Place the bread rounds on top and brush with the remaining butter. Place the ramekins on a baking sheet and bake for 25 minutes.

1 Preheat the oven to 190°C/375°F/ Gas 5. Line the base of four individual 10cm/4in-diameter deep, earthenware ramekin dishes with baking parchment. Brush evenly and thoroughly with a little of the melted butter, then sprinkle each dish with a little of the demerara sugar, rotating the dish in your hands to coat each dish evenly.

VARIATIONS
• Slices of peeled pear or eating apples can be used in this recipe instead of the stoned, sliced plums.
• If using apples or pears substitute the Kirsch in the foamy sauce with Calvados or another apple brandy.
• If you are short on time, drained canned fruit such as pineapple, apricots, pears or plums can be used – simply stir in the ground almonds as in step 2 and add to the prepared ramekins.

3 Cut the crusts off the bread and then use a plain pastry cutter to cut out four rounds to fit the bases of the ramekins. Dip the bread rounds into the melted butter and fit them into the dishes. Cut four more rounds to fit the tops of the dishes and set aside.

4 Cut the remaining bread into strips, dip into the melted butter and use to line the sides of the ramekins completely.

6 Just before the charlottes are ready place the egg yolks and caster sugar for the sauce in a bowl. Whisk together until pale. Place the bowl over a pan of simmering water and whisk in the Kirsch. Continue whisking until the mixture is very light and frothy.

7 Remove the charlottes from the oven and turn out on to warm serving plates. Pour a little sauce over and around the charlottes and serve immediately.

COOK'S TIP
For an extra indulgent dessert, serve the puddings with lightly whipped double (heavy) cream flavoured with extra Kirsch and sweetened to taste with a little sieved icing (confectioners') sugar.

Energy 600Kcal/2513kJ; Protein 9.1g; Carbohydrate 69.6g, of which sugars 44.2g; Fat 32.5g, of which saturates 16.5g; Cholesterol 218mg; Calcium 128mg; Fibre 3.1g; Sodium 467mg.

BAKED MAPLE and PECAN CROISSANT PUDDING

This variation of the classic English bread and butter pudding uses croissants, which give a light fluffy texture. Pecans, brandy-laced sultanas and maple syrup-flavoured custard complete this mouthwatering dessert.

SERVES 4

75g/3oz/generous ½ cup sultanas
   (golden raisins)
45ml/3 tbsp brandy
50g/2oz/¼ cup butter, plus extra for greasing
4 large croissants
40g/1½oz/⅓ cup pecan nuts,
   roughly chopped
3 eggs, lightly beaten
300ml/½ pint/1¼ cups milk
150ml/¼ pint/⅔ cup single (light) cream
120ml/4fl oz/½ cup maple syrup
25g/1oz/2 tbsp demerara (raw) sugar
maple syrup and pouring (half-and-half)
   cream, to serve (optional)

1 Place the sultanas and brandy in a small pan and heat gently, until warm. Leave to stand for 1 hour. Soak a small clay pot in cold water for 15 minutes, then drain, leave for 2–3 minutes and lightly grease the base and sides.

2 Cut the croissants (see Cook's Tip) into thick slices, then spread with butter on one side.

3 Arrange the croissant slices, butter-side uppermost and slightly overlapping in the soaked clay pot. Sprinkle the brandy-soaked sultanas and the roughly chopped pecan nuts over the buttered croissant slices.

4 In a large bowl, beat the eggs and milk together, then gradually beat in the single cream and maple syrup.

5 Pour the egg custard through a sieve, over the croissants, fruit and nuts in the dish. Leave the uncooked pudding to stand for 30 minutes, so that some of the egg custard liquid is absorbed by the croissants.

6 Sprinkle the demerara sugar evenly over the top, then cover the dish and place in an unheated oven. Set the oven to 180°C/350°F/Gas 4 and bake for 40 minutes. Remove the lid and continue to cook for about 20 minutes, or until the custard is set and the top is golden.

7 Leave the pudding to cool for about 15 minutes before serving warm with extra maple syrup and a little pouring cream, if you like.

COOK'S TIPS
• This dessert is perfect for using up leftover croissants. Slightly stale one-day-old croissants are easier to slice and butter; they also soak up the custard more easily. Thickly sliced one-day-old bread or large slices of brioche could be used instead.
• Pecan nuts are an elongated nut in a glossy red oval-shaped shell, but are usually sold shelled. They are native to the USA and have a sweet, mild flavour. Pecans are most commonly used in pecan pie but are also popular in ice creams and cakes. Walnuts can be substituted for pecans in most recipes, and they would be perfect in this one if you don't have any pecan nuts.

COCONUT RICE PUDDING

A delicious adaptation of the classic creamy rice pudding, this dessert is flavoured with coconut milk and finished with a coconut crust.

SERVES 4

75g/3oz/scant ½ cup short grain
    pudding rice
40g/1½oz/3 tbsp caster
    (superfine) sugar
2.5ml/½ tsp vanilla extract
300ml/½ pint/1¼ cups milk
400ml/14fl oz/1⅔ cups coconut milk
105ml/7 tbsp single (light) cream
30ml/2 tbsp desiccated (dry unsweetened
    shredded) coconut or slivers of
    fresh coconut

VARIATION

If preferred, this pudding can be made
with extra milk instead of the single
cream. Use full cream (whole) milk, for
a rich, creamy flavour.

1 Soak a small clay pot in cold water
for 15 minutes, then drain. Add the rice,
sugar, vanilla extract, milk, coconut milk
and cream.

2 Cover the clay pot and place in a cold
oven. Set the oven to 180°C/350°F/
Gas 4 and cook for 1 hour.

3 Remove the lid from the clay pot, stir
the pudding gently, then re-cover and
cook for a further 30–45 minutes, or
until the rice is tender.

4 Remove the lid, stir the pudding, then
sprinkle with desiccated or fresh coconut
and bake uncovered for 10–15 minutes.

Energy 259Kcal/1087kJ; Protein 5.8g; Carbohydrate 34g, of which sugars 19.9g; Fat 11.6g, of which saturates 8.2g; Cholesterol 19mg; Calcium 153mg; Fibre 1g; Sodium 153mg.

CITRUS and CARAMEL CUSTARDS

These Spanish-style custards, made rich with cream and egg yolks, are delicately scented with tangy citrus flavours and aromatic cinnamon.

SERVES 4

450ml/¾ pint/scant 2 cups milk
150ml/¼ pint/⅔ cup single
   (light) cream
1 cinnamon stick, broken in half
thinly pared rind of ½ lemon
thinly pared rind of ½ orange
4 egg yolks
5ml/1 tsp cornflour (cornstarch)
40g/1½oz/3 tbsp caster (superfine) sugar
grated rind of ½ lemon
grated rind of ½ orange
a little icing (confectioner's) sugar,
   for sprinkling

1 Place the milk and cream in a pan. Add the cinnamon stick and the strips of pared citrus rind. Bring to the boil, then simmer for 10 minutes.

2 Preheat the oven to 160°C/325°F/ Gas 3. Whisk the egg yolks, cornflour and caster sugar together. Remove the rinds and cinnamon from the hot milk and cream and discard. Whisk the hot milk and cream into the egg yolk mixture.

3 Stir the grated citrus rind into the custard mixture. Pour into four individual cazuelas, each about 13cm/5in in diameter. Place in a roasting pan and pour warm water into the pan to reach three-quarters of the way up the sides. Bake for 25–30 minutes, or until the custards are just set. Remove the dishes from the water; leave to cool, then chill.

4 Preheat the grill (broiler) to high. Sprinkle the custards liberally with icing sugar and place under the grill until the tops turn golden brown and caramelize.

COOK'S TIPS

• Prepare the grated rind first, then cut a few strips of rind from the ungrated side of the citrus fruits using a swivel-bladed vegetable peeler.
• You can use a special cook's gas-gun or salamander to caramelize the tops instead of grilling (broiling) them.

Energy 225Kcal/939kJ; Protein 8g; Carbohydrate 16.6g, of which sugars 16.6g; Fat 14.6g, of which saturates 7.3g; Cholesterol 229mg; Calcium 197mg; Fibre 0g; Sodium 69mg.

HONEY-BAKED FIGS with HAZELNUT ICE CREAM

This is a delectable dessert – fresh figs are baked in a lightly spiced lemon and honey syrup and served with a gorgeous, home-made roasted hazelnut ice cream.

SERVES 4

1 lemon grass stalk, finely chopped
1 cinnamon stick, roughly broken
60ml/4 tbsp clear honey
200ml/7fl oz/scant 1 cup water
8 large figs

For the hazelnut ice cream
450ml/¾ pint/scant 2 cups double
   (heavy) cream
50g/2oz/¼ cup caster (superfine) sugar
3 egg yolks
1.5ml/¼ tsp vanilla extract
75g/3oz/¾ cup hazelnuts

1 To make the ice cream, place the cream in a pan and heat slowly until almost boiling. Place the sugar and egg yolks in a bowl and beat until creamy.

2 Pour a little of the cream on to the egg yolk mixture and stir. Pour into the pan and mix with the rest of the cream. Cook over a low heat, stirring constantly, until the mixture thickens slightly and lightly coats the back of the spoon – do not allow it to boil. Pour into a bowl, then stir in the vanilla and leave to cool.

3 Preheat the oven to 180°C/350°F/Gas 4. Place the hazelnuts on a baking sheet and roast for 10–12 minutes, or until golden. Leave the nuts to cool, then place them in a food processor or blender and process until they are coarsely ground.

4 Transfer the ice cream mixture to a metal or plastic freezer container and freeze for 2 hours, or until the mixture feels firm around the edge. Remove the container from the freezer and whisk the ice cream to break down the ice crystals. Stir in the ground hazelnuts and freeze the mixture again until half-frozen. Whisk again, then freeze until firm.

COOK'S TIPS
• If you prefer, rather than whisking the semi-frozen ice cream, tip it into a food processor and process until smooth.
• There are several different types of figs available and they can all be used in this recipe. Choose from green-skinned figs that have an amber-coloured flesh, dark purple-skinned fruit with a deep red flesh or green/yellow-skinned figs with a pinky-coloured flesh.

5 Place the lemon grass, cinnamon stick, honey and water in a small pan and heat slowly until boiling. Simmer the mixture for 5 minutes, then leave the syrup to stand for 15 minutes.

6 Meanwhile, soak a small clay pot in cold water for 15 minutes. Cut the figs into quarters, leaving them intact at the bases. Place the figs in the clay pot and pour over the honey-flavoured syrup.

7 Cover the clay pot and place in an unheated oven. Set the oven to 200°C/400°F/Gas 6 and bake the figs for about 15 minutes, or until tender.

8 Take the ice cream from the freezer about 10 minutes before serving, to soften slightly. Transfer the figs to serving plates. Strain a little of the cooking liquid over the figs and then serve them with a scoop or two of hazelnut ice cream.

VARIATION
This recipe also works well with halved, stoned (pitted) nectarines or peaches – simply cook as from step 6 and serve with the home-made ice cream.

Energy 909Kcal/3770kJ; Protein 8.2g; Carbohydrate 48.7g, of which sugars 48.4g; Fat 77.1g, of which saturates 39.6g; Cholesterol 305mg; Calcium 206mg; Fibre 4.2g; Sodium 60mg.

SPICED PEARS with NUT CRUMBLE

*An all-time favourite, this crumble has a crunchy pecan nut and oat topping,
which complements the spicy pears hidden beneath.*

SERVES 4–6

900g/2lb pears
30ml/2 tbsp lemon juice
40g/1½oz/3 tbsp caster (superfine) sugar
5ml/1 tsp mixed (apple pie) spice
2.5ml/½ tsp grated nutmeg
vanilla ice cream, to serve

For the crumble topping
75g/3oz/⅔ cup plain (all-purpose) flour
75g/3oz/6 tbsp butter
50g/2oz/¼ cup light muscovado
    (brown) sugar
50g/2oz/½ cup pecan nuts or
    walnuts, chopped
40g/1½oz/scant ½ cup rolled oats

COOK'S TIP
Look out for golden-skinned Forelle pears,
which are especially good for cooking, or
try Anjou, Williams or Conference pears.

1 Soak a small clay pot in cold water for
15 minutes, then drain. Peel the pears
if wished, then halve them and remove
the cores. Cut each pear into six wedges
and toss in the lemon juice.

2 Place the pears in the clay pot, add
the sugar, mixed spice and nutmeg and
mix together. Place in an unheated oven,
set the oven to 200°C/400°F/Gas 6 and
cook for 25 minutes.

3 Meanwhile, prepare the crumble
topping. Sift the flour into a bowl and
rub in the butter, then stir in the sugar,
nuts and rolled oats.

4 Uncover the clay pot and stir gently to
rearrange the fruit. Spoon the crumble
mixture over the pears, then return the
clay pot to the oven for 25–30 minutes,
or until the crumble is golden. Serve
warm, with vanilla ice cream.

Energy 365Kcal/1523kJ; Protein 3.5g; Carbohydrate 42.9g, of which sugars 33.2g; Fat 21g, of which saturates 7.4g; Cholesterol 27mg; Calcium 57mg; Fibre 4.3g; Sodium 82mg.

NECTARINES BAKED with ALMONDS and PISTACHIO NUTS

Fresh nectarines stuffed with a ground almond and chopped pistachio nut filling, baked in a clay pot until meltingly tender, then served with a passion fruit sauce.

SERVES 4

50g/2oz/½ cup ground almonds
15ml/1 tbsp caster (superfine) sugar
1 egg yolk
50g/2oz/⅓ cup shelled pistachio
   nuts, chopped
4 nectarines
200ml/7fl oz/scant 1 cup orange juice
2 ripe passion fruits
45ml/3 tbsp Cointreau or other
   orange liqueur

1 Soak a small clay pot, if using, in cold water for 15 minutes. Mix the ground almonds, sugar and egg yolk to a paste, then stir in the pistachio nuts.

2 Cut the nectarines in half and carefully remove the stones (pits). Pile the ground almond and pistachio filling into the nectarine halves and then place them in a single layer in the base of the clay pot or cazuela.

3 Pour the orange juice around the nectarines, then cover the pot or dish and place in an unheated oven. Set the oven to 200°C/400°F/Gas 6 and cook for 15 minutes.

4 Remove the lid from the pot or dish and bake for a further 5–10 minutes, or until the nectarines are soft. Transfer the nectarines to individual, warmed serving plates and keep warm.

5 Cut the passion fruits in half, scoop out the seeds and stir into the cooking juices in the clay pot or dish with the liqueur. Spoon the sauce around the nectarines and serve.

Energy 277Kcal/1159kJ; Protein 7.5g; Carbohydrate 27.8g, of which sugars 27.2g; Fat 14.1g, of which saturates 1.5g; Cholesterol 0mg; Calcium 63mg; Fibre 3.8g; Sodium 78mg.

BREAD and BUTTER PUDDING with WHISKEY SAUCE

This is comfort food at its very best. The whiskey sauce is heavenly, but if you are not keen on the alcohol, the pudding can also be served with chilled cream or vanilla ice cream – the contrast between the hot and cold is delicious.

SERVES 6

8 slices of white bread, buttered
115–150g/4–5oz/⅔–¾ cup sultanas
    (golden raisins), or mixed dried fruit
2.5ml/½ tsp grated nutmeg
150g/5oz/¾ cup caster (superfine) sugar
2 large (US extra large) eggs
300ml/½ pint/1¼ cups single
    (light) cream
450ml/¾ pint/scant 2 cups milk
5ml/1 tsp of vanilla extract
light muscovado (brown) sugar, for
    sprinkling (optional)

For the whiskey sauce
150g/5oz/10 tbsp butter
115g/4oz/generous ½ cup caster
    (superfine) sugar
1 egg
45ml/3 tbsp Irish whiskey

1 Preheat the oven to 180°C/350°F/ Gas 4. Remove the crusts from the bread and put four slices, buttered side down, in the base of an ovenproof dish. Sprinkle with the fruit, some of the nutmeg and 15ml/1 tbsp sugar.

2 Place the remaining four slices of bread on top, buttered side down, and sprinkle again with nutmeg and 15ml/1 tbsp sugar.

3 Beat the eggs lightly, add the cream, milk, vanilla extract and the remaining sugar, and mix well to make a custard. Pour this mixture over the bread, and sprinkle light muscovado sugar over the top, if you like to have a crispy crust. Bake in the preheated oven for 1 hour, or until all the liquid has been absorbed and the pudding is risen and brown.

4 Meanwhile, make the whiskey sauce: melt the butter in a heavy pan, add the caster sugar and dissolve over gentle heat. Remove from the heat and add the egg, whisking vigorously, and then add the whiskey. Serve the pudding on hot serving plates, with the whiskey sauce poured over the top.

Energy 757Kcal/3168kJ; Protein 11.7g; Carbohydrate 82g, of which sugars 65.2g; Fat 40.8g, of which saturates 24.3g; Cholesterol 207mg; Calcium 232mg; Fibre 0.9g; Sodium 472mg

FRESH CURRANT BREAD and BUTTER PUDDING

Fresh mixed red- and blackcurrants add a tart touch to this scrumptious hot pudding in which layers of custard-soaked bread are cooked to a crisp golden crust.

SERVES 6

8 medium-thick slices day-old white bread,
  crusts removed
50g/2oz/¼ cup butter, softened
115g/4oz/1 cup redcurrants
115g/4oz/1 cup blackcurrants
4 eggs, beaten
75g/3oz/6 tbsp caster (superfine) sugar
475ml/16fl oz/2 cups creamy milk
5ml/1 tsp vanilla extract
freshly grated nutmeg
30ml/2 tbsp demerara (raw) sugar
single (light) cream, to serve

1 Preheat the oven to 160°C/325°F/Gas 3. Butter a 1.2 litre/2 pint/5 cup ovenproof earthenware dish.

VARIATION

A mixture of blueberries and raspberries would work just as well as the currants.

2 Spread the slices of bread generously with the butter, then cut them in half diagonally. Layer the slices in the dish, buttered side up, sprinkling the currants between the layers.

3 Beat the eggs and caster sugar lightly together in a large mixing bowl, then gradually whisk in the creamy milk and vanilla extract along with a large pinch of freshly grated nutmeg.

4 Pour the milk mixture over the bread, pushing the slices down into the liquid. Sprinkle the demerara sugar and a little more nutmeg over the top. Place the dish in a roasting pan and fill with hot water to come halfway up the sides of the dish. Bake for 40 minutes, then increase the oven temperature to 180°C/350°F/Gas 4 and bake for about 20 minutes more, or until the top is golden. Serve warm, with single cream.

Energy 328Kcal/1377kJ; Protein 10.3g; Carbohydrate 42.2g, of which sugars 25.4g; Fat 14.3g, of which saturates 7.4g; Cholesterol 156mg; Calcium 186mg; Fibre 1.9g; Sodium 321mg.

APRICOT PANETTONE PUDDING

Panettone and pecan nuts make a rich addition to this "no-butter" version of a traditional bread and butter pudding.

SERVES 6

sunflower oil, for greasing
350g/12oz panettone, sliced
 into triangles
25g/1oz/¼ cup pecan nuts
75g/3oz/⅓ cup ready-to-eat dried
 apricots, chopped
500ml/17fl oz/generous 2 cups full-cream
 (whole) milk
5ml/1 tsp vanilla extract
1 large (US extra large) egg, beaten
30ml/2 tbsp maple syrup
nutmeg
demerara (raw) sugar,
 for sprinkling

1 Lightly grease a 1 litre/1¾ pint/4 cup ovenproof earthenware dish. Arrange half of the panettone triangles in the dish, sprinkle over half the pecan nuts and all of the chopped, dried apricots, then add another layer of panettone on top.

COOK'S TIP

Panettone is a light fruit cake originally from northern Italy but now popular all over the world. It is traditionally eaten at festivals such as Christmas or Easter. Panettone is baked in cylindrical moulds, giving it a distinctive shape. You can now find panettone in different flavours – the coffee-flavoured type is particularly good.

2 Heat the milk and vanilla extract in a small pan until the milk just simmers. Put the egg and maple syrup in a large bowl, grate in about 2.5ml/½ tsp nutmeg, then whisk in the hot milk.

3 Preheat the oven to 200°C/400°F/ Gas 6. Pour the egg mixture over the panettone, lightly pressing down the bread so that it is submerged. Leave the pudding to stand for about 10 minutes, to allow the panettone slices to soak up a little of the liquid.

4 Sprinkle over the reserved pecan nuts and sprinkle a little demerara sugar and freshly grated nutmeg over the top. Bake for 40–45 minutes until the pudding is risen and golden brown. Serve hot.

Energy 294Kcal/1237kJ; Protein 9.4g; Carbohydrate 43.2g, of which sugars 21.8g; Fat 10.4g, of which saturates 3.7g; Cholesterol 44mg; Calcium 180mg; Fibre 2.3g; Sodium 248mg.

PEAR, ALMOND and GROUND RICE PIE

Ground rice gives a distinctive, slightly grainy texture to puddings that goes particularly well with autumn fruit. Pears and almonds are a divine combination.

2 Place the butter and caster sugar in a mixing bowl and beat together using a wooden spoon or electric mixer until light and fluffy, then beat in the eggs, one at a time, and the almond extract. Fold in the flour and the ground rice.

3 Carefully spoon the creamed mixture over the quartered pears in the flan or pie dish and then level the surface with a palette knife or metal spatula.

SERVES 6

4 ripe pears
25g/1oz/2 tbsp soft light brown sugar
115g/4oz/½ cup unsalted (sweet) butter, at room temperature
115g/4oz/generous ½ cup caster (superfine) sugar
2 eggs
a few drops of almond extract
75g/3oz/⅔ cup self-raising (self-rising) flour
50g/2oz/⅓ cup ground rice
25g/1oz/¼ cup flaked (sliced) almonds
pouring custard or crème fraîche, to serve

1 Preheat the oven to 180°C/350°F/ Gas 4. Grease a shallow 25cm/10in flan or pie dish, then peel and quarter the pears and arrange them in the dish. Sprinkle with the brown sugar.

4 Sprinkle the flaked almonds evenly over the top of the creamed mixture, then bake the flan for about 30 minutes, or until the topping springs back when touched lightly and is a golden brown colour. Serve warm or cold with custard or crème fraîche.

Energy 396Kcal/1656kJ; Protein 5.2g; Carbohydrate 50.9g, of which sugars 34.8g; Fat 20.2g, of which saturates 10.7g; Cholesterol 104mg; Calcium 92mg; Fibre 2.9g; Sodium 190mg.

SPICED BLACKBERRY and APPLE CRUMBLE

Any fruit can be used in this popular dessert, but you can't beat the favourites of blackberry and apple. Hazelnuts and cardamom seeds give the topping extra flavour.

SERVES 4–6

butter, for greasing
450g/1lb tart cooking apples
115g/4oz/1 cup blackberries
grated rind and juice of 1 orange
50g/2oz/¼ cup soft light brown sugar
custard, to serve

For the topping
175g/6oz/1½ cups plain (all-purpose) flour
75g/3oz/6 tbsp butter
75g/3oz/⅓ cup caster (superfine) sugar
25g/1oz/¼ cup chopped hazelnuts
2.5ml/½ tsp crushed cardamom seeds

VARIATIONS
This pudding can be made with all kinds of fruit. Try plums, apricots, peaches or pears, alone or in combination with apples. Rhubarb is especially good when partnered with bananas.

1 Preheat the oven to 200°C/400°F/ Gas 6. Generously butter a 1.2 litre/ 2 pint/5 cup baking dish. Peel and core the apples, then slice them into the prepared baking dish. Level the surface with the back of a spoon, then sprinkle the blackberries over. Sprinkle the orange rind and light brown sugar evenly over the top, then pour over the orange juice. Set the fruit mixture aside while you make the crumble topping.

2 Sift the flour into a large bowl and rub in the butter until the mixture resembles coarse breadcrumbs. Stir in the caster sugar, hazelnuts and cardamom seeds, then sprinkle the topping over the top of the fruit.

3 Press the topping around the edges of the dish to seal in the juices. Bake for 30–35 minutes, or until the crumble is golden. Serve hot, with custard.

Energy 336Kcal/1413kJ; Protein 4g; Carbohydrate 53.2g, of which sugars 30.8g; Fat 13.4g, of which saturates 6.8g; Cholesterol 27mg; Calcium 72mg; Fibre 3g; Sodium 81mg.

TARTE TATIN

This upside-down apple tart is remarkably easy to make — especially if you use ready-rolled pastry. The apples are cooked in butter and sugar to make a caramel topping.

SERVES 6–8

3 eating apples
juice of ½ lemon
50g/2oz/¼ cup butter, softened
75g/3oz/⅓ cup caster (superfine) sugar
250g/9oz ready-rolled puff pastry
cream, to serve

COOK'S TIPS
• Tarte Tatin is a popular traditional French dessert. It is basically an upside-down apple pie cooked in a pan. The tart is inverted before serving to reveal a rich caramel topping.
• To turn out the tarte Tatin, place the serving plate upside down on top of it, then, protecting your arms with oven gloves, hold both pan and plate firmly together and deftly turn them over. Lift off the pan.

1 Preheat the oven to 220°C/425°F/Gas 7. Cut the apples in quarters and then remove the cores. Toss the apple quarters in the lemon juice.

2 Spread the butter over the base of a 20cm/8in heavy, ovenproof omelette pan. Sprinkle the caster sugar over the base of the pan and arrange the apple wedges on top, rounded side down.

3 Cook over a medium heat for about 15 minutes, or until the sugar and butter have melted and the apples are golden. Cut the pastry into a 25cm/10in round and place on top of the apples; tuck the edges in with a knife. Place the pan in the oven and bake for 15–20 minutes or until the pastry is golden. Carefully invert the tart on to a serving plate, then cool slightly before serving with cream.

Energy 208Kcal/872kJ; Protein 1.9g; Carbohydrate 23.5g, of which sugars 12.4g; Fat 12.8g, of which saturates 3.3g; Cholesterol 13mg; Calcium 25mg; Fibre 0.4g; Sodium 136mg.

BLACK CHERRY CLAFOUTIS

Clafoutis is a batter pudding that originated in the Limousin area of central France. It is often made with cream in place of milk and traditionally uses slightly tart black cherries.*

SERVES 6

butter, for greasing
450g/1lb/2 cups fresh black
    cherries, pitted
25g/1oz/¼ cup plain (all-purpose) flour
50g/2oz/½ cup icing (confectioner's) sugar,
    plus extra for dusting
4 eggs, beaten
250ml/8fl oz/1 cup full-cream
    (whole) milk
30ml/2 tbsp cherry liqueur, such as Kirsch
    or maraschino
vanilla ice cream, to serve

1 Preheat the oven to 180°C/350°F/ Gas 4. Grease a 1.2 litre/2 pint/5 cup baking dish and add the cherries.

2 Sift the flour and icing sugar into a large mixing bowl, then gradually whisk in the beaten eggs until the mixture is smooth. Whisk in the milk until well blended, then stir in the liqueur.

3 Pour the batter into the baking dish and then stir gently to ensure that the cherries are evenly distributed. Transfer to the oven and bake for about 40 minutes, or until just set and light golden brown. Insert a small knife into the centre of the pudding to test if it is cooked in the middle; the blade should come out clean.

4 Allow the pudding to cool for at least 15 minutes, then dust liberally with icing sugar just before serving, either warm or at room temperature. Vanilla ice cream makes a good accompaniment.

VARIATIONS
Try other fruit or nut liqueurs in this dessert. Almond-flavoured liqueur is delicious teamed with cherries, while hazelnut, raspberry or orange liqueurs will also work well. Other fruits that can be used in this pudding include blackberries, blueberries, plums, peaches, nectarines and apricots.

Energy 167Kcal/704kJ; Protein 6.7g; Carbohydrate 23.8g, of which sugars 20.6g; Fat 4.5g, of which saturates 1.5g; Cholesterol 129mg; Calcium 89mg; Fibre 0.8g; Sodium 66mg.

LEMON SURPRISE PUDDING

This is a much-loved dessert that many of us remember from childhood. The surprise is the unexpected sauce concealed beneath the delectable sponge.

SERVES 4

50g/2oz/¼ cup butter, plus extra
 for greasing
grated rind and juice of 2 lemons
115g/4oz/½ cup caster (superfine) sugar
2 eggs, separated
50g/2oz/½ cup self-raising (self-rising) flour
300ml/½ pint/1¼ cups milk

1 Preheat the oven to 190°C/375°F/ Gas 5. Use a little butter to grease a 1.2 litre/2 pint/5 cup baking dish.

COOK'S TIP
Lemons are often waxed before packing. If a recipe uses the rind of the lemons either buy unwaxed lemons or scrub the peel thoroughly to remove the wax.

2 Beat the lemon rind, remaining butter and caster sugar in a bowl until pale and fluffy. Add the egg yolks and flour and beat together well. Gradually whisk in the lemon juice and milk (don't be alarmed – the mixture will curdle horribly). In a grease-free bowl, whisk the egg whites until they form stiff peaks.

3 Fold the egg whites lightly into the lemon mixture using a metal spoon, then pour into the prepared baking dish.

4 Place the dish in a roasting pan and pour in hot water to come halfway up the side of the dish. Bake for 45 minutes until golden. Serve immediately.

Energy 319Kcal/1341kJ; Protein 7g; Carbohydrate 43.1g, of which sugars 33.8g; Fat 14.5g, of which saturates 8.1g; Cholesterol 126mg; Calcium 166mg; Fibre 0.4g; Sodium 190mg.

STRAWBERRY OAT CRUNCH

This simple dessert looks good and tastes delicious. The strawberries form a tasty filling between the layers of oat crumble.

SERVES 4

150g/5oz/1¼ cups rolled oats
50g/2oz/½ cup wholemeal
    (whole-wheat) flour
75g/3oz/6 tbsp butter
30ml/2 tbsp pear and apple concentrate
500g/1¼lb strawberries
10ml/2 tsp arrowroot
natural (plain) yogurt, custard or cream,
    to serve

VARIATIONS
• Use dried apricots (chop half and cook the rest to a purée with a little apple juice) instead of the strawberries.
• Add a few chopped almonds or walnuts to the crumble mixture.

COOK'S TIP
You'll find pear and apple concentrate in good health food stores.

1 Preheat the oven to 180°C/350°F/ Gas 4. Mix the oats and flour in a bowl. Melt the butter with the apple and pear concentrate in a pan; stir into the bowl.

2 Purée half the strawberries in a food processor; chop the rest. Mix the arrowroot with a little of the strawberry purée in a small pan, then add the rest of the purée. Heat gently until thickened, then stir in the chopped strawberries.

3 Spread half the crumble mixture over the base of a shallow 18cm/7in round ovenproof earthenware dish to form a layer at least 1cm/½in thick. Top the crumble with the chopped and puréed strawberry mixture, then add the remaining crumble mixture, patting it down gently to form an even layer. Bake the oat crunch for about 30 minutes until golden brown. Serve warm or cold, with yogurt, custard or cream.

Energy 339Kcal/1425kJ; Protein 7g; Carbohydrate 49.8g, of which sugars 13g; Fat 13.8g, of which saturates 6.5g; Cholesterol 27mg; Calcium 61mg; Fibre 4.3g; Sodium 98mg.

MOIST APPLE CAKE

This delicious cake is perhaps best in autumn, when home-grown apples are in season.
It has a lovely crunchy top and can be served cold, as a cake, or warm with chilled
cream or custard as a dessert.

MAKES I CAKE

225g/8oz/2 cups self-raising
   (self-rising) flour
good pinch of salt
pinch of ground cloves
115g/4oz/½ cup butter,
   at room temperature
3 or 4 cooking apples, such as
   Bramley's Seedling
115g/4oz/generous ½ cup caster
   (superfine) sugar
2 eggs, beaten
a little milk to mix
granulated sugar to sprinkle over

I Preheat the oven to 190°C/375°F/
Gas 5 and butter a 20cm/8in cake
tin (pan).

2 Sieve the flour, salt and ground cloves
into a bowl. Cut in the butter and rub in
until the mixture is like fine
breadcrumbs. Peel and core the apples.
Slice them thinly and add to the rubbed
in mixture with the sugar.

3 Mix in the eggs and enough milk to
make a fairly stiff dough, then turn the
mixture into the prepared tin and
sprinkle with granulated sugar.

4 Bake in the preheated oven for 30–40
minutes, or until springy to the touch.
Cool on a wire rack. When cold store in
an airtight tin until ready to serve.

Per cake Energy 2315Kcal/9717kJ; Protein 37g; Carbohydrate 312.5g, of which sugars 145.3g; Fat 110.9g, of which saturates 64.1g; Cholesterol 702mg; Calcium 948mg; Fibre 10.7g; Sodium 1.68g

APPLE PIE

This is one of the most popular desserts on every informal menu and, when well made, there is nothing to beat it. Bake in a traditional metal pie plate so that the pastry base will be perfectly cooked. Serve with chilled whipped cream, or vanilla ice cream.

SERVES 6

225g/8oz/2 cups plain (all-purpose) flour
130g/4½oz/generous ½ cup butter, or
    mixed butter and white vegetable fat
    (shortening)
25g/1oz/2 tbsp caster (superfine) sugar
45ml/3 tbsp very cold milk or water

For the filling
675g/1½lb cooking apples
75g/3oz/½ cup sultanas (golden raisins)
    (optional)
a little grated lemon rind (optional)
75g/3oz/6 tbsp caster (superfine) sugar
a knob (pat) of butter or 15ml/1 tbsp
    of water
a little milk, to glaze
icing (confectioners') sugar and whipped
    cream, to serve

1 Sieve the flour into a large mixing bowl, add the butter and cut it into small pieces. Rub the butter into the flour with the fingertips, or using a pastry cutter, lifting the mixture as much as possible to aerate.

2 Mix the caster sugar with the chilled milk or water, add to the bowl and mix with a knife or fork until the mixture clings together. Turn on to a floured worktop and knead lightly once or twice until smooth.

3 Wrap in baking parchment or foil and leave in the refrigerator to relax for 20 minutes before using. Meanwhile, preheat the oven to 200°C/400°F/Gas 6.

4 Roll out one-third of the pastry and use to line a 23cm/9in pie plate. Use any trimmings to make a second layer of pastry around the top edge of the pie plate.

5 To make the filling, peel, core and slice the apples and arrange half of them on the pastry base, then sprinkle over the sultanas and lemon rind, if using. Top with the caster sugar, the remaining apples and butter or water.

6 Roll out the remainder of the pastry to make a circle about 2.5cm/1in larger than the pie plate. Dampen the pastry edging on the rim and lay the top over the apples, draping it gently over any lumps to avoid straining the pastry. Press the rim well to seal. Knock up the edge with a knife, and pinch the edges neatly with the fingers to make a fluted edge.

7 Brush the pastry lightly with milk and bake the pie in the preheated oven for about 30 minutes, or until the pastry is nicely browned and crisp, and the fruit is cooked.

8 To serve, dust the pastry with icing sugar and serve hot, warm or cold, but not straight from the refrigerator.

VARIATION
The same filling may be used to make a deep pie in a 25cm/10in deep oval pie dish, although only about three-quarters of the quantity of pastry will be needed for the topping.

Energy 393Kcal/1650kJ; Protein 4.1g; Carbohydrate 56.3g, of which sugars 27.7g; Fat 18.4g, of which saturates 11.4g; Cholesterol 46mg; Calcium 68mg; Fibre 2.5g; Sodium 136mg

SLOW COOKER PRESERVES AND DRINKS

Although the slow cooker isn't suitable for fast-boiling jams, jellies and marmalades to setting point, it is perfect for making rich chutneys and relishes. The long, slow cooking develops their flavour to such an extent that long-maturation is unnecessary and many can be eaten immediately. It is particularly good for making textured preserves because the fruit and vegetables retain their shape well. Fruit curds, such as the traditional fresh lemon curd, are easier than those made conventionally because there is no need for constant stirring. You will also find a number of delicious drinks here including Mexican Hot Chocolate and Hot Spiced Wine.

MANGO CHUTNEY

No Indian meal would be complete without this classic chutney. Its gloriously sweet, tangy flavour complements the warm taste of spices perfectly. It is also great served with chargrilled chicken or duck breasts, and will liven up cheese sandwiches a treat.

3 Stir the sugar, chilli, ginger, garlic, bruised cardamoms, bay leaf and salt into the mango mixture until the sugar has dissolved completely.

4 Cover and cook for 2 hours, then uncover and let the mixture cook for a further 1 hour, or until the chutney is reduced to a thick consistency and no excess liquid remains. Stir the chutney every 15 minutes during the last hour.

5 Remove and discard the bay leaf and the chilli. Spoon the chutney into hot sterilized jars and seal. Store for 1 week before eating and use within 1 year.

COOK'S TIP
To make a more fiery chutney, seed and slice two green chillies and stir into the chutney mixture with the other spices.

MAKES 450G/1LB

3 firm mangoes
120ml/4fl oz/½ cup cider vinegar
200g/7oz/scant 1 cup light muscovado (brown) sugar
1 small red finger chilli or jalapeño chilli, split
2.5cm/1in piece of fresh root ginger, peeled and finely chopped
1 garlic clove, finely chopped
5 cardamom pods, bruised
1 bay leaf
2.5ml/½ tsp salt

1 Peel the mangoes and cut out the stone, then cut the flesh into small chunks or thin wedges.

2 Put the chopped mango in the ceramic cooking pot. Add the cider vinegar, stir briefly to combine, and cover the slow cooker with the lid. Switch to high and cook for about 2 hours, stirring the chutney halfway through the cooking time.

Per 450g/1lb: Energy 1045Kcal/4465kJ; Protein 4.1g; Carbohydrate 272.5g, of which sugars 271.1g; Fat 0.9g, of which saturates 0.5g; Cholesterol 0mg; Calcium 908mg; Fibre 11.7g; Sodium 1002mg.

BUTTERNUT, APRICOT and ALMOND CHUTNEY

Coriander seeds and turmeric add a slightly spicy touch to this rich golden chutney. It is delicious spooned on to little savoury canapés or with melting cubes of mozzarella cheese; it is also good in sandwiches – helping to spice up bland or run-of-the-mill fillings.

MAKES ABOUT 1.8KG/4LB

1 small butternut squash, weighing about 800g/1¾ lb
400g/14oz/2 cups golden granulated sugar
300ml/½ pint/1¼ cups cider vinegar
2 onions, finely chopped
225g/8oz/1 cup ready-to-eat dried apricots, chopped
finely grated rind and juice of 1 orange
2.5ml/½ tsp turmeric
15ml/1 tbsp coriander seeds
15ml/1 tbsp salt
115g/4oz/1 cup flaked (sliced) almonds

1 Halve the butternut squash and scoop out the seeds. Peel off the skin, then cut the flesh into 1cm/½in cubes.

2 Put the sugar and vinegar in the ceramic cooking pot and switch to high. Heat for 30 minutes, then stir until the sugar has dissolved.

3 Add the butternut squash, onions, apricots, orange rind and juice, turmeric, coriander seeds and salt to the slow cooker and stir well.

4 Cover with the lid and cook for 5–6 hours, stirring occasionally. After about 5 hours the chutney should be a fairly thick consistency with relatively little liquid. If it is still quite runny at this stage, cook uncovered for the final hour. Stir in the flaked almonds.

5 Spoon the chutney into warmed sterilized jars, cover and seal. Store in a cool, dark place and allow to mature for at least 1 month before eating. Use within 2 years. Once opened, store the chutney in the refrigerator and use within 2 months.

Per 1.8kg/4lb: Energy 2770Kcal/11723kJ; Protein 41.7g; Carbohydrate 532.6g, of which sugars 524.1g; Fat 67.3g, of which saturates 5.9g; Cholesterol 0mg; Calcium 807mg; Fibre 31.6g; Sodium 5967mg.

SWEET and HOT DRIED-FRUIT CHUTNEY

This rich, thick and slightly sticky preserve of spiced dried fruit is a wonderful way to enliven cold roast turkey left over from Christmas or Thanksgiving dinner.

MAKES ABOUT 1.5KG/3LB 6OZ

350g/12oz/1½ cups ready-to-eat
    dried apricots
225g/8oz/1½ cups dried dates,
    stoned (pitted)
225g/8oz/1⅓ cups dried figs
50g/2oz/⅓ cup glacé (candied) citrus peel
150g/5oz/1 cup raisins
50g/2oz/½ cup dried cranberries
75ml/2½fl oz/⅓ cup cranberry juice
300ml/½ pint/1¼ cups cider vinegar
225g/8oz/1 cup caster (superfine) sugar
finely grated rind of 1 lemon
5ml/1 tsp mixed (apple pie) spice
5ml/1 tsp ground coriander
5ml/1 tsp cayenne pepper
5ml/1 tsp salt

1 Roughly chop the apricots, dates, figs and citrus peel, then put all the dried fruit in the ceramic cooking pot. Pour over the cranberry juice, stir, then cover with the lid and switch the slow cooker on to low. Cook for 1 hour, or until the fruit has absorbed most of the juice.

2 Add the cider vinegar and sugar to the fruit mixture. Turn the slow cooker up to the high setting and stir until the sugar has dissolved.

3 Re-cover and cook for 2 more hours, or until the fruit is very soft and the chutney fairly thick (it will thicken further as it cools). Stir in the lemon rind, mixed spice, coriander, cayenne pepper and salt. Cook uncovered for 30 minutes, until little excess liquid remains.

4 Spoon the chutney into warmed sterilized jars, cover and seal. Store in a cool, dark place. Open within 10 months of making. Once opened, store in the refrigerator and use within 2 months.

VARIATIONS
Stoned dried prunes can be substituted for the dates, and dried sour cherries for the dried cranberries. Apple juice can be used instead of the cranberry juice.

Per 1.5kg/3lb 6oz: Energy 2873Kcal/12248kJ; Protein 32g; Carbohydrate 714.3g, of which sugars 703.5g; Fat 6.8g, of which saturates 0.2g; Cholesterol 0mg; Calcium 1075mg; Fibre 52.1g; Sodium 2358mg.

BEETROOT, DATE and ORANGE PRESERVE

With its vibrant red colour and rich earthy flavour, this distinctive chutney is good with salads as well as full-flavoured cheeses such as mature Cheddar, Stilton or Gorgonzola.

MAKES ABOUT 1.4KG/3LB

300ml/½ pint/1¼ cups malt vinegar
200g/7oz/1 cup granulated sugar
350g/12oz raw beetroot (beets)
350g/12oz eating apples
225g/8oz red onions, very finely chopped
1 garlic clove, crushed
finely grated rind of 2 oranges
5ml/1 tsp ground allspice
5ml/1 tsp salt
175g/6oz/1 cup chopped dried dates

1 Put the vinegar and sugar in the ceramic cooking pot. Cover with the lid and switch the slow cooker to high. Leave until steaming hot.

2 Meanwhile, scrub or thinly peel the beetroot, then cut into 1cm/½in pieces. Peel, quarter and core the apples and cut into 1cm/½in pieces.

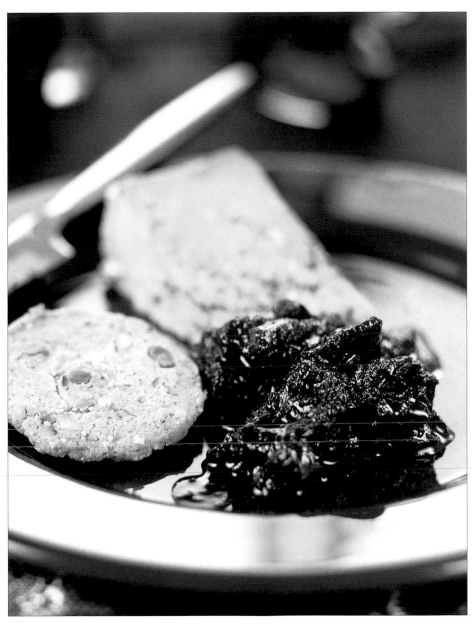

3 Stir the vinegar mixture with a wooden spoon until the sugar has dissolved. Add the beetroot, apples, onions, garlic, orange rind, ground allspice and salt. Stir everything together, then re-cover and cook for 4–5 hours, stirring occasionally until very tender.

4 Stir in the dates and cook for a further hour until the mixture is really thick. Stir once or twice during this time to prevent the chutney catching on the base of the ceramic cooking pot.

5 Spoon the chutney into warmed sterilized jars, cover and seal. Store in a cool, dark place and open within 5 months of making. Refrigerate after opening and use within 1 month.

COOK'S TIP
For really speedy preparation and a deliciously fine-textured chutney, put the peeled beetroot through the coarse grating blade of a food processor. Alternatively, you can simply grate the beetroot by hand.

Per 1.4kg/3lb: Energy 1632Kcal/6949kJ; Protein 16.8g; Carbohydrate 413.7g, of which sugars 406g; Fat 1.5g, of which saturates 0.2g; Cholesterol 0mg; Calcium 278mg; Fibre 23.1g; Sodium 2241mg.

CARROT and ALMOND RELISH

This Middle Eastern classic, usually made with long fine strands of carrot, is available from many supermarkets. This version, using coarsely grated carrots, is just as good.

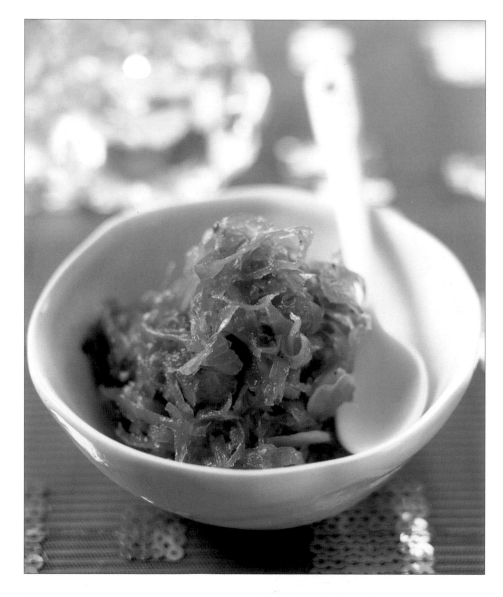

3 Switch the slow cooker to high and cook for about 2 hours, or until the carrots and ginger are almost tender, stirring only if the mixture looks dry around the edges.

4 Stir in the lemon rind and cook for a further 1 hour, until the mixture is thick. Stir once towards the end of the cooking time to prevent the mixture from sticking to the base of the pot.

5 Put the almonds in a frying pan and toast over a low heat until just beginning to colour. Gently stir into the relish, taking care not to break the almonds.

6 Spoon the relish into warmed sterilized jars, cover and seal. Store in a cool, dark place and leave to mature for 1 week. The relish will keep unopened for up to 1 year. However, once the jars have been opened, store them in the refrigerator and use within 2 weeks.

MAKES ABOUT 675G/1½LB

15ml/1 tbsp coriander seeds
500g/1¼lb carrots, grated
50g/2oz fresh root ginger, finely shredded
200g/7oz/1 cup caster (superfine) sugar
120ml/4fl oz/½ cup white wine vinegar
30ml/2 tbsp clear honey
7.5ml/1½ tsp salt
finely grated rind of 1 lemon
50g/2oz/½ cup flaked (sliced) almonds

1 Crush the coriander seeds using a mortar and pestle. Put them in the ceramic cooking pot with the carrots, ginger and sugar, and mix well.

2 Put the vinegar, honey and salt in a jug (pitcher) and stir until the salt has dissolved completely. Pour the mixture over the carrots. Mix well, cover and leave for 1 hour.

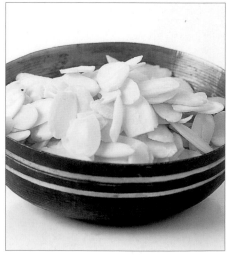

Per 675g/1½lb: Energy 1407Kcal/5947kJ; Protein 13.7g; Carbohydrate 289.6g, of which sugars 285.8g; Fat 29.4g, of which saturates 2.7g; Cholesterol 0mg; Calcium 268mg; Fibre 15.7g; Sodium 2898mg.

PAPAYA and LEMON RELISH

This chunky relish is best made with a firm, unripe papaya. The slow, gentle cooking allows all the flavours to mellow. Serve with roast meats, or with cheese and crackers.

MAKES 450G/1LB

1 large unripe papaya
1 onion, very thinly sliced
175ml/6fl oz/generous ¾ cup red
 wine vinegar
juice of 2 lemons
165g/5½oz/¾ cup golden caster
 (superfine) sugar
1 cinnamon stick
1 bay leaf
2.5ml/½ tsp hot paprika
2.5ml/½ tsp salt
150g/5oz/1 cup sultanas (golden raisins)

1 Peel the papaya and cut it lengthways in half. Remove the seeds, then cut the flesh into small chunks.

2 Place the papaya in the ceramic cooking pot, add the onion slices and stir in the vinegar. Switch the slow cooker to high, cover and cook for 2 hours.

3 Add the lemon juice, sugar, cinnamon stick, bay leaf, paprika, salt and sultanas, and stir thoroughly until the sugar has completely dissolved.

4 Cook the chutney, uncovered, for a further 1 hour to allow the mixture to reduce slightly; the relish should be fairly thick and syrupy.

5 Ladle the chutney into hot sterilized jars. Seal and store for 1 week before using. Open within 1 year of making. Once opened, store in the refrigerator and use within 2 weeks.

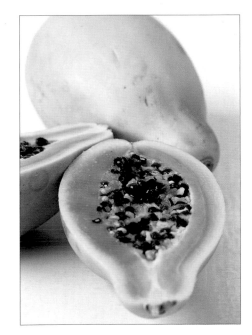

Per 450g/1lb: Energy 1294Kcal/5511kJ; Protein 8.4g; Carbohydrate 332.7g, of which sugars 332.7g; Fat 1.4g, of which saturates 0g; Cholesterol 0mg; Calcium 272mg; Fibre 16.1g; Sodium 1111mg.

CHRISTMAS MINCEMEAT

In many mincemeat recipes, the raw ingredients are simply mixed together. Here, gentle cooking develops and intensifies the flavour, so that the mincemeat may be used straight away without being left to mature. At the same time, heating it to simmering point helps prevent fermentation, and this allows a much longer shelf-life.

MAKES ABOUT 1.75G/4LB

450g/1lb cooking apples
115g/4oz/¾ cup glacé (candied) citrus peel
115g/4oz/½ cup glacé (candied) cherries
115g/4oz/½ cup ready-to-eat dried apricots
115g/4oz/1 cup blanched almonds
150ml/¼ pint/⅔ cup brandy
225g/8oz/1 cup currants
225g/8oz/1⅓ cups sultanas (golden raisins)
450g/1lb/3¼ cups seedless raisins
225g/8oz/1 cup soft dark brown sugar
225g/8oz/1⅔ cups suet (chilled, grated shortening) or vegetarian suet
10ml/2 tsp ground ginger
5ml/1 tsp ground allspice
5ml/1 tsp ground cinnamon
2.5ml/½ tsp grated nutmeg
grated rind and juice of 1 lemon
grated rind and juice of 1 orange

1 Peel, core and chop the cooking apples, then roughly chop the citrus peel, glacé cherries, apricots and blanched almonds.

2 Reserve half the brandy and put the rest into the ceramic cooking pot with all the other ingredients. Stir well until thoroughly mixed.

3 Cover the ceramic cooking pot with the lid and switch the slow cooker to high. Cook for 1 hour.

4 Stir the mixture well, then re-cover the pot and reduce the temperature to low. Cook for a further 2 hours, stirring halfway through cooking to prevent the mixture from overheating and sticking to the sides of the pot.

5 Remove the lid and leave the mixture to cool completely, stirring occasionally.

6 Stir the reserved brandy into the mincemeat and spoon the mixture into sterilized jars. Cover and store in a cool, dry place for up to six months. Once opened, store in the refrigerator and use within two weeks.

Per 1.75g/4lb: Energy 7149Kcal/30087kJ; Protein 55.6g; Carbohydrate 1114g, of which sugars 1088.3g; Fat 267.7g, of which saturates 106.3g; Cholesterol 0mg; Calcium 1228mg; Fibre 47.3g; Sodium 774mg.

CONFIT of SLOW-COOKED ONIONS

This jam of slow-cooked, caramelized onions in sweet-sour balsamic vinegar will keep for several days in a sealed jar in the refrigerator. You can use red, white or yellow onions, but yellow onions will give the sweetest result. Shallots will also make an excellent confit.

2 Cover the pot with the lid, then place a folded dishtowel on top. Cook the onions for 5 hours, stirring the mixture several times during the cooking time to ensure the onions soften evenly.

3 Season well with salt and ground black pepper, then add the thyme, bay leaf, sugar, balsamic vinegar and red wine. Gently stir with a wooden spoon until the sugar has completely dissolved, then stir in the prunes.

4 Re-cover and cook for 1½–2 hours, or until the mixture is thick and sticky. Adjust the seasoning, adding more sugar and/or vinegar to taste. When cool, store the confit in the refrigerator. Serve either cold or warm.

SERVES 6

30ml/2 tbsp extra virgin olive oil
15g/½oz/1 tbsp butter
500g/1¼lb onions, thinly sliced
3–5 fresh thyme sprigs
1 bay leaf
30ml/2 tbsp light muscovado (brown) sugar, plus a little extra
30ml/2 tbsp balsamic vinegar, plus a little extra
120ml/4fl oz/½ cup red wine
50g/2oz/¼ cup ready-to-eat prunes, chopped
salt and ground black pepper

1 Put the oil and butter in the ceramic cooking pot and heat on high for about 15 minutes, until the butter has melted. Add the onions and stir to coat.

Energy 133Kcal/556kJ; Protein 1.2g; Carbohydrate 16.5g, of which sugars 14.6g; Fat 5.9g, of which saturates 1.8g; Cholesterol 5mg; Calcium 26mg; Fibre 1.6g; Sodium 20mg.

FRESH LEMON CURD

This classic tangy, creamy curd is still one of the most popular of all the curds. Delicious spread thickly over freshly baked white bread or served with American-style pancakes, it also makes a wonderfully rich, zesty sauce spooned over fresh fruit tarts.

3 Put the eggs and yolks in a bowl and beat together with a fork. Strain the eggs into the lemon mixture, and whisk well until combined. Cover the bowl with foil, then return it to the slow cooker.

4 Cook the lemon curd on low for 1–2 hours, stirring every 15 minutes, until thick enough to lightly coat the back of a wooden spoon.

5 Pour the curd into small warmed sterilized jars. Cover and seal. Store in a cool, dark place, ideally in the refrigerator, and use within 3 months. Once opened, store in the refrigerator.

MAKES ABOUT 450G/1LB

finely grated rind and juice of 3 lemons
　(preferably unwaxed or organic)
200g/7oz/1 cup caster (superfine) sugar
115g/4oz/½ cup unsalted (sweet)
　butter, diced
2 large (US extra large) eggs
2 large (US extra large) egg yolks

COOK'S TIP
To make sharp, tangy lime curd, replace the lemons with the grated zest and juice of 4 large ripe, juicy limes. Lime curd has a lovely pale greenish hue.

1 Pour about 5cm/2in very hot water into the ceramic cooking pot. Switch the slow cooker to high. Put the lemon rind and juice, sugar and butter in the largest heatproof bowl that will fit inside the slow cooker.

2 Put the bowl into the slow cooker, then pour enough near-boiling water around it to come just over halfway up the sides. Leave for about 15 minutes, stirring occasionally, until the sugar has dissolved and the butter melted. Remove and allow to cool for a few minutes. Turn the slow cooker to low.

Per 450g/1lb: Energy 1968Kcal/8224kJ; Protein 22.4g; Carbohydrate 215.3g, of which sugars 215.3g; Fat 118.9g, of which saturates 66.9g; Cholesterol 1102mg; Calcium 277mg; Fibre 0g; Sodium 895mg.

BLUSHING PEARS

As this pickle matures, the fruits absorb the colour of the vinegar, giving them a glorious pink hue. Their deliciously spicy, sweet-and-sour flavour is especially good with cold turkey at Christmas, or with game pie, well-flavoured cheese or paté.

MAKES ABOUT 1.3KG/3LB

1 small lemon
450g/1lb/2¼ cups golden granulated sugar
475ml/16fl oz/2 cups raspberry vinegar
7.5cm/3in cinnamon stick
6 whole cloves
6 allspice berries
150ml/¼ pint/⅔ cup water
900g/2lb firm pears

1 Using a sharp knife, thinly pare a few strips of rind from the lemon. Squeeze out the juice and add to the ceramic cooking pot with the strips of rind.

2 Add the sugar, vinegar, spices and water, and switch the slow cooker to high. Cover and leave to heat for about 30 minutes, then stir until the sugar has completely dissolved. Re-cover with the lid and heat for a further 30 minutes.

3 Meanwhile, prepare the pears. Peel and halve the pears, then scoop out the cores using a melon baller or small teaspoon. If the pears are very large, cut them into quarters rather than halves.

4 Add the pears to the slow cooker, cover and cook for 1½–2 hours, turning them occasionally to coat them in the syrup. Check the pears frequently; they should be tender and translucent but still retain their shape.

5 Using a slotted spoon, remove the pears from the slow cooker and pack into hot sterilized jars, adding the spices and strips of lemon rind.

6 Remove any scum from the surface of the syrup, then ladle it over the pears. Cover and seal. Store for a few days before eating, and use within 2 weeks.

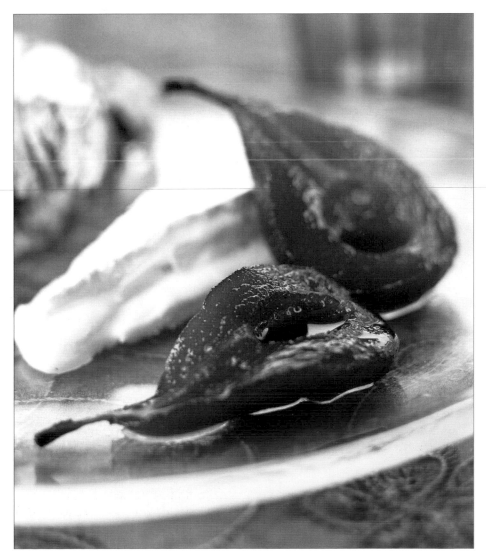

Per 1.3kg/3lb: Energy 2133Kcal/9086kJ; Protein 5g; Carbohydrate 560.3g, of which sugars 560.3g; Fat 0.9g, of which saturates 0g; Cholesterol 0mg; Calcium 230mg; Fibre 19.8g; Sodium 50mg.

HOT SPICED WINE

On a cold winter evening, there is nothing more welcoming than a glass of warm spicy wine. The slow cooker is particularly useful when you are making the wine for guests: you can prepare the spiced wine up to four hours before your guests arrive, and the slow cooker will keep it at the ideal serving temperature until you are ready to serve.

SERVES 8

50g/2oz/¼ cup soft light brown sugar
150ml/¼ pint/⅔ cup near-boiling water
2 small oranges, preferably unwaxed
6 whole cloves
1 stick cinnamon
½ whole nutmeg
1½ bottles red wine, such as Bordeaux
150ml/¼ pint/⅔ cup brandy

1 Put the sugar in the ceramic cooking pot and pour in the near-boiling water. Stir until the sugar has dissolved, then switch the slow cooker to high.

COOK'S TIP
Use heatproof glasses with a handle so that guests can hold the hot wine easily.

2 Rinse the oranges, then press the cloves into one and add it to the slow cooker with the cinnamon, nutmeg and wine. Halve the remaining orange, then slice and set aside. Cover the slow cooker with the lid and cook on high or auto for 1 hour, then reduce to low or leave on auto and heat for 3 hours.

3 Stir the brandy into the spiced wine and add the orange slices. Heat for a further 1 hour.

4 Remove the whole orange and the cinnamon stick. The wine is now ready to serve and can be kept hot for up to 4 hours. Serve in heatproof glasses.

CRANBERRY and APPLE PUNCH

When you are throwing a party, it is good to have a non-alcoholic punch available. Here, the slow cooker extracts maximum flavour from fresh ginger and lime peel.

SERVES 6

1 lime
5cm/2in piece of fresh root ginger, peeled and thinly sliced
50g/2oz/¼ cup caster (superfine) sugar
200ml/7fl oz/scant 1 cup near-boiling water
475ml/16fl oz/2 cups cranberry juice
475ml/16fl oz/2 cups clear apple juice
ice and chilled sparkling mineral water or soda water, to serve (optional)

1 Pare the rind off the lime and place in the ceramic cooking pot with the ginger and sugar. Pour over the water and stir until the sugar dissolves. Cover with the lid and heat on high or auto for 1 hour, then reduce the temperature to low or leave on auto and heat for a further 2 hours. Switch off the slow cooker and leave the syrup to cool completely.

2 When cold, strain the syrup through a fine sieve (strainer) into a large serving jug (pitcher) or punch bowl and discard the lime rind and ginger.

3 Squeeze the juice from the lime and strain through a sieve into the syrup. Stir in the cranberry and apple juices. Cover and chill in the refrigerator for at least 3 hours or until ready to serve.

4 To serve, pour or ladle the punch over plenty of ice in tall glasses and top up with sparkling mineral water or soda water, if using.

COOK'S TIP
You can now buy all kinds of different apple juices made from specific varieties of apple. They have distinctive flavours, and it is well worth searching them out.

Hot Spiced Wine: Energy 162Kcal/675kJ; Protein 0.2g; Carbohydrate 6.8g, of which sugars 6.8g; Fat 0g, of which saturates 0g; Cholesterol 0mg; Calcium 12mg; Fibre 0g; Sodium 10mg.
Cranberry and Apple Punch: Energy 111Kcal/475kJ; Protein 0.1g; Carbohydrate 27.9g, of which sugars 16.5g; Fat 0.1g, of which saturates 0g; Cholesterol 0mg; Calcium 8mg; Fibre 0g; Sodium 2mg.

MEXICAN HOT CHOCOLATE

Blending or whisking the hot chocolate before serving gives it a wonderfully frothy texture. The slow cooker is particularly good for heating the milk in this recipe because the gentle heating process allows the cinnamon and cloves to infuse and flavour the hot chocolate with a deliciously warm and spicy flavour.

SERVES 4

1 litre/1¾ pints/4 cups milk
1 cinnamon stick
2 whole cloves
115g/4oz dark (bittersweet) chocolate, chopped into small pieces
2–3 drops of almond extract
whipped cream and cocoa powder or grated chocolate, to serve (optional)

COOK'S TIP
Traditional Mexican hot chocolate is always warmly spiced. It is a popular breakfast drink, often served with delicious deep-fried *churros*, which are Mexican sugared doughnuts.

1 Pour the milk into the ceramic cooking pot. Add the cinnamon stick and cloves, cover with the lid and switch the slow cooker to high. Leave to heat the milk and infuse the spices for 1 hour, or until the milk is almost boiling.

2 Add the chocolate pieces and almond extract to the milk and stir until melted. Turn off the slow cooker.

3 Strain the mixture into a blender (it may be necessary to do this in two batches) and whizz on high speed for about 30 seconds, until frothy. Alternatively, whisk the mixture in the ceramic cooking pot with a hand-held electric whisk or a wire whisk.

4 Pour or ladle the hot chocolate into warmed heatproof glasses. If you like, top each with a little whipped cream and a dusting of cocoa powder or grated chocolate. Serve immediately.

NORMANDY COFFEE

The Normandy region of northern France is known for its abundant apple orchards, and its name is often given to dishes made with apple juice or apple sauce. This recipe combines the sweet-tart flavour of apples and spices to make a delicious, tangy coffee.

SERVES 4

475ml/16fl oz/2 cups apple juice
30ml/2 tbsp soft brown sugar, to taste
2 oranges, thickly sliced
2 small cinnamon sticks
2 whole cloves
pinch of ground allspice
475ml/16fl oz/2 cups hot, freshly brewed strong black coffee
halved cinnamon sticks, to serve (optional)

COOK'S TIPS
• For a good flavour, use strong coffee – espresso or filter-/plunger-brewed at 75g/3 tbsp/scant ½ cup coffee per 1 litre/1¾ pints/4 cups water.
• To make an alcoholic drink, replace a quarter of the apple juice with the French apple brandy, Calvados. Stir in the brandy after straining the spice-infused apple juice and removing the spices.

1 Pour the apple juice into the ceramic cooking pot and switch the slow cooker on to high.

2 Add the sugar, oranges, cinnamon sticks, cloves and allspice to the pot and stir. Cover and heat for 20 minutes.

3 Stir the mixture until the sugar has dissolved completely, then cover with the lid and heat for 1 hour.

4 When the juice is hot and infused with the spices, switch the slow cooker to low to keep warm for up to 2 hours.

5 Strain the juice into a bowl, discarding the orange slices and spices.

6 Pour the hot coffee into the juice and stir. Quickly pour into warmed mugs or espresso-style cups, adding a halved cinnamon stick to each, if you like.

Mexican Hot Chocolate: Energy 262Kcal/1102kJ; Protein 9.9g; Carbohydrate 30g, of which sugars 29.7g; Fat 12.3g, of which saturates 7.6g; Cholesterol 17mg; Calcium 309mg; Fibre 0.7g; Sodium 109mg.
Normandy Coffee: Energy 85Kcal/363kJ; Protein 0.2g; Carbohydrate 22.2g, of which sugars 22.2g; Fat 0.1g, of which saturates 0g; Cholesterol 0mg; Calcium 11mg; Fibre 0g; Sodium 3mg.

USEFUL ADDRESSES

MANUFACTURERS
Contact the following slow cooker manufacturers for retail advice, online orders and customer services, including parts and repairs.

UNITED KINGDOM

Lakeland Ltd
Customer Services Department
Alexandra Buildings
Windermere
Cumbria LA23 1BQ
Tel: (01539 4) 88100
www.lakeland.co.uk

Morphy Richards
Customer Services Department
Talbot Road
Mexborough
South Yorkshire
S64 8AJ
Tel: (01709) 582 402
www.morphyrichards.com

Prima
Contact shop.prima-international.com for online orders, retail advice and customer service centres in your area.

Russell Hobbs
Customer Services Department
Pifco Ltd
Failsworth
Manchester
M35 0HS
Tel: (0161) 681 8588
www.russell-hobbs.com

TEFAL
Contact www.tefal.co.uk for online orders, retail advice and customer service centres in your area.

UNITED STATES

Farberware Inc
Customer Services Department
Tel: (800) 253-9054
www.farberware.com

Hamilton Beach
Customer Services Department
55353 Lyon Industrial Drive
New Hudson
MI 48165
Tel: (1-800) 851-8900
www.hamiltonbeach.com

Kirby & Allen
Customer Services Department
1330 Livingstone Avenue
North Brunswick
NJ 08902
Tel: (732) 246-1460
Email: customerservice@kirby-allen.com
www.kirby-allen.com

Proctor Silex HB/PS
Customer Services Department
234 Springs Road
Washington, NC 27889
Tel: (US) (1-800) 851-8900
     (Can) (1-800) 267-2826
     (Mexico) (01-800) 71-16-100
www.proctor-silex.com

Rowecraft
Customer Services Department
24 Critchett Road
Raymond, NH 03077
www.rowecraft.com

Russell Hobbs
Customer Services Department
Myers Electric
416 Whalley Avenue
New Haven
CT 06511-3097
Tel: (toll free) 1-888-HOBBS-20
www.russell-hobbs.com

West Bend
Customer Services Department
PO Box 2780
West Bend
WI 53095
Tel: (262) 334-6949
www.west-bend.com

Windmere/Applica
Tel: (1-800) 557 9463
Contact applicaconsumeraffairs@fox-international.com for retail advice and customer service centers in your area.
www.windmere.com

AUSTRALIA

Morphy Richards
Contact www.morphyrichards.com for customer service centres in your area.

Russell Hobbs
Contact www.russell-hobbs.com for online orders, retail advice and customer service centres in your area.

TEFAL
Contact www.tefal.com for customer service centres in your area.

NEW ZEALAND

Morphy Richards
Contact www.morphyrichards.com for customer service centres in your area.

Russell Hobbs
Contact www.russell-hobbs.com for online orders, retail advice and customer service centres in your area.

TEFAL
Customer Services Department
PO Box 64-302
Botany Town Centre
East Tamaki
1730 Auckland
Tel: (0800) 700 711
www.tefal.com

INDEX

A

alcohol 37
  Calvados 326
  cider 222–3, 247, 298–9, 320–1
  drunken chicken 225
  hot spiced wine 502–3
  Kirsch sauce 468–9
  Marsala 324
  octopus and red wine stew 189
  poached pears in red wine 440
  rabbit with red wine and
    prunes 277
  rum 446
  stout 275, 317
  venison sausages with red wine
    gravy 274
  whiskey sauce 478
  wine 136, 155, 203, 263, 269
  winter fruit poached in mulled
    wine 441
anchovies 104–5, 164, 168, 207
apples
  apple pie 488–9
  baked stuffed apples 442
  braised sausages with onions,
    celeriac and apple 265
  cranberry and apple punch
    502–3
  moist apple cake 487
  noisettes of pork with creamy
    Calvados and apple sauce 326
  pot-roast loin of pork with
    apple 328
  roast farmyard duck with apples
    and cider 247
  spiced blackberry and apple
    crumble 482
  tarte tatin 483
apricots
  apricot and almond stuffed
    chicken 216
  apricot panettone pudding 480
  braised lamb with apricots and
    herb dumplings 342
  butternut, apricot and almond
    chutney 493
Asian-style duck consommé 96
asparagus 396–7
aubergines 31

  mixed bean and aubergine
    tagine with mint yogurt 376–7
  moussaka 304–5
  ratatouille 372
avgolemono 91
avocado 211

B

bacon
  braised pheasant with wild
    mushrooms, chestnuts and
    bacon 271
  lamb's liver and bacon casserole
    148
  sausage, bacon and potato
    casserole, 334
  spring chicken slow-braised in
    smoky bacon sauce 220–1
banana and chocolate chip
  pudding 447
banana and pumpkin cake 461
bananas with rum and raisins 446
barley 33, 111, 310, 341
basil 84
beans 33
  bean and pistou soup 107
  black bean chilli con carne 325
  Boston baked beans 291
  bulgur wheat, asparagus and
    broad bean pilaff 396–7
  guinea fowl with beans and
    curly kale 270
  Jamaican black bean pot 379
  lamb shanks with beans and
    herbs 338–9
  mixed bean and aubergine
    tagine with mint yogurt
    376–7
  mushroom and bean pâté 120
  pancetta and broad bean
    risotto 327
  rice with dill and broad beans
    432
  roast lamb with beans and
    green peppercorns 336
  rosemary risotto with borlotti
    beans 360
  spicy hot mixed bean chilli with
    cornbread topping 354
  sweet and sour mixed bean
    hot-pot 352
beef 20–1
  beef and mushroom pudding
    284–5
  beef carbonade 320
  beef hotpot with herb
    dumplings 322
  boeuf bourguignon 321
  braised beef in a rich peanut
    sauce 283
  braised beef with horseradish
    286–7
  calf's liver with slow-cooked

    onions, Marsala and sage 324
  citrus beef curry 314–15
  clay-pot beef with red peppers
    318–19
  fillet of beef stroganoff 149
  Hungarian cholent 288
  pot-roast beef with Guinness
    317
  pot-roast brisket 55
  Provençal beef stew 282
  slow-baked beef with a potato
    crust 323
  spiced beef 289
  steak and kidney pie with
    mustard gravy 280–1
beetroot, cabbage and tomato
  borscht 92
beetroot, date and orange
  preserve 495
beetroot, roasted sweet potatoes
  and onions in coconut and
  ginger paste 417
beetroot with lemon dressing 411
beurre blanc 65
blackberry and apple crumble 482
blueberry muffin pudding 462
bouillabaisse 112
bouquet garni 36
braising 50–1, 74
Brazilian pork and rice casserole
  329
bread 53
bread and butter pudding 61,
  452–3
bread and butter pudding, fresh
  currant 479
bread and butter pudding with
  whiskey sauce 478
brill in red wine sauce 203
broccoli, anchovy and pasta soup
  104–5
buckwheat noodles with cabbage,
  potatoes and cheese 406–7
bulgur wheat, asparagus and
  broad bean pilaff 396–7
butter 144–5, 406–7
butternut, apricot and almond
  chutney 493
butterscotch fondue 69
butterscotch sauce 67

C

cabbage
  braised guinea fowl with red
    cabbage 234
  braised red cabbage 51
  braised red cabbage with
    beetroot 422
  buckwheat noodles with
    cabbage, potatoes and
    cheese 406–7
  cabbage, beetroot and tomato
    borscht 92
cakes 62–3
canned vegetables 31
cannelloni Sorrentina-style 168
capers 208
caramel sauce 67
caraway 354
cardamoms 344–5, 434
  cardamom chicken mousselines
    130
Caribbean peanut chicken 226
carrots
  braised leeks with carrots 421
  carrot and almond relish 496
  carrot and coriander soup 83
  frosted carrot and parsnip cake
    456–7
  lamb and carrot casserole with
    barley 310, 346
casseroles 46–9, 74, 75
cassoulet 266–7
Catalan potato and broad bean
  soup 100–1
cauliflower with tomatoes and
  cumin 412–13
celeriac 265
cheese
  baked scalloped potatoes with
    feta cheese and olives 392
  buckwheat noodles with
    cabbage, potatoes and
    cheese 406–7
  cheese and vegetable pudding
  cheese fondue 68
  cheese-stuffed pears 122
  cheese-topped roast baby
    vegetables 385
  chocolate cheesecake brownies
    458
  fettucine with butter and
    Parmesan 406–7
  French onion soup with cheese
    croûtes 82
  moussaka 304–5
  onions stuffed with goat's
    cheese and sun-dried
    tomatoes 363
  pan haggerty 381
  pasta shells with tomatoes and
    ricotta 405
  pasta with cheese and cream
    409

red lentil and goat's cheese
  pâté 121
spaghetti with cheese and black
  pepper 144–5
tagliatelle baked with
  mushrooms, Gorgonzola and
  walnuts 403
tomato, feta cheese and olive
  tarts 393
truffade 390–1
cherry clafoutis 484
chicken 24–5, 75
  apricot and almond stuffed
    chicken 216
  cardamom chicken mousselines
    130
  Caribbean peanut chicken 226
  chicken and leek soup with
    prunes and barley 111
  chicken and pistachio pâté
    128–9
  chicken and prawn jambalaya
    258
  chicken and split pea koresh 233
  chicken baked with shallots,
    garlic and fennel 251
  chicken biryani 261
  chicken casserole with winter
    vegetables 262
  chicken fricassée 218–19
  chicken gumbo with okra, ham,
    tomatoes and prawns 256–7
  chicken in a cashew nut sauce
    231
  chicken korma 232
  chicken piri-piri 260
  chicken soup with knaidlach 94
  chicken with chickpeas and
    almonds 242–3
  chicken with chipotle sauce 224
  chicken with forty cloves of
    garlic 250
  chicken with tomatoes and
    honey 242–3
  Chinese chicken and chilli soup
    110
  coq au vin 263
  corn-fed chicken with winter
    vegetables 255
  dorowat 229
  drunken chicken 225
  fragrant chicken curry 230
  hen in a pot with parsley sauce
    217
  hunter's chicken 244
  Jamaican jerk chicken 227
  layered chicken and mushroom
    bake 215
  mousseline pâté 59
  mustard baked chicken 246
  oven-roasted chicken with
    Mediterranean vegetables
    248–9
  poaching 56
  pot-roast chicken with lemon
    and garlic 253
  pot-roasting 55
  poussins and new potato pot-
    roast 254
  risotto with chicken 259
  Seville chicken 245
  spicy chicken jambalaya 228
  spring chicken slow-braised in
    smoky bacon sauce 220–1
  stoved chicken 252
  tarragon chicken in cider 222–3
chickpeas 242–3, 349, 362
  Moroccan braised chickpeas 378
  spicy tamarind chickpeas 367
chilli
  black bean chilli con carne 325
  chicken with chipotle sauce 224
  Chinese chicken and chilli soup
    110
  Italian lamb meatballs with chilli
    tomato sauce 343
  parsnips and chickpeas in garlic,
    onion, chilli and ginger paste
    362
  pork ribs with ginger and chilli
    147
  potato wedges with tomato
    and chilli salsa 137
  roast vegetables with fresh
    herbs and chilli sauce 412–13
  spicy hot mixed bean chilli with
    cornbread topping
Chinese chicken and chilli soup
    110
chocolate
  chocolate cheesecake brownies
    458
  chocolate chip and banana
    pudding 447
  chocolate chip walnut cake 455
  chocolate fondue 69
  chocolate sauces 67
  dark chocolate cake 62
  Mexican hot chocolate 504–5
  rich chocolate cake 454
  steamed chocolate and fruit `
    puddings 450
Christmas mincemeat 498
chutneys 70, 492, 493, 494
cider-glazed gammon 298–9
citrus and caramel custards 473
citrus beef curry 314–15

clam, mushroom and potato
  chowder 115
clams and mussels with lemon
  grass and coconut cream 154
clay-pot cooking 8–9, 76–9
  equipment 16–19
cobblers 35
coconut 154, 158, 417
  coconut and seafood soup with
    garlic chives 114
  coconut custard 438
  coconut rice pudding 472
  coconut salmon 171
  coconut, tomato and lentil dhal
    with toasted almonds 368
cod and prawn green coconut
  curry 158
cod with caramelized onions 180
coffee
  Normandy coffee 504–5
  petits pots de crème au mocha
    445
  sticky coffee and pear pudding
    448–9
compôtes 35
coq au vin 263
coriander and carrot soup 83
corn and potato chowder 106
corn-fed chicken with winter
  vegetables 255
cornbread topping with spicy hot
  mixed bean chilli
courgette and mushroom lasagne
  127
courgettes in tomato sauce
  418–19
couscous 347, 399
  couscous-stuffed sweet peppers
    361
cranberry and apple punch 502–3
cream 207, 326, 386–8, 409, 425
  penne with cream and smoked
    salmon 156
crème brûlée 61
crumbles 35, 53
cucumber with salmon risotto
  165
cumin 412–13
custard 66

D

date, beetroot and orange
  preserve 495
date puddings with toffee sauce
  451
dippers 68, 69
dorowat 229
drunken chicken 225
duck 25, 26
  Asian-style duck consommé 96
  cassoulet 266–7
  duck stew with olives 236
  Mediterranean duck with
    harissa and saffron 264
  roast farmyard duck with apples
    and cider 247

stir-fried crispy duck 153
dumplings 52, 94, 320–1, 322,
  342, 354

E

eggs
  avgolemeno 91
  baked egg custard 60–1
  baked eggs with creamy leeks
    124
  dorowat 229
  frittata with leek, red pepper
    and spinach 394
  Hungarian cholent 288
  lentil frittata 395
  pan-fried ham and vegetables
    with eggs 140
  tuna frittata 161
equipment 10–19
essences/extracts 37

F

fennel 251, 430
  baked fennel with a crumb
    crust 418–19
  mushroom and fennel hot pot
    352
  red mullet braised on a bed of
    fennel 174–5
fettucine with butter and
  Parmesan 406–7
figs honey-baked with hazelnut ice
  cream 474–5
fish 28–9
  baked monkfish with potatoes
    and garlic 206
  baked sardines with caper and
    tomato stuffing 208
  baked sea bass with lemon
    grass and red onions 210
  baked sea bream with
    tomatoes 202
  Basque-style tuna 179
  bouillabaisse 112
  broccoli, anchovy and pasta
    soup 104–5
  cannelloni Sorrentina-style 168
  coconut salmon 171
  cod and prawn green coconut
    curry 158
  cod with caramelized onions 180
  creamy anchovy and potato
    bake 164
  fillets of brill in red wine sauce
    203
  fish plaki 193
  fish stew with lemon grass 159
  fish terrine 131
  fish with fregola 199
  fish with spinach and lime 198
  Goan fish casserole 190–1
  green fish curry 185
  haddock and smoked salmon
    terrine 132–3
  hoki balls in tomato sauce 173
  Italian fish stew 188

Jansson's temptation 207
lemon sole and prosciutto
    roulades 178
Mediterranean leek and fish
    soup with tomatoes 113
mixed fish jambalaya 172
monkfish with rocket pesto,
    peppers and onions 204–5
Moroccan fish tagine 192
northern Thai fish curry 184
penne with cream and smoked
    salmon 156
poached fish in spicy tomato
    sauce 170
poaching 57
red mullet braised on a bed of
    fennel 174–5
salmon baked with potatoes
    and thyme 209
salmon risotto with cucumber
    165
seafood chowder 116–17
seafood pie with rösti topping
    194–5
skate with tomato and olive
    sauce 177
smoked trout cannelloni 167
special fish pie 166
spinach and nut stuffed herrings
    182–3
swordfish in barbecue sauce 181
swordfish steaks with mango
    and avocado salsa 211
tuna frittata 161
tuna lasagne 169
fondues 68–9
French onion soup with cheese
    croûtes 82
frittata with leek, red pepper and
    spinach 394
frozen vegetables 31
fruit 34–5
    Christmas mincemeat 498
    dried fruit sauce 66
    fresh currant bread and butter
        pudding 479
    fresh fruit bread and butter
        pudding 452–3
    fresh fruit coulis 68
    fruit curd 70–1
    light fruit cake 459
    poaching 57
    spicy pork casserole with dried
        fruit 296–7
    spicy tamarind chickpeas 367
    steamed chocolate and fruit
        puddings 450
    sweet and hot dried fruit
        chutney 494
    winter fruit poached in mulled
        wine 441

G
Galician broth 89
game 26–7
gammon 57

garlic 155, 206, 251, 253, 311,
    362, 365, 386–7, 414, 430
    chicken baked with shallots,
        garlic and fennel 251
    chicken with forty cloves of
        garlic 250
    lentil dhal with roasted garlic
        and whole spices 431
    prawns with baked garlic and
        roasted tomatoes 157
    roasted potatoes with garlic
        and onions 427
    spaghetti with garlic and oil 143
    Spanish potato and garlic soup
        100–1
garlic chives 114
    garlic chive rice with
        mushrooms 435
Genoese minestrone 88
ginger 147, 362, 417, 443
    gingered seafood stir-fry 160
    moist golden ginger cake 464–5
globe artichoke salad 410
Goan fish casserole 190–1
goose 25
grains 32
Greek meatballs in rich tomato
    sauce 301
grouse with orchard fruit stuffing
    272
guinea fowl
    braised guinea fowl with red
        cabbage 234
    guinea fowl and spring
        vegetable stew 235
    guinea fowl with beans and
        curly kale 270

H
haddock and smoked salmon
    terrine 132–3
haddock with spicy Puy lentils 176
ham
    chicken gumbo with okra, ham,
        tomatoes and prawns 256–7
    glazing 57
    lemon sole and prosciutto
        roulades 178
    pan-fried ham and vegetables
        with eggs 140
hare 27

hare pot pies 239
harissa 264, 399
heat diffusers 76
herbs 36, 83, 84, 307, 222–3, 360
    beef hotpot with herb
        dumplings 322
    braised lamb with apricots and
        herb dumplings 342
    dill 307, 432
    lamb shanks with beans and
        herbs 338–9
    mint 152, 376–7, 420
    parsley 217, 320–1
    roast vegetables with fresh
        herbs and chilli sauce 412–13
    sage 324
    spaghetti with butter and herbs
        144–5
    thyme 209, 429
herrings 182–3
hoki balls in tomato sauce 173
hollandaise sauce 64–5
honey 242–3, 306, 474–5
horseradish 286–7
Hungarian cholent 288

I
ice cream 474–5
icing 63
Irish stew 316
Italian farmhouse soup 103
Italian fish stew 188
Italian lamb meatballs with chilli
    tomato sauce 343
Italian pork sausage stew 292

J
Jamaican black bean pot 379
Jamaican jerk chicken 227
Jansson's temptation 207
juniper 238

K
kale 270
kidneys on brioche croûtes 146

L
lamb 22
    braised lamb shanks 50
    braised lamb with apricots and
        herb dumplings 342

braised shoulder of lamb with
    pearl barley and baby
    vegetables 341
devilled kidneys on brioche `
    croûtes 146
fragrant lamb curry with
    cardamom spiced rice 344–5
Greek meatballs in rich tomato
    sauce 301
Irish stew 316
Italian lamb meatballs with chilli
    tomato sauce 343
lamb and carrot casserole with
    barley 310, 346
lamb and pumpkin couscous 347
lamb in dill sauce 307
lamb pie with mustard thatch
    303
lamb shanks with beans and `
    herbs 338–9
lamb stewed with tomatoes
    and garlic 311
lamb's liver and bacon casserole
    148
Lancashire hot pot 302
Middle Eastern roast lamb and
    potatoes 337
minted lamb stir-fry 152
Moroccan lamb with honey and
    prunes 306
Moroccan spiced lamb soup 109
moussaka 304–5
roast lamb with beans and
    green peppercorns 336
spiced lamb with tomatoes and
    peppers 340
Tuscan pot-roasted shoulder of
    lamb 308–9
Lancashire hot pot 302
leeks 30
    baked eggs with creamy leeks
        124
    braised baby leeks in red wine
        with aromatics 136
    braised leeks with carrots 421
    chicken and leek soup with
        prunes and barley 111
    country-style terrine with leeks
        123
    frittata with leek, red pepper
        and spinach 394
    leeks in cream sauce 425
    Mediterranean leek and fish
        soup with tomatoes 113
lemon 253, 411, 429
    fresh lemon curd 500
    lemon surprise pudding 485
    papaya and lemon relish 497
lemon grass 154, 210, 366
lemon sole and prosciutto
    roulades 178
lentils
    coconut, tomato and lentil dhal
        with toasted almonds 368
    haddock with spicy Puy lentils
        176

lentil and pasta soup 102
lentil dhal with roasted garlic and whole spices 431
lentil frittata 395
pork tenderloin with spinach and Puy lentils 332–3
potage of lentils 93
red lentil and goat's cheese pâté 121
lettuce and peas with mint 420
lime 198, 366
linguine with rocket 142
liver 148, 324

M
mango and avocado salsa 211
mango chutney 493
maple 444, 470–1
marinades 44–5
marmalade 71
Mediterranean baked vegetables 382
Mediterranean duck with harissa and saffron 264
Mediterranean leek and fish soup with tomatoes 113
Mediterranean sausage and pesto soup 108
Mediterranean vegetables baked in a golden batter 389
Mexican hot chocolate 504–5
microwave cooking 78
Middle Eastern roast lamb and potatoes 337
mincemeat 498
minestrone 88
monkfish 204–5, 206
Moroccan braised chickpeas 378
Moroccan fish tagine 192
Moroccan lamb with honey and prunes 306
Moroccan spiced lamb soup 109
moussaka 304–5
mushrooms 30, 271, 403
beef and mushroom pudding 284–5
clam, mushroom and potato chowder 115
field mushrooms with hazelnuts 383
garlic chive rice with mushrooms 435

layered chicken and mushroom bake 215
mushroom and bean pâté 120
mushroom and courgette lasagne 127
mushroom and fennel hot pot 352
pasta with mushrooms 126
wild mushroom and sun-dried tomato soufflés 141
wild mushroom soup 87
mussels and clams with lemon grass and coconut cream 154
mussels with white wine and garlic 155
mustard 246, 280–1, 303

N
nectarines baked with almonds and pistachio nuts 477
Normandy coffee 504–5
North African spiced soup 90
nuts
almonds 216, 242–3, 368, 477, 481, 493, 496
baked maple and pecan croissant pudding 470–1
basmati rice and nut pilaff 398
cashews 231, 358, 369
chestnuts 271
chicken korma 232
coconuts 114, 154, 158, 171, 417, 438, 472
hazelnuts 383, 474–5
peanuts 226, 283, 356
pistachios 128–9, 477
savoury nut loaf 125
spiced pears with nut crumble 476
spinach and nut stuffed herrings 182–3
walnuts 359, 403, 455

O
octopus and red wine stew 189
okra 256–7
okra and tomato tagine 380
olive
baked scalloped potatoes with feta cheese and olives 392
duck stew with olives 236
skate with tomato and olive sauce 177
spaghetti with garlic and oil 143
tomato, feta cheese and olive tarts 393
one-pot cooking 7–9, 74–5
equipment 14–15
onions 30, 204–5, 210, 265, 324, 362, 417, 430
cod with caramelized onions 180
confit of slow-cooked onions 499
fish plaki 193

French onion soup with cheese croûtes 82
onions stuffed with goat's cheese and sun-dried tomatoes 363
oven-roasted red onions 416
pan haggerty 381
potato, onion and garlic gratin 365
saffron rice with onion and cardamom 434
slow-cooked spiced onions 415
orange candied sweet potatoes 364
orange, date and beetroot preserve 495
osso bucco with risotto Milanese 348
ostrich stew with sweet potatoes and chickpeas 349

P
paella 200, 400–1
pan haggerty 381
pancetta and broad bean risotto 327
pan-frying 75
papaya and lemon relish 497
papaya cooked with ginger 443
pappardelle with rabbit 237
parsnips and carrot cake 456–7
parsnips and chickpeas in garlic, onion, chilli and ginger paste 362
parsnips and potatoes baked with garlic and cream 386–7
pasta 33
broccoli, anchovy and pasta soup 104–5
cannelloni Sorrentina-style 168
fettucine with butter and Parmesan 406–7
fish with fregola 199
Genoese minestrone 88
Italian farmhouse soup 103
lentil and pasta soup 102
linguine with rocket 142
mushroom and courgette lasagne 127
pappardelle with rabbit 237
pasta shells with tomatoes and ricotta 405
pasta squares and peas in broth 104–5
pasta twists with pesto 408
pasta with cheese and cream 409
pasta with mushrooms 126
penne with cream and smoked salmon 156
smoked trout cannelloni 167
spaghetti with butter and herbs 144–5
spaghetti with cheese and black pepper 144–5
spaghetti with garlic and oil 143
spaghetti with rocket pesto 404

tagliatelle baked with mushrooms, Gorgonzola and walnuts 403
tuna lasagne 169
pâtés 58, 59, 120, 121, 128–9
pears
blushing pears 501
cheese-stuffed pears 122
pear, almond and ground rice pie 481
poached pears in red wine 440
spiced pears with nut crumble 476
sticky coffee and pear pudding 448–9
peas
braised lettuce and peas with mint 420
chicken and split pea koresh 233
chickpeas 242–3, 349, 362, 367, 378
pasta squares and peas in broth 104–5
spicy tamarind chickpeas 367
penne with cream and smoked salmon 156
pepper 144–5
peppercorns 336
peppers see sweet peppers
pesto 108, 204–5, 408
Mediterranean sausage and pesto soup 108
petits pots de crème au mocha 445
pheasant with wild mushrooms, chestnuts and bacon 271
pigeons 26
marinated pigeon in red wine 269
pigeons in stout 268
pilaff with saffron and pickled walnuts 359
pistou and bean soup 107
plum charlottes with foamy Kirsch sauce 468–9
poaching 56–7
polenta 53
pork 23
Boston baked beans 291
Brazilian pork and rice casserole 329
cassoulet 266–7

cider-glazed gammon 298–9
Galician broth 89
hot and sour pork 290
Italian pork sausage stew 292
lemon sole and prosciutto
    roulades 178
Mediterranean sausage and
    pesto soup 108
noisettes of pork with creamy
    Calvados and apple sauce
    326
pâté 58
pork and potato hot-pot 293
pork chow mein 151
pork cooked in cider with
    parsley dumplings 320–1
pork fillets with prune stuffing
    295
pork ribs with ginger and chilli
    147
pork tenderloin with spinach
    and Puy lentils 332–3
pot-roast loin of pork with
    apple 328
spicy chicken jambalaya 228
spicy pork casserole with dried
    fruit 296–7
sweet-and-sour pork stir-fry 150
pot-roasting 54–5, 74
potage of lentils 93
potatoes 52–3
    baked monkfish with potatoes
        and garlic 206
    baked scalloped potatoes with
        feta cheese and olives 392
    buckwheat noodles with
        cabbage, potatoes and
        cheese 406–7
    clam, mushroom and potato
        chowder 115
    corn and potato chowder 106
    creamy anchovy and potato
        bake 164
    griddle potatoes 426
    Jansson's temptation 207
    Middle Eastern roast lamb and
        potatoes 337
    new potatoes and vegetables
        baked Turkish-style 388
    new potatoes with thyme and
        lemon 429
    pan haggerty 381
    pork and potato hot-pot 293
    potato and sausage casserole
        294
    potato gratin 428
    potato, onion and garlic gratin
        365
    potato wedges with tomato
        and chilli salsa 137
    potatoes and parsnips baked
        with garlic and cream 386–7
    potatoes baked with fennel,
        onions, garlic and saffron 430
    potatoes baked with tomatoes
        390–1

poussins and new potato pot-
    roast 254
roasted potatoes with garlic
    and onions 427
salmon baked with potatoes
    and thyme 209
sausage, bacon and potato
    casserole 334
seafood pie with rösti topping
    194–5
slow-baked beef with a potato
    crust 323
truffade 390–1
poultry 24–5, 75
poussins and new potato pot-
    roast 254
prawns 29, 158, 256–7, 258
    hot and sour prawn soup 97
    prawns with baked garlic and
        roasted tomatoes 157
preserves 70–1, 490–501
Provençal beef stew 282
prunes 111, 277, 295
pumpkins 31
    lamb and pumpkin couscous
        347
    pumpkin and banana cake 463
    spicy pumpkin soup 86
    sweet pumpkin and peanut
        curry 356

R
rabbit 27
    braised rabbit 276
    pappardelle with rabbit 237
    rabbit casserole with juniper 238
    rabbit with red wine and
        prunes 277
raisins 446
ratatouille 372
red mullet braised on a bed of
    fennel 174–5
reheating 51
relishes 496, 497
rice 32
    avgolemono 91
    basmati rice and nut pilaff 398
    basmati rice with vegetables 433
    Brazilian pork and rice
        casserole 329
    brown rice with lime and
        lemon grass 366

bulgur wheat, asparagus and
    broad bean pilaff 396–7
clay-pot risotto with spinach
    and saffron 402
coconut rice pudding 472
garlic chive rice with
    mushrooms 435
osso bucco with risotto
    Milanese 348
pancetta and broad bean
    risotto 327
pear, almond and ground rice
    pie 481
pilaff with saffron and pickled
    walnuts 359
rice pudding 61
rice with dill and broad beans
    432
risotto with chicken 259
roasted squash with rice stuffing
    384
rosemary risotto with borlotti
    beans 360
saffron rice with onion and
    cardamom 434
salmon risotto with cucumber
    165
seafood risotto 201
spiced Indian rice with spinach,
    tomatoes and cashew nuts
    369
rocket 142, 204–5, 404
rosemary risotto with borlotti
    beans 360

S
sabayon sauce 55
saffron 264, 359, 399, 402, 430
    saffron mussels with white wine
        and garlic 155
    saffron rice with onion and
        cardamom 434
salmon 132–3, 156, 165, 171
    salmon baked with potatoes
        and thyme 209
    salmon risotto with cucumber
        165
sardines 208
sauces
    savoury 37, 64–5
    sweet 66–7
sausages

braised sausages with onions,
    celeriac and apple 265
cassoulet 266–7
Mediterranean sausage and
    pesto soup 108
potato and sausage casserole 294
sausage, bacon and potato
    casserole 334
toad-in-the-hole 335
venison sausages with red
    wine gravy 274
sea bass 210
sea bream with tomatoes 202
seafood chowder 116–17
Seville chicken 245
shellfish 29
    bouillabaisse 112
    chicken and prawn jambalaya
        258
    chicken gumbo with okra, ham,
        tomatoes and prawns 256–7
    clam, mushroom and potato
        chowder 115
    coconut and seafood soup with
        garlic chives 114
    cod and prawn green coconut
        curry 158
    gingered seafood stir-fry 160
    hot and sour prawn soup 97
    Italian fish stew 188
    mixed fish jambalaya 172
    mussels and clams with lemon
        grass and coconut cream 154
    octopus and red wine stew 189
    prawns with baked garlic and
        roasted tomatoes 157
    saffron mussels with white wine
        and garlic 155
    seafood chowder 116–17
    seafood paella 200
    seafood pie with rösti topping
        194–5
    seafood risotto 201
    shellfish tagine 196–7
shrimp see prawns
skate with tomato and olive sauce
    177
slow cookers 10–11
    additional equipment 12–13
    bain-marie 58–9
    safety 72–3
slow cooking 6–9
soups 42–3, 80–117
spaghetti with butter and herbs
    144–5
spaghetti with cheese and black
    pepper 144–5
spaghetti with garlic and oil 143
spaghetti with rocket pesto 404
Spanish potato and garlic soup
    100–1
spices 36–7
    fragrant lamb curry with
        cardamom spiced rice 344–5
    haddock with spicy Puy lentils
        176

hot spiced wine 502–3
lentil dhal with roasted garlic
    and whole spices 431
marbled spice cake 460–1
Moroccan spiced lamb soup 109
North African spiced soup 90
poached fish in spicy tomato
    sauce 170
root vegetable gratin with
    Indian spices 424
slow-cooked spiced onions 415
spiced beef 289
spiced blackberry and apple
    crumble 482
spiced Indian rice with spinach,
    tomatoes and cashew nuts
    369
spiced lamb with tomatoes and
    peppers 340
spiced pears with nut crumble
    476
spicy chicken jambalaya 228
spicy hot mixed bean chilli with
    cornbread topping 354
spicy pork casserole with dried
    fruit 296–7
spicy pumpkin soup 86
spicy tamarind chickpeas 367
spicy venison casserole 273
spinach 198, 230, 369, 394, 402
    pork tenderloin with spinach
        and Puy lentils 332–3
    spinach and nut stuffed herrings
        182–3
    spinach and root vegetable
        soup 95
    spinach braised with sweet
        potatoes 423
squash 493
    roasted squash with rice stuffing
        384
squid 29
steak and kidney pie with mustard
    gravy 280–1
steamed puddings 60–1
stews 46–9, 74
stir-frying 75
stock 38–41
strawberry oat crunch 486
sweet peppers 31
    chilled tomato and sweet
        pepper soup 85
    clay-pot beef with red peppers
        318–19
    couscous-stuffed sweet peppers
        361
    frittata with leek, red pepper
        and spinach 394
    monkfish with rocket pesto,
        peppers and onions 204–5
    ratatouille 372
    spiced lamb with tomatoes and
        peppers 340
sweet potatoes
    orange candied sweet potatoes
        364

ostrich stew with sweet
    potatoes and chickpeas 349
roasted sweet potatoes, onions
    and beetroot in coconut and
    ginger paste 417
spinach braised with sweet
    potatoes 423
sweet pumpkin and peanut curry
    356
swordfish in barbecue sauce 181
swordfish steaks with mango and
    avocado salsa 211

T
tagliatelle baked with mushrooms,
    Gorgonzola and walnuts 403
tamarind chickpeas 367
tapioca pudding 439
tarragon chicken in cider 222–3
tarte tatin 483
terrines 59, 123, 131, 132–3
Thai fish curry 184
toad-in-the-hole 335
toffee sauce 451
tofu and vegetable Thai curry
    374–5
tomatoes 31
    baked sardines with caper and
        tomato stuffing 208
    baked sea bream with
        tomatoes 202
    cabbage, beetroot and tomato
        borscht 92
    cauliflower with tomatoes and
        cumin 412–13
    chicken gumbo with okra, ham,
        tomatoes and prawns 256–7
    chicken with tomatoes and
        honey 242–3
    chilled tomato and sweet
        pepper soup 85
    coconut, tomato and lentil dhal
        with toasted almonds 368
    courgettes in tomato sauce
        418–19
    fish plaki 193
    fresh tomato sauce 64
    Greek meatballs in rich tomato
        sauce 301

hoki balls in tomato sauce 173
Italian lamb meatballs with chilli
    tomato sauce 343
lamb stewed with tomatoes
    and garlic 311
Mediterranean leek and fish
    soup with tomatoes 113
okra and tomato tagine 380
onions stuffed with goat's
    cheese and sun-dried
    tomatoes 363
pasta shells with tomatoes and
    ricotta 405
poached fish in spicy tomato
    sauce 170
potato wedges with tomato
    and chilli salsa 137
potatoes baked with tomatoes
    390–1
prawns with baked garlic and
    roasted tomatoes 157
ratatouille 372
roasted tomatoes and garlic 414
skate with tomato and olive
    sauce 177
spiced Indian rice with spinach,
    tomatoes and cashew nuts
    369
spiced lamb with tomatoes and
    peppers 340
tomato and fresh basil soup 84
tomato, feta cheese and olive
    tarts 393
turkey and tomato hot-pot 214
veal stew with tomatoes 300
wild mushroom and sun-dried
    tomato soufflés 141
toppings 52–3, 354
trout cannelloni 167
truffade 390–1
tuna 161, 169, 179
turkey 25
    turkey and tomato hot-pot 214
Tuscan pot-roasted shoulder of
    lamb 308–9

V
veal
    osso bucco with risotto
        Milanese 348

veal stew with tomatoes 300
vegetables 30–1
    basmati rice with vegetables
        433
    braised shoulder of lamb with
        pearl barley and baby
        vegetables 341
    cheese-topped roast baby
        vegetables 385
    chicken casserole with winter
        vegetables 262
    corn-fed chicken with winter
        vegetables 255
    Genoese minestrone 88
    guinea fowl and spring
        vegetable stew 235
    Italian farmhouse soup 103
    Mediterranean baked
        vegetables 382
    Mediterranean vegetables
        baked in a golden
        batter 389
    mixed vegetable soup 42
    new potatoes and vegetables
        baked Turkish-style 388
    North African spiced soup 90
    oven-roasted chicken with
        Mediterranean vegetables
        248–9
    pan-fried ham and vegetables
        with eggs 140
    roast vegetables with fresh
        herbs and chilli sauce 412–13
    root vegetable casserole
        with caraway dumplings
        354
    root vegetable gratin with
        Indian spices 424
    spinach and root vegetable
        soup 95
    tofu and vegetable Thai curry
        374–5
    vegetable and cashew nut
        biryani 358
    vegetable couscous with saffron
        and harissa 399
    vegetable kashmiri 357
    vegetable korma 373
    vegetable paella 400–1
venison 27
    venison casserole 273
    venison casseroled with
        stout 275
    venison sausages with red wine
        gravy 274
Vermont baked maple
    custard 444
vine leaves, braised 138–9

W
white sauce 64
winter fruit poached in mulled
    wine 441

Y
yogurt 376–7